THE CLASSICS OF **WESTERN SPIRITUALITY**

THE CLASSICS OF WESTERN SPIRITUALITY
A Library of the Great Spiritual Masters

Celtic Spirituality

TRANSLATED AND INTRODUCED BY
OLIVER DAVIES

WITH THE COLLABORATION OF
THOMAS O'LOUGHLIN

PREFACE BY
JAMES MACKEY

PAULIST PRESS
NEW YORK • MAHWAH

Cover art: Cross carpet page from Mark's Gospel, found in the Lindisfarne Gospels (c. 698 A.D.)

Cott Nero DIV f.94v St. Mark, cross carpet page Lindisfarne Gospels (c. 698 A.D.) British Library, London, UK/Bridgeman Art Library, London/N.Y. (used with permission).

We have sought wherever possible to gain permission from holders of copyright of the original texts. Thanks are due to the following for the granting of translation rights: the Governing Board of the School of Celtic Studies, the Pontifical Institute of Medieval Studies, and the Royal Irish Academy. I am grateful also to individual editors, including Dr. Marged Haycock, Dr. Iestyn Daniel, Dr. Huw Pryce and Dr. David Howlett.

Library of Congress Cataloging-in-Publication Data

Celtic spirituality / edited and translated by Oliver Davies ; with the collaboration of Thomas O'Loughlin.
    p. cm. — (The classics of Western spirituality ; #96)
    Includes bibliographical references and index.
    ISBN 0-8091-3894-8 (pbk. : alk. paper) — ISBN 0-8091-0505-5 (alk. paper).
    1. Spirituality — Celtic Church Early works to 1800. 2. Spirituality — Ireland Early works to 1800. 3. Spirituality — Wales Early works to 1800. I. Davies, Oliver. II. O'Loughlin, Thomas. III. Series.
BR794.C45 1999
270'.089'916—dc21
                                              99-41570
                                                   CIP

Published by Paulist Press
997 Macarthur Boulevard
Mahwah, New Jersey 07430

www.paulistpress.com

Printed and bound in the United States of America

Contents

CONTENTS

II. THE TEXTS

Hagiography:

Monastic Texts:

CONTENTS

Poetry:

CONTENTS

Devotional Texts:

Liturgy:

Apocrypha:

Exegesis:

CONTENTS

Homilies:

Theology:

Editor of This Volume

OLIVER DAVIES is reader in philosophical theology at the University of Wales, Lampeter, and is author of *Celtic Christian Spirituality* (with Fiona Bowie [New York: Crossroad, 1995]) and *Celtic Christianity in Early Medieval Wales* (Cardiff: University of Wales Press, 1996). He has also written extensively on the medieval mystical tradition.

Collaborator of This Volume

THOMAS O'LOUGHLIN is lecturer in theology at the University of Wales, Lampeter. His research has focused on early medieval biblical exegesis, and he has recently published *Teachers and Code-Breakers: The Latin Genesis Tradition 430–800* (Turnhout, Brepols, Belgium, 1999).

Author of the Preface

JAMES MACKEY is emeritus professor of theology at the University of Edinburgh and visiting fellow of Trinity College, Dublin. He is editor of *An Introduction to Celtic Christianity* (Edinburgh: T&T Clark, 1989) and has recently published *The Critique of Theological Reason* (Cambridge University Press, 1999).

Acknowledgments

I am grateful to my colleagues at Lampeter, especially Tom O'Loughlin, Jonathan Wooding, and Alex Woolf, now at the University of Edinburgh, for their advice and help with this book. I am grateful also to the many tutors, particularly Elva Johnston and Iestyn Daniel, and to the students who have attended the Masters program in Celtic Christianity at Lampeter in recent years, and who have provided me with a marvelous opportunity to test ideas. I owe a particular debt of thanks also to Fiona Bowie, my wife and colleague, for a number of valuable insights into this material from an anthropological perspective, and to Marlene Ablett for her secretarial help in the final production of the manuscript. I am grateful also to Professor Bernard McGinn for his unfailing kindness and sagacity as series editor, and to Kathleen Walsh for her patience and support in the final production of this book.

FOR D.P.

Preface

Spirituality is a word that is not always to everybody's liking. This is partly because, in the Age of Heroic Materialism, still hugely influential all about us, the word *spirit* and its derivatives seem to be reminiscent of a dualistic and obsolescent Christian Platonism and the negative aura set over this word by some of its most determined practitioners. In addition, like mysticism, as that is (mis)interpreted in the experientialist terms that have been with us since the last century, spirituality seems to require and to invite us to seek out and cultivate very esoteric kinds of inner experience that have little or nothing to do with marrying, begetting and rearing children, harvesting land and sea, and the myriad other activities that crowd together under those comprehensive references to making a living, or getting a life here and now in the only world we know for sure to exist. And this despite the fact that mystics like Meister Eckhart and the author of *The Cloud of Unknowing* make no reference to such special experiences, and others such as John of the Cross and Teresa of Avila attach little or no importance to them.

The most effective way of rescuing spirituality from such unwelcome misapprehensions, then, is to present to the public a world in which, as in Hegel, spirit never leaves and never will leave the body. This is a world of eternally immanent, incarnate spirit—spirit that transcends the whole universe of being toward the ultimate and eternal perfection of the universe, precisely because it is immanent in the whole of it. Spirit, which is especially accessible to and particularly immanent in the essentially incarnate human spirit, which is itself increasingly pivotal in the continuous creation and destiny of the only world we know.

Where is such an immanent, incarnate, uncompromisingly this-worldly spirituality in evidence? One answer is the Christian Bible. Follow its logic: the Divine Word, which continuously creates the world, takes human form in Jesus of Nazareth, who, as life-giving spirit, forms his extended body from fellow humans down the ages. It is to this body that the physical world itself looks for a like liberation from evil and finitude, the liberation of the sons of God, until in the eschaton all together share eternal fulfillment in the new heaven-and-earth. Celtic Christianity, then, provides another answer, and not least because it is so thoroughly biblical, and in the end more Antiochene than Alexandrian in its exegesis. It is most obviously biblical in the dominance amongst the genres represented in its surviving literature of commentaries on Scripture, homilies on Scripture and, yes, its profligate and not yet fully audited store of Apocrypha. For the Apocrypha, in addition to increasing our knowledge of noncanonical sources, illustrate also, and much more importantly, that canonical Scripture texts were retold in a manner which simultaneously inculturated the Christian faith and thoroughly formed in scriptural terms the minds of the faithful. One thinks, for instance, of the insertion of the pan-Celtic goddess, Brigid, into the retelling of the infancy narratives.

When one considers another significant genre from Celtic Christian literature—the voyage literature—the this-worldly character of its spirituality is yet more secure. This ancient and fundamental form of religious imagery of exodus and return—in which God travels toward and through creation so that creation can travel to its final and eternal perfection in creative union with God—finds here its cultural equivalent in a visionary journey through the familiar world which all the time tries to envisage a perfected, yet similarly structured world to come, continuous with this world. Obviously, to the Insular Celts, paradise is an island.

Yet Celtic Christianity is a thoroughly embodied spirituality in its general theology, and not just in some of its literary genres. And that is not only a reference to the particular genre constituted of formal theological writings; although it is true of these also, as Pelagius in particular illustrates. For Pelagius all of God's creation, all and everything that comes into being by God's continuous creation is good. Nothing that enters the realm of reality by the universal process of bodily becoming can be evil or sinful by that very fact. True, the world of becoming, the world *in via,* is constantly under siege by demonic, destructive forces, which by God's power we must be protected from daily, and which must finally be overcome. But that is an entirely different matter; and in this matter, Pelagius and his fellow spiritual athletes were undoubtedly as right as Augustine was wrong. Everything that comes into existence is good, and especially the newly conceived human being with its will for life and life more abundant, for God is constantly and creatively at work in all that comes to be.

But general theology in the case of the Celts also has a broader range of reference. Taken in its original sense, let us consider the logos of *theos,* the understanding of God's nature and activity. General theology refers to the shape of this understanding implicit over a wider range of literary genres—in the lives of the saints, for example, and other writings of monastic foundations which were, after all, in insular Celtic realms at least, charged with the spiritual formation of the laity also.

Put in its simplest form this general theology of Celtic Christians thinks of the divine being and act or, better, the divine presence and power, flowing in and through what can only be described as an extended family. At the center of that family, where divine being and act are quintessentially concentrated as it were, is of course the divine presence and power flows in and through Mary (very much one of a Quaternity in medieval Gaelic Bardic poetry), the angels (the archangel Michael, for instance, the Celtic Christian "reincarnation" of the god Lugh), the great holy men and women of the Celtic Christian community (Patrick, Columcille, and especially, perhaps, Brigid, the "reincarnation" of the pan-Celtic goddess of the same name, with all her original creative powers intact), the sacral kings, and right down to the natural elements themselves. An awesomely immanent divine being, presence and power, then, could be experienced and invoked in and through any and all of these varied embodiments.

Some of course who read stories of the more astonishing effects of this very concretely mediated divine power, in the process of conserving and protecting life, of healing and enhancing it, will talk of magic. They may talk correspondingly of charms instead of prayers when Celtic folk invoke such divine power incarnate in saint or element for such purposes, as happens in many a saint's life, in a *Lorica* or other prayer-form. And some will be offended at the miraculous use of such power to destroy the saint's enemies or their possessions. And all of these, on occasion, will be right to talk like this and to be offended. Celtic Christianity is no more innocent of distorted expression than is any other known version of Christianity.

But it is wise to remember that the charge of magic does not lie against the belief in thoroughgoing immanence of the divine power and presence as such, nor against the forms by which it is invoked, even in such instances as its sustaining and creative presence in sun and sea and wind. The charge of magic can only be sustained against a particular kind of mentality that uses such forms of invocation in any or all of these presences of divine power. It is the mentality that invokes the power immanent in creatures and uses the corresponding prayer, particularly in its ritual form, as if that power could be automatically activated. It is against that mentality that thereby attempts to bypass God's gracious will and thus in effect treats the immanent power as other than the free creative grace of the one, true God, that a charge of magic can reasonably be raised. And from that mentality no religious belief, profession or prayer is absolutely safe. "I accept you, Jesus, as my Savior and Lord"; even that can be used magically; and one may well suspect that it sometimes is.[1]

As for the harshness and, as it is sometimes called, vindictiveness with which divinely empowered holy men and women in the Celtic Christian tradition met the opponents of their persons and mission, one can only say that they had ample evidence of such conduct in the biblical sources to which they were so totally devoted. Yahweh quite frequently ordered the utter destruction of such opponents of his "son," Israel; and there is the New Testament example of the fate of Ananias and his wife at the hands of Peter. It may well be, as in the case of magic also, that versions of Christianity which so highlight the utter immanence of the gracious, continually creative God in all ordinary things and events, and which propound a correspondingly this-worldly spirituality, are more prone to these particular distortions than are other versions of Christianity. Then the thing to do is to learn from the special light thrown upon this version of Christianity, while correcting its characteristic, occasional distortions, and to do something similar with other versions of Christianity that may highlight transcendence, for instance, at the expense, at times, of an equally inevitable immanence.

Of course the contention that Celtic Spirituality has the distinctive value of these particular highlights, together with the particular vulnerabilities to which they are exposed, even if the same is claimed for what would then be seen as complementary versions of Christian spirituality, each in its own right, can be and has been opposed by the contrary contention, to wit, that there is no such thing as Celtic Christianity. The case for Celtic Spirituality, with its distinctive affordances, is based then on what might be called the principle of inculturation and on the evidence of a culture shared by a loose family of peoples. And both supports for the case are controverted.

The inculturation principle states that Christianity, like any other religion, inevitably takes shape of the culture—the images and ideas, practices and institutions—in which it is born or to which it travels. Allowance must be made of course for deliberate attempts at times to prevent this natural process from taking effect. So Celtic Christianity has its thoroughly this-worldly spirituality, it is said, because of the character of the already religious culture into which it came. But the inculturation principle entails much more than that. It entails a view of development of religion, or spirituality, and indeed of knowledge which, like the universe itself, is much more evolutionary than static. In short, the much advertised catholicity or universality of Christianity is seen to be achieved, not on the static Englightenment model of a set of abstract truths or doctrines about life and reality that transcend all concrete cultures by being conceptually absolute and unchangeable. Rather, it is based on a more contemporary model of the evolution of reality itself, shaped by the mutations (of religion also) formed in the concrete and local ecological-cultural niche. The ones that promise life and life more abundant spread into other concrete locales in a mutual or rather multiple-interactive process in which universality of application and appropriation are secured, not at the expense of but, quite to the contrary, by very courtesy of the ever increasing enrichment that derives form the distinctive cultural *trans*-formation by each of the mutational *in*-formation each receives from the others.

Toward a further understanding of the inculturation principle, wisdom, which is a way and a life as much as a truth, and all that contributes to wisdom, form science-technology to religion, is conserved and increased, like the evolving creation itself, through a process of mutual enrichment rather than displacement. This process is itself always potentially universal and then practically so, as a result of rather than despite the ability of each ecological-cultural niche to receive the promising transformations of the others into its own native forms. This surely is an acceptable formula, not just for the relationship of religion to culture in general, or for the relationship of Christianity to "primal" religions, or of versions of Christianity to each other, but for the relationship of Christianity to other "world" religions. At the very least it enables the essential, incarnate spirituality of Celtic Christianity, itself due in no small part to the pre-Christian Celtic civilization in which it was (and is) inculturated, to be recommended as an intrinsic part of that process of mutual enrichment by which Christianity is to reach the fulfillment of the ends of the world and of its times.

But there are those who doubt the very existence of a Celtic Christianity or a Celtic spirituality, forged through the inculturation of an incoming Christianity in the "primal" religious culture(s) of peoples called the Celts.[2] Oliver Davies is well aware of these doubts and of even stronger positions along similar lines, and his answer is fair and adequate. Nothing needs to be added, except perhaps some comment on a term that has become quite common in this kind of debate: the term *insular.*

In the summer of 1991, the Palazzo Grassi in Venice mounted what must surely have been the most comprehensive exhibition of Celtic art the world has yet seen. The exhibition was entitled *I Celti; La Prima Europa* and, instead of the usual catalog, there was offered to visitors to the exhibition what must surely be one of the most comprehensive collections of scholarly articles on the Celts ever assembled in one volume—though these articles were all centered upon the objects on display from the various Celtic territories. Hence a section of this scholarly work (published by Bompiani as, in its English version, *The Celts*), was entitled "The Island Celts," for the section dealt with the islands of Ireland and Britain, the territories from which almost all of Oliver Davies's material is drawn. Now the use in this context of the term *insular,* whether used of Celts or of their art, culture, or religion(s), is innocent, informative, and entirely acceptable.

There is another usage of the term *insular* in reference to these same islands, however, that is far from innocent and, rather than being informative, seems designed to carry an unquestioned assumption that in fact no such entities as Celtic peoples, or Celtic art, or culture(s), or religion, or Christianity, and so on, can be detected in these islands. For in these contexts the adjective *insular* is chosen to describe art, or culture, or religion and its constituent parts, so as to deliberately displace the adjective *Celtic.* It is somewhat paradoxical that this second usage of the term *insular* is frequently found amongst those whose professions place them in university departments of Celtic Studies, or Celtic Languages. We might well wonder why, if only in the interests of consistency, we do not hear more often of departments or professors of insular studies, or even insular departments? But the more serious suspicion must be that we are here in the presence of residual imperial rhetoric and its correspondingly (still) colonized minds. For in secular terms, imperial rhetoric is designed to deter the colonized from dwelling on their own identity, which is totally bound up with their culture, and their culture in turn is particularly embodied in their language. And in religious terms, the still colonized mind is unable to see what the great Columbanus so clearly saw and so persuasively argued for, namely, that a Christian faith truly incarnate in a particular culture ("in the condition in which we were saved"), can form a creative part of the true unity of a universal church, even one that stoutly acknowledges the still imperially conceived primacy of Rome.

Celtic Christianity, with its distinctive spirituality, did certainly exist, and it still exists in part and is in part recoverable. It has its contributions to make and even its corrections to offer to the other cultural versions of Christianity that together make up the one ever evolving Christian family in the world. Just as in that true cross-cultural dialogue of equals, which is demanded of all of us in the very name of traveling the Christian road to the final and universal fulfillment, it too must be enriched and corrected by other cultural versions of Christianity, and indeed of other religions and even of some very critical secular humanisms. And this puts all of us in debt to the editor who included this volume in the Classics of Western Spirituality series, and most of all in debt of the scholarship of Oliver Davies, with some help from Thomas O'Loughlin. The fine selection of religious texts, together with an enlightening and judicious introduction to their provenance, nature, and content, meets most admirably the needs of those who would wish to recover something of their native Christian spirituality, and of others who would wish to learn something from it as well as to contribute their own insights to it.

James P. Mackey
The University of Edinburgh
Faculty of Divinity
The Mound
Edinburgh

I.
Introduction

AN INTRODUCTION TO
CELTIC SPIRITUALITY

There is something peculiarly attractive about the Christianity of the early Celtic-speaking peoples, which continues to exercise a considerable fascination on many today. The vivid and complex gospel illustrations, which are perhaps the best known and most frequently reproduced creations of the Christianity of the insular world, suggest a self-confident, brilliantly original civilization in which the skills and ingenuity of the individual artist are given a prominent place. The intricate, interweaving designs and natural motifs convey the impression of a religion that is in close dialogue with nature rather than withdrawn from it, and the rich adornment of the biblical text is a reminder of the great status accorded to the Word of God. If we were to explore further, we would find that such gospel books were often believed to have a mystical power as objects of incarnate grace and that the understanding that the presence of God could be felt and discerned in the natural and human landscapes of our world was widespread among Christians from Celtic cultures. God was present to them in images and signs, in poetry and art, in sacrament and liturgy; and their own response to God was no less direct, for it was commonly a physical one, expressed at the level of the body in the embrace of a life-transforming penance. Indeed, it is these two themes, penance and creativity, that are the guiding motifs of Celtic Christianity. Both speak of incarnation, and of the affirmation and transformation of life, since creativity is the mark of the Spirit and penance is the gate to glory.

THE CONCEPT OF A CELTIC SPIRITUALITY

The claim that there is, or was, a type of spirituality that is generally specific to one particular ethnic group is inevitably a complex one; in the case of the Celts it is one that has also proved

3

highly controversial. Indeed, there can seem to be an unbridge-able gap between historians who protest against the very exis-tence of "a Celtic Church," and a host of more popular writers for whom the existence of such an entity, or variants on it, is entirely axiomatic.[1] It seems wise at this early stage therefore to clarify some of the theoretical issues that underlie the concept of a distinctively Celtic spirituality before proceeding to an analysis of the texts themselves.

One of the critiques commonly made is that the term *Celtic* is itself anachronistic for the periods in question, and indeed there is no evidence that the early Irish and Welsh authors of the source texts included in this volume ever understood themselves to be "Celts" at all.[2] The origins of the term lie in Greek and Roman geographical and ethnographical writings.[3] From the sixth to the fourth century B.C., geographers such as Skylax, Avienus, and Hecataeus of Miletus begin to describe Celts as warlike peoples pushing down to the south of Europe.[4] The evidence is, however, that the term had no precise ethnic signification and that Celts merely designated those peoples who lived in the west: "To the north were the Scythians, to the east the Persians, to the south the Libyans and to the west the Celts."[5] The word *Celtic* itself lay dor-mant for many centuries until it was revived by the linguistic researches of George Buchanan (1506–1582) and Edward Lluyd (1660–1709). In his *Archaeologia Britannica* of 1707, the latter described seven languages as belonging to a distinctive "Celtic" family (Irish, Welsh, Scottish Gaelic, Manx, Cornish, and Breton as well as Gaulish). In 1853, Johann Kaspar Zeuss published his *Grammatica Celtica,* a comparative grammar of the Celtic lan-guages, thus creating the foundation of scientific Celtic philologi-cal studies. Gradually, however, the word came to take on broader ethnic and cultural connotations (e.g., Celtic lands, Celtic litera-ture, Celtic music). The origins of this shift lie in the "Celtic renaissance" in Ireland during the late nineteenth century, its first applications to "church" dating from the end of the nine-teenth century.[6] Latterly, we have seen a further development with the evolution in Ireland, Wales, Scotland, Brittany, and elsewhere of a new and distinctive sense of "being Celtic," which is evident in the flourishing of numerous pan-Celtic organizations. In some degree this may reflect an interiorization of the "Celtic" image projected from without, generated to some considerable extent by communities in the United States and elsewhere that trace their origins to Ireland, Scotland, or Wales. But it is rooted too in the rise of nationalist movements in the Celtic areas over the last one hundred years. For centuries the Celtic-speaking peoples have all experienced a greater or lesser degree of political and economic marginalization and have undoubtedly represented an anomaly within the context of a normative "national" identity imposed by the English or French from without. It is only relatively recently, however, that the multiple identities of the historically Celtic peoples have shown signs of coalescence into a common Celtic cultural and even political front.[7]

The above need not be taken to mean that the use of the term *Celtic* is invalid in the early period, however. Historiography is itself an exercise in interpretation. Anthropologists have coined the terms *emic* and *etic* identities, by which is meant the identity a particular group holds with respect to itself and that which others place on it.[8] This is an important distinction that has far-reaching consequences, especially with regard to early historical periods. After all, many or even most of the cultural and ethnic categories that historians habitually employ function at the etic level and not at the emic one at all. Thus we speak of "American History" before people would have dreamed of calling themselves "American," and "British History" extends back to a period many centuries before the emergence of the modern British state. Such terms are inherently vague (which is probably why they are useful), and can be used to signify cultural, ethnic, geographical, or even chronological categories singly or in combination, according to context. Celtic is another such term, albeit one that is perhaps worked—and overworked—more than most; and if it represents an oversimplification of complex and shifting human realities, then this tendency is inevitably inherent within the use of such generic terms.

A second common criticism is that the very concept of Celticity, or "being a Celt," is hopelessly compromised by forms of ethnic romanticism. This is a trend that is evident even in the classical period. The early experience of the tribes they called Celts on the part of both the Romans and the Greeks was of their destructive incursions into northern Italy during the fourth century and into the Greek peninsula during the third century B.C.E.[9] It was natural therefore that classical authors should also see in the Celts the image of their own uncivilized past, as when Posidonius draws a direct parallel between the reservation of the prime portion to the champion at a Celtic feast and a passage from the *Iliad*.[10] But classical authors also saw the Celts as being exotic and strange, bewitched by the often nomadic and nonurban character of Celtic societies in the early period, which contrasted with their own way of life founded on the *polis* and its more urbane values. Stoic influence can be felt, for instance, in the depiction of the druids as "natural philosophers," which we find in Strabo, and Pliny leaves us a with a distinctly romantic and picturesque vignette of a white-robed druid cutting mistletoe from a sacred oak with a golden sickle.[11] There is much Celtic romance also during the Middle Ages with the appropriation by one European culture after another of the Arthurian legends, or *matière de Bretagne*. During the Tudor period, English writers took over the early Welsh, or "British," legend of how Madoc discovered America in order to lend a historical pedigree to a new power with extensive colonial ambitions.[12] The problem of image and reality in the Celtic world is a persistent one, and it has undoubtedly had a considerable effect in the Celtic countries themselves. In 1760 James Macpherson published a collection of his own compositions with the title *Fragments of Ancient Poetry, Collected in the Highlands of Scotland, and Translated from the Gaelic or Erse Language*. These poems, attributed to the Gaelic bard Ossian, son of Fingal, were greatly influential, especially on the Continent.[13] In Wales during the same period, Iolo Morganwg's editorial liberties with Welsh medieval texts likewise won him great notoriety.[14] The tendency to romance the Celts is still greatly influential today.[15] It is easy to see why many people, disillusioned with the narrow rationalism, demanding technologies, and urban environments of modern existence, should seek consolation in the intriguing image of an ancient and magical "other." Even though such approaches are not historically grounded, they do constitute an interesting phenomenon in themselves and are part of the history of Celticity.[16]

Though anachronistic as an emic category, therefore, the notion of the Celt as an etic category reflects the valid insight of the modern period that the Goidelic ("Q"- Celtic) and Brythonic ("P"-Celtic) languages spoken in the insular world formed a loose-knit linguistic family. Language is the primary expression of culture, and affinities of language bring with them affinities of culture—though whether in the case of the Celtic-speaking peoples such continuities derived from a common cultural inheritance, or from culture contact through geographical proximity, or from both factors and in which proportion, is less easily decided. Nor is the assertion of visible cultural continuities among the Celtic peoples in fields such as poetics, myth, religion, archaeology, and art, as well as language, to be taken as a denial of the powerful influence of *latinitas,* as the quasi-universal medium of cultural thought and practice. Nor is it to deny the extensive and fertile contacts and affinities with other ethnic groups, such as Anglo-Saxons and even Vikings. Above all, the modern reader must beware of projecting back on the diverse Celtic-speaking peoples the concept of a homogeneous and unified cultural area, a notion of nationhood that is a purely modern ideal, supremely exemplified perhaps in the United States, in favor of the altogether more diffuse and untidy picture that more accurately reflects the medieval reality.

The question whether and in what way the religious practices of Celtic-speaking peoples represented a distinctive branch of early Christianity arose some time before the reappearance in the modern age of the concept of "celticity." From its inception this debate took place within the highly charged ideological atmosphere of church reform. The Reformation in England provided the context for the first emergence of the question. In 1572 Matthew Parker, Archbishop of Canterbury, published his important work *De Antiquitate Britannicae Ecclesiae,* in which he argued that the early British Church differed from Roman Catholicism in key points and thus offered an alternative model for patristic Christianity, in which the newly established Anglican tradition could see its own ancient roots. James Ussher, the Anglican Archbishop of Armagh, was prompted by a similar motivation in his *A Discourse of the Religion Anciently Professed by the Irish and the British* of 1631.[17] But it is not only Anglicans who have claimed early Celtic Christianity as their own, against Roman Catholics. Both Congregationalists and Presbyterians have seen in what they perceived to be its anti-hierarchalism an argument against Anglican episcopacy, and in its perceived popularism, a bulwark against Anglican social elitism. In the contemporary period, entirely new agendas have emerged, from those of the New Age, embracing Goddess-religion and shamanism, for instance, to distinctively Christian calls for a more holistic, ecologically sensitive, and inclusivist Christianity. Contemporary interest in Celtic Christianity therefore extends from a concern on the part of the Roman Catholic Church in Ireland to rediscover its roots to a wholesale assimilation into the thoroughly Romantic appropriation of all things Celtic, as the expression in the sphere of religion of a recognizably New Age esotericism and individualism. Although construction is fundamentally a part of all our awareness of history, the various schools of Celtic religious thought in today's world are dramatically divided in the extent to which they hold themselves accountable to historical detail, and in the extent to which they are concerned to be seen as part of an ongoing Christian tradition. It has perhaps been the fate of Celts and the Celtic more than any other ethnic category to engage the imaginations of other cultures and to be taken up into agendas and narratives quite removed from the social realities of the insular world during the early Middle Ages.

Christianity, like many other religions, likes to appeal to tradition for legitimacy. Inevitably, therefore, the past, identified as tradition, becomes a disputed area, reflecting all the cross-denominational variations in theological ideals and values that inform the Christian present, as much as the differences inherent in the denominational structures themselves. The continuing debate surrounding the existence or otherwise of a distinctive Celtic Christianity or spirituality is being conducted against the background of just such a dispute over tradition. But in this case, additional elements come into play, for the work of some of the main opponents of the idea cannot be identified with the perspective of an ecclesial tradition as such but reflect rather an objectively historical approach. Leading historians such as Kathleen Hughes and Wendy Davies have taken issue with advocates of a Celtic Church, attacking the notion of structural continuities between Christianity in Ireland and Wales and also questioning the distinctive character of the Christianity of the region in the context of the period.[18] In matters of "church," however, not a lot is objective. It is after all a very complex phenomenon. Some analytical approaches will focus on the church as an institution, manifesting itself in its economic and political functions within society. They will consider the church as an organized body of people, focusing on its internal structures for maintaining order and cohesion and its various interactions with the economic, social, and political life of the host society. Another approach, that of the historian of spirituality, takes church in a very different sense. Here the center of interest will be on the spiritual reality of *ecclesia* as the gathered people of God. That reality is constructed in the diverse ways in which countless individuals have encountered the gospel and made the Christian narrative their own in the context of their ordinary lives. For all its elusive abstraction, church in this spiritual, or existential, sense is a valid object of study and has its place beside other forms of historical analysis. Understandably, those who pursue such an "existential archaeology" of the Christian Church will inhabit a very different interpretative tradition from those who do not. They will generally engage with different materials, specifically with those that in some way reflect the inner life, including poetry, letters, sermons, devotional texts, the *Lives* of saints, and liturgical and exegetical texts as well as formal theology (all of which are well represented in the present volume). These items tend to be of less interest to historians of the social, economic, and political life of the Church. The historian of spirituality will tend to "see" a very different church therefore, or, rather, the same church under a very different aspect.

9

One of the differences in emphasis between the various historical interpretative traditions will lie in the area of what each considers to constitute a distinctive Christianity in the past. Those with an eye for the political life of the church, for instance, will look at indicators such as relations between secular rulers and clerics, and, in the Celtic context, between bishops and abbots. Historians of spirituality, on the other hand, will consider representations of the sacred, ideals of holiness, attitudes toward the body and the enviroment, particular emphases within the doctrine of the Incarnation, devotional practices, forms of prayer, and so forth. In particular, the historian of spirituality will be interested in the way in which faith determined the world-view of Christians in the past, forming their understanding of self and world, of sin and salvation. The judgment as to the distinctiveness or otherwise of the Celtic tradition will depend, for the historian of spirituality, on these kinds of indicators, which may not come into the purview of other types of historical assessment at all. It is inevitable also that the modern theologian, sensitive to issues concerning the role of nature, women, or the imagination within Christianity today, will tend to place a far greater weight on these dimensions in early Celtic texts than will the social historian, and will more readily value them as the elements of a distinctive tradition. Some may wish to dismiss this as the intrusion of a subjective bias into the "objective" evaluation of history, but, as Michel de Certeau has pointed out, all historical writing is inherently inclined toward the creation of what he calls "learned circularities" or "sociocultural tautologies."[19] The surest safeguard against too narrow a perspective on the Christian past, of whatever kind, is a combination of different approaches, each with its own tasks and sensitivities, and with its own perspective on the complex phenomenon of the religious life of humankind. It is in the service of a broader and more adequate understanding of the church of the past that the study of the spirituality of early Christian sources of Celtic provenance is offered here.

Let me conclude this section with a summary of the positions I have adopted on this range of disputed questions. The first is that

"Celtic," though potentially misleading, remains a useful term in its inclusivity, and is generally to be preferred to "Irish," "Welsh," or even "insular," which—though entirely appropriate in many contexts—are too exclusivist for the survey of literature contained in this volume.[20] This is to advocate a "soft" use of Celtic, therefore, which is to be distinguished from a "hard" use in that it denies neither the real variety of culture in the Celtic world nor the evident continuities with other cultural areas. But it does maintain the principle of an affinity of language, supporting some kind of affinity of culture between the Celtic-speaking areas, reinforced by extensive cultural contact based on close geographical proximity. It should be noted that Welsh saints appear in Irish saints' *Lives,* Irish saints in Welsh saints' *Lives,* and Welsh saints' in Breton saints' *Lives.*[21] A text such as the *Penitential of Gildas,* which is arguably of Welsh provenance, was copied by an Irish scribe and survives in a Breton manuscript (together with many other important works from the early Irish Church), while the body of sermons known as the *Catechesis celtica,* which was written in distinctively Irish Latin, survives also in a Breton manuscript with Welsh or Cornish glosses.[22] Second, I maintain that the Christianity that developed in the Celtic countries during the early Middle Ages is characterized by a strongly incarnational theology, with an emphasis in diverse ways on physicality and materiality that supports both asceticism and sacramentality. Particularly in vernacular sources, nature appears as a theme to an unusual degree, and enjoys its own autonomy, rather than purely serving the human ends of atmosphere and mood as an imitation of the classical mise-en-scène. Human creativity is drawn to the center of the Christian life in Irish art and Welsh poetry, both of which stress the role of the imagination. Features such as the Brigit tradition offer positive and empowering images of women, even if the relation between these and contemporary social realities is complex. At a theological level these different aspects find a unity in the centrality of the doctrine of the Trinity, which profoundly shaped the religious imagination of the early Celtic peoples. Again, it must be stressed, the issue is a particular patterning of emphases, which cohere theologically into what we might describe as a distinctive spirituality. To some extent what we will find in these texts is a type of Christianity that was characteristic of the patristic period, prior to the rise of Benedictine monasticism on the Continent and the centralizing, regulating influence of the papacy, and which survived in the Celtic margins of Europe longer than it did elsewhere. But we also find here a wonderfully life-affirming and exuberant kind of Christianity that must owe something of its spirit to pre-Christian forms of religious life among the Celts. The relative innocence and freshness of early Celtic Christianity is a discovery that the modern observer, wearied by the abstractions and dualisms of body in opposition to spirit that have dogged the Christian tradition in its more classical forms, may find welcome.

THE ORIGINS OF CELTIC CHRISTIANITY

The process of religious change is one that involves a complex dynamic of transference and interdependence as well as the visible structures of transformation. If a world religion is to take root within a community, then it is inevitable that some degree of fusion or coalescence will take place between the new religion and the religious forms it is seeking to replace. This in turn will lead to some degree of subtle adaptation on the part of the world religion to the religious sensibility of the host people. In the context of early medieval Ireland (for which we have the most evidence), we need not ask the difficult question of how much early material is actually of pagan origin, but simply note that pre-Christian religious paradigms and forms will certainly have governed the way in which Christianity was assimilated but also the types of Christianity that became established.[23] A religious sensibility that is associated with primal religion may lead to forms of syncretism, but it will also cause an emphasis on certain aspects of the Christian gospel and the neglect of others. Indeed, it could be argued that part of the strength of the Christian tradition is precisely the way in which it lends itself to different appropriations or realizations through the medium of different cultures while still retaining its essential identity. Contemporary interest in early Celtic Christian texts is to some degree the recognition that aspects of authentic Christianity were more visible to our ancestors than to ourselves.

While recognizing the importance of Celtic primal religion at the earliest and most formative stage of the evangelization of the Celtic-speaking cultures, it must be recognized that the surviving evidence for Celtic religion is sparse, and often comes from widely differing places and times. But something of its general character does emerge.[24] In the first place, early Celtic religion appears to have been in the main local, with a particular focus on place. Early Gaulish religion was cultic, centering on specific sacred sites such as woodland glades, lakes, springs, or mountains.[25] The many ancient deposits of weapons and treasure that have been discovered in lakes, rivers, and springs almost certainly reflect a desire to placate or reward a divinity of place. Indeed, the liminality of such water sources may indicate that they were seen as points of access to another world. There is more than a hint of this too in poetological texts from a medieval Welsh manuscript, which suggest that the poetry that welled up in the inspired bard had its source in the Other World like spring water that bubbles up from the depths below.[26] Speaking of pre-Christian pagan beliefs in his native Wales or Britain, Gildas, a sixth-century writer, ruefully comments on "the mountains and hills and rivers, once so pernicious, now useful for human needs, on which, in those days, a blind people heaped divine honours."[27] The ancient *dindsenchas* or "place-lore" tradition of early Christian Ireland is also testimony to the enduring sense of locality, as is the extensive tapestry of local saints and their folklore, which dominated the popular culture of the Celtic lands.

The important place of birds and animals in early Celtic Christianity may also reflect this concern with locality and the natural environment. Birds may have been in some sense auguries in pre-Christian Ireland, and the religious iconography of the continental Celtic tradition is full of the representation of deities as animals and birds.[28] It is possible that practices that could be classed as quasi-shamanistic formed part of religion in some parts of the early Celtic world and that ancient animal figures

13

are actually men or women dressed up as animals. There is some evidence from Ireland that early bards wore a costume of bird-feathers,[29] and transmogrification plays a significant part in the mythology of both Wales and Ireland.[30]

A second characteristic of original Celtic religion was its orality. It is probably inevitable that a primal religion, rooted in a particular people and locality, will shun the written word since this may seem to compromise the privileged position of the priestly caste who are charged with maintaining the native lore through an oral medium. The Romans noted the reluctance of the continental Celts to use writing in religious matters, and there are again signs in some medieval Welsh poetry of a clash between a native, oral, cosmological tradition and the classical or Christian models that entered the Celtic countries through written texts.[31] Indeed, the flourishing of a Christian poetic tradition in the vernacular languages (amply represented in the current volume) is an indication of the long continuation of an oral tradition that was embodied in the bards.

The particular shape that monasticism took in many parts of the early Celtic Christian world may have reflected the role of extended kinship units in early Celtic society. It has been argued that monastic settlements took root so quickly and firmly in Ireland because they offered a Christianization of the social status quo.[32] It is certainly the case that the successive abbots of major Irish foundations, such as Iona in western Scotland, came from the same geographical and tribal backgrounds and many had family links through royal lineages. It is possible also that it was a surviving sense of Christianity as a tribal religion that to some extent explains the reluctance of the Welsh to evangelize the early English peoples.

We find little of the metaphysical spirituality of the early, highly Origenist, monastic texts from the East, which otherwise enjoyed great influence in the Celtic lands; rather, there is the suggestion of a society in which heroic values were still prominent and that—with a few exceptions—found a straightforward asceticism more congenial than the philosophical abstractions of Hellenistic theology. The Irish *Táin* and Welsh *Gododdin* are classically heroic tales, full of magical powers and the din of battle, which can be dated in written form to around the seventh century C.E.[33] Even allowing for a degree of stylistic archaism, they suggest that the social values of the early Celts with their feasting and warriors were not far removed from those of the Homeric epics.

In view of the down-to-earth character of Celtic society, it may seem strange to the modern reader that the doctrine of the Trinity, often experienced by the student as one of the more esoteric areas of Christian teaching, should have been so widely and popularly received. But it is possible that this also reflected the influence of a pre-Christian cultural and religious fascination with triads and the number three. In the twelfth century Gerald of Wales comments on the enduring Welsh obsession with the number three, and early Irish myth and art is full of triads, trefoils, and triple figures.[34]

If recent anthropological work on modern animist or indigenous religions can offer new interpretive models for understanding Celtic religion, then recent missiological theory can cast a valuable light on the process of inculturation outlined above. Two types of evangelization can be identified: Congolese and Peruvian. The latter is a historical instance of the evangelization of a colony by a major sixteenth-century Christian power that sought to impose its own cultural version of Christianity on a new habitat. In this case Christianity remained to an extent superficial, failing to fuse with the deeper structures of Peruvian society. In the case of Congo, the evangelization, which likewise occurred in the sixteenth century, was achieved through a relatively small number of individuals who did not wish, or who were unable, to impose a system of specific cultural and social values. Christianity therefore fused with native Congolese systems at a deep level, becoming rooted in the society, but also in turn experiencing change as the social and conceptual structures of that society produced new Christian spiritual, cultural, and religious norms.[35] It is not difficult to see therefore that the Christianity that emerged in the Celtic-speaking countries during the early Middle Ages was one that contained elements of the Congolese type, the process of inculturation allowing the emergence of specifically local emphases as well as the integration of the insular cultures into the body of early Christian life, piety, and learning.[36]

CELTIC CHRISTIANITY: MISSION AND MATURITY

Ireland

The written historical record for the history of Christianity in Ireland begins with the entry for the year 431 in the Chronicle of Prosper of Aquitaine to the effect that "Palladius was ordained by Pope Celestine and sent to the Irish believers in Christ as their first bishop."[37] Who these Christians were and how they came to Ireland is a question that has excited much debate, but it is entirely reasonable to suppose that just such a community existed, evolving through contact with the Celtic Christians of Western Britain, prior to the missionary activity of Patrick. It is notable that the foundations that are linked with the name of Palladius by tradition are all in Leinster, in the Eastern part of Ireland, and thus a short sea journey away from the western coast of Britain. Patrick himself is likely to have been a Brythonic Celt from a Christian family in North West Britain (perhaps around Carlisle), from where he was snatched by an Irish raiding party and taken into slavery. He then escaped and made his way back to Britain, but returned later to Ireland with a strong commitment to work as a missionary there. It is likely that he worked mainly in the north of Ireland, among the Ulaid, around the middle of the fifth century. Muirchú's *Life of Patrick* was written in Ireland in the seventh century and marks an upsurge of interest in the figure of Patrick after some two hundred years of silence. This trend culminates in the *Book of Armagh,* written in the north of Ireland in 807, which juxtaposes the writings of Patrick with Muirchú's *Life* and the prestigious *Life of St. Martin of Tours,* in order to reinforce the claim of Armagh to the Primacy of all Ireland. But neither of the two documents attributed to Patrick, the "Declaration" and "The Letter to the Soldiers of Coroticus," sheds much light on the structure of the earliest Irish Church.[38]

A second important, though less well attested, area of influence was Gaul and the Gallican Church. Patrick probably had Gaulish helpers and he may well himself have visited Gaul. The Irish monks who from the sixth century traveled across the continent of Europe were following in the footsteps of ancient Irish traders, and the great monastic foundations of Southern Gaul, such as Marmoutier and Lérins, were seedbeds of monasticism that undoubtedly left their mark on the early Irish Church.[39]

It is to the canons of the church that we should turn, however, for the earliest and most reliable evidence concerning the initial development of Christianity in Ireland. The earliest group of canons attributed to "The First Synod of St. Patrick" may date from the late sixth century,[40] and these depict a church that is neither in the first flush of mission nor yet fully integrated into the host society. The strictures against clergy who exercise their right to "enforce surety" and to use violence against defaulters suggest that at least some of the clergy were "of noble grade" since "enforcing surety" (naidm) was a right reserved for the nobility (grád flatha) in the secular Law Codes, but a reference also to clergy who are slaves is an indication that the clerical class has not yet been integrated into the social system as honorary nobility. The absence of punitive measures (e.g., fines) other than penance and excommunication also suggests that church and secular law had not yet merged as they would do later when clergy, integrated into the native law of status, automatically received certain legal rights. These same canons also abound in references to pagan practices and depict a church that is governed by bishops operating within territorial dioceses, based on the territory of the indigenous tribe.

But later canons show a church that has become more fully part of Irish society and has taken on features that serve to distinguish it from the earlier continental model of church that we see in the canons from "The First Synod of St. Patrick." By the seventh and eighth centuries the power of the bishop was equaled by that of the abbot, especially in major monastic foundations, and the territorial diocese had been partly superseded by the monastic paruchiae, which were the conglomeration of different foundations all of which traced a common lineage.[41] Different reasons have been put forward for this change, apparent already in the vigorous expansion of monasticism during the sixth century, including the view that with the conversion of entire families, substantial areas of land could more easily pass to the monastery than to the church.[42] As we have already noted, the tribal character of the *paruchiae* reflected kinship patterns in society at large, and their pyramidal structure paralleled the phenomenon of a supraregional overlordship within native Irish society. These latter elements could equally have found expression through conventional territorial dioceses, but perhaps there was something in the uncompromising ascetical and communitarian ideals of the monastery that appealed more strongly to the Irish convert Christian.

The second half of the sixth century was the period of the great monastic leaders and founders. Throughout Ireland individual men and women, such as Comgall of Bangor, Ciarán of Clonmacnois, and Brigit of Kildare, came to embody the values of the new religion in a special way, some stressing the role of learning and others the place of asceticism in the Christian life. Another such figure was Colum Cille, who was born around 521. Our knowledge of Columba (as he was also known) derives largely from his *Life*, which was written by his relative Adamnán some one hundred years after his death. Colum Cille was linked with the powerful Uí Néill tribe of Northern Ireland and with the royal dynasty of Leinster. He founded monasteries in Derry and Durrow and, in 563, left Ireland to found a community off the Scottish coast at Iona. The island of Iona was still in the sphere of influence of the Picts at this point, although in course of time Irish language and culture would come to dominate the whole of the western part of Scotland. Iona itself became a greatly influential center of Irish Christianity from where the religion of the Irishmen passed to Northumbria, where it took root at Lindisfarne and elsewhere, and even extended down into parts of East Anglia.[43] The happy coalescence of Irish and early English culture and Christianity during this period, which led to what is termed the "Insular" tradition, suffered a blow with the Synod of Whitby

(664) and controversy over the calculation of Easter. Nevertheless, even after this time, there was still much travel and interchange, with Irishmen holding senior posts in the English Church, Englishmen studying in Ireland or at Irish foundations, and visible cooperation in the fields of learning and art.[44]

Another major figure of this period was Columbanus (543–615), who was born in Leinster, trained in Bangor (Co. Down), and left Ireland in 587 for Gaul. In contrast to Colum Cille, we have a good number of works from the pen of Columbanus that convey the picture of an able, though uncompromising, Christian leader. The *Rule* and *Penitential* of Columbanus are noted for their austerity, although his sermons and letters show him also to have been a discerning and passionate leader of souls with a mystical temperament. His letter to Pope Boniface on the sensitive issue of the dating of Easter shows the extent to which Irish Christianity could be expressly Roman in its orientation. Columbanus was an important mediator of Irish Christianity to the Continent, and he was the founder of monasteries such as Luxeuil in southeast France and Bobbio in northern Italy (there were Irish monks also at St. Gall, in Switzerland). The lifelong and voluntary commitment of Columbanus to exile from his homeland is an outstanding example of *peregrinatio pro christo,* or "wandering for Christ," whereby a monk would cut himself off from his own extended family as an act of ascetical discipline. It is these wandering Irish monks in exile who were responsible for bringing Christianity to large areas of western and central Europe.[45]

The religious vocation of these early monks, with its combination of learning and asceticism, was an ideal that was to reappear time and again in the history of the Irish Church. Its first and major resurgence, however, occurred in the eighth century with the emergence of a movement known as the Célí Dé, or "servants/clients/friends of God." The reform spread out from Munster in southern Ireland to other parts of the country and even beyond, to the western seaboard of Britain. It found its center, however, in the Dublin area, where leaders such as Maelruain of Tallaght and Dublittir of Finglas inspired their followers with a love of renunciation and radical monasticism. The movement is associated also with the flowering of Irish religious poetry, especially the hermit poetry, and with the Stowe Missal, which is a chief source for the early Irish liturgical tradition.[46]

The Irish Church was badly disrupted from the ninth century onward by Viking attacks, as was the case elsewhere in Europe, but it was the advent of the Cluniac reforms in the eleventh century and the Normans in the twelfth that led to the greater integration of Ireland into the forms and ways of continental Christianity.[47]

Wales

The first signs of a Christian presence in Britain date from the early third century. The martyrdoms of Aaron, Julius (these two probably in modern Caerleon), and Alban can be dated to the middle of the third century,[48] and British bishops were present at the Council of Arles in 314. The new religion came to Britain through the Roman forces and administrators, who occupied the greater part of the country from the first century onwards.

Very little is known about the character and quality of the Christian life in Britain in this ancient period, but the scant evidence we have points to the existence of a strongly Romanized church, most prevalent among the Romano-British elite, who were the people most directly in contact with the occupiers.[49] It was a church whose language was overwhelmingly Latin and whose diocesan structure, based on local centers of population, generally reflected the Roman pattern of civil organization. The three British bishops who attended the Council of Arles came from London, York, and either Lincoln or Colchester. Romano-British Christians suffered with the rest of Christendom during the persecutions of the mid-third century and rejoiced when in 313 the Edict of Milan marked a new period of liberation and security for the Christian Church. Whatever the character of this Romano-British Church, however, it was sufficiently developed to generate a sophisticated and influential theological movement that would be judged heretical in course of time. Pelagianism flourished among monastic circles in Britain, as it did elsewhere, especially among the rigorous communities of southern Gaul. Pelagius himself was probably a Brythonic

Celt by birth, and his writings express the deeply communitarian and ascetical values of the early monasticism that flourished throughout the Celtic lands.[50]

The Romano-British Church survived until the first half of the fifth century when, after the withdrawal of the Roman forces in 409, the Romanized, Celtic areas of Britain came under increasing pressure from the vigorous assaults of the Irish from the west, the Picts from the north, and, most importantly, the Germanic or early English peoples who were seizing land from the east. Over a period of time the territory of the Romano-British Church sharply contracted in the face of such pagan advances. The Brythonic lands, largely to the west and north of the country, which offered the invaders most resistance, did so on account of the generally remote and inaccessible character of their terrain, which had served also to restrict the degree of Roman influence in these parts. The Romano-British Church, therefore, which sent no more bishops to continental councils, was cut off from the continental wellsprings of the new religion and increasingly took on the aspect of an insular and archaic foundation. It was not necessarily the case that Christianity was completely extinguished in the eastern, English parts of Britain, but evidence for its survival there, prior to the evangelization of the English in the seventh century, is patchy.[51]

With the collapse of the Romano-British Church in the fifth century, Christianity was restricted to Strathclyde and Cumbria in the north, through Wales to Devon and Cornwall in the south. In addition, there increasingly occurred the movement of peoples from the southwest to Armorica or Brittany in northwest France. But despite the presence of figures such as St. Ninian at Whithorn in the North, it is to the Welsh Church that we must turn for the most numerous British sources in the early period, since we possess almost no literary sources for Christian life in Brythonic Scotland, Cornwall, and Brittany until the later Middle Ages.[52] Indeed, the early Welsh were keen to stress their historical links with the old Roman civilization and with the religion that it had introduced, and it is worth noting that the very term *Welsh* is an early English word that means "Romanized Celt."[53] There is much evidence to support continuity moreover, since there are almost no accounts of conversion in the earliest Welsh literature, the Welsh/British Church that Gildas berates in the early sixth century is apparently already hopelessly corrupt, and there is evidence for at least one sixth-century territorial diocese (along the lines of the Romano-British Church) in either Welsh Bicknor or near Kenderchurch in southeast Wales.[54]

The spiritual inspiration for the early Welsh Church seems to have come in the main from the monks of the Middle East through their counterparts in southern Gaul. The *Lives* of the early Welsh saints are full of references and allusions to the monasticism of the desert, and the Eastern monastic ascetical ideal evidently provided a powerful role model in Wales, as it did in other Celtic lands. It is likely that during the fifth and sixth centuries individuals inspired by these ideals sought solitude and a life of work and prayer, attracting to themselves like-minded followers who established communities about them, as had been the pattern in fourth-century Egypt. In course of time, some such communities developed into small townships while other sites retained their original ascetical and eremetical character. There is some evidence to suggest that the communities of the far west (e.g., Bardsey in the north, Caldy and St. David's in the south), which were closer to Ireland, may have reflected a more ascetical life-style, while those of the east (e.g., Llantwit Major), which were closer to England, may have laid greater stress on learning.[55]

As was the case in Ireland, the "classical" period in Wales came to an end principally with the arrival of the Normans, who brought with them many of the norms of continental Christianity. For the first time the major religious Orders of the Catholic Church, especially the Cistercians, took root. The ancient Celtic foundations either gave way to the new Orders or themselves conformed, frequently by adopting the Augustinian Rule and becoming canons. The new integration into European ways brought change, but it also quickened a Welsh national consciousness and represented a welcome expansion of Welsh cultural horizons. Nor did it necessarily prove inimical to the indigenous religion, since a number of the Welsh Cistercian houses became bastions of Welsh culture and tradition. It is worth noting that the anonymous Dominican author of "Food of the Soul" still reflects a deeply Celtic sensibility in his work despite the European character of his religious formation. But in both Ireland and Wales, following the adoption of continental norms of religious life, the distinctive aspects of the indigenous Christianity were increasingly confined to the sphere of vernacular religion. The *Carmina Gadelica* collections of Gaelic songs from the Highlands and Islands, which were gathered during the second half of the nineteenth century, remain strongly Celtic in kind and are a reminder of the extent to which an oral and minority culture can conserve elements from an earlier tradition.[56]

TOWARD A CELTIC SPIRITUALITY

The reconstruction of the spirituality of medieval Christians is not an easy task. In the first place, it requires an understanding of a cultural world that was very different from our own. But it is precisely the "otherness" of early medieval Celtic Christianity that makes it attractive to us, for it seems to contain perspectives that must have originated in the religious disposition of tribal peoples virtually untouched by the classical tradition. The Welsh highly valued their direct links with Roman civilization and the Irish came to show a keen interest in the literary culture of Greece and Rome, but important aspects of early Celtic Christianity reflect an orientation different from that which came to predominate throughout the Latin world. Of course, there are real parallels with the Anglo-Saxon Church in its earlier period, and in terms of ecclesiastical structure also with the pre-Carolingian Church more generally. There are parallels too with the early Orthodox Church in Syria and Russia, as there are with the Christianity of certain indigenous groups in the world today.[57] It may be that an ancient form of Christianity survived much longer on the western margins of Europe, where there was, for instance, a relative absence of urban centers, than it did elsewhere. And it is arguable also that at least elements of that tradition survived fitfully into the modern period through the intense conservatism of remote monolingual Celtic-speaking communities, whose bards and storytellers preserved early material in an oral medium with a degree of continuity that is unimaginable in the context of an urban environment and a written language.

Whatever the strengths of the classical Christian perspective that became the norm in most parts of western Christendom, many in the world today have become generally skeptical of a number of its key presuppositions. The primacy of the male and the designation of the male as being normative for humanity can be a hindrance to the Christian life. An emphasis on reason to the detriment of the imagination can seem restrictive and diminishing of important human potentialities. The absence of nature, except as literary device or untamed opponent of Christian power, seems counter to a developing ecological consciousness. Also, diverse forms of alienation from the body are visible in modern Western society, from obesity to pornography, for which Christianity (both Protestant and Catholic), with its emphasis on belief and the processes of the mind and persistent tendency to denigrate the physical, must take some responsibility. A number of the Christian texts included in the present volume offer—albeit tentatively in some instances—the outline of alternative paradigms. We see here images of women as agents of power (Brigit); we see implicit and explicit appeals to the place of the imagination at the center of Christian life (art and poetry), and strong images of nature as an autonomous realm that is nevertheless touched by the life of grace (Melangell).[58] Running throughout a number of texts is the awareness of the body as the focus of human existence, not subordinate to the mind in a tortuous relation of subjection and culpability, but thematized as the locus of penance, where penance itself is not self-inflicted mutilation but the reception of new life and the beginning of the transformation that leads to glory ("The Loves of Taliesin").[59]

In many ways Christianity lives by its ability to rediscover its past. The history of Christianity shows a constant tendency toward invigorating revival and rediscovery of its roots as well as to polemics surrounding the varying definitions of tradition. Celtic Christianity offers just such a renewal. But the way to appropriate traditions form the past, originally practiced in this case in social and spiritual contexts very different from our own, is problematic. Not many readers of this book in New York or London will be remotely in touch with the living fragments of the Celtic religious past, which still survive precariously in remote areas of Ireland, Scotland, Wales, and Brittany. Indeed, it may seem an equally alien world to the inhabitants of Dublin, Edinburgh, Cardiff, or Rennes. Nevertheless, one way in which the texts included in this volume are important is that they alert us to possibilities of Christian existence subtly different from our own, which are both ancient and new.

THE SOURCES:
INTRODUCTION TO THE
TRANSLATED TEXTS

HAGIOGRAPHY

If the remote origins of medieval hagiography lie in the biography and edifying literature of the classical world, then it is the accounts of the Christian martyrs and the lives of holy men and women of the desert that represent the immediate source. Among the texts of particular influence in the Celtic world were the *Life of Anthony* by Athanasius and the *Life of Martin of Tours* by Sulpicius Severus.[60] The earliest Celtic hagiography, the *Life of Samson,* which was composed in Brittany probably some time in the late seventh century, already shows the influence of the ascetical ideal of the desert in combination with fabulous and wonder-working motifs whose origins probably lie in the native tradition of Celtic heroic folklore and mythology.[61] This combination of ascetical monasticism on the one hand and magical potency on the other was to remain a characteristic of the Celtic hagiographical tradition for centuries to come.[62]

The traditions of the saints in the Celtic lands, as in many other cultures, began at a point long before the emergence of the formal Latin *Lives* of saints with which the genre is most frequently associated. The earliest surviving traces are vernacular praise-poems or references in calendars, martyrologies, and annals, and with just a few exceptions, Celtic hagiography belongs to the tenth, eleventh, and twelfth centuries.[63] Saints were also deeply ambivalent figures within early Christian Celtic tradition, being on the one hand the supernatural protectors of their communities and powerful emblems of political jurisdiction and, on the other, incarnations of the highest spiritual and ascetical ideals.[64] Through the cult of relics and the hagiographical folklore of story and verse, the presence of the saints touched all parts of Celtic society. It was generally political considerations, however, that precipitated the emergence of

26

respectable Latin *Lives* from the amorphous mass of tradition. In Ireland this had much to do with the competing claims of the different monastic *paruchiae,* or spheres of influence, that were concerned to establish the credentials of their founders, while the Welsh *Lives* of the eleventh and twelfth centuries represented in part a new assertiveness of the native church in the face of Norman encroachments. But such *Lives* not only have a political history; they also functioned as "a catechetical tool much like the stained glass which surrounded and instructed the faithful in their participation in the liturgy." As "sacred narrative," they are calculated statements not only of what the church and the people understood by sanctity but also of how the hagiographers felt sanctity could best be signified.[65] This latter point is of considerable importance, since there is a marked tendency among Celtic hagiographers to signal Christian sanctity by the use of motifs that appear to belong to the iconography of an earlier and pre-Christian age or, alternatively, to that of a surviving paganism.[66] These are magical in kind and stress the Christian saint's access to *power.* The *Lives* of Celtic saints are notoriously amoral in that the power of the saint can often be manifest in destructive ways that sit uneasily with the ethical values of the Christian gospel. Commenting on the saints of Ireland, Gerald of Wales remarks that they are "more vindictive than the saints of any other place."[67] It would be wrong to surmise, however, that Celtic Christians were encouraged to practice magical arts and to strike their enemies dead at a glance; rather these motifs of power often served the greater political purpose of claiming a special status for a particular saint and thus, by implication, for the institution with which he or she was most closely associated. There may also be evidence of a *Religionsstreit* in the *Lives:* a conflict between the old druidic religion and Christianity. It is in the light of this perhaps that the Christian saint is portrayed as an individual who possesses superior powers to the druids and magicians of old.[68]

The Patrick Tradition

Patrick has become almost synonymous with Irish Christianity, and indeed with Ireland. Because of this fame, more attention has been devoted to him—by religious writers, historians of early Irish history, philologists, and individuals from many other disciplines—than to any other individual in Irish history, so much indeed that a forthcoming bibliography will contain several thousand items.[69] The effect of this has been that many become more conversant with "the Patrick Problem" than with our most certain evidence: Patrick's own writings. Therefore, the policy here is to leave the historical problems out of consideration entirely.[70] By introduction we need say only this: Patrick was a fifth-century Christian of the Roman Empire, who crossed the sea to a barbarian land (i.e., one outside the Latin-speaking world of the empire) to bring its people Christianity. There, probably late in life, he wrote an account of his life and ministry (cf. *Confessio* 62). Moreover, at some other time, he wrote a formal warning of their sins to Christians from the island of Britain who were soldiers of a leader called, in Latin, "Coroticus," who had been raiding Ireland and attacking some of Patrick's converts.

The title of Patrick's longer work, the *Confessio* (which we have here translated as "Patrick's Declaration of the Great Works of God"), calls for some comment. While the work does not have this title in some early manuscripts, we can consider it an authentic description of what Patrick wanted to write, as he uses the term at the end of the work: "And this is my declaration *(confessio mea)* before I die." The meaning of the title, in Latin, is also problematic. Our first instinct is to think of it as a confession in the sense of a reply to his critics—an autobiographical work that fulfills a function somewhat like John Henry Newman's *Apologia pro vita sua*—and such a reply to critics does appear to be part of Patrick's motivation in writing. Another way of looking at the work has been to interpret *confessio* in the sense of a declaration or confession of faith *(confessio/professio fidei)*. Again, the expression of his Trinitarian faith lends support to this way of understanding *confessio*. However, neither of these understandings of *confessio* addresses the fact that many events are retold by Patrick simply as they deserve to be known for they are seen by him as significant in that they testify to the work of God in his life and deeds. When we look at various uses of the term *confessio* in the

scriptures in Latin, a different view emerges. It is a praise of the
Lord for his strength (Ps 95:6) and for his majesty and righteousness (Ps 110:3). It involves telling of the glory he shares with his
people (Ps 148:14). A confession is a song of God's works, of his
mighty deeds, and of his mercies toward his people (Ps 88:2). It
is part of the duty of the disciple to offer thanks and acknowledge publicly the gifts of God, that one is in his debt, and that
one belongs to him and seeks to do his will in one's actions (Ezr
10:11). This sense is made even more clear in some passages in
the New Testament. Confession is part of holding fast to the
work of Christ as the high priest who has made all nations
acceptable to the Father (Heb 4:14), and this activity of confession is testimony to Christian hope (Heb 10:23). It is an aspect of
fighting the good fight of the Christian to testify to Christ's saving work in the presence of others (1 Tm 6:12), and in this the
Christian imitates Christ who testified to God's power in the
presence of Pilate (cf. Jn 18:37) (1 Tm 6:13). If we look on
Patrick's account of what God did through him in this light, then
his *confessio* is but another part of his own service of God, which
is the preaching of the gospel to those who have not heard it (cf.
Rom 15:16 and 1 Cor 9:12–3).

The translation is based on the edition of Newport J. D.
White,[71] but it takes account both of the edition of L. Bieler[72] and
the work of D. Howlett.[73] It has long been recognized that Patrick
used written materials, besides the scriptures, in this work.[74]
Recently, this realization has led to a massive study of possible
sources, or at least parallels, for the ideas found in Patrick.[75] However, the concentration here has been on adding a biblical apparatus.[76] This strategy's purpose is twofold: First, it shows the
extent of Patrick's familiarity with the Christian scriptures; and
second, by way of the biblical indices in other works, it enables
the reader to compare his approach to that of other writers in the
Christian tradition regarding the themes on which he touches.[77]

"The Letter to the Soldiers of Coroticus" plunges us into the
world of the fifth century like no other piece of writing from the
insular world. Although we can only guess at the specific events
that prompted this letter, we know that the fifth century was one

of increasing disorder in the West. The withdrawal of the Roman legions from Britain early in the century left a power vacuum among warlords anxious to grab whatever was for the taking, and slaves were an ideal commodity. As the century progressed, raiding, taking captives, and holding people for ransom became commonplace not only on the fringes of the Roman world but wherever the new peoples were establishing themselves, for example, among the Franks in Gaul. Patrick knew the whole business intimately as one taken captive himself, and he speaks in this letter from the basis of that experience. We, moreover, should not forget that he is the only person from that period who survived enslavement and told his story.

The *Book of Armagh* (now in Trinity College Dublin), which dates from A.D. 807, records three "Sayings" as surviving from Patrick. Whether they are genuine statements from Patrick that were later written down, we shall never know. However, there is nothing in the contents that would challenge attributing them to Patrick. In any case, the fact that "sayings" were recorded shows the respect in which the memory of Patrick was held in Armagh.

Muirchú wrote his "Life of Patrick" toward the end of the seventh century. While in many ways it is a typical piece of early medieval hagiography, it merits study in the context of insular spirituality.[78] Muirchú has a developed sense of the relationship between Christian revelation and the pagan religion of his ancestors. That religion was not simply a darkness, but a preparation for the gospel, and hence his people were always in some relationship with the true God and under the protection of his Providence.[79] Apart from its obvious focus, Patrick, the *vita* provides us with information about several concerns in the politics, secular and ecclesiastical, of the time. At the time the Uí Néill [the grandsons of Néill] were the growing dynasty in Ulster and Leinster. Part of their policy was to take over the Patrick cult as their own patron, and to link it with their dynastic center: Armagh. Muirchú's *vita* supports these claims. Within church politics, meanwhile, there was a dispute among those who wished to continue following customs, most notably the method for deriving the date of Easter, which had been abandoned on the Continent. The group that wanted to introduce the newer, and more accurate, system of computistics were known as the *Romani,* and Muirchú was one of their number. However, these concerns should not cause us to forget that this work is our earliest life of Patrick, and that it stands close to the fountain of the Patrick legend, which has manifested itself in so many ways in Irish religious history.[80]

Among later Patrician texts, the *lorica* known as "Patrick's Breastplate" is perhaps the best known. There may be a reference to a connection between this work and Patrick in the ninth-century *Book of Armagh,* though the association is first made explicitly in the eleventh-century *Liber Hymnorum,* where it is said that Patrick sang the *lorica* when ambushed by King Loeguire, with the result that he and his companions took on the form of wild deer. We can speculate that the name "Deer's Cry" *(fáeth fiada)* given to this text may reflect the influence of this legend on an original title, *fóid fiada,* which "is a technical term applied to those charms of druids and *filid* which produced invisibility."[81] The language of the text is not earlier than the eighth century.

The Brigit Tradition

These texts generally date from a later period than the Patrician works, although our earliest work, "Ultán's Hymn," may be a composition of the seventh century and thus be one of the oldest hymns in the Irish language. In the *Liber Hymnorum* it is variously ascribed to Colum Cille, Broccan the Squint-eyed, and Brendan, among others.[82] The hymn reminds us that the earliest evidence for the traditions of the saints often occurs in poetical works rather than in formal hagiography.[83] We almost entirely lack the biographical information for Brigit of Kildare that we have for Patrick, and can only note that the year of her birth is given in the Annals of Ulster as 452, with three different dates for her death.[84] She was the foundress of the double monastery at Kildare, which held jurisdiction over a large part of southwest Ireland until the suppression of the monasteries.[85] In the twelfth century it was visited by Gerald of Wales, who noted the maintaining of a sacred fire, tended by nineteen nuns (with Brigit tending it on the twentieth night).[86] The metaphors applied to Brigit in "Ultán's Hymn," such as "golden, radiant flame" leading the faithful to the "brilliant, dazzling sun," indicate the interplay of pagan and Christian motifs that seems to occur throughout the Brigit tradition. In *Cormac's Glossary* of the ninth century, we are told that Brigit the goddess is daughter of the Dagda, or "Good God," and that she was the goddess of poetry and had two sisters of the same name, who are the patronesses of smithwork and healing.[87] The sacred fire at Kildare, the fire symbolism of "Ultán's Hymn," and the occurrence of a miracle showing a peculiar affinity with the sun in Cogitosus's *Life of St. Brigit* suggest that the Brigit persona may have something of the qualities of a goddess of fire or sun goddess as well.[88] The designation of Brigit, in "Ultán's Hymn," as the "mother of Jesus" (as well as variants on this such as "Mary of the Gaels," the "foster-mother of Christ," and "Mary's midwife") shows the extent to which the symbols and symbolic functions of different religious and cultural systems can be fused together in early Celtic sources.[89]

"The Life of St. Brigit the Virgin by Cogitosus" is the best known of the various *Lives* of Brigit, and it can be dated to the period from 650 to 690.[90] We have little information regarding Cogitosus, but he may have been of the Úi hAedo tribe, from Leinster.[91] There exist further Latin *Lives* of Brigit, including an important text known as the *Vita I*.[92] This contains some very early elements, but the date of its composition is disputed. A further *Life*, in both Irish and Latin, which is included here under the title "The Irish Life of Brigit," has been dated from as early as 774 to the early ninth century. It has been argued that in its Latin sections it seems to draw on some of the sources of the *Vita I*.[93]

In his *Life*, Cogitosus attempts to present Brigit in conventional hagiographical terms. He lays great stress on her power and her virtue (both expressed by the same Latin word, *virtus*). She is a virgin, an able leader, and a fit foundress of the monastic tradition in Kildare of which Cogitosus himself is probably a part and the privileges of which he is keen to maintain. But even this text contains passages that are seemingly borrowed from the early Irish saga tradition, such as the account of Brigit's curing of the giant's appetite and her retrieval of a brooch from a fish.[94] A repeated emphasis on miracles that involve the production of food or animal husbandry, frequently as acts of charity, suggests the combination of the functions of a fertility goddess with the claims of an altruistic Christian sanctity, and we may see some echo of Brigit the goddess of smithcraft in the story of how Brigit smashed a silver dish against a stone, dividing it into three exactly equal parts.[95]

"The Irish Life of Brigit" is far less sophisticated in tone than Cogitosus's version, and generally reads like a catena of miracles. Here we are informed that Brigit's mother, Broicsach, was a slave-woman and that Brigit herself was raised in the house of a druid. In addition to miracles involving food production, we find accounts of wonder-working that are specifically linked with fertility, both animal and human. She is able to turn water into milk, and cures a woman of infertility (providing her with male children she has lost) by treating her with water enriched with her own blood.[96] "The Irish Life" also contains accounts of Brigit's cursing, notably her own brother, who wishes to marry her off against her will. She causes his eyes to burst in his head.[97] Something of the exceptional status of the saint is conveyed by the fact that, according to "The Irish Life," Brigit was consecrated by Mel, who, "being intoxicated with the grace of God there, did not know what he was reciting from his book, for he consecrated Brigit with the orders of a bishop."[98]

The cult of Brigit remained a powerful influence in the social and cultural life of Ireland, and is visible even today. Her feast of February 1 coincides with the ancient festival of *imbolc*, which, by one reading, is an ancient pastoral term that signifies "milking," suggesting again a link with fertility.[99] The theme of fertility is certainly dominant in the cult of Brigit, and finds expression in the many rites and artifacts (including the *brideog*, or doll-like representation of Brigit) that characterize the coming of spring in rural Ireland.[100]

The Voyage of Brendan

Brendan is a saint whose name is remembered in place names particularly from the west of Ireland and who lived, according to the Annals of Ulster, during the sixth century.[101] He founded the monastery of Clonfert in Connacht. He must himself have traveled widely, but his widespread cult is also associated with the journeying of the Ciarraige, a sea-faring people, who carried his name around the west coast of Ireland and as far as Scotland, Wales, and Brittany. *The Voyage of Brendan* probably dates from the early tenth century and, along with the *Life of Brendan,* forms an essential source for the Brendan tradition.[102] *The Voyage of Brendan* is an account of the saint's journeys across the sea in search of the "Promised Land of the Saints," itself a cypher either for the "Promised Land" of Canaan or for the "Kingdom of Heaven."[103] These Christian motifs are evidently intertwined with ancient Irish concepts of the "Other World" embodied in pagan mythological sagas of voyage and discovery. *The Voyage of Brendan* has rightly been called "a Christianized tale of the *Immram,* or 'voyage' literature, a type of pagan romance which itself must have sprung from the folk-lore of the maritime peoples of Ireland who for unknown ages had looked out upon the mystery of the broad Atlantic."[104] In its combination of ancient Irish motifs, Christian apocalyptic vision, biblical reminiscences, early medieval zoological and geographical lore, all combined with exact descriptions of the monastic *regimen* and ascetical ideals, *The Voyage of Brendan* can be regarded as a compendium, or even classical narrative, of the early Irish Church. This extraordinary text was translated into numerous vernacular languages and enjoyed considerable influence on the continent of Europe.[105] St. Brendan's Isle appeared on charts of the Atlantic until the eighteenth century, and has even been seen as an account of an early Irish discovery of America.[106]

Rhigyfarch's Life of David

The first Welsh text to be included is a finely crafted work of the Norman period and breathes the atmosphere of a later age.

Rhigyfarch, author of this "Life of St. David," belonged to a distinguished Cambro-Norman family who had close associations with Ireland. His father, Sulien, was twice bishop of St. David's on the west coast of Wales, and spent some ten years in Ireland. Iwan, Rhigyfarch's brother, likewise spent time in Ireland and was a scribe in the Irish style.[107] Rhigyfarch's "Life" can be dated to around the year 1095.

Rhigyfarch begins his narrative by suggesting that there were all kinds of special omens and events surrounding the birth of David that made him, in a sense proper to hagiography, another Christ. But the fact that David robbed a preacher of his eloquence while still in the womb suggests the bardic rather than the biblical world, for magically silencing his competitors was the characteristic of the chief poet of tradition, Taliesin.[108]

Rhigyfarch conveys to us an image of David as the inspirational organizer of a substantial monastic foundation: He is "a man of eloquence, full of grace, experienced in religion, an associate of angels, a man to be loved, attractive in countenance, magnificent in appearance" who spends his time "teaching, praying, kneeling" as well as caring "for his brethren" and "feeding a multitude of orphans, wards, widows, needy, sick, feeble and pilgrims." But despite the stylistic sophistication of "The Life of St. David," and the complexity of the monastic structures it depicts, Rhigyfarch's text nevertheless contains elements of a primitive ascetical ideal. This is evident in David's own devotional and ascetical practices, as when he immerses himself in cold water after long hours of prayer, but it is primarily to be seen in the account we are given of the *regimen* that was followed by his community and that may, in fact, be based on an original Rule of St. David.

The Life of Beuno

The second Welsh text survives only in a Middle Welsh version from around the fourteenth century, but it may be the translation of an earlier Latin source for Beuno's life, perhaps incorporating primitive tradition. In any case, "The Life of Beuno" appears to contain a number of iconographic motifs that are primitive in feeling and suggest characteristics of the pre-Norman world. Thus on no fewer than four occasions Beuno issues a curse with fatal consequences and, on three occasions, he brings the dead to life. Images of decapitation and the restoration of the head to the body predominate in a way that recalls the significance of the skull in the ancient religion of Gaul. Some echo of druidic religion, and its close association with oak trees, may be preserved in the oak tree that Beuno plants and that is able magically to distinguish between a Welshman who passes beneath it and an Englishman (or pagan in another tradition), striking the latter dead. Beuno controls the elements insofar as water in a cauldron cannot be brought to the boil in his presence and, when accused of practicing "magical arts," Beuno curses the man with swift and fatal consequences. This particular "Life" also responds well to a structuralist interpretation, which would see a binary opposition between the metaphor of fire, associated with dryness, heat, maleness, and Christianity, and that of water, linked with wetness, cold, femaleness, and the old religion.[109] This becomes particularly evident in the account of the death of Gwenfrewi, who has been pursued by the lascivious King Caradoc, and her restoration to life by Beuno. Caradoc is associated with water, since he "melted away into a lake," while Gwenfrewi herself seems to be a symbol of transformation, since her head, struck off by Caradoc, "fell into the church while her body remained outside." When Beuno healed her, the girl "dried the sweat from her face" while "a spring was formed" where her blood fell to the ground. Beuno himself is known as *casulsych,* or "dry-coat," after the magical coat that can never get wet, which Gwenfrewi (according to the *Life of Gwenfrewi*) weaves each year for him.[110] Gwenfrewi's spring, which is situated at Holywell in North Wales (Welsh: *Treffynon,* or "Town of the Spring"), was accredited with healing powers and was an important pilgrimage site in the Middle Ages and later. Arguably holy wells such as this, which were so popular in medieval Wales, represent one of the key points of transformational continuity between the old religion and the new.[111]

THE SOURCES

The Life of St. Melangell

The final text included in this section is a relatively late work, dating in surviving form from the late fifteenth or early sixteenth century although based on earlier written and oral sources that are no longer extant.[112] "The Life of St. Melangell" once again depicts the Celtic saint as a figure who enjoys the particular trust of animals. The cult of Melangell was recognizably present in Pennant Melangell (the village in mid-Wales that bears her name) in the twelfth century and may date from a significantly earlier period.[113] The interpenetration of place and "sacred narrative" through the folklore of the saints is a configuration that is very typical of the Celtic countries, which, prior to the advent of the Normans, steadfastly preferred their own ancient and local saints to those of the universal church.[114]

MONASTIC TEXTS

The monastic movement began in the deserts of North Africa and the Middle East in the third and fourth centuries and became one of the most formative influences on the early church. Monastic bishops such as Athanasius, Augustine, and Basil the Great were prominent among those who shaped early Christian theology and doctrine, and the ascetical ideals of the monks passed over both to the clergy and, in some degree, to the people of God as a whole. From the fourth century onward the new monastic ideal and way of life came to the West, especially through the work of John Cassian, taking root particularly in southern Gaul. Gildas, writing in the sixth century, knew of monks as a minority in Britain, from where the movement may have spread to Ireland.[115]

It is notable, however, that Celtic monks of the early period differed in a number of respects from their continental counterparts, who would eventually come to dominate all over Western Europe. Whereas the Benedictines and their Reforms offered a specific, generally ascetical life-style, Celtic monasticism was altogether a more widespread and therefore inclusive phenomenon.[116] No single Rule, not even that of Columbanus, achieved supremacy, and the various foundations at different stages represent a patchwork of widely differing ascetical ideals. In both Ireland and Wales strict monks are associated in particular with eremeticism and semi-eremetical communities,[117] while at the other end of the spectrum we find unequivocal evidence for the existence of lay abbots and inheritance by their sons of the abbot's office up to the Viking period and beyond.[118] In addition, church and secular canons make accommodation for the wives of both priests and bishops.[119]

The Celtic monastic tradition represented a curious combination of laxity and rigor, inclusiveness and vocation; and, although it is rightly associated with great achievement in the arts, another, more ascetical expression of the spirit of the Celtic monks was the Penitential tradition, which originated in Wales and Ireland, from around the sixth century. Penitentials are remarkable texts that link not only the highest ascetical ideals with pastoral realism but also much that is hyperbolic and bizarre with the punctilious detailing of legal codes.[120] They are as much quarries of information for the psychologist and social historian as they are for those interested in historical Christianity.

The earliest Celtic Penitentials are those for which a Welsh provenance is claimed: "The Preface of Gildas on Penance" (translated here), the Decrees of the *Synod of North Britain,* the *Grove of Victory,* and the *Excerpts from a Book of David.* The Welsh attribution of these works is supported by references to Roman measures in the first and fourth, and by the laying down of severe penances for guiding the "barbarians" (presumably Anglo-Saxons) in the third.[121] "The Preface of Gildas" is an early text, therefore, and is the product of a young and insular church. The sole sanctions it proposes are ecclesiastical (penance and excommunication), whereas the later Penitentials include the sanction of fines, which derives from secular law, and are the product of a church that has become more assimilated into Irish society.

Although "The Preface of Gildas" is more moderate in its penances, the conclusion to "The Penitential of Cummean" is a classic statement of the discretion that underlies the Celtic Penitential tradition, whereby the confessor is urged to weigh up the individual strengths and weaknesses of the sinner and to take these into account when imposing the needful penance. "The Penitential of Cummean" makes considerable use of Welsh sources and is the most comprehensive of the Celtic Penitentials. It follows the eight capital sins of Cassian in its structure (unlike Finnian and Columbanus), and applies Cassian's principle of "healing through opposities." It also includes a short list of commutations. The author was Cummaine Fota, Bishop of Clonfert, who died in 662.[122] "The Penitential of Cummean" may also have been the "Irish book" that much influenced the important English Penitential attributed to Theodore of Tarsus, who was Archbishop of Canterbury from 668 to 690,[123] and it circulated widely on the Continent during the eighth and ninth centuries (as did the "Penitential of Columbanus"). Later Irish Penitentials such as the *Bigotian Penitential* used Cummean, as did a number of other Welsh and Irish texts (as well as the Rule of St. Benedict). It also bears a close resemblance to the vernacular "Old Irish Penitential," a Culdee text that was presumably written in Tallaght in the late eighth century.[124]

The emphasis on frequent confession to a spiritual superior (Irish: *anmchara* or "soul-friend"), the concept of eight deadly sins, and the extensive use of Cassian's "healing through contraries" (which originated in Greek medical theory) are all indications of the influence of the Egyptian desert in the formation of Celtic Penitential practice. Penitential texts passed from Ireland and Britain to the Continent through the work of Irish and Anglo-Saxon missionaries. Although they sparked a good deal of controversy, they also contributed in course of time to the adoption of regular private confession to a priest and private penance, which, at the Fourth Lateran Council of 1215, became part of universal Catholic tradition. On the less positive side, the tables of commutations (whereby lengthy periods of penance could be commuted by shorter periods of more intense austerity or by almsgiving), which were also a creation of the Celtic tradition, certainly laid the foundation for later Penitential abuses such as trafficking in indulgences.

"The Rule for Monks by Columbanus" shows the influence of

Basil the Great, Cassian, and Jerome, but may also, in part, be dependent on an earlier Rule by the ascetical Comgall of Bangor, which no longer survives. It addresses the first principles of monasticism rather than the everyday detail of communal life, and thus differs in balance from the Rule of St. Benedict. It too shows the influence of Egypt, in the emphasis on nocturnal psalmody and solemn vigils, where it again has an affinity with the *Antiphonary of Bangor* and the tradition of Comgall. Columbanus's text, which is noted for its interest in interior states as well as its relative severity, had considerable influence on subsequent monastic Rules, including the *Concordia Regularum* by Benedict of Aniane.[125]

POETRY

One of the most remarkable features of medieval Celtic Christianity is the prominence from an early period of a Christian vernacular poetic tradition. Elsewhere in Europe the role of the vernacular poet was generally suspect and marginal, lying on the periphery of Latin ecclesiastical culture.[126] Moreover, where we do find early vernacular religious lyrics, as in Anglo-Saxon England, they tend to be catechetical and intended in general for a lay audience, whereas the Celtic texts are more centrally located within Christian monastic culture.[127] There are two key factors regarding the role of the poet in medieval Celtic society that reinforce this distinction.

In the first place, recognized poets (who were almost always men) enjoyed an unparalleled social status in the Celtic world, as is evident in the Law Books of both Ireland and Wales. The *ollam* or highest grade of Irish poet enjoyed a status in law equal to that of a bishop or a petty king,[128] and in Wales, the *pencerdd* was similarly honored.[129] Moreover, the medieval Celtic bard was not only the eulogizer of kings, but also genealogist and preserver of tribal lore and cosmology. It has been argued that the high social status of the Celtic poet resulted from his assumption of some of the social functions of the druid, who, with the advent of Christianity, increasingly became *persona non grata*.[130] This same mechanism

40

might also explain why we seem to find a more secure Christian bardism in early medieval Wales, where the power of the druids was substantially reduced in the first century A.D. under the Roman occupation, than in Ireland, where the druids survived to be a major challenge to fifth- and sixth-century Christianity. It is notable also that medieval Welsh makes use of druidic terminology in order to express the sacred elements of Christian life, whereas this particular phenomenon does not occur in Irish.[131] The centrality of the poet within medieval Celtic society can be seen to be a key area, therefore, in terms both of cultural transformation and continuity.[132]

Second, the Celtic poet had an exalted understanding of his own vocation. Medieval Celtic poetics are filled with notions of supernatural power and divine or semi-divine inspiration. According to one Irish text, the most gifted poets are those "who are both divine and secular prophets and commentators both on matters of grace and of secular learning, and they then utter godly utterances and perform miracles."[133] A fourteenth-century book of instruction for Welsh poets reminds the reader that the Holy Spirit himself is the source of poetic inspiration—a theme that was energetically debated throughout the later Middle Ages.[134] The fourteenth-century Welsh *Book of Taliesin,* on the other hand, contains a number of poems that appear to suggest the survival of a pagan and druidic model of bardic inspiration.[135] In sum, the vernacular religious poetic tradition in both Wales and Ireland is one of our most important sources for Celtic Christianity since it was an area of Christian culture that continued to represent a vital point of contact with cultural and religious paradigms that belonged to an earlier pre-Christian world. But the lyric form, in addition, gives access to the minds and hearts of monastic writers from the past who speak in these works of their joys and struggles in the spiritual life.

The first three poems given here are hymns of praise that were written in Old Irish and therefore date from the ninth century or earlier. The first selection contains fulsome praise of God as King "who rules over all," echoing something of the secular praise tradition but also including elements from the doxology found in

Revelation 7:12. The second, on the other hand, praises God as Creator of all, both heaven and earth. The third poem consists of lines that were written in the margin of a manuscript of the Latin grammarian Priscian, copied by monks of St. Gall in the first half of the ninth century. The situation described by those lines is that of a hermit monk living in the woods and surrounded by songbirds. The occurrence in this short poem of three references to bird-song linked with praise may have a certain religious resonance in that the interpretation of bird-song was an important aspect of the diviner's craft.[136] There may be a subtext here, therefore, suggesting the Christian transformation of a pagan motif. A degree of poetic self-reference is notable in this poem also in that the poet implies in the final line that his poetry of praise shall count in his favor on the Day of Judgment. The fourth poem of the selection, which dates from the twelfth century or later, continues the theme of poetry as praise of God; the poet asks God to ensure that his language of praise shall be faultless.

The dominant motif of the next four poems, which are again Old or early Middle Irish, is that of penance and a life orientated toward repentance for past sins, asceticism, and the hope of resurrection. The first three poems (5–7) depict the life of a hermit, living in solitude and passing the day with frequent prayer at the canonical hours, genuflection, and fasting. There is a particular emphasis on the gift of tears as a guarantee of redemption (poem 6), and on the constant struggle with wayward thoughts that distract the monk from his meditation on death and his prayer (poem 7).

The final two poems from this section date in the main from the Old Irish period and reflect the desire to fuse the Christian devotional tradition with the passage of time: the seasons (poem 9) or the days of the week (poem 10). The former is evidently associated with the genre of martyrologies and catalogs of the saints, which were popular in medieval Ireland, existing even in Irish metrical form.[137] In both poems the saints are called on to protect the speaker from dangers, both temporal and spiritual.

We encounter many of the same themes in the work of early Welsh religious poets, although here there are undoubtedly subtle differences in emphasis. The first of these included here (11), which is one of the earliest works in the Welsh language, already seems to speak from an established tradition of Christian bardism. It presents an awareness of the universal creation, and of God as Creator, but appears implicitly to oppose the expressive powers of the poet to those of both the natural world and the world of "letters." Thus we may be able to discern here early signs of conflict between an oral and a literate tradition, with the poet seeming to state the importance of his own role as a focus for the Church's praise. In the following poem, "Padarn's Staff," we return to the theme of the saints, in this case the staff of St. Padarn, who was associated with Llanbadarn Fawr in west Wales, a major center of Welsh learning and Christianity, noted also for its contact with Ireland. The author may be the twelfth-century scholar Ieuan ap Sulien (brother of Rhigyfarch, who wrote "The Life of St. David"), who was well known for his Latin poetry and who copied the text of St. Augustine's *On the Trinity,* which forms the basis of the manuscript in which "Padarn's Staff" was originally written. It is more likely, however, that the poem is an earlier one that Ieuan ap Sulien has simply recorded. The theme of praise is maintained in the following four poems (13–16). The first of these, "Glorious Lord," once again combines the themes of nature, culture ("letters"), the poetry of praise, and the church, to which is added the distinctively human realms of agriculture and morality. The poem itself appears to become a vehicle of praise in which all these disparate dimensions of existence are united. In the hymn-like "Praise to the Trinity" (poem 14) we find that God strongly emerges as Creator again, and as Trinity, and we find, once again, a combination of the diverse elements within an overall framework of praise. In all these early poems there occur motifs of praise that are borrowed from the secular heroic tradition. This is particularly the case in "Praise to God" (poem 15), however, where there is a great emphasis on the saving *action* of God, on his victory, "triumph," and "honor" as well as his largesse. The occurrence of the Latin word *Domini* in the opening phrase of the poem ("In the name of the Lord..."), which is itself a common liturgical formula that is frequently associated with the consecration of the elements in early liturgies, may perhaps serve to evoke the theme of the Eucharist and thus suggest an alignment between this central Christian sacrament, based on the saving death of Christ ("the perfect rite"), and the poet's own sacrament of praise. There are elements in later Welsh poems that support this reading.[138] The fourth praise poem is anachronistically attributed to Alexander the Great and is described as a "breastplate" or *lorica*. Although not actually of the *lorica* type, this poem nevertheless evokes the cross of Christ ("a shining breastplate") as an efficacious form of protection.[139]

Penance is the theme of the following seven poems (17–23), which appear to reflect the simple though rigorous demands of monastic life. In the first three (17–19) we find an emphasis on regular hours of praise, especially vigils, and the certain sense of our own mortality. Sleep and drunkenness are the perils to monastic life. The reference to the *Beati,* or 118th psalm (Vulgate), in "The Advice of Addaon" (18) suggests that the author of this and other of the Welsh monastic poems may have been under the influence of the Célí Dé or Culdees, for whom the 118th psalm played a vital and quite distinctive role in penitential and devotional life.[140] "The First Word I Say" and "Maytime is the Fairest Season" both speak of pilgrimage as an ascetical discipline (21 and 22), while "Fragment of the Dispute Between Body and Soul" subverts the denigration of the body by the soul for being the source of all evil, which is the conventional paradigm of this genre, by insisting that the body is the soul's "companion in glory."

The next two poems (24–25) show an awareness again of the poet's distinctive role and of his dependence on the grace of God for inspiration and skill. Praising God emerges also as the poet's own path to salvation. The conclusion of the second poem again contains an implicit opposition between an oral and a literary tradition.

The following three poems (26–28) belong to a later period, that of the "Poets of the Princes," whose court poetry during the twelfth and thirteenth centuries represents a high point of Welsh cultural life.[141] These were professional poets and laymen in the main whose religious works nevertheless both function as Christian catachesis and convey ascetical ideals that are evidently monastic in origin. The work by Meilyr Brydydd (fl. 1100–1137) is of the "Deathbed Song" type *(marwysgafn),* which expresses both repentance for past sins and an appeal for divine mercy (26). It concludes with a celebration of the remote island of Enlli (English: Bardsey Island), which was a major site of pilgrimage in the Middle Ages and where twenty thousand saints were reputed to be buried. The same theme of repentance occurs in Meilyr ap Gwalchmai's "Ode to God," where it is combined with a fruitful play on "grace," "gift," "flawlessness," and "skill" as images that combine the theme of Christian redemption with the inspiration and technical craft of the poet as singer of sublime praise to God (27). A similar word-play occurs in the final and greatest "Deathbed Song," by Cynddelw Brydydd Mawr (fl. 1155–1200), in which we encounter a magnificent combination of themes to do with the Creation, the Redemption, the End of Time, and the distinctive role of the poet as receiver of divine gifts (28).

The penultimate work, "The Loves of Taliesin," dating from around the thirteenth century, is a classic expression of the spirit of early Celtic Christianity (poem 29). In the manner of the earliest poems it combines the diverse elements of human experience, thus establishing a sense of a universal whole. The thematic center of the poem is penance, which is understood to offer a path to glory and to be a form of beauty. Indeed, this intensely life-affirming poem is an appreciation of beauty in all its forms, including the social and the individual, the natural and the sacred. The final work of the selection is a short poem to the Virgin Mary surviving in a fifteenth-century manuscript.

DEVOTIONAL TEXTS

We think of poetry today as being largely the private expression of personal feeling, and to some extent Celtic lyrics do give us privileged access into the experience of early medieval Celtic Christians, offering insight into the light and shadow of their spiritual lives. But it is also the case that early poetry generally had public functions other than that of personal expression, and was composed in order to edify as well as entertain. Also, a whole branch of lyrics, written in Latin as well as the vernacular, is more appropriately understood to comprise either charms and spells or devotional prayers that were intended to gain spiritual and temporal protection for those who repeated them. The origins of such poems, including litanies and "breastplates" *(loricae),* are often unclear and although they appear from the late eighth century onward in collections of prayers that were essentially intended for private devotional use, they may originally have had some para-liturgical functions.[142] These prayer books of the late eighth and early ninth centuries are of English provenance, showing the continuation of Irish and even some Welsh influence in the Anglo-Saxon kingdoms until the cooling of relations during the course of the ninth century.[143]

The intention of these devotional songs is often to consecrate the whole of human life. Thus "May Your Holy Angels" (text 1) and "O God, Lord of Creation" (text 2) have the appearance of prayers to be sung at nighttime before lying down to rest. There is evidence also that the breastplates were used as morning prayers.[144] The origins of the breastplate lie in the monastic application of texts such as Ephesians 6:11–18, in combination with the strong trend in early monasticism toward the practice of continuous prayer; thus they can be regarded as a development parallel to the Divine Office.[145] The detailed listing of parts of the body may reflect the influence of medical tracts current in early medieval Ireland, and this element can be paralleled in early exorcisms of Celtic provenance.[146] The earliest breastplate poem included here is "The Breastplate of Laidcenn," formerly attributed to Gildas (text 3).[147] This work can be dated to some time before 661, the year in which Laidcenn of Clonfert died.[148] The rich and complex Latin of the original, spiced with foreign terms, is typical of the "Hisperic" style. This breastplate, with its enumeration and repetition, is a fine example of the use of incantation to ward off the manifold forms of evil.[149]

"The Broom of Devotion" (text 4) also includes elements of the breastplate form in its first part. It is one of the most famous of early Irish prayers and is attributed to Colcu ú Duinechda of

Clonmacnois (d. 796). Its two halves may originally have been written separately. The next two pieces are examples of Litanies (texts 5 and 6), for which the early Irish church was noted. Protection from the dangers of traveling is the theme of the next two poems. The first (text 7), which is traditionally attributed to Colum Cille, may reflect the daily life of a traveling trader or, indeed, the experience of a pilgrim priest, seeking souls for God, while the second (text 8) is a charm for protection at the beginning of a journey.

The penultimate text is a confessional prayer composed in Latin by a Welshman (if the attribution to Moucan is correct), which survives in an English manuscript from the second half of the eighth century (text 9). It includes extensive and detailed reference to the Bible and is a plea for mercy before Judgment. Although it is largely a compendium of biblical reference and quotation, a recent editor has shown the extent to which the Old and New Testaments are skillfully made to illumine each other through typology in the poem.[150] "The Prayers of Moucan" also shows the extent to which the author's imagination entered the narrative and penitential imagery of the Bible. The final piece is a Welsh poem, by Gruffudd ap yr Ynad Coch (fl. c. 1280), which is a particularly fine example of the reworking of the *lorica* theme in an overtly literary medium during the thirteenth century (text 10).

LITURGY

The question that runs throughout the study of early Irish liturgy is to what extent "Celtic" practice constituted a separate tradition.[151] With regard to the Divine Office practiced in monastic communities, there is some evidence that in fact there was a significant degree of consistency at least in the early period, with affinities between the late seventh-century *Antiphonary of Bangor* and the account of the Office given in the *Voyage of Brendan*. These two sources together with Columbanus have an ascetical flavor in that they stress the place of the night Office, and they can as a body be distinguished from the liturgical framework of

Benedictine communities on the Continent.[152] But it is evident too that there was divergence of practice with regard to both monastic Rules and the Office in Ireland, on account of the failure of any one Irish monastic family to gain complete ascendancy.[153] With regard to other liturgical practices, there is a hint that Celtic Christians may in the earliest period have followed an anomalous practice of allowing a priest to perform confirmation rather than a bishop, and that the ordination of bishops may have reflected primitive practice that came to be seen as anachronistic.[154]

A number of the pieces included here derive from the circles of the Célí Dé. Sometime in 774, St. Maelruin founded a monastery in Tallaght (now a suburb of Dublin). It was destined to survive for only a short time, but it left its mark on the Irish Church and a rich legacy of theology and devotion. The monasteries of Tallaght and Finglas (now also a Dublin suburb) became known as "the two eyes of Ireland" and spearheaded a major renewal in the church. One of the books that this group produced has come down to us under the title of the "Stowe Missal" and was produced in Tallaght before 800.[155] It consists of fifty-seven leaves of coarse Irish parchment, each 5.5″ x 4.25″ in size, and it shows signs of much use. It contains the ordinary of the Mass in the form of a Mass of the Holy Eucharist (1 Cor 11:26–32 and Jn 6:51–7 are the readings) and the prayers for Masses of the saints, living penitents, and the dead. It also contains a rite of baptism, a formula for visiting the sick, and a short tract on the nature of the Mass in Irish ("The Tract on the Mass in the Stowe Missal"). This depicts an elaborate view of the fraction whereby the bread was broken into many different pieces according to the orders of the church and arranged in the shape of a Celtic cross.[156] One distinct part of this missal is that soon after it was produced, someone called Moél Caích added some additional chants—not a standard part of the Roman Rite—at the places where these were used in the liturgy ("Two Eucharistic Chants"). These are *catenae* of scriptural verses and provide evidence for the view of the Célí Dé regarding the Eucharist, and an insight into how they used scripture.

Irish liturgy was remarkable for its use of many collects of the unusual rhymed quatrain type, also typical of Ireland.[157] Hymns were no less a feature of the Irish Church, and two major collections survive, the *Antiphonary of Bangor* dating from the late seventh century and the Irish *Book of Hymns,* which dates from the late eleventh century. The precise use of the hymns that survive is often not clear, and they may have been sung in the Mass and in other liturgical contexts, or have been used in private devotion. But the final two items in our selection, the "Communion Hymn" *(Sancti, venite)* and "Hymn at the Lighting of the Paschal Candle" *(Ignis creator igneus),* both have evident liturgical associations.[158]

APOCRYPHA

Biblical apocrypha represented an important part of the spiritual vitality of the early church. After the establishing of the biblical canon, many apocryphal texts survived as imaginative reworkings and complementary additions to the canon itself, feeding into popular devotion, religious art, and liturgy. Certain themes predominated, such as miracle stories and dramatic images of the end of time, and many of the texts were attributed to the Apostles, or purported to describe their experiences.

The relative remoteness of Ireland together with the native Irish penchant for "the supernatural and the eschatological...the wonderful and bizarre" led also to a flourishing tradition of Irish biblical apocrypha.[159] Indeed, there are perhaps more apocryphal texts in Irish than in any other European vernacular language, and we possess also a number of important early Latin apocryphal texts from Ireland.[160] Of some interest also are texts that appear to be based on Latin originals that are no longer extant or at least no longer extant in that particular form.

Indeed, the chief text chosen for translation in the present volume is an example of this kind. "The Evernew Tongue," which probably dates from the tenth century, consists of a dialogue between the Hebrew sages who are assembled on the summit of Mount Zion on Easter Eve and the spirit of the Apostle Philip. According to tradition, the Apostle Philip was able to continue preaching although his tongue was cut out seven or nine times.[161] The themes touched on are the classical features of apocryphal and apocalyptic writing, including snatches from the "language of Heaven" and motifs concerned with both the Creation and the End of Time. Whitley Stokes suggested that it may be based on a lost Latin "Apocalypse of Philip," and fragments of original Latin embedded in the Irish text support this view. The author may also have made use of material from medieval Lapidaries and Bestiaries. A sign of the popularity of "The Evernew Tongue" in medieval Ireland is the fact that it survives in three recensions. The first and longest version, from the Book of Lismore, is the one translated here.

The second text, with the title "The Creation of Adam," is an account of the composition of Adam from seven components. The composition of the human body from the elements is an ancient theme that appears in Plato's *Timaeus,* and was later taken up by Philo.[162] But this Irish text represents a significant variation from the form in which the theme generally appears in the Christian tradition. Here Adam is composed of seven components or materials, including "clouds," "wind," and "the light of the world," which is the "Holy Spirit," rather than the four elements of tradition. The immediate source for these images is a Latin text that circulated in Europe from the ninth century,[163] and that was itself probably dependent on a passage from the apocryphon 2 Enoch (30,8). There we read that Adam's body is composed of "earth," "dew," "sea" (or "sun"), "stone," "clouds," "grass," and "spirit or wind." This survives only in an Old Slavonic version.[164] A further variant occurs in "The Evernew Tongue," discussed above, where the human body, as the body of Christ, is composed of six similar or identical materials ("wind or air," "heat and burning fiery matter," "sun and stars," "bitter and salty elements," "stones and the clay of the earth," "flowers and colored things of the earth"). The relatively frequent occurrence in Irish and Welsh literature of the theme of the constitution of the human body (whether as the body of Adam or of Christ) from four, six, seven, or eight components is an indication of the extent to which this motif engaged the imagination of early Celtic authors.[165]

50

The third text is "The Power of Women," which is an adaptation of 1 Esdras 3:1–4:32 and can be dated to the middle of the ninth century.[166] While the origins of this tale again lie outside Ireland, its portrayal of women as figures of power echoes the role of women as agents of power in the Irish hagiographical tradition.

The final text, "The Vision of Adamnán," is a remarkable account of heaven and hell. It is a highly eclectic piece, drawing on native, scriptural, and apocryphal sources, and is a product of the tenth or eleventh century.[167] This piece combines vivid and imaginative imagery with theological ideas having to do with eschatology and the human soul. The sevenfold division of heaven links this text with other works, such as the "Vision of Paul," and locates it in an apocryphal tradition whose roots may lie in the ancient Gnostic or Coptic Christian world.[168]

EXEGESIS

If the earliest Christian exegesis occurs in passages from the New Testament itself, then the remote origins of this great tradition lie in part in the late classical moralizing interpreters of Homer and Virgil and, nearer to hand, in the Jewish exegetical tradition as evidenced by Philo of Alexandria and then by the early rabbis. It was the Alexandrian Origen, however, who developed scriptural interpretation and made of it a marvelous tool for understanding not only the Bible itself but also the principles of Christian spirituality and theology. The multi-layered exegesis of Origen, moving creatively from the literal to the allegorical and from the historical to the mystical, was to remain influential within the Christian church for more than a thousand years.

There is evidence that there was a flourishing school of biblical exegesis during the latter half of the seventh century in southern Ireland, which may have produced the earliest Latin commentary on the Catholic Epistles, as well as other important theological texts.[169] Another persuasive indication of the status of biblical texts in early Ireland is given by the great gospel books of the Insular tradition. The fine and intricate craftsmanship of the family of illuminated texts that culminates in the Book of

Kells can only have been produced at enormous financial cost over several generations, and these marvelous texts are a further sign of the very great esteem in which the scriptures were held within early Irish society. We read in a passage from a homily in the *Leabhar Breac* that the physical body of Christ, his mystical body (the church), and the body of scripture are all one.[170] This is the very essence of Origen's biblical theology, and it again confirms the spiritual status that attached to the physical reality of the Word of God as divine revelation in early Ireland.

An extensive corpus of Irish biblical commentary survives, numbering some thirty-nine pieces or more.[171] Although the process of editing this work is still at a relatively early stage, the general trend seems to be Alexandrian, with a strong emphasis on free or allegorical readings of texts. Much is also repetitive and bizarre since, even by the standards of the Middle Ages, Irish exegetes had a particular delight in tracing random multilingual etymologies. But in a way that typifies the eclecticism of early Irish Christian culture, the tradition of exegesis of the Psalms was deeply Antiochean (i.e., historical) and closely reflected the commentary by Theodore of Mopsuestia, which survives entire in a manuscript of Irish provenance.[172] The biblical texts used in early medieval Ireland were generally of a mixed, though conservative, type, combining many elements of the Old Latin as well as the newer Vulgate version. Greek biblical texts of Irish provenance also survive, though exclusively on the Continent.

The first exegetical text included here is a mystical interpretation of Psalm 118 (Hebrew Psalm 119), which dates from around the tenth century. This Psalm, which was generally known in the Celtic tradition as the *Beati* (cf. Irish *Biáit* and Welsh *Bwyeid*), played an important role within the monastic communities of the Celtic world. It was believed in Ireland that its repetition every day of the year would free a soul from hell, and it was used also as a charm to bring good fortune at the outset of a journey.[173] The commentator plays on the fact that it is an acrostic Psalm that contains 176 verses in all (divided into sections of eight and introduced by each of the twenty-two letters of the Hebrew alphabet in turn). He is aware also of St. Jerome's division of the Hebrew scriptures into twenty-two books (five books of Moses, eight prophets, nine *hagiographa*). Each verse in the Psalm then becomes a single step in a journey, which is repeated 365 times over the course of a whole year. But each pace also contains the twenty-two letters of the Hebrew alphabet (which he allegorically or mystically dubs twenty-two "stadia") and thus, by implication the whole of the Old Law. But in the fourth stanza we find a literal reference also to the conventional category of 125 paces in a stadium. The author's detailed division of the number of paces that the liberated soul is required to take in accordance with the daily repetition of the psalm over the course of a year has something of the esoteric character of medieval Jewish number mysticism.

The second text is a commentary on Psalm 103 from the *Glossa in Psalmos,* a Hiberno-Latin text written around A.D. 700.[174] The form of this commentary is typically Irish in that it includes brief extracts of biblical texts to which a short commentary is attached—a tradition that appears to begin with the commentaries of Pelagius. This particular Psalm contains many allusions to the natural world. The Irish commentator clearly delights in these and embellishes them in a manner that contrasts with the material we find in Theodore of Mopsuestia's *Commentary on the Psalms,* of which otherwise the Irish author is a careful imitator.

HOMILIES

Homilies are a further, vital element in the construction of a tradition, and the early Irish Church has left us a relatively rich inheritance of sermons that survive in several Hiberno-Latin collections, including one from Cracow and another from Verona. The major such collection, however, is the work of Columbanus, and the four sermons translated here show the great rhetorical power of his cultivated style, coupled with his deeply monastic vision of the meaning of human existence. "Sermon Five" and "Sermon Eight" explore the idea that human life is only a "way" to another life and that we should exercise detachment at all times from the world around us, through which we travel to our "true home." Far from being life itself, life on earth contains the promise of death, and we must be wayfarers on its path. "Sermon Eleven" contains counsel on life in community and the spiritual training of the monastic vocation, while "Sermon Thirteen" is a powerful and mystical reverie on the Eucharist.

The next sermon is taken from a collection of Latin sermons to which a modern editor has given the title *Catechesis celtica*. This dates from the ninth century and is of uncertain provenance, surviving in a Breton manuscript with Welsh and Cornish glosses, but containing distinctly Irish material. The particular sermon translated here reflects a Johanine background and may show an affinity with the thought of Scottus Eriugena in its awareness of the presence of the divine in the living forms of the earth.

"An Old Irish Homily," dates from around the middle of the ninth century and speaks of the gratitude we should feel toward God, our Creator. It contains the typically Celtic image of hell as a place that is wintry, wet, and cold, while heaven is like summer with its blossoming and feasting. The sermon, known as "The Cambrai Homily," is a particularly ancient prose text that dates from the seventh or early eighth century; it is notable for its reference to the three martyrdoms: white (exile), green (fasting), and red (death).[175]

The final set of three texts provides examples of catechesis rather than homilies on the theme of Sunday. During the Carolingian period a fuller appreciation of Sunday was seen as part of the "reforms" needed in the church, both to restore the vigor of the church and as part of its missionary expansion in northern Europe.[176] It is in this context of "reform" and missionary activity that these texts were composed.[177] They are paradigms for preachers using short repetitive sentences and an elegantly simple Latin style for catechesis. All three texts are from the ninth century and are found in manuscripts that contain other catechetical and didactic texts. The manuscripts are of Breton, Breton or Welsh, and Anglo-Saxon provenance, and so represent a particular Celtic influence on continental Christianity.[178] These texts can be seen as one way of appropriating the Paschal Mystery. Sunday is the day of narrating God's works. On it, or indeed through it, the events of "then" of which the Christians are beneficiaries become "now." With the church gathered, and the story told, they give thanks for their present reality, which is all of God's creating and redeeming actions.

THEOLOGY

All the pieces included in the present volume contain a degree of what we might term implicit theology, but the texts included in this section discuss theological ideas in a more explicit and discursive manner and are the product of individuals who have received a high degree of formal education. The genre of the theological treatise as such is generally the product of a later historical period than that which is reflected in this volume, and although a number of scholastics were of known Celtic provenance, the Latinity of their culture argues in general against the influence of perspectives embodied in the vernacular Celtic world, although we should note that human thinking, even of the most formal type, never occurs in a cultural and social vacuum.[179] It is notable, for instance, that in the second and fourth of our pieces theology is expressed in strongly poetic terms, while much of what follows in this section appears to reflect a distinctively positive and dynamic view of nature and the natural and thus an optimistic view of the human self. In the case of Pelagius and Eriugena, this is the result of Greek theological influence, which sets both thinkers apart from the dominant, Augustinian current of their age; for our unknown Welsh author the influence may be that of the native bardic schools.

We begin with a text that contains a number of Pelagian themes and that has been attributed to Pelagius himself.[180] Pelagius was either a British Celt by birth or perhaps the product of an Irish community living in Wales.[181] His birth date can be placed in the middle of the fourth century, since he appears in Rome as a mature man in around 380, where he remains until its fall to Alaric in 410. Pelagius and his follower Caelestius were formally condemned by Pope Zosimus in 418. He wrote a substantial body of work, although some considerable controversy surrounds a number of titles that have at some time or other been attributed to him. The Pelagian corpus can be divided into works of an exegetical type, theological treatises, and ascetical texts, of which the final category exists in the main in the form of letters, such as "On the Christian Life," which is a lengthy letter addressed to a Christian widow. As is inevitably the case with a theologian charged with heresy, the greater parts of these texts have been attributed to other authors by tradition, including Jerome, Augustine, Fastidius, and Eutropius. Some of Pelagius's writings survive only in the form of quotations embedded in the texts of Augustine's own anti-Pelagian works.

Pelagius's controversy with Augustine turned on the central issue of human freedom and original sin. In Augustine's text *On Forgiveness of Sins and Baptism,* written in 412, the Pelagians are portrayed as rejecting original sin (i, 26) and holding to the possibility of a sinless life on earth (ii, 24). In *On Nature and Grace* of 415 Augustine argues that the Pelagians deny grace because they have such an elevated view of nature (para. 39, 69). For them, God has already planted the possibility of making right moral choices in all human souls, this choice being guided by the external example and teaching of Christ (para. 59). Against this Augustine argues that faith itself is a consequence of the movement of internal grace (para. 47).

Peter Brown has said of Pelagius that he was "the last, the most radical, and the most paradoxical exponent of the ancient Christianity—the Christianity of discontinuity."[182] Indeed, much of what Pelagius argued in his ascetical rather than his theological writings can be understood as the cry of indignation of an uncompromising rural monastic at the fashionable Christianity of Rome during the onset of a new and liberal age. To this extent at least Pelagius belongs to the Celtic world, on the margins of Europe and deeply imbued with early monastic ideals. From the point of view of his theology, however, he is to be seen against the background of early fifth-century debates in Rome having to do with an anti-Manichean defense of the freedom of the will, reflections on the nature of the soul (following Origen's controversial views on the matter), and the character and transmission of original sin.[183] It is in this context also that we should see the

Pelagian emphasis on the power to choose between good and evil as a God-given faculty of the soul, the right use of which is founded on the example of the Law and the teaching of Christ. His very high theology of Creation led him also to deny original sin on the grounds that neither vice nor virtue is inborn, and thus to oppose the view that unbaptized infants are damned. There is little of this theology in "On the Christian Life" (which is to be found in Augustine's works and in the *Letter to Demetrias*), but we do find here a constant appeal to the life of Christian virtue and to a sense that Christanity is a religion not of name but of fact. There is also a noticeable trend toward the communitarian values of the Christian vocation.

Our second item, the *Altus Prosator* or "The High First-Sower," is traditionally attributed to Columba,[184] and it is one of the literary and theological gems of Hiberno-Latin writing. Written in the late sixth or early seventh century, in all likelihood on Iona, it provides a panorama of Christian faith. Its formal structure is abecedarian: Each stanza begins with the next letter of the Latin alphabet,[185] and it presents as a sequence the history of salvation: the uncreated Trinity; the creation of angels, humans, and matter; the fall and the effects of disobedience and sin; the redemption; and the final times. The work has been a constant challenge to commentators as one notes its changing theological vistas, the number of textual allusions often in unexpected combinations, and the sheer force of its poetry, which has impressed and influenced Latin writers from at least the ninth century.[186] Here a proper commentary cannot be attempted, not even an exhaustive apparatus of its biblical allusions; instead what is intended is an accurate translation that can be used as the basis for further exploration.[187]

The Irish theologian known as John Scottus Eriugena was born not later than 810 and died in around 877.[188] In c. 845 he was present at the court of Charles the Bald where he established himself as one of the leading theological figures of the day. He is the author of a number of scholarly commentaries and of the influential treatise *Divine Predestination* (851), which he was commissioned to write by Hincmar, Archbishop of Reims, in refutation of the work of Gottschalk. From 860 to 862 he translated the works of Pseudo-Dionysius, a formidable task since Greek was virtually unknown in the Latin West at the time, and later wrote a commentary on the *Celestial Hierarchy* by the same author. He devoted himself to the translation of works by Maximus the Confessor *(Ambigua* and *Quaestiones ad Thalassium)* and Gregory of Nyssa *(De imagine).*[189] He also wrote a commentary on the Gospel of John, and composed a number of poems. But Eriugena devoted much of the later part of his life to writing his *Periphyseon* or *The Division of Nature.* This extensive work presents one of the most sophisticated Christian Neoplatonist systems of the Middle Ages, and is founded on a familiarity with the sources of a Greek theology that looks back to Proclus and a deep knowledge of the Augustinian corpus.

The central theme of the *Periphyseon* is the fourfold division of "nature" into "nature which creates and which is not created" (God as the supreme cause of all things), "nature which is created and which creates" (the ideas as primal causes of all things), "nature which is created and which does not create" (entities that are subject to generation in time and space), and "nature which does not create and which is not created" (God as the final end of all things).[190] It presents an understanding of the origin and meaning of the universe that is powerfully governed by the notion of "procession" and "return," which Eriugena takes from his Greek sources. This establishes the created world, both visible and invisible, as a theophany of God, who is unknowable in himself. God is thus simultaneously present in all things and infinitely beyond all things in a dialectical configuration that places the human self at its center. Human beings reflect the divine source in a special way since they alone participate in the nature of God as knowing, and, through the purification of consciousness by contemplation, human beings can reach the third, or highest, stage of return to the divine source where their end is the "supernatural sunset of the most purified souls into God."[191]

Unfortunately, it has been possible to include in this selection only Eriugena's "Homily on the Prologue to the Gospel of John," which was intended originally, in all probability, as the "homily of the day" on Christmas Day.[192] And indeed, even in this relatively brief extract we can see of the role of scriptural exegesis in the formation of his thought, and his debt in particular to Dionysius and Maximus.[193] We can see something also of his theology of light and his understanding of the created world as theophany.

The fourth piece is a Welsh language text, "The Food of the Soul," which was written by a Dominican, probably in the mid-thirteenth century, and which survives in the manuscript known as the *Book of the Anchor of Llanddewibrefi* of 1346. Our text is described as being one of three books that constituted the work *The Holy Sanctuary of Life*. The other books do not survive, although it is likely that they contained the Rule and Constitution of the Dominican Order and that they preceded the surviving book. The first part is a treatise of pastoral theology and contains a discussion of the vices and virtues that is of a conventional type. The second part is a treatise on mystical theology and is distinctive in that it adopts the identification of the Holy Spirit with the love of God and of our fellow human beings. This position was characteristic of the theology of Peter Lombard and it remained highly controversial throughout the Middle Ages. Perhaps the fact that our author was a poet, evident from the third section of his text, can account for his holding this unpopular view. There is a well-attested tradition from this period that the Holy Spirit itself is the source of bardic inspiration. This version of the indwelling of the Holy Spirit in the case of the bard may then have preconditioned our bardic author to follow the Lombardian view that the Holy Spirit itself indwells us whenever and wherever we love.[194]

The third part itself is a vision of the Christian Trinity, which culminates in a lengthy and unusually elaborate description of the physical beauty of Jesus as a twelve-year-old boy. There is a probable debt here to extant Latin material on the twelve-year-old Jesus on the one hand and on the other to the imagery of precious stones employed in the Book of Isaiah and the Book of Revelation, as well perhaps to medieval *Lapidaria*.[195] But the ornate style of the Welsh "Poets of the Princes," who loved to create rich-sounding compound words, is clearly an additional influence. Toward the end of this work we find a rare practical account of the steps to be followed by those who desire a visionary experience. This remarkable text is a fusion of sophisticated literary, theological, and visionary elements, and it appears to seek to translate the beauty of God, discerned through mystical ecstasy, into a highly ornate and extravagantly literary medium.

A NOTE ON THE SELECTION AND TRANSLATION

The selection of texts in the present volume represents only a very small part of the material that survives from the Celtic countries during the early Middle Ages. I have naturally sought to make these as representative as possible, although I freely admit that I have tended to choose those texts that reflect a distinctively Celtic spirituality. Many other texts exist that are entirely within the mainstream of Christian theology and sensibility. The medieval Celtic spiritual tradition was not isolated from continental Christianity, but was rather in constant dialogue with it. This, too, is the reason why some elements distinctive to the Celts could feed in turn into the mainstream and become in time part of the universal tradition.

The selected texts are mainly of Irish or Welsh (British) provenance. This is largely due to the fact that there is little surviving early medieval Christian material from Scotland, with the splendid exception of Adamnán's *Life of Columba*. Unfortunately, this classic of hagiography proved too long for inclusion here.[196] Regrettably, the earliest vernacular material from Brittany and Cornwall is late medieval in date, and thus falls outside the classical period of Celtic Christianity. I should add finally that the allocation of texts to one section rather than another has been in many cases somewhat arbitrary, and I am aware that a number of items could equally well have found a place in an alternative section.

I have aimed to use the best available editions of the texts included here, though some are more satisfactory than others. I have not felt competent to establish editorial readings of my own in the Irish material, though I have done so to a very limited extent with some of the Welsh and Latin texts. While all the translations are my own, I must acknowledge a substantial debt to the work of

many previous skilled and learned translators, including Charles
Plummer, Whitley Stokes, John Strachan, Michael Herren, David
Howlett, Sean Connolly, Donncha Ó hAodha, Gerard Murphy,
and especially Máire Herbert, who has recently published,
together with Martin McNamara, some fine translations of Irish
apocryphal texts. I am indebted to these and other editors also for
many annotations to the texts. The translations for which Thomas
O'Loughlin is responsible are clearly marked in the Table of Contents. He is the author too of all the annotations to these texts and
of the sections from the introduction where they are discussed. In
order not to disrupt the flow of the text, Thomas O'Loughlin has
placed scriptural references in the endnotes.

II.
The Texts

HAGIOGRAPHY

1. THE PATRICK TRADITION

i.

Patrick's Declaration of the Great Works of God[1]

[1][2] I am Patrick. I am a sinner:[3] the most unsophisticated of people; the least among all the Christians;[4] and, to many, the most contemptible. I am the son of the deacon Calpornius, as he was the son of the priest Potitus who belonged to the village on Bannavem Taburniae. Indeed, near it he had a small estate from where, when aged about sixteen, I was taken captive. I was then ignorant of the true God and, along with thousands upon thousands of others, was taken into captivity in Ireland. This occurred according to our merits for we had pulled back from God;[5] we did not keep his commandments;[6] and we did not listen to our priests,[7] who kept on warning us regarding "our salvation."[8] And "so" the Lord "poured upon" us "the heat of his anger"[9] and dispersed us among many peoples,[10] right "out to the very ends of the earth,"[11] where now my smallness[12] is seen among these men of an alien land.

[2] And there the Lord "opened my understanding to my unbelief,"[13] so that however late, I might become conscious of my failings.[14] Then remembering my need, I might "turn with all my heart to the Lord my God."[15] For it was he who "looked on my lowliness"[16] and had mercy on the ignorance of my youth,[17] and who looked after me[18] before I knew him and before I had gained wisdom or could distinguish between good and evil.[19] Indeed, as a father consoles his son,[20] so he protected me.[21]

[3] So it would be neither right nor proper[22] for me to do anything but to tell you all of the many blessings and great grace which the Lord saw fit to give me in the land of my captivity.[23] I tell you these things because this is how we return thanks to God,[24] that after being corrected and having come to an awareness of

67

God,[25] that we glorify and bear witness to his wonderful works[26] in the presence of every nation under heaven.[27]

[4] For there is not, nor ever was, any other God—there was none before him and there shall not be any after him[28]—besides him who is God the Father unbegotten: Without a source, from him everything else takes its beginning. He is, as we say, the one who keeps hold of all things.[29] And his Son, Jesus Christ, whom we profess to have always existed with the Father. He was spiritually with the Father before the world came into being; begotten of the Father before the beginning of anything in a way that is beyond our speech. And through him all things were made, all things visible and invisible.[30] He was made man, and having conquered death was taken back into the heavens to the Father.[31]

"And [the Father] has bestowed on him all power above every name in heaven and on earth and under the earth, so that every tongue may confess that [our] Lord and God is Jesus Christ"[32] in whom we believe. And we look forward to his coming, in the time that is soon to be, when he will be judge of the living and the dead, "who will repay each one according to his works."[33]

And "[the Father] has plentifully poured upon us the Holy Spirit,"[34] the gift and pledge of immortality, who makes those who believe and listen into "sons of God" the Father "and fellow heirs with Christ."[35] [This is] who we confess and adore, One God in Trinity of sacred name.

[5] As he himself said through the prophet: "Call upon me in the day of trouble; I will deliver you, and you shall glorify me."[36] And elsewhere he said: "It is honorable to acknowledge and reveal the works of God."[37]

[6] But even if I am imperfect in many things I want my brothers and relatives[38] to know the sort of man I am, so that they may understand what it is to which I have committed my soul.

[7] I am not forgetting "the testimony of" my "Lord"[39] who testifies in the Psalms: "You destroy those who speak lies"[40] and who elsewhere says: "The lying mouth kills the soul."[41] Again, the same Lord says in the gospel: "I tell you, on the Day of Judgment men will render account for every careless word they utter."[42]

[8] So with all my heart I dread, "with fear and trembling,"[43]

this sentence on that day,[44] which no one can evade or hide
from,[45] when every single one of us shall "render an account" of
even the least sins "before the judgment seat of" the Lord
"Christ."[46]

[9] For these reasons I have thought of writing this account
this long while, but held back until now as I was afraid of the
attack of men's tongues, and because I have not been a student
like other men who in the very best manner have drunk equally in
law and sacred letters.[47] They have never had to change their
speech since infancy; rather they were always adding to the command of language and bringing it to perfection. My words and
speech,[48] however, are translated into an alien language, and you
can easily assess the quality of my instruction and learning from a
taste of my writing. For as the wise man says: "For wisdom
becomes known through speech, and education through the
words of the tongue."[49]

[10] But what use is even a true excuse, especially when there is
an element of presumption in it, since now, as an old man, I desire
to have what I did not acquire in my youth? Then my sins blocked
me from gaining a firm grasp on what I had already read. But will
anyone believe me if I repeat [the reason I came to proper learning
so late in life]? I was young, indeed almost a speechless boy, when I
was taken captive, and at that time did not yet know what I ought to
desire and what I ought to avoid. So today it is with shame and very
great fear that I lay bare my lack of expertise and polish. The situation is this: To the learned I am unable to make my meaning clear[50]
with the brevity my spirit and mind desire and the disposition
toward which my understanding points.[51]

[11] But if I had been given the same chance as the rest, then
without a doubt, "for the sake of the reward,"[52] I would not keep
silent. And, if it seems to some that I am being arrogant in making
my declaration—I with my lack of learning and my "slow
tongue"[53]—then note that it is written: "The tongue of the stam-
merers will learn quickly to speak peace."[54] So how much more
then should we want this, we who are, as it says, "the letter of
Christ for salvation unto the uttermost parts of the earth."[55] And,
although this letter is not a learned one, it is "one delivered" with

strength,[56] "written in our hearts not with ink, but with the Spirit of the living God."[57] And again, "the Spirit bears witness"[58]: "For the Most High also created the things of the farm-yard."[59]

[12] So at first, I was a rustic and a wanderer[60] without any learning "who knew not how to provide for what would come later."[61] But I know one thing without any doubt and with the greatest of assurance: that "before I was punished"[62] I was like a stone lying in the deepest mire;[63] and then, "he who is mighty"[64] came and, in his mercy, raised me up.[65] He most truly raised me on high and set me on the top of the rampart.[66] So I ought to cry out with all my strength and render thanks to the Lord for his blessings are indeed great, here and in eternity, and beyond all that the human mind can imagine.

[13] So now, be amazed "you both small and great that fear God"[67] and all you learned ones, all you clever speakers, listen and examine what you hear. [Now tell me:] Who was it that raised me up a fool from the midst of you who seem to be wise men and "experts in the law"[68] and "powerful in word"[69] and in every other matter? But indeed, [God] inspired me, the detestable of this world[70]—if that is what I am, above others so that I should faithfully serve, "with fear and reverence"[71] and "without blame,"[72] the people to whom Christ's love brought me,[73] and to whom he gave me for the rest of my days should I be found worthy. In effect, that is that I should truly serve them with humility.[74]

[14] And so it is proper and right "in the measure of faith"[75] in the Trinity, to make clearly known "the gift of God"[76] and his "eternal consolation."[77] And, to do this "without hesitating"[78] at the dangers involved. Likewise it is proper to spread abroad the name of God, trustingly and "without fear,"[79] so that even "after my death"[80] I may leave something of value to the many thousands of people, my brothers and sons, whom I have baptized in the Lord.

[15] And I was not worthy[81] in any way for what the Lord was to grant to his servant after tribulations, many setbacks, captivity, and many long years. He gave me a great grace toward that people [among whom I had been captive]. This was something I had never thought of, nor hoped for, in my youth.

[16] But then, when I had arrived in Ireland and was spending every day looking after flocks, I prayed frequently each day. And more and more, the love of God and the fear of him grew [in me], and [my] faith was increased[82] and [my] spirit was quickened,[83] so that in a day I prayed up to a hundred times, and almost as many in the night. Indeed, I even remained in the wood and on the mountain to pray. And—come hail, rain, or snow—I was up before dawn to pray, and I sensed nothing of evil nor any other spiritual laziness in me.[84] I now understand why this was so; at that time "the Spirit was fervent" in me.[85]

[17] And it was there indeed that one night I heard a voice which said to me: "Well have you fasted. Very soon you are to travel to your homeland." And again, not long after that, I heard "a revelation"[86] which said to me: "Behold! Your ship is prepared." But the ship was not nearby, but maybe two hundred miles away where I had never been and where I knew nobody. Soon after that I took flight leaving the man I had been with for six years. And I traveled[87] "in the power of God,"[88] who directed my path[89] toward the good, and I feared nothing[90] until I arrived at the ship.

[18] The ship was about to depart on the very day I arrived and I said [to those on board] that I wanted to sail with them from there. But this was displeasing to the vessel's master, who, with disdain, answered me sharply: "No way can you ask to travel with us!" So having heard that I went away from them toward the hut where I was taking shelter. And on the way I began to pray. And before I finished my prayer I heard one of the crew shouting loudly after me: "Come! Quickly! These men here are calling you." So I turned back toward them at once and they said to me: "Come on, we are taking you on faith. So show your friendship with us according to whatever custom you choose." But on that day I refused to suck their nipples,[91] on account of the fear of God,[92] but despite this I stayed with them for I hoped that some of them would come to faith in Jesus Christ—for they all belonged to "the nations."[93] And without any further ado, we got under way.

[19] We landed after three days and for [the next] twenty-eight days we made our way through a desert. And when their food ran out, starvation overcame them.[94] So one of the days the master

asked me: "So now, Christian, you explain to us why were are in this mess. Your God is great and all-powerful,[95] so why are you not able to pray for us? We who are on the very brink with hunger and it seems unlikely we will ever see another human being." So I boldly said to them: "'Turn' in trust and 'with your whole heart'[96] to the Lord, my God, to whom nothing is impossible,[97] that today he may send food to satisfy you on your journey—for he has an abundance everywhere."[98]

And then, with God's help, it happened. Behold a herd of swine appeared before our eyes on the road,[99] and they killed many of them. They made camp there for two nights,[100] and, with their fill of pork, they were well restored[101] for many of them had dropped out[102] and had been left "half dead" by the roadside.[103] And after this they thanked God mightily, and I became honorable in their eyes.[104] From then on they had an abundance of food. As well as this they came across some wild honey[105] and "offered some of it"[106] to me. Then one of the said: "This has been offered as a sacrifice"[107] But thanks be to God, I tasted none of it.

[20] That very night, while I was sleeping, Satan strongly tried me—I shall remember it "as long as I am in the body."[108] Something like an enormous rock fell on top of me and I lost all power over my limbs. But where did it come to me, for I was ignorant in spiritual matters, that I should call on Helias?[109] And at this point I saw the sun rise in the sky and while I called out "Helia, Helia" with all my strength, behold the sun's splendor fell on me and dispelled immediately all the heaviness from upon me. And I believe that Christ, my Lord, assisted me and his Spirit had already cried out through me. And I hope it will be so "in the day of my distress"[110] as it says in the gospel: "On that day," the Lord declares, "it is not you who speak, but the Spirit of your Father who will speak in you."[111]

[22] [112]And as we traveled [the Lord] looked after us with food, fire, and dry shelter each day,[113] until after fourteen days we came into human society. As I mentioned already, we journeyed for twenty-eight days through the desert and on the very night we reached humanity, we had none of the food left.[114]

[21] And after many years, I was once again taken captive.

But on the very first night I was with them, I heard a divine revelation[115] which said to me: "You will remain with them for two months." This is exactly what happened and on the sixtieth night "the Lord freed me from their hands."[116]

[23] And after a few years I was again with my parents in Britain who welcomed me as a son. They, in good faith, begged me—after all those great tribulations I had been through—that I should go nowhere, nor ever leave them. And it was there, I speak the truth, that "I saw a vision of the night"[117]: a man named Victoricus—"like one" from Ireland—coming with innumerable letters. He gave me one of them and I began to read what was in it: "The voice of the Irish." And at that very moment as I was reading out the letter's opening, I thought I heard the voice of those around the wood of Foclut, which is close to the western sea. It was "as if they were shouting with one voice"[118]: "O holy boy, we beg you to come again and walk among us." And I was "broken hearted"[119] and could not read anything more. And at that moment I woke up. Thank God, after many years the Lord granted them what they called out for.

[24] And on another night, either in me or close to me—"I do not know, God knows"[120]—I heard them using the most learned words. But I could not understand them, except what became clear toward the end of the speech: "He who 'gave his life'[121] for you, he it is who speaks in you." And at that point I woke up, and was full of joy.

[25] And on another occasion I saw him praying in me, and it was as if I was inside my body and I heard [him] over me, that is over "the inner man,"[122] and he was praying there powerfully with sighs.[123] And in my excitement and astonishment[124] I wondered who it could be that was praying in me. But toward the end of the prayer it became clear[125] that it was the Spirit. Just then I awoke and remembered what was said through the Apostle: "Likewise the Spirit helps the weaknesses of our prayers; for we do not know how to pray as we ought, but the Spirit himself intercedes for us with ineffable sighs which cannot be expressed in words."[126] And again it says: "The Lord is our Advocate,[127] he intercedes for us."[128]

[26] And when some of my superiors challenged me coming up with my sins against my toilsome episcopate—for truly on that day "I was struck" mightily "so that I was falling"[129] here and in eternity—then did the Lord in his goodness spare the convert and the stranger "for his name's sake."[130] And he powerfully came to my aid in this battering so that I did not slip badly into the wreckage of sin and into infamy. I pray God that "it may not be charged against them"[131] as sin.

[27] "The charge they brought"[132] against me was something from thirty years earlier which I had admitted[133] before I was even a deacon. Once when I was anxious and worried I hinted to [my] dearest friend about something I had done one day—indeed in one hour—in my youth, for I had not then prevailed over [my sinfulness]. "I do not know, God knows"[134] if I was then fifteen years old, and I was not a believer in the true God nor had I ever been,[135] but I remained in death and nonbelief until I was truly punished[136] and, in truth, brought low by daily deprivations of hunger and nakedness.[137]

[28] Quite the opposite, when I went to Ireland, not of my own volition, I was nearly defeated. But this [captivity] was very good for me for I was corrected by the Lord; and he prepared me for what I am today—a state I was then far away from—when I have the pastoral care, and many duties, for the salvation of others, but at that time I was not even concerned for myself.

[29] And so came the day when I was rejected[138] by those I have mentioned; and on that night[139] "I saw a vision of the night." [I saw] a piece of writing without any nobility opposite my face, and at the same time I heard the divine revelation[140] saying to me: "We have seen with anger the face of [our] chosen one with his name laid bare [of respect]." Note he did not say: "You have seen with anger," but "We have seen with anger" as if in this matter he were joined to his chosen one. As he said: "He who touches you touches the pupil of my eye."[141]

[30] So it is that "I give thanks to him who strengthened me"[142] in all things: that he did not impede me in my chosen journey, nor in my works, which I had learned from Christ my Lord. On the contrary, I felt in myself a strength, by no means small, coming

from him,[143] and that my "faith was proven in the presence of God and men."[144]

[31] And so "I boldly declare"[145] that my conscience is clear both now and in the future. I have "God as [my] witness"[146] that I am not a liar[147] in those things that I have told you.

[32] But I am very sorry for my dearest friend, to whom I trusted even my soul, that he merited to hear this [divine] revelation.[148] And I found out from some of the brethren that at the inquiry he fought for me in my absence. (I was not present at this, nor was I in Britain, nor did the issue arise with me.) He indeed it was who told me with his own lips: "Behold, you are to be given the rank of bishop"—something for which I was unworthy. So how did he later come to the idea of disgracing me in public in the presence of all those people both good and bad, [regarding a matter for] which earlier he had, joyfully and of his own volition, pardoned me, as indeed had the Lord who is greater than all?[149]

[33] Enough said!

However, I must not hide that gift of God which he gave us bountifully in the land of my captivity,[150] because it was then that I fiercely sought him and there found him and he preserved me from all iniquities.[151] I believe this to be so because of his Spirit dwelling in me[152] who has worked in me[153] until this very day.[154] This is something I will boldly repeat.[155] But God knows that if a man had said this to me, perhaps then I would have remained silent because of Christ's love.[156]

[34] And so I thank my God without ceasing who preserved me as his faithful one "on the day of" my "trial"[157] so that today I can offer a sacrifice to him with confidence. [Today] I offer my soul as "a living victim"[158] to Christ my Lord who "preserved me in all my troubles"[159] so that I can say: "'Who am I, O Lord'[160] and what is my vocation, that you have cooperated with me with such divine [power]?" Thus today I constantly praise and glorify your name[161] wherever I may be among the nations[162] both in my successes and in my difficulties. So whatever happens to me—good or ill—I ought to accept with an even temper[163] and always give thanks to God who has shown me that I can trust him without limit or doubt. It is he who "in the last days"[164] heard me, so that

I—an ignorant man—should dare to take up so holy and wonderful a work as this: that I should in some way imitate those men[165] to whom the Lord foretold what was about to occur when "his gospel [of the kingdom will be preached throughout the whole world] as a testimony to all nations" before the end of the world.[166] And this is what we see: It has been fulfilled.[167] Behold! We are [now] witnesses to the fact that the gospel has been preached out to beyond where any man lives.[168]

[35] To narrate in detail[169] either the whole story of my labors or even parts of it would take a long time. So, lest I injure my readers, I shall tell you briefly how God, the all-holy one, often freed me from slavery and from twelve dangers which threatened my life, as well as from many snares and from things which I am unable to express in words.[170] Moreover, I have God as my authority—he who knows all things even before they happen—that he frequently warned me, a poor ignorant orphan, through divine revelations.[171]

[36] So where did I get this wisdom?[172] It was not in me: I neither knew the number of [my] days[173] nor cared about God. Where did I later get that great and health-giving gift that I might know and love God, albeit that I had to leave my country and parents?

[37] And many gifts were offered to me with sorrow and tears. And I offended them and went against the will not only of some of my elders, but, under God's direction, I refused to consent or agree with them in any way. It was not my grace, but God who conquered in me and who resisted them all that I might come to the Irish nations to preach the gospel[174] and put up with insults from unbelievers, that I might hear the hatred of my wanderings,[175] [endure] many persecutions even including chains,[176] and that I be given my freedom for the benefit of others. And, indeed, if I be worthy I am ready to give my life right now[177] "for his name's sake."[178] And, if the Lord should grant it to me,[179] it is there [in Ireland] I want "to spend freely"[180] my life "even until death."[181]

[38] Truly, I am greatly in God's debt.[182] He has given me a great grace, that through me many peoples might be reborn[183]

and later brought to completion;[184] and also that from among them everywhere clerics should be ordained [to serve] this people—who have but recently come to belief—[and] which the Lord has taken [to himself] "from the ends of the earth."[185] He thus fulfilled "what he once promised through his prophets":[186] "To you shall the nations come from the ends of the earth and say: 'Our fathers have inherited nought but lies, worthless things in which there is no profit.'"[187] And in another place:[188] "I have set you to be a light for the nations, that you may bring salvation to the uttermost parts of the earth."[189]

[39] And it is there [in Ireland] that I desire "to wait for the promise"[190] of him who never deceives us and who repeatedly promises in the gospel: "They will come from the east and from the west and from the south and from the north and sit at table with Abraham, Isaac, and Jacob."[191] So we believe that believers will come from the whole world.

[40] So it is right and proper that we should fish well and carefully—as the Lord warns and teaches us saying: "Come after me and I shall make you fishers of men."[192] And again[193] he says through the prophets: "Behold! I send out fishermen and any hunters, says God,"[194] and so forth. So truly it is our task to cast our nets[195] and catch "a great multitude"[196] and crowd for God; and [to make sure] that there are clergy everywhere to baptize and preach to a people who are in want and in need. This is exactly what the Lord warns and teaches about in the gospel when he says: "Go therefore," now, "and teach all the nations, baptizing them in the name of the Father and of the Son and of the Holy Spirit, teaching them to observe all that I have commanded you; and behold, I am with you always even to the close of the age."[197] And again:[198] "Go into all the world and preach the gospel to the entire universe. He who believes and is baptized will be saved; but he who does not believe will be condemned."[199] And again:[200] "This gospel of the kingdom will be preached throughout the entire universe, as a testimony to all nations; and then the end will come."[201] And likewise the Lord foretold this through the prophet when he says: "And in the last days it shall be, says the Lord, that I will pour out my Spirit upon all flesh,

and your sons and your daughters shall prophesy, and your young men shall see visions, and your old men shall dream dreams; and indeed on my menservants and my maidservants in those days I will pour out my Spirit; and they shall prophesy."[202] And the prophet Hosea says: "Those who were not my people I will call 'my people,' and her who was not beloved I will call 'my beloved.' And in the very place where it was said to them, 'You are not my people,' they will be called 'sons of the living God.'"[203]

[41] Such indeed is the case in Ireland where they never had knowledge of God[204] —and until now they celebrated only idols and unclean things.[205] Yet recently, what a change: They have become "a prepared people"[206] of the Lord, and they are now called "the sons of God."[207] And the Irish leaders' sons and daughters are seen to become the monks and virgins of Christ.[208]

[42] Indeed, on one occasion this happened. A blessed Irish woman of noble birth, a most beautiful adult whom I had baptized, came back to us a few days later for this reason. She told us how she had received a divine communication[209] from a messenger of God which advised her to become a virgin of Christ and that she should move closer to God. Thanks be to God, six days after that she avidly and commendably took up[210] that life which is lived by all who are virgins of God. This, of course, is not to the liking of their fathers and they have to suffer persecution and false accusation from their parents.[211] Yet despite this their number keeps increasing and we do not know the number of those born there from our begetting—apart from widows and those who are continent. But of all these women those held in slavery have to work hardest: They are continually harassed and even have to suffer being terrorized. But the Lord gives grace to many of his maidservants, and the more they are forbidden to imitate[212] [the Lord], the more they boldly do this.

[43] This, therefore, is the situation: Even if I were willing to leave them and go to Britain—and I was all set[213] to go there, and wanted to go for it is my homeland and where my family is—and Gaul "to visit the brethren"[214] and see the face of my Lord's saints—God knows how much I wanted to do this; I am "bound in the Spirit," who "testifies to me"[215] that should I do this he would

make me as guilty.[216] Moreover, I fear the loss of the work I have begun here, and so it is not I but Christ the Lord who has ordered me to come [here] and be with these people for the rest of my life. If the Lord wills it,[217] he will guard my way from every evil,[218] that I might not sin in his presence.[219]

[44] However, I hope I have done the right thing, for "as long as I am in this body of death"[220] I do not trust myself because he is strong[221] who daily tries to drag me away from faith and from the genuine religious chastity which I have chosen for Christ my Lord until the end of my life. But the hostile flesh[222] is always drawing me toward death,[223] namely, toward doing those enticing things which are forbidden. While I know in part[224] those matters where I have had a less perfect life than other believers, I do acknowledge this to my Lord and I am not ashamed[225] in his sight[226]—"for I do not lie."[227] From the time I knew him, from youth,[228] the love of God and the fear of him have grown within me, so that, with the Lord's help, "I have kept the faith"[229] until now.[230]

[45] So if there is anyone who wants to laugh [at me] or insult [me] they can. But I will not hide, nor be silent about those "signs and wonders"[231] which were shown to me by the Lord many years before they actually occurred: For he knows everything "from all eternity."[232]

[46] So I should give God thanks without ceasing[233] for he often forgave my stupidity[234] and negligence[235]—on more than one occasion—in that he was not fiercely angry[236] with me who had been appointed his helper.[237] Yet, I was not quick in accepting what he had made clear to me, as "the Spirit reminded me."[238] And the Lord "was merciful" to me "a thousand, thousand times"[239] because he saw what was within me and that I was ready[240] but that I did not know what I should do about my state [of life]. All the while many were forbidding my mission: Behind my back among themselves they were telling stories and saying; "Why does this man put himself in danger among enemies 'who do not know God' ?"[241] I can truly testify that this was not from malice, but because it did not seem right to them that one as rustic as myself should do such a thing. Then, I was not quick to

acknowledge the grace that was in me;[242] now, what I ought to have done before seems right to me.

[47] So now, without any affectation, I have told my brethren and fellow-servants.[243] They believed me because "I warned and I warn"[244] in order to make your faith more sure and robust.[245] Would indeed that you would imitate greater things and do more powerful things![246] This would be my glory,[247] for "the wise son is the glory of the father."[248]

[48] You all know, as does God, how I lived among you from my youth[249] "in the faith of truth"[250] "and with sincerity of heart."[251] Furthermore, I have acted with good faith toward the nations [i.e., non-Christians] among whom I live, and will continue doing so in the future. "God knows"[252] "I have taken advantage of none"[253] of them; and for the sake of God[254] and his church I would not think of doing so, lest I should provoke persecution[255] of them and of us all, and lest the name of God be blasphemed through me—for it is written: "Woe to the man through whom the Lord's name is blasphemed."[256]

[49] "Now even if I am unskilled in everything,"[257] yet I have tried in some small way to guard myself for [the sake of] the Christian brethren and the virgins of Christ and "the religious women"[258] who of their own accord used to give me little gifts. And when they threw any of their ornaments on the altar, I used to return these to them though they were often offended that I should do that. But I did it because of the hope of eternity[259] and so that I could guard myself carefully in everything.[260] Thus, infidels could not, for any reason, catch either me or my ministry of service. And furthermore, by this course of action I did not give unbelievers reason, in even the least matter, to speak against me or to take my character.[261]

[50] Maybe when I baptized all those thousands, I hoped to get even half a penny from one of them? "Tell me and I will return it to you!"[262] Or when the Lord ordained clergy everywhere through me as his mediocre instrument, and I gave my ministry to them for free, did I even charge them the cost of my shoes? "Tell it against me and I will" all the more "return it to you!"[263]

[51] "I spend myself"[264] for you that you might lay hold of me.[265] Indeed I have traveled everywhere for your sake: I have gone amid many dangers; I have gone to places beyond where anyone lived; and I have gone where no one else had gone to baptize people, or ordain clergy, or complete people.[266] With God's help, I have carried out all these things lovingly, carefully, and most joyfully[267] for your salvation.

[52] Sometimes I gave presents to kings—over and above the wages I gave their sons who traveled with me—yet they took me and my companions captive. On that day they avidly sought to kill, but the time had not yet come.[268] Still they looted us, took everything of value, and bound me in iron. But on the fourteenth day the Lord freed me from their control, and all our belongings were returned to us for the sake of God[269] and "the close friends"[270] we had seen earlier.

[53][271] You all know well how much I paid those who are judges in all the areas[272] I visited frequently. I suppose I must have paid out the price of fifteen among them, so that you might enjoy me and I might always enjoy you in God.[273] I am neither sorry about it, nor is it enough for me, so still "I spend and I will spend all the more."[274] The Lord is powerful and so he can grant me afterward that "I might spend" myself "for your souls."[275]

[54] Behold, "I call God as the witness in my soul that I do not lie";[276] nor would I write in such a way that it would be "an occasion of greed or false praise";[277] nor do I do so out of a desire for honor from you. It is enough for me that honor which is not yet seen,[278] but which is believed in by the heart:[279] "For he who promised is faithful"[280] and never lies.

[55] Moreover, I see that already "in this present age"[281] the Lord has highly exalted me. I was not the sort of person [you would expect] the Lord to give this grace to, nor did I deserve it, for I know with the greatest certainty that poverty and woe are more my line than pleasures and riches—after all, Christ the Lord was poor for our sake[282]—and so I too am one who is miserable and unfortunate. Even if I wanted riches, I do not have them "and I am not judging myself"[283] for not a day passes but I expect to be killed or waylaid or taken into slavery or assaulted in some

other way. But for the sake of the promise of heaven "I fear none of these things."[284] Indeed, I have cast myself into the hands of God,[285] the almighty one who rules everywhere,[286] as the prophet has said:[287] "Cast your burden on God, and he will sustain you."[288]

[56] Behold now "I commend my spirit" to my "most faithful God"[289] "whose ambassador I am"[290] in my unworthiness, since "God does not have favorites"[291] and chose me[292] for this task that I might be just one of the least of his servants.[293]

[57] Therefore, "I shall give to him for all the things that he has given to me."[294] But what shall I say to him? What can I promise to give my Lord? I have nothing of value that is not his gift![295] But "he searches the hearts and the inmost parts"[296] and [knows] that it is enough that I exceedingly desire, and was ready indeed,[297] that he should grant to me "to drink his cup"[298] just as he granted it to the others who love him.

[58] So may it never happen to me[299] that my God should separate me from his "people which he has acquired"[300] in the outermost parts of the earth. I pray God that he give me perseverance and deign to grant that I should render him faithful witness until [the moment of] my passing [from this life to the life to come],[301] all for the sake of my God.

[59] And, if at any time I have "imitated something that is good"[302] for the sake of my God whom I love, then I ask him to grant me that I may shed my blood[303] "for his name's sake"[304] with those proselytes and captives, even if this means that I should lack even a tomb,[305] or that my corpse be horribly chopped up by dogs and wild beasts, or that "the birds of heaven devour it."[306] I do hereby declare that should this happen to me, that I should have gained my soul as well as my body.[307] For should any of these things happen, there is no doubt that on the day[308] we shall arise in the brightness of the sun,[309] this is in the glory of Christ Jesus our redeemer,[310] we shall be "sons of the living God"[311] and "fellow heirs with Christ"[312] and "conformed to his image";[313] "for from him and through him and in him"[314] we shall reign.

[60] But this sun which we see, rising each day for us by God's command, it shall never reign, nor shall its splendor last.[315] Likewise all those miserable people who worship it shall end up in a

foul punishment. We, on the other hand, are those who believe in and adore Christ—the true sun.[316] He is the sun which does not perish, and so we too, "who do his will," shall not perish.[317] And, as Christ "will abide forever,"[318] so he [who believes in him] "will abide forever," for Christ reigns with God the Father Almighty, and with the Holy Spirit, before all ages, and now, and "through all the ages to come."[319] Amen.

[61] So here it is! I have, again and again, briefly set before you the words of my declaration. "I bear witness" in truth and joyfulness of heart "before God and his holy angels"[320] that the one and only purpose I had in going back to that people from whom I had earlier escaped was the gospel and the promises of God.[321]

[62] I now pray for anyone who believes in, and fears, God who may perchance come upon this writing which Patrick, the sinner and the unlearned one, wrote in Ireland. I wrote it so that no one might say that whatever little I did, or anything I made visible according to God's pleasure, was done through ignorance. Rather, you should judge the situation and let it be truly believed that it was "the gift of God."[322] And this is my declaration before I die.

ii.
The Letter to the Soldiers of Coroticus

[1] Patrick, a sinner and one truly unlearned, declare myself to be a bishop set up by God in Ireland. I most certainly hold that what I am,[1] I have received from God. And so I live as an alien among the barbarians and a wanderer from the love of God,[2] as God is my witness. Not that I wished to utter anything so harshly or so roughly, but the zeal of God[3] forces me, and the truth of Christ[4] raises me up[5] for the love of neighbors and sons[6] for whom I gave up homeland and parents, and, if I am worthy, even "my life up to the grave."[7] I have sworn[8] to my God to teach the nations,[9] even if I am held in contempt by some.

[2] These words, which I have composed and written with "my own hand,"[10] are to be sent, given, and proclaimed to the soldiers of Coroticus. In doing this I do not speak to my compatriots[11] nor to "fellow citizens with the" Roman "saints";[12] but to those who by their evil deeds are servants of the demons. In a hostile manner these allies of the Irish and of the apostate Picts live in death, and are bloodthirsty for the blood of the innocent Christians I have begotten in countless numbers for God and have strengthened in Christ.

[3] The day after the anointed neophytes—still in their white baptismal garb and with the fragrance of the chrism on their foreheads still about them—were cut down and cruelly put to the sword by these men, I sent to them a holy priest—one I had taught since his infancy—accompanied by other clerics with a letter. In it I asked them to give back to us baptized prisoners they had taken along with some of the loot. They treated the whole matter as a big joke.[13]

[4] So now I do not know whom to grieve for more:[14] those who were killed, those captured, or those whom the Devil has deeply ensnared in his trap.[15] They will be enslaved equally with him in the everlasting punishment of Gehenna.[16] For it is indeed true that "he who commits sin is a slave of sin"[17] and shall be known as "a son of the Devil."[18]

[5] So let everyone who fears God know[19] that [the soldiers of Coroticus] are strangers to me and to Christ, my God, "for whom I am an ambassador."[20] The father-killer and the brother-killer are raging wolves,[21] "eating up" the Lord's "people like bread."[22] As it is said: "The wicked have destroyed your land, O Lord."[23] For [the Lord] has wonderfully and mercifully planted [his law] in Ireland in these final times;[24] and, with God's help, it has grown there.[25]

[6] I do not go beyond my authority for I have a share with those "whom he called and predestined"[26] to preach the gospel with no small measure of persecutions[27] "unto the very end of the earth."[28]

So despite the fact that the Enemy[29] begrudges this through the tyranny of Coroticus, who fears neither God nor his chosen priests, still it is to these priests he has granted the highest, the divine, and the sublime power: "Those whom they shall bind on earth shall be bound in heaven."[30]

[7] So I earnestly entreat [all] "you holy and humble of heart."[31] It is not lawful to seek favor from men such as these nor "to eat food" or drink "with them";[32] nor to accept their alms until they make satisfaction to God with painful penance and the shedding of tears,[33] and free the baptized "servants of God"[34] and the handmaids of Christ—for whom he was crucified and died.

[8] "The Lord rejects the gifts of the wicked. [...] He who offers a sacrifice from the goods of the poor is as one who sacrifices a son in the sight of his father."[35] "The riches," he says, "which he has unjustly gathered will be vomited from his belly, the angel of death will hand him over to be crushed by the anger of dragons, he will be killed with the viper's tongue, and an unquenchable fire will consume him."[36] Hence "woe to him who gathers for himself from the things that are not his."[37] Or [as it says elsewhere], "What does it profit a man if he gains the whole universe and suffers the loss of his soul?"[38]

[9] But it would take too long to describe individual crimes and set out the testimonies from the whole law which deal with such greed.[39] [So here are the basics:]

— Avarice is a deadly crime.[40]
— "You shall not covet you neighbor's goods."[41]
— "You shall not kill."[42]
— A murderer cannot be with Christ.[43]
— "He who hates his brother is a murderer."[44]
— "He who does not love his brother remains in death."[45]

How much more guilty is the man who stains his hands with the blood of "the sons of God"[46] whom [God] had acquired recently in the very ends of the earth[47] through the preaching of us who are so insignificant.

[10] Was it without God, or "according to the flesh"[48] that I came to Ireland? Who forced me to come? "I am one bound in the Spirit"[49] so that I cannot see any of my relatives.[50] Is it from within me that the holy mercy arises which I show toward this people—a people who once took me prisoner and destroyed the servants, male and female, of my father's estate? I was a free man "according to the flesh,"[51] my father a decurion, and I sold my status for the benefit of others.[52] I am neither ashamed of this nor sorry, but thus I have arrived at this point: I am a servant in Christ to a foreign people for the ineffable glory "of the eternal life which is in Christ Jesus our Lord,"[53] [11] even though my own people do not know me, for "a prophet has no honor in his own country."[54]

Perhaps we are not from "the one fold"[55] nor have we "one God and Father,"[56] as he says: "He that is not with me is against me; and he who does not gather with me, scatters."[57] It is not right that "one destroys, another builds."[58] "I am not seeking my own way,"[59] for it is not from me but from God's grace "who put this care in my heart"[60] that I should be one of the hunters and fishers[61] whom long ago he foretold would come "in the last days."[62]

[12] They despise me, oh, how they look down on me! What am I to do, O Lord?[63] Behold around me are your sheep torn to pieces and afflicted by those robbers[64] under the command of the bad-minded Coroticus. Far from the love of God is the man who hands over Christians into the hands of the Irish and the Picts. "Fierce wolves" have devoured the flock[65] of the Lord which with the greatest love and care[66] was truly increasing beautifully

in Ireland. Indeed, I could not count how many of the sons and daughters of the rulers of the Irish had become monks and virgins of Christ. On account of this "do not be pleased with the wrong done by the unjust, knowing that even unto depths of hell it shall not please the wicked."[67]

[13] Which of the saints would not be horrified at the prospect of fun, parties, or enjoyment with the likes of these men? They have filled their homes with plunder taken from dead Christians and they live by this. Wretched men, they do not know the poisonous lethal food that they share with the children and friends. They are like Eve who did not understand that in reality she gave death "to her husband."[68] All who do evil are like this; they work toward the everlasting penalty of death.[69]

[14] This is the practice of the Roman Christians of Gaul. They send suitable holy men to the Franks and other pagan peoples[70] with great piles of money to buy back baptized captives. You, however, kill them and sell them to a foreign "nation which does not know God."[71] You are like someone who hands over "the members of Christ" to a whorehouse.[72] Do you have any "hope in God"?[73] Who can approve of you? Who can address you with any words of praise? God will judge—as it is written: "Not only those who do evil, but those also who approve of it, will be damned."[74]

[15] I do not know "what" more "to say or how to speak"[75] about these dead "sons of God"[76] whom the sword struck so harshly. Indeed, it is written: "Weep with those who weep";[77] and in another place: "If one member suffers, all the members suffer with it."[78] This is the reason the church suffers and mourns for its sons and daughters[79] who have not yet been put to the sword, but who were carried off and brought to distant lands where sin abounds openly,[80] grievously, and without shame. There freeborn men are offered for sale and Christians are made into slaves again,[81] indeed slaves of the worst and most unworthy of men: the apostate Picts.

[16] So with sadness and grief I cry out: O "most beloved" and radiant brothers and "sons"—you are more than I can count—to whom I "have given birth in Christ,"[82] what shall I do with you? I who am not worthy to come to the assistance of God or men. "The wickedness of the unjust has prevailed over us."[83] We have

become like strangers.[84] Perhaps they do not believe that we have received "one baptism" and have "one God and Father."[85] That we were born in Ireland is an unworthy thing to them. As [scripture] says: "Do you not have one God? Why do each of you abandon your neighbor?"[86]

[17] And so my dearest friends, I grieve, grieve deeply, for you, but at the same time I rejoice within myself: "I did not labor in vain"[87] and my journeying has not been useless. For while such an indescribably awful crime has occurred, still, thanks be to God, it is as faithful baptized people that you have left this world to go to Paradise.[88] I can see you, you have not begun your migration to where "there is no night, nor sorrow, and where death shall be no more"[89] and "you shall rejoice leaping like calves let loose from their stalls. And you shall tread down the wicked, for they will be ashes under the soles of your feet."[90]

[18] And then you will reign with the Apostles, prophets, and martyrs and take possession of an eternal kingdom. Of this he himself testifies when he says: "They will come from east and west and sit at table with Abraham, Isaac, and Jacob in the kingdom of the heavens."[91] "Outside are the dogs and sorcerers and murderers" and[92] "liars and perjurers, their lot shall be in the lake of everlasting fire."[93] It is not without good reason that the Apostle says: "If the just man is barely saved, where will the sinner and the impious transgressor of the law appear?"[94]

[19] What then is the case with Coroticus and his criminal band? Where will these rebels against Christ appear? They are the ones who distribute baptized young women as prizes and all for the sake of a wretched temporal kingdom which will vanish[95] in a moment[96] like a cloud,[97] or indeed "like smoke scattered by the wind."[98] "So the" lying "sinner will perish from before the face of the Lord, but the just will feast"[99] in great harmony with Christ. "They will judge the nations and rule"[100] over wicked kings forever and ever.[101] Amen.

[20] "I testify before God and his angels"[102] that it will come about just as he has indicated by one as unlearned as myself. These are not my words but words which never lie: those of God and his Apostles and prophets. I am but the one who has

announced them in Latin.[103] "He that believes will be saved, he who does not believe will be condemned."[104] "God has spoken."[105]

[21] I earnestly request that any servant of God who is capable of bringing these tidings to public notice should do so: Let such a messenger neither hide nor detract from them but read them aloud so that every people and Coroticus himself should hear them. If this happens then God may inspire them, and they might return to him.[106] For though it be very late, it may be they will repent of their impious actions—being the murderers of the Lord's brothers—and release the baptized captives they have taken. Thus they would merit to live[107] in God and be healed for this life and eternity.

Peace to the Father and to the Son and to the Holy Spirit. Amen.[108]

iii.
The Sayings of Patrick (the Dicta)

[1] On my journeys through the regions of Gaul, through Italy, and even among the islands of the Tyrrhenian Sea, I had as my leader the fear of God.[1]

[2] You have rested from this world to go to paradise.[2] Thanks be to God.[3]

[3] The church of the Irish, which is indeed that of the Romans; if you would be Christians, then be as the Romans, and let that the song of praise be sung among yourselves at every hour of prayer: Lord have mercy,[4] Christ have mercy.

Every church which follows me, let it sing: Lord have mercy, Christ have mercy, Thanks be to God.

iv.

The Life of Patrick by Muirchú

Dedication[1]

My lord Aed,[2] many have made an attempt to put order on this historical account[3] according to what their fathers and those who were storytellers have handed down since the beginning. However, because of the great difficulty of this work of narration, the diversity of opinions, and the many suspicions of many people, they never arrived at the one and certain path of history. And so, if I am not mistaken, like boys being brought into the arena, as our proverb has it, I have set out on the dangerous and deep ocean of sacred narration in what is, given my abilities, a little child's coracle.[4] This ocean has towering waves and sharp reefs and no one has sailed it before me except my father, Cogitosus. But lest you imagine that I am trying to make a mountain out of a molehill, I shall only try to expound a selection from the many deeds of Patrick. I shall do it with little expertise from authors whose worth is less than certain, with a frail memory, weak intellect, and in a wretched style.[5] That I do it at all is only in respectful obedience to your command,[6] and with the most pious affection for your holy charity and your authority.

Prologue

In the name of the king of heaven, the savior of this universe, here begins the prologue of the life of St. Patrick the confessor. Time, place, and person are required. Now 436 years are reckoned from the death of our Lord Jesus Christ to the death of Patrick.[7]

In a book belonging to Ultán, bishop of Connor, I have found four names for Patrick: [1] holy Magonus (which means "famous"); [2] Sochet; [3] Patrick his own name; [4] Cothirthiacus, because he served four houses of wise men.[8] One of these wise men, Miliucc moccu Bóin, bought Patrick and he remained in his service for seven years. Patrick, son of Calpornius, had four names: Sochet when he was born, Cothirthiacus while a slave, Magonus when he was a student, and Patrick when he was ordained.

[His life will be treated in Book 1 under these] Headings.[9]

1. Patrick's origins and first captivity.
2. His voyage with the pagans, their anger in a deserted country, and how God granted him and the pagans food.
3. His second captivity when he was held prisoner for sixty days.
4. The reception he received from his parents as soon as they recognized him.
5. About the time when he set out for the apostolic sea and his desire to learn wisdom.
6. How he encountered St. Germanus among the Gauls and so did not go any further.
7. About the time the angel visited Patrick and asked him to come here.
8. About Patrick's return from Gaul, and the ordination of Palladius, who then died.
9. About his ordination by St. Amatorex after Palladius's death.
10. About the king at Tara at the time when Patrick brought baptism.
11. Patrick's first journey on this island to redeem himself from Miliucc, before he redeemed others from the Devil.
12. About Miliucc's death and what Patrick said about his offspring.
12a. About the weekly visit of an angel to Patrick.
13. St. Patrick's teaching when the decision was taken about the celebration of the first Easter in Ireland.
14. About how the first Easter sacrifice took place in Ireland.
15. About the pagan feast at Tara on the same night when Patrick adored the Paschal Lamb.

THE LIFE OF PATRICK

Book 1

[1] Patrick, called Sochet, was a Briton. His father was Calpornius, a deacon, and his father (as Patrick himself tells us) was Potitus, a presbyter, and they lived in Bannavem Taburniae, which is not far from our own sea (I am reliably informed this is what is now called Ventia).[10] His mother's name was Concessa.

Patrick was sixteen when, with others, he was captured and brought to this barbarian island and detained by a cruel pagan king.[11] And for six years, in the manner of the Hebrews,[12] "with fear" of God and "trembling" as the psalmist says,[13] with vigils and many prayers—a hundred by day and the same number by night, he freely "rendered to Caesar the things of Caesar, and to God the things of God."[14] Up to that time he was ignorant of the true God, but, since the Spirit was now fervent in him, he began to fear God and to love the Almighty Lord. Then, after many sorrows, after hunger, thirst, cold, exposure,[15] after pasturing flocks, after many visits of Victoricus (the angel sent to him by God), after many great well-known miracles, after many replies from God[16] (I shall mention just two examples: "It is good that you fast for soon you will be going home," and "Behold, your ship is ready"—but it was not near him but two-hundred miles away where he had never been!), Patrick fled that pagan tyrant "and his practices"[17] and accepted the sacred companionship of the eternal and heavenly God. So, by divine command, he sailed to Britain with pagan barbarian strangers who worshiped false Gods. He was twenty-three years of age.

[2] After sailing, like Jonah,[18] for three days and nights, Patrick had to march, like Moses, for twenty-eight days and nights through a desert[19] forced on by the pagans who, like the Jews, murmured about being almost dead from hunger and thirst.[20] Their leader teased him by asking him to call on his God to save them from perishing.[21] So seeing their need and having pity on them,[22] sharing their suffering, crowned with merit, glorified by God,[23] Patrick supplied them by God's help with an abundance of food from a herd of pigs. These were sent to him by God just as once he sent a flock of quails [to the Israelites].[24] They also, like

93

John [the Baptist], found wild honey, but as the worst of pagans they did not deserve locusts, but only pigs.[25] St. Patrick did not touch this food as it had been sacrificially offered,[26] and he had no ill effects nor any sense of hunger or thirst.[27] And that same night while he was sleeping, Satan attacked him violently—it was as if he were burying Patrick under great stones, crushing his limbs. But Patrick called loudly on Elijah twice[28] and immediately the sun rose over him; its splendor scattered the gloomy darkness,[29] and Patrick's powers returned to him.

[3] Many years later Patrick was again captured by strangers. On the first night of this captivity the Lord gave him a revelation,[30] saying: "You will be with your enemies for two months." And it happened in just that way for the Lord freed him from their hands[31] on the sixtieth day. Moreover, he provided Patrick and his followers with food, water, and fire for ten days until they encountered other people.

[4] After a few years Patrick was at last back home resting with his parents and relatives. He was received as a son, and they begged him that after his trials and tribulations he never go away again. But he would not agree to this, and while he was at home many visions were given to him. He was then nearly thirty, and, as the Apostle says, in "mature manhood, to the measure of the stature of the fullness" of the age "of Christ."[32] Then Patrick went off to visit the apostolic see, the head of all the churches of the whole world. He wanted to learn and understand the divine wisdom, and participate in the holy mysteries to which God was calling him, for he wanted to bring divine grace to foreign nations[33] by converting them to the Christian faith.

[5] So Patrick left Britain for Gaul with his heart set on crossing the Alps to reach his final goal: Rome. On this journey he discovered a great gift in the most holy bishop Germanus of the city of Auxerre. He remained with him for a long time—like Paul at the feet of Gameliel[34]—as a perfect student, patient and obedient. Patrick devoted himself wholeheartedly to wisdom, learning, and chastity—all that is useful for mind and soul. He kept himself, with great fear and love of God, in goodness and simplicity of heart, a virgin in spirit and body.

[6] After a long time there (some say thirty, others forty, years), his faithful old friend Victoricus (who predicted, when he was a slave in Ireland, what would happen to him) began to visit him frequently to say that it was now time for him to fish with the evangelical net among the wild and barbarian nations whom God had sent him to teach.[35] There he was told in a vision: "The sons and daughters of the Wood of Foclut are calling you" etc.

[7] So when an opportune time came he began, with divine help, his journey toward the work for which he was long prepared, that of the gospel.[36] Germanus sent a presbyter, Segitius, with him so that he would have a fellow witness for he had not yet been ordained to the episcopal grade by the holy lord Germanus.[37] They were certain that Palladius, archdeacon of Pope Celestine, bishop of the city of Rome (the forty-fifth successor from St. Peter the Apostle in holding the apostolic see), had been ordained and sent to convert that island, which is situated in the cold and wintry regions. But how could [Palladius] do this when "no one can receive anything except what has been given from heaven"?[38] Those wild and vicious people would not easily accept his teaching, and Palladius did not want to spend long in a land not his own. So he decided to return to Pope Celestine. Having crossed the sea from Ireland to Britain, he died there while making his way back to Rome.

[8] At Ebmoria Patrick and his companions heard of the death, in Britain, of Palladius from the latter's disciples, Augustine and Benedict. So they detoured to meet a wonderful man called Amathorex who lived nearby. There Patrick, "knowing all that was to happen to him,"[39] accepted the episcopal grade from the holy bishop Amathorex. There also, and on the same day that Patrick was ordained, his companions Auxilius and Iserninus received the lesser grades. While they were accepting the blessings and doing everything perfectly according to custom, they sang the verses of the psalmist: "You are a priest forever according to the order of Melchizedek"[40]—something so specifically appropriate for Patrick!

Then in the name of the holy Trinity, our venerable traveler went on the ship that was ready and waiting for him. Arriving in

Britain, he traveled across it as quickly as possible—no one seeks the Lord with idleness[41]—and then with a favorable wind he crossed over our sea.

[9] At that time there was a mighty and fierce pagan king in those parts.[42] This was the Emperor of the Barbarians, who reigned at Tara, which was then the capital of the kingdom of the Irish. This king was Loiguire, son of Níall, whose family ruled almost the whole island. He had with him seers and wise men and augurs and spell-casters and those skilled in every one of the evil arts. They were able to know and predict everything—according to the pagan idolatrous custom—before it occurred. Two of these were preferred by the king above the rest: Lothrock (also called Lochru) and Lucet Máel (also called Ronal). With their magical skill this pair often declared that they could see another way of life about to come to Ireland from outside. It would be like a kingdom, it would come from far away across the seas, and it would bring an unknown and annoying teaching with it. This teaching would be given out by a handful, yet be received by many, and held in honor by all. It would overthrow kingdoms, kill the kings who resisted it, seduce the crowds, destroy all their gods, cast out their own skills and works, and this kingdom would have no end. They also pointed to the man who would bring this new way of life and persuade people [to accept it]. They prophesied in words that made up a kind of poem which was often recited in those days, and especially in the two or three years just before Patrick's coming. Because of their "language's peculiar idiom"[43] the poem's meaning is not very clear, but here it is:

One with shaven head will come here with his curled-headed stick
He will sing foul things from his home with perforated head
From his table in the front part of his house his whole family will reply
to him: "Let it be! Let it be!"[44]

We can say this far more clearly in our own language: When all these things happen,[45] our kingdom—which is pagan—shall not stand.[46] With the advent of Patrick came the destruction of the cult of the idols, and everything was filled with the universal faith of Christ. We have said enough about these things, now back to our story.

[10] His voyage over, the holy man borne down with marvels and spiritual riches from beyond the seas found a suitable landing place in the region of the Cúala—a famous harbor called Inber Dee.[47] There Patrick thought that the best thing to do was to first redeem himself from slavery. So he was eager to go to the northern regions and find the pagan Miliucc, who had held him captive. He brought with him twice the price of his servitude, namely the heavenly and the earthly, that he might free the man he once served as a slave. So before he reached the island that is today named after him, Patrick turned the prow of his ship, and leaving Brega and the regions of the Conaille and Ulaid to one side, traveled to the inlet of Bréne. They eventually landed at Inber Slane. He and his companions hid their little boat there and went a little inland to rest. But the swineherd of Díchu (although a pagan, this man was naturally good, and, by the way, the barn in which he lived is now called after Patrick) found them while they were resting, and thinking them to be thieves or robbers, he went to tell his master. Unawares, the swineherd led Díchu upon them. Díchu's intention was to kill them, but the moment he saw St. Patrick's face the Lord changed his thoughts to the good. So Patrick preached the faith to him, and there and then he believed Patrick. Thus Díchu was the first of all the people [to be converted]. The saint rested with Díchu for some days. But the saint wished to depart quickly to visit Miliucc and bring him his price, for thus he might convert him to the faith of Christ. He left his boat with Díchu and began to make his way by land through the region of the Cruithni until he reached Slíab Mís, the mountain on which he worked as a captive many years earlier and where he had seen the angel Victoricus leave his swift footprint on a stone when, in Patrick's sight, he was ascending into heaven.[48]

[11] But Miliucc heard that his slave was coming to see him to make him, by force as it were, change his ways. He did not want this at the end of his life as he did not want to become a subject to his former servant, nor that the servant should now rule over him. At the Devil's prompting he decided to destroy himself by fire. So he gathered all his possessions in the house where he was once a king, and set fire to them and himself. St. Patrick, standing on the

right hand side of Slíab Mís—where now for the first time since his return he saw where as a slave he had received such grace, saw the fire lit by the chief with his own eyes. (A cross marks the spot where St. Patrick stood to this very day.) Standing there he was speechless, and for two to three hours he wept, sighed, and mourned without saying one word.[49] Then he said: "'I do not know, God knows'[50] this human ruler chose to commit himself to the flames lest he should believe in, and serve, the eternal God at the end of his life. 'I do not know, God knows'[51] none of this king's sons 'shall sit upon his throne'[52] 'from generation to generation.'[53] And indeed his descendants shall be subject to others forever." This said, he prayed and armed himself with the sign of the cross, and quickly turned about and went back to the region of the Ulaid along the same route he came. On his return to Mag Inis he remained with Díchu for many days. While there he traveled about the whole region and chose it as a place he loved; and faith began to grow there.

[12] Now back to the story. Every week on the seventh day an angel visited Patrick, who enjoyed speaking with him as one man speaks to another.[54] Even when he was sixteen, and spending six years in slavery,[55] the angel visited him, and Patrick enjoyed the angel's advice and conversations on thirty occasions before leaving Ireland for the land of the Latins. Once he lost the pigs he was herding and the angel came and showed him where they were. The next day, having talked about several things, the angel put his foot on the rock of Scirit, beside Slíab Mís, and ascended in his presence.[56] The imprint can still be seen in that place where the angel visited him thirty times. It is now a place of prayer for the faithful for prayers said there obtain the most happy fruit.

[13] It was coming close to the time of the Passover.[57] This was the first Passover to be celebrated to [the glory] of God in this Egypt which is our island, resembling as it were the Passover, of which we read in Genesis, in the Land of Goshen.[58] Patrick and his companions discussed with the pagans amongst whom God had sent them where they should celebrate this first Passover. After many suggestions were put to them, St. Patrick, by divine inspiration, finally decided that this great solemnity of

the Lord—since it was the head of all the solemnities—should be celebrated in the great plain of Brega, for there was the greatest kingdom of these pagan peoples,[59] the head of all their paganism[60] and idolatry. There, as the psalmist says, he "crushed the head of the dragon."[61] There an unstoppable spike would be driven into the head of all idolatry[62] with the hammer of a work joined to strong faith[63] by the spiritual hands of St. Patrick and his companions. "And so it happened."[64]

[14] So they put to sea leaving that good man Díchu in full faith[65] and peace, and went to Mag Inis. Now in the fullness of ministry the coast was on their right hand, as was fitting, unlike earlier when it was on their left. After a good and swift trip they landed at Inber Colpdi. Leaving their boat they walked to the great plain and by evening they had reached the burial mounds of Fíacc. These, so the old story goes as it was told by Ferchertne (one of the nine wise-man prophets of Brega), were dug by the men, that is the servants, of Fíacc. And there Patrick and his companions made camp and offered, with the every devotion of spirit, "to the most high God"[66] the Passover "sacrifice of praise," and so fulfilled "the word of the prophet."[67]

[15] Now that year another solemnity, this one of idolatry when the pagans gathered with many spells, feats of magic, and idolatrous superstitions, was being held at the same time. Hence the king, his satraps, leaders, princes, and the nobles of the people had gathered there.[68] King Loíguire had also called to Tara all the wise men, those who can predict the future, and those who were trained or could teach every skill and art.[69] Loíguire at Tara was like Nebuchadnezzar at Babylon who had done likewise.[70] And on the very night St. Patrick was celebrating the Passover, they were partaking of the worship of their great pagan festival. Now there was a custom among the pagans—made clear to all by edict[71]—that it would be death for anyone, wherever they were, to light a fire on that night before the fire was lit in the house of the king (i.e., the palace of Tara). So when St. Patrick celebrating the Passover lit the great bright and blessed divine fire, it shone out clearly and was seen by nearly everyone living in the plain of Tara.[72] And those who saw it viewed it with

great wonder. All the elders and nobles of the nation were called in the king's presence and he spoke to them:[73] "Who is this man who has dared to commit such a crime in my kingdom? Let him perish by death!" And the answer from those around him was that they did not know. Then the wise men answered: "'O king, live forever!'[74] This fire, which we see lit this night before the fire of your own house, must be quenched this night. Indeed, if it is not put out tonight, it will never be extinguished! You should know that it will keep rising up and will supplant all the fires of our own religion. The one who lit it, and the kingdom he is bringing upon us[75] this night, will overcome us all—both you and us—by leading away everyone in your kingdom. All the kingdoms[76] will fall down before it,[77] and it will fill the whole country and it 'shall reign forever and ever.'"[78]

[16] Just as with Herod, "when the king heard this he was" very "troubled, and with him the whole city" of Tara.[79] So he said this in reply: "This will not happen! But let us go there to see what is going on, and then we can capture or kill the people who are committing this crime in our kingdom." So, following a practice they had received from their gods, the king ordered three times nine chariots made ready, and he took with him Lucet Máel and Lochru, since they were his greatest wise men and more excellent than all the rest in a conflict.

It was at the end of the night that Loíguire left (and as was appropriate to the occasion the heads of both men and horses were turned to the left[80]) Tara for the burial ground of the men of Fíacc. Traveling along, the wise men with the king said: "O king, you should not yourself go into the place where the fire is burning in case this would later cause you to adore the man who lit it. Instead, you should remain outside and let the man be called to you so that he can adore you, and you be in charge of him. Then in your sight we can dispute with this man, and you can judge between us." The king replied that "this is a wise policy and I shall follow it." When they arrived they dismounted from their chariots and horses,[81] but they did not go within the circle of the place of the fire; rather they sat down nearby. [17] So Patrick was called to come out into the king's presence outside the place of light. Meanwhile, the wise men said to the group: "Let us not get up when he comes, for anyone who gets up at his coming will later believe him and adore[82] him." Patrick, seeing all the horses and chariots as soon as he got up, went toward them. The appropriate verse of the psalmist was on his lips and in his heart:[83] "Some take pride in chariots, and some in horses, but we shall walk in the name of [the Lord] our God."[84]

When Patrick came out they did not rise. But one man, with the Lord's help, was unwilling to obey the wise men's dictates. He was Ercc, son of Daig, whose relics are now adored in the city called Slane. When he arose, Patrick blessed him, and he believed in the eternal God. Then the duel of words began. The wise man Lochru wanted to provoke the saint, so within earshot of him he started to insult the Catholic faith with vile and filthy words. At that moment Patrick caught him with his eye (like what Peter said about Simon) and let out a mighty, powerful, and confident cry to the Lord: "O Lord, who can do all things, and in whose power all things are held in existence, and who has sent me here, grant that this unholy man who blasphemes your name may now be lifted up and cast outside, and die speedily."[85] This said, the wise man was lifted up into the sky, and then he fell back down to earth, splitting his skull on a rock. Thus he died in their presence and the pagans feared.[86]

[18] So angered were the king and his group by Patrick's actions that they wanted to kill him. The king shouted: "He is going to destroy us: Grab him!" When St. Patrick saw that the blasphemous pagans were about to strike, he stood up and cried out: "Let God rise up, let his enemies be scattered; let those who hate him flee before him."[87] At once, darkness descended on them so that those blasphemers fought and clashed with one another in a horrible commotion. The earth shook,[88] the axles of their chariots were crunched together, while horses and chariots were driven headlong over the plain, and only a handful, half-alive,[89] reached mount Monduirn. In this curse by Patrick seven times seven men perished in the presence of their king, and all at the fruit of the king's own words. The curse continued until there were just four people left: the king himself, his wife, and two Irishmen. They stood there

trembling with fear. Then the queen went and spoke to Patrick: "O righteous and powerful one, do not destroy the king for he is coming to kneel and adore your Lord."

Terror-driven, the king came into the holy presence and made a display of adoration with his knees, but not with his will. Just after they had departed, the king called St. Patrick over to him. His words were deceptive, for he wanted to kill Patrick no matter what. But Patrick, knowing the thoughts[90] of this most evil king,[91] blessed his company of eight men and a boy in the name of Jesus Christ and began to go toward the king. The king was counting them as they approached, when in an instant he could no longer see them. All that the pagans could see was eight deer and a fawn going as if to the desert. So in the early light the king, and the others who had escaped Patrick's curse, turned back toward Tara. He was downcast, fearful, and conscious of his ignominy.

[19] The next day, which [for us] was the Day of the Passover [Easter Day], was for the pagans the day of their greatest festival; and many kings, princes, and wise men had gathered with Loíguire for a feast.[92] While they were eating and drinking in the palace of Tara,[93] some speaking about what had happened, others turning it over in their minds, Patrick with only five companions appeared among them, having come in through "closed doors" in the way we read about Christ.[94] He went there to proclaim and demonstrate the holy faith in Tara in the presence of all nations.[95] As he entered the dining hall of Tara, only one out of the whole group stood to salute his arrival. This was Dubthach maccu Lugir, the greatest of the poets. (With him there was another poet called Fíacc, who was then no more than a boy. But Fíacc later became a famous bishop, and today his relics are adored in Sléibte.) When Dubthach stood to honor St. Patrick, the saint blessed him and he was the first who believed in God on that day,[96] "and it was reckoned to him as righteousness."[97] Seeing Patrick, the pagans asked him to eat with them so that they could test him later. And he, "knowing all that was going to happen,"[98] accepted their invitation.

[20] "While they were" all "eating,"[99] one of the wise men, called Lucet Máel, despite having taken part in the nocturnal conflict when his colleague perished, still wanted to challenge Patrick. His first move was to slip something into Patrick's cup from a flask he had with him.[100] Those around him watched to see what Patrick would do. When St. Patrick recognized what kind of test this was, he blessed his cup. Its contents now became like ice. Then he turned it upside down and only the drop added by the wise man fell out. Blessing it again, the contents returned to their natural liquid form, "and they were all amazed."[101]

After the cup test, the wise man said: "Let us perform signs in this great field."[102] So Patrick asked him which kind they should perform. The wise man said: "Let us call down snow upon the earth." But Patrick said: "I do not wish to do anything which is contrary to the will of God."[103] So the wise man said: "I will bring it upon the earth for all to see." Then sending forth magical spells he covered the whole field with snow. It reached the height of a man's belt in depth, and all saw it "and were amazed."[104] Then the saint said: "Behold we have all seen this, now get rid of it!" The wise man replied: "I am unable to get rid of it until the same time tomorrow." So the saint declared: "You are capable of doing ill, but not of doing good. This is not the case with me." Then as he cast his blessing around the field, the snow disappeared. Without rain or mist or wind it went in a moment. "The crowd" applauded and "were amazed,"[105] and "it touched their hearts."[106] A little later the wise man, by invoking the demons, was able to produce another sign. This time he called down the deepest darkness over the land so that all the people grumbled.[107] Then the saint said: "Get rid of the darkness!" As before, the wise man could not do this. So the saint prayed, blessed it, and at once the darkness was driven out, the sun shone, and the people cried out and "gave thanks."[108]

After all these clashes between Patrick and the wise man had taken place before him, the king said to both of them: "Throw your books into water, and we shall worship the man whose books escape undamaged." Patrick answered: "I will do this," but the wise man said: "I refuse to submit to the judgment of water with this man, for he holds water as a god."[109] Presumably the wise man had heard that baptism was given through water by Patrick. So the king then replied: "Then send them through fire." Patrick said: "I am prepared to do this." But the wise man was unwilling and stated: "This man worships fire and water in alternate years as god: Now water is his god, now fire." The saint replied: "This is not true. What should happen is this: You should go with one of the boys who accompany me into an enclosed house which is divided into two separate parts.[110] You put on my vestment,[111] while my boy puts on yours. Then let both of you be set on fire 'in the sight of the Most High.'"[112] The scheme was acceptable and they set about building the house: One half was made from green wood, the other from dry wood. Into the green part stepped the wise man, while in the dry part was placed Benignus, one of Patrick's boys, wearing the magical robe [of the wise man]. Then with the house closed up from outside, it was set ablaze while the whole crowd looked on. "And it came to pass in that hour,"[113] through Patrick's praying, that the flaming fire[114] consumed the wise man and the green wood entirely,[115] St. Patrick's chasuble alone surviving intact as the fire did not touch it. Happily, the exact opposite result happened to Benignus. Although he was in the dry part of the house, in his case it was like what was said about the three boys [in the fiery furnace]: "The fire did not touch them at all and caused them no pain or distress."[116] Only the wise man's chasuble, which the boy was wearing, was burnt—and this happened by God's command.

The king "was greatly infuriated"[117] with Patrick over the death of his wise man and would have killed him except he was prevented by God. At Patrick's bidding and by his word the anger of God came down upon that blasphemous people,[118] and many of them perished.[119] Then St. Patrick spoke thus to the king: "Unless you now believe, you shall quickly die, for the anger of God has come down upon your head."[120] And the king feared greatly and his heart was in turmoil,[121] and with him that of the whole city.[122]

[21] So King Loíguire gathered his elders and whole senate and said to them: "It is better that I believe, rather than that I die."[123] So having held the meeting, on the counsel of his fellows

he believed on that day and he turned to the eternal Lord God, and in that place many others believed.[124] And Patrick told the king: "Because you have resisted my teaching and have put obstacles in my way, although the day of your reign shall be prolonged, none of your descendants shall ever be king."[125]

[22] So then St. Patrick, according to the precept of the Lord Jesus, "went off teaching all the nations and baptizing them in the name of the Father and of the Son and of the Holy Spirit."[126] He "went out" from Tara "and proclaimed the good news everywhere, while the Lord worked with him and confirmed the message by the signs that accompanied it."[127]

[23] Now, god willing, I want to try to narrate a few of the many wonders of Patrick, bishop and eminent teacher of the whole of Ireland.

At that time when the whole of Britain was held rigid in unbelief, one of its kings had a noble daughter called Monesan. She, "full of the Holy Spirit,"[128] refused with God's help all the proposals from those who wanted to marry her. Despite frequent drenchings with water, they could not force her to do what she did not want and considered of lesser worth. Now between the beatings and the drenchings, her mother and her nurse sought to persuade her to marry, but Monesan kept questioning them if they knew who made the sphere of the heavens by which the universe is given light. When she got the answer that the maker of the Sun was he whose seat is in heaven,[129] she when frequently asked to join in the bond of marriage said: "I shall never do this." And in this she was enlightened with the most luminous counsel of the Holy Spirit. So she searched, like Abraham before her, "through nature for the maker of all that is created."[130] Her parents took advice on her behavior and heard that Patrick was a just man[131] who was visited by the eternal God every seventh day. So they went to Ireland with their daughter and after much labor they encountered Patrick, who asked where they had come from. So the travelers began to shout loudly and tell him: "It is the intensity of the desire of our daughter to see God that has made it necessary for us to travel to you." So Patrick, "full of the Holy Spirit,"[132] lifted his voice and asked her: "Do you believe in God?"

She replied: "I believe!" Then he washed her with the washing of water and the Holy Spirit.[133] Just after that, without any delay, she lay on the ground and handed her spirit over into the hands of the angels.[134] Where she died, there she was joined [to Christ]. Then Patrick foretold that after twenty years her body would be taken with honor to a little chapel that was near that place. And later this happened. Indeed, the relics of this woman from across the sea are worshiped there to this day.

[24] I must not omit mention of another of Patrick's wonderful deeds. He had heard of the most wicked act committed by one of the kings of the British. This was that foul and cruel tyrant Coroticus, who was a great persecutor and killer of Christians. Patrick sent him a letter in which he attempted to call him back to the way of truth.[135] But Coroticus only sneered at these saving admonitions. When it was conveyed to Patrick that sneering was the only outcome of his letter, he prayed to the Lord and said: "O Lord, if it be possible,[136] cast out this traitor[137] from the present life and from the life to come."[138] Only a little time had passed after this when Coroticus heard someone singing in accompaniment to music that he should move off his throne. And then all who were dearest to him burst out in one voice with this song. There and then, in the midst of them all, he miserably took on the form of a fox. At once he left that place and since that very hour and day he has never been seen. It was as if Coroticus was like water: Once it has flowed away it is never seen again.

[25] We must make brief mention of [another] miraculous deed of Patrick, that apostolic man of the Lord, while he still stood here in the flesh. Indeed it is so wondrous that it is only written about him and Stephen.[139] Once just before he went to his usual nightly place for solitary prayer, Patrick saw the wonders of the heavens.[140] The saint then wishing to test his most beloved and faithful boy, Benignus, said to him: "O my son, tell me, I beg you, if you see those things which I see." The little fellow replied with confidence: "It is known to me already what you sense, for I see heaven opened and the Son of God and his angels."[141] The Patrick said: "I now realize that you are worthy to be my successor."[142] Then without delay and with hastened step they arrived at

the usual place of prayer, which was a riverbed in mid-river. During the prayers the young fellow said: "I cannot take the cold of this water any longer!" for the water was exceedingly cold for him. Patrick told him to move down from the upper part of the river to a place lower down. But Benignus could not stand there either for he declared that now he felt the water to be exceedingly hot. So not being able to stay there any longer, he got up out of the river and onto the land.

[26] In Patrick's time, one of the men in the Ulaid region of Ireland was Macc Cuill Greccae. He was such a wild and wicked tyrant that he was named "the Cyclops." He was depraved in his thought, intemperate in his words, evil in his actions, bitter in spirit, angry in soul, impious in body, unfeeling in mind, a gentile in life-style, and stupid in conscience.[143] This tyrant used to operate from a barren fastness called Druim moccu Echach, which was high in the mountains. Every day he used to cruelly ambush and kill travelers moving through that region. Indeed, he was so cruel that he adopted cruelty as his trademark. So deeply had he fallen into wickedness that one day when he was sitting on his hilltop and saw St. Patrick approaching, his first thought was to kill him. Patrick walked along the way radiating the clear light of faith and sparkling with the wondrous halo of heavenly glory, and with the untroubled trust that comes with Christian teaching. Macc Cuill then said to his partners in crime: "Look! Here comes the seducer and perverter of the people! His game is to make a mighty display of 'power' so that he can deceive and lead astray crowds of people. Let us set out and ensnare him, and then we will know whether or not this god he keeps talking about has any power." So they tempted the holy man thus. They placed a healthy member of their gang in the middle of the group with a cloak over him. This man then pretended to be fatally ill. In this manner they wanted to prove that the saint was a fraud, and then they thought they could call the saint a seducer, his miracles could then be called illusions, and his prayers described as spells and witchcraft.

As Patrick and his disciples got closer, the bandits said to him: "Look over here! One of us has just taken ill. So come closer and sing some of the spells of your sect over him for you might be able to heal him."[144] Patrick, knowing all[145] their deceits and lies, stoutly and bravely said to them: "If he had been ill [his death] would be no surprise." Then the gang uncovered the face of the one who pretended illness and they discovered that he was dead. Stupefied and bewildered by this great miracle, the pagans said to one another: "Truly this is a man of God,[146] and we have done evil in tempting him."

Then St. Patrick turned toward Macc Cuill and asked him: "Why did you want to tempt me?" The cruel tyrant replied: "I am repentant of this deed, and whatever you order me to do I will do. Now I deliver myself into the power of this high god of yours whom you preach." And St. Patrick said: "Then 'believe in my Lord' and God 'Jesus,'[147] and 'confess your sins'[148] and be baptized 'in the name of the Father and of the Son and of the Holy Spirit.'"[149] And, "at that very hour"[150] he was converted, and he believed in the eternal God, and was baptized. Then Macc Cuill told the saint even more: "I confess to you, Patrick my holy lord, that I had proposed to kill you. So judge what is the debt that I owe for so great a crime." Patrick replied: "I am unable to judge, but God will judge. You must now go down to the sea, unarmed, and leave this part of Ireland. You can take none of your riches except one piece of clothing. Something poor and small which just about covers you. You are not to taste or drink any of the fruits of this island, and you shall bear this as a mark of your sin upon your head.[151] When you arrive at the shore bind your feet with an iron fetter and throw its key into the sea. Then get into a one-hide boat[152] and put to sea without a rudder or an oar. You can then accept wherever the wind and sea take you. In whichever place divine Providence lands you, there you are to swell and keep God's commandments." Macc Cuill said: "I shall do as you have said. But what shall we do about this dead man?" Patrick replied: "He shall live and rise without pain." And at that hour Patrick raised him and he returned to life healthy. Meanwhile Macc Cuill departed in silence. He went to the southern shore of Mag Inis having the untroubled trust of faith. He bound himself on the seashore and threw the key into the sea as he had been ordered. He then took to the sea in a small boat. The north wind blew and propelled him toward the south. Finally, it cast him ashore on the island called Euonia. There he encountered two truly wonderful men, splendid in faith and in teaching. These two had been the first to teach the Word of God and [give] baptism on Euonia, and the island's people had been converted to the Catholic faith through their teaching. Their names were Conindrus and Rumilus. When these two saw the man with only one short garment they were amazed and sorry for him. So they lifted him from the sea and received him with joy. He, on the other hand, having discovered spiritual fathers in this place picked for him by God, trained his body and soul in accordance with their rule. He passed the rest of his time on earth in that place with these two holy bishops, and eventually was their successor in the episcopate. This is Macc Cuill, bishop of Mane and prelate of Arde Huimnonn.[153]

[27] On another occasion St. Patrick was resting on the Lord's Day. He was beside a marsh up above the seashore not far north of Druimm Bó. There he heard the sound of some pagans nearby who were working on the Lord's Day busily digging the ditch that runs around a rath. So Patrick called to them and prohibited them working on the Lord's Day.[154] But far from listening to the words of the saint, they began to laugh at him and make fun of what he said. Then St. Patrick said: "Mudebroth,[155] though you labor hard, it will benefit you nothing!" And this happened exactly as the saint had said: On the very next night a great wind came and tossed up the sea, and the tempest wrecked the entire work of those pagans.

[28] "There was once a rich man"[156] honored in the eastern region [Airthir] "who was named"[157] Dáire. St. Patrick asked him to give a particular piece of land over to him for the practice of religion. So the rich man said to the saint: "Which piece are you asking for?" "I request," said the saint, "that you give me the piece of high ground named Druimm Sailech, and I can build in that place." But [Dáire] did not want to give that piece of high ground to the saint, so he gave him another piece of low-lying

land—what is now the burial mount of the martyrs near Armagh—and St. Patrick lived there with his companions.

Some time after that one of the men who looked after Dáire's horses brought one of those horses to pasture in the very grassy place belonging to the Christians. This letting loose of a horse in his place offended Patrick, who said: "Dáire has done a stupid thing in sending brute animals to upset this little place which he has given to God." But the handler "did not hear as if he were deaf, and like one who is dumb he opened not his mouth"[158] and said nothing. However, he left the horse there for the night and went off. On the following morning, however, when he came back to check on the horse he found that it was dead. He then went back to his master's house full of sadness and said to him: "Behold that Christian killed your horse, because it offended him that his place was disturbed." Then Dáire said to his men: "That man also shall be killed. Away now and kill him!" Just then as his men went outside, Dáire was gripped in death. His wife then said: "This death is caused by the Christian. Someone must go quickly and bring us his blessings and we will be well.[159] Those who have gone off to kill the Christian are to be stopped and called back here." So two men went off and, not letting on what had occurred, said to [Patrick]: "Behold Dáire has just been taken ill. We want to carry back something from you which might be able to heal him." But St. Patrick, knowing what had happened, said: "You don't say?" So he blessed water and gave it to them saying: "Go, sprinkle some of this water on your horse and take it with you." So they did this and the horse came back to life. Then they brought the water with them and when Dáire was sprinkled with this holy water he was restored to health. After this Dáire came and paid homage to St. Patrick, and he brought along with him a wondrous bronze bowl from across the seas which could hold three measures. Then Dáire said to the saint: "Behold this bronze is yours." And St. Patrick responded: "Grazacham!"[160] On returning home, Dáire said: "This man is a fool if he can say nothing more than "grazacham" for such a wonderful bronze as can take three measures!" So Dáire told his servants: "Go off and carry back to us our bronze." They went away and said to Patrick: "We shall carry away this bronze." Nevertheless, this time Patrick [again] said: "Grazacham, carry it away!" And the servants carried it off. Later Dáire questioned his fellows: "What did the Christian say when you carried off the bronze?" They told him: "He said 'grazacham.'" Dáire then said in response to this: "'Grazacham' in giving, 'grazacham' in taking away.[161] His statement is such a good one that with these uses of 'grazacham' his bronze shall be carried back to him again!" This time Dáire himself came to Patrick carrying the bronze. [Dáire] said to him: "Let this be your bronze. You are a steady and unflappable man. Moreover, that part of the land which I have, but which you once asked for, that I now give to you so that you can dwell there." This is the place of the city we call Armagh. And both St. Patrick and Dáire went out and surveyed that wonderful offering and most pleasing gift. They then ascended to that high ground and found there a deer with its little fawn lying in the place where now the altar is in the northern church of Armagh. Patrick's companions wanted to catch and kill the fawn, but the saint did not want this to happen and would not permit it. Instead, the saint himself took hold of the fawn and carried it in his arms and the deer followed him like a loving lamb until he set the fawn free in another valley on the northern side of Armagh.[162] There even today, as those who know about these thing relate, some signs of his power still remain.

[29] It is reported by those who know these things that there was once a tough and very greedy man in Mag Inis. Indeed he was so greedy he had become stupid in his avarice. Thus one day when the two oxen which drew Patrick's cart after the holy work of the day were resting and grazing in one of his meadows, this silly man chased them off with force. And he did this in the presence of St. Patrick. St. Patrick was so angered by this that he uttered this curse: "Mudebroth![163] You have done evil. This field will never again be of any use to you nor to your descendants forever. From this moment forth it will be useless." "And it was so."[164] On that very same day there was a mighty inundation from the sea which washed over the whole field. It was like what is described in the prophet's words: "A fruitful land [is turned] into

a salty waste, because of the wickedness of its inhabitants."[165] The result is that it has been sandy and infertile ever since that day when St. Patrick cursed it "down to today."[166]

[His life will be treated in] Book 2 [under these] Headings.

1. Patrick's diligence in prayer.
2. How someone who was dead spoke with him.
3. How a Sunday night was lit up so that they could find horses.
4. About the angel preventing him for choosing to die in Armagh.
5. About the burning bush with the angel in it.
6. Concerning Patrick's four requests.
7. About his day of death and his life-span of thirty years.
8. How a barrier was placed against the night and so for twelve nights there was no darkness.
9. How it received the Eucharist[167] from Bishop Tassach.
10. About the angels who kept the vigil beside his body on the first night of his funeral.
11. About the advice given by an angel regarding where Patrick's tomb should be.
12. How fire came out from his tomb.
13. How the sea level rose so that there could not be a war over his body.
14. How the people were happily led astray.

[1] Of his diligence in prayer, we shall try to write down only a few details out of the many things that might be said about Patrick. Daily, whether he was staying in one place or traveling along the road, he used to sing all "the psalms and hymns" and the Apocalypse of John "and" all "the spiritual songs"[168] of the scriptures. No less than a hundred times in each hour of the day and each hour of the night he made the sign of the triumphant cross upon himself; and at every cross he saw as he traveled, he used to get down from his chariot and turn toward it in order to pray.

[2] While traveling in his chariot one day, Patrick passed by a cross which had been erected alongside the road without observing it. But the charioteer, though he said nothing at the time, did see it. After further traveling, Patrick and the charioteer arrived

at the inn where they were to spend the night. They were inside and about to pray before eating when the charioteer commented to Patrick: "I saw a cross placed alongside the road we have just traveled." At once Patrick got up, left the inn, and went back along the road. When he arrived at the cross, Patrick began to pray before it, and then noticed that it was located over a tomb. So Patrick questioned the dead man about who he was, about the sort of death he had suffered, and as to whether he was a believer who lived within the faith. The dead man replied to Patrick in this way: "When I was alive I was a pagan, yet now I am buried here as a Christian. In another province there was a woman whose son died in these parts. The area was quite foreign to her and she did not know where he had been buried. Afterward while mourning her sad loss she traveled here to find his grave. But she was so upset that she thought my grave was that of her son. So she set up that cross beside me by mistake." Once Patrick heard this and that the cross was located on a pagan tomb he could understand how it had happened that he failed to see the cross when he first passed it.[169] But what is most interesting about this event, and which really shows us the power of the saint, is that he could raise up a dead man in order to converse with him. And moreover, the grave of a man who died in the faith of Christ became known, and the nourishing cross came to be placed in its true location beside him who deserved this sign.

[3] Now Patrick had a custom that he would not move onward on his journeys from the evening[170] of the night of the Lord's Day[171] until the morning of the Second Day of the Week.[172] Now on the Lord's Day on one occasion, when in honor of the sacred time he was passing the night in a field, a mighty rainstorm began. But while heavy rain fell over the whole peopled area of our fatherland, in that place where the holy bishop was spending the night the ground was bone dry. It was just like what happened to Gideon's bowl and fleece.[173]

[Another time, Patrick's] charioteer realized that the horses had gone astray and was grieving about this as if he had just lost close friends! [He told Patrick this,] but as it was dark he could not go and search for them. So Patrick was moved to kindness

113

like a godly father[174] and said to the tearful charioteer: "God is always ready to help us in our difficulties and he grants us his mercy in all our misfortunes,[175] so you shall find these horses that you are crying over." Then holding out his hand, and drawing clear his sleeve, Patrick raised his hand and his five fingers shone out like spotlights. They lit up all the area round about them and in that light the man was able to find his missing horses, and to stop crying. But [we should note] this miracle was not known about during Patrick's lifetime because the charioteer told no one about it until after Patrick's death.

[4] Finally, after all the miracles [some recorded here,] others written about elsewhere, and not to mention those which are piously passed on by word of mouth, the day of Patrick's death was drawing near. Indeed, an angel came to speak to him about it. So Patrick sent word to Armagh since that was the place he loved above all the lands. He ordered that many men should come to him and bring him to where he wanted to go. So with his company about him he began his desired journey to Armagh, to the land of his great longing. [5] However, as he traveled he saw near the road, just like Moses before him, "a bush that was burning, but not consumed."[176] Victor, the angel who used to visit Patrick, was in the bush. Victor [sent] another angel to prevent Patrick traveling to where he wanted to go, and this angel said to him: "Why are you setting out on this journey without the advice of Victor? Victor is calling you now, so deviate from your route and go to him." In response to this message, Patrick changed direction as ordered, and asked what he ought to do. The angel answering his questions said: "Return to where you have come from[177] (namely Saul), and the four petitions you have prayed for are granted to you."

"The first petition was this: that you [Patrick] shall rule in Armagh.

The second petition was this: that anyone who on the day of his death sings the hymns you [Patrick] composed shall have the correct penance for his sins judged by you.

114

The third petition was this: that the offspring of Dichú, who received you in such a generous fashion, shall deserve mercy and not perish.

The fourth petition was this: that 'on the Day of Judgment'[178] all the Irish shall be judged by you. Just as once it was said to the Apostles: 'And you shall sit judging the twelve tribes of Israel,'[179] so may you judge those people whose Apostle you have been."[180]

[6] "So turn back now as I have told you, and in death you will enter into the way of your fathers."[181]

And the death of Patrick took place on the sixteenth day of the Kalends of April [i.e., 17 March] and the years of his life numbered one hundred and twenty years in all. [His feast] is celebrated by all the Irish each year [on that day].

[7] "And you shall set a barrier against the fall of night."[182] So on the day Patrick died there was no night, nor was there night in that province for the following twelve nights while they celebrated his passing. With its dark wing night did not embrace the earth; nor was there even dusk; and the Evening Star did not bring in its train the star-bearing shadows. The people of the Ulaid tell that until the end of that entire year the nights were not as dark as they had been. All this happened to declare the merit of so great a man. If anyone should doubt that these things took place at the time of Patrick's funeral, let him listen to the scriptures and carefully attend to what happened to Hezekiah. As a sign of health he was shown the Sun moving backward over "ten lines" "on the sundial of Ahaz" so that the day was almost doubled in length.[183] Or let him note [what Joshua said]: "Sun, stand still at Gibeon, and Moon, in the valley of Aijalon."[184]

When the hour of his death was drawing near, Patrick received the sacrifice from Bishop Tassach—as the angel Victor had told him that he would—as food for his journey[185] to the blessed life.[186]

[8] Angels kept vigil over his holy body with prayers and Psalms during the first night of his funeral, while all those who came for this vigil slept that night.[187] But on the other nights men watched over the body praying and singing Psalms. When the angels departed to heaven they left behind in that place the

sweetest of smells: It was like honey and had the sweet smell that comes from wine. Thus it was fulfilled[188] what was said in the blessing of the patriarch Jacob: "Behold the smell of my son is like the scent of a fruitful field blessed by the Lord."[189]

[9] When the angel visited him he gave him advice on where his tomb was to be located: "Two unbroken oxen are to be selected. Then let them wander while drawing a cart on which lies your body. Wherever they come to rest, in that place let a church be built in honor of your relics." And as the angel had directed, two untamed young bullocks, with a cart haltered around their necks, steadily pulled the holy body. The chosen, and now famous, cattle belonged to the herd of Conal from the place called Clocher to the east of Findabair. These cattle, ruled directly by the will of God, went out as far as Dún Lethglaisse, and there Patrick is entombed.

[10] The angel also told him this: "So that your relics will not be taken out of the earth, let your body be covered with one cubit of earth." That this instruction came directly from the will of God was clearly demonstrated in the very recent past. When some men were digging up the ground near the body in the process of building a church over it, they saw a flaming fire rise up out of his tomb and they immediately pulled back for they feared the flaming fire.[190]

[11] At the time of Patrick's death the struggle for his relics was so great that the Uí Néill allied with the Airthir ("Easterners") came to the brink of war with the Ulaid. Once they had lived close by as neighbors; now they are the most bitter of enemies. However, so that bloodshed might be avoided, through the merit of Patrick and the mercy of God, the inlet of the sea known as Druimm Bó rose up with billowing waves and flooded backward and forward as if to quench the hatred of these embittered peoples—for bitter people is the sort they are. Thus the fierce sea's rising stopped the warfare of these peoples.

[12] Later on, when Patrick was buried and the inlet of the sea had subsided, the Uí Néill and the Airthir again wanted to do battle with the Ulaid. Fully fitted out for war, they burst into the area where the holy body was located. But they were happily led

astray through false thinking. They imagined they had found the two oxen with the cart, and that they were grabbing the holy body [of Patrick]. Then with the body, and all their arms and equipment, they traveled as far as the river Cabcenne. Just then the body vanished from their sight. It would have been impossible to have peace over so blessed a body as Patrick's except they were seduced by this vision at that time. If they had not been so seduced, by the directly expressed will of God, the health of innumerable souls[191] would have been turned to death and ruin. It was similar to the time when the Syrians were blinded lest they would kill the holy prophet Elisha, and by divine Providence were led by Elisha as far as Samaria.[192] So here in the case of Patrick through this distracting vision was established the concord of the peoples.

Patrick's Breastplate

I rise today:

in power's strength, invoking the Trinity,
believing in threeness,
confessing the oneness,
of Creation's Creator.

I rise today:
in the power of Christ's birth and baptism,
in the power of his crucifixion and burial,
in the power of his rising and ascending,
in the power of his descending and judging.

I rise today:
in the power of the love of Cherubim,
in the obedience of angels
and service of archangels,
in hope of rising to receive the reward,
in the prayers of Patriarchs,
in the predictions of prophets,
in the preachings of Apostles,
in the faith of confessors,
in the innocence of holy virgins,
in the deeds of the righteous.

I rise today:
in Heaven's might,
in Sun's brightness,
in Moon's radiance,
in Fire's glory,

    in Lightning's quickness,
    in Wind's swiftness,
    in Sea's depth,
    in Earth's stability,
    in Rock's fixity.

I rise today:
    with the power of God to pilot me,
    God's strength to sustain me,
    God's wisdom to guide me,
    God's eye to look ahead for me,
    God's ear to hear me,
    God's word to speak for me,
    God's hand to protect me,
    God's way before me,
    God's shield to defend me,
    God's host to deliver me:
        from snares of devils,
        from evil temptations,
        from nature's failings,
        from all who wish to harm me,
        far or near,
        alone and in a crowd.

Around me I gather today all these powers:
    against every cruel and merciless force
    to attack my body and soul,
    against the charms of false prophets,
    the black laws of paganism,
    the false laws of heretics,
    the deceptions of idolatry,
    against spells cast by women, smiths, and druids,
    and all unlawful knowledge
    that harms the body and soul.

May Christ protect me today:
    against poison and burning,
    against drowning and wounding,

so that I may have abundant reward;
Christ with me, Christ before me, Christ behind me;
Christ within me, Christ beneath me, Christ above me;
Christ to right of me, Christ to left of me;
Christ in my lying, Christ in my sitting, Christ in my rising;[1]
Christ in the heart of all who think of me,
Christ on the tongue of all who speak to me,
Christ in the eye of all who see me,
Christ in ear of all who hear me.

I rise today:
    in power's strength, invoking the Trinity,
    believing in threeness,
    confessing the oneness,
    of Creation's Creator.

For to the Lord belongs salvation,
and to the Lord belongs salvation
and to Christ belongs salvation.

May your salvation, Lord, be with us always.

2. THE BRIGIT TRADITION

i.
Ultán's Hymn

Brigit, woman ever excellent, golden, radiant flame,
Lead us to the eternal kingdom, the brilliant, dazzling sun.

May Brigit guide us past crowds of devils,
May she break before us the attack of every plague.

May she destroy within us the taxes of our flesh,
The branch with blossoms, the mother of Jesus.

The true virgin, easy to love, with great honor,
I shall be forever safe with my saint of Leinster.

One of the columns of the land with Patrick preeminent,
The adornment above, the royal queen.

May our bodies when we are old be in sackcloth,
From her grace may Brigit rain on us.

We pray to Brigit by the praise of Christ
That we may be worthy of the heavenly kingdom.

The Life of St. Brigit the Virgin by Cogitosus

PROLOGUE

You urge me, my brothers, to attempt a description of the virtues and works of Brigit of blessed and sacred memory, drawing upon both personal memories and written records in the manner of the learned. My lowliness, lack of knowledge and eloquence do not qualify me for such a demanding task with such delicate and difficult material, but God can make much of little, as when he filled the poor widow's house from a drop of oil and a handful of flour (3 Kgs 16; 4 Kgs 4).

And so, driven by your requests, I am content only to obey and therefore propose to put before you without any ambiguity or obscurity a few from the many things which have been handed down by those who are greater and more learned than I, in order not to incur the guilt of disobedience. These will reveal to the eyes of all to what extent numerous and diverse virtues blossomed in this virgin. Not that my poor memory, unexceptional skill, and rustic style are equal to such a task, but the blessing of your faith and the long hours of your prayer deserve more than the skills of the author can provide.

This woman therefore grew in exceptional virtues and by the fame of her good deeds drew to herself from all the provinces of Ireland inestimable numbers of people of both sexes who willingly made their votive offerings. On the firm foundation of faith she established her monastery on the open expanses of the planes of Mag Liffe, which is the head of almost all the churches of Ireland and holds the place of honor among all the monasteries of the Irish.[1] Its jurisdiction extends over the whole of the land of Ireland, from coast to coast. Her concern was to provide for the orderly direction of souls in all things and to care for the churches of the many provinces which were associated with her, and she reflected upon the fact that this could not be without the help of a high priest, who could consecrate churches and perform ordinations. She summoned a famous hermit, therefore, who excelled in all ways, and through whom God had manifested many powers, telling him to leave his retreat and his solitary life and to make his way to join her, so that he might govern the church together with herself in episcopal dignity and there might be no lack of priestly order in her churches.

Afterward this anointed head and principal of all the bishops and most blessed head of all women established their chief church in felicitous and mutual cooperation under the guidance of all the virtues, and by both their merits their episcopal and feminine see spread throughout the whole island of Ireland, like a fertile vine pushing its burgeoning branches out on all sides.

It has always been ruled over by the Archbishop of the Irish and by the abbess, whom all the abbesses of the Irish venerate, by a blessed line of succession and by perpetual rites. And so, under pressure from my brothers, as I have said, I shall attempt to give an account of the miracles of this blessed virgin, Brigit, as they were revealed both before she became abbess and after, although, in my desire to be succinct, it may be that I change their order.

THE LIFE OF ST. BRIGIT

Holy Brigit, whom God knew beforehand and predestined to be formed in his image, was born in Ireland of noble Christian parents who belonged to the good and wise sept of Echtech. Dubthach was her father and Broicsech her mother, and from her childhood she was dedicated to all good things. Chosen by God, the girl was of a sober disposition, modest and mature and constantly increasing in virtue.

And who could give a complete account of the works that she performed even at this young age? I shall select only a few as an example from the countless number at hand.

In due course, when she had reached maturity, she was sent by her mother to churn cow's milk and to make butter so that she too should carry out the same tasks as other women were accustomed to do and, at the appointed time, have ready with the others a plentiful return of produce from the cows, including the usual measure of butter. But this most beautiful and generous girl, who wished to obey God rather than his creatures, gave both the milk and the butter to the poor and to wayfarers. When the time came for them all to have ready the produce from the cows, her own turn came, and when those who were working with her displayed their produce, she too was asked to show the fruit of her labor. She was pale with fear of her mother, since she had nothing to show, having given it all away to the poor, unmindful of the morrow. But burning with the flame of an inextinguishable faith, she turned to the Lord in prayer. The Lord immediately heard the voice and prayers of the virgin and, by the generosity of his divine power, he who is our help in adversity answered her faith in him and provided a plentiful amount of butter. Marvelously, no sooner was her prayer said than her share of work was seen to be done and even to exceed those of the other women who worked with her. Seeing such a great miracle with their own eyes, all praised the Lord who had done this and were filled with wonder that there should be such power of faith in the virgin's heart.

Not long afterward, her parents wished to betroth her to a man, as is the way of the world. But filled with heavenly inspiration, she wished to offer herself as a chaste virgin to God and sought out the most holy bishop Macc Caille, of blessed memory. Seeing her heavenly desire and modesty and such a love of chastity in such a virgin, he placed a white veil and pure white garment over her saintly head. She knelt before God, the bishop, and the altar and, offering her virginity to God the Almighty, she touched the wooden base of the altar. That wood remains fresh even to the present day as a result of her pure virtue and is green as if it had not been cut down and stripped of its bark, but was still rooted in the ground. Even today it drives out the infirmities and diseases of the faithful.

Nor should I fail to mention another miracle which this renowned handmaid is said to have performed in her unceasing service of God. On one occasion she was moved by pity to give the pork that she was cooking in the cauldron for guests to a dog that came fawning and begging. But when the pork was removed from the cauldron and was divided up for the guests, it was found to be complete, as if nothing had been taken from it. Those who saw this were filled with admiration for the girl who was incomparable in her faith and in the merit of her good works, and they spread fitting praise of her.

Again she gathered reapers and workers together for the harvest, but as they assembled, clouds and rain set in upon them. The rain poured down in torrents all over the surrounding land and rivers of water flooded through the valleys and gulleys. Only her own crops remained dry, unaffected by the rain or the storm. While all the other reapers throughout that region were stopped from working by the downpour, her own workers, with no hint of rain, labored all day, from dawn to dusk, by the power of God.

Among her other marvels, this one also seems worthy of admiration. Once when bishops were coming together as her guests, she had nothing with which to feed them. But her need was richly met in the usual way by the manifold grace of God. She milked a cow three times in a single day, contrary to custom. And on this marvelous occasion she gained from the one cow what she would normally have expected to get from three of the best cows.

And I shall reveal this miracle too for your delight, in which her pure, virginal mind and willing hand were united as one. When she was pasturing her sheep on rich and level ground that was thick with grass, she was caught in heavy rain and returned home soaked to the skin. Finding little gaps, the sun shone into the house. Her eyes deceived her and mistaking the sun's ray for a solid beam of wood, she hung her wet clothes upon it, as if that were what it really was. But the clothes did indeed remain hanging on the delicate sunbeam. And when those who were living in the same house spread the news of this great miracle round about, they praised this incomparable girl fittingly.

And this next feat must not be passed over in silence. Once when St. Brigit was in a field with her grazing sheep and was preoccupied with their care, a certain young man, who knew of her generosity to the poor, skillfully disguised himself and carried off seven sheep during the course of the day, hiding them in a secret place. But when the flock was driven as usual to the sheepfold as evening fell, and was counted very carefully two or three times, their number was amazingly found to be complete, without any loss. Those who were accomplices were astonished at the power of God displayed through the virgin, and they decided to return the seven sheep to the flock, which now numbered exactly the same as it had before.

The name of the handmaid of God was on the lips of all on account of these and other miracles beyond number, and she was seen to be worthy of the highest praise.

On another extraordinary occasion some lepers asked this venerable Brigit for some beer, but she did not have any beer to give them. Seeing water that had been prepared for baths, she blessed it in the strength of her faith and turned it into the very best beer, which she generously dispensed to the thirsty. It was indeed he who turned water into wine in Cana of Galilee who turned water into wine here through the faith of this most blessed woman.

But speaking of this miracle, it is fitting to recall another one.[2] In the potent strength of her ineffable faith, Brigit blessed a woman who, though she had taken a vow of chastity, fell through weakness into youthful lust so that her womb swelled with child. The fetus disappeared, without coming to birth or causing pain, and the woman was restored to health and to penance.

One day, when a certain person came asking for salt, just as other poor and destitute people used to come to her in crowds beyond number on account of their needs, the blessed Brigit promptly made salt from rock, which she had blessed, in order that she might be able to answer their need. That person joyfully parted from her, carrying home a generous portion of salt.

And it seems to me that this additional most powerful and divine miracle should be included with the others, in which in imitation of the Savior she worked a sublime feat in the name of God. Following the Lord's example, she opened the eyes of someone who had been blind from birth. The Lord bestowed upon his Apostles his own powers and works since when he said of himself "I am the light of the world" (Jn 9:5), he also said to his Apostles, "You are the light of the world" (Mt 5:14), and speaking

126

to them, said, "The works that I do they also do, and greater works than these they shall do" (Jn 14:12).

Brigit's faith, like a grain of mustard seed, worked upon the one born blind and, like the Lord, she gave that person full and normal sight through a great miracle. And so, celebrated for such great feats, for her humility of heart and purity of mind, for her temperate way of life and spiritual grace, she merited the great authority and renown that came to her above all the virgins of her day.

One day, a woman who was one of her followers from outside her community came to visit her with her twelve-year-old daughter who had been dumb from birth. Showing her great reverence and respect, as everyone was accustomed to do, she bowed and inclined her neck to receive her kiss of greeting. Brigit, who was joyful and welcoming to all, encouraged her with words seasoned with divine salt and, following the example of our Savior who commanded the little children to come to him, she took the daughter's hand in her own and, not knowing that the girl was dumb, asked her what it was that she desired, that is, whether she wanted to take the veil and remain a virgin or be given away in marriage. Her mother advised her that her daughter would not be able to reply, at which Brigit said that she would not let go of her daughter's hand until she had given her reply. When she asked the girl a second time, the daughter answered: "I wish to do only what you wish." When the girl's mouth had been opened, she began to speak without hindrance or impediment to her tongue.

Who can fail to be moved by this further feat of hers, of which so many have heard? Once, when she was caught up in heavenly meditation, as was her custom, and her thoughts were raised from earth to heaven, she let a dog take away a piece of bacon of some considerable size. After a month had passed the meat was found whole and untouched exactly where the dog normally lay. Not only had the dog not dared to devour what the blessed virgin had left, but since its usual nature had been subdued by a divine miracle, it had patiently guarded the bacon.

The number of her miracles increased daily, so that they are now almost beyond counting, so many acts of pity and righteousness did she perform, answering the needs of the poor, whether it was convenient to do so or not. For example, when a certain poor person asked her for some food for the poor, she hurried to those who cook the meat in order to get something for the poor from them. One of the servants, himself a cook, stupidly tossed a piece of raw meat into the white fold of her apron, but when she carried this food to the poor man, her garment was neither stained nor ruffled.

Nor is the following particularly exceptional among her saintly acts. Among all the pilgrims and poor people who were drawn to her from all parts by the great fame of her virtue and exceeding generosity, there was a certain unpleasant leper who requested that the best cow of the herd together with the best of all the calves be given to him. Far from refusing his request, she gladly and promptly gave the best of all the cows and the prime calf of another cow to this sick man. Out of pity she also sent her chariot with him for the lengthy journey across the spreading plain in case he should be wearied by having to drive the cow on the long journey. She also commanded that the calf be put in the chariot behind him. And so the cow spontaneously followed them all the way to their destination, licking the calf with her tongue and tending it as if it were her own. You see, dearest brothers and sisters, how brute animals served her, contrary to their own nature.

After some time had passed, some evil robbers, who had no respect for either God or their fellow human beings, came from another province to carry out a raid. They crossed the wide bed of a river on foot and stole her cow. But as they returned the same way, they were caught by the sudden flooding and rush of the huge river. The river which stood up like a wall did not permit the most wicked theft of blessed Brigit's cow to pass through but knocked the thieves down and pulled them along, freeing the cows from their grasp, which then returned with the thongs hanging from their horns, back to their own herds. See how the power of God is revealed!

One day holy Brigit needed to attend a gathering of the people for a compelling practical reason, and she sat in her chariot, which was drawn by two horses. As she sat in the vehicle, she practiced on earth the life of heaven, as was her custom, by contemplative meditation, and prayed to her Lord. As they came down a slope, the second horse reared in fear and, out of all control, it wrenched itself free of the harness and took off in terror across the plain. But the hand of the Lord held up the yoke and prevented it from falling. She remained praying in her chariot, drawn by just a single horse, and, in full view of the crowd who had followed her after this sign of divine strength, she arrived unhurriedly and unharmed at the assembly of the people. Here she exhorted the people with teaching and words of salvation, seasoned with divine salt, which were amply confirmed by these signs and miracles.

And it seems to me that this feat too demands to be reported on account of its virtues. On one occasion a single wild boar, which was being hunted, came running out of the woods in terror and suddenly landed in the midst of blessed Brigit's pigs. She noted its arrival and pronounced a blessing upon it. Thereupon it lost its terror and settled down among the herd. See, brothers and sisters, how even brute animals and creatures were unable to resist her words and her will but served her tamely and obediently.[3]

One day an uninformed man saw the king's fox walking into the palace and, in his innocence, believed it to be a wild animal, not knowing that it was a pet which lived in the king's hall and entertained the king and his companions with the various tricks it had learned, relying upon the agility of its body and quickness of its mind. He killed it therefore in full view of a crowd and was immediately bound by the people who had seen what he had done, accused, and dragged off to the king. When the king learned what had happened, he was furious and said that he would order the man, together with his wife and children, to be killed and all his household to be taken into slavery unless he could produce for him a fox that had all the same skills.

When the holy and venerable Brigit heard this story, she was so moved to pity that she ordered her chariot to be yoked. Filled with deep grief for the unfortunate man who had been unfairly condemned and pouring out prayers to the Lord, she traveled across the plain and followed the road that led to the royal palace. And the Lord did not delay in answering her prayers, but sent one of his wild foxes to her. When it came running toward her at speed and approached blessed Brigit's chariot, it sprang nimbly into the chariot and sat peacefully beside her, nestling out of sight beneath her cloak.

When she arrived at the palace, she began to beseech the king to release the poor man, who had incurred guilt through his own ignorance, and to free him from his chains. But the king would not listen to her pleas, confirming that he would not release the man until he was provided with another fox which was just as tame and clever as the other fox had been. Even as she spoke, she produced the fox, which in the presence of the king and the whole crowd proceeded to display the same skills and clever tricks of the previous fox and entertained everyone in exactly the same way. Seeing this, the king was now satisfied as were his nobles, and with the crowd applauding with admiration for the marvel that had been done, he ordered the man who had previously been under sentence of death to be unbound and set free.

Not long afterward, when St. Brigit had returned home, having secured the man's release, the same cunning fox became oppressed by the crowds and artfully slipped away, fleeing to the deserted woodland places and to its lair. It was chased by many horses and hounds, but it made fools of them and, fleeing across the open fields, the fox safely made its escape.

Everyone venerated St. Brigit, who performed ever greater deeds, and marveled at what she had done by the excellence of her holiness and the prerogative of her many virtues.

On another day, the blessed Brigit saw some ducks swimming on the water, occasionally taking wing, and being moved with affection for them, she commanded them to come to her. A great flock of them flew over to her on feathered wings with eager obedience to her words and showing no fear, as if they were used to people. She touched them with her hand and caressed them for a while, before allowing them to fly back into the sky. She praised the Creator of all things, to whom all creatures are subject, and for whom all things live, as is said in the Office of the Dead.[4]

From all these examples it is evident that all animals, flocks, and birds were subject to her will. Now this miracle of hers, which must be celebrated in all ages, also needs to be told to the faithful. Once, when she was sowing among all the most salutary seed of the Word of the Lord, as was her custom, she saw nine men in the particular guise of a vain and diabolical cult who shouted loudly and were greatly disturbed in mind. They walked the ways of wickedness and misfortune, and through the ancient enemy who reigned in them they had determined with the most perfidious vows and oaths (since they thirsted for the spilling of blood) upon the murdering and killing of others before the beginning of the forthcoming month of July. The most reverent and kindly Brigit preached to them with many sweet words, urging them to abandon their mortal errors and to expunge their crimes by heartfelt contrition and true repentance. But they stupidly went their own way, determined to fulfill their empty vows, while the reverend virgin poured forth prayers to God that all may be saved, by the Lord's example, and come to the knowledge of the truth.

The wicked men went out and saw what they thought was the man whom they wished to kill. They immediately pierced him with their spears and struck off his head with their swords and returned with blood-stained weapons in the sight of many as if they had destroyed their enemy. But miraculously they had killed no one, although it seemed to them that they had fulfilled their vows. When no one was found to be missing in that region, where they thought they had triumphed, all knew the abundance of the divine favor that had been wrought through most holy Brigit. And thus those who had previously been murderers turned back to God through penance.

In the following miracle by St. Brigit too the power of God was manifested through her indescribable piety and sacred devotion. There was a certain man called Lugaid, who was exceptionally stout and the strongest of all men. He could do the work of twelve men in a single day, when he wished to, and could eat enough for twelve men too (just as he could do the work of many on his own, so too could he eat their rations). He beseeched Brigit to pray to Almighty God to reduce his appetite, which led him to eat too much, but without reducing his physical strength. Brigit gave him her blessing and prayed to God on his behalf;

thereafter he was content with the food for one and yet was still able to do the work of twelve as before, since his former strength was still in him.

Similarly there was a certain huge tree which had been cut down for some purpose by skilled woodmen with their axes. A number of strong men were gathered together on account of its great bulk and size and the difficulty of its position with many broken branches, in order to take down the tree and to transport it with the help of many oxen and contraptions to its required destination. But despite the great number of men, the strength of the oxen, and the various devices, in no way were they able to move or drag the tree, and so they all drew back from it. But by the most strong faith of blessed Brigit, like a mustard seed, by which faith, as the Master teaches by the medium of the heavenly gospel, mountains are moved, so that all things are possible to those who believe (Mt 17:20), they were able to move this great tree by the divine mysteries of the power of the gospel with no one's help and were able to bring it without any difficulty to the place designated by Brigit. Such excellence of divine power was made known throughout all the provinces.

But it occurs to us that we should not remain silent about the next miracle either. There was once a man of the world, noble by birth and deceitful in character, who burned with desire for a certain woman. Cunningly planning how he might possess her, he entrusted a silver brooch to her safe-keeping, only to take it back from her secretly and throw it into the sea. Since she could not return it to him, she would have to serve as his maid to be used as he desired. He planned this evil deed for no other reason than to be able to demand either that his brooch should be returned to him or that the woman herself should become his slave on account of her guilt and should be subject to his lust. In her fear the chaste woman fled to St. Brigit as to a most secure city of refuge. When she had learned of the reasons for the woman's plight, and even before she had finished speaking, St. Brigit called to herself a man who had fish which had been caught in the river. When their innards had been cut open and removed, they found the silver brooch in the belly of one of them, the same brooch that the cruel man had thrown into the sea. Then, with an easy mind, she took the same brooch and went with the infamous tyrant to a meeting of the people that was gathering to consider who was to blame. There she showed them the brooch in the presence of many witnesses who recognized that it was the very same one of which all had been speaking, and thus she was able to free the chaste woman from the clutches of the cruel tyrant. He for his part confessed his guilt and submitted himself in humility to St. Brigit. Then, when she had received the accolade of all on account of the great miracle which she had performed, she gave thanks to God, having done everything for his glory, and returned home.

We should include an account of her marvelous hospitality toward a certain faithful woman amongst these miracles. St. Brigit was journeying across the wide plain of Mag Breg in accordance with God's will and, just as evening fell, she arrived at the woman's dwelling where she spent the night. The woman received her joyfully with outstretched hands and gave thanks to the Almighty for the safe arrival of the most holy Brigit, virgin of Christ.

Since she did not have anything with which to entertain Brigit or with which to make her a meal on account of her poverty, she broke up the loom on which she had been weaving for firewood and, placing her calf, which she had killed, on the wood, she lit the fire with a willing heart. When they had eaten dinner and had passed the night with vigils, the woman rose early (who had taken the calf from her cow in order that there should be nothing lacking for the welcome and entertainment of St. Brigit) and found the cow with another calf at its side, of exactly the same form, which she loved just as she had done before. And there was a wooden loom similarly restored, that was of exactly the same shape and size as the other.

And thus, her miracle performed, St. Brigit bade farewell to those living in the house and, cheerfully setting out, continued on her journey in the manner of a bishop.

Amongst so many miracles this one is particularly to be admired. When three lepers came, asking her to give them alms of any kind, she gave them a silver dish. And in case this should be the cause of conflict and disagreement among them when they came to divide it between themselves, she asked someone who was expert in weighing out gold and silver to break it into three parts of equal weight. When he began to make excuses, saying that it could not be done, blessed Brigit took the silver dish and broke it against a stone, dividing it into three equal parts, as she had wished. Marvelously, when these three pieces were then weighed on the scales, not one of them was found to be a fraction greater or less than any other. And so the three poor people departed joyfully with their gifts, with no reason for grievance or envy.

Following the example of blessed Job, no poor person ever left her presence empty-handed. Indeed, she even gave to the poor the foreign and exotic robes of the illustrious Bishop Conleth, which he wore when celebrating the mysteries at the altar on feasts of the Lord and vigils of the Apostles. When the time of the feast returned again, and for the high priest of the people to change into his vestments, St. Brigit, who had already given them to Christ in the form of a poor person, passed to the bishop another set of vestments, similar in both weave and color, which she had just received from Christ, whom—as a beggar—she had clothed, draped over a two-wheeled chariot. She had willingly given the other vestments to the poor, and now received these just when they were needed. For as she was the living and most blessed member of the highest head, she was able to bring about all that she wished.

St. Brigit brought distinction to herself also with the following miracle. The king of her country where she lived issued a decree for all the peoples and provinces who lived under his rule to the effect that all the people were to gather from every region and province in order to construct a wide road, strengthened with the branches of trees and with foundations of stone, in the deep and impassable marsh, passing through wet places, including bogs, where there ran a large river. Once built, it was to be able to support four-wheeled vehicles, horsemen, chariots, wagon-wheels, and the movement of ordinary people as well as forces to attack the enemy on all sides.

When the people had arrived from every place, the road was divided into separate sections, each of which was to be built by a particular clan or family. But when the most difficult part of the river fell by chance to a certain clan, this group avoided the hard labor by forcing it upon a weaker clan, the one to which St. Brigit herself belonged. Choosing for itself an easier section, this cruel clan could then begin their work without the obstacle of the river.

St. Brigit's blood relations came and prostrated themselves before her, to whom, it is said, she replied: "Go away. It accords with God's will and power that the river shall be moved from its present course, where you are weighed down by heavy labor, to the place which the others have chosen for themselves." And when at the dawn of that day all the people rose to work, the offending river was seen to have left its former place and valley, where it used to run between two banks, and to have moved from the section where St. Brigit's clan had been forced to work to that of the proud and strong people who had unjustly imposed their will upon the weaker and less numerous group. As proof that the miracle happened, traces of the river which moved elsewhere can still be seen, as can the empty valley through which the powerful river once flowed; but the place itself is dry and with no hint of water.

But it was not only during her life on earth, but also after she had laid down the burden of the flesh, that she performed many miracles. The abundance of the divine gift never ceased to work in the monastery where her venerable body was laid to rest. We have not only heard of these miracles but have even seen some of them with our own eyes.

For instance, the prior of that great and most illustrious monastery of St. Brigit, which we have briefly mentioned at the outset of this work, sent workmen and stonemasons to look for a rock to cut as a millstone wherever they might find it. But without knowing the way, they climbed up a steep path and arrived at the top of a rocky mountain, where they chose a great boulder at the very top of that very high mountain. They carved it on all sides into a round shape and cut a hole in it to make a millstone. But when they requested the prior to bring a team of oxen to that mountain, where the stone shaped like a millstone lay, he could not drive them to the top on account of the steep mountain path and could scarcely ascend the very difficult track himself with just a small number of companions.

Together with all his workmen, the prior pondered how they could transport the millstone from the ridge of the high mountain since it was not possible for the oxen to be yoked or to pull a load on such a steep slope. They began to despair and, as some left the mountain, decided to abandon the stone and to accept that their effort in rounding the stone off had been in vain. But after careful thought and consultation with his workers, the prior said: "This is not what we should do. But lift the stone up instead with all your strength and cast it from the highest peak, calling upon the name and power of the most holy St. Brigit. For we cannot succeed in carrying this millstone over these rocky places by strength or devices unless Brigit, to whom nothing is impossible—all things being possible to those who believe—shall transport it to a place from where the strength of oxen can carry it on." And so, with a firm faith, they cast it into the valley below, and watched it slowly descend the mountain side, sometimes passing to the side of rocks and sometimes bouncing over them, and roll across patches of marshy land at the bottom of the mountain where neither man nor beast could stand on account of the depth, until it came marvelously and without suffering any damage to a flat area where their oxen were waiting to carry it on. From there it was transported to the mill by the team of oxen, where it was skillfully joined to the other stone.

And there is another wonderful, though previously unknown, story to be added to the account of the millstone that was guided by the blessed Brigit, which is now familiar to all. A certain pagan who lived near the mill sent a simple man with his grain to be ground at the mill, without the miller's knowledge. And when it was cast between the millstones, neither the force of the stream nor the flood of the water nor any effort of skill could make them move. And when those who were there thought about this, they were perplexed, but when they learned that the grain belonged to a druid, they had no doubt at all that the millstone upon which Brigit had exercised her divine power had refused to grind the grain of a pagan man into flour. They immediately removed the pagan's grain and replaced it with grain from their monastery, whereupon the mill began to work perfectly again in the usual way.

After a while it happened that the mill caught fire. It was no small miracle that when the whole millhouse was destroyed by fire, including the other stone that was paired with the one we have spoken of above, the latter was completely unharmed by the flames, which did not dare to touch it. It remained unscorched in the ashes of the millhouse.

Afterward, in the light of this miracle, they brought the stone to the monastery and set it beside the door of the inner cashel that surrounds the church, where people come to venerate St. Brigit. It was given a place of honor at that entrance and it drives out the diseases of the faithful who touch it.

Nor should we fail to mention the miracle during the rebuilding of the church in which the bodies of that glorious pair, Bishop Conleth and this holy virgin Brigit, rest to the right and the left of the ornate altar, in shrines decorated with different kinds of gold, silver, gems, and precious stones, with crowns of gold and silver suspended above them.

In order to accommodate increasing numbers of the faithful of both sexes, the church is spacious in its ground area and imposing in its height. It is decorated with painted pictures and contains three chapels within it, which are of good size and divided from each other by wooden partitions but sharing the single roof of the cathedral church; one of these decorated partitions which is painted with images and draped with wall-hangings traverses the eastern part of the church from one wall to the other and has a doorway at either end. By the door on the right the archbishop enters the sanctuary and draws near to the altar where he offers the sacrifice together with his monastic chapter and those who have been appointed to the sacred mysteries. Through the other entrance, situated on the left-hand side of the transverse partition, only the abbess with her faithful virgins and widows enters in order to enjoy the feast of the body and blood of Jesus Christ. The second of these partitions divides the floor of the church into two equal parts and extends across from the east to the transverse wall. The church has many windows and a finely decorated door on the right-hand side through which the priests and the faithful of the male sex enter, while the virgins and faithful of the female sex come in through another door on the left-hand side. And so in one large basilica a great mass of people of varying status, rank, sex, and provenance, and separated by partitions, pray with a single spirit—though different in status—to the almighty Lord.

Now when the ancient door of the left-hand gate, through which St. Brigit was accustomed to enter the church, was hung on its hinges by the craftsmen, it did not completely fill the new entrance of the rebuilt church. A quarter of the gate was left open. It needed only another quarter to be added to its height for the gap to be closed. The craftsmen debated whether they should make another larger door which would fit the opening, or whether they should attach a board to the old door in order to increase its size. The aforementioned master, who was the leading craftsman of the Irish, gave this wise advice: "This night we should pray to the Lord at St. Brigit's side so that she can guide us in the morning as to what we should do." And so he spent the whole night praying beside St. Brigit's shrine.

Having offered his prayer, he rose in the morning, brought the old door, and placed it on its hinges. He found that it now filled the opening entirely. There was no gap or overlap. And so St. Brigit increased the length of the door so that it completely filled the opening, and no gap could be seen except when the door was pushed back as people entered the church. This miracle of the Lord's power is visible to the eyes of all who see this doorway and door.

But who can find the words to express the great glory of this church and the countless wonders of her monastic city? "City" is the right word and is justified by the many people who live there. This city is a great metropolis within whose borders, which St. Brigit marked out as a clear boundary, no earthly enemy nor hostile attack is to be feared. For the city is the safest place of refuge of all the towns anywhere in the whole of Ireland, with all its fugitives, where the treasures of kings are kept safe, and it is regarded as being the most excellent on account of its illustrious supremacy.

And who could count the various multitudes and innumerable crowds of people who swarm here from all provinces? Some come for the abundance of the festivals, some to have their illnesses cured, some come to see the spectacle of the crowds, and others come with great gifts for the feast of St. Brigit, who fell asleep on the first of February, safely casting off the burden of the flesh, and followed the Lamb into the heavenly mansions.

I beg the indulgence of my brothers and of those who read these things, since I was compelled by obedience and not by any puffed-up pride of knowledge to skim the great sea of St. Brigit's wonderful works—a daunting task even for the strongest—with these few examples recounted in rustic speech from her great miracles beyond number.

Pray for me, Cogitosus, the blameworthy descendant of Aed, and I beseech you to commend me to the good Lord in your prayers; and may God grant you the peace of the gospel.

Here ends the life of St. Brigit the virgin.

The Irish Life of Brigit

News of the miracles spread. One day Broicsech went to milk there, leaving no one in the house but the holy girl who was asleep. They saw that the house had caught fire behind them. The people ran to help, thinking that they would not find a single post still standing. But they found the house intact and the girl asleep, her face like….And Brigit is honored there….

One day the druid was asleep and he saw three clerics wearing garments with white hoods baptizing Brigit, and one of the three said to him: "Let Brigit be your name for the girl."

The druid, the female slave, and her child were at Loch Mescae, and the druid's mother's brother was there too, the latter being a Christian. They were there at midnight and while the druid was watching the stars, he saw a fiery column rising up from the house, from the very place where the slave and her daughter were. He woke his uncle, who saw it too and said that she was a holy girl. "That is true," he said, "if I were to tell you all the things she has done."

On another occasion when the druid and his uncle were in a house and the girl asleep, wherever her mother was, they heard the girl's quiet voice at the side of the house, even though she had not yet begun to speak. "See on our behalf," the druid said to his uncle, "how our girl is, for I do not dare to do so since I am not a Christian." He saw her lying in the position of a cross-vigil and praying. "Go again," the druid said "and ask her something this time, for now she will say something to you." He went and spoke to her: "Say something to me, girl." The girl then spoke to him: "This will be mine. This will be mine." The druid's uncle did not understand that. "Show me what this means," he said to the druid, "for I do not understand it." "You will not be pleased with it at all," the druid said, "for she has said that this place will be hers until the Day of Judgment." The maternal uncle of the druid was disturbed at the idea that Brigit would keep the land. The druid said: "Truly it shall be fulfilled. This plain shall be hers even though she accompanies me to Munster."

When it was time to wean her, the druid became anxious for her, since she vomited anything he gave her to eat, though her appearance was none the worse. "I know what is wrong with the girl," the druid said. "It is because I am impure." Then a white cow with red ears was assigned to sustain her, and she was healed as a result.[1]

Then the druid went to Munster, to Úaithne Tíre, to be precise. There the saint was fostered and said after a while to her fosterer: "I do not wish to serve here, but send me to where I may meet my father." This was done, and her father Dubthach took her away to his own patrimony in the two plains of Uí Fhailgi. She remained there among her relatives, and while still a girl, she performed miracles.

But then she was taken to a certain virgin to be fostered by her. Later Brigit became her cook. She would find out the number of guests who would come to her fostermother, and whatever it might be, the supply of bread would not run out during the night.

On one occasion her fostermother was seriously ill. She was sent with another girl to the house of a certain man called Báethchú to ask for a drink of ale for the sick woman. They got nothing from Báethchú....They came to a certain well where she filled three containers. The liquid was tasty and intoxicating, and her fostermother was healed immediately. This is what God did for her.

One day Dubthach made her herd pigs. Thieves stole two of the boars. When Dubthach went in his cart from Mag Lifi, he met them and recognized his two boars. He seized the thieves and claimed damages for his pigs on them. He brought his two boars home and said to Brigit: "Do you think you are herding the pigs well?" "Count them," she said. He counted them then and found their number complete.

One day a guest came to Dubthach's house. Her father entrusted her with a good piece of bacon to be boiled for the guest. She gave one-fifth of the bacon to a hungry dog which approached her. When the dog had eaten this, she gave it another fifth. The guest, who was watching, remained silent as though overcome with sleep. On returning home again the father found his daughter. "Have you boiled the food well?" he asked. "Yes," she said. And he himself counted the pieces of bacon and found them all there. Then the guest told Dubthach what the girl had done. "After this," said Dubthach "she performed more miracles than can be told." Then that portion of food was distributed among the poor.

On a subsequent occasion, an old pious nun who lived near Dubthach's house asked Brigit to go and address twenty-seven Leinster saints in a single gathering. It was then that Ibor the bishop told the gathering of a vision which he had seen the night before. He said: "I thought that I saw the Virgin Mary last night in my sleep, and a certain venerable cleric said to me: 'This is Mary who will dwell among you.'" Then the nun and Brigit arrived. "This is the Mary whom I saw in a dream." The people who were there rose to their feet and spoke with her. They blessed her. The gathering took place where Kildare is now, and there Ibor the bishop said to the brothers: "This site is open to heaven, and it will be the richest of all in the whole island; and today a girl, for whom it has been prepared by God, will come to us like Mary." This is how it happened.[2]

On another occasion she wished to visit her mother who was in slavery in Munster, and her father and fostermother were opposed to her going. She did go however. Her mother was engaged in dairy work at that time in…away from the druid, and she was suffering from a disease of the eye. Brigit was working in her place, and the druid's cart driver was herding the cattle; and she used to divide every churning she made into twelve portions with its curds, placing a thirteenth portion in the middle, which was larger than all the others. "What is the advantage in doing that?" the driver asked. "Not difficult," said Brigit. "I have heard that there were twelve Apostles with the Lord, he himself being the thirteenth. One day God will send me thirteen poor people, the same number as Christ and his Apostles." "And why do you not store up some of the butter," asked the driver, "for that is what every dairy worker does?" Brigit said: "It is difficult for me to deprive Christ of his own food." Then baskets were brought to her from the wife of the druid to be filled. She only had the butter from one and a half churnings. But that filled the baskets, and the guests, that is the druid and his wife, were satisfied. The druid said to Brigit: "The cows shall be yours and give the butter to the poor. Your mother shall not be in service from today and it shall not be necessary to buy her. I shall be baptized and shall never leave you." "Thanks be to God," said Brigit.

On one occasion Dubthach brought Brigit to Dúnlang, the king of Leinster, in order to sell her as a serving slave since her stepmother had accused her of stealing everything in the house for the servants of God.[3] Dubthach left her to guard his cart on the green of the fort, leaving his sword with her. But she gave it to a leper who came to her. Dubthach said to the king: "Buy my daughter from me to serve you, for her behavior has deserved it." "In what way has she offended you?" said the king. "Not difficult," replied Dubthach. "She does things without asking permission; whatever she sees, her hand takes." When Dubthach, returned, he asked her about the precious sword. She replied: "Christ has taken it." Having learned that, he said: "Why did you give the value of ten cows to a leper, my daughter? It was not my sword but belonged to the king." The girl replied: "Even if I had the power to give the whole of Leinster, I would give it to God." Therefore the girl was left in slavery and Dubthach returned home. Marvelously, the virgin Brigit was raised by divine power and placed behind her father. "Truly, Dubthach," the king said, "this girl can neither be sold nor bought." Then the king gave a sword to the virgin, and....After the miracles we have already described, they returned home.

Shortly afterward a man came to Dubthach's house as Brigit's suitor. His name was Dubthach moccu Lugair. This pleased her father and brothers. "It is difficult for me," Brigit said, "since I have offered up my virginity to God. I will give you some advice. There is a wood behind your house where there lives a beautiful girl. She will be betrothed to you, and this is how you will know it. You will find a wide open enclosure and the girl washing her father's head, and they will give you a warmer welcome, and I will bless your face and your speech so that whatever you say will be pleasing to them." It happened as Brigit said.

Her brothers were saddened at being deprived of the dowry. There were poor people living close to Dubthach's house, and one day she carried a small load for them. She was met by her brothers, her father's sons, who had come from Mag Lifi. Some of them laughed at her, and others were not pleased with her. Bacéne said: "The beautiful eye in your head will be betrothed to a man whether you like it or not." Thereupon she immediately thrust her finger into her eye. "Here is that beautiful eye for you," said Brigit. "I think it unlikely that anyone will ask you for the hand of a blind girl." Her brothers rushed around her at once, but there was no water to wash the wound. She said to them: "Push my staff into the ground here." When this was done, a stream gushed out of the earth. Then she cursed Bacéne and his descendants, saying: "Your two eyes will soon burst in your head." That is what happened.

Dubthach said to her: "Take the veil then, my daughter, for this is your wish. Give this holding away to God and man." "Thanks be to God," said Brigit.

One day she went to a foundation on the side of Cróchán of Brí Éile with seven virgins to take the veil; she believed that Mel the bishop lived there. There she greeted two virgins, Tol and Etol, whose home was there. They told her: "The bishop is not here but in the churches of Mag Taulach." Even as they spoke, they saw a young man called Mac Caille, who was a pupil of Mel the bishop, and they asked him to lead them to the bishop. But he replied: "There are no paths there, but marshes, deserts, bogs, and pools." The saint said: "Help us in our difficulty." As they proceeded on their way, he could afterward see a causeway there.

When the hour of consecration had arrived, the veil was raised by angels from the hand of Mac Caille, the minister, and was placed on St. Brigit's head. As she bent down during the prayers, she held the ash beam which supported the altar, which was later changed into acacia, which is neither consumed by fire nor grows old during the passing of the centuries.[4] Three times the church was burned down, but the beam remained intact under the ashes.

The bishop, being intoxicated with the grace of God there, did not know what he was reciting from his book, for he consecrated Brigit with the orders of a bishop. "Only this virgin in the whole of Ireland will hold the episcopal ordination," said Mel. While she was being consecrated a fiery column ascended from her head.

Afterward the people gave her a place called Ached hÍ in Saltus Avis. While staying there for a short while, she managed to persuade three pilgrims to remain there and donated the place to them. She performed three miracles there, namely the flowing of the spring in dry land, the meat turning into bread, and the healing of the hand of one of the three men.

Once during Eastertide Brigit asked her virgins: "What shall we do? We have one sack of malt, which we should prepare so that we shall not be without ale over Easter. But there are seventeen churches in Mag Tailach. If only I could keep Easter for them with respect to the ale for the sake of the Lord whose feast it is, so that they would at least have something to drink if they have no food. It is unfortunate for us only that we have no containers." That was true, for there was one barrel in the house and two tubs. "They are good; let it be prepared." In one of the tubs it was mashed and in another it was left to ferment, and the barrel was filled from what was fermented in the second tub before being taken to each church in turn. The barrel was quickly returned, but it always held ale. Eighteen barrelfulls had come from the one sack and enough for herself over Easter. And there was no lack of feasting in every single church from Easter Sunday to Low Sunday as a result of Brigit's preparations.

A woman from Fid Éoin who was a believer donated her cow on that Easter Day. Two of them drove the cow, the woman and her daughter....They had lost their calf as they came through the wood, and they petitioned Brigit then. That prayer aided them, and their cow now led the way to the settlement where Brigit was. "This is what we must do," said Brigit to her virgins, "for this is the first offering to us since we have been in this hermitage. It should be taken to the bishop who blessed the veil on our head." "It is of little use to him," the virgins said, "the cow without the calf." "That does not matter," said Brigit. "The little calf will come to meet its mother so that they will arrive at the enclosure together." And it happened as she said.

On the same Easter Sunday there came to her a certain leper who was losing his limbs, and asked for a cow: "For God's sake Brigit, give me a cow." "Leave me alone," said Brigit. "I would not let you alone even for a single day," he said. "My son, let us await the hand of God," said Brigit. "I will go away," said the leper. "I will get a cow from somewhere else." Brigit said: "...and if we were to pray to God for the removal of your leprosy, would you like that?" "No," he said. "I get more this way than if I were clean." "It is better," said Brigit, "...and you shall take a blessing and be cleansed." "All right then," he said, "for I am in much pain." "How will this man be cleansed?" Brigit asked her virgins. "Nun, this is not a difficult question. You should bless a cup of water, and then the leper should be washed in it." This is what they did, and the leper was completely cured. "I shall not leave the cup that has healed me," he said. "I shall be your servant and your woodman." And that is what happened.

On the following day, that is Monday, Mel came to Brigit to preach and to say Mass for her during the Easter Octave. A cow had been brought to her on that day too and it was given to Mel the bishop, the other cow having been taken. One of Brigit's virgins had an attack of fever, and she was given Communion. "Is there anything you wish for?" said Brigit. "There is," she answered. "If I do not get some fresh milk, I shall die immediately." Brigit called a virgin and said: "Bring me my own cup from which I drink, full of water. Bring it without anyone else seeing what you do." It was brought to her then, and she blessed it so that it became warm fresh milk. As soon as she tasted it, the virgin was healed. These then are two simultaneous miracles: the changing of water into milk and the healing of the girl.

On the following day, Tuesday, there was a good man nearby who was related to Brigit. He had been ill for a whole year. "Take for me today," he said, "the best cow in my byre for Brigit, so that she will pray for me to see if I shall be healed." They brought the cow, and Brigit said to them: "Take it straight away to Mel." They returned it to their house and exchanged it for another cow, without the sick man knowing. When Brigit was told this, she was angry at the deception. She said to Mel: "By the morning wolves shall eat the good cow which was given to me and which was not brought to you, and they shall eat seven oxen as well." The sick man was then told this. He said: "Go and take her seven of the best oxen from the byre." This was done. "Thanks be to God," said Brigit. "Take them to Mel in his church. He has been preaching and saying Mass for us throughout the Easter Octave. He shall have a cow for each day of labor, for this is no more than he has given us. And take a blessing with all eight, a blessing on him from whom they were brought," Brigit said. As soon as she had spoken, he was immediately healed.

During the Easter Octave Brigit had a painful headache. "That does not matter," said Mel. "When we go to visit our first settlement in Tethbae, Brigit and her virgins will go with us. There is a wonderful healer in Mide, Áed mac Bricc. He will cure you." It was then that she healed two paralytic virgins of the Fothairt.

Then the two blind Britons with a young leper of the sept of Eochaid came and begged to be healed. Brigit said to them: "Wait a while." But they replied: "You have healed the sick of your own people and you neglect the healing of foreigners. But at least heal our boy who is of your people." And by this the blind were given sight and the leper was cleansed.

Low Sunday drew near. "I do not think it fortunate now," Brigit told her virgins, "not to have beer on Low Sunday for the bishop who will preach and say Mass." As soon as she had spoken, two virgins went to fetch water with a large churn, though Brigit was not aware of this. Brigit saw them when they returned. "Thanks be to God," said Brigit. "God has given us beer for our bishop." The nuns became frightened then. "May God help us!" "Whatever foolish thing I said, I have not said anything evil, my nuns." "God did what you desired, and the water that was brought in, since you blessed it, was immediately turned into beer with the fragrance of wine, and better beer than has ever been brewed in all the world." The one churn was enough for them with all their guests and the bishop.

On the Monday after Low Sunday Brigit went in her cart,

together with her virgins, to the plain of Mide to see a healer, hoping to go on afterward to the plain of Tethbae to visit a foundation which Mel and Melchú had there. On Tuesday, as night fell, they turned aside to the house of a certain Leinsterman of the Uí Brolaig. He welcomed them and with respect and kindness entertained holy Brigit and the bishops. That good man and his wife complained. The wife said: "All the children I have given birth to have died, except two daughters, who have been dumb since they were born." She went to Áth Firgoit. Something frightened the horses, and holy Brigit fell in the middle of the ford. Her head struck a stone and was injured on top, so that her blood stained the waters red. Holy Brigit said to one of the two dumb girls: "Pour the water mixed with blood over your neck in the name of God." She did so and said: "You have healed me. I give thanks to God." "Call your sister," Brigit said to the girl who had been healed. "Come here, sister," she said. "I shall come indeed," said her companion, "and though I go I have already been healed. I bowed down in the track of the cart and was cured." "Go home," Brigit said to the girl, "and you shall give birth again to as many male children as have died on you." They were delighted at that. And that memorable stone often heals many. Any diseased head which is placed upon it is cured. It was then that they met the learned physician, Áed mac Bricc. The bishop said: "...the head of the holy woman." He touched it and addressed the virgin with these words: "Virgin, the vein of your head has been touched by a physician who is much better than I am."

They went to Tethbae, to the first foundations of the bishops, namely Ardagh. The king of Tethbae was feasting nearby. A servant in the king's house had done a terrible thing. He had dropped a valuable goblet which belonged to the king so that it smashed to pieces against the table before the king. The goblet was a wonderful one and was one of the king's rare treasures. He seized the wretch then and there was nothing for him but death. One of the two bishops came to beseech the king. "I shall not give him to anyone," the king said, "nor shall I give him in exchange for any compensation, but he shall be put to death." "Give me the broken goblet," the bishop said. "You shall have it," said the king. The bishop then carried it to Brigit, and told her everything. "Pray to the Lord for us that this goblet may be mended." She did so, and restored it and gave it to the bishop. On the following day the bishop took the goblet to the king and said: "If your goblet were returned to you as before, would you release the prisoner?" "Not only that, but I would give him whatever gift he would desire." The bishop showed him the goblet and spoke these words to the king: "It was not I who performed this miracle but holy Brigit."

When Brigit's fame had spread throughout Tethbae, a certain devout virgin, Bríg daughter of Coimloch, sent a message to Brigit asking her to visit her. Brigit went and Bríg herself rose to wash her feet. At that time there was a devout woman who was sick. While they were washing Brigit's feet, that sick woman sent a servant girl to fetch from the tub some of the water which had washed over Brigit's feet. It was brought to her and she washed her face with it so that she was completely healed at once. Having been ill for a year, she was the only servant that night. When their dishes were placed in front of them, Brigit began to stare intently at them. "If it please you," said Bríg, "holy virgin, what do you see on your dish?" "I see Satan sitting on the dish in front of me." "If it is possible," said Bríg, "I should like to see him too." "It is possible," said Brigit, "provided that you make the sign of the cross over your eyes first; for anyone who sees the Devil without blessing themselves first or...will go mad." Bríg blessed herself then and saw that fellow. His appearance seemed ugly to her. "Brigit, ask him why he has come," said Bríg. "Give me an answer," said Brigit. "No, Brigit," Satan said. "You are not entitled to it, for it is not to harm you that I have come." "Answer me, then," said Bríg. "What in particular has brought you onto this dish?" The demon replied: "I always live here with a certain virgin, whose sloth has given me a place." Bríg said: "Let her be called." When she had come, Bríg said: "Sign her eyes with the cross, so that she may see him whom she has nourished in her own bosom." When this was done, she saw the awful monster. Brigit said to the virgin, now filled with fear and trembling: "Behold, you see him whom you have cherished for many years and seasons." "Holy virgin," said

Bríg, "may he never enter this house again." "He shall not enter this house," said Brigit, "until the Day of Judgment." They ate their meal and gave thanks to God.

Once she was hurrying along the bank of the Inny. There were many apples and sweet sloes in that church. A certain nun gave her a small gift in a basket of bark. When she brought it into the house, lepers came straightaway into the middle of the house to beg from her. "Take those apples," she said. Then she who had presented the apples said: "I did not give the gift to lepers." Brigit was displeased and said: "You do wrong in preventing gifts to the servants of God; therefore your trees shall never bear any fruit." And as she went out, the donor saw that all at once her garden bore no fruit, which had just before had much fruit. It remained barren forever, except for foliage.

Another virgin brought her apples and sweet sloes in large quantities. She immediately gave them to some lepers who were begging. "She who brought it will be well," said Brigit. "O nun, bless me and my garden." "May God indeed bless that big tree which I see in your garden," Brigit said. "May it bear sweet apples and sweet sloes as to one-third, and that twofold fruit shall not be lacking from it and its offshoots." And that is what happened. As the nun went into her garden she saw the alder tree with its fruit and sweet sloes on it as to one-third.

In a certain place, Aicheth Fir Leth, two lepers followed Brigit. They became very jealous of each other and began to quarrel, but their hands and feet grew stiff. Seeing this, Brigit said, "You should do penance." They did so. Not only did she release them but she also cured them of leprosy.

It was then that the two virgins came to Brigit to ask her to go with them to consecrate their foundation and house together with them. Their names were Induae and Indiu. On the way they met a young man who had come to speak to the nuns whom Brigit was accompanying. "I have come to you," he said, "from this sick man, so that a cart might be brought to him and he may die in the same enclosure with you." "We have no cart," said the nuns. "Bring my cart to him," Brigit said. This was then done. They waited until matins until the sick man came. Lepers came to them afterward in the morning. "Brigit," they said, "give us your cart, for the sake of Christ." "Take it," Brigit said. "But leave me alone for a while, you servants of God, so that we may bring the sick man first of all to our house which is nearby." "We will not leave you alone even for a single hour, unless our cart is being taken from us anyway." "Take it away," said Brigit. "What shall we do," said the nuns, "with our sick man?" "Not difficult," Brigit said. "Let him come with us on foot." That is what happened then; he was completely healed on the spot.

It was then she washed the feet of the nuns of Cúl Fobair, and healed four of them while washing them, one who was paralyzed, one who was blind, a leper, and one who was possessed.

It was then that she healed the dumb paralytic boy at the house of Mac Odráin. It happened that Brigit and the dumb boy were left alone. When some poor people came and asked for a drink, Brigit looked for the key of the kitchen and could not find it. Not knowing of the boy's affliction, she addressed him with these words: "Where is the key?" And by this, the dumb paralytic boy spoke and ministered.

Shortly afterward at the beginning of summer, Mel and Melchú said to Brigit: "We have been told that Patrick is coming from the south of Ireland to Mag mBreg. We will go and speak to him. Will you go too?" "I will," said Brigit, "so that I may see him and speak to him and so that he may give me his blessing." As they set out, a certain cleric with many servants and a retinue followed them on the way to ask them to go with him to Mag mBreg. "It is a matter of urgency for us," Mel said, "that our cleric may not escape us." "Tell me the place where we are to meet in Mag mBreg, and I will wait for this pitiful gathering." Later Brigit waited for the wandering band. "There are twenty virgins coming with me along the road," Brigit said. "Give them some of the loads to carry." The wretched ones said: "Do not let that happen, for you have granted us a greater favor since in your company the road is safe for us." "Are there not two carts coming along the road?" Brigit asked. "Why do they not carry the loads?" She had not looked to see what was in them. Since Brigit entered the religious life, she had never looked to the side but only straight ahead. The cleric said: "There is a brother of mine in one of the carts who has been paralyzed for fourteen years. In the other there is a sister of mine who is blind." "That is a pity," Brigit said. That night they came to a certain stream called the Manae, and they all ate their meal with the exception of Brigit. The following morning she healed the two sick people who were traveling with her, and the loads were put into the carts. They all gave thanks to God.

It was then that she healed the household of a plebeian on the shore of the sea.[5] This is what happened. A certain man was working in a cow pasture, and the saint asked why he was working alone. He replied: "My whole family is ill." Hearing this, she blessed some water and immediately healed twelve sick members of the man's family.

They then came to Tailtiu. Patrick was there. An obscure question was being debated there, for a certain woman had come to return her son to a cleric of Patrick's household. The cleric's name was Brón. "How did this happen?" everyone asked. "Not difficult," said the woman. "I had come to Brón to have the veil blessed on my head and to offer my virginity to God. But my cleric seduced me so that I have given birth to his son." Brigit approached the assembly as they were debating. Then Mel said to Patrick: "The holy virgin Brigit is approaching the assembly, and she will find out for you by the greatness of her grace and the timeliness of her miracles whether this is true or false, for there is nothing in heaven or earth which Christ will refuse her if she requests it. That is what should be done in this case," said Mel. "She should be called away from the others and asked about this question, for she will not perform miracles in the presence of holy Patrick." Brigit then arrived. The crowd rose to their feet. She was immediately called apart from the assembly to speak to the woman and the clerics, apart from Patrick, who accompanied her. "Whose is that child over there?" Brigit asked the woman. "Brón's," the woman answered. "That is not true," said Brigit and she made a sign of the cross over the woman's face so that her head and tongue swelled up. Patrick came to them then into the great place of assembly. Brigit spoke to the child in the presence of the assembled people, though it had not yet begun to speak. "Who is your father?" Brigit asked. The infant replied: "Brón the bishop is not my father but a certain base and ugly man who is sitting at the edge of the assembly. My mother is a liar." They all gave thanks to God, and cried out that the guilty woman should be burned.[6] But Brigit refused, saying "This woman should do penance." This was done, and the swelling of her head and tongue disappeared. The people rejoiced, the bishop was freed, and Brigit was praised.

At the end of the day everybody left the assembly for hospitality. There was a good man living on the bank of the river called Seir. He sent his slave to the gathering to call Brigit, saying to his household: "I want the holy virgin who performed the wonderful miracle in the assembly place today to consecrate my house tonight." He welcomed her. "Let water be poured on our hands," said her virgins to Brigit, "here is our food." "It is of no use now," said Brigit, "for the Lord has shown me that this is a heathen home, with the sole exception of the slave who summoned us. Therefore I shall not eat now." The good man found this out, namely that Brigit was fasting until he was baptized. He said: "I have indeed declared that Patrick and his household would not baptize me. But for your sake, I will believe." "I do not mind provided that you are baptized," Brigit said. "It happens that there is no man in orders with me. Let someone go from us to Patrick so that a bishop or priest may baptize this man." Brón came and baptized the man with his whole household at dawn. They ate their meal at midday and gave thanks. They came to holy Patrick. Patrick said: "You should not go about without a priest. Your driver should always be a priest." And that was observed by Brigit's abbesses until recent times.

After that she healed the old peasant woman who was placed in the shadow of her cart at Cell Shuird in the south of Brega.

She healed the possessed man...who had gone round the borders. He was brought to Brigit afterward and, when he had seen her, was cured.

Brigit later went to Cell Lasre. Lassar welcomed her. There was a single milch ewe there which had been milked, and it was killed for Brigit. Toward the end of the day they saw Patrick coming toward the farm. "May God help us, Brigit," Lassar said. "Give us your advice." Brigit replied: "How much do you have?" She said: "There is no food except for ten loaves, a little milk which you have blessed, and a single lamb which has been prepared for you." This is what they did; they all went into her refectory, including both Patrick and Brigit, and they all had their fill. Lassar gave her her church, and Brigit is venerated there.

She remained the next day at Cell Lasre. A certain man of Kells, who was hated by his wife, came to Brigit for help. Brigit blessed some water. He took it with him and, when his wife had been sprinkled with it, she loved him passionately.

A certain pious virgin sent to Brigit in order that Brigit might go to visit her. Her name was Fine. Cell Fhine was named after her. That is where she went and where she remained. One day wind and rain, thunder and lightning set in. "Which of you virgins will go today with our sheep into this terrible storm?" All the virgins were equally reluctant. Brigit answered: "I like pasturing sheep very much." "I do not want you to go," said Fine. "Let my will be done," said Brigit. Then she left and chanted a verse as she went:

> "Grant me a clear day
> For you are a dear friend and royal youth;
> For the sake of your mother, loving Mary,
> Banish rain, banish wind.
>
> My king will do it for me,
> Rain will not fall till the night,
> On account of Brigit today,
> Who is going here to the herding."

She stilled the rain and wind.

3. THE VOYAGE OF BRENDAN

St. Brendan, son of Findlug, descendant of Alta of the line of Eogan, was born in the marshy region of Munster.[1] He was a very ascetical man, famed for his miracles and spiritual father to almost three thousand monks.[2]

One evening, a monk by the name of Barinthus,[3] a kinsman of his, came to visit him while he was engaged in spiritual warfare in a place which is called Brendan's "Meadow of Miracles."[4] When the holy monk asked him all kinds of questions, he began to weep and prostrate himself on the ground, where he remained for a long time. But St. Brendan lifted him to his feet and kissed him, saying: "Father, why does your arrival make us sad, when you came to comfort us? Rather, you should give joy to your brothers. Proclaim the word of God to us and refresh us with an account of the many wonderful things you saw when at sea."

Then, when St. Brendan had finished speaking, St. Barinthus began to tell them of an island he had seen, saying: "My son, Mernoc,[5] the steward of Christ's poor, fled from my sight in order to be a hermit. He discovered an island, called the Island of Delights, beside a rocky mountain. A long time later I learned that there were many monks with him there and that God had worked many miracles through him. And so I went to visit my son. As our boat drew near after three days travel, he rushed out to meet me with his brothers. The Lord had revealed to them my approach. As we went around the island, monks swarmed like bees to meet us from their various cells. Their dwelling places were scattered around the island, but the monks lived with one mind and heart in faith, hope, and love, sharing a common table and remaining always united in singing the praise of God. They ate nothing but fruit, nuts, roots, and other kinds of greens. But after compline, each went back to his own cell and remained there until cockcrow or until the bell was rung. But I wandered around the whole island all night with my son Mernoc. He led me to the western shore where there was a little boat, and said to

155

me: "Father, get into the boat and let us sail to the island which is called the Promised Land of the Saints, that land which God will give us and our successors on the last day."

As we boarded the boat and sailed away, clouds descended upon us from all sides so thickly that we could scarcely make out the prow or stern of the boat. But when we had sailed for an hour or so, a bright light shone about us and there appeared before us a land that was spacious, green, and lush. When we had landed the craft, we alighted and began a fifteen-day tour around the island, without ever coming to its end. We saw only flowering plants and trees that bore fruit, and even the stones were precious ones. On the fifteenth day we came to a river flowing from east to west. As we considered all these wonders, it was not clear to us what we should do, although we wished to make our way across the river. But we waited for a sign from God. As we pondered the matter in our hearts, there suddenly appeared a man in great radiance before us, who immediately called us by our own names and greeted us, saying: "Be of good heart, my brothers. The Lord has shown this land to you, which shall be given to his holy ones.[6] This river divides the island in two. You may not cross to the other side. Go back therefore to the place from which you have come." When he had finished speaking, I immediately asked him where he came from and what his name was. He said: "Why do you ask me where I come from and what my name is? Why do you not ask me about this island? It has remained unchanged just as you see it now since the beginning of the world. Do you need any food, drink, or clothing? You have been here a whole year already without having anything to eat or drink. You have never felt drowsy, nor has night fallen. For day is never-ending here, and there is no obscuring dark. Our Lord Jesus Christ himself is the light."

We set out at once and the man accompanied us as far as the shore, where our boat was tied up. But as we entered the boat, the man vanished from our gaze and we sailed back through the same darkness as before to the Island of Delights. When the brothers caught sight of us, they rejoiced greatly at our approach and openly grieved at our long absence. "Why, fathers, did you leave your sheep to roam freely in this wood without their shepherd? We are growing used to our abbot leaving us often for some other place, though we do not know which, where he stays sometimes for a week, a fortnight, or even a month." When I heard this, I tried to comfort them, saying: "Brothers, do not let evil thoughts enter your minds. Here you dwell, beyond doubt, at the gates of Paradise. Nearby there is an island which is called the Promised Land of the Saints, where neither night falls nor day ends. It is to this place that Mernoc, your abbot, so often goes. It is guarded by an angel of the Lord. Can you not tell from the fragrance of our clothes that we have been in Paradise?" Then the brothers answered, saying: "Father, we know that you have been to God's Paradise over the sea, but we do not know where exactly it is. We have often been able to smell the fragrance of our abbot's clothes for forty days after his return."

I remained there with my son for two whole weeks without eating or drinking anything, yet we felt so replete that anyone would have thought that we were full of new wine. After forty days I received the blessing of the brothers and the abbot, and set off on the journey home with my companions in order to return to my cell—I shall go there tomorrow.

When he had heard these words, St. Brendan and all his community prostrated themselves on the ground and glorified God, saying: "'The Lord is righteous in all his ways: and holy in all his works' (Ps 144:17) because he has revealed to his servants such great wonders, and is blessed in his gifts, for today he has nourished us with such spiritual delight." Then St. Brendan said: "Let us take some refreshment now, and carry out the new commandment of the Lord (Jn 13:34)." The following morning St. Barinthus received his brothers' blessing and departed for his own cell.

St. Brendan selected seven monks from his community, shut himself in an oratory with them, and said to them: "My most beloved fellow-warriors, I look to you for advice and help, for my heart and all my thoughts are united in a single desire. I have resolved in my heart, if only it be God's will, to seek that Promised Land of the Saints, of which St. Barinthus has spoken. How does this seem to you, and what advice do you wish to give me?"

As soon as they knew their holy father's intention, they said with one voice: "Father, your will is our will. Have we not left our families, have we not set aside our inheritance and put ourselves in your hands? And so we are ready to follow you to either death or life. We seek one thing only: the will of God."

And so St. Brendan and those who were with him completed a forty-day fast, in three-day periods, before they set out.[7] When the forty days were up, he bade farewell to his brothers, commending them all to the charge of the prior (who later became his successor in that same place), and set out in a westerly direction together with fourteen of his monks toward the island of a holy monk called Enda.[8] There they remained for three days and nights.

When he had received the blessing of the holy father and of all the monks who were with him, he set out toward the furthest part of the region, where his family lived. He did not wish to see them, but pitched his tent on the top of a mountain that extended far into the ocean, in the place that is called Brendan's Seat, where there was access for only one boat.[9] St. Brendan and his companions constructed a coracle with iron tools. The ribs and frame were of wood, as is the custom in those parts, and they were covered with cowhide tanned with the bark of oak. They greased all the external seams of the skin with fat and stored away two more sets of skins inside the coracle together with supplies for forty days, fat for preparing the skins as covering for the boat, and other bits and pieces which are necessary for human life. They fixed a mast in the middle of the boat, a sail, and the other things that are required for navigation. Then St. Brendan commanded his brothers in the name of the Father, Son, and Holy Spirit to enter the boat.

As Brendan was standing alone on the shore, blessing the harbor, three of his brothers arrived who had followed him from the monastery. They immediately fell at the feet of the holy monk and said: "Father, let us come with you, or we shall die in this place of hunger and thirst, for we are determined to be wandering pilgrims all the days of our lives." When the man of God saw their need, he told them to enter the boat. "Your will be done, my sons," he said and added: "though I know why you have come.

One of you has done well and God has prepared for him the place that he deserves. But for the other two he shall prepare a terrible judgment."

St. Brendan entered the boat, and with hoisted sail they set off westward into the summer solstice. They had a favorable wind and needed to do no more than trim the sail. But after fifteen days the wind dropped and they rowed and rowed until their strength failed. Then straightaway St. Brendan began to give them words of comfort and encouragement: "Brothers, you have nothing to fear, for God is our helper. He is our navigator and helmsman, and he shall guide us. Pull in the oars and the rudder. Spread the sail and let God do as he wishes with his servants and their boat." Every day they ate in the evening. Every now and again a wind sprang up, but they could not tell from which direction it came or in which direction the boat was driven.

Forty days had passed and they found themselves without food when an island appeared to them from the north, very rocky and high. As they approached its shore, they saw a towering wall of rock from which there gushed many streams of water, rushing down from the peaks of the island into the sea. But they could find no harbor at which to land. By now the monks were tormented with hunger and thirst and some of them tried to catch water from the streams with their flasks. When St. Brendan saw this, he said: "Stop that at once. You are acting foolishly. God does not yet want to show us a way in, and you are forcing yourselves upon the place! In three days times our Lord Jesus Christ will show his servants a harbor and a place to rest and refresh our weary bodies."

For three days they circled the island, and then, on the third day at about three o'clock, they found a harbor which was just big enough for a single boat. Brendan immediately got to his feet and blessed it. On both sides there loomed a soaring and jagged cliff like a sheer wall. When they had all left the boat and were standing on dry land, Brendan forbade them to unload any equipment from the boat. Then, when they were making their way along the shore, a dog came running toward them and sat at Brendan's feet, as dogs are accustomed to sit at the feet of their master. St. Brendan said to his brothers: "Has God not sent us a good messenger? Let us follow him." Then St. Brendan and his brothers followed the dog as far as the settlement.

They entered and saw before them a large hall lined with couches and chairs and with water to wash their feet. When they had sat down, St. Brendan said to his companions: "Take care, brothers, that Satan does not lead you into temptation. For I see him inciting one of those three brothers who followed us from the monastery to a dreadful crime. Pray for his soul, for his body is given over into the power of Satan." The walls of the house in which they were sitting were lined with pots made from different kinds of metal, together with bridles and drinking horns cased in silver.

Then St. Brendan said to the monk whose job it was to serve the brethren with bread: "Bring the food which God has sent us." As soon as he was on his feet, this monk found a table with linen coverings, loaves of wonderfully white bread, and fish. When everything was ready, St. Brendan blessed the food and said to his brothers: "Let us praise the God of Heaven, who gives food to all creatures." And so the monks sat back in their seats and glorified God. Similarly they had plenty to drink, as much as they wanted. When dinner was over and they had concluded the day's prayer with compline, St. Brendan said: "Take your rest now. There is a well-made bed here for each one of you. It is right that you should rest, for you are exhausted by all your efforts." But when sleep had come upon the monks, St. Brendan saw the Devil at work, like a little Ethiopian boy, holding a bridle in his hand and playing with it in front of the monk. St. Brendan immediately got to his feet and remained in prayer until dawn. Early in the morning, when the brothers had quickly said their office and made their way to the boat, a table appeared before them, already laid, just as had happened the day before. And so for three days and three nights God prepared food for his servants.

Then St. Brendan set off with his brothers, saying to them these words: "You must be careful not to remove anything from this island." They all replied: "Far be it from us that our journey should be spoiled by any theft." Then St. Brendan said: "See, just as I predicted yesterday, our brother has a silver bridle hidden in his breast. A Devil gave it to him last night." When the brother heard these words, he flung the bridle away and fell down at the feet of the man of God, saying: "I have sinned, father; forgive me. Pray for the salvation of my soul." Immediately all the monks threw themselves to the ground, beseeching the Lord for their brother's soul.

As the brothers got to their feet again, and Brendan lifted the monk up, they saw a little Ethiopian boy leap forth from his breast, shrieking loudly: "Man of God, why are you driving me out from my home in which I have lived now for seven years, depriving me of my inheritance?" St. Brendan replied: "I command you in the name of our Lord Jesus Christ not to harm anyone from now till the Day of Judgment."

Then he said to the monk: "You must receive the body and blood of the Lord, for your soul is soon to leave your body. This shall be your burial place. But the brother who followed you from the monastery shall remain forever in hell." And so, when he had received Communion, his soul departed form his body and was received by angels of light before the gaze of his brothers. Brendan buried his body in that very place.

Brendan and his brothers arrived at the shore of the island where their boat was moored. As they entered the boat, a young man arrived, carrying a basket full of bread and a jug of water. He said to them: "Accept this blessing from the hand of your servant. You have a long journey ahead of you until you find refreshment and rest. But this bread and water will last you until Easter." They accepted his gift and sought the open seas, partaking of food and water every two days. Thus their boat was borne this way and that across the face of the deep.

One day they caught sight of an island not far from where they were. A favorable wind came to their aid as they began to sail toward it, so that they did not have to row more than their strength allowed. When they had arrived at the harbor, the man of God ordered them all to leave the boat, he himself being the last to disembark. Their walk around the island revealed many springs that formed gushing rivers full of fish. St. Brendan said to his brothers: "Let us sing the Divine Office here. Let us sacrifice the Spotless Victim to God, for today is Maundy Thursday." There they remained until Holy Saturday.

As they walked around the island, they came upon various flocks of sheep, all of which were the same color, that is white, and which quite obscured the ground from view.[10] St. Brendan called his brothers together and said to them: "Take from the flock what you will need for the feastday." The monks hastened to the flock as they had been told and removed from it a single sheep. And when they had fastened it by its horns, it followed the monk holding the tether in his hand to where the man of God was standing as if it were tame. Again the man of God said to one of his brothers: "Take a lamb without blemish from the flock." He promptly carried out the command.

When they had prepared everything for the following day, there suddenly appeared before them a man carrying a basket full of bread baked in hot ashes and other kinds of food and drink. When he had placed these before the man of God, he made three full prostrations at the feet of the holy father, saying: "What have I done to deserve the honor, O pearl of God, of providing you with food and drink by the work of my hands during these holy days?" St. Brendan raised him from the ground and kissed him, saying: "My son, Our Lord Jesus Christ has shown us a place where we can celebrate his Holy Resurrection," to which the man replied: "Father, you will celebrate Holy Saturday here, but God has determined that tomorrow you shall celebrate the vigils and Masses of his Resurrection on that island which you can see."

While speaking, he began to wait upon the servants of God and to prepare everything that was required for the following day. When all was ready and had been taken down to the boat, the man said to St. Brendan: "This is all that your boat can take. In eight days time I shall bring across all the food and drink you need to last until Pentecost."

"How do you know where we shall be in eight days time?" asked St. Brendan. He replied: "By tonight you shall be on that island which you can see nearby, and there you shall remain until midday tomorrow. Then you will sail westward to another island, called the Paradise of Birds, which lies not far from the first.

There you will remain until the octave of Pentecost." St. Brendan also asked him how it was possible for the sheep to grow to such a size there. They were bigger even than cows. He replied: "There is no one on the island to milk them, nor winter to slim them down, and so they graze all day and night. That is why they are bigger than the sheep in your country." They blessed each other, made their way to the boat, and set out to sea.

But when they arrived at the other island, their boat came to a stop before they could beach it. St. Brendan told his brothers to leave the boat and to stand in the shallows, which they did. They then attached ropes to the boat from either side and dragged it ashore. The island was rocky and bare. There were only occasional trees to be seen, and there was no sand on the shoreline at all. Brendan remained on the boat while the brothers passed the night in the open in prayer and vigil. For he knew the nature of the island, but did not want to tell them in case they should be afraid.

In the morning, he told the priests to say their own individual Masses, which they did. When Brendan too had sung his Mass on the boat, the brothers began to unload the pieces of raw meat to cover them with salt, and the fish that they had brought with them from the other island. Then they put a cooking-pot on the fire. When they had fed the fire with wood and the pot had begun to boil, the island started to heave like a wave. The brothers started to run to the boat, begging the abbot for his protection. He hauled them in one by one and they set out, leaving behind all that they had unloaded onto the island. Then the island began to move across the surface of the sea, and the fire, still alight, could be seen from over two miles away. St. Brendan explained to his brothers what was happening, saying: "Brothers, are you amazed at what the island has done?" They said: "Indeed we are, and it fills us with fear." He said to them: "My little children, do not be afraid, for last night God revealed to me by a vision the meaning of this thing. The island that we were on was nothing other than a sea animal, the foremost of all that swim in the oceans. It always seeks to make its tail and head meet, but cannot do so on account of its length. Jasconius is its name."[11]

When they were sailing close to the island where they had previously stayed for three days and climbed its highest point, which faced westward across the sea, they caught sight of another island only a short distance away. It was covered with grass and filled with flowers and groves of trees. They began to sail around it, looking for a harbor, and eventually came to a south-facing shore where a river flowed into the sea. There they landed the boat. The monks got out of the boat, and St. Brendan told them to pull the boat with ropes upstream as hard as they could. The river was as wide as their boat. The father sat in the boat as they hauled it along for a mile until they came to the source of the river. St. Brendan said to them: "See, our Lord Jesus Christ has given us a place in which to stay and celebrate his Resurrection." And he added: "Even if we had brought no supplies with us at all, this spring, I believe, would provide us with sufficient food and drink."

Overhanging that spring there was a tree of astonishing girth and height that was full of pure white birds. There were so many of them there that it was hardly possible to see its branches and leaves.[12] When the man of God saw them, he began to ponder and to weigh within himself what it was that had caused so many birds to come together in a single flock. He was so tormented by this that he threw himself to the ground in tears and called upon God, saying: "O God, who knows all that is unknown and who reveals all that is hidden, you know the suffering of my heart. I beseech you by your majesty that you may deign through your great mercy to make known to me, a sinner, this mystery of yours that I see before me. I ask this not by my own merits or worth but by your infinite mercy."

When he had said this to himself and had sat down again, one of the birds, its wings sounding like the chiming of a handbell, flew down from the tree to the boat where the man of God was sitting. It settled on the tip of the prow, stretched out its wings, as if making a sign of joy, and gazed peacefully upon the holy father. The man of God knew at once that God had answered his prayer, and he said to the bird: "If you are the messenger of God, tell me where all these birds have come from and why they have all gathered here."

164

The bird replied: "We are part of the fall of the ancient enemy, not through our own sin but by agreement with theirs. But when we were created, his fall, together with his followers, led to our own ruin. Our God is just and true. It is by his great justice that we were placed here. We are not punished with suffering. Here we can see the presence of God, but he has cut us off from those who stand before his throne. We wander the different paths of the air, of heaven, and of earth, just like the other messengers of God. But on feast days and on Sundays we receive bodies like the ones you see and we celebrate our Creator here, singing his praises. But you with your brothers have completed one year of your journey. Six more years remain. Every year you will celebrate Easter in the same place where you are going to celebrate it today, and later you will find your heart's desire, that is the Promised Land of the Saints." When it had spoken, the bird took off from the prow of the ship and flew back to the others.

As the hour for vespers approached, all the birds in the tree began to sing as if with a single voice, beating their wings against their sides: "Praise is due to you, O God, in Zion, and to you shall vows be performed" (Ps 64:1). They continued to sing this verse antiphonally for a whole hour. To the man of God and his companions, this singing and rhythmic beating of wings seemed as sweet as a song of lamentation.

Then St. Brendan said to his brothers: "Take nourishment for your bodies, for today our souls have already been filled with divine food." When supper was over they sang the Divine Office, and then slept till the third hour of the night. But St. Brendan stayed awake and summoned his brothers to the vigil of the Holy Night with the verse: "O Lord, open my lips" (Ps 50:17). When the holy man had finished praying, all the birds started to flap their wings and sing: "Praise the Lord, all his angels, praise him, all his host" (Ps 148:2). They continued to sing for an hour, just as they had at vespers.

As the sun rose, they began to sing: "And may the splendor of the Lord come upon us" (Ps 89:17) with the same rhythm and chant that they had used at lauds. And then at terce, the same verse: "Sing Psalms to our God, sing Psalms; sing Psalms to our king, sing Psalms with understanding" (Ps 46:7). At sext: "Let thy face, O Lord, shine upon us and take pity on us" (Ps 66:2). At nones they sang: "Behold how good and pleasant it is when brothers dwell in unity" (Ps 132:1). And so, day and night, the birds praised the Lord. St. Brendan nourished his brothers on the feast of Easter until the octave day.

When the days of the feast were over, he said: "Let us make use of this spring, because so far it has served only for washing our hands and our feet." No sooner had he said this than the man with whom they had spent three days before Easter and who had given them their supplies arrived with his boat full of food and drink. When everything had been unloaded from his boat, he spoke before the holy father, saying: "Men and brothers, here you have enough to last you until Pentecost; do not drink therefore from this spring. It is too potent for drinking. Let me describe its nature to you: Whoever drinks from it shall immediately fall into a deep sleep and shall not awake for twenty-four hours. But when it has been taken out from the spring, it has the flavor and nature of ordinary water." He received the blessing of the holy father, and returned home.

St. Brendan remained in the same place until the octave of Pentecost; their refreshment was the song of the birds. On Pentecost itself, when the holy man had sung the Mass with his brothers, their steward arrived with all that they needed for celebrating the feast. But when they had all sat down for their meal, he said to them: "You still have a long journey ahead of you. Fill your flasks from this spring and take dry bread with you that shall keep for a year. I shall give you as much as your boat can carry." Then he received a blessing and returned home.

After the eight days, St. Brendan loaded the boat with all that the steward had brought them and ordered their flasks to be filled with water from the spring. When everything had been carried down to the shore, the same bird that had once spoken to Brendan quickly flew down and sat again on the prow of the boat. The man of God realized that it had something to tell them. The bird spoke to them in a human voice: "Next year you will celebrate Easter Sunday and the Easter period with us. And you will be in the same place you were for Maundy Thursday. Similarly you will celebrate the Easter vigil where you celebrated it before, on the back of Jasconius. After eight months you will find the island which is called the Island of the Community of St. Ailbe, and there you shall celebrate the Nativity of the Lord."[13]

When the bird had said this, it flew off home. The monks began to set sail into the open sea, and the birds all sang, as if with one voice: "Hear us, O God of our salvation, hope of all the ends of the earth and of the farthest seas" (Ps 64:6).

The holy father and his community spent three months sailing this way and that across the face of the deep. Nothing met their eyes but the open sky and the sea. Every second or third day they took food and drink. Then one day there appeared to them an island close to hand but, as they approached the shore, a wind blew them away from the harbor. And so for forty days they sailed around the island without being able to find a landing-place. The monks who were in the boat began to beseech the Lord with tears and to implore his help, for they were overwhelmed with weariness and exhaustion. But after three days of prayer and fasting, they saw a narrow inlet, so small that only a single boat could enter it, and two springs nearby, one muddy and the other clear. The monks hastened with their flasks to drink the water, but seeing what they were doing, the man of God said: "My sons, do nothing that is forbidden without the approval of the elders who live on this island. They will willingly grant to you the water which now you wish to drink without their knowledge."

Then as they left the boat and began to consider in which direction they should go, an elderly and very dignified man with snow-white hair and a shining face came to meet them. He prostrated himself on the ground three times before kissing the man of God in greeting. St. Brendan and those who were with him lifted him from the ground. After exchanging kisses, the old man held the holy father's hand and walked the two hundred yards to the monastery with him. Then St. Brendan stood with his brothers at the monastery door and said to the old man: "Whose monastery is this, and who is in charge here? Where do those who live here come from?" Thus the holy father put different questions to the old man but could elicit no response from him but only the gentlest of gestures to indicate that silence should be maintained.

As soon as the holy father understood the rule of that place, he warned his brothers, saying: "Guard your tongues in case you should disturb these monks with your shamelessness." As he spoke, eleven monks came to meet them bearing reliquaries and crucifixes and singing hymns, repeating to them the following verse: "Rise up, you holy ones of God, from your abode and set out on the way of truth. Sanctify this place, bless your people and deign to keep us, your servants, in peace."[14] As soon as they had finished this verse, the abbot of the monastery greeted St. Brendan and each one of his brothers with the kiss of peace. Each group greeted the other with the kiss of peace.

They then led them to the monastery, singing prayers as they went, as is the custom in western parts. Then the abbot of the monastery together with the monks began to wash the feet of their guests, while singing the antiphon "A new commandment I give to you" (Jn 13:34). When this was done, the abbot led them to the refectory in total silence, where a bell was rung; they washed their hands and were shown to their seats. Then, at another ring of the bell, one of the community rose from his place and began to place loaves of wonderfully white bread upon the table and certain root vegetables that had an amazing taste. The seats of the guests alternated with those of the community, and there was a whole loaf for each pair of monks. At a further ring of the bell they were served with drink.

The abbot also encouraged the monks with great good humor, saying: "Now you can take your fill, with joy and fear of the Lord, of that spring from which you secretly drank earlier today. The monks wash their feet every day in that other, muddy stream which you saw, since it is always warm. We do not know who bakes the bread that you see, nor who brings it to our cellar. But we do know that they are provided for us, his servants, by the great generosity of God through one of his creatures. We are twenty-four monks in all here. Every day we receive twelve loaves to eat, a loaf between every pair. On feast days and on Sundays God increases the supply to one loaf each for everyone, so that there is enough left for dinner. And now, with your arrival, we have received double the amount.[15] Christ has been feeding us in this way since the time of St. Patrick and St. Ailbe, our holy father, for eighty years. But we never seem to grow old or weak. On this island we have no need for cooked food, nor do we ever suffer from cold or heat. And when the time for Mass or vigils comes, the lamps which we brought from our own country by divine Providence are lit and they burn until day, with an undiminished flame."

They drank three times and then the abbot rang the bell, as was his custom. The monks solemnly rose together from the table in complete silence and led the way to the church, followed by St. Brendan and the abbot of the monastery. As they entered the church, another group of twelve monks departed from them, genuflecting hastily as they left. When he saw them, St. Brendan said: "Father abbot, why did these monks not eat with us at the same time?" The father replied: "That was because you are here and there is not enough space at our refectory table for all of us together." They will have their meal now, and will not go hungry. Meanwhile we shall sing vespers in the church so that those of our brethren who are now eating can sing vespers after us.

When the evening office was over, St. Brendan began to reflect upon the way the church had been built. It was square, of the same length as breadth,[16] and it contained seven lamps, (cf. Rv 1:12), three hanging before the central altar and two before each of the other two altars. The altars were constructed of cubes of crystal, and the sacred vessels too were of crystal, including the patens, chalices, and cruets and other liturgical objects, as were the twenty-four seats positioned around the church. (cf. Rv 4:4). The abbot's seat was placed between two choirs of monks. Both groups would begin and end their chant with him. No monk in either choir would presume to begin a line of chant; that was reserved for the abbot alone. No one in the monastery presumed to speak or to make a noise. If any monk needed anything, he would go to the abbot, kneel before him, and ask him in his heart for what he required. The abbot would immediately take a tablet and stylus and write down what God had revealed to him, granting the same to the monk who had petitioned him.

When St. Brendan had considered all these things in his heart, he said to the abbot: "Father, now it is time for us to return to the refectory so that we may do everything in daylight." This is what they did. When the day's routine was complete, everyone went swiftly to compline. After the abbot had begun the verse "O God, come to our aid" and had sung the "Glory be to the Father," the monks added: "We have acted wrongly and done evil. You who are a faithful father, spare us, O Lord. Now may I lie and rest in peace, for you alone, O Lord, make me dwell in safety." Then they sang the Office which belongs to this hour.

When the round of Psalms was over, all the brothers went out to their respective cells, taking their guests with them. The abbot remained behind in the church with St. Brendan, waiting for the approach of the light. St. Brendan inquired of the holy father about the keeping of silence in the monastery and about their way of life, asking how this was possible in the flesh.

Then the abbot replied with great reverence and humility: "Father, I testify before Christ that we first came here eighty years ago and yet it is only when we sing praise to God that we hear a human voice. All twenty-four of us never make a sound, and only those who are older will make a sign with their fingers or eyes. After our arrival here none of us have ever suffered any of the afflictions of spirit or flesh that visit the human race."

St. Brendan said: "May we too stay here?" But the abbot replied: "No, you may not, for that is not God's will. Why do you ask me that, father? Did God not reveal to you what you should do before you came to us? You must return to your own monastery with fourteen of your brethren. There God has prepared your burial place. Of the other two monks, one will go to the island which is called the Isle of the Anchorites while the other is doomed to a terrible death in hell."

As they were speaking of these things, a flaming arrow shot through the window before their eyes and lit all the lamps that were positioned before the altar. Then it shot back out the way it had come. But the precious light remained in the lamps. "Who puts out the lamps in the morning?" asked blessed Brendan, to which the holy father replied: "Come and see the mystery of the thing yourself. Do you see the candles burning in the middle of the lampstands? They never burn down, nor do they leave any ash, for their light is spiritual." St. Brendan said: "How can an immaterial light burn physically in a material object?" "Have you not read of the burning bush on Mount Sinai?" the old man replied. "The bush itself was untouched by fire."

They remained in vigil right through the night until morning came, and when it was day, St. Brendan asked permission to continue on his journey. The old man said: "No, father. You should stay with us to celebrate the Nativity of the Lord until the octave of the Epiphany." The holy father remained therefore with his brothers in the monastery of twenty-four monks, who are known as the Community of St. Ailbe.

When the feast was over, St. Brendan and his followers received both supplies and blessings from these holy men and put out to sea in their little boat with all possible speed. Sometimes by the power of sail and sometimes by their own efforts, they voyaged from one place to another until the beginning of Lent.

One day they caught sight of an island not so far away and immediately began to row swiftly toward it, since they were now greatly in need of food and drink. Three days before their supplies had run out. When St. Brendan had blessed the harbor and all had left the boat, they found a spring of wonderfully clear water surrounded by every kind of plant and vegetable and all kinds of fish swimming downstream to the sea.

St. Brendan said to his brothers: "It is God who has given us this refreshment after our labors. Catch enough fish for our supper, cook them on the fire, and pick the plants and vegetables which God has prepared for his servants." This they did. But as they poured out the water to drink, the man of God said to them: "Brothers, take care not to drink too much of this water in case it makes you ill." Not all the monks heeded his warning equally, and so some drank a single cupful, some two cupfuls, and others three. A deep sleep descended upon them, some for three days and nights, some for two days and nights, and others for one day and night. And the holy father prayed to God unceasingly on their behalf since they had fallen into such danger through their ignorance.

When the three days were over, the holy father said to his companions: "Brothers, let us flee this death before it has an even worse effect upon us. The Lord gave us sustenance, but you have turned it into a source of harm. Let us leave this island, therefore, taking enough fish with us to last for one meal every three days until Maundy Thursday. Take a cup of water per day for each monk and one vegetable." They loaded the boat with all that St. Brendan had ordered, hoisted the sail, and set out to sea in a northerly direction.

After three days and nights the wind dropped and the sea began to look as though it were almost solid on account of the great calm. The holy father said: "Pull in your oars and let down the sail. Let God take us where he will." And so the ship was carried to and fro for twenty days until God raised another fair wind for them, from west to east. Then they began both to hoist the sail and to row. Every three days they consumed some of their supplies.

One day an island appeared to them in the distance, like a cloud on the horizon, and St. Brendan said to them: "My sons, do you recognize that island?" They answered that they did not. "Well, I recognize it. This is the island on which we celebrated Maundy Thursday last year, where our good steward lives." Then the monks were filled with joy and began to row as quickly as they could. When the man of God saw this, he said: "Don't row so hard, or you will exhaust yourselves. Is almighty God not the helmsman and captain of our ship? Do not strain yourselves, since he guides us where he will."

But when they drew near to the shore of this island, the same steward came running out to meet them and led them into the harbor where they had disembarked the previous year. He praised God all the time and kissed the feet of each and every one, beginning with the holy father and ending with the lowliest monk. "God is wonderful in his saints. The God of Israel is he who will give power and strength to his people. Blessed be God" (cf. Ps 67:36). When the ship had been unloaded, he put up a

tent, prepared a bath for them—for it was Maundy Thursday—
and dressed them all in new clothes, serving them for the next
three days. The monks also celebrated the Passion of the Lord
with great reverence until Holy Saturday.

When they had completed the ceremonies of Holy Saturday,
offered Mass, and received Holy Communion, the steward said
to St. Brendan and his followers: "Return to your craft so that you
can celebrate the holy night of the Lord's Resurrection where
you celebrated it last year, remaining there until midday. Then
set out for the island which is called the Paradise of Birds, where
you spent from Easter to the octave of Pentecost last year, taking
with you all that you need of food and drink. I shall come and
visit you the Sunday after Easter." This they did. The steward
loaded the boat with as many loaves and as much drink, meat,
and other delicacies as it could hold. And then, when St. Brendan had blessed the boat and joined them in it, they set out
toward the other island.

As they approached the place where they were to disembark,
they saw a cooking-pot that they had left there the previous year.
When they had landed, St. Brendan began to sing the *Benedicite*
right through to the end.[17] When he had finished, he warned his
monks with these words: "My dear sons, watch and pray in case
you should enter into temptation. Remember how God tamed
that terrible beast beneath us without any difficulty." Accordingly
the monks scattered themselves around the island and kept vigil
until it was time for matins. Later each priest individually offered
a Mass to God until nine o'clock. Then St. Brendan offered the
unblemished Lamb to God and said to his brothers: "Last year I
celebrated the Resurrection of the Lord here. I want to do the
same this year." Then they went on to the Island of the Birds.

At their approach to the harbor of this island, all the birds
began to sing, as if saying with one voice: "Victory to our God
who sits upon the throne and to the Lamb" (Rv 7:10). And again:
"The Lord God has shone upon us. Bind the sacrifice with cords,
as far as the horns of the altar" (Ps 117:27). They sang with their
voices and flapped with their wings for almost half an hour until

everything had been unloaded from the boat and the holy father and all his holy community were settled in their tent.

When he had celebrated the Feast of Easter with his community, the steward arrived, as he had promised, on the first Sunday after Easter, bringing with him all the essential supplies.

As they sat at the table, the bird who had spoken to them last year settled on the prow of the boat, extended its wings, and made a noise like the sound of a great organ. The man of God knew that it wanted to tell them something. The bird said: "God has appointed four places for you for each season of the year where you shall stay until the seven years of your pilgrimage are over. You shall spend Maundy Thursday with your steward who is there each year, the Easter vigil on the back of a whale, the Feast of Easter until the octave of Pentecost with us, and the Nativity of the Lord with the community of Ailbe. At the end of seven years, after great trials of different kinds, you will find the Promised Land of the Saints which you seek and there you shall live for forty days before God shall lead you back to the land of your birth." The holy abbot and his brothers threw themselves to the ground, thanking and praising their Creator. When the venerable old man rose to his feet, the bird flew back to its place.

Later, when the steward had finished his meal, he said: "I shall return to you with provisions with God's help on the day of Pentecost." He returned home with the blessing of the holy father and of all who were with him. They remained there until Pentecost and, when the feast was over, St. Brendan instructed his brothers to prepare the boat for sailing and to fill their flasks from the spring. The steward arrived with a boat laden with food just as they were dragging their vessel down to the sea. And when he had transferred everything to St. Brendan's boat, he bade farewell to all with a kiss and returned from where he had come.

The venerable father and his companions sailed out to sea, where they voyaged for forty days. Then one day they saw a creature of immense size following them at a distance; it blew spray from its nostrils and cut through the waves at high speed as if coming to devour them. Even as the monks saw this, they raised a shout to the Lord: "Save us from being eaten by this beast, O

Lord!" St. Brendan consoled them, saying: "Do not be too frightened, you of little faith. God, who is always our defender, shall save us from the jaws of this animal and from all other dangers."

And indeed, as it drew near to them, it sent waves crashing against the boat which only increased the monks' fear. St. Brendan raised his hands to heaven and said: "O Lord, save your servants, as you saved David from the hand of the giant Goliath. Rescue us, as you rescued Jonah from the belly of the great whale."

After these three pleas for deliverance, another sea monster, appearing from the west, rushed to meet the first animal and, spewing fire from its jaws, immediately attacked it. The old man said to his brothers: "See, my sons, the wonderful deeds of our Redeemer. See how the beasts obey their Creator. The matter will soon be over, and you will not be harmed by this battle in any way, but it will be remembered as having been to the glory of God." Almost as he spoke, the wretched creature that had pursued the company of Christ was cut into three pieces before their eyes, and the other animal returned victorious to the place from where it had come.

On another day they saw a large island in the distance covered with trees. As they drew near to its shore to land, they saw the rear section of the beast which had been killed. St. Brendan said: "See the creature that wished to devour us. Now it shall be your food. You shall remain here for a long time. Drag your boat higher onto the shore and look for a safe place in the wood to pitch your tent." The holy father himself chose the place where they would live.

But when they had carried out the instructions of the man of God and had carried all their belongings to the tent, St. Brendan said to his brothers: "Cut enough meat from the beast to last you for three months. For tonight the body will be eaten by animals." They worked away until the time for vespers came, storing as much meat as they would need, just as Brendan had told them. And when their work was done, the brothers said: "Father, how shall we be able to survive here without water?" He replied: "Do you think it is more difficult for God to supply you with water than with food? Walk toward the southern shore of the island, where you will find a spring of the clearest water with many plants and vegetables. Bring me a reasonable supply." They found everything just as the man of God had said. St. Brendan remained there for three months, since there was a great storm at sea, with gales and squalls of rain and hail.

The monks went to see whether what Brendan had said about the beast had come true. When they came to the place where it had been, they could find nothing but a pile of bones. They returned to the man of God, and said: "Father, it has happened just as you said it would." He replied: "I know, my sons, that you wished to test me, to see if what I said was true or not. I shall give you another sign: A large piece of fish shall be washed up there tonight, which shall be your food for tomorrow." The following day the monks went and found that what he had said was true, bringing back with them as much as they could carry. The venerable father said to them: "Preserve it carefully in salt. You will have need of it. God will give us fine weather today, tomorrow, and the day after, and the swell will die down. Then we shall leave."

When these days had passed, St. Brendan instructed his monks to load the boat, filling their water bottles and other containers and gathering the necessary plants and vegetables, for St. Brendan had not eaten the meat of any creature since his ordination. When all had been loaded onto the boat, they hoisted the sail and set out in a northerly direction.

One day they saw an island in the distance. "Do you see that island?" St. Brendan asked, and they replied that they did. "There are three kinds of people who live on that island: boys, youths, and older men. One of your party will remain on pilgrimage here." The monks wondered which one of them it might be. When they persisted and he saw that they were disheartened, he said: "This is the monk who will remain there," and pointed to one of the three who had left the monastery to follow him at the beginning of the journey and concerning whom he had made a prediction when they had joined the boat in their native land.

They drew close to the shore of the island. The island was astonishingly flat and seemed to them to be scarcely higher than the sea, without trees or anything standing into the wind. It was very broad and covered with white and purple vegetation.[18] Three groups could be seen, just as the man of God predicted, standing roughly a stone's throw apart. They moved from one place to another until one group stopped and sang: "The saints shall go from strength to strength, the God of gods shall be seen in Zion" (Ps 83:8). When one group came to the end of a verse, another stopped and took it up again, and so they continued without pause. The first group of boys were clothed in pure white garments, the second in blue garments, and the third in purple dalmatics.

It was ten o'clock by the time they reached the island's harbor. At midday they began to sing these Psalms in unison: "God be merciful to us" to the end, "O God, come to my aid," and, thirdly, "I believed and therefore I have spoken" (Pss 66, 69, 115), followed by a prayer. At none they sang another three Psalms: "From the depths," "Behold, how good," and "Praise the Lord, O Jerusalem" (Pss 129, 132, 147). At vespers they sang: "You are worthy of praise, O God, in Zion," "Bless the Lord, O my soul," "O Lord, my God," and "Praise the Lord, you servants" (Pss 64, 103, 112), followed by the fifteen Gradual Psalms, which they sang sitting down.[19]

When their singing was ended, the island was enveloped by a cloud which was astonishingly bright and so dense that they could no longer see anything at all. But they could still hear the voices of people singing without break until it was time for matins. Then they took up the songs: "Oh, praise the Lord from the heavens," "Sing to the Lord a new song," and, thirdly, "Oh, praise God in his holy ones" (Pss 148, 149, 150). Then they sang twelve Psalms in order from the psalter.

As day came, the cloud lifted from the island and they sang three more Psalms: "Have mercy on me, O God," "O God, my God, from dawn I shall seek you" and "Lord, you have been our refuge" (Pss 50, 62, 89). At terce they sang another three: "Oh, clap your hands together, all you people," "Save me, O God, for your name's sake," and "I love the Lord because he has heard my voice" (Pss 46, 53, 114), with the Alleluia. Then they offered the sacrifice of the unblemished Lamb, and all came to receive Communion, saying: "Receive this sacred body and blood of our Lord and Savior for life everlasting."

When the Mass was over, two young men left the group and brought a basket full of the purple plants, saying: "Take with you some of the produce of this Island of Strong Men. Let our brother return to us, and go in peace." St. Brendan called the monk concerned to him and said: "Kiss your brothers and go with those who are calling you. Blessed was the hour in which your mother conceived you in her womb, for you have been found worthy of living with a community such as this." When he had kissed his brothers and the holy father, St. Brendan said to the monk: "My son, remember how many good things God has given you in this world. Go now, and pray for us." The monk immediately went with the two young men back to their school.

The venerable father set out to sea with his companions. At three o'clock, he told his brothers to make themselves a meal of the plants from the Island of Strong Men. The man of God took one of them and was amazed to see how big and succulent it was. "Never have I seen or even read of such large plants," he said. They were all the same size, round and large. He asked for a cup and squeezed from just one a whole pound of juice, which he shared among the twelve. For the next twelve days they lived on a single fruit each every day, and the savor of honey remained always upon their tongue.

When this period was over, the holy father ordered a three-day fast. At the end of the third day an enormous bird flew toward the boat, with a branch from some unknown tree in its beak. At the tip of the branch hung a large bunch of grapes of a wonderful purple color. The bird dropped the branch into the lap of the holy man. St. Brendan called his brothers together and said: "Look at the food that God has sent us!" Each grape was the size of an apple. The man of God gave the grapes individually to the monks, and thus they had enough to last them for another twelve days.

Then St. Brendan again imposed a fast upon his brothers. On the third day they saw an island close at hand, densely covered with trees upon which there grew such an amazing crop of the same fruit, exactly the same type and color, that the branches almost touched the ground. There was not a single bare tree there, nor was there a tree of any other kind. Then the monks reached the harbor. The man of God left the boat and began to walk around the island. There was a fragrant odor on the island, just like the smell of pomegranates pervading a house. The monks remained in the boat to wait for St. Brendan's return. Meanwhile they caught the scent of this sweetest fragrance and almost forgot their fast. Brendan discovered six springs surrounded by a thick growth of green plants and vegetables of various types. He returned to his brothers, carrying with him the first fruits of the island's produce, and said: "Leave the boat, put up the tent, and refresh yourselves with the wonderful fruits of this land, which God has shown to us." For forty days they lived on the grapes and plants and vegetables from the springs. And then they returned to the boat, taking with them as much as their craft could hold.

Once on the boat, they set sail and drove before the wind. As they made their way, they saw a bird in the distance, known as the gryphon, flying in their direction.[20] The monks said to the holy father: "This creature is coming to eat us up." But St. Brendan replied: "Do not be afraid. God is our helper, and he shall save us this time too." As the bird stretched out its talons to seize the monks, the other bird that had brought them the branch of grapes suddenly swooped down upon the gryphon, which immediately tried to devour it. But the other bird defended itself successfully and tore out the eyes of the gryphon, which then flew upward until the monks could hardly see it. It pursued the gryphon and finally killed it. The carcass fell into the sea near their boat, and the other bird returned from whence it came.

It was many days before St. Brendan and his mariners glimpsed the island of the Community of St. Ailbe. He celebrated Christmas there with his brothers. When the feast was over, the venerable father received the blessing of the abbot and his monks and sailed the ocean for a long time, until the feasts of Easter and Christmas returned, which they spent at the places already mentioned.

On one occasion, when St. Brendan had celebrated the feast of St. Peter the Apostle on board the boat, the sea was so clear that they could see right down into it. In the depths they saw various kinds of creatures lying on the seabed. They seemed close enough to touch, so clear was the sea. They were like flocks at pasture, and there were so many of them, lying head to tail, that they looked like a city on the march.[21] The monks asked the venerable father to celebrate Mass silently in case the creatures should hear them and rise up to attack them. But the holy father smiled and said to them: "I am amazed at your foolishness. Why are you afraid of these animals when you were not afraid of the monarch of the deep, who devours all the creatures of the sea, but sat many times on his back, singing Psalms? You even gathered sticks, lit a fire, and cooked meat. Why then are you afraid of these? Surely our Lord Jesus Christ is God of all these creatures, and can subdue them all?"

When he had said this, he began to sing at the top of his voice. Meanwhile his brothers continued to watch the sea creatures which, when they heard his voice, rose up from the seabed and began to swim around the boat so that these same creatures were all the monks could see about them. They did not approach the boat but swam to and fro some distance away until the man of God had completed his Mass. Then all the creatures vanished from sight, turning tail in all directions along the many paths of the sea. Then for eight days, with a favorable wind and sail extended, St. Brendan journeyed across the crystal-clear sea.

One day, when they had celebrated their Masses, they saw a column rising up out of the sea which seemed not to be far from them. But still it took them three days to reach it. When they drew near, the man of God looked up at the highest point of the column but could hardly see it on account of its great height. It was higher even than the sky. The column was wrapped in a wide-meshed net. Indeed, the mesh was so wide that the boat could pass right through it, but no one could tell what it was made of. It was silver-colored, but seemed to them to be harder than marble. The column was of the clearest crystal.[22]

St. Brendan said to his brothers: "Ship the oars, lower the mast and sail, while some of you hold back the meshes of the net." It was so vast that it extended for almost a mile on all sides from the column and plunged down a similar distance into the sea. When they had done this, the man of God said to them: "Steer the boat in through any of the openings so that we can see for ourselves the wonders of our Creator." They entered and looked this way and that, and the sea seemed to them as clear as glass so that they could see all that moved beneath it. They could view the foundations of the column below and yet see the top of the column reflected on the surface of the sea. The sun shone as brightly within as it did outside.

St. Brendan measured four sides of the opening of the net and found it to be some six feet long on all sides. They spent the whole day sailing along one side of the column and, despite its shade, could still feel the sun's rays even until three o'clock. This was how the man of God measured the dimensions of all four sides, over the course of four days, finding that each was just over two thousand feet long.

On the fourth day they discovered a chalice made of the same substance as the covering, together with a paten that was of an identical color to the column; both were lying in a reveal on the southern side. Brendan immediately picked these objects up and said: "It is our Lord Jesus Christ who has shown us this miracle, and these gifts have been given so that many others may believe my words." He ordered his brothers to sing the Divine Office and then to take some food, for they had not found the time to eat or drink since catching sight of the column.

When dawn came the monks set out northward. As they passed through an opening, some monks raised the mast and sail as others held open the mesh of the covering. When all was ready, a favorable wind sprang up so that there was nothing they had to do but manage the sail and the steering. Thus they sailed for eight days in a northerly direction.

On the eighth day they saw an island nearby, which was very rocky and bare, with neither trees nor grass, and covered in slag heaps and forges. The venerable father said to his brothers: "Truly, brothers, this island frightens me. I do not want to visit it or even to approach it, but the wind is driving us straight in that direction." When they had advanced just a little, no more than a stone's throw, they could hear the heaving of bellows like the sound of thunder and the pounding of hammers against iron and anvil.[23] As these sounds reached his ears, the venerable father made the sign of the victory of the Lord in all four directions and said: "Lord Jesus Christ, deliver us from this island."

When the man of God had spoken, one of the inhabitants of the island emerged, as if going about some task outside. His hair was shaggy and his face was both fiery and dark. When he saw the servants of God passing by the island, he went back into the forge. The man of God crossed himself again and said to his brothers: "My sons, raise the sail higher and row as hard as you can, so that we can escape this island." No sooner had he said this than the savage rushed down to the facing shore carrying a massive and fiery piece of smouldering slag in a pair of tongs, which he immediately threw at the servants of God. It did not harm them, but passed over their heads and landed two hundred yards beyond them. Where it entered the sea, the water began to boil as if there were a volcano there, with smoke rising from the sea as if from a flaming furnace.

But when the man of God had put almost a mile between them and the place where the piece of slag had fallen, all the inhabitants of the island ran down to the shore, each carrying yet more pieces. Some tossed them at the servants of God, the one throwing his piece over the other. They ran back to their forges, setting them on fire, and soon it appeared as if the whole island was one big furnace while the sea boiled like a cooking pot full of meat when plied well with glowing rocks.[24] And all day long they could hear the sound of loud wailing on the island. Even when the island was no longer in sight, the wailing of its inhabitants still reached their ears and the stench of the island still filled their nostrils. Then the holy father encouraged his brothers with these words: "O soldiers of Christ, be firm in your true faith and arm yourselves with spiritual weapons since we are on the very edge of hell. Remain vigilant and act courageously."

On another day there appeared a high mountain to the north before them which seemed to be swathed in thin clouds but which, from a closer view, turned out to be smoke rising from its summit. The wind impelled them quickly toward this same island until the boat was standing just off the shore. The cliffs were so high that they could hardly see the summit; they were as black as coal and amazingly sheer, like a wall.

One monk, who was one of the three who had followed Brendan from the monastery, leapt from the boat and walked to the foot of the cliff. Then he began to shout, saying: "I am being dragged away from you, father, and cannot return to you." The monks immediately drew the boat away from the shore and appealed to the Lord with a cry: "Have pity on us, O Lord, have pity on us." Then the venerable father with his companions saw how the poor man was dragged off to torments by a host of demons and how he was consumed by fire, and he said: "Alas, my son, that you have met the end you deserved while still living."

Again a fair wind took them in a southerly direction. But when they looked back from afar at that island, they saw the mountain emerge from the smoke, spewing flames high into the air and sucking them back in again so that the whole mountain burned like a pyre, right down to the sea.

When St. Brendan had sailed southward for seven days, they saw a shape in the sea, like that of a man sitting on a rock. From a distance the sail that was suspended between two uprights seemed like a cloak. The object was being tossed around by the waves like a boat caught in a hurricane. Some of the monks said that it was a bird and others a ship. When the man of God heard them saying these things among themselves, he said: "Stop arguing. Let us sail the boat in that direction."

When the man of God drew near, the waves formed a circle, as if turned solid, to keep them out, and they found a shaggy and disfigured man squatting on a rock. The waves rushed toward him from all sides, crashing over his head, then left the bare rock exposed as they receded, on which the wretched man was sitting. The sheet of cloth, which was hanging in front of him, would billow out one moment and would beat him about the eyes and head the next.[25]

Blessed Brendan began to ask him who he was and what he had done to be sent to that place and to deserve such a penance.

He replied: "I am Judas, most wretched, and the greatest traitor. I am here not on account of my own merits but because of the mysterious mercy of Jesus Christ. For me this is not a place of torment but rather a place of respite granted me by the Savior in honor of his Resurrection." It was the Lord's own day. "It seems to me when I sit here that I am in the Garden of Delights in comparison with the agonies which I know I shall suffer this evening. For I burn like molten lead in a crucible day and night at the heart of the mountain which you see, where Leviathan lives with his companions. I was there when that brother of yours was devoured; the mountain was so delighted that it spat out huge flames, as it always does when it consumes the souls of the wicked. I have a respite here every Sunday from first to second vespers, from Christmas until Epiphany, from Easter until Pentecost, and on the Feast of the Purification and the Assumption of the Mother of God. The rest of the year I am tortured in the depths of hell with Herod and Pilate, Annas and Caiaphas. Therefore I beseech you by the Savior of the world to be kind enough to intercede for me with the Lord Jesus Christ that I may be allowed to remain here until sunset tomorrow and that the devils may not torment me, seeing your arrival here, and drag me off to the hideous destiny which I purchased with so terrible a price." St. Brendan replied: "The Lord's will be done. You shall not be consumed by devils tonight until dawn."

Again the man of God asked him: "But what is the purpose of that cloth?" "I once gave this cloth to a leper when I was chamberlain of the Lord. But it was not my cloth that I gave; it actually belonged to the Lord and to his brothers. Therefore it gives me no protection but is rather a great hindrance. The metal uprights from which the cloth is suspended are the ones I gave to the priests of the temple to hang their cooking pots on. The rock on which I sit is the one with which I filled the trench beneath the feet of passers-by on the public highway before I was a disciple of the Lord."

As soon as the evening closed in, a great host of demons began to wheel over the face of the deep, screeching: "Move away, man of God, since we cannot draw near to our friend until you withdraw and we dare not face our prince without him. You have stolen our tidbit from us. Do not stand in our way tonight." The man of God replied: "I do not defend him, but our Lord Jesus Christ has allowed him to remain here until morning." "How can you use the name of the Lord in the presence of the one who betrayed him?" "I command you in the name of our Lord Jesus Christ not to lay hand on him until tomorrow."

When the night was over and the man of God was preparing to set out on his journey again in the early morning, an innumerable host of demons covered the face of the deep, emitting hideous yells: "Man of God, a curse on your going out and your coming in. All night long our prince lashed us most severely for not bringing him this damned prisoner." The man of God replied: "Your curses do not fall upon us but upon yourselves, for whoever you curse is blessed and whoever you bless is cursed." The demons said: "For the next six days the unfortunate Judas shall suffer twice as many torments just because you have defended him this night," but the venerable father replied: "Neither you nor your prince has the authority to do this; God alone has that power. Therefore I command you and your prince in the name of our Lord Jesus Christ not to inflict any more suffering upon him than before." "So you are the Lord of all, are you, that we should obey your words?" the demons asked, to which the man of God replied: "I am his servant, and can command in his name by the power that he has invested in me." The demons followed Brendan until Judas was out of sight, and then returned and snatched up his wretched soul with a great howl and cry.

St. Brendan sailed southward with his companions, glorifying God in all things. On the third day they caught sight of a small island far to the south. As his monks began to pull more strongly toward the island, St. Brendan said to them: "Do not exhaust yourselves, men, too quickly. There is work enough ahead. The coming Easter will soon mark the seventh anniversary of our departure from our native land. Soon you will see Paul, a holy hermit, who has lived on this island without anything to eat for sixty years.[26] For thirty years before that an animal used to bring him food."

But when they approached the shore, they found access difficult due to the high cliffs. The island itself was small and very round, some hundred yards across. There was no soil higher up on its surface, only bare rock like flint. It was as long and broad as it was high. They sailed around the island until they found a narrow harbor, scarcely wide enough to take the prow of the ship, and a difficult ascent. Then St. Brendan said to his brothers: "Wait here until I return to you. You should not enter this place without the permission of the man of God who dwells here."

The venerable father reached the summit of the island where he saw two caves facing each other on the eastern side, and a spring of water gushing from the rock in front of the cave in which the soldier of Christ was sitting. The water that sprang up was immediately absorbed again by the rock. As St. Brendan approached the mouth of one cave, the old man emerged from the other and came to meet him, saying: "Behold how good and joyful it is when brothers dwell together in unity" (Ps 132:1).

Paul told Brendan to call all the monks up from the boat. He kissed each one in turn and addressed them all by their own names. As they listened to him, the monks marveled not only at his foreknowledge but also at his appearance, for he was covered from head to foot with his own hair, which was snow white with age. His face and eyes were all that was visible of him. He wore no clothing at all except his own body hair. But when he saw this, Brendan was saddened within himself and said: "How ashamed am I who bear responsibility for many monks in our order that I wear a monk's habit when I see this mortal man living like an angel and untouched by the vices of the flesh." The man of God replied: "Venerable father, God has revealed to you such varied marvels and in such abundance, which he has shown to none of the holy fathers. And yet you say in your heart that you are not worthy to wear the monk's habit, although you are greater than any monk. A monk has to feed and clothe himself by the work of his own hands, but for seven years God has fed and clothed your family of monks by his mysteries. I, a poor man, sit here like a bird on my rock, clothed only by my hair."

Then St. Brendan questioned him about his arrival there, where he had come from, and for how long he had led this way of life. The latter replied: "For fifty years I lived in the monastery of St. Patrick, where I maintained the cemetery. One day the prior told me to dig a grave for a dead man in a certain spot, and an old man, whom I did not recognize, appeared to me and said: 'Do not dig the ground there, brother, since that will be the burial place for someone else.' 'Who are you, father?' I asked. 'Why do you not know me? Am I not your abbot?' 'St. Patrick is my abbot,' I said, to which he replied: 'I am he. Yesterday I passed from this world, and this is to be the place of my burial. Dig the brother's grave over there, and tell no one what I have told you. Go down to the shore tomorrow and you will find a small boat there. Climb into it, and it shall take you to the place where you are to wait for the day of your own death.'

"Early the next morning I did as the holy father said and went down to the shore where I found a boat just as he had predicted. I climbed into it and sailed for three days and three nights. Then I gave the boat to the wind and went wherever it took me. On the seventh day I saw this island and immediately landed on it, pushing the boat away with my foot, which returned from whence it came. I watched it cut a swift passage through the waves back to its own land. And I remained here. At about three o'clock in the afternoon a sea otter would bring me food from the sea walking on its hind legs, carrying a fish in its jaws and with a bundle of twigs for making a fire between its front legs.[27] When it had placed before me the fish and the twigs, it returned to the sea. I lit a fire with flint and iron and prepared a meal from the fish. This continued for thirty years with the otter bringing me food, a fish, every three days. I ate a third of the fish each day and, thanks be to God, never suffered thirst for every Sunday a trickle of water flowed from that rock from which I could drink and fill my flask for the rest of the week. Then, after thirty years, I found these two caves and this spring. From then on I lived for sixty years, as I still do, from spring water and nothing else. I have been on this island therefore for ninety years, for thirty years living on fish and for sixty living on the water from this spring, and I did not leave my homeland until I was fifty. And so I am now one hundred and forty years old. And here I must soon expect the Day of Judgment in my mortal flesh. Depart now for your homeland and take with you flasks filled with water from this spring. You will need it, for you still have a journey of forty days ahead of you, that is until Holy Saturday. You will celebrate Holy Saturday, Easter Sunday, and the Easter octave where you have celebrated them for the last six years and then, when your steward has blessed you, you will travel to the Promised Land of the Saints. You will remain there for forty days, and then the God of your fathers will bring you back, safe and sound, to the land of your birth."

When St. Brendan and all his monks had received the blessing of the man of God, they set off in a southerly direction and sailed for the whole of Lent, being blown this way and that in their little boat. Their only nourishment was the water which they had brought with them from the island of the man of God, but a single drink every three days satisfied them completely, quenching all their hunger and thirst.

Then, as the man of God had predicted, they arrived at the island where they had left the steward on Holy Saturday. As they entered the harbor, he came running to meet them with great jubilation and even lifted them one by one from the boat with his own arms. When they had sung the Office of that holy day, he placed a meal before them and then, when evening came, they all boarded the boat again, the steward traveling with them.

As they sailed they immediately came across the sea monster again in the usual place, and sang praises to God through the night and celebrated their morning Masses on the monster's back. When the last Mass was over, Jasconius began to swim away and all the monks who were with Brendan began to cry out to God, saying: "Hear us, O God of our salvation. You are the hope of all the ends of the earth and of the distant sea" (Ps 64:6). St. Brendan encouraged his brothers with the words: "Do not be afraid. No harm will befall you, but you will arrive at your destination more quickly." The monster made directly for the shore of the Island of Birds. There they remained until the octave of Pentecost. When the solemnities were over, the steward who had accompanied them said to St. Brendan: "Fill your flasks from this spring and return to the boat. This time I shall be your companion and shall guide you, for without my help you will never find the Promised Land of the Saints." As they climbed into the boat, all the birds of the island sang out in one voice: "May the God of our salvation grant you a safe and speedy journey."

St. Brendan and his companions took the steward to his island where they boarded provisions for forty days for the journey ahead. The steward himself led the way and guided their path. When forty days had passed, evening came and enveloped them in a gloom so great that they could scarcely see one another. The steward said to St. Brendan: "Do you know what this fog is?" "What is it?" Brendan asked. "It surrounds that island which you have been seeking for seven years." And then, after an hour had passed, they were again bathed in an intense light, and they found their boat standing off the shore.

As they left the boat, they saw open land stretching out before them covered with trees laden with autumnal fruit. They walked all around the island, but night did not fall. They ate as much fruit as they wished and drank from the springs, and so for forty days they wandered across the whole land, without ever coming to the farther shore. One day they came upon an immense river which flowed through the middle of the island. Then St. Brendan said to his brothers: "We cannot cross this river, and we do not know the size of this land." But while he was reflecting upon this, a young man came toward them and greeted them joyfully with a kiss. He called each one by name and said: "Blessed are they that dwell in your house, O Lord. They shall praise you forever and ever" (Ps 83:5).

Then he said to St. Brendan: "This is the land which you have sought for so long. You were not able to find it immediately because God wished to show you his many wonders in the great ocean. Return now to the land of your birth, taking with you fruit from this land and as many gems as your boat can carry. The day of your final journey is approaching, when you shall sleep with your fathers. After the passage of many years, this land will be revealed to your successors when Christians will be suffering persecution. This river which you see divides the island into two halves, and you can see nothing but ripened fruit, which is how it remains all the year round, with no shadow of night, for Christ himself is our light."

They gathered fruit and all kinds of precious stones, and when they had received the blessing of the steward and of the young man, St. Brendan and his monks climbed into the boat and began to sail out into the heart of the gloom. When they had passed through this, they came to the isle which is called the Island of Delights. There they were entertained for three days until, after receiving another blessing, St. Brendan returned directly to his homeland.

Brendan's community welcomed him back with great rejoicing, glorifying God for not wishing to deprive them any longer of their father who had been away from them for so long. Then the saintly man, reciprocating their love, gave an account of all that had happened on his journey and all the wonders that God had deigned to show him. Finally he made known to them the prophecy of the young man in the Promised Land of the Saints, assuring them that he would shortly depart this life. Events proved him right for when he had put all his affairs in order and had been strengthened by the sacraments of God, he soon gave up his spirit as he lay in his disciples' arms, and passed over to the Lord, to whom be honor and glory for ever and ever. Amen.

4. THE LIFE OF ST. DAVID BY RHIGYFARCH

lthough our Lord loved and knew his own before creating the world, still there are some whom he makes known with many signs and revelations. And so that saint who was baptized David, but who is known as Dewi by the common people, was not only foretold by the true prophecies of angels, thirty years before he was born, first to his father and then to St. Patrick, but was also proclaimed as one endowed with secret gifts and blessings. For, on a certain occasion, his father, Sanctus by name and merits, who exercised royal power over the people of Ceredigion (which he later laid down for the sake of a heavenly kingdom), heard in a dream the voice of an angel warning him: "Tomorrow you will awake and go hunting, and when you have killed a stag near the river, you will find three gifts, namely the stag that you will pursue, a fish, and a hive of bees. Of these three you will set aside the honeycomb and part of the fish and stag, which you will send to Maucannus's monastery (which is still known as the Monastery of the Deposit) to be kept for your son who will be born to you."[1] These three gifts predict his life. The honeycomb declares his wisdom, for just as the honey lies embedded in the wax, he has perceived the spiritual meaning in a literal statement.[2] The fish declares his life of self-denial, for as the fish lives by water, he rejected wine and cider and everything intoxicating, and led a blessed life for God on bread and water only; for which reason he has been called "David the water-drinker." The stag signifies his power over the ancient serpent, for just as the stag, when it has fed on serpents, longs for a spring of water and is refreshed with renewed strength as if by youth, so he too, standing on the heights as with a stag's feet, deprived the ancient serpent of the human race of its power to injure him, and chose the spring of life with an unceasing flow of tears and was renewed day by day. Thus in the name of the Holy Trinity and by the abstinence of purer food, he acquired the saving knowledge of how to overcome demons.

Later Patrick, who was learned in the Roman arts and who possessed a host of virtues, was made bishop and went in search of the people among whom he had been exiled. There, by refurbishing the lamp of fruitful endeavor with the oil of double charity through unflagging effort, and then desiring not to place it under a meal tub but on a lampstand so that it might shine out to all to the glory of the Father of all (cf. Mt 5:15), he came to the country of the people of Ceredigion. He remained there a short time and then entered the land of Dyfed. He crossed this and finally reaching a place called Rosina Vallis and seeing that it was a pleasing place, he vowed to serve God there. But when he was pondering this in his mind, an angel of the Lord appeared to him and said: "Not to you has God assigned this place, but to a son who is not yet born, and will not be born until thirty years have passed."[3] Patrick was grieved and bewildered when he heard this, and turning it over in his heart, he said: "Since in the sight of my Lord my work is made fruitless, and one not yet born is set above me, I will depart and from this time on not submit myself to such labor." As he thought upon this, he received from the angel soothing words of comfort: "That shall not be; the Lord has appointed you leader in the island of the Irish. It has not yet received the word of life. It is there that you must serve, and there the Lord has prepared a seat for you. You shall be radiant with signs and virtues, and you shall bring the whole nation into subjection to God. I will be with you; and let this be a sign to you. I shall show you the whole island: The mountains shall be moved, the sea shall be brought low, and your gaze, raised above everything and looking out from this place, shall see the promised land." This said, Patrick raised his eyes and from the place where he stood, which is now known as Patrick's seat, he surveyed the whole island.[4] Straightaway, when everything was prepared, he sought a ship; and after he had raised to life a man who had died twelve years previously, he entered the promised land. As for the rest of his life, it is written in the literature of Ireland, where anyone who wishes shall find it.

Thirty years passed and Sanctus, who was king of the people of Ceredigion, departed for Dyfed and, while passing through it, chanced on a girl called Nonita, who was exceedingly beautiful and modest. The king, who was filled with desire, violated her. She for her part knew no man either before or after but continuing in chastity of mind and body, led a most faithful life, for from the time of her conceiving she lived on bread and water alone. There, in that very place where she was violated, and where she conceived, was a small meadow, pleasing to the eye and, by grace, covered with heavenly dew.[5] In that meadow there also appeared two large stones, one at her head and one at her foot, which had not been seen before, for the earth, rejoicing at the conception, opened its bosom in order both to preserve the girl's modesty and as a sign of the importance of her child.

The mother, as her womb grew, followed the usual custom and entered a church in order to offer alms and oblations for the child's birth; and here a certain teacher was preaching the Word to the people. As the mother entered, he was suddenly struck dumb, as if by an obstruction in his throat. When he was asked by the people why he had interrupted his sermon and fallen silent, he replied: "I can talk to you in ordinary conversation, but cannot preach to you. Go outside, and I shall remain here alone to see if I shall then be able to preach." The people went outside while the mother concealed herself and hid in a corner. She did not disobey the command but remained on account of the great thirst she felt for the commandments of life and to prove the privilege of so great a child. Then although he strove with all his heart, he could again do nothing, as if he were prevented by heaven. Terrified by this, he cried out with a loud voice: "I beg anyone who may be hiding from me to reveal themselves and to make themselves known." Then she answered: "Here I am, hiding." Under divine guidance he said: "Go out and let the people come back into the church." As soon as this was done, he preached as usual with a fluent tongue. The mother confessed, when she was asked, that she was pregnant. It was quite clear to all that she was about to bring into the world a child who would excel all the learned men of Britain with the privilege of his honor, the splendor of his wisdom, and the eloquence of his speech.[6] This was borne out by the subsequent merits of his life.

Meanwhile, there lived a certain ruler nearby who learned from the prophecies of his magicians that a boy would be born within his kingdom whose power would extend over the whole country (cf. Mt 2). This man, his mind set only on earthly things in which he found his highest good, was tormented by a great hatred and jealousy. And so, discovering from the oracles of the magicians where the boy was later born, he said: "Let me keep watch over that site on my own for so many days, and whoever I find resting there, even for only a short while, shall fall, struck down by my sword." The nine months came around, as had been preordained, and the time for the birth drew near. One day the mother went out along that very same road which led to the place of the birth, where the tyrant kept watch in accordance with the prophecies of his magicians. Driven on by her approaching time, the mother sought the place prophesied. But on that same day there was such turbulence of the air, with such great flashes of lightning and terrifying crash of thunder and so excessive a downpour of hail and rain, that no one could even go outdoors. But the place where the mother groaned in labor was bathed with so clear a light that it shone in God's presence, as if lit by the sun behind the clouds. During the birth the mother had a certain stone near her on which she pressed with her hands when the pain came upon her. The marks of her hands, as though impressed on wax, have identified that stone for those who have gazed upon it; it split down the middle in sympathy with the mother in her pains. On that spot a church was built, and in the foundations of its altar this stone lies concealed.[7]

He was then baptized by Ailbe, a bishop of the Munstermen; and he opened the eyes of blind Movi, who held him under the water, and whose own eyes were splashed with water, revealing to him the light of day which he had never known.[8] In that same place there suddenly appeared a spring of very clear water, bursting forth to serve for the ministration of baptism. The boy was reared in the place that is called the Ancient Blackberry Bush and he grew up full of grace and of pleasing appearance. There he was taught to read and write and learned the rites of the church; and his fellow pupils saw a dove teaching him and singing hymns with him. But as time went by, his virtues and merits increased, and keeping his body free from a wife's embraces, he was ordained and raised to the dignity of a priest. He then left that place and went to Paulinus, a disciple of Germanus and a teacher, who led a life pleasing to God on an island in Wincdilantquendi.[9] Now it so happened that the same Paulinus was at that time troubled with his eyes (holy Dewi remained there many years, reading and assimilating what he had read), and it was arranged that the disciples should assemble and, as their master called them, should individually bless his eyes, making the sign of the cross upon them, so that he should be healed by their prayer and blessing. After the other pupils had risen in turn to touch the master's eyes, making the sign of the cross upon them, holy Dewi was asked to touch the master's eyes. But he said in reply: "I have not yet looked upon my master's face. I have been here reading with him for ten years, but I do not know his face." Overwhelmed by shyness and modesty, he had avoided looking upon his master's face. His master then said to him: "Raise your right hand and touch my eyes without looking, and I shall be healed." When this was done, the light of day was clearly revealed to him. The darkness banished from his eyes, the master received the lofty light. They then thanked God, and holy Dewi was indeed praised and blessed by each one of them. Not long after an angel appeared to Paulinus and said: "It is time that Dewi, who has doubled his talents by putting them to good use (cf. Mt 25:17), should not bury the talent of wisdom entrusted to him in the earth and become sluggish with the slow torpor of indolence but should add to his Lord's money, which he has received, by a greater increase in profit, so that, established in the joy of his Lord, he may gather in and collect the sheaves of the harvest of souls into the heavenly granaries of eternal bliss." How many seeds of wheat did he sow and plow in with the plowshare of exhortation, then gathering in the fruit of an abundant harvest, sometimes a hundredfold, sometimes sixtyfold, and sometimes thirtyfold (cf. Mt 13:23). For he did not plow with a strong ox and a weak ass together (cf. Dt 22:10), but gave to some the strong bread of life and to others the milk of godly encouragement. He gathered some within the precincts of monastic communities but warned others with a different kind of instruction, who walked along the broader road of life, in order to wean them from the slippery desires of worldly delights. He became all things to all people. He founded in all twelve monasteries. First he reached Glastonbury and built a church; next Bath, where he made the deadly water health-giving by blessing it, making it suitable for the bathing of bodies and endowing it with an unfailing warmth. Then came Crowland and Repton, Colva and Glascwm; from here he founded the monastery of Leominster, then Raglan in the region of Gwent; afterward the monastery of Llangyvelech in which he later received the altar sent to him. He also cured Proprius, King of Erging, by restoring sight to his eyes. These he founded in the usual way, distributing to each the articles required by canonical order and laying down the rules of monastic conduct; he then returned to the place from where he had set out. There lived Bishop Guisdianus, an uncle of his. As they were cheering each other with godly conversation, holy Dewi said: "My angel companion has told me: 'From the place where you intend to serve, hardly one in a hundred shall receive their heavenly reward. But there is another place nearby where scarcely one of those buried in the cemetery in the saving faith shall pay the penalties of hell.'"

One day there came to him three of his most faithful disciples, that is Aidan, Eliud, and Ismael, together with a crowd of fellow disciples. Of one mind and heart, they went to the place which had been foretold by the angel. When they had lit a fire in the name of God, the smoke rose up to the heights and seemed to engulf the whole island, and even Ireland itself. But a certain man called Baia, who lived nearby and was sitting within the walls of his fortress, saw the sun's rays grow dim everywhere and he began to falter and to tremble at such a portent. He was so angered by this that forgetting his meal, he passed the whole day with a heavy heart. His wife approached him and asked why he had forgotten his food contrary to his normal custom. "Why are you so upset and bemused," she asked, "brooding by yourself?" "I have been disturbed by the sight of this smoke rising from Rosina Vallis, which has engulfed the whole land, for I am convinced that he who lit that fire will surpass all in power and glory. As if by some omen, this smoke predicts his fame." His wife said to him: "Rise up, take the band of slaves, and with swords drawn attack these men who have dared to do such a wicked thing, and kill them all." He did so, and his companions set out with evil intent but were struck down with fever and sapped of their strength. But although their strength had gone, they assaulted the men with the filthiest and most blasphemous taunts; for they did not lack the will to do them harm, even if the means to accomplish it had been drained from them, thwarted by the eternal power. As they returned home, they met Baia's wife coming to meet them. She said: "Our cattle have all died suddenly. Let us turn back and beg for mercy on bended knees, showing respect to God's servant so that he may thus take pity on us and on our cattle." Retracing their steps, they approached the man of God and asked for mercy with tears and prayers: "The land upon which you stand shall be yours forever."[10] The servant of God answered kindly: "Your cattle shall come to life again"; and they found that it was as he said.

On another day, his wife, inflamed with jealousy, called her maids together and said: "Go and deport yourselves with naked bodies in front of the monks, using crude words." The maids obeyed, playing lewd games, imitating sexual intercourse, and displaying love's seductive embraces. They drew the minds of some of the monks toward desire, while to others they were an annoyance. The monks sought to leave the place. But the holy father, steadfast with long-suffering patience and whose spirit could not be undermined or corrupted by riches, nor intimidated and exhausted by adversity, said to them: "You know that the world hates you, but now know that the people of Israel, accompanied by the Ark of the Covenant, entered the Promised Land, worn down by the continual dangers of battles but not defeated, and destroyed the uncircumcised people who lived there and held it their own. That struggle is a clear sign of our own victory. For they who seek a promised heavenly homeland must be exhausted by adversities but not overcome and, with Christ as their ally, must finally conquer the impure blemish of their sins. We must not be overcome by evil, then, but must overcome evil with good because, if Christ is for us, who can be against us? Be strong therefore and invincible in the struggle, in case your enemy should rejoice in your flight. We must stand fast; it is Baia who must give way." With these words he strengthened the resolve of his disciples. The next day this same wife slew her innocent stepdaughter (on the site of whose martyrdom a health-giving spring issued forth) and, having become mad, was nowhere to be found. Baia perished, struck down by an enemy who took him by surprise, while his fortress was burned down and gutted by fire sent from heaven. It was fitting that the man who had threatened the man of God with death by the sword should suffer the same fate, and that he who showed no mercy toward God's servants should himself have been punished without mercy.

Now that the malice of enemies had been repelled by the favor of God, the monastic community built in the Lord's name a fine monastery in the place that the angel had previously shown them. When this was finished, the holy father decreed such austerity in his zeal for the monastic ideal that every monk toiled at his daily work and spent his life in manual labor for the good of the community.[11] "For whoever does not work," says the Apostle, "let him not eat" (2 Thes 3:10). Knowing that leisure was the source and mother of vices, he burdened the shoulders of his monks with godly tasks, for those who bow their heads and minds in leisurely repose give birth to the unstable spirit of apathy and to the restless promptings of desire.[12] Thus they work with feet and hands with more eager fervor. They place the yoke upon their shoulders and are unflagging as they dig the ground with mattocks and spades; they carry in their holy hands hoes and saws for cutting, and by their own efforts provide for all the requirements of the community. They scorn possessions, reject the gifts of the wicked, and despise wealth. They use no oxen for plowing; each one is his own ox and his own wealth both to himself and to his brothers. When the work was done, no complaint was heard, and there was no conversation beyond what was strictly necessary, but everyone carried out their allotted task mindfully or with prayer. When the labor in the fields was done, they would return to the cloisters of the monastery and would pass the rest of the day until vespers reading, writing, or praying. When evening came and the bell was rung, everyone left what they were doing. Even if someone heard the bell when they had only just begun a character, or had only half completed it, he would quickly rise and leave his work, making his way silently to the church without any idle chatter. When they had sung the Psalms, in unity of heart and voice, they devoutly remained on bended knees until the appearance of the stars in the heavens marked the close of day.[13] When the others had left, David alone remained to pour forth secret prayers for the state of the church. Finally they gathered at the table and refreshed their tired limbs with their supper, though not too much, for an excess even of bread fosters self-indulgence; but at that meal, each took his food according to the condition of his body and age. They did not serve dishes of various flavors, nor the finer kinds of food; but bread and vegetables seasoned with salt is their fare and they quench their thirst with a temperate kind of drink. For the infirm, the elderly, and those wearied by traveling, however, they provide more appetizing dishes, since it is not right to give equal measures to all. When they have given thanks to God, they go to the church in accordance with canonical rule and devote themselves to vigils, prayers, and genuflections for around three hours. While at prayer in the church, no one was so bold as to yawn, sneeze, or spit. When this is over, they prepare for sleep. Rising at cock crow, they apply themselves to prayer and to genuflections and spend the rest of the night till morning without sleep, serving throughout the other nights in a similar way. From Saturday evening until break of day at the first hour of Sunday, they devote themselves to vigils, prayers, and genuflections, except for one hour after matins on Saturday. They make known their thoughts to the father, and even seek his permission to answer the call of nature. They have all things in common, with no "mine" or "yours," for if anyone were to say "my book" or "my anything else," he would be immediately subjected to a severe penance. Their clothing was humble, mostly skins. They offered unfailing obedience to the father's command, carrying out their duties with great perseverance and maintaining uprightness in all things.

Whoever desired this saintly way of life and sought to enter the company of the brethren had first to remain for ten days outside the doors of the monastery, as if rejected and reduced to silence by words of abuse. If he exercised patience and stood there until the tenth day, he was first admitted and put to serve under the elder who had charge of the gate. When he had labored there for a good while, and resistance in his soul had been broken down, he was finally judged to be ready to enter the company of the brethren. They possessed nothing in excess, but loved poverty by their own free will, for the father would not take for the monastery any of the property (which he renounced when leaving the world), not even a single penny, from a man who desired their way of life; but he was received naked, as if escaping from a shipwreck, in case he should raise himself above his brethren in any way or refuse his equal share of labor on grounds of his wealth or, in the event that he cast aside his monastic habit, seize by force what he had left to the monastery, and thus turn his brothers' patience into anger. But the father himself, overflowing with daily fountains of tears, fragrant with the sweet-smelling offerings of prayers and burning with the fire of a twofold love, consecrated with pure hands the due oblation of the Lord's body. After matins he proceeded alone to commune with the angels, and then immediately sought out cold water where he remained for a sufficient length of time to quell the ardor of the flesh. He spent all day, one after another, steadfastly and untiringly teaching, praying, and kneeling, and caring for his brethren, as well as feeding a host of orphans, wards, widows, the poor, the sick, the weak, and pilgrims. This is how he began, continued, and ended. The brevity of this summary does not allow us to expound upon the remaining aspects of his rigorous discipline, although a necessary ideal for imitation. But he imitated the monks of Egypt, and lived a life like theirs. When they heard report of his good reputation, kings and princes of the world left their kingdoms and sought out his monastery. Hence it happened that Constantine, King of Cornwall, left his kingdom and bent his proud and hitherto unbowed head in humble obedience in this father's cell. There he lived long in faithful submission until finally he departed for another land far away and built a monastery there. But since we have said enough about his way of life, let us return to the theme of his miracles.

One day the brothers gathered together and complained: "In this place there is running water, but in summer there is hardly a trickle." When he heard this, the holy father set out for the place nearby where the angel spoke to him. There he prayed long and hard with his eyes raised to heaven, petitioning for the greatly needed water. As he was praying, a spring of sweetest water gushed forth, and because vines did not grow in that land, it was turned into wine for the celebrating of the sacrament of the Lord's body. But we know also of other springs of fresh water which were bestowed by disciples, in imitation of the father, and which have proved both useful and beneficial for health.

It also happened one day that a certain countryman by the name of Terdi begged his kindly help with much pleading, saying "There is no more water left in our land, and our life is full of labor because we have to fetch water from a distant river." The holy father sympathized with the needs of his neighbors and applied himself in humility, believing that he could find water by the prayers and entreaty of the request and by his own humble compassion. He went out and made a hole in the ground with the tip of his staff, and a spring of the clearest water gushed out, which bubbled forth continuously and gave very cold water even in hot weather.

On another occasion, when holy Aidan, one of his disciples, happened to be reading a book outside in order to confirm the meaning of a doctrine, the prior of the monastery appeared and commanded him to fetch wood from the valley and to take two oxen, for the forest was a long way off. Aidan, the disciple, hastened to the forest without even pausing to close his book, so eager was he to obey the command. When the wood had been prepared and the oxen harnessed, he set off back. Now the road led to an abrupt precipice overhanging the sea. When the cart reached the precipice, it fell headlong toward the sea, taking the oxen with it. But he made the sign of the cross over them as they fell, and thus was able to retrieve them safe and sound from the waves, together with the cart, and joyfully set out again. As he continued his journey, however, there was such a cloudburst that the ditches were flooded. When he arrived back and released the oxen from their labor, he went to where he had left his book and found that the rain had not harmed it, although it had been left open. When the brethren learned of this, they praised both the graciousness of the father and the humility of the disciple equally, for the graciousness of the father revealed the book untouched by the rain and preserved for the obedient disciple, while the humility of the disciple preserved the oxen safely for the father.[14]

Now when St. Aidan had completed his studies and when the virtues in him had been purified and the vices overcome, he left for Ireland, where he founded a monastery which is called Guernin in the Irish language, and lived a holy life. One Easter night, when he was absorbed in prayer, an angel appeared to him and said: "Do you know that tomorrow at dinner poison will be given to the venerable saint Dewi, your father, by certain of his brothers?" "No," replied St. Aidan. The angel said: "Send one of your servants to tell him of it." But the saint responded: "No ship is ready, nor is the wind right for sailing." The angel answered: "Let your fellow disciple, Scuthinus by name, go down to the seashore, and I will convey him there." The disciple obeyed and went down to the seashore, entering the sea up to his knees, and a sea animal took him up and conveyed him to the outskirts of the city. The ceremonies of the Easter festival were now over, and the holy father Dewi was making his way to the refectory for dinner together with his brothers when he was met by his former disciple Scuthinus. He told Dewi all that had happened concerning him, and all that the angel had commanded with regard to him, and together they joyfully took their place in the refectory, giving thanks to God. After the prayer the deacon, whose custom it was to serve the father, got to his feet and placed the poisoned bread upon the table; both the cook and the steward were in the plot. Scuthinus, whose other name was Scolanus,[15] arose and said: "Today, brother, you will not wait on the father, for I shall serve him." Confused, the deacon stepped back, aware of what he had done. But the holy father blessed the bread and divided it into three parts. He commanded them to give one part to a dog, another to a crow, and both perished in the sight of all upon eating the bread. The father himself took the third part and consumed it with a blessing. They all watched him intently for the next three hours, thinking that he was about to die, but there was no sign of the effects of the fatal poison, and so he courageously preserved his life from harm.

Also, on another occasion, when the Irish burned with an unquenchable desire to visit the shrines of the saintly Apostles Peter and Paul, among their number was the most faithful abbot Barre, who with unflagging steps walked the pilgrims' hallowed road. After fulfilling his saving vow, he turned back to his own monastic precincts and visited the holy man. There he tarried for some while in holy conversation, in accordance with his desire, extending the delay since there was no wind for the ship which had been prepared for his return home. He was concerned that quarrels, disagreements, and brawls might break out among the brothers while the abbot was away, and that the bond of love would be broken (just like bees which, when their king dies, pull apart and break up the cells of the honeycomb which they had firmly cemented together), and so he anxiously sought out and found a marvelous way to travel. He asked for and received for one day the horse which the holy father was accustomed to ride when going about on church business. When the father had blessed him, he went to the harbor and entered the sea, placing his trust in the father's blessing and using the horse like a ship to carry him. The horse plowed its way through the heavy seas as if over a flat field. But when he had gone further out to sea, he came to where St. Brendan was leading a marvelous life on the back of a sea monster. When St. Brendan saw a man crossing the sea on horseback, he was amazed and said: "God is wonderful in his saints." (cf. Ps 68:35). The rider approached the spot where he was so that they could greet each other. When they had exchanged greetings, St. Brendan asked him from where and from whom he had come, and how it was that he rode the sea on horseback. Barre told him of the reasons for his pilgrimage and said: "Since my ship's delay was keeping me from my brothers, father Dewi gave me the horse which he was accustomed to ride to use in my need. And so, armed with his blessing, I set out like this." "Go in peace," said Brendan to him. "I shall come and see him." Barre returned to his country safe and sound and told his brothers all that had happened to him. They kept the horse in the service of the monastery until its death, after which they made a statue of it in memory of the miracle. This remains in Ireland to this day, covered in gold, and is famous for its many wonders.

On a further occasion, another of his disciples, Midunnauc by name, was digging a road with his brothers on an incline near the boundary of the monastery in order to improve the access for those bringing the necessities of life. He said to one of the men working with him: "Why are you so lazy and half-hearted in your work?" But the latter was roused to anger by his words and lifted up the iron tool he was holding to strike him on the head. But the holy father saw this from afar, made the sign of the cross, and raised his hand toward them, with the result that the man's hand was withered. Later the same disciple, who had devoted himself to a life of humble obedience and who had grown in virtue, left for Ireland. But as he entered the boat, a whole multitude of bees followed him and settled in the place where he had sat. For in addition to his other tasks in the community, this disciple had tended the beehives, in order to nourish the swarms of young bees, so that he could provide some tasty items of a more delectable food for those who were in need. Unable to tolerate any loss to the community of his brethren, he returned again to the holy father, followed by the entire swarm of bees, who flew back to their hives. He took his leave of the father and the brethren once again, but again the bees followed him, and so it happened that whenever he went out, the bees would follow him. He went back to the father a third time in the hope that they might be tired and might stay in their hives, and thus would not be denied to his brethren for his convenience. In return for such great consideration and sense of duty, he was commended to God with innumerable prayers and blessings, and he received the father's blessing to sail and to take the bees with him. The holy father blessed the bees with these words: "May the land to which you are going abound with your offspring. May your progeny never be lacking in it. But may our monastery be forever deserted by you; may your offspring never increase in it." We have learned from experience that this remains the case even today, for we have discovered that swarms of bees brought to the monastery of the same father quickly decrease and die. Ireland, however, where until that time no bees could survive, is now rich with an abundance of honey. And so, by the holy father's blessing they have increased on the island of Ireland, although it is well known that they were unable to survive there previously. Even if you threw a piece of Irish earth or a stone into the midst of bees, they would scatter and fly away from it.

As he increased in virtues, so too did he increase in the esteem of good men and women. For one night an angel appeared to him and said: "Prepare yourself tomorrow, put on your sandals and depart for Jerusalem. Set off on the journey you have longed to make. I shall call two others to be your traveling companions, namely Eliud" (now known as Teilo, since he was once a monk in his monastery) "and also Paternus" (whose manner of life and virtues are contained in his own story). But the holy father, amazed at the authoritative command, said: "But how shall this be? For those whom you promise as companions are three or more days distant from us and from each other. It is impossible for us to gather here tomorrow." The angel replied: "Tonight I shall go to each of them, and they shall come to the meeting place that I shall now show you." Without delay the saint disposed of the contents of his cell and set out early in the morning with his brothers' blessing. He arrived at the meeting place, where he found his promised companions, and they all set out together. As fellow travelers they were equals and no one considered himself superior to another; each of them was servant and each of them was master. They were diligent in prayer, and watered their way with tears; their merits increased with each step they took. They were one in mind, in joy, and in sorrow. They sailed across the Channel and came to Gaul, where they heard the foreign languages of different peoples, and father David, like the Apostles themselves, was endowed with the gift of tongues, so that they had no need of an interpreter even while traveling among strange peoples, and could also strengthen the faith of others with words of truth.

Finally they approached the city of Jerusalem, the goal of their desire. But in the night before their arrival an angel appeared to the Patriarch in a dream, saying: "Three Christian men from the lands of the West are approaching whom you will receive with joy and hospitality. Bless them and consecrate them as bishops for me." The Patriarch then prepared three thrones of greatest distinction, and when the holy men reached the city, he greatly rejoiced and warmly welcomed them to the thrones prepared for them. Refreshed by spiritual conversation, they give thanks to God. Then, on the grounds of this divine selection, the Patriarch advanced David to the archbishopric. When this was done, he addressed them: "Obey my words and follow my command. The power of the Jews against the Christians is on the increase. They harass us and reject our faith. Prepare yourselves therefore and go out to preach every day so that their aggression may be restrained and dispelled when they know that the Christian faith has been proclaimed in western lands and promulgated to the furthest ends of the earth." They obeyed his command, and each one preached every day. Their preaching was well received; many converted and many were confirmed in their faith.

Having completed everything, they decided to return to their own land. Then the Patriarch bestowed four gifts upon Dewi, namely a consecrated altar on which he consecrated the body of the Lord, which possesses innumerable powers and which no one has seen since the bishop's death, for it lies hidden beneath many skins; also a famous bell, itself celebrated for its powers; a staff and a tabard of woven gold—the staff, glorious with miraculous powers, is proclaimed throughout the whole land. "But," the Patriarch said, "since they would be a heavy burden for you on your journey back to your own country, return in peace. I will send them after you." They said farewell to the Patriarch and returned home. Each of them awaited the promise of the Patriarch and received the gifts conveyed by angels, Dewi in the monastery called Llangyvelech, Paternus and Eliud in their own monasteries. Therefore the common people say that they came down from heaven.

Since even after St. Germanus had come to our aid a second time, the Pelagian heresy was recovering its strength and obstinacy, again implanting the poison of a deadly serpent in the heart of our country, a general synod of all the bishops of Britain was called. And so one hundred and eighteen bishops came together, as well as an innumerable multitude of priests, abbots, clergy of other ranks, kings, princes, lay men and women, so that this very great crowd completely covered the surrounding land. The bishops conferred among themselves, saying: "The crowd is too great. It is impossible not only for a voice but even for the sound of a trumpet to carry to the ears of them all. Hardly anyone will hear the words of our preaching, and the crowd shall take the infection of the heresy home with them." Therefore they arranged to preach by making a mound of clothes on a small rise upon which they would preach one at a time. Whoever was endowed with such a gift of speech that his words could reach the ears of all who were furthest away, that man would be made archbishop and metropolitan by common consent. Then a place called Brefi was chosen, the garments were piled high, and they preached with all their might. And yet, as though their throats were restricted, their voices could hardly reach those who were nearest. The people awaited the Word, but the majority could not hear it. One after another tried to preach, but to no avail. They felt a great anxiety and fear that the people would return with the heresy still unopposed. "We have preached," they said, "but with no effect. And so our efforts are rendered useless." But then one of the bishops rose up (called Paulinus, with whom holy Dewi the bishop had once studied) and said: "There is one, who was made bishop by the Patriarch and who is not present at our synod. He is a man of eloquence, full of grace, of proven religion, a friend of angels, a lovable man, with an attractive face, magnificent in appearance, six feet in stature. It is he whom, in my view, you should summon here." Messengers were immediately sent out and, arriving at the holy bishop, they announced the reason for their coming. But the holy bishop declined, saying: "Let no one tempt me. Who am I to succeed where others have failed? I know my own limits. Go in peace." Messengers were sent a second and third time, but still he withheld his consent. Finally the holiest and most faithful men are sent, the brothers Daniel and Dubritius. But the holy bishop Dewi foresaw this with prophetic spirit and said to his brethren: "Today, my brethren, very holy men are coming to visit us. Receive them gladly, and procure fish to have with the bread and water for their meal." The brothers arrived, all exchanged greetings and conversed about holy things. The meal was laid on the table, but they insisted that they would never eat a meal in his monastery unless he returned with them to the synod. To this the saint replied: "I cannot refuse you. Eat, and I will go with you to the synod. But I cannot preach there, though I shall assist you, however little, with my prayers."

Setting out, they drew near to the synod, and heard the sound of mournful weeping near at hand. The saint said to his companions: "I will go to the scene of this great wailing." But his companions replied: "But let us go to the assembly in case our late arrival should grieve those who are waiting for us." The man of God approached the place of mourning, and there he found a bereaved mother keeping watch over the dead body of a young man (to whom with barbaric misjudgment she had given a very long name). He consoled the mother and lifted her spirits with good counsel. But the mother, knowing of his fame, threw herself at his feet and pleaded with him with cries of entreaty to take pity upon her. Filled with compassion for human weakness, he approached the body of the dead boy and watered his face with tears. Finally the limbs grew warm, the soul returned, and the body quivered. He took hold of the boy's hand and returned him to his mother. But she, her sorrowful weeping turning into tears of joy, said: "My son was dead to me, let him from now on live to God and to you." The holy man accepted the boy, laid on his shoulder the gospel book that he always carried on his heart, and took him with him to the synod. That boy subsequently lived in a holy manner for as long as his life lasted.

He then entered the synod, the company of bishops rejoiced, the people were glad, and the whole assembly exulted. They asked him to preach, and he did not spurn the council's will. They asked him to climb up upon the mound of garments and, before the eyes of everyone, a snow-white dove from heaven settled upon his shoulder and remained there all the time that he was preaching. While he preached to all in a clear voice, being heard equally by those who were near and those who were far away, the ground beneath him rose up and turned into a hill and, since he was on the top, he was visible to all as if standing on the summit of a mountain. He raised his voice until it rang out like a trumpet; a church was built on the top of that hill. The heresy was driven out, the faith was strengthened in sound hearts, and all were of one accord. Thanks were given to God and to holy David.

Later, blessed and glorified by all, he was constituted archbishop of the whole British race by the unanimous consent of all the bishops, kings, princes, nobles, and those of every rank. His monastic city was also declared the metropolitan seat of the whole country so that whoever rules it should be regarded as archbishop.[16] The heresy was driven out therefore and the decrees of Catholic and ecclesiastical governance were confirmed, which had been disregarded and almost entirely forgotten during the frequent and cruel outbreaks of the enemy. As if waking from a deep sleep, all have earnestly fought the battles of the Lord through these decrees, which can still in part be found in the most ancient documents of the father, and which were written down by his own holy hand.

In later years another synod, the Synod of Victory, was called in which many bishops, priests, and abbots came together and confirmed the decrees of the earlier synod, also adding to them certain other necessary matters, after firm and vigorous scrutiny.[17] From these two synods all the churches of our land have received their usage and rule by Roman authority; the decrees of the synods which he had confirmed by word of mouth, the bishop and he alone committed to writing with his own holy hand. Throughout the whole of the land, the brothers then built monasteries; everywhere the sounds of churches were in evidence, everywhere voices were raised to heaven in prayer, everywhere the virtues were unweariedly brought back to the bosom of the church, everywhere the offerings of charity were distributed to the needy with an open hand. The holy bishop Dewi was the supreme overseer, the supreme protector, the supreme preacher, from whom all received the content and structure of virtuous living. For all people he was the order, the dedication, the benediction, the absolution, the correction. He was instruction to the studious, life to the needy, an upbringing to orphans, support to widows, a leader to fathers, a Rule to monks, a way of life to secular clergy; he was all things to all people. What swarms of monks he engendered! What great benefits he brought to all! With what splendor of virtue he shone! Thus he was brought to a ripe old age and was praised as the leader of the whole British race and the ornament of his country; and the number of his years was one hundred and forty-seven.

When the day was approaching which had been set apart for weighing the rewards of his merits (cf. Heb 11:26), the eighth day before the first day of March, and the brothers were keeping the hour of matins, an angel spoke to him with a clear voice: "The day which you have long desired is now close at hand." The holy bishop, recognizing the voice of a friend and greatly rejoicing in his spirit, said to him: "Now let your servant, Lord, depart in peace" (Lk 2:29). But the brothers, hearing only the sound and not being able to make out the words as they conversed, all fell to the ground in terror. Then the whole of the monastery was filled with angelic harmonies and with a delightful and scented fragrance, and the holy bishop, his mind raised up to heaven, cried out with a loud voice: "Lord Jesus Christ, receive my spirit." The angel spoke again, in an audible voice, so that the brothers could understand: "Make ready and gird yourself; for on the first day of March our Lord Jesus Christ, in the company of a great host of angels, shall come to meet you." Upon hearing this and sobbing with sudden grief, they made great lamentation. A mighty sadness

arose; the monastery resounded with weeping and with the words
"Holy bishop, take away our sorrow!" But he comforted and sustained them with consoling words: "My brothers, be steadfast and
bear to the end the yoke that you have accepted." From that hour
onward, until the day of his death, he remained in the church to
preach. News of this spread through the whole of Britain and Ireland, borne by an angel who said: "Do you know in this coming
week that the holy bishop Dewi shall pass into heaven?" Then,
crowds of saints hastened from all sides to visit the holy father, just
like bees that make their way to the hives at the approach of a
storm. The monastery overflowed with tears, the wailing echoed
to the stars, the young mourned as for a father, the old as for a
child. On the intervening Sunday, in the presence of a vast multitude, he preached a most excellent sermon and, with unblemished hands, consecrated the Lord's body. But when he had
partaken of the Lord's body and blood, he was soon seized with
pains and became ill. The service ended; he blessed the people
and addressed everyone in these words: "My brethren, persevere
in those things which you have learned from me and have seen in
me. In three days time, on the first day of March, I shall go the way
of my fathers. May you fare well in the Lord. I shall depart." From
that Sunday night until the fourth day after his death, all who had
come remained weeping, fasting, and keeping watch. Accordingly, when the third day arrived, the place was filled with choirs
of angels, and was melodious with heavenly singing, and replete
with the most delightful fragrance. At the hour of matins, whilst
the monks were singing hymns, Psalms, and canticles,[18] our Lord
Jesus Christ deigned to bestow his presence for the consolation of
the father, as he had promised by the angel. On seeing him, and
entirely rejoicing in spirit, he said, "Take me with Thee." With
these words, with Christ as his companion, he gave up his life to
God, and, attended by the escort of angels, he sought the gates of
heaven. His body, borne on the arms of holy brethren and accompanied by a great crowd, was committed to the earth with all
honor and buried in the grounds of his own monastery; but his
soul, set free from the bounds of this transitory life, was crowned
throughout endless ages. Amen.

These and many other works the father did, whilst a perishable body weighed down the soul which it carried (cf. Wis 9:15). But from the many that exist, we have provided only a few examples in order to satisfy the thirst of the ardent, by means of the vessel of my humble narrative. For, just as one can never drain a river dry which issues from an everlasting spring with a narrow vessel of too limited capacity, so no one can commit to writing all the father's signs and miracles, his most devout practice of virtues and observance of precepts, even if he were to use a pen of iron. But as I have stated, these few I have gathered together as an example to all and for the father's glory from the very many that are scattered in the oldest manuscripts of our country, and chiefly in those of his own monastery. These, though eaten away along their edges and backs by the continuous gnawing of worms and the ravages of passing years, and written in the manner of the elders, have survived until now, and are gathered together and collected by me to the glory of the great father and for the benefit of others, that they shall not perish, as the bee sucks delicately with its mouth from the different blooms in a garden filled with flowers. Indeed, as for those works which he performs with the passage of time and has carried out more effectively since he cleaved more closely to God, having laid aside the burden of the flesh and having gazed upon the Deity face-to-face, those who wish may discover them through the witness of many. But as for myself, Rhigyfarch by name, who have somewhat rashly applied my slender mental abilities to this task, may those who read this work with a devout mind assist me with their prayers, so that, since the Father's mercy, like that of spring, has carried me through the summer heat of the flesh to the scanty flowering of my understanding, it may in the end, when the vapors of desire have vanished and before my course is ended, bring me the fruit of a good harvest through due and proper works. Then, when the tares of the enemy are separated, and the reapers shall have filled heaven's garners with purified sheaves (cf. Mt 13:29–30), they may find a place for me, as a gleaning of the latest harvest, within the portals of the celestial gates, there endlessly to behold God, who is blessed above all things, forever and ever. Amen.

5. THE LIFE OF BEUNO

There was once a man of lineage[1] in Powys in the place that is called Banhenic, near to the river which was known then as Sabrina and now as Hafren.[2] Bugi was the name of that gentleman and his wife was Beren, daughter of Llawdden. They were people who were true of heart and their way of life was good. They kept God's commandments in every way they could, without ever being accused of worldly wickedness. But they had no male heir. They were an elderly couple and would never have children, for they had already lived for many years. And they slept together for twelve years without having intercourse, by mutual agreement.

One day, when they were conversing with each other, they saw an angel approaching them, his garments as white as snow, and he said to them: "Be joyful and glad for God has heard your prayer." Then the angel said to the man: "Let there be intercourse tonight between you and your wife. She shall conceive and give birth to a son who shall be honored before God and all people." They did as the angel had commanded. And Beren conceived on that night, and gave birth to a son. The son was called Beuno.

They reared the child until the time came for him to receive an education. Then they sent him to a holy man who was in Caerwent. Tangusius was the name of the saint. His parents gave him over, and they did so by making a vow. He remained with that saint, by the help of God, and learned the whole of the scriptures. Then, having learned the liturgy and rules of the church, he was ordained and became a priest.

And then Ynyr Gwent began to take note of him. He was the king in that place. He was humble, chaste, and generous and kept God's commandments in all things. He received Beuno with honor and generously gave him a gold ring and a crown. He devoted himself as a pupil and a monk to St. Beuno, granting him three tracts of land in Ewas together with all the people who lived on this land and all their worldly goods.

213

And at that time Beuno's father was struck down with a fatal illness and sent a messenger to his son, Beuno, asking him to visit him in his weakness and his passing away. Then Beuno said to his companions and his disciples: "Let three of you (he said) remain in the monastery while I go to visit my father who lies seriously ill."[3] That is what they did. St. Beuno commended them to the king and to the nobles of the country and went himself to the place where his father was ill. When his father had made his Communion, his confession, and a perfect end, he died.[4]

Afterward Beuno lived on the land he had inherited from his father and built a church there, consecrating it in the name of Christ the Lord. He planted an acorn by the side of his father's grave, which grew into an oak tree of great height and thickness. From the crown of this tree there grew a branch right down to the ground and from the ground back up to the top of the tree so that the bend in the branch was touching the ground. This is how it always remained. If an Englishman passes between the branch and the trunk of the tree, he shall drop dead on the spot, but if a Welshman does so, he shall be none the worse.[5]

When Beuno had lived on his inherited land for some while, he finally left this land and went by foot to Mawn, son of Brochwel. He received Beuno kindly and graciously on account of his friendship, his generosity, and his humility in carrying out God's commandments. And then Mawn made a donation to God and to Beuno for the sake of his own soul and that of his father Aberriw.

One day, when Beuno was walking around his corn, near the river Severn, he heard from the other side of the river the cry of an Englishman, who was encouraging his dog in pursuit of a hare. At the top of his voice the Englishman shouted: "Charge, charge." These were words of encouragement to his dog in his own language. When Beuno heard the shout of the Englishman, he immediately turned and went straight back to his disciples, saying to them: "Put on your clothes, my sons, and your shoes, and let us leave this place. The people of the man of foreign speech whom I heard calling to his dogs across the river shall invade this place. It shall be theirs, and they shall keep it in their possession." Then Beuno said to one of his disciples (Rithwlint was his name): "My son, be obedient to me. I wish you to remain here, may my blessing be with you, and I shall leave a cross, which I made." The disciple received his teacher's blessing and remained there.

Beuno came, together with his disciples, as far as Meifod, where he remained with St. Tysilio for forty days and forty nights. From there he went to King Cynan, son of Brochwel, and asked of him a place where he could pray for his soul and his friends. Then the king gave him Gwyddelwern, a place which took its name from the Irishman whom Beuno raised from the dead there, when his wife had killed him. Beuno maintained a church there until such time as the nephews of Cynan came to Beuno from their hunting to ask for food from him, who had been living there in peace. Beuno told his servants to bring a young ox down from the mountain and to kill it in order to provide food for them. That is what the servants did. The meat was placed in a pot to boil on the fire at the third hour of the day, and it remained on the fire until the afternoon with the men ceaselessly feeding the fire. And when the afternoon came, the water had not yet warmed nor the meat changed color.[6] Then one of the laymen said: "It is this clerk," he said "who is doing this by his magical arts so that we should get nothing to eat." When Beuno heard this from his mouth, he put a curse upon him and the man died within the day. Then Beuno turned to the sons of Selyf and said: "What your fathers gave freely to God, you seek to tax and restrict. May God grant this to me, may he whom I serve bring it about for me that your children never own it and that you yourselves be destroyed from this kingdom and from the kingdom to come." And Beuno received what he had asked for in his prayer.

Thereupon Beuno left that place and walked to the bank of the River Dee in search of a place where he could pray to God. Nor did he find anywhere until he came to Temic, son of Eiludd, who granted Beuno a home in perpetuity. There Beuno built a church and consecrated it to God. Before much time had passed, Temic left that deserted place to Beuno.

One day Temic and his wife came to the church in order to hear Mass and Beuno's sermon, leaving his daughter behind to guard their home. She was the most beautiful girl in the world, and had not yet been given to a man. And as she remained on guard, she saw the king, who ruled that place, approaching her. His name was Caradoc. She rose up to greet him and was pleasant to him while the king, for his part, asked her where her father had gone. "He went," she said, "to the church. If you have any business with him, wait for him and he will soon be here." "I will not wait," he said "unless you become my mistress." The girl said: "I am not fit to become your mistress since you are a great king and are from a line of kings. My blood is not noble enough for me to be your mistress. But wait here," she said "until I come from my room and I shall do what you desire." Pretending to go to her room, she fled and made for the church where her father and mother were. The king saw her fleeing, and gave chase. As she reached the door of the church, he caught her up and struck off her head with his sword, which fell into the church while her body remained outside. Beuno and her mother and father saw what had happened, and Beuno stared into the face of the king and said: "I ask God not to spare you and to respect you as little as you respected this good girl." And in that moment the king melted away into a lake, and was seen no more in this world.

Then Beuno took the girl's head and placed it back with the body, covering the body with his cloak and saying to her mother and father who were mourning for her: "Be quiet for a little while and leave her as she is until the Mass is over." Then Beuno celebrated the sacrifice to God. When the Mass was finished, the girl rose up entirely healed and dried the sweat from her face; God and Beuno healed her. Where her blood fell to the earth, a spring was formed, which even today still heals people and animals from their illnesses and injuries. And that spring is called after the girl and is known as Ffynnon Wenfrewi. Many who had seen what had happened began to believe in Christ. One of those who believed was Cadfan, King of Gwynedd. He gave much land to Beuno.

After the death of Cadfan, Beuno went to visit Cadwallon, Cadfan's son, who became king after Cadfan, and asked of him a tract of land since he had nowhere nearby to live and to pray. The king gave Beuno a place in Arfon which is called Gwaradoc. Beuno gave the king a broach of gold which Cynan, son of Brochwel, had given him when he was dying. That broach was worth sixty cows. Then Beuno built a church, and began to erect a wall around it. One day when he was building that wall, together with his disciples, they saw a woman approaching them carrying a newly born child and asking Beuno to baptize her son.[7] Beuno said: "Wait a little while, woman, until we have finished this." But the child began to cry so that it was unendurable. "Woman," said Beuno, "why does the child cry so hard?" "Holy man," said the woman, "he has good reason." "Good woman," said Beuno, "what reason does he have?" "In truth," said the woman, "the land that you have taken and upon which you are building is his inheritance." Then Beuno said to his disciples: "Leave your work and, while I do the baptism, make ready for me my chariot. We will go with this woman and her child to see the king who gave me his inheritance."

Then Beuno and his disciples departed with the woman and her child and came to Caer Seint, where the king was.[8] That place is now known as Caernarfon. Then Beuno said to the king: "Why did you give me the inheritance of another, which was wrong?" "Where is the person who is entitled to it?" said the king. "The child," said Beuno, "who is in the lap of the woman over there is entitled to the land and is heir to it." Beuno said: "Give the child the piece of land and give me another in exchange, or give me back the gift I gave you, that is the broach of gold."[9] But this is the answer that the proud and arrogant king gave to Beuno: "I will not give you any land in exchange. And the gift you gave me I have given to someone else." Beuno became angry and said to the king: "I ask God that your rule over this land and terrain shall not last long." And Beuno went away, leaving him under a curse.

The king had a cousin who was called Gwideint, who followed Beuno and caught him up on the other side of the river which is called Seint, where Beuno was sitting upon a stone on the river bank. For the sake of his own soul and the soul of Cadwallon, his cousin, he gave to God and Beuno his own inheritance, which is called Clynnog, for all eternity without tax or tribute and with neither rights of possession nor any claim over it being held by any other person in the world. There Beuno performed so many miracles by the power of God that none could count their number.

At that time it happened that one of the workmen of Aberffraw went to the court of Ynyr Gwent, and there was no youth more handsome than he in all the world. And when Ynyr Gwent's daughter saw the young man, she loved him so much that she could not be without him. The king recognized this on the spot and decided to give the lad to his daughter as a husband in case she should find some other means to get him. He knew for certain on account of his fairness and good looks that he was the son of a king and of noble birth.

After a while he returned, together with that youth and his wife, to his country, and they came to a place that is called Pennardd in Arfon. There they dismounted from their horses and rested. Her great fatigue and weariness brought sleep upon the princess. For his part, while the princess slept, he was filled with an excess of shame that he was going to his country with a wife as noble as she was and there was nowhere he could take her. He would have to go back to the work from which he had previously earned his living. And then, prompted by a Devil, he cut off her head with his sword while she slept, and set off toward his country, taking the good horses, the gold, and silver to the king. And with these goods he purchased possessions and an office from the king, namely that of his chief steward.

Beuno's shepherds discovered the body and went straightaway to tell him of it. Beuno went swiftly with them to the place where the body was. There he picked up the head and pressed it back upon the body, and, falling upon his knees, he prayed to God like this: "Lord, Creator of Heaven and Earth, to whom nothing is unknown, raise this body up in health." There the maiden rose up, restored to full health, and told Beuno of all her misfortune. Then Beuno said to her: "You must choose either to return to your country or to stay here and serve God." The good and gentle girl said to him: "I wish to remain here, close to you and serving God, who raised me up from the dead." And where her blood had fallen to the ground, a pure spring appeared, which was called after the girl, namely Ffynnon Digiwc.

Some while later Idon, the brother of the princess and son of Ynyr Gwent, came to Beuno in search of his sister. When he arrived, the girl was with Beuno, serving God. He asked his sister whether she would come with him to his country, but she replied that she did not wish to go and to leave the place where she had been raised from the dead. And when Idon saw that he was unsuccessful, he pleaded with Beuno to go with him to Aberffraw and to force the king to return the horses, the gold, and the silver that the man had taken with his sister. Then they both walked to the court of the king, where Idon recognized the man he was looking for and immediately drawing his sword, rushed at him and cut off his head. The king became angry and demanded that the man who had killed the other should be seized. But Beuno said: "Do not lay your hands on the man who has come with me." In his wrath, the king dragged him away and swore that he would have the man struck down straightaway if Beuno did not bring the man he had killed back to life. Undaunted and trusting in God, Beuno then raised to life the man who had been killed. And then the king, repenting of having put the saint to the test, gave Beuno the mansion which is called Aelwyd Veuno.[10]

There are many other things we have left out, not mentioning them, in case this book should seem long-winded. These are only a few of Beuno's miracles. No one knows what God did for Beuno except God himself. And God shall come to the aid of whoever is known to do good. Beuno performed all the commandments of God. He gave food and drink to anyone he saw who was hungry and thirsty, clothing for the naked, lodging for the stranger. He visited the sick and those in prison. He performed every good thing that holy scripture tells us to do.

And as Beuno's life was drawing to an end and his day approaching, on the seventh day after Easter he saw the heavens opening and the angels descending and ascending. Then Beuno said: "I see the Trinity, the Father, the Son, and the Holy Spirit, Peter and Paul and pure David, Deiniol, the saints and the prophets, the Apostles and the martyrs, appearing to me. And in the midst there I see seven angels standing before the throne of the highest Father and all the fathers of heaven, singing: "Blessed is the one you have chosen and have received and who shall dwell with you always." I hear the cry of the horn of the highest Father summoning me and saying to me: "My son, cast off your burden of flesh. The time is coming, and you are invited to share the feast that shall not end with your brothers. May your body remain in the earth while the armies of heaven and the angels bear your soul to the kingdom of heaven, which you have merited here through your works."

This hour shall be the Day of Judgment when the Lord says to the saints: "Blessed sons of my Father, come to the kingdom that was prepared for you from the beginning of the world, where there shall be life without death, youth without old age and health without suffering, joy without grief, the saints in the highest rank with God the Father, in unity with the angels and archangels, in unity with the disciples of Jesus Christ, in unity with the nine grades of heaven, who did not sin, in the unity of the Father and the Son and the Holy Spirit, Amen."

Let us too beseech the mercy of the all-powerful God by the help of St. Beuno so that we may receive with him everlasting life in all eternity, Amen.

This is the line of Beuno. Beuno, son of Bugi, son of Gwynlliw, son of Tegid, son of Cadell Drynlluc, son of Categyrn, son of Gortheyrn, son of Gorthegyrn, son of Rhyddegyrn, son of Deheuwynt, son of Eudegan, son of Eudegern, son of Elud, son of Eudos, son of Eudoleu, son of Afallach, son of Amalech, son of Belim, son of Anna. The mother of that Anna was cousin to Mary the Virgin, the mother of Christ.

6. THE LIFE OF ST. MELANGELL

In Powys there was once a certain most illustrious prince by the name of Brychwel Ysgithrog, who was the Earl of Chester and who at that time lived in the town of Pengwern Powys, which means in Latin the head of Powys marsh and is now known as Salop, and whose home or abode stood in that place where the college of St. Chad is now situated. Now that very same noble prince gave his aforesaid home or mansion for the use of God as an act of almsgiving both by his own free will and from a sense of religious duty, making a perpetual grant of it for his own sake and for the sake of his heirs. When one day in the year of our Lord 604, the said prince had gone hunting to a certain place in Britain called Pennant, in the said principality of Powys, and when the hunting dogs of the same prince had started a hare, the dogs pursued the hare and he too gave chase until he came to a certain thicket of brambles, which was large and full of thorns. In this thicket he found a girl of beautiful appearance who, given up to divine contemplation, was praying with the greatest devotion, with the said hare lying boldly and fearlessly under the hem or fold of her garments, its face toward the dogs.

Then the prince cried "Get it, hounds, get it!" but the more he shouted, urging them on, the further the dogs retreated and, howling, fled from the little animal. Finally, the prince, altogether astonished, asked the girl how long she had lived on her own on his lands, in such a lonely spot. In reply the girl said that she had not seen a human face for these fifteen years. Then he asked the girl who she was, her place of birth and origins, and in all humility she answered that she was the daughter of King Jowchel of Ireland and that "because my father had intended me to be the wife of a certain great and generous Irishman, I fled from my native soil and with God leading me came here in order that I might serve God and the immaculate Virgin with my heart and pure body until my dying day." Then the prince asked the girl her name. She replied that her name was Melangell. Then the prince, considering in his innermost heart the flourishing though solitary state of the girl, said: "O most worthy virgin Melangell, I find that you are a handmaid of the true God and a most sincere follower of Christ. Therefore, because it has pleased the highest and all-powerful God to give refuge, for your merits, to this little wild hare with safe conduct and protection from the attack and pursuit of these savage and violent dogs, I give and present to you most willingly these my lands for the service of God, that they may be a perpetual asylum, refuge, and defense, in honor of your name, excellent girl. Let neither king nor prince seek to be so rash or bold toward God that they presume to drag away any man or woman who has escaped here, desiring to enjoy protection in these your lands, as long as they in no way contaminate or pollute your sanctuary or asylum. But, on the other hand, if any wrongdoer who enjoys the protection of your sanctuary shall set out in any direction to do harm, then the independent abbots of your sanctuary, who alone know of their crimes, shall, if they find them in that place, ensure that the culprits be released and handed over to the Powys authorities in order to be punished."

This virgin Melangell, who was so very pleasing to God, led her solitary life, as stated above, for thirty-seven years in this very same place. And the hares, which are little wild creatures, surrounded her every day of her life just as if they had been tame or domesticated animals. Nor, by the aid of divine mercy, were miracles and various other signs lacking for those who called upon her help and the grace of her favor with an inner motion of the heart.

After the death of the said most illustrious prince Brochwel, his son Tyssilio held the principality of Powys, followed by Conan, the brother of Tyssilio, Tambryd, Gurmylk, and Durres the lame, all of whom sanctioned the said place of Pennant Melangell to be a perpetual sanctuary, refuge, or safe haven for the oppressed (thereby confirming the acts of the said prince). The same virgin Melangell applied herself to establish and instruct certain virgins with all concern and care in the same region in order that they might persevere and live in a holy and modest manner in the love of God, and should dedicate their lives to divine duties, doing nothing else by day or by night. After this, as soon as Melangell herself had departed this life, a certain man called Elissa came to Pennant Melangell and wishing to debauch, violate, and dishonor the same virgins, suddenly perished and died there in the most pitiful manner. Whoever has violated the above-mentioned liberty and sanctity of the said virgin has been rarely seen to escape divine vengeance on this account, as may be seen every day. Praises be to the most high God and to Melangell, his virgin.

MONASTIC TEXTS

1. THE PREFACE OF GILDAS ON PENANCE

1. A priest or a deacon who has previously taken the monastic vow and who has committed natural fornication or sodomy shall do penance for three years.[1] He shall ask for pardon once an hour and shall miss the main meal[2] once a week except during the fifty days that follow the Passion.[3] On Sunday he shall have an unlimited supply of bread and a tidbit smeared with butter.[4] On other days he shall have a portion of dry bread, a meal enriched with a little fat, garden vegetables, a few eggs, British cheese, a Roman half-pint of milk on account of the frailty of the body in this age, and a Roman pint of whey or buttermilk for his thirst and some water if he does hard physical work. His bed shall be made of only a little straw. During the three forty-day periods[5] he shall increase his penance as far as his strength allows. At all times he shall bewail his guilt from the bottom of his heart. Above all things let him show the readiest obedience. After a year and a half he may receive Communion, come for the kiss of peace, and sing the Psalms with his brethren, in case his soul should utterly perish after going without the heavenly medicine for such a long time.

2. If the culprit is a monk of lower rank, he shall do penance for three years, but his allowance of bread shall be increased. If he labors with his hands, he shall take a Roman pint of milk and another of whey and shall take as much water as he needs to quench his thirst.

3. But if it is a priest or a deacon without monastic vow who has sinned, he shall do the same penance as a monk not in holy orders.

4. But if a monk merely intended to commit such a sin, he shall do penance for a year and a half.[6] But the abbot has the authority to moderate this if his obedience is pleasing to God and the abbot.

227

5. The ancient fathers set twelve years penance for a priest and seven for a deacon.

6. A monk who has stolen an article of clothing or any other thing shall do penance for two years as stated above, if he is a junior; if he is a senior, for one complete year. If he is not a monk, then also for a year, especially during the three periods of forty days.

7. If a monk vomits the Host during the day from an overful stomach, he shall not presume to take his supper, and if illness is not the cause, he shall expunge his offense with seven special fasts,[7] but if illness is the cause rather than gluttony, then with four special fasts.

8. But if it is not the Host, he is to be punished with a special fast of one day and with much reproach.

9. If anyone loses a Host through carelessness,[8] leaving it to be consumed by wild animals and birds, he shall do penance for three forty-day periods.

10. If on account of drunkenness someone is unable to sing the Psalms, being benumbed and speechless, he shall be deprived of his supper.

11. He who sins with an animal shall expiate his guilt for a year; if by himself alone, for three forty-day periods.

12. He who holds communion with someone who has been excommunicated by his abbot, forty days.

13. He who unwittingly eats carrion, forty days.

14. It is to be understood, however, that the penance is to be increased in proportion to the length of time that someone remains in sin.

15. If a particular task has been imposed upon someone which he does not do on account of contempt, he shall go without supper, but if it is only through an oversight, he shall go without half his daily portion.

16. But if he undertakes someone else's task, he shall modestly make this known to the abbot, without anyone else hearing, and shall carry it out if ordered to do so.

17. He who holds anger for a long time in his heart is in a state of death. But if he confesses his sin, he shall fast for forty days,

and if he persists in sin, for two periods of forty days. And if he does the same thing again, he shall be cut off from the body like a putrid member, since anger breeds murder.[9]

18. He who has been offended by anyone should make this known to the abbot, not in the spirit of an accuser but of a physician, and the abbot should decide.

19. He who has not arrived by the end of the second Psalm shall sing eight Psalms one after another. If, when he has been woken up, he comes after the reading,[10] he shall repeat in order whatever the brethren have sung. But if he comes at the second reading,[11] he shall go without supper.

20. If in error anyone has changed any of the words where "danger" is noted,[12] he shall do penance for three days or perform three fasts.

21. He who allows the Host to fall to the ground through carelessness shall go without supper.

22. He who has willingly been defiled in sleep, if the monastery is well stocked with beer and meat, shall make a standing vigil for three hours at night, if his health is good. But if it has poor fare, he shall sing twenty-eight or thirty Psalms while standing as a suppliant, or shall make satisfaction with extra work.

23. We should celebrate Mass for good rulers but certainly not for bad ones.

24. Priests are indeed not forbidden to celebrate Mass for their bishops.

25. He who is accused of any fault and answers contemptuously[13] shall go without supper.

26. He who has broken a hoe which was not broken before shall make amends either by extra work or by a special fast.

27. Anyone who sees one of his brethren breaking the commands of the abbot should not conceal the fact from the abbot. But first he should urge the sinner to confess his wrongdoing to the abbot of his own accord. Let him not be found so much an informer as one who truly practices the rule.

Thus far Gildas.

2. THE PENITENTIAL OF CUMMEAN

H ere begins the prologue on the medicine for the salvation of souls.

1. As we are about to speak of the remedies for wounds according to the rulings of the fathers before us, of sacred utterance to you, my most faithful brother, let us first indicate in a concise manner the medicines of Holy Scripture.

2. The first remission then is that by which we are baptized in water, according to this passage: "Unless we are born again of water and of the Holy Spirit, we cannot see the Kingdom of God" (Jn 3:5). 3. The second is the feeling of charity, as this text has it: "Many sins are forgiven her for she has loved much" (Lk 7:47). 4. The third is the fruit of almsgiving, according to this: "As water quenches fire, so too do alms extinguish sin" (Sir 3:33). 5. The fourth is the shedding of tears, as the Lord says: "Since Ahab wept in my sight and walked sad in my presence, I will not bring evil things in his days" (1 Kgs 21:29). 6. The fifth is the confession of crimes, as the psalmist testifies: "I said, I will confess against myself my injustice to the Lord and you have forgiven the iniquity of my sin" (Ps 32:5). 7. The sixth is the affliction of heart and body, as the Apostle comforts us: "I have given such a man to Satan for the destruction of his flesh, that his spirit may be saved in the day of our Lord Jesus Christ" (1 Cor 5:5). 8. The seventh is the amending of our ways, that is, the renunciation of vices, as the gospel testifies: "Now you are whole, sin no more, in case something worse happens to you" (Jn 5:14). 9. The eighth is the intercession of the saints, as this text states: "If any be sick, let him bring the priests of the church and let them pray for him and lay their hands upon him, and anoint him with oil in the name of the Lord, and the prayer of faith shall save the sick man and the Lord shall raise him up, and if he be in sins, they shall be forgiven him" and so forth, and: "The continual prayer of a just man avails much before the Lord" (Jas 5:14–16). 10. The ninth is

the reward of mercy and faith, as this says: "Blessed are the merciful for they shall obtain mercy" (Mt 5:7). 11. The tenth is the conversion and salvation of others, as James assures us: "He who causes a sinner to be converted from the error of his life[14] shall save his soul from death and cover a multitude of sins" (Jas 5:20); but it is better for you, if you are weak, to lead a solitary life than to perish with many. 12. The eleventh is our pardon, as he that is the truth has promised, saying: "Forgive and you shall be forgiven" (Lk 6:37). 13. The twelfth is the passion of martyrdom, as the one hope of our salvation then grants us pardon; and God replies to the cruel robber: "Truly I say to you this day you shall be with me in Paradise" (Lk 23:43).

14. Therefore since these things are quoted on the authority of the canon,[15] it is right for you also to seek out the decrees of the fathers who were chosen by the mouth of the Lord, according to this passage: "Ask your father and he will declare to you, your elders and they will tell you" (Dt 32:7); indeed, "Let the matter be referred to them." And so they determine that the eight principal vices contrary to human salvation shall be healed by the eight remedies that are their contraries. For it is an old proverb: Contraries are cured by contraries. For they who do what is forbidden without restraint ought to restrain themselves even from what is allowed.

1. ON GLUTTONY

1. Those who are drunk with wine or beer, contrary to our Savior's prohibition (as it is said: "See that your hearts are not overburdened with excess and drunkenness or with the cares of this life in case that day should come upon you suddenly; for it shall come as a snare upon all those who live on the face of the earth" [Lk 21:34–35], and as the Apostle says: "Do not be drunk with wine in which there is indulgence" [Eph 5:18]), if they have taken the vow of sanctity, they shall expiate the fault for forty days with bread and water; laity however for seven days.

2. He who compels anyone for the sake of good fellowship to get drunk shall do penance in the same way as someone who has

been drunk. 3. If he does this on account of hatred, then he shall be judged a murderer.

4. He who is not able to sing Psalms, being groggy and unable to speak, shall perform a special task.

5. He who anticipates the canonical hour,[16] or only on account of appetite takes finer food than the others have, shall go without supper or live for two days on bread and water.

6. But he who suffers excessive distension of the stomach and the discomfort of satiety shall do penance for one day. 7. If he suffers to the point of vomiting, without being in a state of ill health, for seven days.

8. But if he vomits the Host, forty days. 9. If he does this on account of illness however, for seven days. 10. If he ejects it into the fire, he shall sing a hundred Psalms. 11. If a dog licks up this vomit, he who has vomited shall do penance for one hundred days.

12. He who steals food shall do penance for forty days; if he does so again, for three forty-day periods; if a third time, for a year; but if a fourth time, he shall do penance in permanent exile under another abbot.

13. A boy of ten years who steals anything shall do penance for seven days. 14. But if afterward at the age of twenty years he happens to commit a small theft, for twenty or forty days.

2. ON FORNICATION

1. A bishop who commits fornication shall be degraded and shall perform penance for twelve years.

2. A priest or deacon who commits natural fornication, having previously taken the vow of a monk, shall do penance for seven years. He shall ask pardon every hour and shall perform a special fast every week except in the fifty days from Easter to Pentecost. After the special fast he shall have bread without limit and a tidbit smeared with some butter [that is to say a quarter measure] and he shall live like this on Sundays, while on other days he shall have a portion of dry bread [made from a twelve-*polentae* vessel of flour] and a meal enriched with a little fat, garden vegetables, a few eggs,

British cheese, a Roman half-pint [equal to twelve hen's eggs] of milk on account of the frailty of the body in this age, a Roman pint of whey or buttermilk [equal to twelve hen's eggs] for his thirst, and some water if he does hard physical work.[17] His bed shall be made of only a little straw. During the three forty-day periods he shall increase his penance as far as his strength allows. At all times he shall bewail his guilt from the bottom of his heart. Above all things let him show the readiest obedience. After a year and a half he may receive Communion, come for the kiss of peace, and sing the Psalms with his brethren, in case his soul should utterly perish after going without the heavenly medicine for such a long time.[18]

3. If the culprit is a monk of lower rank, he shall do penance for three years but his allowance of bread shall not be increased.[19] If he labors with his hands, he shall take a Roman pint of milk and another of whey and shall take as much water as he needs to quench his thirst.[20]

4. But if it is a priest or a deacon without monastic vow who has sinned, he shall do the same penance as a monk not in holy orders. 5. But if after the offense he wants to become a monk he shall do penance in the strict form of exile for a year and a half. But the abbot has the authority to moderate this if his obedience is pleasing to God and the abbot.

6. He who sins with a beast shall do penance for a year; if on his own, for three forty-day periods; if he has [clerical] rank, a year; a boy of fifteen years, forty days.

7. He who defiles his mother shall do penance for three years, with perpetual exile.

8. Those who befoul their lips shall do penance for four years; if they are used to the habit they shall do penance for seven years.

9. So shall those who commit sodomy do penance for seven years.

10. For femoral intercourse, two years.

11. He who merely desires in his mind to commit fornication, but who cannot do so, shall do penance for one year, especially in the three forty-day periods. 12. He who is polluted by a shameful

word or glance, yet did not wish to commit bodily fornication, shall do penance for twenty or forty days according to the nature of his sin. 13. But if he is polluted by the violent assault of a thought, he shall do penance for seven days. 14. He who for a long time is tempted by the thought of fornication, and does not resist the thought strongly enough, shall do penance for one or two or more days, according to the duration of the thought. 15. He who is willingly polluted during sleep shall rise and sing nine Psalms one after another, on bended knees; the following day he shall live on bread and water. Or he shall sing thirty Psalms, bending his knees at the end of each. 16. He who desires to sin during sleep, or is unintentionally polluted, fifteen Psalms. He who sins but is not polluted, twenty-four.

17. A cleric who commits fornication once shall do penance for one year on bread and water; if he begets a child, he shall do penance for seven years as an exile; so also a virgin.

18. He who loves any woman but is unaware of any evil beyond a few conversations shall do penance for forty days. 19. But if he kisses and embraces her, one year, especially in the three forty-day periods. 20. He who loves in mind only, seven days. 21. If however he has spoken but has not been accepted by her, forty days.

22. A layman repenting of fornication and the shedding of blood shall do penance for three years; in the first and in the three forty-day periods of the others, with bread and water, and in all three years without wine, without meat, without bearing arms, without his wife.

23. A layman who defiles his neighbor's wife or virgin daughter shall do penance for one year with bread and water, without his own wife.

24. But if he defiles a woman of God and begets a child, he shall do penance for three years without bearing arms; in the first with bread and water, in the others without wine and meat. 25. If, however, he does not beget a child, but defiles, he shall do penance for a year and a half without delicacies and without his wife.

26. But he who has intercourse with his slave-woman shall sell

her and shall do penance for one year. 27. If he begets a child by her, then he shall set her free.

28. In the case of one whose wife is barren, both he and she shall live in continence.

29. If any man's wife deserts him and returns again, he shall receive her without payment,[21] and she shall do penance for one year with bread and water, or he shall do so if he has taken another wife.

30. He who is married should be continent during the three forty-day periods of the year and on Saturday and Sunday, night and day, and on the two appointed weekdays,[22] and after conception, and to the very end of the menstrual period.

31. After birth, he shall abstain for thirty-three days, if it is a son, and for sixty-six days, if it is a daughter.

32. A man whose child dies on account of neglect without baptism shall do penance for three years; in the first with bread and water, in the other two without delicacies and marital intercourse.

33. If a cleric from the same parish does not accept him, he shall do penance for one year; if he is not of the same parish, for half a year.

3. ON AVARICE

1. He who commits theft once shall do penance for one year; if a second time, for two years. 2. If he is a boy, forty or thirty days, according to his age or education.

3. He who hoards the leftovers until the following day through ignorance shall give them away to the poor; but if he acts through contempt for those who accuse him, he shall be healed by almsgiving and fasting according to the judgment of a priest. But if he persists in his avarice, he shall be sent away.

4. He who recovers his own property from someone who is carrying it off, against the command of the Lord and the Apostle, shall give to the poor what he recovers.

5. He who steals someone else's property by any means shall restore four times as much to him whom he has injured. 6. If he

cannot make restitution, then he shall do penance as stated above. 7. He who steals sacred things shall do penance as stated above, but in confinement.

8. He who swears a false oath shall do penance for four years. 9. But he who makes another commit perjury unknowingly shall do penance for seven years. 10. He who is led into perjury unknowingly and later finds it out shall do penance for one year. 11. He who suspects that he is being led into perjury and nevertheless swears on oath shall do penance for two years on account of his consent.

12. He who bears false witness shall first satisfy his neighbor, and with what he has wrongly charged his brother, with such judgment shall he be condemned, a priest being the judge.

13. He who fails to fulfill any of those things for which the Lord says: "Come, you blessed of my father…" (Mt 25:34),[23] for whatever time he has remained thus, he shall do penance and shall be generous in his gifts to the end of his life; otherwise he shall be cut off.

14. A cleric who has an excess of goods shall give them to the poor; otherwise he shall be excommunicated. 15. If he afterward repents, he shall live for the same length of time in solitary penance as he was recalcitrant.

16. One who lies on account of greed shall make satisfaction through generosity to the one he has cheated. 17. He who lies through ignorance, however, and does not know it, shall confess to him to whom he has lied and to a priest, and shall be condemned to an hour of silence or fifteen Psalms. 18. But if he did it intentionally, he shall do penance with three days of silence or thirty Psalms if he holds a position of authority.[24]

4. ON ANGER

1. He who causes distress to his brother, justly or unjustly, shall pacify his anger with a recompense, and so he shall be able to pray.[25] 2. But if it is impossible to be reconciled with him, then at least he shall do penance, with a priest as judge. 3. But he who

refuses to be reconciled shall live on bread and water for as long as he has been implacable.

4. That "murderer who hates his brother" (cf. 1 Jn 3:15) shall go on bread and water for as long as he has not overcome his hatred, and he shall be joined to him whom he hates in sincere charity. 5. He who commits murder with malicious premeditation shall give up his weapons until his death and, dead to the world, shall live for God. 6. But if he has already taken the vows of perfection, he shall die to the world by perpetual exile. 7. But he who does this through anger and not with premeditation shall do penance for three years with bread and water, with almsgiving and prayers. 8. But if he kills his neighbor unintentionally, by accident, he shall do penance for one year.

9. He who incapacitates or maims a man with a blow in a quarrel shall meet his medical expenses and shall make good the damages for the injury and shall do his work until he has recovered and shall do penance for half a year. 10. If he does not have the resources to make restitution for these things, he shall do penance for one year. 11. He who strikes his neighbor without injuring him shall do penance on bread and water for one, two, or three forty-day periods.

12. He who curses his brother in anger shall make satisfaction to him whom he has cursed and shall live alone on bread and water for seven days. 13. He who speaks harsh but not injurious words in anger shall make satisfaction to his brother and keep a special fast. 14. But if he expresses his anger with pallor or flush or tremor, yet remains silent, he shall go for a day on bread and water. 15. He who merely feels incensed in his mind shall make satisfaction to the one who is the object of his anger. 16. But if he does not wish to confess to him who is the object of his anger, then that pestilential person shall be cut off from the company of the saints. If he repents, he shall do penance for as long as he was recalcitrant.

5. ON DEPRESSION

1. He who harbors bitterness in his heart for a long time shall be healed by a cheerful face and a light heart. 2. But if he

does not quickly lay this aside, he shall correct himself by fasting according to the judgment of a priest. 3. But if he returns to it, he shall be cut off until, on bread and water, he willingly and gladly acknowledges his fault.

6. ON APATHY[26]

1. The idler shall be given an additional burden of work, and the indolent an extended vigil, that is, he shall occupy himself with three or seven Psalms.[27]

2. Any wandering and unstable man shall be healed by remaining in one place and by application to work.

7. ON VANITY

1. The contentious man shall also subject himself to the decision of another; otherwise he shall be anathematized since he is among those who are strangers to the Kingdom of God.

2. One who boasts of his own good deeds shall humble himself; otherwise any good he has done he has lost on account of human glory.

8. ON PRIDE

1. Whoever takes up any novelty outside the scriptures, which might lead to heresy, shall be sent away. 2. But if he repents, he shall publicly condemn his own opinion and convert to the faith those whom he has deceived, and he shall fast at the decision of a priest.

3. He who through pride charges others with any kind of contempt shall first make satisfaction to them and then fast according to the judgment of a priest.

4. The disobedient shall remain outside the assembly without food and shall humbly knock until he is received, and shall live on bread and water for as long a time as he has been disobedient.

5. The blasphemer too shall be healed by a similar decree.

6. He who grumbles shall be cut off and his work rejected; he shall remain with the due half loaf of bread[28] and water.

7. The envious shall make satisfaction to him whom he has envied, but if he has does him harm, he shall make it up to him with gifts and shall do penance. 8. He who disparages another on account of envy or willingly listens to disparaging talk shall be cut off and shall fast for four days on bread and water. 9. If the offense is against a superior, he shall do penance thus for seven days and shall serve him willingly thereafter. 10. But, as someone says, to speak the truth is not to disparage; but according to the gospel, first "tell him his fault between you and him alone" and afterward, "if he does not listen," call another, and if he still will not hear you, "tell it to the church" (Mt 18:15–17).

11. He who is informed on and he who is the informer are persons of the same status. If he who is informed on denies his guilt, they shall both do penance for one year, two days a week on bread and water, and two days at the end of each month, while all the brethren hold them in subjection and call upon God as their judge. 12. But if they persist in obstinacy when the year has lapsed, they shall be readmitted to the communion of the altar at the risk of eternal fire, and shall be left to the judgment of God. 13. If at any time one of them confesses, his own hardship shall be increased by the degree to which he has inflicted hardship on the other.

14. If anyone injures the good name of a brother whom he loves through idle gossip, he shall do penance in silence for one or two days. 15. But if he did it in conversation, he shall sing twelve Psalms.

16. He who relates the evils of those who have not embraced sanity, in case others should consent to them, or in order to blame evil and confirm the good, or in grief and pity, is to be considered a healer; but if none of these motives are present, then he is a detractor and shall sing thirty Psalms one after another.

17. He who offers an excuse to the abbot or the steward, if he is ignorant of the Rule, shall do penance for one day; if he knows the Rule, he shall do a special fast.

18. He who deliberately disdains to bow to any superior shall go without supper.

19. He who is silent about a brother's sin, which is a mortal one, shall rebuke him with confidence, and shall live on bread and water for the same length of time that he was silent. 20. If it was a slight sin that he kept silent about, he shall indeed rebuke him, but shall do penance with Psalms or fasting according to the judgment of a priest. 21. He who rebukes others boldly shall first pacify them and then sing thirty Psalms. 22. He who imputes a shameful sin to a brother, before he rebukes him in private, shall make satisfaction to him and do penance for three days.

23. He who speaks with a woman alone or remains under the same roof as her at night shall go without supper. 24. If he does this after being forbidden to do so, then he shall do penance on bread and water.

25. Some authorities rule that twelve three-day periods are the equivalent of a year, which I neither praise nor blame.[29] 26. Others, one hundred days with half a loaf of dry bread and an allowance of water, and salt, with fifty Psalms sung every night. 27. Others, fifty special fasts, with one night intervening. 28. Others rule that the penance of the sick shall consist in the giving of alms, that is, the price of a man or maidservant; but it is more fitting if someone gives half of all that he possesses and, if he has wronged anyone, that he pay him back fourfold.

9. ON MINOR CASES

1. If by some accident someone negligently loses the Host, leaving it for animals and birds to devour, if it is excusable, he shall do penance for three forty-day periods; if not, for a year.

2. He who knowingly gives Communion to someone who is excommunicate shall do penance for forty days.

3. So shall he do penance who innocently eats carrion; but if he knows what he does, he shall do penance for a year.

4. Now let it be understood that someone should do penance for the same length of time that he remains in sin.

5. If a particular task has been imposed upon someone

which he does not do on account of contempt, he shall go without supper. 6. He who has not arrived by the end of the second Psalm shall sing eight Psalms one after another. 7. If he is woken after the reading, he shall repeat in order whatever the brethren have sung and shall beg for pardon. 8. If however he does not come a second time, he shall go without supper.

9. If in error anyone has changed any of the words of the Mass where "danger" is noted, he shall do three special fasts.

10. He who allows the Host to fall to the ground through carelessness shall do a special fast.

11. We should celebrate Mass for good rulers but certainly not for bad ones.

12. Priests are indeed not forbidden to celebrate Mass for their bishops.

13. Those who show barbarians the way shall do penance for fourteen years, provided that there is no massacre of Christians. But if there is, they shall give up their weapons and shall live for God until they die, being dead to the world.

14. He who despoils monasteries, falsely saying that he is redeeming captives, shall go for one year on bread and water, and everything that he has taken he shall give to the poor, and he shall do penance for two years without wine and meat.

15. He who loses a consecrated object shall do penance for seven days.

16. He who eats the flesh of a dead animal, whose manner of death he does not know, shall live for a third of a year on bread and water and for the rest of it without wine and meat.

10. LET US NOW SET DOWN THE DECREES OF OUR FATHERS BEFORE US ON THE SINFUL PLAYING OF BOYS

1. Boys who talk alone and break the regulations of the elders shall be corrected by three special fasts. 2. Those who kiss simply shall be corrected with six special fasts; those who kiss licentiously without pollution, with eight special fasts; if with pollution or embrace, with ten special fasts. 3. But if at twenty years of age or older, that is as adults, they commit the same sin, they

shall live at a separate table on bread and water, excluded from the church, for forty days.

4. Children who imitate acts of fornication and stimulate one another, but are not defiled because of their immature age, twenty days; if frequently, forty.

5. A boy who receives communion at Mass, although he has sinned with a beast, one hundred days.

6. But boys of twenty years who practice masturbation mutually and confess before they take communion shall do penance for twenty or forty days. 7. If they repeat it after penance, one hundred days; if more frequently, they shall be separated and shall do penance for a year.

8. If one of the above age practices femoral intercourse, one hundred days; if he does it again, a year.

9. A small boy misused by an older one, if he is ten years of age, shall fast for a week; if he consents, for twenty days.

10. If a small boy eats anything he has stolen, he shall do penance for seven days. 11. If, after his twentieth year, he happens to commit some small theft, he shall do penance for twenty days. 12. If, however, at the age of manhood he happens to do anything similar, forty days; if it is repeated, one hundred days; if it becomes a habit, a year.

13. A man who practices masturbation by himself, for the first offense, one hundred days; if he repeats it, a year. 14. Men guilty of femoral intercourse, for the first offense, a year; if they repeat it, two years. 15. Those practicing homosexual intercourse, if they are boys, two years; if men, three or four years. But if it has become a habit, seven years, and the kind of penance shall be decided by a priest. 16. Those who satisfy their desires with their lips, four years. If it has become a habit, seven years.

17. A boy who has only recently come from the world who seeks to commit fornication with some girl and has not been polluted shall do penance for twenty days; but if he has been polluted, one hundred days. But if, as is often the case, he has his way, a year.

18. He who eats the skin of his own body, that is, a scab, or the vermin which are called lice, and also he who eats or drinks his

own urine or feces, shall do penance for a whole year on bread and water with the imposition of hands of his bishop.

19. He who instead of baptizing only blesses a little infant shall do penance for a year separated from the community, or shall atone with bread and water. 20. If, however, the infant dies having only had such a blessing, that murderer shall do penance according to the judgment of a council.

21. Small boys who strike each other shall do penance for seven days; but if they are older, for twenty days. If they are adolescents, they shall do penance for forty days.

11. ON QUESTIONS CONCERNING THE HOST

1. He who fails to guard the Host carefully so that a mouse eats it shall do penance for forty days. 2. But he who loses it in the church, that is, so that a part falls and is not found, twenty days. 3. But he who loses his chrismal,[30] or only the Host in whatever place, and it cannot be found, three forty-day periods or a year. 4. He who pours anything from the chalice onto the altar when the linen is being removed shall do penance for seven days; or if he has spilled it liberally, he shall do penance with special fasts for seven days. 5. If the Host falls from the hand into the straw, he shall do penance for seven days from the time of the accident. 6. He who spills the chalice at the end of the solemn Mass shall do penance for forty days.

7. He who vomits the Host having gorged his stomach with food, if he ejects it into the fire, twenty days, but if not, forty. 8. If, however, dogs consume this vomit, one hundred. 9. But if it is with pain, and he ejects it into the fire, he shall sing one hundred Psalms.

10. If anyone neglects to receive the Host and does not ask for it, and if there is no reason to excuse him, he shall keep a special fast. And he who, having been polluted in sleep during the night, receives the Host shall do penance likewise.

11. A deacon who forgets to bring the oblation until the linen is removed when the names of the departed are recited shall do penance likewise.[31]

12. He who gives anyone a beverage in which a mouse or a weasel is found dead shall do penance with three special fasts. 13. He who later discovers that he tasted such a drink shall keep a special fast. 14. But if those animals are found in the flour or in any dry food or in porridge or curdled milk, whatever is around their bodies shall be thrown out, and all the rest shall be taken on good faith.

15. He who touches liquid food with unfit hand shall be corrected with one hundred lively blows.[32] 16. But if any of the liquid is discolored, the distributor shall be corrected with a fast of seven days. 17. He who takes this without realizing and afterward discovers it shall torture his empty stomach for fifteen days with fasting.

18. Whoever eats or drinks what has been soiled by a household animal, namely the cat, shall be healed with three special fasts.

19. He who acts with negligence toward the Host, so that it dries up and is consumed by worms until it comes to nothing, shall do penance for three forty-day periods on bread and water. 20. If it is whole, but a worm is found in it, then it shall be burned and the ashes concealed beneath the altar, and he who neglected it shall make good his negligence with forty days of penance. 21. If the Host loses its taste and is discolored, he shall keep a fast for twenty days; if it is stuck together, for seven days.

22. He who wets the Host shall straightaway drink the water that was in the chrismal; and he shall take the Host and shall amend his fault for ten days. 23. If the Host falls from the hands of the celebrant and is lost, everything that is found in the place where it fell shall be burned and the ashes concealed as above. Then the priest shall be sentenced to half a year of penance. 24. If the Host is found, the place shall be swept clean with a broom, and the straw, as we have said above, burned with fire, and the priest shall do penance for twenty days. 25. If it only fell on the altar, he shall keep a special fast. 26. If he spills anything from the chalice onto the floor through carelessness, it shall be licked up with the tongue, the board shall be scraped and the result consumed with fire, the ashes being concealed as we said above. He shall do penance for fifty days. 27. If the chalice drips upon the altar, the minister shall suck

up the drop and do penance for three days, and he shall wash the linens which the drop has touched three times, the chalice being placed underneath, and he shall drink the water used in washing. 28. If the chalice drips when it is washed inside, the first time twelve Psalms will be sung by the minister; if it happens a second time, twice that number; if a third time, three times that number.

29. If the priest stammers over the Sunday prayer where "danger" is noted, if once he shall be purified with fifty strokes; if a second time, with a hundred; if a third time, he shall keep a special fast.

1. But this is to be carefully observed in all penance: the length of time anyone remains in his faults, what education he has received, with what passion he is assailed, with what courage he resists, with what intensity of weeping he seems to be afflicted, with what pressure he is driven to sin. 2. For Almighty God, who knows the hearts of all and has made us all different, will not weigh the burden of sins in an equal scale of penance, as this prophecy says: "For dill is not threshed with a threshing sledge, nor is a cart wheel rolled over cummin; but dill is beaten out with a stick and the cummin with a rod, but bread corn shall be broken small" (Is 28:27–28), or as in this passage: "The mighty shall be mightily tormented" (Wis 6:7). 3. For which reason a certain man, wise in the Lord, said: "To whom more is entrusted, from him more shall be exacted" (cf. Lk 12:48). Thus the priests of the Lord who preside over the churches should learn that their share is given to them together with those whose faults they have caused to be forgiven. 4. What does it mean to cause a fault to be forgiven then unless, when you receive the sinner, by warning, exhortation, teaching, and instruction, you lead him to penance, correcting him from error, improving him from his vices, and making him such a person that God becomes favorable to him after his conversion, you are then said to cause his faults to be forgiven? 5. When you are a priest like this, therefore, and this is your teaching and your word, there is given to you the share of those whom you have corrected, that their merit may be your reward and their salvation your glory.

Here ends this book written by Cummean.

3. THE RULE FOR MONKS BY COLUMBANUS

Here begin the chapters of the rule.

1. On Obedience
2. On Silence
3. On Food and Drink
4. On Poverty and Overcoming Greed
5. On Overcoming Vanity
6. On Chastity
7. On the Choir Office
8. On Discernment
9. On Mortification
10. On the Monk's Perfection

Here begins the Rule for Monks of St. Columbanus the Abbot.

First of all we are taught to love God with all our heart, all our mind, and all our strength, and our neighbor as ourselves; and then our works.

1. ON OBEDIENCE

On hearing the first word of a senior, all should rise to obey since their obedience is shown to God, as our Lord Jesus Christ says: "He who hears you, hears me" (Lk 10:16). Therefore if anyone who hears the word does not rise at once, he is to be found disobedient. But he who answers back incurs the charge of insubordination, and so is not only guilty of disobedience but also, by providing an example of answering back to others, is to be regarded as the destroyer of many. But if anyone grumbles, then he too must be considered to be disobedient for not obeying willingly. And so his work must be rejected until his good will is known. But up to what point is obedience laid down? It is certainly prescribed as far as death, since Christ obeyed his Father for our sakes up to his own death. And this is what he suggests to us through the words of the Apostle: "Take to heart among yourselves what you found in Christ Jesus, who though he was in the form of God, thought it no robbery to be equal with God; but emptied himself, taking the form of a servant, and being found in human form, humbled himself, being made obedient to the Father to death, even death on a cross" (Phil 2:5–8). Thus nothing must be rejected by Christ's true disciples in their obedience, however hard and difficult it may be, but it must be grasped with enthusiasm and with joy, since if obedience is not of this kind, then it shall not be acceptable to the Lord, who says: "And he who does not take up his cross and follow me is not worthy of me" (Mt 10:38). And so he says of his worthy disciple: "Where I am, there too is my servant" (Jn 12:26).

2. ON SILENCE

The rule of silence is decreed to be carefully observed, since it is written: "The cultivation of righteousness is silence and peace" (Is 32:17). And so, in case anyone is seen to be guilty of talking too much, it is right that he should keep silence except concerning those things that are beneficial or necessary, since scripture tells us that sin will not be lacking in many words (Prv 10:19). Therefore our Savior says: "By your words you shall be justified, and by your words you shall be condemned" (Mt 12:37). Those people will justly be condemned who refused to say just things when they could, but preferred to say with garrulous verbosity what is evil, unjust, irreverent, shallow, harmful, dubious, false, provocative, disparaging, base, fanciful, blasphemous, unkind, and contorted. Therefore we must remain silent about these matters and their like and speak with care and prudence in case either disparagement or arrogant argumentativeness should break out in pernicious verbosity.

247

3. ON FOOD AND DRINK

The monks' food and drink should be poor and taken in the evening, in order to avoid satiety and inebriation, so that they sustain life without harming it: vegetables, beans, flour mixed with water, together with a small loaf of bread in case the stomach is burdened and the mind confused. For those who desire eternal rewards should take account only of serviceability and use. Use of life must be moderated just as labor must be moderated, since this is true discretion that the possibility of spiritual progress may be kept alive by an abstinence which punishes the flesh. For if abstinence goes too far, then it will be a vice and not a virtue, for virtue sustains and contains many goods. Therefore we must fast every day, just as we must take food every day, and while we must eat every day, we should gratify the body poorly and sparingly. And we must eat every day because every day we must advance along our path; every day we must pray, labor, and read.

4. ON POVERTY AND OVERCOMING GREED

Monks, to whom for Christ's sake the world is crucified as they are to the world, must avoid greed when it is not only wrong for them to have things superfluous to their needs but also to desire them. In their case it is not possessions that are required but will; taking leave of all things and every day following the Lord Christ with the cross of fear, they have treasure in heaven. Therefore, while they shall have much in heaven, they should be satisfied on earth with the bare minimum, knowing that greed is a leprosy for monks who imitate the sons of the prophets, for the disciple of Christ it is betrayal and ruin, and for the uncertain followers of the Apostles also it is death. Thus nakedness and disdain of riches are the first perfection of the monk, but the second is the purging of vices, the third the most perfect and perpetual delight in God and unceasing love for the things of God which follows on the forgetting of earthly things. Since this is the case, we have need of few things according to the Word of the Lord, or even only of one. For few things are true necessities of life, or even one thing, like food according to the letter. But we require purity of feeling by the grace of God, that we may reach a spiritual understanding of those few gifts of love which are offered to Martha by the Lord.

5. ON OVERCOMING VANITY

How dangerous vanity can be is shown also by a few words of our Savior who said to his disciples when they rejoiced in this vanity, "I saw Satan fall like lightning from heaven" (Lk 10:18), and who said to the Jews when once they offered excuses for themselves, "But what is highly esteemed among men is an abomination in the sight of the Lord" (Lk 16:15). By these and by that most notorious case of the Pharisee who tried to make excuses for himself, we can conclude that vanity and arrogant self-esteem are the destroyers of all good things when the Pharisee's goods, praised in vain, perish and the publican's self-confessed sins vanish away. Let no long word proceed from a monk's mouth in case his own long labor should be lost.

6. ON CHASTITY

The chastity of a monk is judged by his thoughts, for whom, along with the disciples who drew near in order to be able to hear, the words of the Lord were doubtlessly intended: "He who looks at a woman to lust after her has already defiled her in his heart" (Mt 5:28). For while his vow is weighed by the one to whom he is consecrated, it is to be feared that he may find in the monk's soul something abominable, that they may perhaps have eyes full of wantoness and adultery as St. Peter says (cf. 2 Pt 2:14). And of what value is it if he is a virgin in body but not in mind? For God, being spirit, lives in that spirit and in that mind which seems to him undefiled, in which there is no adulterous thought, no stain of a polluted spirit, and no spot of sin.

7. ON THE CHOIR OFFICE

Concerning the synaxis, that is, the Office of Psalms and prayers in canonical manner, some distinctions must be drawn, since different traditions have been preserved about this. Thus, in accordance with the nature of life and the succession of the seasons, I shall suggest in writing the same thing in different ways. For it should not be uniform in view of the mutual changes of the seasons, but it is right that it should be longer on long nights and shorter on short ones. Accordingly, in agreement with our predecessors, from the twenty-fourth of June, when the nights grow longer, the Office begins to grow gradually from twelve chants of the shortest measure on the night of the Sabbath or the Lord's Day until the beginning of winter, that is, the first of November. Then they sing twenty-five antiphonal Psalms, which always follow in third place after two blocks of Psalms, of twice the same number,[33] in such a way that they sing the whole psalter over the two aforementioned nights, while they modify the remaining nights for the whole winter with twelve chants. At the end of winter, gradually with each week through the spring, three Psalms are always dropped so that only twelve antiphons remain on the holy nights, that is, the thirty-six Psalms of the daily winter office, but through the whole spring and summer until the autumn equinox, that is to say the twenty-fourth of September, it is twenty-four. Then the synaxis is like that on the spring equinox, that is, the twenty-fifth of March, while by mutual changes it slowly increases and decreases.[34]

Thus we must match our watching in vigil with our strength, especially when we are told by the Author of our salvation to watch and pray at all times (cf. Lk 21:36), and when Paul ordains: "Pray without ceasing" (1 Thes 5:17). But since we must know the manner of canonical prayers, in which all gather together in common prayer at appointed hours, at the end of which each should pray in his own cell, our predecessors have appointed three Psalms at each of the daytime hours, as an interruption of work, together with added versicles which intercede first for our own sins, then for all Christian people, then for priests and the other orders of the holy flock who are consecrated to God, and finally for those who give alms, next for the peace of kings, and lastly for our enemies, that God may not count it as their sin that they persecute and slander us, since they know not what they do (cf. Lk 23:34). But at nightfall twelve Psalms are chanted, and at midnight twelve more, but toward the morning twice ten and twice two are appointed, as has been said, during the seasons of short nights, while more, as I have already said, are always ordained for the night of the Lord's Day and Sabbath vigil, on which seventy-five are sung individually in the course of one Office.

These things are said with reference to the communal synaxis. For the rest, as I have said, the tradition of prayer is that the potential of a monk who is devoted to this without being too burdened by his vow should be realized, as far as the excellence of his potential permits, or the capacity of his mind considering his limitations, or the quality of his life can allow, and that it should be realized as far as the zeal of each demands, according to whether he is free and alone, the extent of his learning, the leisure of his position, the depth of his study, the type of his work, and the length of his years. But this is to be counted as the excellence of a single work in such diverse ways, since it varies with labor and circumstance. And so, although the length of standing or singing may vary, the identity of prayer in the heart and the unceasing concentration of the mind with God will be of a single excellence. There are some Catholics who have the same canonical number twelve of Psalms, whether on short nights or long ones, but they perform this canon in four sections during the night; that is, at nightfall and at midnight, at cock-crow and at morning.[35] And as this Office seems small to some in winter, so in summer it is found burdensome and heavy enough, while with its frequent risings during the short night it causes not so much tiredness as exhaustion. But on the most holy nights, that is on those of the Lord's Day or the Sabbath, three times the same number are performed at morning, that is, with three times ten and six Psalms. The great numbers of these men and their holy way of life have attracted many to this canonical number with sweet delight, as well as to the rest of their discipline, in the belief that no one is found to be wearied under this Rule. And though their numbers are so great that a thousand fathers are said to live under a single archimandrite, yet it is said that no quarrel has broken out between two monks since the foundation of the community, and this clearly could not be if God did not dwell there who says: "I will dwell with them and walk among them, and I will be their God and they will be my people" (2 Cor 6:16). Therefore they have deservedly increased and daily increase in numbers—thanks be to God—in whose midst God dwells and through whose merits may we merit salvation through our Lord and Savior. Amen.

8. ON DISCERNMENT

How necessary discernment is for monks is shown by the mistake of many and the ruin of some who, lacking discernment at the beginning, continue without guiding knowledge and thus cannot live a praiseworthy life. Just as error overtakes those who have no path, so for those who live without discernment excess is near at hand, always contrary to the virtues, which lie between the extremes. Its onset is dangerous when beside the straight path of discernment our enemies place the stumbling blocks of wickedness and the temptations of various kinds of error. Therefore we must pray to God continually to illumine with the light of true discernment this way that is surrounded on all sides by the deep darkness of the world so that his true worshipers may be able to come to him through this darkness without error. The word *discernment* comes from distinguishing, therefore, since in us it distinguishes between good and evil, the mediocre and the perfect.[36] For from the beginning good and evil have been divided like light and dark after evil began to exist through the Devil by the corruption of the good, but through God who first illumines and then divides. Thus righteous Abel chose the good, but unrighteous Cain fell upon evil. God made all the things that he created good, but the Devil sowed evils over them by crafty cunning and the sly persuasion of dangerous design. What things then are good? Doubtlessly those which are as whole and uncorrupted as they were when they were created; these God alone "created and prepared," according to the Apostle, "so that we should walk in them"; which are "the good works in which we were created in Jesus Christ" (cf. Eph 2:10), namely, goodness, innocence, righteousness, justice, truth, compassion, love, the peace of salvation, spiritual joy, together with the fruits of the spirit—all these with their fruits are good. But to these the evil qualities stand in opposition: wickedness, seduction, unrighteousness, injustice, lying, greed, hatred, discord, bitterness, together with their many and diverse fruits which are born from them. For those things which are born from these two opposites, from good and evil, are beyond number. But the first evil, which is the pride of primal wickedness, is that which departs from its original goodness and innocence, the opposite of which is the humility of a righteous goodness that acknowledges and glorifies its Creator and which is a rational creature's first good. Thus the rest have gradually grown to be a huge forest of names in two parts. Since this is the case, the good must be firmly held by those who enjoy divine help, for which we should always pray in prosperity and adversity in case we should be puffed up with vain pride in prosperity and sink down into despair in adversity. Thus we must always restrain ourselves from both dangers, that is, from all excess by wonderful moderation and true discernment, which cleaves to Christian lowliness and opens the way of perfection to the true soldiers of Christ, by always judging rightly where there is doubt and everywhere discerning between good and evil, whether between both externally and internally, between flesh and spirit,[37] good works and character, action and contemplation, or the public and the private. Therefore evil things are to be equally avoided, pride, envy, lying, seduction, unrighteousness, immoral acts, gluttony, fornication, avarice, wrath, despair, inconstancy, vainglory, boasting, slander; while the good things, the virtues, are to be pursued, humility, kindness, purity, obedience, temperance, chastity, generosity, patience, cheerfulness, constancy, zeal, persistence, vigilance, silence, which through patience, fortitude, and moderation are to be weighed in the performance of our usual work as if in the scales of discernment, according to the extent of our efforts, who everywhere seek sufficiency. For no one doubts that those for whom sufficiency is not enough have overstepped the measure of discernment, and evidently whatever lies beyond that measure is a vice.

Thus there exists a reasonable measure between being too small and being too large, which always calls us back from any excess on either side, providing in every case what is consonant with need and opposing the unreasonable demands of superfluous desire. And this measure of true discernment, weighing all our actions in the scales of justice, does not allow us to err from what is just or to make a mistake, if we follow it closely as our guide. While we must always keep ourselves from either side according to the saying "Keep yourselves from the right and from the left" (cf. Dt 5:32), still we must always proceed straight ahead by discernment, that is, by the light of God, saying and singing time and again the victorious psalmist's verse: "My God, enlighten my darkness, since in you I am rescued from temptation. For temptation is the life of man on earth" (Ps 18:29–29; Jb 7:1).

9. ON MORTIFICATION

The main part of the monks' rule is mortification since they are indeed commanded by scripture: "Do nothing without counsel" (Sir 32:24). Thus if nothing is done without counsel, then everything is to be asked for by counsel. Thus we are commanded by Moses also: "Ask your father and he will show you, your elders and they will tell you" (Dt 32:7). But although this discipline may seem hard to those who are hard of heart, namely, that we should always hang upon the words of another, to those who are secure in their fear of God it will seem sweet and safe if it is kept wholly and not just in part, since nothing is sweeter than security of conscience and nothing safer than exoneration of the soul, which no one can achieve through their own efforts since it properly belongs to the estimation of others. For what the judge's scrutiny has already tried protects from the fear of judgment, and the weight of another's burden is laid upon his shoulders as are all the risks that he runs since, as it is written, the peril of the judge is greater than that of the accused. And so he will never err who always ask advice of others, as long as he follows it, since if it is the other's reply that is wrong, then the faith of him who believes and the efforts of him who obeys cannot be in error, nor shall he lack the reward of seeking counsel. For if he has considered anything by himself when he should have sought counsel, then he is proved guilty of error in the very fact that he presumed to judge when he should have been judged, and even though it may turn out right, it will be counted to him as a wrong, since he has departed from the right course in this. For the monk whose duty it is only to obey presumes to judge nothing on his own account.

Since these things are the case, monks must everywhere beware of a proud independence and learn true humility as they obey without murmur or hesitation, by which, according to the Word of the Lord, the yoke of Christ may be sweet to them and his burden light. Otherwise while they are learning the humility of Christ, they will not feel the sweetness of his yoke or the lightness of his burden. For humility is the repose of the soul when wearied with vices and effort, its only refuge from so many evils, and insofar as it is drawn to consideration of this from so many errant and empty things without, to that extent it enjoys repose and recuperation within, so that even bitter things are sweet to it and things which it previously found difficult and demanding it now feels to be plain and easy. Mortification too, which is intolerable to the proud and hard-hearted, becomes the comfort of those who take pleasure only in what is humble and gentle. But we should realize that no one can perfectly enjoy either this joy of martyrdom or any other benefit that follows unless he has paid particular attention to not being found unready.[38] For if along with this aim, he has wished to pursue or to nourish any of his desires, both entirely preoccupied and thrown into confusion by these intrusions, he will not always be able to follow thankfully where the commandment leads, nor can someone who is stirred up and lacking in gratitude act as he should.

Thus there are three different ways of mortification: not to argue back in the mind, not to speak with an unbridled tongue, not to go wherever we wish. It demands that we should always say to a senior monk, however unwelcome his instructions, "Not as I will, but as you will" (Mt 26:39), following the example of our Lord and Savior, who says: "I came down from heaven, not to do my will but the will of him who sent me" (Jn 6:38).

10. ON THE MONK'S PERFECTION

Let the monk live in a monastery under the direction of a single father, in the company of many, so that he may learn humility from one, and patience from another. One may teach him silence and another gentleness. Let him not do as he wishes, let him eat what he is told to eat, let him keep what he has received, let him carry out his duties and be obedient to someone he would not have chosen. Let him come tired to his bed and sleep while he is still walking, and let him be made to rise before he has slept enough. Let him be silent when he suffers wrong, let him fear the superior of the monastery as a lord, and love him as a father, believing that whatever he commands is for his own good. Let him not pass judgment on the opinion of an elder; his duty is to obey and carry out what he is commanded to do, as Moses says: "Hear, O Israel," and the rest (Dt 6:4). THE END OF THE RULE.

POETRY

IRISH POEMS

1.
A HYMN OF PRAISE

Blessing and brightness,
Wisdom, thanksgiving,
Great power and might
To the King who rules over all.[1]

Glory and honor and goodwill,
Praise and the sublime song of minstrels,
Exceeding love from every heart
To the King of heaven and earth.

To the chosen Trinity has been joined
Before all, after all, universal
Blessing and everlasting blessing,
Blessing everlasting and blessing.

2.
THE LORD OF CREATION

Let us adore the Lord,
Maker of marvelous works,
Bright heaven with its angels,
And on earth the white-waved sea.

3.
THE SCRIBE IN THE WOODS

A hedge of trees surrounds me, a blackbird's lay sings to me,
    praise I shall not conceal,
Above my lined book the trilling of the birds sings to me.
A clear-voiced cuckoo sings to me in a gray cloak from the tops of
    bushes,

259

May the Lord save me from Judgment; well do I write under the greenwood.

4.

MY SPEECH—may it praise you without flaw: May my heart love you, King of heaven and earth.

My speech—may it praise you without flaw: Make it easy for me, pure Lord, to do you all service and to adore you.

My speech—may it praise you without flaw: Father of all affection, hear my poems and my speech.

5.

ALL ALONE IN MY LITTLE CELL, without the company of anyone; precious has been the pilgrimage before going to meet death.

A hidden secluded little hut, for the forgiveness of my sins: an upright, untroubled conscience toward holy heaven.

Sanctifying the body by good habits, trampling like a man upon it: with weak and tearful eyes for the forgiveness of my passions.

Passions weak and withered, renouncing this wretched world; pure and eager thoughts; let this be a prayer to God.

Heartfelt lament toward cloudy heaven, sincere and truly devout confessions, swift showers of tears.

A cold and anxious bed, like the lying down of a doomed man: a brief, apprehensive sleep as in danger, invocations frequent and early.

My food as befits my station, precious has been the captivity: My dinner, without doubt, would not make me full-blooded.

260

Dry bread weighed out, well we bow the head; water of the many colored hillside, that is the drink I would take.

A bitter meager dinner; diligently feeding the sick; keeping off strife and visits; a calm, serene conscience.

It would be desirable, a pure and holy blemish: cheeks withered and sunken, a shriveled leathery skin.

Treading the paths of the gospel; singing Psalms at every hour; an end of talking and long stories; constant bending of the knees.

May my Creator visit me, my Lord, my King; may my spirit seek him in the everlasting kingdom where he dwells.

Let this be the end of vice in the enclosures of churches; a lovely little cell among the graves, and I there alone.

All alone in my little cell, all alone thus; alone I came into the world, alone I shall go from it.

If by myself I have sinned through pride of this world, hear me lament for it all alone, O God!

6.

GRANT ME TEARS, O LORD, to blot out my sins; may I not cease from them, O God, until I have been purified.

May my heart be burned by the fire of redemption; grant me pure tears for Mary and Ite.

When I contemplate my sins, grant me tears always, for great are the claims of tears on cheeks.

Grant me tears when rising, grant me tears when resting, beyond your every gift altogether for love of you, Mary's Son.

Grant me tears in bed to moisten my pillow, so that his dear ones may help to cure the soul.

Grant me contrition of heart so that I may not be in disgrace; O Lord, protect me and grant me tears.

For the dalliance I had with women, who did not reject me, grant me tears, O Creator, flowing in streams from my eyes.

For my anger, my jealousy, and my pride, a foolish deed, in pools from my inmost parts bring forth tears.

My falsehoods, my lying, and my greed, grievous the three, to banish them all from me, O Mary, grant me tears.

7.
ON THE FLIGHTINESS OF THOUGHT

Shame on my thoughts, how they stray from me! I fear great danger from this on the Day of eternal Judgment.

During the Psalms they wander on a path that is not right: they run, they distract, they misbehave before the eyes of the great God.

Through eager assemblies, through companies of lewd women, through woods, through cities—swifter they are than the wind.

One moment they follow ways of loveliness, and the next ways of riotous shame—no lie!

Without a ferry or a false step they cross every sea: Swiftly they leap in one bound from earth to heaven.

They run—not a course of great wisdom—near, far: Following paths of great foolishness they reach their home.

Though one should try to bind them or put shackles on their feet, they are neither constant nor inclined to rest a while.

Neither the edge of a sword nor the stripe of lash will subdue them; as slippery as an eel's tail they elude my grasp.

Neither lock nor well-constructed dungeon, nor any fetter on earth, neither stronghold nor sea nor bleak fastness restrains them from their course.

O beloved, truly chaste Christ, to whom every eye is clear, may the grace of the sevenfold Spirit come to keep them, to hold them in check!

Rule this heart of mine, O swift God of the elements, that you may be my love, and that I may do your will!

That I may reach Christ with his chosen companions, that we may be together: They are neither fickle nor inconstant—they are not as I am.

8.

THREE WISHES I ask of the King when I part from my body: May I have nothing to confess, may I have no enemy, may I own nothing!

Three wishes I ask this day of the King, ruler of suns: may I have no dignity or honors that may lead me into torment!

May I not work without reward before the Christ of this world! May God take my soul when it is most pure! Finally, may I not be guilty when my three wishes have been spoken!

9.

THE SAINTS' CALENDAR OF ADAMNÁN

The saints of the four seasons,
I long to pray to them,
May they save me from torments,
The saints of the whole year!

The saints of the glorious springtime,
May they be with me

263

By the will
Of God's fosterling.[2]

The saints of the dry summer,
About them is my poetic frenzy,
That I may come from this land
To Jesus, son of Mary.

The saints of the beautiful autumn,
I call upon a company not unharmonious,
That they may draw near to me,
With Mary and Michael.

The saints of the winter I pray to,
May they be with me against the throng of demons,
Around Jesus of the mansions,
The Spirit holy, heavenly.

The other calendar,
Which noble saints will have,[3]
Though it has more verses,
It does not have more saints.

I beseech the saints of the earth,
I beseech all the angels,
I beseech God himself, both when rising and lying down,
Whatever I do or say, that I may dwell in the heavenly land.

10.
A PRAYER TO THE ARCHANGELS FOR EVERY DAY OF THE WEEK

May Gabriel be with me on Sundays, and the power of the King of
  heaven.
May Gabriel be with me always that evil may not come to me nor
  injury.

Michael on Monday I speak of, my mind is set on him,
Not with anyone do I compare him but with Jesus, Mary's son.

If it be Tuesday, Raphael I mention, until the end comes, for my
     help,
One of the seven whom I beseech, as long as I am on the field of
     the world.

May Uriel be with me on Wednesdays, the abbot with high nobil-
     ity,
Against wound and against danger, against the sea of rough wind.

Sariel on Thursday I speak of, against the swift waves of the sea,
Against every evil that comes to us, against every disease that
     seizes us.

On the day of the second fast, Rumiel—a clear blessing—I have
     loved,
I say only the truth, good the friend I have taken.

May Panchel be with me on Saturdays, as long as I am in this yel-
     low-colored world.
May sweet Mary, with her friend, deliver me from strangers.

May the Trinity protect me! May the Trinity defend me!
May the Trinity save me from every hurt, from every danger.

WELSH POEMS

11.

ALMIGHTY CREATOR, it is you who made
The land and the sea...

The world cannot comprehend in song bright and melodious,
Even though the grass and trees should sing
All your wonders, O true Lord!

The Father created the world by a miracle;[4]
It is difficult to express its measure.
Letters cannot contain it, letters cannot comprehend it.

Jesus created for the hosts of Christendom,
With miracles when he came,
Resurrection through his nature for them.

He who made the wonder of the world
Will save us, has saved us.
It is not too great a toil to praise the Trinity.

Clear and high in the perfect assembly,
Let us praise above the nine orders of angels
The sublime and blessed Trinity.

Purely, humbly, in skillful verse,
I should love to give praise to the Trinity,
According to the greatness of his power.

He has required of the host in this world
Who are his, that they should at all times,
All together, fear the Trinity.

The one who has both wisdom and dominion
Above heaven, below heaven, completely;
It is not too great toil to praise the Son of Mary.

12.
PADARN'S STAFF

May his staff, bright and much loved,[5] offer protection,
Its holy power reaching three parts of the world,[6]
No other relic is like Cyrwen,
A wonderful gift was Padarn's staff.

13.
GLORIOUS LORD

Hail to you, glorious Lord!
May church and chancel praise you,
May chancel and church praise you,
May plain and hillside praise you,
May the three springs praise you,
Two higher than the wind and one above the earth,
May darkness and light praise you,
The cedar[7] and the sweet fruit tree.
Abraham praised you, the founder of faith,
May life everlasting praise you,
May the birds and the bees praise you,
May the regrowth and the grass praise you.
Aaron and Moses praised you,
May male and female praise you,
May the seven days and the stars praise you,
May the lower and upper air praise you,
May books and letters praise you,
May the fish in the river praise you,
May thought and action praise you,
May the sand and the earth praise you,
May all the good things created praise you,
And I too shall praise you, Lord of glory,
Hail to you, glorious Lord!

14.
PRAISE TO THE TRINITY

I praise the threefold
Trinity as God,
Who is one and three,
A single power in unity,
His attributes a single mystery,
One God to praise.
Great King, I praise you,
Great your glory.
Your praise is true;
I am the one who praises you.
Poetry's welfare
Is in Elohim's care.
Hail to you, O Christ,
Father, Son,
And Holy Ghost,
Our Adonai.

I praise two,
Who is one and two,
Who is truly three,
To doubt him is not easy,
Who made fruit and flowing water
And all variety,
God is his name as two,
Godly his words,
God is his name as three,
Godly his power,
God is his name as one,
The God of Paul and Anthony.[8]

I praise the one,
Who is two and one,
Who is three together,
Who is God himself,
He made Mars and Luna,[9]

Man and woman,
The difference in sound between
Shallow water and the deep.
He made the hot and the cold,
The sun and the moon,
The word in the tablet,
And the flame in the taper,
Love in our senses,
A girl, dear and tender,
And burned five cities[10]
Because of false union.

15.

PRAISE TO GOD

In the name of the Lord, mine to praise, of great praise,
I shall praise God, great the triumph of his love,[11]
God who defended us, God who made us, God who saved us,
God our hope, perfect and honorable, beautiful his blessing.
We are in God's power, God above, Trinity's king.
God proved himself our liberation by his suffering,
God came to be imprisoned in humility.
Wise Lord, who will free us by Judgment Day,
Who will lead us to the feast through his mercy and sanctity
In Paradise, in pure release from the burden of sin,
Who will bring us salvation through penance and the five wounds.
Terrible grief, God defended us when he took on flesh.
Man would be lost if the perfect rite had not redeemed him.[12]
Through the cross, bloodstained, came salvation to the world.
Christ, strong shepherd, his honor shall not fail.

16.

ALEXANDER'S BREASTPLATE[13]

On the face of the world
There was not born
his equal.

Three-person God,
Trinity's only Son,
Gentle and strong.[14]
Son of the Godhead,
Son of humanity,
Sole Son of wonder.
The Son of God is a refuge,
Mary's Son is a blessed sanctuary,
A noble child was seen.
Great his splendor,
Great Lord and God
In the place of glory.
From the line of Adam
And Abraham
We were born.
But from the line of David
—the fulfillment of prophecy—
The host was born again.
By his word he saved
The blind and the deaf,
From all suffering.
The ragged,
Foolish sinners,
And those of impure mind.
Let us rise up
To meet the Trinity,
Following our salvation.
Christ's cross is bright,
A shining breastplate
Against all harm
And all our enemies,
May it be strong:
The place of our protection.

17.
PRAISING GOD AT THE BEGINNING AND END

He shall not refuse or reject whoever strives
To praise God at the beginning and end of the day,
Mary's only son, the Lord of kings.
Like the sun he shall come, from east to north.
Mary, Christ's mother, chief of maidens,
Call for the sake of your great mercy
Upon your son to chase away our sin.
God above us, God before us, may the God who rules,
Heaven's king, grant us a share of his mercy.
Royal-hearted one, peace between us
Without rejection, may I make amends
For the wrong I have done before going
To my tomb, my green grave,
My place of rest, in the dark without candle,
My burial place, my recess, my repose,
After enjoying the horses and new mead,
Feasting and women's company.
I shall not sleep; I shall consider my end.
We live in a world of wretched vanity,
Which shall pass away like leaves from a tree.
Woe to the miser who gathers great wealth;
Though the world's course lets him be,
He shall, unless he gives all to God,
Face peril at his end.
The fool does not know to tremble in his heart,[15]
Nor to rise early in the morning, pray and prostrate,[16]
Nor to chant prayers or petition mercy.
He will pay in the end bitterly
For his pomp, his pride and arrogance.
For the toads and snakes he feeds his body,
And for lions, and he performs iniquity,
But death shall enter in and greedily
Devour him, bearing him away.
Old age draws near and senility;

Your hearing, your sight, your teeth grow weak,
And the skin of your fingers is wrinkly.
It is old age and gray hairs that cause this.
May Michael intercede for us with the Lord of Heaven
For a share of his mercy.

18.
THE ADVICE OF ADDAON

I asked all the priests of the world,
The bishops and judges,
What most profits the soul.

The Lord's prayer, the *Beati* and holy creed,
All sung for the sake of the soul,
Are best practiced until Judgment Day.

If only you shape your own path
And build up peace,
You shall see no end to mercy.

Feed the hungry and clothe the naked,
Sing out in praise,
For you have escaped the Devil's number.

But the proud and idle, pain on their flesh
On account of excess,
Must be winnowed until they are pure.

Too much sleep, drunkenness and sipping of mead,
Too much pandering to the body,
That is their sweet bitterness before Judgment Day.[17]

They who commit perjury for land and deceive their Lord,
Who pour scorn on the humble,
Shall know regret on Judgment Day.

By rising for matins and by midnight vigils,
By praying to the saints,
Every Christian shall receive forgiveness.

19.
ELAETH'S ENGLYNION

Since my clothes are as battered as my spirits,
On account of sin, I confess it,
May God not punish me twice.

May God not punish a man twice
In his wrath and sadness,
Those cursed by heaven are cursed on earth.

Let the man of earth and sin pray to God,
And keep vigil in the dark,
Let him who offends Christ not slumber.

Let the son of man not slumber for the Son of God's Passion,
Let him be awake at matins,
Then he will win heaven and forgiveness.

He will gain forgiveness who remembers God,
And does not neglect him,
And heaven too on the night he dies.

If he dies unreconciled with God,
Then for the sin he may have done,
It was unfortunate that he was born.

The wicked man does not practice prayer to God,
Against the day of tribulation,
The foolish man does not ponder his end.

20.
THE SONG OF ELAETH

Not to remember God's gracious defense of the pure,
Nor the angels,
Is excess of wicked pride.
Woe to those who do so openly in the world.

I have no love for wealth, its trace is always passing.
All the world is a dwelling by summer pasture.
I am God's servant; highest praise to him,
The God it is best to follow.

I love praise of Peter who governs just peace,
And his long-lasting blessing.
There is hope in him in every nation,
Gentle and praiseworthy, generous keeper of heaven's gate.

I seek from God who grants what is asked of him,
Elohim, our protector,
For my soul against pain,
The protection of all the saints.

I seek from God a worthy petition,
Against the wounds of enemies,
For my soul, because of its thoughts,
The protection of Mary and all the virgins.

And I seek from God a just petition,
Who can be my defender,
For my soul against terrible pain,
The protection of all Christians in the world.

I seek from God a fine and constant petition,
Earnestly, at every matins,
For my soul against suffering,
The highest protection of each and every saint.

21.
THE FIRST WORD I SAY

The first word I say
In the morning, when I arise:
May Christ's cross be my armor about me.

I shall put on the Lord's protection today,
A sneeze I hear.
It is not my God; I will not believe in it.

I shall arm myself splendidly,
And not believe any superstition, for it is not right.
He who created me shall give me strength.

My mind is set on a journey,
My intent is to put to sea.
A beneficial plan, a gift it will be.

My mind is set on a plan,
My intent is to put to sea.
A beneficial plan, O Lord, it will be.

A crow shall raise its wing,
Intending to go far.
A beneficial plan, it will be better.

A crow shall raise its wing,
Intending to go to Rome.
A beneficial plan, it will be fine.

Saddle the bay with white nostrils,[18]
Eager to run, with a rough coat.
King of Heaven, we would need God's aid.

Saddle the short-haired bay,
With easy gait and ambling pace.
Where there is a nose, there will be a sneeze!

Saddle the bay with the long leap,
With easy gait and keen pace.
An unlucky sneeze shall not check the brave.

Earth's company is burdensome, and thick the briar's leaves,
Bitter the drinking horn of sweet mead.
Lord of Heaven, smooth the way of my journey.

O royal offspring, victorious Redeemer,
Peter, head of every nation,
St. Brigid, bless our journey.

Sun of intercession, Lord of petition,
Christ of Heaven, pillar of grace,
May I atone for my sin by my deed.

22.
MAYTIME IS THE FAIREST SEASON

Maytime is the fairest season,
With its loud bird-song and green trees,
When the plow is in the furrow
And the oxen under the yoke,
When the sea is green,
And the land many colors.

But when cuckoos sing on the tops
Of the lovely trees, my sadness deepens,
The smoke stings and my grief is clear
Since my brothers have passed away.

On the hill and in the valley,
On the islands of the sea,
Whichever path you take,
You shall not hide from blessed Christ.

It was our wish, our Brother, our way,
To go to the land of your exile.
Seven saints and seven score and seven hundred
Went to the one court with blessed Christ,
And were without fear.

The gift I ask, may it not be denied me,
Is peace between myself and God.
May I find the way to the gate of glory,
May I not be sad, O Christ, in your court.

23.

FRAGMENT OF THE DISPUTE BETWEEN BODY AND SOUL

While we walk together, companion in glory,
Be perfect in what you do.
Let us seek salvation
Through faith, religion, and creed.

Companions in faith, by the friendship of faith
Comes great and long penance daily;
Soul, when you ask me what my end shall be:
The grave or eternity.[19]

24.

TO THE TRINITY I make my prayer,
O Lord, grant me the skill to sing your praise,
For the bustle of this world is perilous,
And our deeds and decisions cause irate concern
Among the company of the saints, that is the heavenly family,
King of Heaven, may I be eloquent in my praise of you,
Before my soul parts from my body,
Grant me to pray for my sins,
And to sing entreaty before your glory.
May I be part of the merciful Trinity,
I seek and desire, O people of the earth,
The nine orders of heaven, the feast of the hosts,
And the tenth, which is the blessed company of the saints.
The nations shall be glorious,
A great host, their noble victory clear to see,
The ranks who look upon God.[20]
In heaven, on earth, at my end,
In times of joy and sorrow, in tribulation,
In my body, in my soul, in austerity,
Long preparation before the approach of glory,
I shall beseech you, Lord of the land of peace,

That my soul may rest in life
For all eternity, in the highest place,
In the land of heaven, I shall not be refused.

25.

LORD OF HEAVEN, grant me my prayer to you,
May my praise of you free me from punishment.
God asks me well:
"Did you see the Lord's grave prophecy?"
He released the spoils of hell,
And gathered the imprisoned host to himself.
Before I am powerless,[21]
Let me be steadfast for the God of strength,
Before I suffer a bloody death,
Before my mouth slavers,
Before I am joined to wooden boards,
May my soul be filled with his good food.
The script of books tells me little
Of hard affliction after the deathbed.
May those who have heard my song
Come to heaven, finest dwelling.

26.
THE DEATHBED SONG OF MEILYR THE POET

King of kings, leader easy to praise,
I ask this favor of my highest Lord:
Realm-mastering ruler of the sublime and blessed land,
Noble chief, make peace between you and me.
Feeble and empty is my mind, since
I have provoked you, and full of regret.
I have sinned before the Lord my God,
Failing to attend to my due devotion;
But I shall serve my Lord King
Before I am laid in the earth, stripped of life.
A true foretelling (to Adam and his offspring

The prophets had declared
That Jesus would be in the womb of martyrs),
Mary gladly received her burden.
But a burden I have amassed of unclean sin
And have been shaken by its clamor.
Lord of all places, how good you are to praise,
May I praise you and be purified before punishment.
King of all kings, who knows me, do not refuse me,
On account of wickedness, for the sake of your mercy.
Many a time I had gold and brocade
From fickle kings for praising them,
And after the gift of song of a superior power,
Poverty-stricken is my tongue at the prospect of its silence.
I am Meilyr the Poet, pilgrim to Peter,
Gatekeeper who measures right virtue.
When the time of our resurrection comes,
All who are in the grave, make me ready.
As I await the call, may my home be
The monastery where the tide rises,
A wilderness of enduring glory,
Around its cemetery the breast of the sea,
Island of fair Mary, sacred isle of the saints,
Awaiting resurrection there is lovely.
Christ of the prophesied cross, who knows me, shall guide me
Past hell, the isolated abode of agony.
The Creator who made me shall receive me
Among the pure parish, the people of Enlli.

27.
MEILYR SON OF GWALCHMAI'S ODE TO GOD

May God grant me, may I be granted mercy,
May no evil lack defeat me,
May being righteous on account of my gift cleanse me
And the world, which I know well, be shaken.
May I deserve God's favor, the Lord glorify me,
And give me entrance to the home of heaven.

Heaven shall be sure for those who seek freely
The royal growth of the religion of the Creed.
May the king of seas and stars hear me,
Privileged is the cause of one who petitions.
May the honor of the land of Paradise admit me;
That is the genuine kingdom and true.

With fullness of wisdom may my spirit reflect
On the wise fusion of skills that shall make me skillful.
A skilled man does not approach him who speaks
The glib and lying word, for all he may preach it.
I believe in Christ, blessed teacher,
No skilled believer it is who does not believe in him.

May I believe and reflect, and may the wise one see that

I believe in God and the saints and their land's honor,
A Christian am I with unshakable right to a gift;
Christ, may I be granted gifts when he gives.
May Christianity's nurture release me,
The Lord Christ my King bring me freedom.

And may heaven's King protect me from error;
May his gift and his understanding cure my faults.
May God, who is flawless, not destroy me;
Undarkened is the mind that praises him,[22]
Undeceived is the love that loves him,
Unblemished glory for all who believe in him.

May God, creator and ruler, guide me till judgment,
May he desire the ways of sinlessness for me,
And may it be his majestic desire to give me
Bright gifts that can purify me:
May rites of remission accompany my end,
And gifts of counsel guide me.

The counselor of man, gentle to all who desire him,
Bears no ill will to those who love him.
Love for me it is that can clear my blame;

May love and his concern for me not fail.
May the friend of our true cause elect me,
May I have the friendship of the Lord forever.

28.

THE DEATHBED SONG OF CYNDDELW

From God I beseech guardianship of the gift
Of praising my generous and gracious Lord,[23]
Mary's single son who makes morning and afternoon,
And fertile streams,
Who made forest and field and true measure,
Fruit and God's abundant gifts,
Who made grass and trees, heather on the hills,
Who made one person blessed for just judgment
And another flawed, bereft of gifts,
Destitute and full of anger.
I beseech God's Son, since he is sufficient,
For expiation of sin, it is wrong to sin,
For our welcome in heaven under his protection;
Let us go to the land of our desire.

I hail God, I hail you, may there be
Fair praise upon the declaration I declare,[24]
Thousands praise you, Prince,
Of your hosts to the furthest limit.
I would wish, my Lord, by your leave
(I believe in you for your love,
I shall sing you a song of praise,
Dispenser of gifts), may I make no error.
There was more than was needed of greatest grace,
Ruler of the strong, guarding the farthest limit.
The thought terrifies me
Of the sinfulness of Adam's sin.
I am a foolish exile wandering in your blessed land,
With your fair hosts about me,
Brightest bards of the church,

Their sustenance has been shared with me.
Lovely is the path to the place I seek,
Hope I ask from the chief judge of virtue.
All peoples' King, be my Savior,
After wandering the world, may blessing be mine,
By leave of the most sovereign Father,
Son, and Spirit, holiness most bright,
In the law's light blessed I shall be,
In the home of angels pure and most gentle,[25]
In the blessed land of heaven's Lord, whom I petition.

Greatest Lord, when you were born
Love came to us, there came salvation,
Adam's children took leave of the party of paganism,
Of vile lawlessness and of captivity.
There came the object of our keen desire,
Courage came and great plenty.
Christ entered the flesh, his the primacy,
He came to Mary's womb, the desired Son.
The world's five ages emerged from the pain of perdition,
From deceit, from the darkness of a false home,
Of grievous captivity, from harsh grief,
From the enemy's prison, when they were freed.
He is our leader and our perfect protection,
Who will judge our achievement by our labor.
He is the Lord of Heaven, destiny of peace,
Who led us from destruction when he was pierced,
He rises for us and offers his merits,
He is the Lord who shall not impede our welfare,
And as a gift has been given,
Entirely mortal, infinite his rights.[26]
Those who give God his tithe with their hand
Deny him not his due.
I am a bard who has been made flawless
In my Creator's protection, Lord of hosts,
I am Cynddelw, singer of verse, grace has been given me,
May Michael, who knows me, give me welcome.

Greatest Lord, when I sang of you,
Not without worth were my words,
Nor bereft of fair features,
Not wanting the grace wherever I received it.
Unshakable God did not make me
To pursue folly, deceit, or violence.
Such a one, I considered, shall not be woken,[27]
Nor be given heaven, who seeks it not.
I did not serve too keenly,
Nor profit too greatly,
Nor let arrogance grow in my breast,
Nor did I pursue too much penance,[28]
But to be in my Lord's dwelling was my desire,
And freedom for the soul, the need for which I prayed.

Greatest Lord, take to yourself
This tribute of praise and well-formed poetry.
Perfect is the speech-skill and shape
Of my extolling song, candle of a hundred lands,
For you are master and great monarch,
You are counselor and light's lord,[29]
You are the heart of the prophet, and judge,
You are my generous ruler, the giver,
You are teacher to me; drive me not from your heights,
In your wrath, or from your lovely land,
Nor deny me your favor, my Lord creator,
Nor refuse my submission and lowly plea.[30]
Nor deliver me by your hand to a wretched home,
Nor let me run with the black host of the rejected.

29.

THE LOVES OF TALIESIN

The beauty of the virtue in doing penance for excess,
Beautiful too that God shall save me.
The beauty of a companion who does not deny me his company,
Beautiful too the drinking horn's society.

The beauty of a master like Nudd, the wolf of God,[31]
Beautiful too a man who is noble, kind, and generous.
The beauty of berries at harvest time,
Beautiful too the grain on the stalk.
The beauty of the sun, clear in the sky,
Beautiful too they who pay Adam's debt.[32]
The beauty of a herd's thick-maned stallion,
Beautiful too the pattern of his plaits.
The beauty of desire and a silver ring,
Beautiful too a ring for a virgin.
The beauty of an eagle on the shore when tide is full,
Beautiful too the seagulls playing.
The beauty of a horse and gold-trimmed shield,
Beautiful too a bold man in the breach.[33]
The beauty of Einion, healer of many,[34]
Beautiful too a generous and obliging minstrel.[35]
The beauty of May with its cuckoo and nightingale,[36]
Beautiful too when good weather comes.
The beauty of a proper and perfect wedding feast,
Beautiful too a gift which is loved.[37]
The beauty of desire for penance from a priest,
Beautiful too bearing the elements to the altar.
The beauty for a minstrel of mead at the head of the hall,
Beautiful too a lively crowd surrounding a hero.
The beauty of a faithful priest in his church,[38]
Beautiful too a chieftain in his hall.
The beauty of a strong parish led by God,
Beautiful too being in the season of Paradise.
The beauty of the moon shining on the earth,
Beautiful too when your luck is good.
The beauty of summer, its days long and slow,
Beautiful too visiting the ones we love.
The beauty of flowers on the tops of fruit trees,
Beautiful too covenant with the Creator.
The beauty in the wilderness of doe and fawn,
Beautiful too the foam-mouthed and slender steed.
The beauty of the garden when the leeks grow well,

Beautiful too the charlock in bloom.
The beauty of the horse in its leather halter,
Beautiful too the king's retinue.
The beauty of a hero who does not shun injury,
Beautiful too is elegant Welsh.[39]
The beauty of the heather when it turns purple,
Beautiful too pasture land for cattle.
The beauty of the season when calves suckle,
Beautiful too riding a foam-mouthed horse.
And for me there is no less beauty
In the father of the horn in a feast of mead.
The beauty of the fish in his bright lake,
Beautiful too its surface shimmering.
The beauty of the word which the Trinity speaks,
Beautiful too doing penance for sin.
But the loveliest of all is covenant
With God on the Day of Judgment.

30.
POEM TO THE VIRGIN MARY

Virgin who bore God on her breast,
Bright, with goodness full,
Mary miracle, the Lion's precious love,
Virgin once and virgin still.

DEVOTIONAL TEXTS

1.

MAY YOUR HOLY ANGELS, O Christ, son of the living God, tend our sleep, our rest, our bright bed.

Let them reveal true visions to us in our sleep, O High Prince of the universe, O great and mysterious King.

May no demons, no evil, no injury or terrifying dreams disturb our rest, our prompt and swift repose.

May our waking, our work, and our living be holy; our sleep, our rest, without hindrance or harm.

2.

O GOD, LORD OF CREATION, I invoke you. You are my gracious counselor. Do not turn your face toward me, for you are my judgment without betrayal.

You are my king. You are my law. Yours is my flesh, my body. I love you, blessed Christ, for my soul is yours tonight.

Let me not conceal it, O King. May I be in your royal dwelling all my days. May I eat the feast from your table. Do not leave me behind, O God.

3.
THE BREASTPLATE OF LAIDCENN

Help me, Unity in Trinity,
Trinity in Unity, take pity.

Help me, I beseech you, since I am
As if in peril on the great sea,
So that this year's plague does not
Drag me off, nor the world's vanity.

And this too I ask of the high powers
Of the host of heaven,
Not to leave me to be torn by the enemy
But to defend me now with powerful arms.

Let them go before me in the battle-line,
The armies of the heavenly host:
Cherubim and seraphim in their thousands,
Gabriel and Michael and their like.

I beseech the Thrones, Virtues, Archangels,
Principalities, Powers, and Angels
To defend me with their massed ranks
And to scatter my enemies.

Then I beseech the other champions,
The Patriarchs and the sixteen prophets,
The Apostles, pilots of the ship of Christ,
And all the martyrs, athletes of God,[1]

That with their aid safety may surround me
And every evil pass from me.
May Christ make a firm covenant with me.
Let fear and fright fall on the foul fiends.

O God, defend me everywhere
With your impregnable power and protection.
Deliver all my mortal limbs,
Guarding each with your protective shield,
So the foul demons shall not hurl their darts
Into my side, as is their wont.

Deliver my skull, hair-covered head, and eyes,
Mouth, tongue, teeth, and nostrils,[2]
Neck, breast, side, and limbs,
Joints, fat, and two hands.

Be a helmet of safety to my head,
To my crown covered with hair,

DEVOTIONAL TEXTS

To my forehead, eyes, and triform brain,
To snout, lip, face, and temple,

To my chin, beard, eyebrows, ears,
Chaps, cheeks, septum, nostrils,
Pupils, irises, eyelids, and the like,
To gums, breath, jaws, gullet,

To my teeth, tongue, mouth, uvula, throat,
Larynx and epiglottis, cervix,
To the core of my head and gristle,
And to my neck may there be merciful protection.

Be then a most protective breastplate
For my limbs and innards,
So that you drive back from me the unseen
Nails of the shafts that foul fiends fashion.

Protect, O God, with your powerful breastplate
My shoulders with their shoulderblades and arms,
Protect my elbows, cups of the hand and hands,
Fists, palms, fingers with their nails.

Protect my spine and ribs with their joints,
Back, ridge, and sinews with their bones;
Protect my skin and blood with kidneys,
The area of the buttocks, nates with thighs.

Protect my hams, calves, femurs,³
Houghs and knees with knee-joints;
Protect my ankles with shins and heels,
Shanks, feet with their soles.

Protect my toes growing together,⁴
With the tips of the toes and twice five nails;
Protect my breast, collarbone and small breast,
Nipples, stomach, and navel.

Protect my belly, loins, and genitals,
Paunch and the vital parts of my heart;

291

Protect my three-cornered liver and groin,
Pouch, kidneys, intestine with its fold.

Protect my tonsils, chest with lungs,
Veins, entrails, bile with its eruption,
Protect my flesh, loins with marrow,
And spleen with twisting intestines.

Protect my bladder, fat, and all
The rows beyond number of connecting parts;
Protect my hair and the remaining members
Which I have perhaps omitted.

Protect the whole of me with my five senses,
Together with the ten created orifices,[5]
So that from soles of feet to crown of head
I shall not sicken in any organ inside or out.

In case the life should be forced from my body
By plague, fever, weakness, or pain,
Until I grow old, if it be God's will,
And expunge my sins with good deeds.

So that leaving the flesh I may escape the depths,
And be able to fly to the heights,
And by the mercy of God be borne with joy
To be made anew in his kingdom on high.
Amen

4.

THE BROOM OF DEVOTION[6]

I beseech you, O Holy Jesus, by your four Evangelists who wrote your divine gospels, that is, Matthew, Mark, Luke, and John.

I beseech you by your four chief prophets who foretold your Incarnation: Daniel and Jeremiah and Isaiah and Ezekiel.

I beseech you by the nine orders of the church on earth, from psalm-singer to episcopate.

I beseech you by all the chosen ones who have received these orders from the beginning of the New Testament until now, and who shall receive them from now till the Day of Judgment.

I beseech you by the nine orders of the church in heaven, that is, Angels and Archangels, Virtues, Powers, Principalities, Dominations, Thrones, Cherubim, Seraphim.

I beseech you by the twelve Patriarchs who foretold you through spiritual mysteries.

I beseech you by the twelve minor prophets who foreshadowed you.

I beseech you by the twelve Apostles who loved you and entreated you and followed you and attached themselves to you, choosing you above everyone.

I beseech you by all your sons of true virginity throughout the whole world, of both the Old and New Testament, with John the Youngman, the fosterling of your own breast.

I beseech you by all the holy penitents[7] with Peter the Apostle.

I beseech you by all the holy virgins throughout the whole world, with Mary the Virgin, your own holy mother.

I beseech you by all penitent widows, with Mary Magdalene.

I beseech you by all lawfully wedded couples, with suffering Job, who faced many trials.

I beseech you by the holy martyrs of the whole world, of both the Old and New Testament, from the beginning of the world to Elijah and Enoch, who will suffer the last martyrdom on the brink of Judgment, with Stephen, Cornelius, Cyprian, Lawrence, George, and Germanus.

I beseech you by the holy monks who waged war for you throughout the whole world, with Elijah and Elisha in the Old Testament, with John, Paul, and Anthony in the New Testament.

I beseech you by all those who had understanding in the law of nature, with Abel, with Seth, with Elijah, with Enoch, with Noah, with Abraham, with Isaac, with Jacob.

I beseech you by all those who had understanding in the written law, with Moses, with Joshua, with Caleb, with Aaron, with Eleazar, with Jonah.

I beseech you by all those who had understanding in the prophetic law, with Elijah, with Elisha, with David, and with Solomon.

I beseech you by all those who had understanding in the law of the New Testament, with your own holy Apostles and all your saints to the end of the world.

I beseech you by all the holy bishops who founded the ecclesiastical city in Jerusalem, with James of the knees, your own brother.

I beseech you by all the holy bishops who founded the ecclesiastical city in Rome, with Linus and Cletus and Clement.

I beseech you by all the holy bishops who founded the ecclesiastical city in Alexandria, with Mark the Evangelist.

I beseech you by all the holy bishops who founded the ecclesiastical city in Antioch, with Peter the Apostle.

I beseech you by all the holy infants of the whole world who endured the cross and martyrdom for your sake, with two thousand, one hundred and forty children who were slain by Herod in Bethlehem of Judah, and with the child Cyricus.[8]

I beseech you by all the hosts of the venerable, perfect, and righteous men, who completed their old age, their perfection and righteousness for your sake with Eli in the Old Testament, with the righteous, perfect, and venerable old man, Simeon, at the beginning of the New Testament, who embraced you with his arms, knees, and elbows, caressing you, and said: "Now Lord, you have kept your word: let your servant go in peace. With my own eyes I have seen the salvation which you have prepared in the sight of every people: a light to reveal you to the nations and the glory of your people Israel."

I beseech you by all the holy disciples who acquired the spiritual knowledge of both the Old and New Testaments with the seventy-two disciples.

I beseech you by all the perfect teachers who taught the spiritual meaning of Scripture with Paul the Apostle:

That you will take me under your protection, defense, and care, to preserve and protect me from devils and all their promptings against all the elements of the world, against lusts, against transgressions, against sins, against worldly crimes, against the dangers of this life and the torments of the next, from the hands of enemies and every terror, against the fire of hell and judgment, against shame before the face of God, against the attacks of devils, that they may have no power over us at our entry into the next world; against the dangers of this world, against everyone whom God knows to bear us malice under the ten stars of the world.

May God keep far from us their rage, their violence, their anger, their cruelty, their enmity.

May God kindle kindness and love, affection, mercy, and tolerance in their hearts and in their thoughts, in their souls and in their minds and in their bowels.

O holy Jesus,
Gentle friend,
Morning star,
Midday sun adorned,
Brilliant flame of righteouness, life everlasting and eternity,
Fountain ever-new, ever-living, ever-lasting,
Heart's desire of Patriarchs
Longing of prophets,
Master of Apostles and disciples,
Giver of the Law,
Prince of the New Testament,
Judge of doom,
Son of the merciful Father without mother in heaven,
Son of the true virgin Mary, without father on earth,
True and loving brother,

For the sake of your affection, hear the entreaty of this mean wretch for the acceptance of this sacrifice on behalf of all Christian churches and on my own behalf,

For the sake of the merciful Father from whom you came down to us on earth,

For the sake of your divinity, which was obedient to the father for the reception of your humanity,

For the sake of the pure and holy flesh which you received from the womb of the virgin,

For the sake of the spirit of seven forms, which governed this flesh together with yourself and your Father,

For the sake of the holy womb from which you received that flesh without loss of dignity,

For the sake of the holy stem and genealogy from which you took this flesh, from the flesh of Adam to the flesh of Mary,

For the sake of the seven things that were prophesied for you on earth: your conception, your birth, your baptism, your crucifixion, your burial, your resurrection, your ascension into heaven, your sitting at the right hand of God the Father in heaven, your return as Judge,

For the sake of the holy tree on which your sides were stretched,

For the sake of the truth-loving blood which was shed on us from that tree,

For the sake of your own body and blood which is offered on all holy altars in the Christian churches of this world,

For the sake of the whole scriptures in the ordaining of your gospel,

For the sake of all righteousness in the ordaining of your Resurrection,

For the sake of your love, which is the head and summit of all commandments, as it is said: "Love excels all."

For the sake of your kingdom with all its rewards, precious stones, and songs,

For the sake of your mercy, your forgiveness, your kindness, and your own generosity, which is greater than any treasure, that I may have forgiveness and the expunging of my past sins from the beginning of my life to the present day, according to the word of David, who said "Blessed are they whose sins are forgiven…" (Ps 32).

Give, grant, and impart to me your holy grace and your Holy Spirit, to protect and preserve me from all my sins, present and future, and to kindle in me all righteousness and to establish me in that righteousness to the end of my life. And may he receive me at my life's end into heaven in the unity of Patriarchs and prophets, in the unity of Apostles and disciples, in the unity of angels and archangels, in the unity which excels every unity, that is, in the unity of the holy and exalted Trinity, Father, Son, and Holy Ghost, for I have nothing unless I have it according to the words of Paul the Apostle: "Who shall deliver me from the body of this death of sin?" Amen.

5.

LITANY OF THE VIRGIN AND ALL SAINTS

May Mary and John the youth and John the Baptist and all the saints of the world intercede with the fount of true purity and true innocence, Jesus Christ, Son of the Virgin, that the grace and compassion of the Holy Spirit may come to forgive us all our past sins, and protect us from future sins, to subdue our fleshly desires, and to control our unseemly thoughts;

To kindle the love and affection of the Creator in our hearts that it may be he that our mind searches for, desires, and meditates upon forever;

That our eyes may not be deceived by idle glances, and by the profitless beauty of perishable things;

That our hearing may not be perverted by idle songs, nor by the harmful persuasion of devils and evil men;

That our senses of taste may not be beguiled by dainties and many savors;

That he may free our tongues from denigration and insult and unkind chatter;[9]

That we may not barter the true light and true beauty of the life eternal for the deceitful phantasy of the present life;

That we may not forsake the pure wedlock and marriage of our husband and noble bridegroom, Jesus Christ, Son of the King of heaven and earth, for the impure wedlock of a servant of his, so that our soul and body may be a consecrated temple to the Holy Spirit, that we may accompany the blameless lamb, that we may sing the song that only the virgins sing, that we may merit the crown of eternal glory in the unity of the company of heaven, in the presence of the Trinity, forever and ever. Amen.

6.
LITANY OF THE CREATION

I beseech you by the tenth order on the compact earth;[10] I beseech praiseworthy Michael to help me against demons.

Together with Michael, I beseech you by land and by sea unceasingly; I beseech you respectfully by every quality of God the Father.

I beseech you, O Lord, by the suffering of your body, white with fasting;[11] I beseech you by the contemplative life, I beseech you by the active life.

I beseech the people of heaven, with Michael, for my soul; I beseech the saints of the world to help me on earth.

I beseech the people of heaven with bright-armed Michael; I beseech you by the triad of wind, sun, and moon.

I beseech you by water and the cruel air; I beseech you by fire, I beseech you by earth.

I beseech you by the threesome of the vaulted and fiery zone, I beseech you by the two temperate zones, I beseech you by the two frozen zones.

I beseech you by the compass of the harmonious firmament; I beseech every order dignified in its divisions, the host of the bright stars.

I beseech you by the kings with their royal and mighty line of kings; I beseech all mysteries, I beseech the glories of Michael.

I beseech you by every living creature that ever knew death and life; I beseech you by every inanimate creature because of your fair and lovely mystery.

I beseech you by your love, deeper than the ocean; I beseech your very self, O King of the fierce sun.

Every saint that is, was, and shall be, and every holy virgin without deceit, with Michael the fair guardian, to help me without....[12]

May this host protect me! I beseech you, Father. I beseech you.

I beseech you, Father, that I may be in your ranks; this in summary the wise "broom of devotion."

Though brief in words, it is a pure, brightly ordered song; it is full of devotion, it is perfect in learning.

It is a summons to saints, it is a...to elements, it is an entreaty to angels,...breastplate.

It is a breastplate to my soul, it is a fortress to me, body and heart, it is a pleasant and prompt proximity,[13] it is praise to the King of Heaven.

It is sanctification to those who recite it continually; it is a judgment of those who recite it; it is devotion and suffering.

It is partaking of the body of Christ and it is a bitter conflict; it is fair and perfect faith, it is converse with angels.

Every angel, every song, every creature under your power, every saint of fair color,[14] by them I beseech you, O Father. I beseech you.

I beseech you by time with its clear divisions, I beseech you by darkness, I beseech you by light.

I beseech all the elements in heaven and earth that the eternal sweetness may be granted to my soul.

Your infinite pity, your power over battles, your gentleness to your debtors, O beloved and swift King.

To help me out of every conflict, by them I beseech you, O Father.

I beseech you.

7.

MAY THIS JOURNEY BE EASY, may it be a journey of profit in my hands! Holy Christ against demons, against weapons, against killings!

May Jesus and the Father, may the Holy Spirit sanctify us!
May the mysterious God not hidden in darkness, may the bright King save us!

May the cross of Christ's body and Mary guard us on the road![15]
May it not be unlucky for us, may it be successful and easy!

8.

THE PATH I WALK, Christ walks it. May the land in which I am be without sorrow.

May the Trinity protect me wherever I stay, Father, Son, and Holy Spirit.

Bright angels walk with me—dear presence—in every dealing.

In every dealing I pray them that no one's poison may reach me.

The ninefold people of heaven of holy cloud, the tenth force of the stout earth.

Favorable company, they come with me, so that the Lord may not be angry with me.

DEVOTIONAL TEXTS

May I arrive at every place, may I return home; may the way in
which I spend be a way without loss.

May every path before me be smooth, man, woman, and child
welcome me.

A truly good journey! Well does the fair Lord show us a course, a
path.

9.

THE PRAYERS OF MOUCAN

(1.)

I pray to God the Father, God the Son,
And to God the Holy Spirit,
Whose infinite greatness
Enfolds the whole world,
In Persons three and one,
In essence simple and triune,
Suspending the earth above the waters,
Hanging the upper air with stars,
That he may be favorable to me, a sinner,[16]
Who righteously justifies all who err,
Who ever-living lives.
May God be blessed for ages. Amen.
Let it be so. Let it be so.
Eloe, Sabaoth, Ya, Adonai,
Eli Eli lama sabacthani.

(2.)

Grant my head the water of lament
And the water of tears to my eyes,
Since the gold of the temple is darkened
Which you have built in me,
And scattered are the stones of the sanctuary,
Once most beautiful and square.
Chaldean flame has shaken
Two gilded cherubim,

The candelabrum of knowledge
And the veil of chastity are almost rent,
And the oil of unction for the table
Prepared for the Father, Son, and Spirit.
Two columns of the altar
Wonderful works inside and out,
The sea of bronze, many cauldrons with lavers,
Souls in their own fashion,
Light shields, stringed instruments, badges, flat dishes,
Countless vessels of silver and gold,
These things of my soul are demolished
And scattered through the streets.
Woe to me, for my dwelling,
Cedar, with its houses, is far away.
My soul dwelt there for a long time.
I have used up the goods of my father with adulterers.
Eloe. Sabaoth.

(3.)

Now the careful words of repentance
Must be said for me.
He from whom I hope for the stole of immortality
And the ring of dignity,
Who for my arrival slays
The fattened calf from the herd,
Whose blood restored
The structure of the whole world,
And whose blood in the figure of a lamb
Sprinkled and painted on thresholds,
By whom the hand of Didymus is pressed in[17]
And the house of Rahab the harlot is saved.
Eloe.

(4.)

Father, I have sinned against heaven and before you,
Have mercy upon me and hear me.
I am now not worthy to be called your son,
Come to my aid, O God.

Make me like one of your hired servants,
Forgive me and spare me my sins.
Because I greatly hunger for you,
Wipe out the wickedness of my sin.
Show favor to me, Lord, a sinner
Snatch my soul from the hand of hell.
Remember me, Lord, in your kingdom.
Raise me up from the filth of sin,
And do not remove your Holy Spirit from me
Nor in your anger rebuke me.
To you I flee, most holy Father,
And have no refuge but you.
Sons are accustomed to flee to their fathers,
It is allowed after wounds or beatings.
Place me beside you, Lord God of powers,
Since I know my sin.
Lord God, the power of my salvation,
Do not utterly abandon me.
Eloe.

(5.)

You are my strength, Lord, I will love you,
Under the shadow of your wings protect me.
Jesu, son of David, have mercy on me,
That you may open the eyes of my heart.
I shall call to you with the Canaanite widow,
Since my soul has been wounded.
"Even the pups eat the scraps
Which fall from the lord's table (Mt 15:27)."
Speak, health of the world, and my soul shall be healed.
Remit the wickedness of my sin.
If I touch the fringe of your garment,
I shall be saved from my sin.
Eloe. Sabaoth.

(6.)

Hosanna, King from Nazareth! Perfect the praise of my mouth.

Since I have been silent, my sins have matured
And grown strong.
Foreigners have risen up against me,
And the gates of death have closed on me.
My sins have covered my head,
And my soul is bowed down.
The sorrows of death have disturbed me,
And floods of wickedness have choked me.
Why have you abandoned me far from my salvation?
My God, turn to me.
Eloe. Sabaoth.

(7.)

Pull my soul from the spear,
And release it from the paw of the dog.
Have mercy on me, O God, have mercy on me,
Forgive me, Almighty, for I have sinned.
Accept repentance from my heart,
Raise up the poor man from the dung.
If you look upon my wickedness,
I shall melt like wax in the face of fire,
Like a burden of lead that weighs me down
Are the sands of my sins.
The shoots of harmful thorns choke in me
The Word of my God, the seed.

(8.)

Burn my loins and my heart,
That you may not enter into judgment with me,
Until from the dirt I am born to new life.
Over the natural elements of my soul
A hostile man has sown scattered tares.
Troubles face me everywhere.
Against you only have I sinned, wretch that I am.
Who will free me from the body of this death
If not the grace of the Lord the Savior?
Who has removed from us the vessels of the giant,
The tyranny of the vengeful man?

Praising God, I shall call upon the Lord
And shall be safe from my enemies.
It is good for me, Lord,
That you have humbled me,
So that I am not lifted up in your sight.
Lord, since we are perishing, rise up in the shipwreck
Of this world at night.
Give me, Lord, your hand, when the frail
Boat was almost sunk, stretched out to Peter.
Answer the complaint from my closed mouth
As you did with Moses.
Because I have been wounded on the way to the desert,
Lift me up even onto your breast,
O Lord my God.

(9.)

I wandered on the mountains, Good Shepherd,
Place me upon your shoulders.
As the hart desires a spring of living water,
So my soul thirsts for you.
And may you rest, O Holy One,
Between my breasts.
You who feed and lie down at midday,
Guard me as the pupil of your eye,
And bring me into the house of wine
With the bunches of grapes in the vineyards of Eingedi.
My uncle is for me and I for him.
My soul is like a land without water.
My bowels burned as if with fire.
May my heart burn with the fire of your love and fear,
Your love and holy fear which knows not how to yield.
Give me, Jesus, water springing up into eternal life,
I have sought only my soul from the Lord, this I require,
That I shall never thirst in eternity. Lord Jesus,
Receive my spirit, since my soul is greatly troubled.
Into your hands I rightly commend my spirit
So that I may not sleep in death,

So that I may not be filled with the nighttime fear,
Nor with the fear of the midday demon.
Receive me into the peace of Abraham,
Where the souls of the fathers rest,
You who live and reign with the Father together
And with the Holy Spirit for ages secure.
Eloe. Sabaoth. Ia. Adonai.
Eli Eli lama sabacthani.

10.

THE PROTECTION OF THE FATHER AND THE SON of grace
   between me and my enemies,[18]
The protection of the Holy Spirit is my mind's intent,
The protection of beloved Jesus, crown of peace,
The punishment of sin and its followers.
The protection of the cross that grants the gifts of our desire,[19]
Which you accepted, God, for your people,
Against the faithless, enslaving fiends of hell,[20]
Its vicious and malicious hordes.
The protection of love's grace between me and my enemies,
The protection of the seas and of Mary and her maidens,
The protection I implore of the great archangels,
Lord of Heaven and earth, that they may bless me,
The protection of peerless Peter, throne of teaching,
Best of all keepers of the gate.
The protection of the gentle four, virgin and pure,
The Evangelists together, singers of the canon.
The protection of John of noble expression, chief disciple,
Whom Christ blessed with signs of the cross.
The protection, gentle and confessed, constant their prayer,
Of the sovereign prophets of God.
The protection of the triune unity of the three Persons,
The protection of all the saints, sinless senate,
The protection of all the praise of all the angels of heaven,
And the virgins' true confession.
The protection I invoke of the blessed;
Refuge, for their part, may they give me,

The protection of God's martyrs, eternal nobility,
The protection, which is humble, of innocent Abel.
Before I suffer death's great grief,
May two, who are generous, be my friends,
Michael and Gabriel, as rewards of praise,
Spiritual and bountiful companions.
For the sake of the chosen rule of the wise men,
For the freedom of heaven's home they shall protect me,
Freely they shall grant glory to my soul,
And place me in a wealth of light.

LITURGY

1.

THE TRACT ON THE MASS IN THE STOWE MISSAL

1. The altar represents the persecution which is inflicted. The chalice represents the church which has been established and founded on the persecution and martyrdom of the prophets and others.

2. Water first, into the chalice, and this is sung at the same time: "I beseech you, Father; I entreat you, Son; I implore you, Holy Spirit"—that is, the figure of the people who have been poured forth in the church.

3. The Host then above the altar, that is, the turtle-dove. And this is chanted: "Jesus Christ, Alpha and Omega, who is the beginning and the end." A figure of Christ's body which was laid in the linen sheet of Mary's womb.

4. Wine then on water into the chalice, that is, Christ's divinity on his humanity and on the people at the time of begetting. This is chanted: "Forgive us, Father; be generous to us, Son; have mercy on us, Holy Spirit."

5. What is chanted of the Mass after this, Introit, prayers, and addition, as far as the Lesson of the Apostles and the Gradual, represents the law of nature in which the knowledge of Christ has been renewed, through all his members and deeds. But the Epistle and the Gradual, as far as the uncovering of the chalice, is a commemoration of the law of the Letter in which Christ has been prefigured, although that which was figured in it was not yet known.

6. The uncovering as far as half of the Host and the chalice, and what is chanted at the same time, both gospel and Alleluia as far as the oblation, is a commemoration of the law of the prophets in which Christ was explicitly foretold, except that this was not seen until he was born.

7. The elevation of the chalice, after it has been fully uncovered, when the oblation is sung, is a commemoration of Christ's birth and of his glory through signs and miracles.

8. When "Jesus took the bread" is sung, the priest bows three times to repent of his sins. He offers the chalice to God and

chants "God, have mercy on me." The people kneel and no one speaks in case it should disturb the priest, for it is right that his mind does not turn from God while he chants this lesson. Hence it is called the "dangerous address."

9. The three steps backward which the priest takes and the three steps forward is the triad in which everyone sins, that is, in word, thought, and deed, and this is the triad whereby we are renewed again and move toward Christ's body.

10. The priest's examination of the chalice and the Host, and the effort he makes to break it, represent the insults and the beating and the seizing of Christ.

11. The Host on the paten is the body of Christ on the tree of the cross.

12. The breaking of the Host on the paten is the breaking of Christ's body with nails on the cross.

13. The bringing together of the two halves after the breaking of the Host represents the wholeness of Christ's body after the Resurrection.

14. The submerging of the two halves in the chalice represents the submersion of Christ's body in his blood after his wounding on the cross.

15. The piece which is cut from the half on the right-hand side of the priest represents the wounding with the lance in the right armpit, for Christ faced westward on the cross, that is, "toward the city," while Longinus faced eastward, his left being on Christ's right.

16. The confraction is of seven kinds, that is, five pieces of the common Host as a figure of the five senses of the soul; seven of the Host of saints and virgins, except the chief ones, as a figure of the seven gifts of the Holy Spirit; eight pieces of the martyrs' Host as a figure of the eight sections of the New Testament;[1] nine of the Host of Sunday as a figure of the nine households of heaven and the nine grades of the church;[2] eleven of the Host of the Apostles as a figure of the incomplete number of the Apostles after the sin of Judas; twelve of the Host of the Calends (the Circumcision) and of Maundy Thursday, in commemoration of the complete number of Apostles; thirteen of the Host of Low

Sunday[3] and the feast of the Ascension formerly, although later something less is distributed at Communion as a figure of Christ with his twelve Apostles.

17. The five and the seven and the eight and the nine and the eleven and the twelve and the thirteen make sixty-five, and that is the number of the pieces which are in the Host of Easter and Christmas and Whitsunday, for Christ contains all, and all is set on the paten in the form of a cross, and the upper part inclines to the left, as was said: "He bowed his head and gave up the ghost" (Jn 19:30).

18. The arrangement of the confraction at Easter and Christmas: thirteen pieces in the stem of the crosses, nine in its crosspiece, twenty pieces in its circle-wheel, five pieces in each angle, sixteen both in the circle and in the body of the crosses, that is four for every part. The middle piece is that to which the priest goes, that is, the figure of the breast with the mysteries. What lies upward of the shaft to bishops; the cross-piece on the left to priests; that on the right to all lower orders; that from the cross-piece downward to anchorites and penitents; that which is in the upper left corner to true young clerics; the upper right to innocent children; the lower left to people of repentance; the lower right to people lawfully married and to those who go to Communion for the first time.[4]

19. This is what God deems worthy, the mind to be in the symbols of the Mass and that this should be your mind: the piece of the Host that you receive as a member of Christ from his cross, and that there may be a cross of labor on each of us in our own course, since it unites us to the crucified body. It is not right to swallow the piece without tasting it, as it is improper not to seek to introduce savors into the mysteries of God. It is not right for it to go under the back teeth, which symbolizes that it is not proper to dispute God's mysteries too much in case this should lead to an increase in heresy.

The End. Amen. Thanks be to God.

2.
TWO EUCHARISTIC CHANTS FROM THE STOWE MISSAL

Chant 1 *(Cognouerunt Dominum)*
[For use during the Fraction (fol. 34ᵛ–35ʳ)]

> They recognized the Lord, Alleluia;
> In the breaking of bread, Alleluia (Lk 24:35).
> For the bread that we break is the body of our Lord Jesus
> Christ, Alleluia;
> The cup which we bless is the blood of our Lord Jesus Christ,
> Alleluia (1 Cor 10:16–7);
> For the remission of our sins, Alleluia (Mt 26:28).
> O Lord, let your mercy come upon us, Alleluia;
> For how have we hoped in you, Alleluia (Ps 31:1).
> They recognized the Lord, Alleluia;
> In the breaking of bread, Alleluia (Lk 24:35).
>
> We believe, O Lord, we believe that in this breaking of your
> body and pouring out of your blood we become redeemed
> people;
> We confess that by our sharing of this sacrament we are
> strengthened to endure in hope until we lay hold and enjoy its
> true fruits in the heavenly places.

Chant 2 *(Pacem meam)*
[For use during the distribution of Communion (fol. 36ʳ–37ʳ)]

> My peace I give to you, Alleluia;
> My peace I leave with you [Alleluia] (Jn 14:27).
> The lovers of your law have great peace, Alleluia.
> They never stumble, Alleluia (Ps 119:165).
> The king of the heavens [comes] with peace, Alleluia;
> Full of the odor of love, Alleluia.[5]
> Oh, sing him a song that is new, Alleluia (Ps 33:2);
> Come, all his holy ones, Alleluia.[6]
> Come, eat of my bread, Alleluia;
> And drink of the wine I have mixed for you, Alleluia (Prv 9:5).

314

"The Lord is my shepherd" (Ps 23) is recited.[7]
He who eats my body,[8] Alleluia;
And drinks my blood, Alleluia;
Abides in me and I in him, Alleluia (Jn 6:56).

"The Lord's is the earth and its fullness" (Ps 24) is recited.[9]

This is the living bread which comes down from heaven,
   Alleluia (Jn 6:50);
He who eats of it shall live forever, Alleluia (Jn 6:51).

"To you, O Lord, I lift up my soul" (Ps 25) is recited.[10]

The Lord gave them bread from heaven, Alleluia;
Men ate the bread of angels, Alleluia (Ps 78:24–25).

"Defend me, O God" (Ps 43) is recited.[11]

Eat, O my friends, Alleluia;
And drink deeply, O beloved ones, Alleluia (Sng 5:1).
This is the sacred body of our Lord, [Alleluia];
The blood of our Savior, Alleluia;
Feast, all of you, on it for eternal life, Alleluia.[12]
Let my lips proclaim your praise, Alleluia;
Because you teach me your commands, Alleluia (Ps
   119:171–172).
I will bless the Lord at all times, Alleluia;
His praise always on my lips, Alleluia (Ps 34:1).
Taste and see, Alleluia;
How sweet is the Lord, Alleluia (Ps 34:8).
Where I am, Alleluia;
There shall my servant be, Alleluia (Jn 12:26).
Let the children come to me, Alleluia;
And do not stop them, Alleluia;
For to such belongs the Kingdom of Heaven, Alleluia (Mt
   19:14).
Repent, Alleluia;
For the Kingdom of Heaven is at hand, Alleluia (Mt 3:2).
The Kingdom of Heaven has suffered violence, Alleluia;

And violent men have taken it by force, Alleluia (Mt 11:12).
Come, O blessed of my Father, inherit the kingdom, Alleluia;
Prepared for you before the foundation of the world, Alleluia
    (Mt 25:34);
Glory be to the Father, [and to the Son, and to the Holy Spirit];
Come, O blessed of my Father, inherit the kingdom;
As it was in the beginning, [is now, and ever shall be, world
    without end];
Come, O blessed of my Father, Amen, Alleluia.

3.
COMMUNION HYMN

Come, you holy ones, receive the body of Christ,
Drinking the holy blood by which you were redeemed.

You who are saved by the body and blood of Christ,
Let us praise God, by whom we are made anew.

By this sacrament of the body and blood,
All have escaped from the jaws of hell.

Giver of salvation, Christ, the Son of God,
Has saved the world by his cross and blood.

The Lord has been sacrificed for all,
Himself both priest and victim.

The law commanded the sacrifice of victims,
Foreshadowing the mysteries divine.

Bestower of light and Savior of all,
He granted most noble grace to his holy people.

Let all draw near with pure and faithful minds,
Let all receive the protection of eternal salvation.

Guardian of the saints, you are leader, O Lord,
And dispenser of life eternal to those who believe.

He gives heavenly bread to the hungry,
And to the thirsty water from the living spring.[13]

Christ the Lord himself comes, who is Alpha and Omega.[14]
He shall come again to judge us all.

4.
HYMN AT THE LIGHTING OF THE PASCHAL CANDLE

Fiery Creator of fire,
Light Giver of light,
Life and Author of life,
Salvation and Bestower of salvation,
In case the lamps should abandon
The joys of this night,
You who do not desire our death,
Give light to our breast.

To those wandering from Egypt,
You bestow the double grace,
You show the veil of cloud,
And give the nocturnal light.
With a pillar of cloud in the day,
You protect the people as they go,
With a pillar of fire at evening,
You dispel the night with light.[15]

You call out to your servant from the flame,[16]
You do not spurn the bush of thorns,
And though you are consuming fire,[17]
You do not burn what you illumine.
Now it is time that the cloudy bee-bread
Should be consumed, all impurity boiled away,
And the waxen flesh should shine
With the glow of the Holy Spirit.[18]

LITURGY

You store now in the recesses of the comb
The sweet food of the divine honey,
And purifying the inmost cells of the heart,
You have filled them with your word;
That the swarm of the new brood,
Chosen by your mouth and spirit,
May leave their burdens and win heaven
On wings now free from care.

APOCRYPHA

1. THE EVERNEW TONGUE (1–22)

In the beginning God made heaven and earth. It was the High-King of the world, who is mightier than any king, higher than any power, more fierce than any dragon, gentler than any child, more radiant than suns, holier than any saint, more vengeful than all men, more loving than any mother, the only Son of God the Father, it was he who gave this account of the formation and creation of the world to the many nations on earth, since no one but God knew what any visible thing in the world was like, for it was as if the race of Adam had its head in a bag or lived in a dark place. And so it was because no one had any understanding of the form of the world, or of its Creator, that this account came from heaven to open the hearts and minds of all so that all might find the way of life and salvation.

Everything was hidden to the eyes of Adam's race except that they saw the movement of the constellations, the moon, sun, and stars, which used to go round every day without ceasing. Furthermore, they saw that the springs and rivers of the world at no time ceased to flow. They saw the dejection of the earth, the fading and slumbering of light and produce at the coming of winter. They also saw the revival of the earth with warmth and light, flowers and fruit, at the reawakening of the summer.

But they did not know who caused this until there came this account of the creation and of forms and motions of the world,[1] as God had ordained it. Before this story was told, before the Evernew Tongue revealed it, speaking from the height of heaven above the assembly of Mount Sion, all this was hidden. For the multitudes of the eastern world had come together, those from the mountains of Abian as far as the shores of the Red Sea, and from the Dead Sea as far as the island of Sabarn. They numbered three thousand, four hundred and eighty-five bishops, fifty-four thousand, nine hundred and sixty-nine kings of the world.

The gathering continued for a year and four months, summer, winter, spring, and autumn, under nine hundred awnings of white sheets, decorated with gold insignia, on the summit of Mount Sion. Five thousand, nine hundred and fifty tower-torches and jewels cast their light upon the gathering, so that proceedings could not be disrupted by bad weather at any time. There were two hundred and fifty bishops, five hundred priests, three thousand in ecclesiastical orders, one hundred and fifty innocent youths, and five hundred high-kings with their retinues. At midnight they would enter Jerusalem with their singing,[2] and at each matins they would gather to sing the greetings which resound in the holy heavens, *Glory in the highest.*

Then the crowds of the assembly would come up between two plains, as the milling throngs and concourse returned to Mount Sion with the music of their joyful greeting combining with the music of angels from the righteous ranks of the High-King.

Later, when Easter Eve was almost over, a noise like thunder, or like the crackle of fire, was suddenly heard in the clouds. There was a peal of thunder, and a solar glow, like a bright sun, suddenly appeared in the midst of the crowds. That solar glow spun round and round so that the eye could not look upon it, for it was seven times brighter than the sun.

Immediately afterward, as the eyes of the crowd awaited the crash, for they thought it was a sign of Doomsday, a clear voice was heard speaking in the language of angels: *"Haeli habia felebe fae niteia temnibisse salis sal,"* which means: "Hear this account, children of the human race. I have been sent from God to speak to you."

Then weakness and terror suddenly fell upon the crowds, and not without good cause. The sound of the voice was like the shout of a crowd, but more distinct than human voices. It echoed over the host like the cry of a great wind, yet did not seem louder to each one than the voice of a friend in the ear, and was sweeter than any melody.

The Hebrew sages replied: "Tell us your name, your status, and your message." They heard the Evernew Tongue speaking in an angelic voice: *"Nathire uimbae o lebiae ua un nimbisse tiron tibia am biase sau fimblia febe ab le febia fuan,"* which means: "I was born among the peoples of the earth, conceived by procreation of man and woman. Philip the Apostle is my name. The Lord sent me to preach to the heathen. Nine times heathens cut my tongue from my head, and nine times I was able to continue preaching again. That is why the people of heaven know me as the Evernew Tongue."

The Hebrew sages said: "Tell us in what language you are speaking to us." He replied: "I speak to you in the tongue of angels and of all the ranks of heaven. Even the creatures of the sea, beasts, four-footed animals, birds, serpents, and demons know it. It is the language that all will speak at the Judgment.

"It is this which has made me come to you, to explain to you the wonderful story which the Holy Spirit told through Moses, son of Amram, concerning the creation of earth and heaven and all that can been seen there. For the story tells of the making of heaven and earth. In the same way, it concerns the creation of the world made possible by Christ's rising from the dead on this Easter Eve. For every substance, every element, and every essence to be seen in this world were all combined in the body in which Christ rose, that is, in the body of every human being.

"Firstly there is the material of wind and air. This is what gives breath in human bodies. Then there is the material of heat and burning fire. This is what makes the red heat of blood in the human body. Furthermore, there is the material of the sun and the stars of heaven. This makes the shine and the light in the human eye. Then there is the material of bitterness and saltiness, which forms the bitterness of tears, the gall of the liver, and great anger in people's hearts. Then there is the material of stones and the clay of the earth, which binds flesh and bones and limbs together in people. Then there is the material of flowers and the beautiful colors of the earth, which gives variety of complexion and pallor in the face, and color in the cheeks.

"All the world rose with him, for the essence of all the elements was in the body that Jesus assumed. For if the Lord had not suffered on behalf of the race of Adam, and risen from the dead, then Judgment Day would mean the destruction of the whole world and all the descendants of Adam. No creature of sea or land would be reborn, but up to the third heaven the skies

323

would burn. All but three heavens of the Heavenly Kingdom would be consumed. There would be neither land nor kindred, living or dead, in the world, only hell and heaven, if the Lord had not come to redeem them. All would be destroyed without hope of restoration.

"This is why I have come to you," Philip said, "to give you this knowledge, for the formation of the world, according to ancient tradition, is obscure to you." The Hebrew sages said: "Tell us about the wonders without number which happened then, for unless it is explained clearly to us, we shall not understand it."

They heard the Evernew Tongue speaking in the language of angels: *"Lae uide fodea tabo abelia albe fab"* (which means in Latin: "In the beginning God created heaven and earth"), and he says: *"Ambile bane bea fabne fa libera salese inbila tibon ale siboma fuan."* Let us be spared a translation into Hebrew of all that was said there: that there was no ordering of the colors, no earth with mountains and peoples, no sea with islands, no hell with torments, before he said that these elements should exist. There were no circuits of the seven heavens, no clouds to water the earth, no sparks, no storms. There were no lands for them to pour on, for there was neither rain nor snow. There was no lightning, nor gusts of wind, nor thunder. The course of the sun did not exist, nor were there any changes of the moon, nor variation of the stars. There were no sea-monsters, nor sea for them to swim in. There were no streams, herds, animals, birds, dragons, or snakes.

The sages of the Hebrews answered: "What did exist at that time, since none of the things you mention existed then?" The Evernew Tongue replied: "The wonder of all elements existed, which is to say God, who neither begins nor ends, who knows neither sorrow, age, nor decay. There was no hour, no time, and no space when he did not exist. He is neither younger nor older than at first. There was nothing that was difficult for him to do. He conceived a thought, and that thought had no beginning. He meditated upon the existence of something more splendid whereby his power and unutterable dignity might be revealed, for these did not exist in anything other than himself.[3]

"Finally, he immediately created light with these thoughts. And the circuit of the heavens with the nine orders of angels was the light that he created. There were seventy peoples with six hundred and twenty-four sun-filled holdings with melodies and colors in the seven forms of heaven. He fashioned the circuit of those forms in a single day, that is, the material of which the world is made, for God first formed the world in the shape of a round circle."

Then the Hebrew sages said: "Tell us now what kind of dispositions there are in the world, for we are in ignorance about them all."

The Evernew Tongue answered: "Although you do not see it, every element is made round, in harmony with the shapes of the world. For the heavens were created round, as were the seven seas about them, and the earth itself. It is in circular motion that the stars traverse the round wheel of the universe. It is as round shapes that souls appear when they leave the body. The high vault of heaven appears to the gaze as a circle, and the orbit of sun and moon is circular. All of this is appropriate, for the Lord himself is a circle, having neither beginning nor end, he who always was and always will be, and who created all of these things. It was for this reason that the world was created as a rounded form."

The Hebrew people said: "A question: What was there in the round multiform circuit which was the material from which the universe was made?"

The Evernew Tongue replied: "The orbital circuit contained the material of which the universe was made, that is cold and heat, light and dark, heaviness and lightness, wet and dry, high and low, bitter and mild, strong and weak, the roar of the sea and noise of thunder, the fragrance of flowers, chant of angels, and pillars of fire.

"The round, multiform mass which was formed from the material of the universe contained all these," he said. "There too the stuff of hell was formed, for hell was not created until the archangel transgressed and abandoned the law of the King who had created him together with the multitude of angels beyond number. Only then was hell made," he said, "but its material was contained in the round, multiform mass from which the earth was formed and all the peoples of the world. And if the angels who sinned had preserved the nature in which they were created, their angelic radiance, the material of hell would have been changed into a beautiful and radiant realm, like that of the holy angels."

2. THE CREATION OF ADAM

Adam was created in the third hour, was without sin for seven hours, and was driven out from Paradise in the tenth hour.

These are the seven components from which Adam was made. The first was of earth, the second of sea, the third of sun. The fourth was of clouds, the fifth of wind, and the sixth of stones. The seventh was the light of the world.

Let us continue. The first part, formed from earth, was the trunk of his body. The second part, formed from sea, was his blood. The third part, formed from the sun, was his countenance and face. The fourth part, formed from the clouds, was his thoughts. The fifth part, formed from wind, was his breath. The sixth part, formed from stones, was his bones. The seventh part, formed from the light of the world, that is, the Holy Spirit, was his human soul.

If in someone the part that is earth is dominant, then that person will be indolent. If it be the sun, they will be attractive and vivacious. If it be clouds, they will be irresponsible and lustful. If the wind dominates, they will be fiery and irascible. If it be the stones, they will be severe, both thieving and grasping. If it be the sea, they will be likable and placid, and will be beautiful. If it is the light that is strongest, they will know their own mind, and will be filled with the grace of the Holy Spirit and divine scripture.

3. THE POWER OF WOMEN

There was a famous king of the Greeks called Solomon. A king from one of his tribes prepared a great feast for him and they all got very drunk. But there were traitors close to the king and so he said to three friends from his own household: "You should guard me tonight." "We will do so," they said. And so they were at watch, with a cask of wine at their side, and a servant holding a candle toward them. They were all conversing. "We are well off here," said one of the three. "Let us give thanks to our Lord. Our senses are in a state of well-being, with one exception. The feet delight in being stretched out without any exertion. The hands delight in serving food to the body. The eyes delight in watching it being prepared. Noses delight in the aroma and lips in the taste. The one area not to be pleased is our hearing, for none of us hears the pleasant exchange of words."

The question is asked: "What shall we discuss?" "The answer is not difficult. We shall seek to decide which is the strongest power on earth." "I know that it is wine," said the Roman soldier. For it is wine that intoxicated the army, robbing them of their reason and sense, so that they were wildly drunk, sunk into a stupor, and at the mercy of their enemies."

"That is a good argument," said the Greek, "but in my opinion the ruler who gave the wine has the stronger power. The ruler is stronger than other men, and the human race is more worthy than the rest of creation. It is on account of his power that we are sober and awake now, even though we are drinking wine."

"Well, those were good suggestions," said the Jewish soldier, whose name was Nemiasserus. "But it seems to me that the power of women is the greatest. And it would not be surprising if this is what you remember tomorrow." They remained there until morning came.

"So now, what decisions did you come to last night?" the king asked. "This one we made, when discussing what was the greatest power on earth." "I said that it was the power of wine," said the Roman. "I said it was the power of a king," said the Greek. "And I said it was the power of women," said the Jew.

The queen was at the king's side, and the king himself was wearing his golden crown. "Wine is the stronger," one man said. "The power of the king is stronger," said another. "Is it then the case that I have no power?" said the queen, knocking the crown from the king's head with the palm of her hand so that it fell to the ground. "She should be put to death," everyone said. The king looked across at her, and she smiled. The king returned her smile. "The woman will not be harmed," he said. "There you are then," said Nemiasserus, "that is a great power." "It is true," said the king, "the power of woman is greater than all others. For on her brow is her companion spirit, so that she is beyond blame in all that she does."

4. THE VISION OF ADAMNÁN

Glorious and magnificent is the Lord of the elements, great and marvelous are his strength and power. He is kind and gentle, full of mercy and good will, for he calls to heaven those who are loving, compassionate, humane, and merciful. But he humbles the irreligious, wretched host of the damned, casting them down into hell. He grants the mysteries and manifold rewards of heaven for the blessed and many diverse kinds of torments for the sons of death.

As well as the Apostles and disciples of Jesus Christ, there are very many saints and righteous followers of the Lord of the elements to whom have been revealed the mysteries and secrets of the Kingdom of Heaven, and the glorious rewards of the just, together with the various torments of hell and those upon whom they are inflicted. The Apostle Peter was shown the four-cornered ship lowered from heaven with four ropes. Its sound was as sweet as any music. The Apostle Paul was caught up to the Third Heaven where he heard the ineffable words of the angels and the wonderful converse of the company of heaven. Moreover, on the day of Mary's death, all the Apostles were shown the sufferings and miserable punishments of the unblessed, when the Lord commanded the angels of the west to open the earth before the Apostles, revealing hell to their sight with all its torments, as he himself had promised them long before his Passion.

Finally these things were revealed to Adamnán, grandson of Tinne, the great scholar of the western world, of whom we are speaking here, when on the feast of John the Baptist his soul left his body and he was borne to the Kingdom of Heaven with its angels and to hell with its rabble. When his soul left the body, then the angel who had been its guardian while it was in the flesh appeared straightaway, guiding him first to the sight of the Kingdom of Heaven.

They first came to the Land of the Saints, which is a fertile and radiant land. Various splendid companies are there, with cloaks of shining linen and their heads covered with bright hoods. The saints of the eastern world gather in the east of the Land of the Saints, while the saints of the western world congregate in the west. The saints of the northern world and the saints of the southern world form two great gatherings to the north and the south. Therefore everyone in the Land of the Saints is equally near to hear the music and to contemplate the place[4] in which the nine orders of heaven are ranked according to their honor and dignity.

At times the saints sing marvelous songs in praise of God, and at other times they listen to the song of the people of heaven, for the saints have no other need than to listen to the music in their ears, to contemplate the brilliance before them, and to delight at the fragrance of the land. To the southeast a wonderful kingdom opens before them with a porch of gold to the south, cut off from them by a sheet of crystal through which they see the outline and movements of the heavenly host. But neither shade nor screen separates the people of heaven and the saints; rather they are always visible and present before them. A circle of fire rings the land, but all pass in and out without harm.

The twelve Apostles and the Virgin Mary form a separate group around the mighty Lord. Patriarchs, prophets, and the disciples of Jesus are near the Apostles, and there are other virgins to the right of Mary, only a short distance away. All around them are infants and children, and the song of the birds of the heavenly host is music for them. Bright companies of the guardian angels of souls continually do obeisance as they serve those groups in the presence of the King.

No one living could describe or give an accurate account of those companies. The assemblies and gatherings in this Land of the Saints shall remain in that great glory until the mighty congregation of the Day of Judgment when the righteous judge on the Day of Judgment shall assign them to the places and posts where they are to remain, gazing upon the face of God with neither screen nor shade separating them through all eternity.

Yet although the radiance and the glory of the Land of the Saints is so immense, as we have said, the brilliance which is in the plain of the people of heaven is a thousand times greater, round the throne of the Lord himself. This throne is like an ornate chair with four columns of precious stones beneath it. If someone had no other music but the harmony of those four columns, then they would still enjoy the fullness of sublimity and delight. There are three magnificent birds on the throne before the King, whose minds are intent upon the Creator for all time, for that is their vocation.[5] They sing the eight canonical hours, praising and glorifying the Lord, accompanied by the harmonies of the choir of archangels. The birds and the archangels lead the song, and all the people of heaven, both saints and holy virgins, sing the response.

There is a huge arch over the head of the All Highest on his royal throne, like an ornamented helmet or a king's crown. Any human eye that looked upon it would immediately dissolve. There are three circles around it, separating it from the host, whose nature cannot be known by description. There are six thousand creatures in the forms of horses and birds around the fiery chair, which glows without end.

No one can describe the mighty Lord who is on that throne, unless he himself were to do it, or unless he were to command the ranks of heaven to do so. For no one could depict his ardor and his power, his glowing radiance, his splendor and his loveliness, his constancy and his steadfastness, the multitude of his angels and archangels, making music for him, his numerous messengers coming and going to each company in turn with brief reports,[6] his gentleness and great lenience to some, his firmness and great severity to others.

If anyone were to look long around and about him, from east and west, south and north, they would find in every direction a wonderful face seven times brighter than the sun, but they would not discern a human form there, with head or foot, but a fiery mass blazing throughout the world, with everyone in fear and trembling before it. His brilliance fills the whole of heaven and earth, and a ray of light, like that of a magnificent star, is all about him. Three thousand different melodies are chanted by each choir around him, and every single one of their songs is as sweet as the many songs of this world.

And this is what the City is like in which that throne stands: seven crystal walls of various colors surround it, each wall higher than the next. The floor and the foundation of the City are of bright crystal, like the sun in appearance, shot through with blue, crimson, green, and every other color.

Those who live in that City are a mild, most gentle and kindly people, lacking in no virtue, for no one ever comes there or lives in it but holy virgins and pilgrims for God. But it is difficult to understand how their order and arrangement was established, for none of them has their back or side toward another, but the inexpressible power of God has set them face-to-face in rows and circles of equal height, around the royal throne in glory and joy, every face turned toward God.

A crystal chancel screen stands between every two choirs, finely worked with red, gold and silver, with exquisite rows of precious stones interspersed with rare gems and with settings and circles of carbuncle. Between every two of the major groupings there are three precious stones making soft sounds and sweet music, their surfaces bright as burning lamps. Like great candles, seven thousand angels shine upon and illumine the surrounding City, and seven thousand more are in the very center, casting light for all eternity around the royal City. If everyone in the whole world were gathered in a single place, however many they may be, the fragrance from just one candle would be enough to sustain them.

Now those inhabitants of the world who do not immediately enter that City at the point of death, but for whom a place there is allotted after the Last Judgment, pursue a restless and unsettled existence on hills and high ground, in marshes and remote bogs. A guardian angel ministers to each and every soul among these companies and gatherings.

At the main entrance to the City there is a screen of fire and a screen of ice which clash against each other perpetually. The noise of these screens crashing against each other can be heard everywhere in the world. If the descendants of Adam were to hear that noise, then fear and trembling would come upon them. That noise grieves sinners and bewilders them, while the people of heaven hear very little of it, and it seems to them to be as sweet as any music.

That City is amazing and wonderful to describe, for we have given an account of only a small part of its ranks and marvels.

It is difficult for the soul, after its close proximity to the body, in rest and ease, freedom and well-being, to find its way to the throne of the Creator unless it is guided by the angels, for the seven heavens are not easy to ascend. Not one of them is easier than the rest, and there are six doors guarding the Kingdom which face mortals who approach there. Each door is guarded by a porter and watchman from the heavenly host.

The Archangel Michael is stationed at the gate of the nearest heaven together with two virgins who hold iron rods in their laps to flog and beat sinners as they pass through this place of their first anguish and torment.

Ariel is guardian at the gate of the second heaven, together with two virgins holding fiery whips in their hands with which they strike sinners across their face and eyes. In front of that door there flows a stream of fire, its surface a sheet of flame. Abersetus is the name of the angel who keeps watch over that river and who purifies souls, washing away the sin that clings to them until they are as pure and luminous as the light of stars. There is a pleasant well there, mild and fragrant, to clean and refresh the souls of the righteous, although it torments and sears the souls of the wicked and removes nothing from them, only increasing their pain and affliction. Sinners emerge from it in grief and infinite sadness, but the righteous pass in joy and delight to the door of the third heaven.

A fiery furnace burns continually there, its flames reaching a height of twelve thousand cubits. The souls of the righteous pass through there in the twinkling of an eye, but the souls of sinners are seared and burned there for twelve years. Then they are taken by their guardian angel to the fourth door.

A stream of fire flows around the gateway to the fourth heaven, like the one described above. A wall of fire circles it, whose breadth can be measured at twelve thousand cubits. The souls of the righteous pass through it as if it did not exist, while the souls of sinners are caught there for another twelve years of pain and torment until their guardian angel brings them to the door of the fifth heaven.

In that place there is another stream of fire but one which is unlike the others for it has at its center a strange kind of whirlpool in which the souls of the wicked are spun round and round for a period of sixteen years. But the righteous are able to get over it immediately without any delay. When the time comes to let the sinners go, the angel strikes the stream with a rod, which is as hard as stone, and lifts the spirits out with its tip. Then Michael takes them to the entrance of the sixth heaven.

But no suffering or torment awaits them in that place, which is lit up with the brilliance and luster of gems. Michael then meets the Angel of the Trinity and together they flank the soul and bring it into the presence of God.

The welcome of the people of heaven that follows, and the Lord's own welcome for the soul, if it is righteous and without sin, is infinite and beyond all description. But a wicked and imperfect soul faces a harsh and severe reception from the mighty Lord, who says to the angels of heaven: "Seize this wicked soul, you angels of heaven, and hand it over to Lucifer to be plunged and extinguished in the depths of hell forever." Thereupon the wretched soul is cut off fearfully and without mercy from the Kingdom of Heaven and from the sight of God. Then it utters a groan more deeply felt than any other as it departs to face the Devil, having already glimpsed the joy of the Kingdom of Heaven, and it loses the protective company of the archangels who guided it to heaven. Twelve flaming dragons then suck in each soul, one after another, until the lowest dragon delivers it into the maw of the Devil. Then in the presence of the Devil, it eternally suffers the consummation of all evil.

When the guardian angel had shown to Adamnán's soul these visions of the Kingdom of Heaven and of what first happens to the soul when it leaves the body, it then led Adamnán's soul to the depths of hell, with its immense torments, tortures, and sufferings.

The first land that they came to was black and burnt, empty and scorched, where there was no punishment at all. On the far side was a valley full of fire. Vast flames broke from it on all sides. Its floor was black, while the middle and upper sections were red. Eight monsters lived there, their eyes like flaming coals. A huge bridge, rising in an arch, extended from one side of the valley to the other.

Three groups are attempting to cross over it, and not all succeed. For one group the bridge is wide all the way across so that they traverse the fiery abyss without danger, feeling no fear or terror. But another group find that it is narrow at first and then widens out so that they finally make their way across that same valley after great danger. For the last group the bridge is wide at first but then narrows half way across so that they are pitched into the same terrible abyss, right into the throats of those eight fiery monsters who live in the valley.

Those for whom that path was easy are the chaste virgins, the committed penitents, and the bloody martyrs who died willingly for God. The group who found the path narrow at first but then wide are those who first do the will of God under compulsion but then learn to serve him willingly. Those who found the bridge broad at first and then narrow are the sinners who listen to the teaching of the Word of God but do not follow it when they have heard it.

Very many stand in suffering on the shore of eternal torment opposite the land of darkness. Every other hour their pain is eased only to return in the next. Those who are in this state are the people in whom good and evil are equally present. On Judgment Day it will be judged between them, and the goodness in them will outweigh the evil, and they will then be led to the place of life, in the presence of God for all eternity.

There is another large group in great pain nearby. They are fastened to pillars of fire and are plunged into a sea of fire up to their chins. Around their wrists are wound fiery chains, like snakes. The sinners who suffer in this way are those who have murdered their own kin, those who destroy the church of God, and unpitying church leaders who by their rule over the shrines of the saints profit from the gifts and tithes of the church, using this wealth for themselves and not for the guests and poor ones of the Lord.

Furthermore there are large crowds standing forever in black mire up to their belts, clothed in short and icy cloaks. The belts burn them unceasingly with both cold and heat. A host of demons surround them with flaming clubs, beating them about the head and haranguing them without end. The faces of all these wretches are turned northward and a sharp and biting wind catches them directly on the forehead, along with every other ill. Burning fire rains down on them every night and every day which they cannot escape but must suffer for all eternity, weeping and grieving.

Some of them have streams of fire in their sunken cheeks, some have their tongues pierced with spikes of flame and others their heads. It is thieves, perjurers and traitors, slanderers, robbers and despoilers, false judges, unruly people, female sorcerers and satirists, renegade brigands and learned men who teach heresy, who are tormented in this way.

Another large group is gathered on islands in the middle of the sea of fire with a silver wall around them made from their clothing and their alms. These are those who never failed in their acts of mercy but who still indulged in loose living and the desires of the flesh until the day of their death. Their almsgiving comes to their aid in the middle of the fiery sea until the Day of Judgment, when they will be sent to the shore of life.

Then there is another great crowd there, with red flaming cloaks around them, which hang down to the ground. Their shuddering and their cries reach to the heavens. A host of demons without number choke them, urging the stinking and mangy dogs that they hold with their hands to devour and consume them. Around their necks hang red and fiery collars that blaze perpetually. Every other hour they are carried up to the heavens and then in the next are pitched down again into the depths of hell. Those who suffer in this way are clergymen who sin against their holy orders, hypocrites, imposters who deceive and mislead the people and who claim to perform wonders and miracles which they cannot do. The children who tear at the clergymen are those who were entrusted to them to be reformed, but they neither reformed them nor corrected them for their faults.

337

But there is a further large group there who ceaselessly move back and forth across the fiery flagstones, wrestling with hordes of milling demons. The showers of red and glowing arrows that the demons rain upon them are past counting. They run headlong without pausing for rest until they reach a black lake and a black river in order to quench the arrows that have pierced them. The cries of the sinners in those waters are miserable and pitiful for their pain is only increased. It is dishonest smiths, fullers and traders, false judges both among the Jews and in general, irreligious kings, crooked and sinful religious leaders, adulterous women and the go-betweens who lead them into wrongdoing, who suffer in this way.

On the other side of the land of torments there is a wall of fire, seven times more terrifying and fierce than the land of torments itself. But souls do not dwell there, for the demons alone keep it until the Day of Judgment comes.

Alas for those who have to endure these torments and the company of the Devil's host, and alas for those who do not avoid that host! Alas for those whose master is a fierce and savage demon. Alas for those who listen to the wailing and weeping of the souls, beseeching the Lord for Judgment Day to come quickly so that they might discover whether their sufferings are to be eased, for their only respite comes for three hours on Sundays.[7] Alas for those who shall dwell in that land forever! For this is what it is like: There are broken and thorny mountains in that place, scorched bare plains and stinking lakes full of monsters. Rough sandy earth, rugged and icebound, strewn with wide fiery slabs, great seas with terrible storms. It is the home and dwelling place of the devil for all eternity. Four great rivers traverse it: a river of fire, a river of snow, a river of poison, and a river of black, murky water. In these the savage hosts of demons bathe when they have had their fill of their sport of tormenting souls.

The blessed companies of the heavenly hosts sing the harmonious melodies of the eight canonical hours, and praise the Lord with joy and gladness, but the souls groan wretchedly under the ceaseless lashings of the hordes of demons.

These are the torments and the sufferings which the guardian angel showed to Adamnán's soul after its visit to the Kingdom of Heaven. Then, in the twinkling of an eye, his soul was led through the porch of gold and the screen of crystal to the Land of the Saints, to where he had first been guided when his soul left the body. But when he wished to stay and to remain in that land, an angel spoke to him from behind the screen, commanding him to return again to his body and to speak in gatherings and assemblies, and at the meetings of laymen and of clerics, telling them of the rewards of heaven and the sufferings of hell, just as his guardian angel had revealed to him.

And so this was the teaching which Adamnán always preached to the crowds all his life long, and which he taught at the great concourse of the men of Ireland when the Law of Adamnán was imposed upon the Irish people and the women were emancipated by Adamnán and by Finnachta Fledach, King of Ireland, and by the princes of Ireland. The rewards of heaven and the sufferings of hell were the first message that Patrick son of Calpurnius used to impart at the dawn of the gospel to those who believed in the Lord through his teaching and who accepted his spiritual guidance for their souls.

This too was the most constant teaching of Peter and Paul and the other Apostles, that is concerning the rewards and sufferings which had been similarly revealed to them. It was this too that Silvester, abbot of Rome, preached to Constantine, son of Helen, High-King of the world, in the assembly in which he offered Rome to Peter and Paul. And Fabian, who followed Peter, gave Philip, son of Gordian, King of Rome, the same teaching through which he came to believe in the Lord as did many thousands of others at the same time. Indeed, he was the first king of the Romans who believed in our Savior, Jesus Christ.

This is also the message that Elijah imparts to the souls of the righteous beneath the tree of life in Paradise. As soon as Elijah opens his book to teach the spirits, the souls of the righteous gather toward him in the form of brilliantly white birds.[8] First he speaks to them of the rewards of the righteous, the joys and delights of the Kingdom of Heaven, which gives them great joy. But then he tells them of the sufferings and torments of hell and the terrors of the Day of Judgment, at which a look of sorrow is clearly visible on his face and on that of Enoch, who then are the two sorrows of the Kingdom of Heaven. Then Elijah closes the book, and the birds give out a great cry of grief and press their wings against their bodies until streams of blood flow from them, so great is their fear of the sufferings of hell and the Day of Judgment.

Now since the souls of the blessed, to whom has been allotted an eternal place in the Kingdom of Heaven, grieve in this way, how much more appropriate it is that people on earth should reflect, even weeping tears of blood, upon the Day of Judgment and the sufferings of hell. For at that time the Lord will give each his or her due, rewarding the righteous and punishing sinners. At that time sinners shall be plunged into the depths of eternal pain and shall be imprisoned by the Word of God, under the curse of the Judge of Domesday, for all eternity. But the saints and the righteous, those who have given alms and have shown mercy, shall be borne to God's right hand, to dwell eternally in the Kingdom of Heaven, where they shall be in great glory, without age or death, knowing neither end nor term, forever and ever.

This then is the character of that City: a realm without pride or arrogance, without untruth or misdeed, without deception or penitence, without aggression or shame or disgrace, without reproach or envy, without haughtiness, without sickness or disease, without poverty or nakedness, without death or extinction, without hail or snow, without wind or rain, without noise or thunder, without darkness or cold. It is a fine, wonderful, delightful realm, filled with fruit and light and with the fragrance of a perfect land in which every excellence is enjoyed.

EXEGESIS

1. A MYSTICAL INTERPRETATION OF THE *BEATI* (PSALM 118)[1]

The question is further raised here how many days the children of Israel journeyed from Babylon to Jerusalem. This is not difficult to answer: three hundred and sixty-five, for that is the distance from the mystical Babylon (that is, from hell, where all strife and all confusion dwell) to the heavenly Jerusalem, which is the home of all peace and all blessing. Now there are one hundred and seventy-six paces in every journey and twenty-two stadia in every pace. As it is said:

1. Seven times fifty journeys, with power, fifteen without miscalculation,[a] from Babylon,[b] cause of conflict,[c] to the city of Jerusalem.[d]

2. One hundred and seventy-six paces[e] in every journey,[f] a vast amount, by the reckoning[g] of the wise,[h] it is clear, but the type of each pace is different.[i]

3. Twenty-two stadia,[j] unconcealed, in each pace, with mysteries of scripture which are not base, the forms of the old law.[k]

4. One hundred and twenty-five paces[l] in each stadium,[m] which signifies paths; philosophers testify to this, for the measuring of the world.

5. This is the argument that precedes the one hundred and eighteenth psalm; may every wise man who hears it examine it carefully at all times.

6. David, by the will of the King of Heaven, the king-prophet and king-poet, looked upon this mystery with grace through the Spirit of seven forms.

Seven times...

This then is the journey the soul makes while the *Beati* is being recited, that is, one step for every verse, namely one hundred and seventy-six, and the substance of the twenty-two books is in every verse of the *Beati*. That is why the *Beati* brings a soul out of hell after a year, for more than any other prayer it is in harmony with the twenty-two books of the Old Testament, that is, the fullness of them all is in each single verse, and it contains twenty-two sections in accordance with the number of the Hebrew alphabet. And so it was God who fulfilled David's prophecy through their journeys, and not they themselves who ordained them.[2]

a. i.e., three hundred and sixty-five journeys altogether
b. i.e., from hell
c. i.e., which causes teeth to chatter[3]
d. i.e., to heaven
e. i.e., the number of verses in the *Beati*
f. i.e., in every step of the *Beati*
g. i.e., counting
h. i.e., learned
i. i.e., literal and mystical pace
j. i.e., the twenty-two books of the Old Testament
k. i.e., the twenty-two books
l. i.e., the eighth part of a mile
m. i.e., in every single book

2. GLOSS ON PSALM 103

BLESS THE LORD, MY SOUL. That is, "Bless the Lord, all his hosts" (Ps 103:21). THE PSALM OF DAVID HIMSELF. The voice of David, filled with wonder and praise of the Lord, as he gazes upon his creatures.[4] The voice of the church, praising the Lord and recounting his works to his faithful people.

1. BLESS THE LORD, MY SOUL. That is, David utters his praise of God, speaking from his soul. YOU HAVE PUT ON MAJESTY AND SPLENDOR. That is, we owe the acts of grace and the ornament of the offices of the law to you.

2. YOU ARE CLOTHED IN LIGHT AS WITH A ROBE. That is, our minds praise the divine nature thus since we know nothing more excellent than light. YOU HAVE SPREAD OUT THE HEAVENS LIKE A HIDE. That is, the heavens stretch out like the skin of a tent between our eyes and the mysteries and wonders above.

3. YOU COVER WITH WATERS ITS UPPER PARTS. That is, you place it in the waters above the heavens, you cover the upper parts of the heavens, and its furthest parts in the ocean. YOU MAKE THE CLOUDS YOUR CHARIOT. That is, because you descend and ascend in cloud; cloud covered Mount Sinai as it did the tabernacle of Moses. YOU WHO WALK UPON THE WINGS OF THE WIND. That is, an analogy for speed of movement is drawn from birds; the wings of the wind are clouds.

4. YOU WHO MAKE YOUR ANGELS SPIRITS. That is, angels are called spirits on account of the speed of their travel; angel is the name of an activity, while spirit denotes a nature.[5] YOUR MINISTERS A FLAMING FIRE. That is, seraphim, whose name means burning.[6]

5. YOU WHO FOUNDED THE EARTH UPON ITS FIRMNESS. That is, your power is secured as if with a support, and

cannot be moved; it has been established on a firm base from the time of the creation. IT SHALL NEVER BE MOVED. That is, as it is said: "The earth shall stand for all eternity" (Eccl 1:4).

6. THE DEEP, LIKE A GARMENT, IS ITS CLOTHING. That is, the great ocean facing the earth. THE WATERS SHALL STAND ABOVE THE MOUNTAINS. That is, the swelling waves of the sea rise up like mountains.

7. FROM YOUR REBUKE THEY SHALL FLEE. That is, for fear of you, when they rise up and when they fall silent, as it is said: "You rule the raging of the sea" (Ps 89:9). Alternatively: THEY SHALL FLEE, as did the Red Sea and the Jordan, FROM THE VOICE OF YOUR THUNDER. That is, your voice was like thunder to them on account of their fear; for the psalmist the voice or word represents the power of God, which performs what it will by means of the voice or word. THEY SHALL HASTEN AWAY. That is, the waters.

8. THE MOUNTAINS ASCEND. That is, in the storm. AND THE PLAINS GO DOWN. That is, in peace and calm. TO THE PLACE WHICH YOU HAVE FOUNDED FOR THEM. That is, they enter the borders laid down for your kingdom.

9. YOU HAVE SET A BOUND THEY MAY NOT PASS OVER. That is, a shore facing the land on all sides; even if they seem uncontrolled and tower above the land, they do not pass the limit you have set down.

10. WHO SENDS OUT SPRINGS INTO THE VALLEYS. That is, something remarkable: you who cause the waters to run out from the sides of mountains and down into low-lying places. THE WATERS SHALL FLOW BETWEEN THE MOUNTAINS. That is, from the springs, that they may give drink to people and beasts and may irrigate the solitary places.

11. ALL THE BEASTS OF THE FIELD SHALL DRINK FROM THEM. That is, the mountains are so filled with water that flowing down the valleys the waters irrigate the earth and provide

drink for the animals. THE WILD ASSES SHALL WAIT IN THEIR THIRST. That is, the water that must be given them at the right time; the wild ass, an animal that drinks the wind on account of its thirst.

12. THE BIRDS ABOVE THEM. That is, above the rivers. THEY CALL OUT FROM THE MIDST OF THE ROCKS. That is, they give thanks to God from the crags for the water he gives them.

13. HE WATERS THE HILLS FROM THE HEIGHTS. That is, he makes streams flow from the tops of mountains so that they spread over the earth and under the earth. THE EARTH SHALL BE FILLED WITH THE FRUIT OF YOUR WORKS. That is, by the abundance of waters which fructify the earth.

14. AND HERBS FOR THE SERVICE OF PEOPLE. That is, which shows how much God is concerned for our welfare in that he nourishes four-footed animals and birds which serve our needs. THAT BREAD MAY BE PRODUCED FROM THE EARTH. That is, not only does the rain-soaked earth put forth hay for beasts of burden but also produce that is suitable for human consumption.

15. AND OIL TO MAKE THE FACE SHINE. That is, he adds to the gifts of bread and wine the oblation of oil, the use of which enriches and cheers the body. AND BREAD TO STRENGTHEN THE HEART. That is, not that these three suffice alone, but that they are more excellent than anything else.

16. THE TREES OF THE FIELD SHALL BE FILLED. That is, fruit-bearing orchards clothe the fields, nourished by the downpour of showers. Fittingly, each is planted separately.

17. THERE SHALL THE SPARROWS MAKE THEIR NESTS. That is, in the cedars spoken of above. THEIR LEADER IS THE HOUSE OF THE STORK. That is, the sparrow and the stork are birds which build their nests in the trees of the field, and the stork rules over the birds, that is to say, the sparrows. Alternatively,

the bird referred to here is a certain large bird that is leader of all the birds, which incubates its egg in the mountains, together with the heat of the sun, above a river estuary for forty days and then, when this period is over, pushes it down from the mountain with its beak and, having destroyed it, carries half of it across the estuary and displays it for the admiration of all.[7] Alternatively, THE HOUSE OF THE STORK, which being built in the high trees is the leader of the sparrows; for if the sparrows go forth beyond the reach of the shade of the stork's house, then they cannot find their nests again. Thus it is said that it is THEIR LEADER.

18. THE HIGH HILLS ARE A REFUGE FOR THE WILD GOATS. These are elusive animals that live in high and remote mountains. AND THE ROCKS A REFUGE FOR THE ROCK-BADGERS. That is, little creatures which live in rocky caves since they cannot climb up mountains; the rock-badger is like a round hedgehog, covered in spines. It climbs into the vine, drops its eggs onto the earth, and carries them away on its spines.

19. HE APPOINTED THE MOON FOR CERTAIN SEASONS. That is, for the twelve months, whether waning or waxing. Also: To whose advantage is it that the moon wanes rather than the sun? That is an image of the Lord and his church.[8] Also: What literal benefit is there here? That is, for the feeding of those other animals which do not dare to emerge from their dens during the daytime or when the moon is full.

20. YOU BRING DARKNESS, AND IT IS NIGHT. That is, because wild animals go out more at night and fall into the snares of men, and as soon as the sun rises again, they return to their lairs.[9] Thus if anyone is afraid, it is that demons and vices may fall upon them. WHEN ALL THE BEASTS OF THE FOREST GO PROWLING. That is, because they fear to go forth during the day.

21. THE YOUNG LIONS ROAR FOR PREY. That is, it is a characteristic of lions that they provide prey for themselves with the sound of their voice; for animals are trapped by their fear of the

lion's roar. SEEKING THEIR FOOD FROM GOD. That is, because God has provided small animals for the lion's food.

22. WHEN THE SUN RISES. That is, night is beneficial for the repose of men and women, and for the feeding of animals. THEY SEEK REST IN THEIR LAIRS. That is, the young animals for the fear of man.[10]

25. HERE IS THE VAST IMMEASURABLE SEA. That is, here is a marvel; he passed to the sea on account of his wonder for the things of heaven and earth. IN WHICH MOVE CRAWLING THINGS. That is, creatures in the sea. WITHOUT NUMBER. That is, for men and women, since this is not the case for God. LIVING CREATURES, SMALL. That is, fish, AND GREAT, that is, shoals.

26. HERE SHIPS SAIL TO AND FRO. That is, small boats and fast sailing vessels. Alternatively: HERE IS THE VAST IMMEASURABLE SEA. That is, the ocean of the world is vast and they who live in it are called reptiles, and their number is great; there are both small creatures and large creatures in it, whereby all, no matter how great they are, know themselves to be only reptiles for as long as they remain in the ocean of the world.[11] HERE IS A MONSTER. That is, Leviathan; this monster was created to play in the sea and to reign in the world.[12] Leviathan means an addition,[13] that is, all the creatures of the sea. Leviathan is a creature of the sea which the Mediterranean cannot hold, and so he moves this way and that in the Indian Ocean, as if at play. Behemoth, the creature of the fields, means many: that is, all the creatures of the land.[14]

28. WHAT YOU GIVE THEM THEY GATHER UP. That is, they grow by an analogy with human nourishment. THEY EAT THEIR FILL OF GOOD THINGS. That is, in abundance.

29. WHEN YOU HIDE YOUR FACE. That is, your help. THEY ARE DISMAYED. That is, afflicted with hunger. WHEN YOU TAKE AWAY THEIR SPIRIT. That is, afflicted with hunger. THEY PERISH. That is, they die. AND RETURN TO THE

DUST FROM WHICH THEY CAME. That is, to the earth from which they were made; that is, as is the way with human beings.

30. WHEN YOU SEND FORTH YOUR SPIRIT, THEY ARE CRE-ATED. That is, he utters his spirit as the enactment of divine power; that is, other new animals. AND YOU RENEW THE FACE OF THE EARTH. That is, the many different kinds of animals that adorn the earth.

31. MAY THE GLORY OF THE LORD STAND FOREVER. That is, he who did all these things is worthy of our praise. THE LORD SHALL REJOICE IN HIS WORKS. That is, the renewal of his works shall please the Lord.

32. WHEN HE TOUCHES THE MOUNTAINS, THEY POUR FORTH SMOKE. That is, as happened on Mount Sinai.

33. I SHALL SING TO THE LORD. That is, I shall pay honor to the Creator in the unceasing office of Psalms. I SHALL SING PSALMS TO MY GOD. That is, in the psalter.

34. MAY MY PRAISE OF HIM BE SWEET. That is, may my praise be sweet.

35. BLESS THE LORD MY SOUL. That is, for all these gifts and wonders.

HOMILIES

1. SERMONS OF COLUMBANUS

i.

Sermon Five

Human life, fragile and marked for death, how many have you deceived, beguiled, and blinded? While in flight, you are nothing; while in sight, you are a shadow; while you rise up, you are but smoke. Every day you depart and every day you return; you depart in returning and you return in departing, different ending, same beginning, different pleasure, the same passing, sweet to the foolish and bitter to the wise. Those who love you do not know you, and those who condemn you really understand you. Thus you are not true but false; you present yourself as true but prove yourself false. What are you then, human life? You are the wayfaring of mortals and not their living;[1] your beginning is in sin and in death your end. You would be true if the sin of the first human transgression had not cut you short so that you became unsteady and mortal and marked all who tread your way for death. And so you are the way that leads to life, but not life itself, for you are a true way, but not an open one: brief for some and long for others, broad for some and narrow for others, joyful for some and full of grief for others, but for each and every one, you hurry on and cannot be called back. A way is what you are, a way, but you are not evident to all. Though many see you, few understand that you are indeed a way. You are so cunning and alluring that it is given to few to know you as a way. Thus you are to be questioned and not believed or credited, you are to be traversed and not inhabited: wretched human life. For a road is to be walked on and not lived in, so that they who walk upon it may dwell finally in the land that is their home.

And so, mortal life, it is the foolish and the lost, spurned by those with sense and avoided by those to be saved, who dwell in you, who love you, and who believe in you. Therefore, human life, you are to be feared and much avoided, for you are so fleeting, shifting, dangerous, brief, and uncertain that you shall be dissolved like a shadow, a mirage, a cloud, a nothingness, or an emptiness. Thus while you are nothing, mortal life, but a way, a fleeting and empty mirage, or a cloud, uncertain and frail, or a shadow, like a dream, we must journey through you so anxiously, so carefully, so hastily, that all those with understanding should press on, like wayfarers, to their true homeland, untroubled at what has been and concerned as to what is to come. For there is no advantage for us in reaching the height we have attained unless we escape what is still to come; for this life is to be thought of as a way and an ascent. We should not seek in the way what shall only be in our homeland, for effort and fatigue are to be found on the journey, while peace and safety are prepared in the land that is our home. We should be careful therefore in case we are complacent on the way and fail to reach our true home. Indeed, there are many who are so at ease on this journey that they seem not so much to be wayfarers as to be already at home, and they travel unwillingly rather than freely toward a home that is for them already lost. These people have exhausted their home in the journey, and with a brief life have bought eternal death. Unfortunate creatures, they delight in their disastrous exchange. They have loved the transitory things of others, and neglected their own eternal possessions. And so, however wonderful they may be, however enticing and beautiful, we should avoid the earthly goods of others so that we do not lose our own inheritance. Let us be found faithful in the property of others so that we may be made inheritors in those things that are truly ours, by the gift of our Lord Jesus Christ, who lives and reigns from age to age. Amen.

ii.

Sermon Eight

Now we must speak of the end of the way, for we have already said that human life is like a road and by comparing it to a shadow, we have shown that it is dubious and uncertain, and that it is not what it seems to be. In the same way, we have said before how unpredictable and how blind it is, but we must speak further, with the help of the Holy Spirit, about our life's end. It is natural for travelers to hurry on to their homeland; it is natural too that they should experience anxiety on the roadway and peace when they arrive home. And so we too who are on the road should hasten on, for the whole of our life is like one day's journey. Our first duty is to love nothing here, but to love the things above, to desire the things above, to relish the things above and to seek our home there, for the fatherland is where our Father is. Thus we have no home on earth, since our Father is in heaven. And indeed, if he is everywhere by virtue of his power and the greatness of his divinity, he is deeper than the ocean, more stable than the earth, broader than the world, purer than the air, higher than the sky, and more brilliant than the sun. But he dwells openly in the heavens, where he is the "bread of angels" (cf. Ps 78:25) who, as his retinue, inhabit the blessed region of the first heaven and enjoy the sight of God. But since our weaker nature could not endure the pure nature of the invisible God, God, who contains all things and outside whom there is nothing, allotted to the highest virtues the first region of the knowledge of himself, enclosed by the first heaven and tempered by the waters above. For unless that nature of the first heaven were tempered by the waters, it would be set on fire by the virtue of the highest God and could in no way be endured by lower natures. And so, while being present to everyone everywhere, God remains invisible. For he who created all things from nothing is greater than all that can be seen whole, and greater than all that is, and thus when he is seen, he is invisible, since he alone knows who he is and how great he is. But let us pray to him, for although he is invisible and unfathomable, God the Trinity is still known and present to us, according to the degree of our purity. Let us pray to him, I say, while we are here, so that there we may enter in more intimately and understand more clearly. Singing as we progress on our journey, let us say: "Let us run after you, toward the scent of your perfumes" (Sg 1:3) and "my soul has cleaved to you" (Ps 63:8), and "draw me after you" (Sg 1:3), so that with the help of these songs we may pass more swiftly through this world and governed from above we may spurn the things of the present, and thinking only of the things of heaven, may turn our back on earthly things. Unless we are filled with the urgent longing of heavenly desires, we shall necessarily be ensnared in earthly ones.

And then, in case we should concern ourselves with human things, we should concern ourselves with those that are divine, and just like pilgrims continuously sigh for and long for our homeland, for travelers are always filled with hope and desire for the road's end. And so, since we are travelers and pilgrims in this world, let us think upon the end of the road, that is of our life, for the end of our way is our home. But there the fate of all who pass through this world varies according to their merits, the good travelers finding peace in their home, while the evil ones perish and cannot enter it. Many lose their true home because they have greater love for the road that leads them there. Let us not love the road rather than our home, in case we should lose our eternal home, for our home is such that we should love it. Let us keep to this principle, therefore, that we should live as travelers and pilgrims on the road, as guests of the world, free of lusts and earthly desires, but let us fill our mind with heavenly and spiritual forms, singing with grace and power: "When shall I come and appear before the face of my God? For my soul thirsts for the mighty and living God" (Ps 42:2), and "My soul is like a parched land before you" (Ps 143:6), and saying with Paul: "I desire to be dissolved and to be with Christ" (Phil 1:23). Let us know that although we are strangers to the Lord while in the body, we are present to the eyes of God. And so, turning our back on all evil and laying aside all apathy, let us strive to please him who is everywhere, so that we may joyfully and with a good conscience pass over from the road of this world to the blessed and eternal home of our eternal Father, moving from present things to absent ones, from sad things to joyful ones, from passing things to eternal ones, from earthly things to heavenly ones, from the region of death to the sphere of the living, where we shall see heavenly things face-to-face, and the King of Kings, ruling his realms with an upright rule, our Lord Jesus Christ, to whom be glory from age to age. Amen.

iii.
Sermon Eleven

Moses wrote in the Law, "God made man in his own image and likeness" (Gn 1:26). Consider, I beg you, the weight of these words: God, the all-powerful, invisible, unfathomable, ineffable, and unsearchable, when making man of clay, ennobled him with the dignity of his image. What does the human race have in common with God? What does earth have in common with spirit? For God is spirit. It is a great honor that God bestowed on men and women the image of his eternity and likeness to his own character. And it is a great adornment for men and women if they can preserve a likeness to God, while the defiling of the image of God is a great condemnation. For if they abuse what they have received from the breath of God, and corrupt the blessing of their nature, then they distort their likeness to God and destroy its presence in them. But if they use the virtues implanted in them appropriately, then they shall be like God. Whatever virtues God sowed in us in our primal state, therefore, he has commanded us to return to him. This is the first, to love the Lord with the whole of our heart (cf. Mt 22:37), since he first loved us from the beginning (cf. 1 Jn 4:10). For to love God is to restore his image. But they love God who follow his commands, for he said: "If you love me, keep my commandments" (Jn 14:15). This is his commandment, a mutual love, according to the saying: "This is my commandment, that you love one another, as I also have loved you" (Jn 15:12). But true love is not in word only but also in action and truth. And so let us restore to God our Father his own image undefiled in holiness since he is holy, according to the words: "Be holy, since I am holy" (Lv 11:44); in love, since he is love, according to the words of St. John, "God is love" (1 Jn 4:8), in righteousness and truth, since he is righteous and true.

Let us not paint the image of another; for they who are fierce, full of anger and pride, paint the image of a tyrant. Just as false knowledge is uncovered, so too a false image is revealed to be a phantom. For truth is distinguished from falsehood, justice from unrighteousness, love from malevolence, commitment from carelessness, fairness from injustice, affection from pretense, and both paint images upon us which are mutually opposed. For righteousness and unrighteousness, peace and conflict are opposites. In case we should introduce tyrannical images into ourselves, let Christ paint his own image in us, as he does when he says: "My peace I give you, my peace I leave you" (Jn 14:27). But what is the point of knowing that peace is good if still it is not preserved? For the best gifts are usually the most fragile, and the most valuable things require the greatest care and safe-keeping; and something is exceedingly fragile if it is lost by light talk and the slightest injury by a brother. There is no one who is not harmed when others fawn, and to rebuke someone is not to fawn upon them. For you should say: "Fool, you have broken the peace and have become ready for hell." For those who train themselves in the perfection of brotherly love should not speak as they please, letting the tongue follow the mind, since we shall be called to account not just for harmful words but also for words that are idle. Therefore we should train ourselves not to speak too much, but to say only what is necessary. For there is nothing more pleasant for us than to speak of others and their concerns, to speak idle words everywhere, and to criticize those who are not present. Thus those who cannot say "The Lord has given me a discerning tongue, that I can support him who is weary with a word" (Is 50:4) should keep silent, and if they say anything, it should be constructive. However wise we may be, we give less offense when we speak less than when we speak more, for when someone lies, curses, criticizes, then they cut their own throat with their sword. And what else would our enemies have desired but that we should fall victim to our own weapons? Do not be detractors, says scripture, in case you are destroyed. See what is done in the works of unrighteousness; settling and planting, which we can only establish with long hours of work every day, are destroyed by a single word of negative criticism, and what can hardly be constructed by lengthy labor is brought down by the beginning of a single act of speech. Let everyone beware therefore in case their root be torn up from the land of the living on account of their hateful and negative words. For no one ever undermines those whom they love, and belittling others is the firstborn son of hatred. Thus the son of such a father merits destruction.

It is a dangerous dwelling, my dearest friends, where these things are not guarded against. For as the Apostle says, "If you envy each other and bite each other," (Gal 5:15), if you belittle each other, I say, beware in case you are devoured by one another. For if they who do not love are in death (cf. 1 Jn 3:14), then where shall they who undermine others be? Tears are more necessary in this than words. What has the law of God commanded more carefully or more fully than love? And yet you will rarely find anyone who does love. How shall we explain this away? Can we really say that it is difficult and hard? Love is not difficult; love is more pleasant, restorative, and good for the heart. For if vice has not made the heart apathetic, love is its own health and is that which is dear to God. There is nothing that is more precious to God than love, especially spiritual love, since it is the sum of his law and all his commandments, according to the words of the Apostle: "But he who loves his neighbor has fulfilled the law" (Rom 13:8). They who have fulfilled the law by the practice of law have eternal life, as John also says: "Brothers, we know that we have passed from death to life because we love our brethren, for he who does not love is in death." But if anyone is filled with hate, he is a murderer (1 Jn 3:14–15). And you know that no murderer has eternal life in him. Then we must either love or expect nothing but punishment; for "love is the fulfillment of the law" (Rom 13:10). May the Righteous One, our Lord and Savior Jesus Christ, deign to inspire us with love, who deigned to be offered as the founder of peace and the God of love, to whom be glory forever and ever. Amen.

iv.

Sermon Thirteen

Having grasped the wretchedness of human life from reflections upon everyday experience, and at the same time having been dismayed by divine prophecies, we have long had the temerity to display in earlier sermons the poverty of our skill. And although some may find our many words altogether excessive, this discourse seems to us to be a timely event at least for ourselves, for we are not seeking to banish others' indolence so much as our own. In addition, although a theology which has been only partially thought through may have proved less satisfactory to those who are already perfectly wise, for those who are beginners and who share our own lack of fervor, it will seem both necessary and suitable enough. For that which it is harmful to conceal and harmful to cover up cannot profitably be hidden and shrouded in silence. Therefore it seemed better to us to speak, however crudely, than to remain silent, for we judged it safer to discuss these things rather than others which are either frivolous or irrelevant. And so, dearest brothers, do listen attentively to our words in the belief that you will hear something that needs to be heard, and refresh the thirst of your mind from the waters of the divine spring of which we now wish to speak. But do not quench that thirst; drink, but do not be filled. For now the living fountain, the fountain of life, calls us to himself and says: "Let him who is thirsty come to me and drink" (Jn 7:37). And take note of what it is that you shall drink. Let Isaiah tell you, let the fountain himself tell you: "But they have forsaken me the fountain of living water," says the Lord (Jer 2:13). Thus the Lord himself, our God Jesus Christ, is the fountain of life, and so he calls us to himself, the fountain, that we may drink of him. They who love drink of him, they drink who are filled with the Word of God, who love enough, who desire enough, they drink who burn with the love of wisdom. Then let us gentiles eagerly drink what the Jews have forsaken. For perhaps it was said of us with the gentiles: "He breaks off in amazement of mind, the heads of the mighty shall be moved, while they open not their jaws, like a poor man eating in secret" (Hb 3:14); and as if it were said of us also with all the perfect, of whom this was written, let us open the jaws of our inner man, as when eating that bread which came down from heaven, that we may eat hungrily and swiftly, in case anyone should see us, as if we ate in secret. Let us eat the same Lord Jesus Christ as bread, let us drink him as a fountain, who calls himself the "living bread, who gives life to this world" (Jn 6:33), as if to be eaten by us, and who likewise shows himself to be a fountain when he says: "Let him who is thirsty come to me and drink" (Jn 7:37), of which fountain the prophet also says: "since with you is the fountain of life" (Ps 36:9).

Observe from where that fountain flows; for it comes from that place from where the bread also came down, since he is the same who is bread and fountain, the only Son, our God Christ the Lord, for whom we should always hunger. Although we eat him when we love him, though we feast on him when we desire him, let us still desire him like people who are ravenous. Likewise with the fountain, let us always drink of him with an overflowing love, let us always drink of him with a fullness of longing, and let the sweet savor of his loveliness ravish us. For the Lord is sweet and lovely; and although we eat and drink of him, let us still always hunger and thirst, since our food and drink can never be completely consumed, for though he is eaten, he is not eaten up; though he is drunk, he is not drained; since our bread is eternal and our fountain is everlasting, our fountain is sweet. Therefore the prophet says: "Go you who thirst to the fountain" (Is 55:1); for that is the fountain of those who thirst not of those who are replete, and so he calls to himself the hungry and the thirsty, whom he blessed elsewhere, who never have enough of drinking, but who thirst the more, the more they consume. We are right, my brothers, to desire the fountain of wisdom, the Word of God on high, to seek him, always to love him, in whom are hid, according to the Apostle's words, "all the treasures of wisdom and knowledge" (Col 2:3), which he calls those who thirst to enjoy. If you thirst, drink the fountain of life; if you hunger, eat the bread of life. Blessed are they who hunger for this bread and thirst for this fountain; though they are always eating and drinking, they still long to eat and drink. For that is lovely to excess which is always eaten and drunk, for which there is always a hunger and a thirst, always tasted and always desired. Therefore the Prophet-King says, "Taste and see how lovely, how pleasant is the Lord" (Ps 34:8). Therefore, my brothers, let us follow this calling, by which we are called to the fountain of life by the life who is the fountain, not only the fountain of living water, but also of eternal life, the fountain of light, indeed the fountain of glory; for from him come all these things, wisdom, life, and eternal light. The Author of life is the fountain of life, the Creator of light, the fountain of glory. Therefore, spurning the things that are seen, journeying through the world, let us seek the fountain of glory, the fountain of life, the fountain of living water, in the upper regions of the heavens, like rational and most wise fishes, that there we may drink the living water which springs up to eternal life.

If only you would deign to admit me to that fountain, merciful God, righteous Lord, so that there I too might drink with your thirsting ones the living stream of the living fount of the living water and, ravished by his too great loveliness, might hold to him always on high and say: How lovely is the fount of living water, whose water does not fail, springing up to life eternal. O Lord, you are yourself that fountain ever and again to be desired, although ever and again to be consumed. Give this water always, Lord Christ, that it may be in us too a fountain of water that lives and springs up to eternal life. I ask for great things; who does not know that. But you, King of Glory, know how to give great things and have promised great things. Nothing is greater than you yourself, and you have given yourself to us, you gave yourself for us. Therefore we ask that we may know what we love, for we ask for nothing other than that you should be given to us; for you are our all, our life, our light, our salvation, our food, our drink, our God. I ask that you inspire our hearts, our Jesus, with that breath of your Spirit, and wound our souls with your love, so that the soul of each one of us may be able to say in truth: "Show me him whom my soul has loved" (Sngs 1:6), for by love am I wounded. I desire that those wounds may be in me, O Lord. Blessed is such a soul which is thus wounded by love. Such a soul seeks the fountain, such a one drinks, but always thirsts when drinking, it always drinks when desiring, and always drinks when thirsting. Thus it always seeks by loving and is always healed by its wounding. And with this healing wound may our God and Lord Jesus Christ, that Physician of righteousness and health, deign to wound the inward parts of our soul, who with the Father and the Holy Spirit is one forever and ever. Amen.

2. CATECHESIS CELTICA: COMMENTARY ON MATTHEW XVI, 24

"Anyone who wishes to be a follower of mine must renounce self."

Jesus Christ was the only son of God from the human race, who had been condemned to death by the ancient fault of the first parent, and through the teachings of the disciples the sweet-sounding doctrine of the gospel made known these secret things both singly and together to every creature, for "their words went out to the end of the world" (cf. Ps 19:4). He who is the sole blessed and powerful King of Kings and Lord of Lords, possessing immortality (cf. 1 Tm 6:15–16), from the Creator himself all things together are created, through him they are fashioned and ordered and in him they are governed in the world. He created the elements, formed them, and now he governs them. For, as the Apostle says, "from him and through him and in him are all things" (cf. Rom 11:36), namely from the Father, through the Son, and in the Holy Spirit, as John attests "all things were made through him" (Jn 1:3), and David too "in wisdom you made all things" (cf. Ps 104:24), that is, in the Son, and elsewhere: "The heavens are established by the Word of the Lord," that is, by the Father's Son. A word is the word of someone who is speaking, and he who speaks does so by uttering the word that he has brought forth. He entrusts all that is in himself to be governed in the word. For the Father still acts in the Son (cf. Jn 5:17), since the world unfolds through governance, when angels carry out their commands, when the stars revolve, when the winds alternate, when the depths of the waters are stirred by currents and by various movements of the air, when vines[2] put forth straight shoots and produce their seeds, when animals are born and live out their lives by their various appetites, when the wicked are allowed to put temptations in the way of the righteous. The Apostle says: "In

him we live and move and have our being" (Acts 17:28), for neither heaven nor earth and all that are in them, that is every spiritual or corporeal creature, dwells in itself but rather in him, that is,
in God. Everything that exists either lives by reason and the senses,
such as angels and human beings (life that lives, feels, and thinks
in men and women), or is moved by the senses without reason,
such as the brute creatures (for life lives and feels but does not
think in brute creatures), or lacks both senses and reason, such as
trees, vegetables, and the like, although they have a lower form of
life, for if they had no life at all, they would doubtlessly fall into
nothingness. But life that lives, feels, and thinks cannot be reckoned to be in them. Also, all things can be created in God through
governance, as we have contended. The life of whatever has been
created is in him; not only of all the creatures that exist in the present, but also of those things which were and which shall be, for in
God they have neither past nor future, but only present existence,
since whatever all creatures shall be and whatever their movements, they shall certainly not be nothing. Accordingly, the creature always remains in the Creator, and therefore he knew his
creatures before he made them. For before they were created,
they were life in him, and that life was not created but is itself Creator. For the Word in which it exists is not created, since the Word
was God and all things were created through him (Jn 1:1–3). If he
had been created, then all things could not have been created
through him, since indeed all substance which is not God is creature and what is not creature is God. Therefore because the Word
is God, then the life which is in him is God, and in that life is the
light of men and women, a light indeed of rational minds which
sets men apart from sinners, but the light shines in the darkness,
and the darkness did not comprehend it (Jn 1:5), because just as
the vehicle of reason and mental discipline is destroyed when the
sharpness of the mind is blunted,[3] the minds of the foolish can in
no way understand the seven disciplines, although they are irre-
movably implanted in them, so the minds of men when they have
cast aside the religion of the true faith, with base desire and blind
infidelity, shall never posses the all-powerful Lord, that is the true
light, poured out over each one of us, above, below, around,

364

within all things. It was because the Creator of all wished to heal these people that the Word through whom all things were made became flesh and dwelt among us. For just as the word of a man is signified by a sound or some other sign, by assuming which it becomes manifest to the human senses, thus the Word of God became flesh, and assumed that by which he himself could be manifest to the human senses. This is therefore the mediator of God and man, who is both God and man, since the form of God took on the form of a servant (cf. Phil 2:6–7), that is, both God on account of the God who assumes and man on account of the man who is assumed, and who cured those diseased and laid low by the malign poison of sin by speaking the saving word of the true vine.

3. AN OLD IRISH HOMILY

We give thanks to Almighty God, Lord of heaven and earth, for his mercy and forgiveness, for his love and his blessings which he has bestowed upon us in heaven and on earth. It is of him that the prophet says: "All your works shall give thanks to you, O Lord, and all your saints shall bless you" (Ps 145:10). For it is the duty of all the elements to give thanks to God and to bless him, as it is said: "Bless the Lord, all you works of the Lord" (Ps 103:22). For God does not deny his present blessings even to sinners, as scripture says: "God is good who bestows his gifts equally upon the righteous and the wicked" (cf. Mt 5:45), that is, God is devoted and excellent who gives to the good and the evil the good things of the earth equally. For he is the one excellent God who is without beginning or end. He it is who has created all things, who has formed them and sustains them by the might of his power. He it is who nourishes and preserves and gladdens and illumines and rules and has redeemed and renews all things. In him they trust; he it is for whom they wait, for he is King of Kings and Lord of Lords, Creator of heaven and earth, Maker of the angels, Teacher of the prophets, Master of the apostles, Giver of the Law, Judge of the men and women of the world. He is higher than the heavens, lower than the earth, wider than the seas.

It is our duty to give thanks to that Lord for his gifts. For the grateful soul who gives thanks to God for his grace is a temple and dwelling place of God; as Peter says: "God makes the soul grateful and familiar to him." That is, the man or woman who gives thanks to God for his blessings is an estate that belongs to the King of all. But they who are not grateful for the blessings of God are a temple and dwelling place of the Devil; as Peter says: "The ungrateful soul is in the possession of a demon." The evil demon possesses and inhabits the soul of the ungrateful who do not give thanks to God for his blessings. It is that thanksgiving which is meant when they say: "Our souls give thanks to you for your blessings without number." That is, our souls give thanks to you, O Lord, for your blessings without number on heaven and earth.

And so may the blessing of the Lord of heaven and earth be on everyone with whom we have come into contact, on their possession of field and house, on their property both animate and inanimate, and on everyone who serves them and is obedient to them. May the earth give its fruits, may the air give its rainfall, may the sea give its fishes, may there be more grain and milk, more honey and wheat for everyone whose labor and goodwill we enjoy. May God give them a hundredfold on this earth and the kingdom of heaven in the life to come. For they who receive Christ's people actually receive Christ, as he himself says: "Whoever hears you, hears me and whoever rejects you rejects me" (cf. Lk 10:16). That is, he who receives you receives me, he who despises you despises me.

But there are analogies to the kingdom of heaven and to hell in this world. First the analogy to hell, that is winter and snow, stormy weather and the cold, old age and decay, disease and death. The analogy to the kingdom of heaven however is summer and fair weather, flower and leaf, beauty and youth, feasts and feastings, prosperity and an abundance of every good thing.

But it is into hell that God shall cast sinners on Judgment Day, saying: "Go, you who are cursed, into the eternal fire which has been prepared for you by the Devil and his angels." Woe to them to whom the Lord shall say on the Day of Judgment that they shall dwell forever in hell with its many and great torments. For its setting is deep, its surrounds are solid, its jaws are dark, its company is sorrowful, its stench is great, its monsters are everlasting, its earth is sunken,[4] its surface is poisonous, it is an abyss to restrain,[5] it is a prison to hold, it is a flame to burn, it is a net to hold fast, it is a scourge to lash, it is a blade to maim, it is a night to blind, it is smoke to suffocate, it is a cross to torture, it is a sword to punish.

In this way, then, these punishments are to be avoided: by hard work and study, by fasting and prayer, by righteousness and mercy, by faith and love. For whoever fulfills these commandments, God shall call them to himself on the Day of Judgment, saying to them: "Come, you blessed of my Father, possess the kingdom which has been prepared for you from the beginning of the world" (Mt 25:34).

We should strive then for the kingdom of heaven which is unlike the human dominion of the present world, which earthly kings love. It blinds like mist, it slays like sleep, it wounds like a point, it destroys like a blade, it burns like fire, it drowns like a sea, it swallows like a pit, it devours like a monster. But not like that is the kingdom which the saints and the righteous strive for. It is a bright flower in its great purity, it is an open sea in its great beauty, it is a heaven full of candles in its true brilliance, it is the eye's delight in its great loveliness and pleasantness, it is a flame in its fairness, it is a harp in its melodiousness, it is a feast in its abundance of wine, it is a...in its true radiance.[6] Blessed are they who shall come into the kingdom where God himself is, a King, great, fair, powerful, strong, holy, pure, just, knowing, wise, merciful, loving, beneficent, old, young, wise, noble, glorious, without beginning, without end, without age, without decay. May we enter the kingdom of that King, may we merit it and may we dwell there forever and ever. Amen.

4. THE CAMBRAI HOMILY

On gifts which are not to be received on account of the revealing of truth. "Daniel replied, 'Your majesty, I do not look for gifts from you; give your rewards to another. Nevertheless I shall read your majesty the writing and make known to you its interpretation'" (Dn 5:17). Jerome says about this: Let us imitate Daniel in his contempt for the world. In the name of the highest God. "If anyone wishes to come after me, let them renounce themselves, pick up their cross and follow me" (Mt 16:24).

This is the word that our Lord Jesus Christ says to every member of our race, that we should banish from ourselves our vices and sins, and that we should develop virtues and receive stigmata and signs of the Cross for Christ's sake, for as long as we are in harmony of body and soul, and that we should follow our Lord with good deeds. Therefore he says: "If anyone wishes to come after me, let them renounce themselves, pick up their cross and follow me." To deny ourselves means not giving in to our desires and turning our back on our sins. To take our Cross upon ourselves means to accept loss and martyrdom and to suffer for Christ's sake, as has been said: The name of the Cross comes from the word for torture, and we bear the cross of the Lord in two ways, either when we afflict abstinence upon the body or when we believe through compassion that the need of our neighbor is our own need. Whoever suffers through the suffering of others carries the Cross in their minds, as St. Paul says: "Bear one another's burdens, and so fulfill the role of Christ" (Gal 6:2). And as the Apostle says: "Weep with those who weep, rejoice with those who rejoice" (Rom 12:15). "If one member suffers, all suffer together" (1 Cor 12:26).

For this is its use, if there should be any sickness in someone's body, an inflammation somewhere, on the foot, hand, or fingers, then the sickness inflames the whole body. Thus it is appropriate for us ourselves that every sickness or disease that afflicts our

369

neighbors should inflame every part, for we are all members of God, as the Apostle says: "Who is offended and I do not blush? Who sickens and I do not grow sick?" (cf. 1 Cor 9:22–23).

There is not...the holy Apostle has said this from his great love; everyone's sickness was his own, everyone's offense was his own, everyone's weakness was his own. In the same way it is right for each one of us to share in the suffering of all, in hardship, poverty, or weakness. In these wise words of the wise man we see that fellow-suffering is a kind of Cross. Now there are three kinds of martyrdom that are counted as a cross to us, namely, white, blue, and red martyrdom.[7]

The white martyrdom for someone is when they part for the sake of God from everything that they love, although they may suffer fasting and hard work thereby.

The blue martyrdom is when through fasting and hard work they control their desires or struggle in penance and repentance.

The red martyrdom is when they endure a cross or destruction for Christ's sake, as happened to the Apostles when they persecuted the wicked and taught the law of God.

These three kinds of martyrdom take place in those people who repent well, who control their desires, and who shed their blood in fasting and in labor for Christ's sake.

Now there are three kinds of martyrdom which are precious in the eyes of God and for which we obtain rewards if we perform them: chastity in youth, moderation in abundance,[8] or not receiving gifts that corrupt right judgments.

5. THREE SUNDAY CATECHESES

Text I

L et us now begin to recount the wonderful things the Lord did on the Lord's Day (cf. Mt 1:8 and 13:58).

  [i] Now it is impossible to doubt that the Lord's Day is the first day, for it is written that in six days the world was made and that God rested on the seventh day (cf. Gn 1:1–2:6); this seventh day is called the Sabbath (cf. Ex 20:8–11). Now as the Mother of the Lord holds the first place among all women (cf. Lk 1:42), so among all the days, the Lord's Day is greatest; thus we do not call the Lord's Day the eighth day, but the first day.

  [ii] The Lord's Day is the source which contains all the other days, and it renews the Resurrection.

  [iii] The Lord's Day it was when Christ, bringing the thief with him, reopened Paradise (cf. Lk 23:43).

  [iv] The Lord's Day it was when Christ said to the angels: "Open the gates of justice, that I may enter through them and give praise to the Lord" (Ps 117:19[9]; cf. Rv 22:14).

  [v] The Lord's Day it was when the age of the synagogue of the Jews ended and on the Lord's Day the church was born.[10]

  [vi] The Lord's Day it was when our Lord rose from the dead on the third day (cf. Mt 16:21 and parallels; and cf. the Nicene Creed).

  [vii] The Lord's Day it was when the Lord was born.[11]

  [viii] The Lord's Day it was when the Lord sent the Holy Spirit upon the Apostles (cf. Acts 2).

  [ix] The Lord's Day it was when the Lord divided the Red Sea (cf. Ex 14).

  [x] The Lord's Day it was when God performed his wonders at Cana in Galilee (cf. Jn 2:1–11).

371

[xi] The Lord's Day it was when the Lord satisfied the hunger of five thousand people[12] with five loaves and two fishes (cf. Mt 14:15–21).

[xii] The Lord's Day it was when for the first time the manna rained from heaven, and this continued for forty years in the desert (cf. Ex 16:4, 35).[13]

[xiii] The Lord's Day it was when all these things happened so who can doubt that it is the first of all days!

Text II

[i] Why is it that on this day all things were created, namely "heaven and earth, the sea and all that is in it" (Ex 20:11), for it is said that on this day "God created all things at once" (Sir 18:1); so are his works not divided?[14] They are divided by language, for what God can do in moment are divided temporally in the scriptures.[15]

[ii] The Day of the Lord, oh, day of joy, blessed day, venerable day, on which the people come together to the church.

[iii] On the Lord's Day are created the angels and archangels from the mouth of God: the virtues and powers, the principalities, the dominations, the thrones, the cherubim and seraphim (1 Thes 4:15; Col 1:16; Eph 1:21; Gn 3:24; Is 6:6; and cf. the conclusion of the eucharistic prefaces).

[iv] On the Lord's Day the ark comes to rest after the flood (cf. Gn 8:4).

[v] On the Lord's Day he rescued his people from Egypt and carried them through the Red Sea into the desert (cf. Ex 14).

[vi] On the Lord's Day he rained manna from heaven for forty years for the benefit of the Israelites in the desert (cf. Ex 16:4; 35).

[vii] On the Lord's Day four fountains flowed from a rock (cf. Ex 17:1–7): wine, honey, oil, and milk (cf. Dt 8:1; 32:13–4).[16]

[viii]   On the Lord's Day our Lord Jesus Christ was born.

[ix]   On the Lord's Day the boy is circumcised and "they called his name Jesus" (Lk 2:21).

[x]   On the Lord's Day Christ is baptized and the Holy Spirit comes upon him in the form of a dove (cf. Mk 1:9–11).

[xi]   On the Lord's Day "wise men from the east offered him gifts of gold, frankincense, and myrrh" (Mt 2:1, 11).

[xii]   On the Lord's Day Jesus makes wine from water at Cana in Galilee (cf. Jn 2:1–11).

[xiii]   On the Lord's Day from five loaves and two fishes the Lord satisfied with food "five thousand" human beings, "not counting women and children" (Mt 14:15–21).

[xiv]   On the Lord's Day the church is founded by the hand of the Apostle Peter.

[xv]   On the Lord's Day the Lord threw light into the underworld and rescued the souls from "the mouth of the lion" (Ps 21:22).

[xvi]   On the Lord's Day the Lord rose from the dead (cf. Mt 28:1).

[xvii]   On the Lord's Day, after the Resurrection, he sits at the right hand of God the Father Almighty (cf. Col 3:1; and the Nicene Creed).

[xviii]   On the Lord's Day the law is given to Moses on Mount Sinai (cf. Ex 19).

[xix]   On the Lord's Day the Lord sent the Holy Spirit on his Apostles (cf. Acts 2).

[xx]   "On the Lord's Day" the Lord gave the revelation to the Apostle John on the island of Patmos (Rv 1:10).[17]

[xxi]   Thus to all who believe him he gives eternal life (cf. Jn 3:15). Amen.

Text III

[i]   The Day of the Lord is a blessed day because it is the first day (cf. Gn 1:1)

[ii]   The Day of the Lord is a blessed day because the Lord did not stop from his works on it (cf. Jn 5:17).[18]

[iii] The Day of the Lord is a blessed day because on that day God breathed a soul into Adam (cf. Gn 2:7).

[v][19] The Day of the Lord is a blessed day because on that day Abel offered the gifts from his hands to God (cf. Gn 4:4; and the eucharistic liturgy).

[vi] The Day of the Lord is a blessed day because on that day Noah, after the flood, saw a light from out of the ark (cf. Gn 8).

[vii] The Day of the Lord is a blessed day because on that day Israel went through the Red Sea with dry feet (cf. Ex 14).

[viii] The Day of the Lord is a blessed day because on that day the rock is struck and ten rivers flow out from it and the thirst of the people is drowned (cf. Ex 17:1–7).

[ix] The Day of the Lord is a blessed day because on that day manna rains from heaven for forty days for the people of God (cf. Ex 16:4 and 35).

[x] The Day of the Lord is a blessed day because on that day Jesus the son of Nun, the successor of Moses, went through the river Jordan with dry feet (cf. Jos 3:7–17).

[xi] The Day of the Lord is a blessed day because on that day the Lord came to the house of Abraham, and there were four "middles" *(mediae)* in one day: in the middle of the world, and the middle of the age of Abraham, and the middle of the day (cf. Gn 18:1, 28:7).[20]

[xii] The Day of the Lord is a blessed day because on that day the first bishop, named Aaron, is ordained (cf. Ex 40:12–5; Lv 16:32).[21]

[xiii] The Day of the Lord is a blessed day because on that day God blessed the wine in Cana in Galilee (cf. Jn 2:1–11).

[xiv] The Day of the Lord is a blessed day because on that day Christ "came into the world" (Jn 1:9).

[xv] The Day of the Lord is a blessed day because on that day God began the fast which lasted until the Passover (cf. Mt 4:2).

[xvi] The Day of the Lord is a blessed day because on that day the Lord rose from the dead (cf. Mt 28:1), when the

374

whole world is freed from out of the mouth of the Devil (cf. Ps 21:22).

[xvii] The Day of the Lord is a blessed day because on that day the Holy Spirit descended on the Apostles (cf. Acts 2).

[xviii] The Day of the Lord is a blessed day because on that day the Lord will come to judge the living and the dead (cf. Acts 10:42, and the Nicene Creed).

[xix] The Lord said: "If you make the Lord's Day holy, I shall open the cataracts of heaven (cf. Gn 7:11) to you and multiply your fruits (cf. Gn 1:22) and bless your house for all your days until death, and after death I shall give you my kingdom, and that which you seek, I shall give you. There will be joy on account of you (cf. Lk 15:7) and "you will know that I am the Lord" (Ex 6:7). I adjure you by the patience of God, and by my angels, if you do not turn back the Lord's Day to holiness, I shall lead you to a great punishment, and I will hold good before your face and you will be miserable. I shall burn you with heavenly fire."

[xx] They who do works on the Lord's Day, who shave their heads on the Lord's Day, who clean the house on the Lord's Day, these are they whom God will throw into outer darkness. And we ought to preach these things to all humanity, that we might have eternal life without end forever and ever (cf. Rv 22:5). Amen.

THEOLOGY

1. ON THE CHRISTIAN LIFE
BY PELAGIUS

he author's humble opinion of himself. It is purely the occasion of your love (which I have grasped in heart and mind by God's power) and not faith in my own righteousness, nor the experience of wisdom, nor the glory of knowledge that has compelled me, a sinner first and last, more foolish than others and less experienced than all, to dare to write to you at length in order to counsel you to continue along the path of holiness and justice. And it is this too that so drives me and challenges me to speak, though I am sinful and ignorant, that even if I lack the knowledge to speak, still I may not remain silent. And so it is my desire and wish that you should be introduced to those whose wisdom is more abundant, whose eloquence is greater and knowledge fuller, whose conscience is freer from stain of sin, and who can rightly instruct you with words and examples. For not only has the darkness of foolishness and ignorance so blinded our mind that it can neither sense nor utter anything divine, but also conscience has convicted it of all sins, so that we believe the darkness will conceal any light that our mind might possess. And so it is not only that we have nothing to say, but also that we lack the confidence to offer what it is that we do have, since conscience prevents us. But you should nevertheless be content with our crude counsels, for as long as it seems wiser to you and better to do so, and consent to love. Do not weigh what we offer you, or inquire into what it is that we lack; all that we have, we willingly share. Do not look at the appearance of our gift so much as the intent of our soul, and note what we have been able to deny you even though we wished to give you all that we have. We have offered you all that we can and would have offered you what we do not have, had we been able to do so. And so they thirst, but too little, who cannot be content with the water of a shallow stream but must come to a purer and more abundant spring. Nor do I believe them to feel hunger enough who, when they have coarse bread, still wait for bread that is white and refined. And so you too, most beloved sister, who, I am sure, hunger and thirst immeasurably for the things of heaven: Eat coarse bread for the moment, until you find bread of the whitest wheat, and drink the water of a shallow and muddy stream until such time as you find one that is purer and more abundant. And do not for the moment disdain our bread, although it may seem rustic to you. For although rustic bread seems less refined, it is more substantial and more swiftly fills a hungry stomach, restoring strength to the weak, than white bread made from finely ground flour. I shall now give an account, to the best of my abilities, and an explanation, as far as I am able, of how a Christian should act. I can find no better beginning to my treatise than first to discuss the very word *Christian* and why it is that anyone should bear this name.

I. *The name and dignity of the Christian. The Christian's role.* No one among the wise and faithful can fail to know that Christ means "the anointed one." And it is evident that no one is anointed unless they are holy and sufficiently worthy in God's eyes, being no different from prophets, priests, and kings. And so great was the mystery of this anointing that not all the Jewish people but only very few of them merited it before the coming of our Lord Jesus Christ whom God anointed with the oil of gladness, which is the Holy Spirit, above his fellows (cf. Ps 45:7). Since that time those who believe in him and who have been purified by the sanctification of his baptism do not live, as before, under the Law but all are anointed as prophets, priests and kings. We are reminded of how we should be after this anointing by the example of those whose way of life is no less holy than the anointing itself. For it is from the sacrament of this anointing, both of Christ and of all Christians (that is, those who believe in Christ), that the name and term have come, which name those people have been wrongly given who imitate Christ hardly at all. How can you be called something you are not, and falsely take another's name? But if you wish to be a Christian, then do those things that are of Christ and worthily bear the name of Christian. Or perhaps you do not wish to *be* a Christian but only to be called one? Wanting to be called something without actually being it is both base and wretched. No one comes over to Christ in order to be called a Christian but only to be one. Whoever is called a Christian acknowledges that they have Christ as their Lord. And truly they do possess him if they serve and follow him in all things. If they do not do so, then such people are not Christ's servant at all, but rather they mock and deride him; although they declare themselves to be his servant, their service is no more than a pretense. A twofold judgment shall befall such people, firstly on account of their mocking of God, whom for no reason they have called their Lord, and secondly on account of their sinful state.

II. *Sinners. For two reasons God does not punish them immediately. God's good will toward men and women.* But the long patience of God's mercy allows many unbelieving, shameless, and wicked people brazenly to believe that God shall not punish those who sin against him since he does not wish to punish sinners immediately. Wretched, ungrateful, and blind to their own salvation are those who impute this of God because their destruction is deferred. They do not know that God saves them for two reasons: firstly, so that the human race may reflect upon his long patience and, secondly, so that he does not judge rashly by damning sinners straightaway. For if he were not so patient, then the human race would long since have been expunged, and, if God had wished to punish those who sin straightaway, none would have become righteous. For we know and read of several who, either through the blindness of ignorance or on account of wickedness or deceived by the vanity of youth, were previously enslaved by many different kinds of sin and who later, by the most merciful patience of God, were converted from their error: Their works of righteousness are now greater than their earlier sins. God does not pardon sins but rather defers judgment, nor does he deliver from death those who persevere in sin but waits patiently so that even late in the day they may be converted and may live. As blessed Peter the Apostle said: "The Lord is not slow to keep his promise but is patient toward you, not wishing that any should perish, but that all should reach repentance" (2 Pt 3:9).[1] He is kind, generous, and merciful toward you, as it were, since he does not strike you immediately in order that you may see how great his kindness is toward you and how great his mercy, who prefers to wait for you, though you are unfaithful and a sinner, and to deliver you when you have converted, than to punish you as a sinner. God himself says through his prophet how much mercy and kindness he wishes to bestow upon the human race, declaring with the gentleness of his own voice: "But if a wicked man turns away from all his sins which he has committed and keeps all my statutes and does what is lawful and right, he shall surely live; he shall not die. None of the transgressions which he has committed shall be remembered against him; for the righteousness which he has done he shall live. Have I any pleasure in the death of the wicked, says the Lord God, and not rather that he should turn from his way and that I should make him live?" (Ez 18:21–23). And elsewhere he says: "The wickedness of the wicked shall not harm him on the day that he turns from his wickedness" (Ez 33:12). And again: "Return, O faithless sons, and I will heal your grief" (Jer 3:22).

This is how God warns you and provokes you so that you may finally turn away from your sins and be saved. This is how he encourages those who are now subject to death in order that they may live. How gently, how mercifully he invites them that even as sinners they should not deny the generosity of the Father, even calling them sons and daughters, who have lost God the Father by their sins, just as he laments with a plangent and wretched voice in another place that he himself has lost those who have sinned, saying "I am without children, I have lost my people on account of their sins" (cf. Jer 15:7). Know from this then how much God loves you, who prefers that you should live and not die. But you deride him and despise him who loves you more than you love yourself, who wishes that you who desire death should live. The Lord says: "I do not desire the death of mortals, but rather that they should turn to me and live" (cf. Ez 18:32). You wished to die therefore by sinning, while he wishes you to live by conversion. How foolish, irreverent, and ungrateful you are since you do not yield to God in this, though he wishes to take pity on you, and prefers to save you by his mercy than that you should die on account of your sin.

III. *Those who take advantage of God's kindness shall be punished on earth. They are false judges.* Let no one delude themselves, deceiving themselves with a foolish and vain notion, let no one make the mistake of supposing that divine wrath and judgment shall not come upon sinners soon enough, so that they who have not been destroyed on the spot might think that they have got away with their sinning. Let them know rather that God is not overlooking the sin but only deferring his response and that his anger, although delayed, shall come upon sinners suddenly and unexpectedly, as it is written: "Do not say: 'I sinned, yet nothing happened to me.' It is only that the Lord is very patient" (Sir 5:4), and also "Come back to the Lord without delay, do not put it off from one day to the next, or suddenly the Lord's wrath will come upon you" (Sir 5:7).[2] This is fulfilled in the case of many who, on account of their many sins, are overtaken by the wrath of God in the present as they shall be again in the future. But no one understands this, no one realizes it, nor does anyone believe that when they suffer adversity it is on account of their wickedness. They believe rather that what they have endured is more the result of the natural course of things than any crime they have committed.[3] And therefore God does not appear to punish sinners in the present, since when he does punish them, it is not recognized as such. But there are many, whom no one sees, who are judged even now on account of their multitude of sins before the day of judgment. Is there anyone who can say that they have seen someone live a long time who has committed sacrilege, assault, pillage, perjury, murder, theft, extortion, adultery, or who has been guilty of any other crimes? For we see very many examples by which we can prove that wicked and sinful people are judged even in this time, when their sins have run their full course, and their present life is destroyed no less than their future one.

But this is more easily understood by those who have observed in different times and with different judges the destruction of those who live in vice and impiety. Among these, the first place falls to those who sin most boldly and believe that all things are allowed them which it is in their power to do. While they do not fear the judgment of another but themselves stand in judgment over others, they are swift to commit sin. And so it is that those who do not fear the judgment of others as they sin know God as both judge and avenger. Some of their number, who often spilled the blood of innocent souls, knew the wrath and judgment of God in such a way that they were later compelled to spill their own blood—they who had previously willingly spilled the blood of others. Some, who did similar things, were so destroyed by God's wrath that they remained lying on the ground without burial and became food for wild beasts and birds of the air. Others again, who had unjustly killed a great number of men, have been cut to pieces bit by bit so that there should be no fewer cuts in their limbs than those they killed, the number of their avengers. Standing in judgment over them are the many women who have been widowed by the undeserved loss of their husbands, many orphans left behind by their murdered fathers, who shall be forced now to beg and to suffer a lack of clothing, in addition to their orphaned state, for these people perfected their wickedness and cruelty by reducing to poverty the dependents of those whom they killed. But now it is their own widowed spouses and orphaned children who stand in daily need of other people's bread. Surely you can see that this is the perfect testimony of God, who warns us, saying: "You shall not afflict any widow or orphan. If you do afflict them and they cry out to me, I will surely hear their cry; and my wrath will burn, and I will kill you with the sword, and your wives shall become widows and your children fatherless" (Ex 22:22–24).

What a terrible sin! What a grievous outrage! This is cruelty too great to bear. Two savage and brutal things are perpetrated at the same moment. Murder takes place so that robbery may follow. Husbands are killed, fathers are killed, so that widows and orphans may be more easily robbed, and so one person rejoices in the death of another, as if they were not themselves certain to die. It is just therefore that God should be moved by such acts of cruelty and wickedness. It is just that he should reveal his judgment in the case of certain people even before the time. It is just that life should be denied such people both in the present and in the future. And in them we have an example which warns us against thinking that those who live in wickedness and vice can avoid the judgment of God even in the present time.

IV. *God shall punish the sinner when their sins have reached a certain number.* But it is good for us to be told repeatedly that we are preserved by the patience of God until such time as the measure of our sins is complete, at which point we shall be destroyed straightaway and no remission shall be given us. God declares by his own testimony that there is a certain limit and measure to sin.[4] And that sooner or later a person shall be judged as the measure of their sins becomes complete is most clearly demonstrated when God says to Abraham concerning the destruction and the burning of the people of Sodom and Gomorrah, whose sins have now become complete: The cry of the people of Sodom and Gomorrah is full, and their great sins have attained their measure (cf. Gn 18:20). And what does he say of the Amorites, whose sins were not yet complete, and who were burned like the above-mentioned cities after many years: "The sins of the Amorites are not yet complete" (Gn 15:16)? This example clearly instructs and teaches us that each single sin contributes to their full number and that a person is preserved so that they may convert for as long as their sins can still be added to the whole. And so let no one, I say, deceive themselves, let no one delude themselves. God does not love the wicked, he does not love sinners, he does not love the unrighteous, those who are thieving, cruel, and wicked. But he loves those who are good, just, devout, humble, innocent, and gentle, as it is written: "For you are not a God who delights in wickedness, evil can be no guest of yours. The arrogant may not stand before your eyes; you hate all doers of evil. You destroy those who speak lies" (Ps 5:4–6).

V. *The wicked are punished by an early death, but the good are brought into safety.* Someone might say: Why is it that we see good people perish with the wicked? But the former do not perish, but are released, rather, for they are set free from persecutions and from contact with wicked people and are brought into a state of peace. Those people really die and perish who, departing from this world, await the suffering and punishment of still greater judgment. The good are called before their time so that they are no longer exposed to the power of the wicked, while the wicked are removed so that they can no longer persecute the good. The just are summoned to peace from affliction, hardship, and danger, while irreligious people are snatched away from their self-indulgence, wealth, and sensual pleasures. The former pass over in order to judge, and the latter in order to be judged; the former that they may be set free, and the latter that they may face punishment, as is written: "But the good man, even if he dies an untimely death, shall be at peace" (Wis 4:7), and again: "A living man was snatched away from among sinners" (cf. Wis 4:10), and again: "He was pleasing to God who removed him early from a wicked world" (Wis 4:14), and again: "While the irreligious journey into death, the others are in peace" (Wis 3:3). You can see therefore that the destruction of the body means peace and rest, and not suffering, to the just and to those who worship God; as they are released, they are set free rather than subjected to death. For that reason those who are faithful have no fear of this end but rather desire and look forward to its coming, by which they believe that peace shall be theirs and not punishment. But the wicked and the irreligious, and those who are aware of their own crimes, fear death greatly with good reason and by natural foreknowledge, by which they know that they shall be judged. On account of this, once we have grasped this idea, we should commit no sins at all since we know full well that sinners face judgment both in this world and in the next.

VI. *It is improper to arrogate to oneself the name of Christian. The true Christian.* Let us not only boast this name by which Christians are known, but let us believe that we shall also be judged if we claim this name for ourselves without justification. Is there anyone who is so foolish, so lacking in faith, so obstinate, so stiff-necked, so reckless, that they do not fear the anger and fury of God's judgment, which shall at some point come, or do not blush in the presence of their fellow men and women? Let them see how stupid and foolish they are in the eyes even of their own people if their vanity and their folly are so great that they take a name which is not rightly theirs. Who is vain and wretched enough to profess to be a lawyer if they cannot even read? Who is mad and foolish enough to profess to be a soldier when they do not even know how to bear arms? No one is given a particular name without good reason. In order for someone to be called a shoemaker, it is necessary that they should make shoes; knowledge of a craft gives someone the name of craftsman or artisan, and someone is called a tradesman who sells what he has bought for a profit. Examples of this kind teach us that there can be no name without particular actions and that all names depend upon actions. How can you call yourself a Christian since you do not act like one? "Christian" is the name of justice, goodness, integrity, patience, chastity, prudence, humility, humanity, innocence, and true religion. How can you claim this for yourself when you possess only a few of so many virtues? That person is a Christian who is so not only in name but also in deed; who imitates and follows Christ in all things; who is holy, innocent, and pure; who is uncorrupted; in whose heart there is no place for evil; in whose heart there is only true religion and goodness; who is incapable of hurting or wounding anyone, but can only come to the aid of everyone. That person is a Christian who, with Christ as an example, cannot even hate their enemies but does good to those who oppose them, praying for their persecutors and enemies. For if anyone is ready to wound or harm another, then they falsely call themselves Christians. They are Christians who can truly say: I have harmed no one and have lived in righteousness with all.

VII. *God has always been pleased with justice and offended by injustice. Enoch snatched away into immortality.* But in case anyone should judge or think that I am voicing my own ideas here, or in case they should think that they can easily condemn me for speaking according to my own will rather than by the authority of scripture, I shall now offer examples from the same scripture, both from the Old and the New Testament, whose precepts open for us the entrance to life. I shall show how God has exhorted the human race right from the beginning of the world to observe what always pleases him and what gives him offense. For I read that after Adam, who was the first to be formed by God (but about whom it is not appropriate now to speak), there came the brothers Cain and Abel at the beginning of the world. One of them was pleasing to God, for he was innocent and righteous, while the other failed to please God, since he was wicked and unrighteous. Thereupon, after a while, scripture describes Enoch as someone who was righteous enough to whom justice granted that he should not know death in this present life but should be snatched away into immortality from the midst of those who are condemned to die. By his example it is shown that a single just person is dearer to God than many sinners. And there is Noah, too, who was also a just man and of whom we know that the merits of justice determined that life should be given to him alone and to those with him following the flood when the world was condemned. And then scripture testifies how Abraham attained the rewards of faith and righteousness when he was the only friend of God upon the earth at that time, who alone was found to be just. And when, from among all those facing death in Sodom, Lot alone was spared the fire—was this not also the reward of justice? It would take us a long time to go through all the cases one by one and to recount the rewards of all.

VIII. *God afflicted the Israelites with many troubles in order to teach them to perform works of piety. The perfector of the Law.* It is right for us to know how God taught the Jewish people, who were the first that he chose to belong to himself from the seed of Abraham before all other peoples, and what it was that he taught them to observe and to do in order to be pleasing to him. In the first place, I do not think that it was without reason or without the Providence of God that he determined that they should live in a deserted place, making them leave their homeland and journey to a foreign land, that is, to Egypt. And I believe this was the reason—that God had chosen his people and, desiring to teach them mercy, true religion, justice, and all other good works, he wished them to be exiles and captives for a time outside their homeland so that they would learn the misery and hardship of exile and captivity and would later more easily feel pity for others who endure exile and hardship, since they themselves had already learned the misery of exile. For no one is more ready to pity the exile or the stranger than someone who knows the effects of exile. No one offers lodging to a homeless guest so much as someone who has themselves been dependent on the generosity of others. No one is more likely to feed the hungry or to give a drink to the thirsty than someone who has themselves suffered hunger and thirst. No one is so ready to cover the naked with their own clothes than someone who knows the pain of nakedness and cold. No one is more likely to come to the aid of people who face troubles, misery, and hardship than those who have themselves experienced the misfortune of troubles, misery, and hardship. With good reason, then, God, who is the master of mercy and true religion and who would later produce the Law by which he would convey to his people the precepts of mercy and true religion and all good works, wished that they should first themselves endure all afflictions, troubles, and griefs in an alien land so that later they would take pity on those who suffer such things and would follow his commandments. As a good farmer, in your view, is one who prepares the earth with plows and hoes before planting the seed, in case any of the seed should perish, so too God softened and prepared his people over a long period of time before giving them the seed of his saving commandments. So that it may finally be even more clear that this is why they suffered these things, let us consider the commandments of the Lord himself, who said: "You shall not wrong a stranger or oppress him, for you were strangers in the land of Egypt" (Ex 22:21). And again we read: "The mighty God is not partial and takes no bribe, he executes justice for the stranger, the orphan, and widow. Love the stranger, giving him food and clothing, for you too were strangers in the land of Egypt" (cf. Dt 10:17–19). And elsewhere he says: "When you reap your harvest in your field, and have forgotten a sheaf, you shall not return to it; it shall be for the stranger, the orphan, and the widow, that the Lord your God may bless you in all the work of your hands. You shall remember that you were a slave in the land of Egypt; therefore, I command you to do this" (Dt 24:19, 21). And so it may easily be seen and recognized that it was for this reason that his people were afflicted with all kinds of hardship, that by this example he would teach them to pity the sufferings of others, as it is written: "You taught your people by such acts, since it is right that they should be righteous and humane" (Wis 12:19). It is, I believe, quite clear what kind of people he wished his own people to be, and many examples serve to show the nature of the acts with which he is able to achieve this.

But if what we have said scarcely seems to show God's will, we can add the precepts of the Law and the prophets. Let us prove with examples from both the Old and the New Testament what pleases God and always has pleased him, showing what he commands to be done and observed very frequently: "You should love the Lord your God with all your heart, with all your soul, with all your mind, and with all your strength, and you should love your neighbor as yourself" (Dt 6:4–5). That the rule of the Law and the prophets is paramount is shown by the words of our Lord and Savior: "In these two commandments hangs the whole of the Law and the prophets" (Mt 22:37–40). He can neither abolish nor change the fact that the whole rule of the Law and the prophets are in these two commandments, and those who fulfill these things have fulfilled the Law, for you should seek nothing in the old Law except that you should love God and your neighbor. Truly that person is the perfector and author of the Law who sins neither against God nor against their neighbor.

IX. *On those who love God. How the people of God should be.* But the last topic I should ignore and pass over is the question of what it means to love God and our neighbor. They love God who follow all his commandments. They love God who keep his laws and precepts. They love God who are holy as he is holy and who sanctify themselves, as it is written: "Be holy, for I the Lord your

God am holy" (Lv 19:2). They love God who fulfill the words of the prophet: "You who love the Lord hate evil" (cf. Ps 97:10). They love God who think only upon the things of heaven and of God. For God is the lover only of holiness, righteousness, and true religion, and they love God who do nothing but what God seems to love. The teaching of our Lord and Savior shows us what loving God means when he says: "It is they who hear my words and act upon them who love me" (Jn 14:21). If then it is they who carry out what God commands who love him, those who do not do so do not love him. And indeed, those who do not love are filled with hate. For which reason it is clear and evident that God is hated by those who do not keep his commandments, concerning whom I believe it has been said by the prophet: "Do I not hate them that hate you, O Lord? Am I not grieved with those who rise against you? I hate them with perfect hatred; I count them my enemies" (Ps 139:21–22). The righteous prophet hates sinners, adulterers, and evildoers, and those who spurn the commandments of God. As it says in another place: "I have seen those who break your covenant and I have grieved," and "I hate the wicked but I love your law" (Ps 119:158, 113). See therefore how righteous, perfect, and holy we should be, to whom it is not allowed to live in wickedness, nor indeed to keep the company of those who live in wickedness. This is clearly shown to us by the blessed Apostle who tells us not to break bread with sinners, saying: "If anyone who is called a brother amongst you is a fornicator, or covetous, or an idolater, or a reviler, or a drunkard, or an extortioner, with such a one do not even eat" (1 Cor 5:11).

God wished his people to be holy and to be free from any stain of unrighteousness or evil. That is how he wished them to be, so righteous, so devout, so pure, so uncorrupted, so simple, that the gentiles might find nothing culpable in them but only things to admire, saying: "Blessed is the nation whose God is the Lord, and the people whom he has chosen for his own inheritance" (Ps 33:12). Those who worship and serve God should be gentle, serious-minded, prudent, devout, blameless, undefiled, uncorrupted, so that if any should see them, they would be astonished and filled with admiration and would say that these men and women

391

are truly of God, who live like this. The man or woman of God should show themselves to be such and should act in such a way, so that there might be no one who does not wish to see them, who does not desire to hear them, no one who, looking upon them, does not consider them to be the sons and daughters of God, so that the words of the prophet might truly be fulfilled in them: "His mouth is most sweet and altogether lovely" (Sg 5:16).

But if Christians, if the servants of God, show themselves to be like those who devote themselves to demons and idols, then God begins to be blasphemed through them and it is said: O Christian servant of God, whose deeds are so evil, whose works are so shameful, whose behavior is so wretched, whose life is so irreligious, so wicked, so indulgent, so sordid. And they will be accused by these prophetic words: "God's name is blasphemed among the gentiles through you" (Rom 2:24). But woe to those by whom the name of God is blasphemed. For God neither desires nor demands anything more of us than that his name should be praised by all on account of our actions, as it is written: "Offer to God the sacrifice of praise" (Ps 50:14). This is the sacrifice which God seeks and loves above all other sacrifices, so that by our works of righteousness his name may be everywhere praised, and God be proved to be true by the acts and works of his servants. Those people truly love God who do only those things by which his name is glorified.

X. *Love of our neighbor. Avoid causing harm, aim at doing good. Innocence commended.* We have said, as far as we could, how God should be loved; now we shall say, as far as we can, what it is to love one's neighbor as oneself, although the explanation of this is stated more briefly in another place where it is said: "Do not do to another what you would not want to be done to you" (Tb 4:15). Our Lord and Savior says: "So whatever you wish that others should do to you, do so to them" (Mt 7:12). For there is no one who wishes that another should do evil to them. Those people love their neighbor as themselves therefore who do no evil to them since this is not what they would wish for themselves. But they gladly share the good things which they themselves wish to receive from everyone else, since a Christian is expected not only to refrain from doing evil but also actively to do good. There are some who do not receive the reward of heaven but are banished to the fires of hell, although they neither do anything evil nor anything good; just as, so we read in the gospel, our Lord said of those who do neither evil nor good: "Depart from me, you cursed ones, into the eternal fire prepared for the Devil and his angels, for I was hungry and you gave me no food, I was thirsty and you gave me no drink, I was a stranger and you did not welcome me, naked and you did not clothe me, sick and in prison and you did not visit me" (Mt 25:41–44). They are condemned not for doing evil, but on account of the good they did not do.

Anyone who is prudent and wise can see from this what hope there is for those who follow evil ways, when life is denied even to those who, though they did no evil, also did nothing good. For God not only demands of us that we should not be evil but also that we should do good. They are called evil who do evil things, while those who do good are called good. And there are two masters who are served by the good and the bad: the good God, who is served by all who do good, and the wicked Devil, whose servants are those who do evil things. It is not only asked of us that we should cease to be servants of the Devil by the evil we do but also that we should be seen to serve God by doing good. For if there is anyone who is seen neither to do evil nor good, and it is not known which master they serve, how shall they hope for eternal life from God, which they have not earned by good deeds? Let none deceive or delude themselves in their own minds, I say; let none lead themselves astray with empty reasonings. Those who have not been good do not have life. Those who have not done works of justice and mercy cannot reign with Christ. Those who have not been humane, devout, hospitable, full of good will, and compassionate shall not escape the fires of hell. God does not love wicked people, he does not love sinners. Whoever has done evil is the enemy of God. Whoever has not been without malice cannot share with Christ. For nothing is more proper for a Christian, nothing more necessary, nothing to be more striven for with all our might, than that we should banish malice from our spirit, not allowing wickedness into the conscience of our heart, and that we should hold to goodness, preserve righteousness, and maintain purity of mind. Be innocent if you wish to live with God. Be simple if you wish to reign with Christ. What good to you is evil if it shall drag you to your death? Of what use wickedness if it prevents you from reigning with Christ and destroys those who possess it? As it says in scripture: "Evil passion ruins the one who harbors it" (Sir 6:4). If you wish to live, listen to the prophet who says that if you love the kingdom of Christ, you should listen to how you may earn it: "Who is there who desires life and wishes to see good days? Keep your tongue from evil and your lips from speaking deceit. Depart from evil and do good; seek peace and pursue it" (Ps 34:12–14). God honors and loves men and women of this kind, who know nothing of evil, who do not know how to tell lies, whose lips do not speak deceit, and in whom nothing can be seen but goodness and purity.

It is innocence that commends us to God, and simplicity that makes us reign with Christ. How God loves only the innocent, and wishes them to be joined to himself, is shown by many passages, as we find written in the Psalms: "The innocent and righteous have clung to me" (cf. Ps 25:21). And elsewhere it is commanded and said: "Guard innocence, mark justice, for there is posterity for the man of peace" (cf. Ps 37:37). How beneficial and advantageous innocence is for us, even when we are saved late on in life, is shown by the witness of the prophet David, who no longer feared judgment, even though he had previously sinned grievously, from the moment that he knew innocence: "Judge me, O Lord, since I have entered into my innocence" (cf. Ps 35:1). Therefore he knew that he need not fear judgment any more, for he had known innocence, albeit late in the day. And in another place he says: "You have received me on account of my innocence" (cf. Ps 41:12). God later received him on account of his innocence, whom previously he had rejected on account of his sinfulness. Indeed, it is evident that the innocent cannot be confounded in the presence of God from the words: "For as long as the innocent preserved their righteousness, they were not confounded" (cf. Prv 13:6). For nothing is more acceptable to God, nothing more precious, than when innocence is wholeheartedly maintained. Although some may appear to be devout in other works, if they do not have this, then they are subject to vain delusions concerning their devotion. If the Jews, who lived under the Old Covenant, were commanded to preserve this, when they were still permitted to hate their enemies, then what is it now right for you to do, you who are a Christian and obliged to love your enemy? For when shall you not be innocent, or to whom can you do evil, if you are commanded to do good to your enemies (cf. Mt 5:44)? But perhaps you hate even your neighbor, although you are not permitted to hate strangers, and persecute your brother, though you are commanded to love your enemy, and hold yourself to be a Christian, though you keep the commandments neither of the New Covenant nor the Old? But in case you should falsely regard yourself as a Christian and be deceived by the name, listen to the words of the Apostle on how you should be:

Let the thief no longer steal, rather let him labor, doing honest work with his hands, so that he may be able to give to those in need. Let no evil talk come out of your mouths, but only such as is good for edifying, as fits the occasion, that it may impart grace to those who hear. And do not grieve the Holy Spirit of God, in whom you were sealed for the day of redemption. Let all bitterness and wrath and anger and clamor and slander be put away from you, with all malice, and be kind to one another, tenderhearted, forgiving one another, as God in Christ forgave you. Therefore be imitators of God, as beloved children. And walk in love, as Christ loved us and gave himself up for us, a fragrant offering and sacrifice to God. But fornication and all impurity or covetousness must not be even named among you, as it is fitting among saints. Let there be no filthiness, no silly talk, nor levity, which are not fitting, but instead let there be thanksgiving. Be sure of this, that no fornicator or impure man, or one who is covetous (that is, an idolator), has any inheritance in the kingdom of Christ and of God (Eph 4:28–5:5).

That person properly judges himself to be a Christian who keeps these precepts, who is holy, humble, chaste, and righteous, and whose way of life is founded on the works of mercy and of justice.

XI. *Concerning those prayers to which God does not listen. They who pray should be righteous.* Do you consider that person to be a Christian in whom there is no Christian act, in whom there is no righteous way of life, but only wickedness, lack of devotion, and sinfulness? Do you consider that man or woman to be a Christian who oppresses the downtrodden and the poor, who desires the possessions of others, who impoverishes others in the pursuit of wealth, who rejoices in ill-gotten gains, who feeds upon the tears of others, who grows rich through the destruction of the poor, whose mouth is continually dishonored by lies, whose lips utter nothing but unworthy, obscene, sinful, and disgraceful things, and who, when urged to give away his or her own possessions, falls upon those of others? Such a person boldly enters the church, brashly and without a thought stretching out hands which are dishonored with illicit gains and with the blood of the innocent, pouring forth prayers to God with a mouth that is polluted and made unholy with the recent utterance of untruths and shameful things, as if wholly unaware of anything amiss. Why do you act so wretchedly and shamelessly? Why do you heap upon yourself the weight of still greater sins? Why do you inflict injury upon God beyond contempt? Why do you stretch out your hands to God (which he shall not look upon since he has said that only clean and holy hands should be offered to him) and thus more quickly provoke his wrath, as a sign of the punishment of your crime? Why do you beseech God with that mouth which only a short while before uttered evil things? Although they may be many, he disdains your prayers, as it is written: "When you spread forth your hands, I will hide my eyes from you; even though you may make many prayers, I will not listen; your hands are full of blood. Wash yourselves; make yourselves clean" (Is 1:15–16). They who extend and spread forth their hands to God should be sure of themselves and self-aware, trusting in their innocence, as the Apostle says: "I desire then that in every place the men should pray, lifting holy hands" (1 Tm 2:8). They who worthily raise their hands to God, pouring forth prayers with a good conscience, can say: "You know, O Lord, how holy, how innocent, and how free of all deception, harm, and theft are the hands that I stretch out to you, how righteous, clean, and free of all deceit are the lips with which I pray to you, that you may have mercy upon me." Such a one swiftly merits to be heard and, even before they penitently utter their prayers, they can gain what it is they ask for.

XII. *Alms from illicit gains.* I know that there exist those who are so blinded by the deep darkness of wickedness and avarice that, when they have ceased to prosper, they either defeat the poor with their power or oppress the innocent with false testimony or overwhelm the weak with brute force or commit robbery and pillage. Then they give thanks to God, with whose aid, they believe, they have been able to commit such outrages. They judge God to be so wicked that they think he has shared in their crimes. Foolish and wretched, they are so blinded by their wrongdoing that they fail to understand that what God prohibits cannot be pleasing to him and, as if one crime were not enough, yet another is added by speaking badly of God. Some truly believe themselves to be justified in giving scant support to the poor in material things, and others dispense minimally what they have taken from many. One person eats and so many go hungry, and only a few are clothed by the garments of many. But God does not desire almsgiving of this kind, nor does he want the piety of one to depend upon cruelty to another. It is better that you give no alms at all, if doing so means to clothe a few and to leave many naked, robbing many of their garments in order to clothe only one. God approves of the kind of almsgiving which is founded upon honest work, as it is written: "Honor the Lord with your substance and with the first fruits of all your produce" (Prv 3:9). For God despises and condemns almsgiving that is made possible by the tears of others. Of what value is it if you are blessed by one but cursed by many? Of what benefit is almsgiving which comes from others' wealth? Are you really afraid that God will not have anything with which to feed his poor unless you steal from others?

XIII. *Faith without works has no value. A passage by the Apostle on faith without works is explained. Another passage of the same. Faith is not sufficient.* But I know others whom the dark ignorance of folly and thoughtlessness so beguiles and deceives that they pretend that they have faith and judge themselves to be justified in the eyes of God without works of righteousness, and on account of this kind of error they brashly commit heinous crimes, believing that God revenges not crimes but only a lack of faith. And in the same way, not only are they content that they themselves should perish, but they strive also to catch others in their snares in whom there is no light of godly knowledge. In them is fulfilled the words of our Savior who says: "If a blind man leads a blind man, both will fall into a pit" (Mt 15:14). For if no crimes but only a lack of faith is condemned, then we can freely and safely commit sins. And God has given his commandments of justice in vain if faith is sufficient without works. We cannot know from where such an irreligious, shameful, and iniquitous error of ignorance has crept upon us, unless perhaps from those who led the people astray in the Old Testament by this example and delivered them into eternal death and everlasting destruction, concerning whom it is written: "Do not listen to the words of the prophets, who prophesy to you, filling you with vain hopes; they speak visions of their own minds, not from the mouth of the Lord. They say continually to those who despise the Word of the Lord, 'It shall be well with you,' and to everyone who stubbornly follows his own heart, they say 'No evil shall come upon you'" (Jer 23:16–17). But there are many examples available to us, indeed the testimony of the whole of scripture, by which we have been able to destroy and bury so pernicious an error, but in case we should weary the reader any longer, a handful shall suffice. But perhaps you who take a different view will respond to me by asking whether it was on account of a lack of faith or on account of sin that Adam was condemned, who was created the first man by God at the beginning of the world. Here I find there was no lack of faith but only disobedience, which was the cause of his condemnation and by which all were condemned. Cain too was condemned not for his lack of faith but because he killed his brother. What others are there? I read that the whole of this world was destroyed by a flood not because of a lack of faith but because of crimes. When Sodom and Gomorrah were suddenly destroyed by fire, I find that it was not on account of a lack of faith but because of sinners and shameless people, which scripture shows most clearly when it says: "Now the men of Sodom were wicked, great sinners in the sight of the Lord" (Gn 13:13). Did the Jewish people themselves, who were so frequently subject to attack and destruction, not also excel in sin?

But someone may say that they can accept the evidence of the Old Testament only if I support it with examples from the New. Take Ananias and Sapphira, for instance, who were condemned by Peter not on account of their faithlessness but because they had stolen and told lies (Acts 5:49). Perhaps you will say then: "But why does Paul say: 'For we hold that a man is justified by faith apart from works of law' (Rom 3:28)?" And I read that the very one who speaks here condemned a man in his absence for having taken the wife of his father (1 Cor 5:1). It must be understood that scripture, which seems to agree in all things, does contain some minor contradictions. Peter says that we are justified by faith without the works of law, but not without those works concerning which I hear another Apostle say: "Faith without works is dead" (Jas 2:20). For the Apostle Paul spoke of the works of the Law, that is, circumcision of the flesh, observing the new moon, the sabbath, and other matters of this kind, which had previously been prescribed by the Law and now, since the coming of Christ, were no longer necessary. He was really speaking of the works of righteousness which, if someone does not do them, this means that they are dead, although they may pretend to be one of the faithful.

But someone might say, with Paul: "Man believes with his heart and so is justified, and he confesses with his lips and so is saved" (Rom 10:10). You fool, this is accomplished at the point of baptism, for which someone need only have faith and make public confession of it. But of what use is the washing of baptism if it is only faith without righteousness that is required? Everyone believes by faith that sins are washed away by baptism. But if the sinning may continue, what point is there in having washed the sins away? Listen to what our Lord says to the man once healed: "See, you are well! Sin no more, that nothing worse befall you"

(Jn 5:14). This is what the blessed Peter most clearly teaches when he says that something worse will happen to those who have sinned after knowing the way of righteousness: For if, after they have escaped the defilements of the world through the knowledge of our Lord and Savior Jesus Christ, they are again entangled in them and overpowered, the last state has become worse for them than the first. For it would have been better for them never to have known the way of righteousness than after knowing it to turn back from the holy commandment delivered to them. It has happened to them according to the true proverb: "The dog turns back to his own vomit, and the sow is washed only to wallow in the mire" (2 Pt 2:20–22). The blessed Apostle Paul testifies to this too when he says that we cannot be saved without great penance if we sin again after being healed of our former sin by baptism: "For it is impossible to restore again to repentance those who have once been enlightened, who have tasted the heavenly gift, and have become partakers of the Holy Spirit, and have tasted the goodness of the Word of God and the powers of the age to come, if they then commit apostasy, since they crucify the Son of God on their own account and hold him up to contempt" (Heb 6:4–6).

The Evangelist tells us of how a certain person approached the Savior and asked what he should do to receive eternal life, to whom the Lord replied in this way: "If you would enter life, keep the commandments" (Mt 19:17). He did not say: "Only keep faith." For if faith alone is necessary, then it is superfluous to demand that the commandments should be kept. It would be wrong for me to say that our Lord commanded anything superfluous, but that is what those people assert whose sinning has now made them the children of perdition, and who believe that their only solace consists in dragging others down with themselves into eternal death. For if God does not punish sinners, then what of the words: "If the righteous is scarcely saved, where will the impious and sinner appear?" (1 Pt 4:18), and elsewhere: "But the wicked perish" (Ps 37:20), and again: "Let sinners and the wicked be consumed from the earth, so that they are no more" (Ps 104:35), or: "As smoke is driven away, so drive them away; as wax melts before the fire, let the wicked perish before God!" (Ps 68:2). There is no one who is so lacking in faith and belief that they do not think that sinners are to be condemned. And in one place I read that our Savior said: "Not everyone who says to me 'Lord, Lord' shall enter the kingdom of heaven, but he who does the will of my Father who is in heaven" (Mt 7:21). Certainly those people believe in Christ who call him Lord, but the doors of the kingdom of heaven are not opened to them who confess him with their mouths and deny him with their actions. God can be denied with actions no less than he can with words, as the Apostle said: "They profess to know God but deny him by their deeds" (Ti 1:16). And in the gospel our Lord says: "On that day many will say to me, 'Lord, Lord, did we not prophesy in your name, and cast out demons in your name, and do many mighty works in your name?' And then will I declare to them, 'I never knew you; depart from me, you evildoers'" (Mt 7:22–23).[5] Up to this point they are said to have believed and to have performed their virtues in the name of the Lord; but their faith shall do them no good, since they have not done works of righteousness. And so if faith alone is beneficial, why are they consigned forever to the fires of hell together with the angels of Satan, having been judged not for a lack of faith but because they have done nothing good? It is written: "Then he will say to those at his left hand, 'Depart from me, you cursed, into the eternal fire prepared for the Devil and his angels; for I was hungry and you gave me no food, I was thirsty and you gave me no drink...'" (Mt 25:41–42). Indeed, he did not say: "Because you have not believed in me," which leads us to think that they have been condemned not because they did not believe but because they did not perform good works.

XIV. *Who is truly a Christian?* Let no one deceive another, let no one lead anyone else astray: If we have not been righteous, we shall not have life; if we have not served the commandments of Christ in all things, we shall not share with him; if we have not turned our back on earthly things, we shall not receive the things of God; if we have not spurned human things, we shall not possess the things of

401

heaven. Nor should any hold themselves to be Christians unless they follow the teaching of Christ and imitate his example. But do you actually consider that person to be a Christian whose bread never fills the stomachs of the hungry, whose drink never quenches anyone's thirst, whose table is unfamiliar to all, whose roof never affords protection either to the stranger or to the pilgrim, whose clothes never cover the naked, who never comes to the aid of the poor, whose good is unknown to all, whose mercy no one knows, who imitates good people in nothing, but rather mocks and derides and never ceases to persecute the poor? Let the spirits of all Christians be free of these things; let no one say that Christians are like this; let those who are like this not be called the children of God. Those people are Christians who follow the way of Christ, who imitate Christ in all things, as it says in scripture: "He who says he abides in Christ ought to walk in the same way in which he walked" (1 Jn 2:6). That person is a Christian who is merciful to all, who is not motivated by injustice, who cannot endure the oppression of the poor before their very eyes, who comes to the aid of the wretched, who helps the needy, who mourns with those who mourn, who feels the suffering of others as if it were their own, who is moved to tears by the tears of others, whose house is open to all, whose doors are closed to none, whose table is familiar to all the poor, whose food is offered to all, whose goodness is known to all, and at whose hands no one suffers injustice, who serves God day and night, who ceaselessly considers and meditates upon his commandments, who makes themselves poor in this world that they may be rich in God, who is without honor in society that they may appear glorified before God and his angels, who seems to have nothing false or untrue in their heart, whose soul is simple and unstained, whose conscience is faithful and pure, whose mind is wholly in God, whose hope is all in Christ, who desires the things of heaven rather than the things of earth, who leaves behind human things that they may have the things of God. Hear what is said to those who love this world and who vaunt themselves and are satisfied in this present time: "Do you not know that friendship with the world is enmity with God? Therefore whoever wishes to be a friend of the world makes himself an enemy of God" (Jas 4:4).

402

XV. *There are three kinds of widows. How a Christian widow should be.
I have explained to you as well as I could, dearest sister, what it is that a
Christian should do.* Now if all generally who call themselves Christians ought to be like this, let your prudence decide which kind of widow you should show yourself to be, who should serve as an example to all who live good lives. I do not think that you are ignorant of the three different types of widow. The first, which is most perfect, is destined for a heavenly reward because, after the fashion of the widow in the gospels, she serves God with prayers and fasts day and night. The second, who is said to have the care of sons and the home, is not quite so worthy but neither is she subject to sin. But the third kind pursues feasts and pleasures, and she shall face eternal death and suffering. As it is written: "Honor widows who are real widows" (1 Tm 5:3). It is these first widows who are said to be the real ones and who, according to a great priest, that is, Timothy, are to be honored. We are not told to honor the second kind, but neither shall life be denied them, concerning whom it is said: "If a widow has children or grandchildren, let them first learn their religious duty to their own family and make an equal return to their parents" (1 Tm 5:4). Those truly are of the third kind of whom it is written: "She who is self-indulgent is dead even while she lives" (1 Tm 5:6). From this we should understand that not all widows are the same and that those are not pleasing to God who seem only to be widows from their state of life and not by virtue of what they do.

But the Apostle tells us how the widow of Christ should be: "She who is a real widow has set her hope on God, and continues in prayers day and night" (cf. 1 Tm 5:5). Nor do I wish you to pass over that which, when the Apostle defines true widows, shows others to be false; false, that is, in their deeds, their minds, and their way of life, if not in their physical state. Elsewhere the same Apostle describes the behavior and way of life of a true and elect widow, saying: "Let the widow be elected who is well attested for her good deeds, as one who has brought up children [here 'for God' is understood], shown hospitality, washed the feet of the saints, relieved the afflicted, and devoted herself to doing good in every way" (1 Tm 5:10). He has judged this woman to be a true widow whose works are such. How does that woman call herself a widow of Christ who has never done anything of the like? But there are some rich, high-born, and powerful women to whom perhaps it seems unworthy to educate their children for God and not for the world, to offer hospitality to the stranger or to wash the rude feet of the saints, grimy with toil, touching them with their hands, so delicate and white. But such women shall not be worthy to be in the company of the saints in the time to come, to whom they have shown such contempt while on earth, nor shall they be able to share with Christ, whom they did not wish to receive and to whose feet they were frightened to stretch out their hands, for whoever rejects his servants, rejects Christ, as he himself says: "He who rejects you, rejects me" (Lk 10:16). Mary's tears flowed in such abundance that she was able to wash Christ's feet with them, but our women today do not even have sufficient water to wash the feet of pilgrims. You, therefore, who are a most holy and chaste woman, do not wish to imitate those women of this kind who, when they have brazenly done evil, blush to do good; who are confounded by right living but not by sin; and who have exposed themselves to death of their own accord; and who, when they are called back, do not return to life; who fear more the laughter, derision, and tale-telling of society than the judgment of God and for whom it is more important to please wretched men and women than Christ. But be as the Lord has commanded you to be, as the Apostle instructed the Christian widow to be: holy, humble, and calm, and ceaseless in the performance of the works of righteousness and mercy. And regardless of whoever disapproves of you, mocks and derides you, you should please only God, and do those things which are of Christ. Above all, you should ceaselessly meditate upon the commandments of your Lord, apply yourself wholeheartedly to prayers and Psalms, so that if it is possible, you shall always be found to be reading or in prayer. And when this is what you have become, remember us, who love you so much that we give you in our absence what we cannot give by our presence.

2. "THE HIGH FIRST-SOWER" (THE *ALTUS PROSATOR*) BY COLUMBA

A[1]   THE HIGH FIRST-SOWER, the Ancient of Days[2] and unbegotten,

was without any source,[3] limit, or foundation in the beginning,[4] and is,

and will be throughout unending ages forever;[5]

With him is the only-begotten one,[6] the Christ;

And the co-eternal Holy Spirit in the constant glory of the Godhead.

We do not claim that there are three gods; rather we declare that God is one,

but not at the expense of believing in three most glorious Persons.[7]

B.   Blessed Angels and Archangels did he create,

Along with the orders of Principalities, Thrones, Powers, and Virtues.[8]

This happened so that the goodness and majesty of the Trinity in all the gifts of largesse should not remain idle; for in these celestial ranks God could mightily express his generosities through a capable word.[9]

C.   From the peak of the kingdom of heaven,

where the angels are located in brightness,[10]

Lucifer,[11] whom God created, fell down[12] though pride[13]

in the resplendent light and radiant beauty of his own form.

He, the author of silly pride[14] and ingrained envy, brought with him in that same sad fall all the apostate angels;

While the rest remained in their first-rank[15] places of origin.

D. The great Dragon, most foul, terrible, and ancient,[16] was wiser than all beasts and more ferocious than the animals of the earth.[17]
He was the slippery serpent[18] who pulled down with himself into the abyss[19] of the lower places and its many dungeons one-third of the stars of heaven.[20]
Those who flee the true light[21] are there thrown down headlong[22] by the Parasite.

E. The High One, looking forward to the system of the universe[23] and its harmony, made the heaven and the earth;[24]
Brought forth the sea, the waters, the shoots of grass, the trees of the woods, the sun, moon, stars, fire, and all things needed, birds, fish, cattle, beasts, and everything that lives.[25]
Then, at the end of his works, [he made] the first-formed[26] human so that he could rule with knowledge.[27]

F. The stars and the great lights of the upper regions were made together,[28]
So viewing this wonderful and immense created body the angels burst forth in praise of the Lord, the architect of the heavens;[29]
And they with a constant and worthy song of praise rendered thanks to the Lord.[30]
This noble harmony in song was not some by-product of their nature, but sprang by choice from their love [of God].

G. Having loitered around and seduced our two first parents,[31]
the Devil and his horde fell a second time.[32]
The ugliness of their [demonic] faces and the sound of their flying strikes fragile humans with such terror that they cannot see with their eyes of flesh those who are now bundled in the bonds of prison labor camps.[33]

H. The proud one was cast down by the Lord from the human globe,
for it was crowded with his hoards of invisible and wild rebels,[34]

for fear that men influenced by their evil manners,
as they are never enclosed by fences or walls,
should fornicate[35] openly before the eyes of all.

I. From out of their northern sources in the deeper parts of
the ocean,
from the three-quarters[36] of earth covered in sea, the clouds
carry in the rains.[37]
In blue whirlwinds the sea reaches up to the heavens,
so that the grains, vines, and grasses may all benefit,
and then these clouds are moved by the winds coming from
their storehouses,
and these in turn drain out the water from the marshes.

K. The glory of the kings of this world is fragile and cruel,
it passes in a moment struck down at God's nod.
Look, even "the giants" being held "beneath the waters
weep."[38]
They are held there in great pain from being singed with fire
and torments.
They are strangled in the maelstrom of Cocytus, and thrown
about between the rocks of Scylla and Charybdis.

L. The Lord often shakes down the waters bound up in the
clouds,[39]
in case they burst their retainers in a single eruption.
On the earth the more fruitful streams of water flow slowly in
their paths, as if flowing from udders.
Freezing and flowing with the turning seasons, they flow
everywhere without faltering.

M. The sphere of the earth is hung
by the sovereign powers of the great God;
and the circle of the great Abyss is placed and supported
by the powerful will of almighty God.
They are held as if by columns or bars;
and based on a firm foundation as if on an outcrop of
rock.[40]

N. It appears that no one doubts that hell is in the lowest regions,[41]
where darkness, worms, and dreadful beasts are held;[42]
where sulphurous fire burns[43] with consuming flames;
where men's faces are contorted, and there is "weeping and gnashing of teeth";[44]
where the terrible and ancient sighing of Gehenna[45] occurs;
and where from the fiery burning there comes a horrible hunger and thirst.[46]

O. We know,[47] for we have read it, that there are those who dwell beneath the earth,
who often bend the knee in reverence to the Lord;[48]
but they cannot open[49] "the written book"[50] sealed with the seven seals[51] of Christ's warnings.[52]
He broke these seals when he rose again victorious,[53]
fulfilling what was prefigured in prophecy[54] about his coming.

P. In the beginning the Lord planted a paradise,[55]
From the opening of the most noble Genesis we read this.
A paradise from whose source four rivers are flowing outward,[56]
and in whose floral midst is the tree of life.[57]
This tree's leaves do not fall,[58] but bring healing to the nations,[59]
and its delights[60] are both plentiful and beyond words.[61]

Q. Who has ascended Sinai,[62] the Lord's chosen mountain?[63]
Who has heard the thunder that is beyond the measure of sound,
Or the noise of the immense trumpet?[64]
Who has seen the lightning flashing around the sky,
Or the lights,[65] the thunderbolts,[66] or the smashing of rocks?[67]
Only Moses, judge of the Israelite people.[68]

R. "The Day of the Lord," the King of Kings,[69] "is near."[70]

[That will be] "the Day of Wrath,"[71] "of vengeance,"[72] of dark-
ness[73] and clouds;
The day of thunders, mighty and wonderful;
The day of affliction,[74] mourning, and sadness;
On which will cease women's loving and desiring,[75]
And men's worldly competition and desire.[76]

S. Before the Lord's tribunal[77] we shall stand shivering with
fear.[78]
We shall offer an explanation for all our undertakings,
While we see our crimes placed before our sight,
With the books of conscience laid open in front of us.[79]
Then we shall break into the most bitter crying and gasping;
For the possibility of doing something about [our crimes]
will have been taken away.

T. On the trumpet signal of the first[80] most admirable
archangel,[81]
The most fortified dungeons and cemeteries burst open.
Then the deadly chill of the men of this world turns to liq-
uid;
With bones coming together into nodules of sinew from
every side,
While airy souls are coming down to join with them,
Returning again to their proper stations.

U. The Evening Star wanders from the height of Orion at the
turning point of heaven;[82]
The Pleiades, most splendid of stars, are left behind.[83]
It moves over the sea's bounds westward to the sea's
unknown eastern limit following its determined track;
It returns again and again upon its appointed path in a two-
year cycle to rise once more in the east.
But we study this complex movement for what it mystically
tells us.[84]

X. The banner of the cross,[85] the brightest sign, will shine
resplendent,[86]

When Christ, the celestial Lord, descends from the heavens.
The two great lights will be darkened;
The stars will drop on the earth like figs from a tree;[87]
And the whole space of the universe [will be] filled with fire like the inside of a furnace.[88]
Then armies will flee away in the caverns and recesses of the mountains.[89]

Y.   Then the Trinity will be praised;
With the singing of hymns rung out with prayer;
With thousands of lively angels dancing;
With "four living creatures, full of eyes,"[90]
Along with the twenty-four happy elders,[91]
Throwing down their crowns at the feet of the Lamb of God;[92]
And all unite in the eternal triple chorus[: "Holy, holy, holy!"].[93]

Z.   The furious zeal of the fire[94] will consume the adversaries,
Those who will not have faith that Christ came from God the Father.
But we, by contrast, shall fly at once to meet him,
And so shall be with him[95] in the various ordered ranks,
According to the eternal rewards we deserve,
Remaining in glory forever and ever.[96]

Refrain:
Who can please God "in the final time,"[97]
With the various orders of truth made plain?
Only those who have contempt for the present world.

410

3. HOMILY ON THE PROLOGUE TO *THE GOSPEL OF JOHN* BY JOHN SCOTTUS ERIUGENA

1

The voice of the spiritual eagle resounds in the ears of the church.[1] May our external senses grasp its fleeting sounds, and our interior mind penetrate its enduring meaning. This is the voice of the high-flying bird, not the one that flies above the material air or ether or around the whole of the sensible world, but the bird which soars above all theory, on the swift wings of the most profound theology and with the insights of the clearest and most sublime contemplation, passing beyond all that is and all that is not.

By "all that is," I mean those things that do not entirely escape human or angelic knowledge, since they are below God and are limited in their number by the one cause of the whole universe. By "all that is not," I mean those things which transcend the powers of all understanding. And so John, the blessed theologian, soars above not only what can be grasped and spoken of but also those things which exceed all understanding and meaning. By the ineffable flight of his mind, he is raised beyond all things and penetrates to the heart of the one Origin of all. Clearly grasping the incomprehensible and united superessentiality and the distinct supersubstantiality of the Origin and the Word,[2] which is to say the Father and the Son, he begins his gospel with the words: *In the beginning was the Word.*

2

O blessed John, it is not without reason that you bear the name of John. John is a Hebrew name, which is translated into Greek as ᾧ ἐχαρίσατο, meaning "to whom is given."[3] For which of the theologians has been graced with your gifts of penetrating the hidden mysteries of the greatest Good and to intimate to the human mind and senses what was revealed and declared to you there? Tell me then who was granted so great a gift of such a kind. Perhaps some will say that such a gift was granted to Peter, chief of the Apostles, who, when Christ asked him who he thought he was, replied: "You are the Christ, the Son of the living God" (Mt 16:16). But I think we may say without fear of contradiction that Peter spoke here more as an example of faith and action than knowledge and contemplation. Why? For the reason that Peter is always seen as the model of faith and action while John is the example of contemplation and knowledge. The one reclined on the breast of the Lord, which signifies contemplation, while the other hesitated, which symbolizes restless action. For before it becomes habitual, the execution of divine commands may at one moment discern the pure essences of the virtues and in another misjudge them, clouded by the fog of human thinking. The keenness of profound contemplation, on the other hand, once it has gazed upon the face of truth, is neither denied access by anything, nor is deceived, nor is ever blinded by any cloud.

3

But the two Apostles run to the tomb. The tomb of Christ is holy scripture in which the mysteries of his divinity and humanity rest on the solidity of letters as if supported by stone. John, however, ran ahead of Peter. For the power of contemplation, wholly purified, penetrates more keenly and swiftly the profound secrets of divine letters than does action, which still stands in need of purification. But it is Peter who is first to enter the tomb, followed by John. Thus both of them run there and both enter in. Peter is the figure of faith, while John symbolizes understanding. And since it is written "Unless you believe, you will not understand" (cf. Is 7:9), faith is necessarily the first to enter the tomb of holy scripture, followed by the understanding, whose path is prepared by faith.

Peter recognized Christ, who had been made both God and man in time, and cried out: "You are the Christ, the Son of the living God" (Mt 16:16). He did indeed fly high, but higher still flew the one who, when he had grasped Christ with his understanding as God from God, born from before all time, said: "In the beginning was the Word" (Jn 1:1). But it should not be thought that we prefer John to Peter. Who would dare to do that? Which of the Apostles could be higher than the one who both is, and is called, the chief of the Apostles? We do not prefer John to Peter. But we are comparing action with contemplation, the soul which still requires purification with the soul which is already pure. We are only comparing the virtue which is still ascending to an unchanging state to virtue which has already attained it. We are not considering the personal worth of the two Apostles, but are reflecting upon the beautiful diversity of divine mysteries.

And so Peter, which is to say the action of virtues, perceives how the Son of God is enfolded in flesh in a wonderful and ineffable manner, by the power of faith and action, while John, who is the highest contemplation of truth, wonders at the Word of God as it is in itself, prior to the flesh, absolute and infinite in its own origination, which is to say in the Father. Peter is truly led by divine revelation when he sees the eternal and the temporal united in Christ, but it is John who leads the faithful souls to knowledge of what in Christ is purely eternal.

4

The spiritual bird, whose flight is rapid and who sees God—I mean John the Theologian—is above all creatures both visible and invisible, penetrates all thought, and, deified, enters the God who deifies him. O blessed Paul, you were caught up, as you yourself tell us, to the third heaven, to Paradise; but you were not taken up above every heaven and every Paradise. Yet John went beyond every created heaven and Paradise, which is to say beyond every human and angelic nature.[4] In the third heaven, O vessel of election and teacher of the gentiles, you heard words which it is not permitted for mortals to repeat. But John, who gazed into the depths of truth, beyond every heaven and in the Paradise of Paradises, that is, within the cause of all things, heard the single word by which all things were made. He was allowed to repeat this word and to proclaim it to mortals to the extent that it could be proclaimed to human beings. In faith and confidence he declares: *In the beginning was the word.*

5

John was not only a human being but was more than human when he rose above himself and all that is. Transported by the ineffable power of wisdom and by the most pure apex of the mind, he entered into that which is above all things, that is, the secret of the one essence in three substances and of three substances in one essence. He could not have ascended to God if he had not first become God. For, as the gaze of our eyes cannot perceive the forms and colors of sensible things until it has been joined with the rays of the sun, being united in them and with them, so the souls of the saints cannot receive the pure knowledge of spiritual things, which transcends all understanding, unless they have first been made worthy to participate in the incomprehensible truth. And so the holy theologian, changed into God and participating in truth, proclaims that God as Word subsists in God as Principle, that is, God the Son in God the Father. "In the beginning," he says, "was the Word."

Behold the heavens open and the mystery of the most high and holy Trinity and Unity revealed to the world! See the divine angel ascend above the Son of Man, proclaiming to us that he is the Word which exists in the beginning before all things. See the angel then descend upon the Son of Man and cry: "And the Word was made flesh." He descends when he declares the good news that the divine Word has become human and has been born supernaturally of the Virgin Mary into the world. He ascends when he proclaims that the Word was born superessentially of the Father before and beyond all things.

6

In the beginning was the Word, he writes. It should be noted that the holy Evangelist is applying the word "was" *[erat]* at this point with reference to substance and not to time. The verb *sum,* from which we derive the irregular form *erat,* has two meanings. Sometimes it simply denotes the subsistence of some thing, without any suggestion of temporality, in which case it is called a substantive verb, and sometimes it denotes temporality, in line with other verbs. Therefore, "In the beginning was the Word" means "the Son subsists in the Father." Who in their right mind would say that the Son ever subsisted temporally in the Father? For eternity can exist only where immutable truth dwells.

And in case anyone should think that the Word subsists in the Principle in such a way that there is no distinction of substances between them, the Evangelist adds: "And the Word was with God." This means to say that the Son subsists with the Father in unity of essence and distinction of substance.[5]

And again, in case the venomous contagion should infect anyone with the belief that the Word is only in the Father and with God but does not itself subsist substantially and coessentially as God with the Father (which was the error of the faithless Arians), he immediately adds: "And the Word was God."

Foreseeing also that there would be no lack of those who maintain that the Evangelist was not referring to one and the same Word when he wrote "In the beginning was the Word" and "the Word was God," but that he meant that these two were different, the Evangelist added, in order to undermine this heretical view, the phrase: "This was in the beginning with God." This means to say that this Word which is God with God is the same and no other than the Word which was in the beginning. This may be understood more clearly from the Greek versions. There it says αὐτός, which means "the same" and which may refer either to the Word or to God, for these two words *theos* and *logos* are both masculine in Greek. And so we may understand "the Word was God," which Word was with God in the beginning, as if the Evangelist had said as clearly as the day is bright: This God-

Word which is "with God" is the same of which I have said "In the beginning was the Word."

7

All things were made through him. All things were made through the God-Word, through the Word himself who is God. And what does "all things were made through him" mean if not: At the moment the Word was born of the Father before all things, all things were made with him and through him. For the generation of the Word from the Father is the creation of all causes and is the effective production of all things which proceed from the causes as genus and kind. Indeed, all things were made through the generation of God the Word from God who is Principle and beginning. Hear the divine and ineffable paradox, the impenetrable secret, the unfathomable depths, the mystery which transcends understanding. Through him who was not made but begotten, all things were made but not begotten.

The Father is the Principle or beginning from which all things were made, while the Son is the Principle through whom all things were made. The Father speaks forth his Word, which is to say, he brings forth his wisdom, and all things are made. The prophet says: "You made all things in wisdom" (Ps 103:24). And elsewhere, speaking in the person of the Father, he says: "My heart has brought forth." What did his heart bring forth? He explains it himself: "I speak a good word" (Ps 44:2). I utter a good Word, I bring forth a good Son. The heart of the Father is his own essence, from which came the Son's own essence.

The Father precedes the Word, not with respect to nature but with respect to cause. Hear what the Son himself says: "My Father is greater than I am" (Jn 14:28), which means that his essence is the cause of my essence. The Father precedes the Son causally, I say, while the Son precedes by nature all that was made through him. The essence of the Son is coeternal with the Father. The essence of those things which were made through him began to exist in him before all the ages of the world, not in time but with time.[6] Time indeed was created together with all

416

other things that were made, and not before; it is not prior to them, but was created together with them.

8

And what is the consequence of the Word uttered by the mouth of the Most High? For the Father has not spoken in vain, nor did his utterance lack fruit or great effect, since even human beings produce an effect in the ear of another when we speak among ourselves. There are three things therefore in which we should believe and which we should understand: the Father who speaks, the Word who is uttered, and the things which are made by the Word. The Father speaks, the Word is born, and all things are made. Listen to the prophet: "For he spoke and it was done" (Ps 32:9). That is, he brought forth his Word, through whom all things were made.

And in case you should think that some of the things which were created by God's Word while others were created from outside him or exist in themselves, so that it is not the case that all that is and all that is not can be traced back to a single principle or beginning, the Evangelist concluded his preceding theology with the words: "And without him was not anything made which was made" (Jn 1:3). This means that nothing was created outside him, since he contains all things within himself, comprehending all, and nothing can be considered to be coeternal, consubstantial, or coessential with him except his Father and his Spirit, which proceeds from the Father through the Word.

All this can more easily be understood in the Greek language. Where the Latin has *sine ipso* ["without him"], Greek has χωρὶς αὐτοῦ, which means "outside him." Similarly the Lord himself says to his disciples: "Without me you can do nothing" (Jn 15:5). In other words, he says you who without me have not been able to make yourselves, what can you do without me? Here again the Greek says not ἄνευ, but χωρίς, not "without" but "outside." Therefore I say that it is easier to understand this point in the Greek since if anyone says "without him," then the meaning is "without his help or counsel," and there is no suggestion that all

417

things are to be attributed to him. The phrase "outside him," on the other hand, makes it clear that there is nothing whatsoever that was not created in him and through him.

9

What was made in him was life. Far removed from the power of all reason and intellect, the blessed Evangelist has revealed to us divine mysteries. He has shown us the God-Word in the God who speaks, leaving those who contemplate holy scripture the task of discovering the Holy Spirit in both. Whoever speaks emits breath in the word that he utters; so too God the Father, at one and the same time, gives birth to his Son and, by the birth of the Son, produces the Spirit. The Evangelist goes on to say that all things were made through God the Son and that nothing exists outside him, as if developing his theology from another point of departure with the words "What was made in him was life." Previously he said: "All things were made by him." As if he had been asked about those things which were made by God the Word, how and what they were in him through whom they were made, he replied: *What was made in him was life.*

This sentence can be read in two ways. We can say either "What was made," adding "was life in him," or we can say "what was made in him," adding "was life." Thus by virtue of this ambiguity, we can discern two meanings here. The interpretation: What was made fragmented in space and time, distinct in kind, form, and number, whether of sensible or intelligible substance, combined or separate, all this was life in him, is not the same as: What was made in him was nothing other than life. Let our meaning be the following therefore: All those things which were made through him are life in him and are one in him. For all things existed—or subsisted—in him as causes before they came into existence in themselves as effects. The mode of existence beneath him of those things which were made through him is not that of those things in him which are his very self.[7]

418

10

All things therefore that were made through him live immutably in him and are life. In him all things neither existed nor shall exist according to intervals of time or space, but all things in him are above time and space and are one. Visible and invisible, corporeal and incorporeal, endowed with reason and without reason, all subsist universally in him, heaven and earth, the abyss and whatever is in them, these things live in him and are life, and they subsist eternally. Even those things which seem to us to lack all power of movement have life in the Word. And if you wish to know how and in what way all things which were made through the Word subsist vitally, uniformly, and causally in him, then take the nature of creatures as an example and learn to see the Creator in those things which were made in him and through him: "For the invisible things of him," as the Apostle says, "are clearly understood by the intelligence, being understood from the things which are made" (Rom 1:20).

See how the causes of all things which the sensible sphere of this world contains all subsist simply and uniformly in this sun which we call the great luminary of the world. From there the forms of all bodies proceed, the beauty and diversity of colors and all the other things which can be said of sensible nature. Consider the manifold and infinite power of seeds, and how a great number of plants, shrubs, and animals are all contained at once in individual seeds, how there rises from them a lovely multiplicity of forms beyond number. See with your inner eyes how the many rules of a science become one in the artistry of an expert, and how they have life in the spirit of the person who masters them. See how the infinite number of lines becomes as one in a single point, and take note of other examples from nature. Raised up by these beyond all things, as if by the wings of the contemplation of nature, you can gaze into the secret places of the Word with the pinnacle of your mind, aided and illumined by divine grace, insofar as this is granted to human beings who seek their God by rational arguments, and see how all the things which are made through the Word live in him and are life in him.

419

"In him," as the divine voice says, "we live and move and have our being" (Acts 17:28). And as the great Pseudo-Dionysius says: "The being of all things is the superessential deity."[8]

11

And the life was the light of men. Blessed theologian, the Son of God, whom you previously called "Word," you now call "life" and "light." Nor were you wrong to introduce different names in order to convey new meanings to us. You called the Son of God "Word" since the Father uttered all things through him: "He spoke and it was done." You have called him "light" and "life" since the same Son is the light and life of all things which were made through him. And what does he illumine? Nothing other than himself and his Father. He is light therefore and illumines himself, revealing himself to the world, manifesting himself to those who do not know him.

The light of divine knowledge departed from the world when humankind abandoned God. Now the eternal light manifests itself to the world in two ways, through the Bible and creatures. For the divine knowledge cannot be restored in us except by the letters of scripture and the sight of creatures. Learn the words of scripture and understand their meaning in your soul; there you will discover the Word. Know the forms and beauty of sensible things by your physical senses, and see there the Word of God. And in all these things Truth itself proclaims to you only he who made all things, and apart from whom there is nothing for you to contemplate since he is himself all things. He himself is the being of all things. Indeed, just as there is no substantial good outside him, neither does any essence or substance exist outside him.

And the life was the light of men. Why did he add "the light of men"? It is as if the light of the angels, the light of the created universe, the light of all visible and invisible existence, were specifically and peculiarly the light of humanity. Might it be that the Word which gives life to all things is said to be specifically and peculiarly the light of humanity since it was in a man that he proclaimed himself not only to other men and women but also to angels and to all creatures who possess the power of participation in divine knowledge? For he appeared not through an angel to angels, nor through an angel to human beings, but through a human being to both humankind and angels, not as an apparition but in true humanity, with which he wholly united himself in substance, and manifested himself to all creatures endowed with knowledge. And so the light of humanity is our Lord Jesus Christ, who revealed himself in his human nature to all creatures that possess reason and knowledge and showed to them the hidden mysteries of his divinity, by which he is equal to the Father.

12

And the light shone in the darkness. Listen to the Apostle: "Once you were darkness, now you are light in the Lord" (Eph 5:8). Listen to the words of Isaiah: "The light has shone on those who sat in the land of the shadow of death" (Is 9:2). The light shines in the darkness. On account of original sin, the whole of the human race was in darkness—not the darkness of the outer eyes, which sense the forms and colors of sensible things, but of the inner eyes, which discern the beauty and kind of intelligible things; not in the darkness of gloomy skies, but in the darkness which is the ignorance of truth; not the absence of light which illumines the physical world, but the absence of light which falls upon the immaterial world. Born of the Virgin Mary, the light shines in the darkness, that is, in the hearts of those who know it.

The whole of the human race is, as it were, divided into two parts: those whose hearts have been illumined by the knowledge of the truth and those who still remain in the deepest darkness of irreligion and wickedness. The Evangelist adds: "And the darkness comprehended it not." It is as if he clearly said: The light shines in the darkness of the souls of the faithful, and the light increases, beginning with faith and ending with vision. But the hearts of the unfaithful and the ignorant have not understood the light of the Word of God which shines in the flesh. "Their foolish hearts were darkened," as the Apostle says, "professing themselves to be wise, they became fools" (Rom 1:21–22). This, at least, is the moral sense.

13

But the natural understanding of these words is the following. Even if it had not sinned, human nature could not shine by its own powers, for it does not itself possess the nature of light but participates in light. Although it is capable of wisdom, it is not itself wisdom, participation in which makes someone wise. Just as the air does not shine by itself (to which has been given the name "darkness"), and yet is still capable of receiving sunlight, so too our human nature, when considered in itself, is a certain dark substance, but one that is capable of receiving and participating in the light of wisdom. The air, when it participates in the sun's rays, is not said to shine of itself; it is the radiance of the sun which is manifest in it so that it does not lose its natural obscurity but only receives the light from elsewhere into itself. In the same way the rational part of our nature, when the Word of God is present to it, knows intelligible things and knows its God not by its own power but by the infusion of divine light. The Word himself says: "It is not you who speak, but the Spirit of your Father who speaks in you" (Mt 10:20). With this single sentence he intended to teach us a general principle. He wished that the following words should sound ineffably in the ear of our hearts: It is not you who shine, but the Spirit of your Father shines in you. In other words, it is he, the Father, who manifests me to you, shining upon you, since I am the light of the intelligible world, that is, of rational and intellectual nature (cf. Jn 8:12). It is not you who know me, but I who know myself by my own spirit in you, since you are not substantial light but only participate in the self-subsisting light.

Thus the light shines in the darkness since the Word of God, which is the light and life of men and women, does not fail to shine in our human nature, although this, considered in itself, is formless and dark. Nor does the Word wish to forsake it, although it has erred, nor shall he ever abandon it. He forms it, by maintaining it through nature, and reforms it, by deifying it through grace. And since the light itself is beyond the comprehension of all creatures, "the darkness comprehended it not." God transcends all thought and understanding, and he alone possesses immortality. His light is called darkness on account of its excellence, since no creature can understand its nature.

14

There was a man sent by God whose name was John. See the eagle relaxing its wings of highest contemplation as it descends in gentle flight from the most sublime heights of the summit of theology to the deep valley of history, leaving the heavens for the earth of the spiritual world. Sacred scripture is in a sense an intelligible world, consisting of its four parts, just as the sensible world is composed of the four elements. Its earth, which is at the mid-point, and at the lowest level, as if at the center of this intelligible world, is history. Around it and embracing it, as the waters circle the earth, is the deep of moral exegesis, which the Greeks call ἠθική. Around history and ethics, as if around the two lower parts of the intelligible world, is the encircling air of the knowledge of nature: that which I call natural science and which is known to the Greeks as φυσική. Outside and beyond all that is the ethereal and burning fire of the empyrean heaven, that is, the sublime contemplation of the divine nature which the Greeks calls theology, beyond which no intelligence can penetrate.

And so the great theologian, I mean John, at the beginning of his gospel, touching the highest peaks of theology, penetrates the secrets of the heaven of spiritual heavens, ascending beyond all history, ethics, and physics. As if descending to earth, he turns the flight of his mind to those things which occurred shortly before the incarnation of the Word and which demand an historical narrative, and says: "There was a man sent by God."

15

John introduces John into his theology: "Deep calls unto deep" (Ps 41:8) in the voice of the divine mysteries. The Evangelist narrates the history of his namesake; the one, to whom it was given to know the Word in the beginning, commemorates the other, to whom it was given to precede the incarnate Word. "There was," he says and not simply, "sent from God," but "there was a man," in order to distinguish between the man, who participated merely in human nature and was the precursor, from the man who united in himself human and divine nature as one, and who came after; in order to separate the voice which passes from the Word which remains always and is unchanging; in order to suggest that the one is the morning star, which appears at the dawn of the kingdom of heaven, and that the other is the sun of righteousness which takes its place. He distinguishes the one who witnesses from him to whom he witnesses, the message from him who sends it, the light of the lamp that flickers in the night from the brilliant light which fills the world, destroying the darkness of death and sin of the whole human race. And so the forerunner of the Lord was a human being, not God, while the Lord, of whom he was the forerunner, was both a human being and God. The forerunner was a man called to become God by grace, while the one he preceded was God by nature, who was called to become a man by humility and by the desire to effect our salvation and redemption.

A man was sent. By whom? By God the Word, whom he preceded. His mission is that of being forerunner. In a loud cry he sends his voice out before: "the voice of one crying in the wilderness" (Jn 1:23). The herald prepares the approach of the Lord. *His name was John,* to whom it was given to become the forerunner of the king of kings, to proclaim to the world the incarnate Word, to baptize him for the spiritual adoption of all, and to bear witness to the eternal light by his voice and his martyrdom.

16

*He came as a witness, to bear witness to the li*ght, which is to say, to Christ. Hear his witness: "Behold the Lamb of God, who takes away the sins of the world" (Jn 1:29). And again: "He who comes after me was created before me" (Jn 1:27). The Greek text is clearer here: ἔμπροσθέν μου, which means "in my presence," "before my eyes." It is as if he had openly said: "I saw the one before my eyes who was born in the flesh after me according to the chronological order, in a prophetic vision I saw him, conceived before me and made man in the virgin's womb, when I was still in the barren insides of my own mother."

"He was not that light, but was sent to bear witness to that light." This must be read with the above in mind: "He was not that light, but *was sent* in order to bear witness to that light." He was the forerunner of the light and not the light itself. But why then is he called "a burning light" and "morning star"? He was a burning light, but he did not burn with his own flame, nor shine with his own light. He was indeed the morning star, but did not generate his own light. It was the grace of the one whom he preceded that burned and shone in him. He was not the light but participated in the light. That which shone in and through him was not of him. As stated above, no creature endowed with reason or intelligence is substantially light of itself, but rather participates in the one, true, substantial light which shines forth intelligibly everywhere and in all things.

That is why the Evangelist adds: "That was the true light which illumines everyone who comes into the world." The self-subsisting Son of God, born of the self-subsisting Father before all ages, he calls the true light, and he calls the same Son who became a human being among the human race for the sake of humanity. He is the true light, who said of himself: "I am the light of the world; whoever follows me will not walk in darkness, but shall have the light of eternal life" (Jn 8:12).

17

That was the true light which illumines everyone who comes into the world. What does "who comes into the world" mean? And "everyone who comes into the world"? From where do they enter the world? And which world do they enter? And if those are meant who come into the world from the hidden recesses of nature through their generation in space and time, then what kind of illumination is there for those who are born, only to die, who grow only to decay, who become composite beings only to be dissolved again, and who fall from the peace of silent nature into the unrest of tumultuous misery? I ask you, what true and spiritual light can there be for those born into a false and passing life? Is this world not a fitting dwelling place for those who are cut off from the true light? Is it not appropriately called the region of the shadow of death and the vale of tears, the abyss of ignorance, the earthly habitation which weighs down the human soul and which prevents the inner eyes from the seeing the true light?

The words "which illumines everyone who comes into the world" should not be taken to refer to those who proceed from hidden seminal causes to corporeal species, but rather to those who spiritually enter the invisible world through the regeneration of grace which is imparted in baptism, to those who forsake that birth which is by corruptible flesh for the birth which is by the spirit. They tread underfoot the world below and rise up to the world above, leaving behind the shadows of ignorance and death in their desire for the light of wisdom and life. They cease to be human children and become the children of God. They leave behind them the world of vices, destroying it in themselves, and fix their gaze on the world of virtues, striving to attain it with all their energy. Thus the true light illumines those who enter the world of virtues, not those who rush into the world of vices.

18

He was in the world. Here it is not only the sensible creation in general that the Evangelist calls "the world," but also, and specifically, the substance of rational nature which is in the human self. In all these things and, to state it simply, in the whole created universe, the Word was the true light; that is, it subsists and always has existed, for it could never cease to subsist in any thing. Just as when someone is speaking, if he should fall silent, then his voice will fade and disappear, so too if the heavenly Father ceases to utter his Word, then the effect of the Word, that is, the created universe, will cease to exist. For it is the Word of God the Father which brings the universe into existence and maintains it in being, that is, the eternal and unchanging generation of his Word.

And the following sentence can only be applied—not without good reason—to the world of the senses: *He was in the world, and the world was made by him.* In case anyone should think, under the influence of the Manichaean heresy, that the world of the physical senses was created by the Devil and not by the Creator of all that is visible and invisible, our theologian adds: *He was in the world,* that is, he who contains all things exists in this world; *and the world was made by him.* For the Author of the universe exists only in his own works and not in the works of another.

19

We should note that the blessed Evangelist named the "world" four times. But we should understand that there are three worlds. The first of these is the one which contains absolutely nothing but the invisible and spiritual substances of the angelic powers; whoever enters this world will fully participate in the true light. The second world is diametrically opposed to the first since it is constituted wholly of visible and corporeal natures. And although this world is situated at the lowest point of this universe, the Word was still in it and it was created by the Word. It is the first stage for those who wish to ascend through the senses to knowledge of the truth, for the different kinds of visible things draw the contemplative soul on to the knowledge of invisible things. The third world is that which, like a middle term, unites in itself the higher, spiritual world and the lower, physical world, and makes both one. It is only in the human person that this world is found, in whom all creatures are united. For we are composed of both body and soul. Holding together the body of this world and the soul of the other world, we form a single universe. The body possesses the whole of corporeal nature and the soul the whole of incorporeal nature; united in a single whole, they constitute the entire universe of the self. That is why "man" is called "the whole," for all creatures are combined in him as in a vessel.[9] Therefore the Lord himself tells his disciples: "Preach the gospel to every creature" (Mk 16:15).

This world, therefore, which is the human self, has not known its own Creator; nor has it desired to know its God either by the symbols of the written Law or by the examples of visible creation, being shackled by the chains of carnal thought: *And the world did not know him.* The human race did not know God the Word, either before he became incarnate, when he was still in a pure state of divinity, or when clothed only in the Incarnation, after he became a man. They did not know the invisible, and denied the visible. They did not wish to seek him who sought them, nor to listen to him who called out to them, nor to revere him who deified them, nor to receive him who received them.

20

He came to his own, which is to say, to that which he had himself made and which therefore is rightly said to be his own. *And his own received him not.* The words "his own" refer to all men and women, whom he wished to redeem and did redeem.

But as many as received him, and believed in his name, to them he gave the power to become sons of God. But now there appears a division, not with regard to the human nature of the rational world but with regard to the will. Those who receive the incarnate Word are distinguished from those who reject him. The faithful believe that the Word has come, and they willingly welcome their Lord. Nonbelievers deny him and willfully reject him, the Jews through envy, the pagans through ignorance. To those who received him, he gave the power to become the sons of God, while to those who do not receive him, he gives the opportunity to change their mind. For no one is denied the possibility of believing in the Son of God and of becoming a child of God, for this is embedded in the human will and in the cooperation of grace. To whom has he given the opportunity to become a child of God? To those who receive him and who believe in his name. The Arians, for instance, receive him but do not believe in his name. They do not believe that he is the sole begotten Son of God, consubstantial with the Father. They deny the ὁμοο ύσιος, that is being of one essence with the Father, but maintain that he is ἐτερούσιος, which means of a different essence from the Father. Accordingly, it does not profit them to receive Christ, since they strive to deny his truth. But to those who receive Christ, as truly human and truly divine, and believe this most firmly, to such is given the possibility of becoming children of God.

21

Which were born not of blood, nor of the will of the flesh, nor of the will of man, but of God. In ancient Greek manuscripts it says merely: "Which were born not of blood but of God." Those who have gained adoption as sons of God through their faith are not born of blood, the Evangelist says, which means not by physical procreation. But they are born of God the Father through the Holy Spirit as co-heirs of Christ, that is, as sharers in the sonship of the only begotten Son of God.

Neither of the will of flesh, nor of the will of man. Here both sexes are introduced, from which the multitude of those propagated in the flesh are born. By the word "flesh" the Evangelist signified the female sex and by "man" he meant the male sex.

You might say it is impossible that mortals should become immortals, that corruptible beings should be free of corruption, that mere mortal beings should become the children of God, and that temporal creatures should possess eternity; but for whichever of these you doubt the most, accept the contrary argument with which you can support doubt with faith: *And the Word was made flesh.*

If what is greater has certainly gone before, why does it seem incredible that what is less should follow? If the Son of God became a human being, which no one who receives him doubts, why is it so astonishing that those who believe in the Son of God should themselves also be destined to be children of God? The Word became flesh so that the flesh, that is, the human race, should ascend to him by believing in the Word through the flesh, so that through the natural, only-begotten Son many should be adopted as sons. Not for his own sake did the Word become flesh, but for our sake, who could not be changed into the sons of God except by the flesh of the Word. He came down alone but ascends with many. He who made of God a human being makes gods of men and women. *And dwelt among us,* that is, he took possession of our nature so that he might make us participators in his own nature.

22

And we beheld his glory, the glory of the only begotten of the Father. Where did you see, O blessed theologian, the glory of the incarnate Word, the glory of the Son of God made a human being? When did you see him? With what eyes did you see? With bodily eyes, I believe, on the mountain at the time of his transfiguration. You were there as the third witness to the divine glorification. I believe that you were present, too, at Jerusalem, and heard the voice of the Father glorifying his Son with these words: "I have glorified him and I shall glorify him again" (Jn 12:28). You heard the crowds of children crying: "Hosanna to the son of David" (Mt 21:15). And what can I say about the glory of the Resurrection? You saw him rising from the dead, when he entered through the closed door to where you waited with the other disciples. You saw his glory ascending to the Father, when he was gathered into heaven by the angels. But above all these things, you saw him, that is the Word, by the most sublime vision of your mind, at his origin, with the Father. There it is that you saw his glory, as the only-begotten of the Father.

Full of grace and truth. This phrase has two meanings. The humanity and divinity of the incarnate Word can be understood here, so that the fullness of grace refers to the humanity and the fullness of truth to the divinity. Indeed, the incarnate Word, our Lord Jesus Christ, received the fullness of grace according to his humanity, since he is the head of the church, the firstborn of all creatures, that is of the whole of humanity, which was healed and restored in him and through him. I say "in him" because he is the supreme and chief example of that grace by which human beings, not by their own merit, become God, and it is this which becomes primordially manifest in him. I say "through him" since "we have all received of his fullness" (Jn 1:16) the grace of deification through the grace of faith, by which we believe in him, and the grace of action, by which we keep his commandments.

By the fullness of the grace of Christ we can understand the Holy Spirit. For the Holy Spirit is indeed often called grace, since it dispenses and effects the gifts of grace. The sevenfold operation of this Spirit filled the humanity of Christ and rested in him, as the prophet says: "And the Spirit of wisdom and understanding, the Spirit of counsel and might, the Spirit of knowledge and devotion shall rest upon him; and he shall be filled with the fear of the Lord" (Is 11:2). If you wish to apply to Christ himself the words "full of grace," then know that it refers to the fullness of his deification and his sanctification according to his humanity. By his deification I mean that process whereby humanity and God are united in the unity of a single substance, and by his sanctification, that not only was he born of the Holy Spirit but he was also filled with the gifts of the Spirit and, as if placed at the top of the mystical candelabrum of the church, the lamps of grace shine in him and from him.[10]

But if you wish to understand that the fullness of grace and truth of the incarnate Word refers to the New Testament, as the Evangelist himself seems to have thought a little later when he says: "The Law was given by Moses, but truth and grace came by Jesus Christ" (Jn 1:17), then you have grounds for saying that the fullness of grace of the New Testament was given through Christ and that the truth of the symbols of the Law was fulfilled in him. As the Apostle says: "In him the fullness of divinity dwells bodily" (Col 2:9). He calls the fullness of divinity the hidden meanings of the shadows of the Law. Christ, who came in the flesh, taught and revealed that these meanings dwell bodily in him, since he himself is the source and fullness of graces, the truth of the symbols of the Law, and the end of the visions of the prophets. To him be glory with the Father and the Holy Spirit for now and forever. Amen.

4. THE FOOD OF THE SOUL

> Let praise and glory be sung—a hymn
> To the Trinity, Unity, One Divinity,
> Let marvelous rejoicing be given—together
> To Father, Son, and Spirit of splendor.

This is the third book in a work called the *Holy Sanctuary of Life,* which has the title "The Food of the Soul," and is divided into three parts. The first discusses the vices which are to be avoided and the virtues which are to be practiced, the second is a discussion of divine love which unites God and the soul, and the third part treats of the sweet ecstasies which that love brings and the visions which the Holy Spirit bestows during the ecstasies, and of the nine orders of angels. And of these, we shall speak first of the vices, so that they may soon be avoided, for someone who is full of vice is not worthy to receive the divine love which the virtuous person can enjoy, as shall be explained later.

There are seven major vices, which are known as deadly sins, being called thus since they bring death to the soul. The death of the soul is being separated from God, who is life to the soul, for as the soul gives life to the body, which is dead without it, so God gives life to the soul, which is dead without him. And so being separated from God through deadly sins is death to the soul. There are seven major vices, which are forms of deadly sin, and which can be represented by one word of seven letters, that is BAKAGILL, in which each letter stands for a whole word. The B stands for *Balchder* (pride), the A for *Anghawrder* (avarice), the K for *Kynghoruynt* (envy), the second A for *Aniweirdeb* (lust), the G stands for *Glythineb* (gluttony), the I for *Irllonedd* (anger) and the LL for *Llesgedd* (indolence). And so all the major sins are represented by a single word: BAKAGILL.

We shall speak now of each of them individually, and show what is known about each together and its branches, starting with pride, which is the beginning of all evil. Pride is an excess of puffed-up desire in the glorification of one's own person through corrupt arrogance of mind, despising those who are lower and rebelling against those who are higher, desiring to draw them down to the same level and to lord oneself over them. Pride has sixteen branches, that is self-love, boasting, self-exaltation, insubordination, presumption, puffing oneself up, abuse, impatience, disobedience, negligence, presumption, mockery, hypocrisy, flippancy, ambition, and vainglory.

Self-love is not being able to bear someone else to be above us or equal to us. Boasting is claiming that we possess something which is not ours. Self-exaltation, or pomposity, is excelling others in words, deeds, or clothes and despising them accordingly. Insubordination is stubbornness of mind from the presumption of not yielding to our better or superior. Presumption is contemplating evil. Puffing ourselves up is disrespectfully contesting the authority or commands of prelates or elders. Abuse, or wrangling, is screaming or shouting dissent against the truth. Impatience is unbridled, turbulent, wild agitation of mind without restraint. Disobedience is insubordination toward prelates or superiors with regard to their commands. Negligence is failing or not taking care to do those things which it is our duty to do. Presumption is refusal of due honor to prelates or elders. Mockery is dissolute and shameful cursing through derision, especially against the Creator. Hypocrisy is concealing forbidden vices by parading strong virtues which do not exist. Flippancy is showing lightness of mind by saying too many empty and foolish things. Ambition is a lust for the honor of fleeting fame. Vanity or vainglory is the wicked glorying in virtues which we do not ourselves possess, or if we do possess them, praising ourselves without giving praise to God for them.

Let us discuss avarice next and its branches. Avarice is too much desire, too much greed to collect worldly goods, without concern as to how they are obtained, preserving them poorly and not giving the excess to the poor. Avarice has sixteen branches, that is, simony, usury, robbery, perjury, theft, lying, rape, compulsion, disturbance, false judgment, presumption, deceit, betrayal, falseness, self-indulgence, and injustice. Simony is buying or selling a spiritual thing, or something that belongs to it. Usury is taking more than what is due by selling the time. Theft is taking someone else's property without their knowledge. Robbery is snatching someone else's property secretly against the will of the owner. Perjury is supporting a lie with an oath. Lying is to tell an untruth to someone in order to deceive them. Rape is despoiling someone of their possessions by compulsion. Compulsion is forcing someone illegally to do what they should not do. Disturbance is exciting another wrongly and without cause. False judgment is giving judgment illegally, on account of love, fear, or desire. Presumption is keeping too much company with evil. Betrayal is cheating another deceitfully, or crafty cunning to cheat someone through flattering dissimulation. Deceit is hidden trickery by cheating someone through feigned friendship. Falseness or cunning is to conceal an evil life by deceitfully parading the appearance of holiness. Self-indulgence is selfishly devoting oneself to collecting worldly goods without entertaining shame or concern for how they are obtained. Injustice is imputing to others vices, weaknesses, or faults in the knowledge that they do not possess them.

Let us discuss envy next and its branches. Envy is poisonous and malign hatred for someone through rejoicing at their misfortune and regretting their good fortune. Jealousy, or envy, has fifteen branches, namely slander, disparagement, backbiting, detraction, defamation, calumny, evil inventions, concealing or oppressing the good, hatred, dishonesty, enmity, bitterness, disunity, ridicule, and accusation. Slander is disparaging someone when they are not present, through reducing their good reputation and increasing their bad one. Disparagement is deceitfully slandering another in their absence. Backbiting is wrangling and slanderous disparagement about the words or actions of others in their absence. Detraction is the malign slander of evil inventions to those in authority or to officers in order to cause another's loss on account of hatred. Defamation is opposing the reputation of another for good deeds and trying to conceal them. Calumny is casting suspicion upon a good deed and putting it in a false light. The concealing or suppression of praise

435

is to hide the good of another when it should be applauded. Evil inventions is knowingly to impute or invent slander against another. Hatred is grudging another's advantage or good fortune. Dishonesty is failing to give credit to another for something good. Bitterness is a poisonous and base thought, lacking all joy. Ridicule is false delight in bringing another down through an intemperate and hateful sense of humor. Accusation is reporting the vice or crime of another to a judge in order to harm them. Enmity is disliking another by wishing them ill. Disunity is hating someone else so much that we do not wish to be one with them in anything whatsoever.

Let us discuss lewdness next, and its branches. Lust is a slippery wildness, a sliding of the mind into filthy, polluting, and carnal desires. Lust has seven branches, that is, fornication, adultery, incest, sin against nature, lechery, obscenity, bestiality. Fornication is all intercourse outside the marriage bed. Adultery is when a married man couples with another woman, or a married woman with another man. Incest is sinning with an immediate male or female relative, or with a relative by marriage, with whom we have a physical or spiritual bond. Sin against nature is spilling male seed in any place other than the one intended for it. Lechery is a sliding of the mind into forbidden and effeminate desires. Obscenity is exhibiting the lewdness of the mind in external signs. Bestiality is sinning with brute animals. There are eight things which induce and excite adultery or lewdness, namely, indolence, rich food, costly drinks, flirting, kissing, amorous words, secret gifts, conversing in private, and the ninth is frequent glances at young women.

Let us treat gluttony next, and its branches. Gluttony is an infinite desire to eat or drink excessively. Gluttony has twelve branches, namely greediness, drunkenness, extravagance, intemperance, incontinence, shamelessness, frivolity, licentiousness, excess, ostentation, repletion, and vomiting. Greediness is consuming too much food. Drunkenness is having too much to drink. Extravagance is squandering what should and should not be given. Intemperance is exceeding the limit laid down for the consumption of food and drink by breaking the fasts set by the

Catholic Church. Incontinence is lusting after too much food or drink. Shamelessness is the use of obscene and irreligious words. Frivolity is saying empty and meaningless words on account of the vanity of indolence. The licentiousness of gluttony is showing external signs of the internal lust of the mind for gluttony. Excess is seeking too many courses of dainty food or too many costly drinks. Ostentation is clothing the body in too much expensive apparel. Repletion is burdening the heart with too many dainties. Vomiting is consuming too much food or drink until it is necessary to bring it up again by vomiting.

Let us discuss anger next and its branches. Anger is a raging and virulent desire immediately to avenge one's wrath against another. Anger has fourteen branches, namely hatred, disunity, abuse, injury, self-love, impatience, ribaldry, maliciousness, wickedness, malevolence, fury, turbulence, ill-nature, murder. Hatred is mental disturbance about someone else on account of being incorrigibly ill-natured. Disunity is distance between those who used to love one another. Abuse is causing injury through words, like growling. Injury is causing harm to another illegally through word or deed. Self-love is wounding each other by reviling each other with angry words. Impatience is an unrestrained and untempered fury of the mind. Ribaldry is breaking out with unseemly and obscene language through sudden agitation of the mind. Maliciousness is causing loss to another by deceitful cunning. Wickedness is daring to harm another with cruelty. Malevolence is wishing another person evil without necessarily being able to carry it out. Fury is losing your reason on account of rage. Turbulence, or excitability, is the slippery instability of the flesh which comes from the frailty of the mind. Ill-nature is showing by facial expression and wicked behavior bitterness and deadliness of mind. Murder is a branch of anger which is expressed in action as when one person takes the life of another.

Murder has six branches. One is that which has been mentioned, actually taking the life of another. The second is harboring a deadly hatred toward somebody else. The third is the evil intention of wishing someone were dead to the extent of not caring if he actually were killed. The fourth is failing to forewarn someone as when someone knows that another intends to commit murder but fails to alert the victim, and lets him go on unwarned. The fifth is giving someone advice on how to kill another. The sixth is stealing food from those who are needy as if someone were to see another dying of hunger, without helping that person despite the power to do so.

Let us discuss indolence next and its branches. Indolence is indifference of mind in failing to do good, being too weary to finish a good act which has been begun, or to fight what is evil. Indolence has nine branches, namely trepidation, laziness, listlessness, neglect, imprudence, indiscretion, drowsiness, stupidity, and vanity. Trepidation is being afraid to embark on a good work. Laziness is being too weary to complete the good work that has been begun. Listlessness is fearing to begin something great and virtuous. Neglect is failing to do what we are bound to do. Imprudence is when we fail to anticipate things which we could have foreseen. Indiscretion is avoiding one kind of sin while we fall into another. Drowsiness is being slow to finish something which we should finish. Stupidity is when we refuse to work to complete the work which we are obliged to do. Vanity is idle chatter.

There are three ways in which sin is committed through these seven vices, that is, in thought, word, and deed, and thereby in one's whole body. An analogy to this can be shown with pride, which is the stem of all vices and which is bred in three ways, namely in respect of the three kinds of good that God has given the human race. These are natural good, accidental good, and spiritual good. In the case of natural good, pride is bred from strength or physical beauty, courage or fluency of speech, voice, or genius. Natural good therefore is those virtues which nature bestows upon us. In the case of accidental good, pride is bred from skill or knowledge or wealth or honor or dignity or lineage or the favor of great men or the praise of nobility or abundance of expensive clothing. All these are accidental and accidental, blessings are those which come by accident. In the case of spiritual good and grace, pride is bred from obedience or patience or civility or nobility or gentleness. Blessings of spirit and grace are powerful spiritual virtues which are granted by the Holy Spirit.

As pride is bred from each one of these, in word, thought, and deed, each one of the other vices is bred from pride in the same way. And just as each one of the vices is a stem to its branches, so too pride is a stem to the seven cardinal vices.

Let us discuss the spiritual virtues next, which are opposed to the vices. There are seven virtues that are contrary to the seven vices and which can be denoted with the single seven-lettered word KUCHADE. *Karyat* (love) gives us the K, which is opposed to envy, the branches of love being opposed to each one of its branches, as is the case with all seven virtues and vices. *Uvuddawt* (obedience) gives us U and is opposed to pride. *Cymhedrolder* (moderation) gives us C and is opposed to gluttony. *Haelyoni* (generosity) gives us H and is opposed to avarice. *Anmyned* (patience) gives us A and is opposed to anger. *Diweirdeb* (chastity) gives us D and is opposed to lust. *Ehutrwyd* (zeal) gives us E and is opposed to indolence.

The cardinal vices are fatal stings which can kill the soul unless there is a remedy to save it. There are three kinds of remedy, that is, repentance by the mind, confession by the tongue, and penance by action, since the vices are bred by thought, word, and deed. And so ends the first part of this book concerning the vices that are to be avoided and the virtues that are to be practiced.

We continue with a discussion of divine love, which serves to join God the Creator with humanity his creation. Firstly, we must know what love is, what the different kinds of love are, and where the source of righteous love lies.

St. Augustine defines love in this way, saying that love is a certain life that joins two things, or desires to join them.[1] There are two kinds of love, that is, affective love, which lasts from eternity, and demonic love, which is transient and of the Devil. The former is directed toward an eternal object and is joined to it in eternity, while the latter is directed toward something which is passing and certain to die, with which it shall itself pass and die. The first love is perfect, since its object is itself perfect and eternal, and is God. The second love is imperfect, since it is imperfect to love something which we could equally well hate and reject. It is necessary to part from what is itself passing. The former is called tender or affectionate love, for the love which eternally unites the lover and his love should be tender and affectionate. But the second is called foolish love, since that love which shall vanish with its lover is indeed foolish. And so that kind of love is to be rejected as being a love that deceives. The first is perfect and honorable desire for it is godly while the other is of the flesh.

And this is the source of this blessed and affectionate love: the Holy Trinity of Heaven, Creator of all things, visible and visible, in him all things are since all things are contained by these three, that is, power and knowledge, or wisdom, and goodness. And these three are attributed to the three Persons of the Trinity. To the Father belongs power, for he is all-powerful and almighty. To the Son belongs wisdom and knowledge, since he is true wisdom and knowledge who assumed human form and who knows all things. And to the Holy Spirit belongs goodness and mercy, since he is all-merciful and since through him and his mercy the Son assumed the human body which was born of the Virgin Mary.

Although each one of these three Persons is perfect God, they are one God in eternal divinity without there being any more or any less divinity in any one of them than another, or in all three Persons together rather than in just one Person, or previously or subsequently in one rather than another, but rather all three Persons are equal in age and exist from eternity. The Trinity is called by a secret name, which is Alpha and Omega. This means *A* and *O*, the beginning and the end. *A* is a triangular letter and signifies the three Persons of the Trinity. At the top point is the Father, while the Son is at the lower point, to the Father's right, since he sits on the right hand of the Father. At the other lower point and to the left is the Holy Spirit, since it is he who conveys the affectionate love between the Father and the Son. *O* is a round letter with neither beginning nor end, since the beginning and end are present everywhere in something that is round, although there is no beginning or end to it. Therefore, there is both beginning and end in the circle, which signifies the one divinity of the three Persons, who are the beginning and end of all things, although there is neither beginning nor end in it. This too is the circle of the Three and the One who is all things, since from him all things come, through him all things come, and in him all things dwell, as the Apostle Paul says.

You can make a model of this by cutting a round block in the following way, namely by cutting a circle in the form of an *O* in which a triangular *A* is cut, placing God the Father at its highest point. Put God the Son at the lower point, on the Father's right. This is Jesus Christ. In the other corner, to his left, place the Holy Spirit in the form of a fiery dove, who signifies the affectionate love that conveys the loving tenderness that is between the Father and the Son, the Son and the Father. The *O* is a round letter, which has neither beginning nor end, since the beginning and end is everywhere on its circumference. This signifies the one divinity of the Three Persons. Mark the place of the Father at the highest point of the circle, in the eastern position, and at the north, to the right of the Father, place the Son. Mark the place of the Holy Spirit on the right, to the left of the Father, emitting or conveying the sparks of fiery love which is the tender love between the Father and the Son. Place the Holy Catholic Church, which is the wedded bride of the only Son of God, in the west, that is at the bottom. She is the Church Triumphant, which is made up of the general hosts of Christ's faithful, the men and women of the Church Militant on earth and the angels of the Church Triumphant which is above.

Further, from the tender love which flames between the Father and the Son (to which the Holy Spirit has been likened, and which he truly is) come the sparks of the Church Triumphant, and from there they pass to the hearts of the faithful who are the Church Militant here below. However small these sparks may be, they cannot be any less but only greater than the whole of creation since, although they are called sparks, they are not less than the whole of the fire from which they come, which is to say the Holy Spirit, who is no less than the unity of the Three Persons together.

This affectionate love is divided into two kinds, the first of which is loving God more than anything, while the second is loving your neighbor as much as you love yourself. It is right to love God more than anything in four ways, namely with the whole of your heart, your soul, your strength, and your mind. "With the whole of your heart" means to love him wisely, until there is nothing in your heart which opposes his love but your whole heart is given to him. This is what he himself commands when he says: "My Son, give me your heart" (Prv 23:26), which is to say the whole of the will of your heart until there is no blood in your heart which would not be shed on account of this love if need be. "With all your soul" means with sweetness and delight until there is no sweetness or delight left in the soul but God himself and no one is loved with righteous love but God himself, or one who should be loved for the sake of his love. "With the whole of your strength" means steadfastly so that there is nothing that shall separate you from the love of God. "With the whole of your mind" means mindfully so that his love never passes from your mind and you never forget that you should love God more than anything.

You should love your neighbors as much as yourself. This means that you should not wish them ill any more than you do yourself, and what you wish for yourself, you should wish also for them. Do not allow your neighbors to suffer more want or need than you do yourself, insofar as you are able, nor should you let yourself be corrupted by loving them more than you do yourself to the extent of leaving nothing in your possession to sustain yourself but giving it all to ease their need. You should love no one more than you love yourself, except God, although you should love your neighbor as much as you do yourself.[2]

Your neighbor is each one of Christ's faithful people, that is, every faithful Christian, but primarily everyone who has done you good, although you are more bound to your parents and family than you are to strangers. You are more bound to love your spiritual parents and family too, such as clerics and religious, than your own physical family, since the spirit is superior to the flesh. But chiefly, if you are yourself the member of an Order, then you should love your brethren and your spiritual fathers.

Every other kind of love which is fixed upon another creature,

442

and not upon God, is foolish love, which does not come from the sparks of the Holy Spirit. And since it does not come from the circle of the Trinity, which is everything, it is centered on nothingness and with nothingness it is lost. For nothingness is the absence and contrary of everything that is. For this reason it is outside the circle of everything, and with it is sin, for sin and nothingness are the same thing.[3] This is why persistent sinners are lost forever in their sins, in nothingness, since they turn from what is something by fixing their foolish love on nothingness and are thus united with it. Further, just as the foolish love, which is as insubstantial as impermanence and sin, unites the lover with nothingness, so too the affectionate love, which is eternal and substantial, unites the lover to God, who is all that is, from eternity. Therefore, through that tender love which comes from the sparks of the Holy Spirit, who is the tender love of the Father for the Son and the Son for the Father, humanity, the creature, is united with the Creator, who is God Almighty. Thus the second part of this book comes to a close, namely that which treats of divine love.

Let us continue with the third part, which concerns the ecstasies and trances that come from the divine love, and the nine orders of angels.

When you have practiced the virtues of which we have spoken, by escaping the vices and renouncing them, and, if you have fallen into them, have healed their stings through the remedies mentioned above, then you must give yourself wholly, heart, soul, and mind, to the precious and divine love of which we have spoken. While you should love each of the Three Persons as much as the others, and all three together as much as any single one, and each single one as much as all three together, nevertheless, on account of kinship, proximity of relation, and the recognition of your own fleshly being and likeness, it is easier for you to put your trust in the Son than in the Father or Holy Spirit. For he it was who took on our flesh and was begotten by the Holy Spirit and was born of the Virgin Mary. Because of this, he is our brother, while God the Father is a father to us and the Holy Spirit is a foster-father to us, for his love is food for our soul.

THE FOOD OF THE SOUL

This is what the friar was told in his dreams. For a certain friar of the Order of Friars Preacher was doing penance, placing all his trust in the Trinity of heaven and with all his heart's desire was accustomed in his mind to kiss repeatedly the feet of each of the Three Persons individually, just as if he had held them in his hands. Then one day, in the morning, when he was in a trance, he heard a voice which was clear and sweet, loving and fair, speaking to him, saying: "You do well to love each of us separately, but since it is difficult for you to conceive of the feet of the Father and of the Holy Spirit and to know these, delight lovingly in the Son and caress him since he is one of your own kind, who was born for you and suffered for you. What you do for him is acceptable to us and you do it for us as well as for him, for we are one with him, and three together." And then the friar lovingly beseeched the Trinity of heaven to show him something to treasure perpetually in undying memory of the blessed child, holy and divine, by trusting steadfastly in the Trinity that he would indeed receive that for which he asked intensely and righteously by worthy prayer.

And then, after some time had lapsed and the Feast of the Trinity came in the summer, one morning, when the friar had been praying fervently to the Trinity after community matins until the break of day, the friar, who had long since been released from his penance, fell into a spiritual trance. And in this trance he saw, as it seemed to him, that the whole world was on the top of a high hill and everyone was quaking with fear at the mighty vision that was about to appear. The friar saw how the whole sky parted and opened, releasing a brilliant sun of immense splendor. On its highest part he saw something like a shining sky, which filled everyone with great fear, for it could be brilliant or dark as it wished. On the left-hand side of that bright shining sky there was a radiant flame, slow, fair, and lovely, which conveyed the burning light between the sun and its rays. On the right-hand side of the first sky the rays of the sun shone brightly and illumined the whole of the world.

And then the friar was told: "The round sun that you saw without end and without beginning is the unity of the Three Persons of the Trinity. The highest shining sky of which everyone was afraid is the Father of heaven, whom we should all fear like a child, fearing, that is, that we might oppose him or offend him, as a child fears its father, through love, in case he should offend him. The radiant flame of fire of the other sky is the Holy Spirit, which is fire that conveys the tender love between the Father and the Son, and the brilliant shining ray on the right-hand side is the one Son of God, who is the radiance and light of the whole world. And in this way too the circle could and should be inscribed, as was explained above.

And then the friar prayed passionately, with tears, that he might be shown the Son more clearly than before. The next moment, he heard a sweet and clear voice saying: "Come, behold the Son appearing to you." And immediately he could see in the brilliant shining light a ray in the image of a Son of Man, an infinite, boundless, and eternal love, a great radiance of his perfect beauty, as if twelve years old, the age at which the blessed Lord Jesus first began to teach in the Temple, and the varied splendor of the precious loveliness of his radiant and rosy cheeks increasing to such an extent that no creature could look upon him without falling immediately into a faint of love and great desire for such perfect, noble, and divine beauty. And no wonder, for it is eternal life, unending immortality, to look upon that divine and noble face. And while no creature could keep in its memory or mind a hundred-thousandth part of the brilliance of the shining beauty that was his, nevertheless the following is what the friar could retain of the loveliness of the Heavenly Son and his glorious form.

THE BEAUTY OF THE SON

The Son was a fair, blond child of slender build, twelve years old and of medium height, the appearance and dimensions of his body being those of a child of that age. His head was graceful and almost perfectly round, covered with shining curls of golden yellow hair, just as if you could make or envisage two hanks of fine yarn or thin leaves of burnished gold extending more than a span on either side of the two bright faces, with the hair on the forehead cut in the shape of a horseshoe. The hair was cut high

445

enough on the side of the head to expose the two ears, and on the nape of the neck leading up to the fair and graceful crown of the head as far as the front. Smooth, clean-combed, and lustrous, it supported the golden crown, with a white forehead, level and smooth, even and broad, the color of mother of pearl, and as wide as a hand-breadth of the largest man on earth and a large span in length from one temple to the other. Beneath the forehead there were two pure, bright eyebrows, long, fine, and black, like two slivers of gleaming jet set in a huge surround of crystal or pearl, the brightest possible, or like two slender plaits of fine black silk gleaming against two sleeves of the most brilliant scarlet. And between both eyebrows there was a radiant mark, like a bright pearl, shining at the center of a mace of gleaming balsam wood. And then, beneath the eyelids, brilliant with different colors, as on the eyebrows, there were two ruby-colored eyes, red as pomegranate and like a hawk's eyes, from which there flowed the tears of tender love, like tiny drops of dew in the month of May, or tiny beads of quicksilver, and all because of his affectionate love toward his faithful creatures. These tears were called the dew of the Holy Spirit, and they fell into the hearts of penitents who performed their penance worthily. This was the certain sign that they received the grace of the Holy Spirit and his perfect tender love. Between his ruby eyes there was a small, round, delicate mouth and a nose that was symmetrical and straight, emitting affectionate love by the slow, sweet movements of his divine nostrils. And around that heavenly nose there was a radiantly shining face as round as the span of the biggest man and as broad. So blessed was that face and so fair that no bodily creature of heaven or earth could be likened to it. It was like white snow at Epiphany, or white roses, or lilies, or apple-blossom, or highland gossamer, or fresh shoots, or a splendid sun in the sky, or an evening moon, or the sailors" star, or Venus when it is most beautiful in the firmament, or a summer's sun when it shines most clearly and brightly at midday in June. And then there were two pure bright red cheeks, round and rosy, as radiant as the dawn on a summer's day, or as two red roses, or an evening sun setting over a mountain of shining gold, or a bright red wine

446

sparkling through fine glass. And so the clear redness of his two cheeks perfected the brilliance of his blessed face, and the brilliance of his blessed face highlighted the beauty of his clear red cheeks, and all together intensified the radiance of his yellow hair, thick and flowing, which in turn drew out the gentle beauty in them. And then the shining blackness of his eyebrows and eyelids increased each other's brightness, and both together intensified the beauty of his whole body, just as the beauty of his whole body intensified their beauty. Then the noble child had two lips which excited perfect love for everyone and perfect love in everyone for the child, protruding a little in the desire for loving kisses from his faithful creatures, and shining out of them, when the protrusion of the loving lips quivered, were what looked like sparks that rise from a scented fire of dry bundles of wood, with all manner of savor and taste so that no sugar nor digestive powder nor first crop of honey nor claret could compare with it. These are called the loving sparks of the Holy Spirit, and where they fell into the hearts of the faithful, they caused the intense desire of the precious love of the Holy Spirit. And then, in his small, rounded, and delicate mouth there were small, white, well-spaced teeth with bright red gums and a smooth, sweet tongue eloquent of speech. And below the short, round, graceful mouth there was a round, smooth, and even chin and beneath this a round neck, long and comely, and beneath that long white arms, rounded and shapely, with shoulders equally rounded and fine. And below that two long white hands, bright and smooth with short pink nails and long, slender, elegant fingers, immeasurably bright and lustrous. A rising, martial breast and a noble, lion-like body with a slender and noble waist. Then stout white thighs of strong build with rounded knees between them with long white legs of regular and symmetrical shape except that their calves were thicker near the knees than in their thin part. And beneath these, there were long, white, and delicate feet with white, dainty, and rounded toes. And then the tenderness of all the spiritual flesh was graceful and bright, begotten of the Holy Spirit and blessedly born of the Virgin Mary, fulfilling the correspondence of all faithful flesh with him in eternal love of affection.

And that child of such lovely beauty was clothed in this way, with a gown and trousers of fine, shimmering Stinos (a precious stone from farthest Spain that can be spun and garments made of the thread which, when soiled, are cleansed in fire—they last forever and are called Uriel since the Hebrew word *Ur* means "fire" in Welsh). On both sleeves were buttons of pure gold, from the wrist to the elbow, and precious rubies in each button. And so the garment lay on his chest, from his chin to his waist, with a shirt and breeches of fine white bissum, bissum being a fine linen from Egypt. He wore shoes of finest black Spanish leather, which signify the human flesh which he put on from the dark earth, with golden buckles tied around his instep and plates of gold covered in bright gems extending from the instep to the tips of his toes. And over that bright white coat, which signified the radiant innocence of the virgins, there was a robe of brocaded silk, red as flame, died in the blood of one hundred and forty-four thousand martyrs, innocent children who were killed in seeking Christ in his name before one of them was two years old.

And all these children surrounded him, singing praise to him, as no one above or below the earth could sing him praise. And the meaning of the praise they sang, as far as the friar could tell, was this:

> We thank you, O Lord, for your gifts,
> We children, of powerless youth,
> Had we become old, or grown into men,
> We would without mercy have been lost.
> You defended us when you gave to us.
> You made our blood, fruitful creation.
> Great was your love for us, you baptized us
> From our bloodstained bodies, highest state.
> Christ, heavenly Lord, when we praise you,
> Hear our prayer, our blood petitions.
> Before being tried, we won,
> By you grace, the test of victory.
> Blood, lacking tongue or strength of flesh,
> And heart's strength of the human race,
> Sings praise to God of the Trinity,
> Excellent unity, divine dwelling.

True praise to the generous Father,
And to the Holy Spirit, perfect song.
Childhood praise by the children of the world
For blessed Mary's Son of joy.
The outpouring of our splendid praise
Sings a song, blood without a word;
To a communion of Three Persons
Of everlasting unity it is made. Amen.

That is what the children, virgin martyrs, sang constantly and without pause. And on that robe of flame-red brocaded silk there was a fur of ermine with fine spots: Some signified the priests, some brilliant ones the virgins, some piercing ones the celibate penitent. A cord of gold thread ran from shoulder to shoulder, supported by a garnet on each shoulder, and the robe was edged with a border of gold of a hand's width covered with rubies and jewels embedded in the gold. Around his body there was a band of exquisite work, woven from fine golden thread, studded with precious jewels, with a pin of shining garnet, a clasp of red gold, and a brilliant pearl at its end. There was nothing attached to it except a golden seal engraved with a shield, the cross, the nails, the crown of thorns, the spear, and other instruments of Christ's suffering. It is with this that the hearts of Christ's faithful are sealed as are their names in the Book of Life. Upon the head of the excellent child there was a crown of perfect gold and, set in the gold, twelve stones of the most precious imperial kind. The lovely child was sitting in an ornate chair of brilliant white ivory to which were attached on all sides the blades of spears of refined red gold, covered with every kind of imperial and most precious stone. Beneath him, around him, and under his feet there were a variety of brocaded pillows, some of silk and some of threaded gold. In his right hand he held a shining gold scepter and under his hand on top of the staff there was a bright, clear garnet, with another upon his hand. From that point upward the staff was divided into three sections to show the Three Persons of the Trinity who, from the one body of an undivided divinity, rule the three regions of the universe: heaven, earth, and hell. And when the lovely child breathed the

449

spirit of his divine love, sweet perfumes fell on all around, to which neither the scents of roses or lilies, or any fruit or herb, neither myrrh nor gum nor balm, cinnamon nor cassia nor any precious oil, could be compared. And thus the blessed and heavenly child filled the five senses with love for his merits: his infinite beauty filling sight, the delight of his slow, sweet speech filling hearing, the sparks of sweetness which came from the rise of his lips and the small tears from his eyes that fell into their hearts filling taste, the spiritual exhalation of his breath filling smell, and the tenderness of his spiritual flesh, conceived by the Holy Spirit and born of the Virgin Mary, filling the fifth sense of the whole body, which is touch. And no wonder that the Creator should fill the five senses with his merits.

And then the friar fell down before the golden boy in a faint of great love for that divine child, who raised him up compassionately, saying: "Arise and love me further as much as you can." "O Lord," said the friar, "it is no credit to me that I love you for no one could look upon you without loving you." "Not so," he said, "since I would not have appeared to you if you had not loved me. You do not love me as much as I love you, but you have not seen me wholly. When you do see me, you will love me differently. And tell the poets, to whom I have given a share in the spirit of my delightfulness, that it would be better for them to return to this spirit to worship me rather than praising foolish love for the vain and transient things that all pass away."

"Further, since by the divine love of his precious affection the Holy Spirit grants spiritual visions in trances and ecstasies which come from that affectionate love, you should know how it is that they can come.

"Firstly, when you desire them to come, you should be certain that you are without sin by believing the true faith of the Holy Catholic Church and have complete hope in the Creator, winning merit in his eyes by your deserving religious works and true love toward God and your neighbor. You should turn from vices and practice efficacious deeds, preparing and ordering yourself in your bed after matins or after midnight following the first sleep or the second. And you should be sure that your spirit is calm and collected, with neither excess or need.

"Then through true love and the whole desire of your heart, you should let your mind dwell on the great beauty of the divine child mentioned above, imagining that he is between your arms and you between his arms, embracing and caressing him in steadfast faith and trust. And then, by praying to him, call lovingly upon the Holy Spirit by saying this hymn to him and letting your heart dance and hop for him with the whole will of affectionate love:[4]

Come Spirit, holy Creator of the world, illustrious Lord of worlds, into our hearts and breasts, privileged ruler. Visit our mind, turn our purpose, gloriously mighty pledge. Fill all of us with your love with a strong hand. You bless us and comfort us, the most comforting, the fountain of living grace, the gift of the Lord, the Father, from the highest region above; fire of love and purity of the holy golden temple; finger of God's right hand; fair harvest of wise words; seven-fold gift of diverse kinds; most heavenly blessing, which grants us fluid speech, measured and slow. Kindle for us, mysterious One, bright light of heaven, the color of a summer's sun; pour kindly most lively affection into our senses; strengthen us against arrogance through valiant strength. Drive the enemy far away from all, human harm; give us peace through joy by a term of rich service, so that we may shun every deceit and bad feeling, every hurt and all wickedness of the fierce dragon; grant us to know the Father through you, most divine service, and the Blessed Son, and the most spiritual Holy Ghost. Praise and honor to the Father, abundance and most gentle dominion; praise without ceasing to the only Son of Mary, fairest virgin; and may the Son of the Lord of Christendom, Highest Creator, send us the beloved fire of the Holy Spirit, most precious jewel.

"And then devote yourself to caressing the blessed child with all your might, just as if he were physically between your arms, until by the power of that affectionate love you begin to feel a kind of tingling in the nerves and veins and through the whole of your body, and in the throat like sips of honey from the comb of the first swarm, and in the heart as a pleasant, gentle love, causing it

451

to sing hymns or dance from the strength of the pleasure of that precious, sweet, and affectionate love.

"You should know too that the small sparks of the Holy Spirit mentioned above which rise from the protruding lips of the holy child land on your neck and breast, and the tiny drops of dew of the Holy Spirit mentioned above, which well like small tears from his red eyes, enter your heart. Devote yourself more and more to that sweet love by closely embracing the dear child. It is arrogance for anyone to think of embracing him; remember then that his affectionate mercy loves to embrace you more, to love you more, than you can think of embracing and loving him. And then remember clearly that your mind must not turn to anything carnal or to anything else but to him alone. Then call as constantly as you can upon these mystical names, revering them truly and lovingly in your mind and believing in their potency: Messias + Sother + Emanuel + Tetragrammaton + Sabaoth + Adonai + Alpha + & O + Agios + Amen Alleluia +. And by calling constantly and lovingly upon these precious names, devote yourself still more to the affectionate love of the heavenly child until you begin to feel all about you the sweet and delicate fragrance of incense, filling the whole of your nostrils and your soul with delight in that savor.

"Then know that his spiritual breath comes to you until you know that he is physically present with you, although you cannot see him.

"Then call constantly upon the above names with all your will until you begin to fall into frequent ecstasies which mean more to you than the whole world.

"Then, if you cannot do this on account of some affectionate love, call upon all the names, calling always upon the blessed name of Jesus, the only son of the Virgin Mary.

"And then, if you hear some delightful and most sweet singing, know that it is the angels who sing. And if you see a brilliant white cloud suddenly filling your whole gaze and your whole heart with the tender love of eternal life, vibrantly radiant as a flash of lightning, know that it is he himself in his spiritual and triumphant incarnation who is there.

THE FOOD OF THE SOUL

"And then call upon Jesus, the only son of the Virgin Mary, until you fall into a sweet and delightful trance from the frequent sweet ecstasies mentioned above.

"And then, if you see in that trance a sleep sweeter and deeper than the first coming upon you, know that you are outside your physical being in spiritual and divine sleep.

"And then, if your senses return before the agreeable sweetness of that sleep, call lovingly upon the name of Jesus in your mind, since you cannot utter it.

"And then, if you see that you seem to receive in that slumber another unbroken sleep which is sweeter and deeper than all the others, then give yourself wholly to the Spirit, and the vision that you see in it will be true, for it comes from the Holy Spirit. You must not speak of it to anyone except your private companion in faith, nor should you boast about it in case it does not come again. That sleep is called the sleep victorious, since it is a victory to receive it and they who do so are themselves victorious. The chief time for you to seek it is on Saturday after midnight, close to dawn, or between night and day, after you have prepared yourself by fasting and prayer on Friday and Saturday and by holy confession have devoted yourself to the blessed Trinity of heaven.

"And then, on that day, that is, Sunday, receive the Communion of the body of Christ. And on that night, by the honor of the Trinity and by the power and miracles of the body of Christ, it may be that you will receive another sleep, sweeter than the first, with a vision that is more perfect.

"And then, thank the Trinity by saying these words:

> Let praise and glory be sung—a hymn
> To the Trinity, Unity, One Divinity,
> Let marvelous rejoicing be given—together
> To Father, Son and Spirit of splendor."

THE NINE ORDERS OF ANGELS

Let us turn now to the nine orders of angels and what sort of men and women should be compared with each of those orders.

The Hebrew word for angels is *Malaoth,* that is, "messengers," for they convey and spread abroad God's will for his people. Holy Scripture says that they have nine orders, namely Angels, Archangels, Thrones, Lordships, Principalities, Dominions, Powers, Cherubim, and Seraphim.[5]

Angels reveal to men and women the small messages that they are commanded to tell, and with them are placed those who know a little of divine things and who teach this with love and mercy to others.

Archangels are the princes of the angels, for they tell the greatest things. Some of them received their names according to their services, such as these three: Michael, Gabriel, and Raphael. Michael is translated as "one like God," or the "power of God." He is sent to where there are miracles or marvelous things. Gabriel is translated as "the strength of God." He is sent where divine strength is shown, as he was sent to tell the Virgin Mary that she was full of the power of the Holy Spirit. Raphael is translated as "the remedy of God." He is sent to where the soul or the body needs healing, as he was sent to heal old Tobias's blindness. With the archangels are placed those who know the secrets of heavenly commandments and who tell and teach them to others with love and mercy.

Principalities are those that have hosts of angels and archangels under them, performing the services of God, and who were seated with him. With them are classed those who practice spiritual virtues beyond all others and who by their virtues govern their fellow-elect.

Dominions are those to whom the strength of all the opposing angels is subject so that they cannot harm the world at will. With these are classed those people to whom the Holy Spirit gives power to cast out devils and evil spirits from the hearts of others.

Thrones are seats on which the Creator sits when passing judgments and laws. With these are classed those men and women who control themselves, their actions and thoughts, by giving themselves to the fear of God so that they can fairly judge others and the Lord God may be able through them to excel the works of their brothers.

Lordships are those who surpass principalities, and with them are classed pure men and women who by their purity and love overcome all vices and desires of the flesh.

Heavenly powers are certain virtues or wonderful miracles performed by the host of angels in this world and with them are classed men and women who perform miracles and wonders and signs of virtues.

Cherubim are high authorities over the angels, and they are called the angels of miracles or wonders and are, when translated, a multitude of forms of knowledge or abundance of forms of skill, and with them are classed those who are full of heavenly knowledge and spiritual skill in knowing the Trinity of heaven.

Seraphim are the multitude or abundance of affectionate love for God, excelling all the orders of angels, and, when translated, mean a kindling fire, for between them and God there is no other order of angels, since the nearer to God the greater the burning light of the fire of love. With these are classed men and women who so burn with affectionate love that they forgive all things for his sake. Therefore they are closest to God who love him most.

It is through that love, therefore, that God and man are united. And as God is life to the soul, so too his love is food for the soul, for as the human soul departs from the physical body if the body does not have its earthly food, in the same way God departs from the soul if the soul does not receive its heavenly food, that is divine, sweet, and worthy love. May the Holy Spirit grant us that perfect love, who is true love, conveying affection between the Father and the Son and who dwells in unity with them forever and ever. Amen.

And so ends the book called "The Food of the Soul," which is the third book of the volume which is called the *Holy Sanctuary of Life*. Let a circle be drawn here of the nine orders of angels, as is fitting for each, and in the highest order the only Son of God, as he has been described above, eagerly embracing his faithful.

Abbreviations

Apocrypha	McNamara, M., *The Apocrypha in the Irish Church* (Dublin, 1975).
B	*Bulletin of the Board of Celtic Studies.*
Blodeugerdd	Haycock, M., *Blodeugerdd Barddas o Ganu Crefyddol Cynnar* (Cyhoeddiadau Barddas, 1994).
CCSL	*Corpus Christianorum Series Latina* (Turnhout, 1953–).
Celtic Christianity	Davies, O., *Celtic Christianity in Early Medieval Wales* (Cardiff, 1995).
Church	Hughes, K., *The Church in Early Irish Society* (London, 1966).
CMCS	*Cambridge Medieval Celtic Studies.*
CSEL	*Corpus Scriptorum Ecclesiasticorum Latinorum* (Vienna, 1866–).
DS	*Dictionnaire de Spiritualité ascétique et mystique* (Paris, 1932–).
E	*Ériu.*
EC	*Etudes celtiques.*
ECA	*Encyclopaedia of Cultural Anthropology* (ed. D. Levinson and M. Ember) (New York, 1996).
GPC	*Geiriadur Prifysgol Cymru* (Cardiff, 1950–).
HGC	Lewis, H., ed., *Hen Gerddi Crefyddol* (Cardiff, 1931).
IBA	Herbert, M., and McNamara, M., *Irish Biblical Apocrypha* (Edinburgh, 1989).

ABBREVIATIONS

JRSAI	*Journal of the Royal Society of Antiquaries of Ireland.*
Liturgy	Warren, F. E., *The Liturgy and Ritual of the Celtic Church* (2nd ed. by J. Stevenson) (Woodbridge, 1987).
LlC	*Llên Cymru.*
LlD	Jarman, A. O. H., ed., *Llyfr Du Caerfyrddin* (Cardiff, 1982).
LThK	*Lexikon für Theologie und Kirche* (Freiburg, 1957–).
L&S	Lapidge, M., and Sharpe, R., eds., *A Bibliography of Celtic-Latin Literature 400–1200* (Dublin, 1985).
MWRL	McKenna, C. A., *The Medieval Welsh Religious Lyric: Poems of the Gogynfeirdd 1137–1282* (Belmont, Mass., 1991).
PBA	*Proceedings of the British Academy.*
PL	*Patrologiae cursus completus, series latina,* (ed. J.-P. Migne) (Paris, 1844–1864).
PRIA	*Proceedings of the Royal Irish Academy.*
RC	*Revue celtique.*
Sources	Kenney, J. F., *The Sources for the Early History of Ireland: Ecclesiastical* (Dublin, 1979).
Th. Pal.	Stokes, W., and Strachan, J., *Thesaurus Palaeohibernicus* vol. II (repr. Dublin, 1975).
YB	Williams J. E., Ysgrifau Beimiadol (Denbigh, Flintshire; 1965–)
ZCP	*Zeitschrift für celtische Philologie.*

Notes

NOTES TO THE PREFACE

1. See my "Magic and Celtic Primal Religion," ZCP 45 (1992): 62–84.

2. The term *primal* seems to have been imported into the study of Celtic Christianity from Edinburgh University's Centre for the Study of Christianity in the Non-Western World, in the course of arguing the case for a distinctive version of Christianity truly incultured in pre-Christian religio-cultural categories. But it is not an uncontroversial term. See my "Christian Past and Primal Present," EC 29 (1992): 285–97; James L. Cox, "The Classification 'Primal Religions,'" and David Turner, "Aboriginal Religion as World Religion," both in *Studies in World Christianity* 2 (1996): 55–76 and 77–96.

NOTES TO THE INTRODUCTION

1. The existence of a "Celtic Church" has been questioned in particular by Kathleen Hughes, "The Celtic Church: Is This a Valid Concept?" in CMCS (1981), pp. 1–20, and Wendy Davies, "The Myth of the Celtic Church," in *The Early Church in Wales and the West,* ed. Nancy Edwards and Alan Lane (Oxbow, 1992), pp. 12–21.

2. E.g., Patrick Sims-Williams, "Some Celtic Otherworld Terms," in *Celtic Language, Celtic Culture: A Festschrift for Eric P. Hemp* (Oxford California, 1990), pp. 57–81. Gerald of Wales in the twelfth century certainly recognized Breton as a language cognate with Welsh, and the author of the ninth-century *Cormac's Glossary* notes some similarities in vocabulary between the Irish and Welsh languages of his day (Whitley Stokes, ed., *Cormac's Glossary* [Calcutta, 1868]). Although early Irish and Welsh were far from mutually comprehensible, we may assume that knowledge of either language facilitated acquisition of the other, just as it does today.

3. It was used primarily of the ancient inhabitants of Gaul, though not of Britain. See J. Rhys, "Celtae and Galli," PBA (1905–1906), pp. 71–134.

4. H. D. Rankin, "The Celts through Classical Eyes," in *The Celtic World,* ed. M. Green (London, 1995), pp. 21–33, especially pp. 22–23.

5. Colin Renfrew, *Archaeology and Language* (Harmondsworth, 1987), p. 219.

6. E.g., G. T. Stokes, *Ireland and the Celtic Church: A History of Ireland from St. Patrick to the English Conquest in 1172* (London, 1886); and John Dowden, *The Celtic Church in Scotland* (London, 1894). See also *Sources,* pp. 108–109, for a bibliographical overview.

7. This has found fresh expression recently in the emergence of a new geopolitical term: "the Atlantic Arc." This designates the northwestern European seaboard from the British Isles and Ireland down to southwest Portugal, which constitutes a vulnerable economic periphery within the European Union.

8. A good discussion of these terms and their origin can be found in ECA, pp. 382–385.

9. Aristotle and Polybius attributed the quality of *thymos* to the Celts, a word Plato employs in the sense of "passionate arousal" or "excitability" (Aristotle, *Eudemian Ethics* 1229b.28; Polybius II. 22). See H. D. Rankin, *Celts and the Classical World* (London, 1987), pp. 55–56.

10. Rankin, "The Celts through Classical Eyes," p. 28.

11. Pliny, *Natural History,* xvi, 95.

12. Gwyn A. Williams, *Madoc* (Oxford, 1987).

13. For an account of the Ossian controversy and the evolution of Celtic romanticism in general, see Malcolm Chapman, *The Celts* (New York, 1992), pp. 120–145.

14. Gwyn A. Williams, *When Was Wales?* (Harmondsworth, 1985), pp. 159–172.

15. For a history of this theme, see in particular Patrick Sims-Williams, "The Visionary Celt: The Construction of an Ethnic Preconception," in CMCS 11 (1986), pp. 71–96; and Stuart Piggott, *Ancient Britons and the Antiquarian Imagination* (London, 1989).

16. See Malcolm Chapman, *The Celts* (New York, 1992); and Marion MacDonald, *"We Are Not French!" Language, Culture and Identity in Brittany* (London, 1989). Both examine the romantic roots of "Celtic" as an ethnic signifier today. But in the case of Celtic communities today, neither takes due account of the role of language in the preservation of culture. A minority language that is linked to a subversive oral culture

can—far more than is the case with majority languages—prove a formidably conservative force in the construction, or preservation, of cultural perspectives and traditions.

17. Interestingly, Ussher believed that the religion of the Irish and Scots was the same as that of the Britons. Neither author, of course, uses the term *Celtic*. Glanmor Williams surveys this literature in "Some Protestant Views of Early British Church History" in his *Welsh Reformation Essays* (Cardiff, 1967), pp. 207–219.

18. See note 1 above. G. Márkus and Th. O. Clancy are also skeptical (*Iona: The Earliest Poetry of a Celtic Monastery* [Edinburgh, 1995] pp. 8–9).

19. See Jeremy Ahearne, *Michel de Certeau: Interpretation and Its Other* (Cambridge, 1995), p. 17.

20. Literary and theological texts written in Welsh in the thirteenth century, which are well represented here, cannot be said to be "insular."

21. See *Sources*, pp. 170–182, for the relevant bibliographies.

22. L. Bieler, *Irish Penitentials* (Dublin, 1975), pp. 3, 12–13; A. Wilmart, *Reg. Lat 49: Catéchèses Celtiques*, in *Studi e Testi*, Vol. 59 (Vatican, 1933), pp. 30–31. For a discussion of a number of points of contact between the Irish and British churches, especially the Hiberno-Breton link, see D. Dumville, "Some British Aspects of the Earliest Irish Christianity," in *Irland und Europa*, ed. P. Ní Catháin and M. Richter (Stuttgart, 1984), pp. 16–24.

23. K. McKone has argued that the contribution of native culture to the Christianity of early Ireland is minimal in his monumental, though controversial, study *Pagan Past and Christian Present in Early Irish Literature* (Maynooth, 1991). McKone gives a useful summary of the "nativist and nonnativist" debate (pp. 1–28).

24. For early Celtic religion in general, see Graham Webster, *The British Celts and Their Gods under Rome* (London, 1986); Miranda Green, *The Gods of the Celts* (New Haven, 1993); and Nora Chadwick, *The Celts* (London, 1971), pp.141–185.

25. Jean Louis Brunaux, *The Celtic Gauls: Gods, Rites and Sanctuaries* (London, 1988); and Barry Cunliffe, *The Celtic World* (London, 1992), pp. 88–95. For a counter view, see Jane Webster, "Sanctuaries and Sacred Places," in *The Celtic World*, M. Green ed. (London, 1995), pp. 445–464.

26. Marged Haycock, *Rhai Agweddau ar Lyfr Taliesin*, University of Wales Ph.D., 1982, Vol. 2, p. 620. See also *Celtic Christianity*, pp. 77–79.

27. *Gildas: The Ruin of Britain and Other Works*, ed. and trans. Michael Winterbottom (London, 1978), p. 17.

28. Miranda Green, *Symbol and Image in Celtic Religious Art* (London and New York, 1989), pp. 131–168.

29. *Dictionary of the Irish Language*, Royal Irish Academy, s.v. *tuigen.*

30. In Wales this is represented most clearly by the Taliesin tradition; see Patrick K. Ford, *Ystoria Taliesin* (Cardiff, 1992), pp. 1–46. For shamanism in general, see ECA, pp. 1182–1186.

31. For a discussion of a number of poems from the *Book of Taliesin* in which this seems to be the case, see *Celtic Christianity*, pp. 79–80.

32. Kathleen Hughes, *The Church in Early Irish Society* (London, 1966), pp. 65–78.

33. There is a parallel here with the German work *Der Heliand*, which dates from the early ninth century, though here heroic age motifs are incorporated into an essentially Christian text.

34. Gerald of Wales, *Description of Wales*, I, 10, 18. On triple figures in Celtic religion in general, see Green, *Symbol and Image in Celtic Religious Art*, pp. 169–205.

35. The anthropologist Aloysius Pieris has set up an opposition between "cosmic religions" (where religion is the product of an integral environment) and "metacosmic" or world religions, and has argued that it is only when a worldwide religion fuses with a cosmic one that the former will take root. This process is not necessarily to be identified with syncretism, which implies a coexistence or amalgam of religious forms, but can in fact lead to a particular instantiation of the world religion, which acquires new emphases under the influence of the earlier religious beliefs and structures (A. Pieris, *An Asian Theology of Liberation* [Edinburgh, 1988]).

36. On the role of Iona as center of continental learning in the insular world, see Thomas O'Loughlin, "The Library of Iona in the Late Seventh Century: The Evidence of Adomnán's *De Locis Sanctis*," E 45 (1994), pp. 33–52.

37. For this and other historical texts, see Liam de Paor, *St. Patrick's World* (Dublin, 1993).

38. For a good general discussion of the Patrick tradition and recent bibliography, see D. Dumville, ed., *St. Patrick. AD 493–1993* (Woodbridge, England 1993).

39. J. N. Hillgarth, "Old Ireland and Visigothic Spain," in *Old Ireland*, R. McNally ed. (Dublin, 1965), pp. 200–227; and "Ireland and Spain in the Seventh Century," in *Peritia* 3 (1984), pp. 1–16.

40. Hughes, *The Church in Early Irish Society*, pp. 44–56.

41. We still await a comprehensive and up-to-date study of the organizational aspects of the early Irish Church. R. Sharpe has challenged the received view, which derives from the work of K. Hughes, in his article "Some Problems concerning the Organization of the Church in Early Medieval Ireland," *Peritia* 3 (1984), pp. 230–270. On the situation in Wales, see Hughes, "The Celtic Church: Is This a Valid Concept?" and T. Charles-Edwards, "The Seven Bishop-Houses of Dyfed," *Bulletin of the Board of Celtic Studies* 24 (1970–1972), pp. 247–262.

42. Hughes, *The Church in Early Irish Society,* pp. 75–78.

43. For a history of the monastic *familia* of Columba, see M. Herbert, *Iona, Kells and Derry* (Oxford, 1988).

44. Michael Richter, *The Enduring Tradition* (London, 1988), p. 95.

45. P. Riché, "Columbanus, His Followers and the Merovingian Church," in *Columbanus and Merovingian Monasticism,* ed. H. B. Clarke and M. Brennan (Oxford, 1981), pp. 59–72.

46. P. O'Dwyer, *Céli Dé: Spiritual Reform in Ireland 750–900* (Dublin, 1981).

47. A. Gwynn, "Irish Monks and the Cluniac Reform" and "The Coming of the Normans," repr. in *The Irish Church in the Eleventh and Twelfth Centuries* (Dublin, 1992), pp. 1–16 and pp. 271–311.

48. Charles Thomas, *Christianity in Roman Britain to AD 500* (London, 1981), pp. 42–50.

49. E. A. Thompson, *St. Germanus of Auxerre and the End of Roman Britain* (Woodbridge, 1984), pp. 15–19.

50. Alternatively, he may have been born in the Irish-speaking communities of southwest Wales. See *Sources,* pp. 161–163 for texts and discussion.

51. Thomas, *Christianity in Roman Britain,* pp. 249–294; Patrick Sims-Williams, *Religion and Literature in Western England* (Cambridge, 1990), pp. 79–83; and Margaret Gelling, *The West Midlands in the Early Middle Ages* (Leicester, 1992), pp. 86–92.

52. Kathleen Hughes, "Where are the Writings of Early Scotland?" in *Celtic Britain in the Early Middle Ages,* ed. D. Dumville, (Suffolk, 1980), pp. 1–21.

53. Dafydd Jenkins, "Gwalch-Welsh," in CMCS 19 (1990), pp. 56–67.

54. Wendy Davies, *Wales in the Early Middle Ages* (Leicester, 1982), p. 158.

55. Nora Chadwick, "Intellectual Life in West Wales in the Last Days of the Celtic Church," in *Studies in the Early British Church,* ed. K.

Hughes, C. Brooke, K. Jackson, and N. K. Chadwick (Cambridge, 1958), p. 161.

56. For a brief discussion of the *Carmina Gadelica* and issues of cultural continuity, see O. Davies and F. Bowie, *Celtic Christian Spirituality: an Anthology of Medieval and Modern Sources* (London and New York, 1995), pp. 17–18.

57. A major characteristic of the Syrian Church was theological expression in poetic form, leading to a rich tradition of hymnology, and both Syria and Russia proved initially resistant to the metaphysical dimension of monastic life while adopting its ascetical and communitarian ideal.

58. Richard Kearney, who has written extensively on the imagination as a form of cognition, has made a case for the privileging of the imagination in the Irish tradition (*The Irish Mind* [Dublin, 1985], pp. 35–36).

59. The exceptionally positive designation of penance as "blue martyrdom" in the Irish tradition, for which Clare Stancliffe argues in her "Red, White and Blue Martyrdom" (in *Ireland in Early Medieval Europe*, ed. D. Whitelock, R. McKitterick, and D. Dumville [Cambridge, 1982]), especially pp. 44–46), supports the view that penance can carry life-affirming connotations in the Celtic world.

60. Clare Stancliffe offers a detailed analysis of the latter in her *St. Martin and His Hagiographer: History and Miracle in Sulpicius Severus* (Oxford, 1983). Further hagiographical texts known to Adamnán, for instance, were Constantinus's *Life of Germanus* and the *Life of Benedict* by Gregory the Great (G. Bruning, "Adamnáns Vita Columbae und ihre Ableitungen," ZCP 11, 1916–1917, pp. 213–304).

61. This is the date suggested most recently by Ian. N. Wood in "Forgery in Merovingian Hagiography," in *Fälschungen im Mittelalter. Internationaler Kongress der Monumenta Germaniae Historica. München 16–19 September, 1986*, Teil V (Hannover, 1988), pp. 369–384. Nora Chadwick has a discussion of the complex historical issues surrounding the composition and dating of this work in her *Early Brittany* (Cardiff, 1969), pp. 250–256.

62. On the Celtic hagiographical tradition in general, see *Sources*, pp. 288–304. J-M. Picard discusses the structure of early Celtic *Lives* and the influence of classical prototypes in his "Structural Patterns in Early Hiberno-Latin Hagiography," *Peritia* 4 (1985), pp. 67–82. For an analysis of the distinctive role of the miraculous in Celtic hagiography, see C. Stancliffe, "The Miracle Stories in Seventh-Century Irish Saints' Lives," in *The Seventh Century: Change and Continuity*, ed. J. Fontaine and J. Hillgarth (London, 1992), pp. 87–115.

63. P. Ó Riain discusses the evolution of hagiographical texts from oral tradition in his "Towards a Methodology in Early Irish Hagiography," *Peritia* 1 (1982), pp. 146–159.

64. For the social background of the saints and their foundations, see Lisa M. Bitel, *Isle of the Saints: Monastic Settlement and Christian Community in Early Ireland* (Ithaca, 1990).

65. Thomas J. Heffernan, *Sacred Biography: Saints and Their Biographers in the Middle Ages* (New York and Oxford, 1988), pp. 6 and 17. Other recent overviews of the topic include Richard Kieckhefer, "Imitators of Christ: Sainthood in the Christian Tradition," in *Sainthood: Its Manifestations in World Religions*, ed. Richard Kieckhefer and George D. Bond (Berkeley, California, 1988), pp. 1–42; and Donald Weinstein and Rudolph M. Bell, *Saints and Society* (Chicago, 1982).

66. Kenney notes that the later *Lives* possess more magical elements than the earlier ones and suggests that this may show "the fuller acceptance of Christianity by the people" (*Sources*, p. 303).

67. Gerald of Wales, *The History and Topography of Ireland*, II, 83 (Harmondsworth, 1982), p. 91.

68. On this theme, see Charles Plummer, *Vitae Sanctorum Hiberniae* (Oxford, 1910, repr. 1968), Vol. I, pp. cxxxix–clxxxviii.

69. Due to appear as *Clauis Patricii III: An Annotated Bibliography of St. Patrick—D.M.L.C.S. Ancilliary Publication 6.* It is the work of Anthony Harvey of the Royal Irish Academy.

70. For a survey, cf. D. Ó Cróinín, *Early Medieval Ireland: 400–1200* (Dublin, 1995), ch. 1.

71. *"Libri Sancti Patricii:* The Latin Writings of St. Patrick," PRIA 25c (1905), pp. 201–326.

72. *Libri Epistolarum Sancti Patricii Episcopi* (Dublin, 1952).

73. *The Book of Letters of Saint Patrick the Bishop* (Dublin, 1994).

74. For example, L. Bieler wrote: "It would certainly be a gross exaggeration to say that he knew no other book than the Bible. There is evidence of his acquaintance with the writings of Sts. Cyprian and Augustine" (*The Works of Saint Patrick,* Ancient Christian Writers 17 [Washington, 1953], p. 15).

75. D. Conneely, *The Letters of Saint Patrick* (Maynooth, 1993).

76. While every edition and translation of Patrick has provided some biblical apparatus, that of Conneely far outstripped them. Conneely has been used extensively, but selectively, here; and other references have been added.

77. In every case, the biblical numeration followed is that of the LXX/Vulgate. While this is inconvenient, especially with regard to the Psalms, the alternative would have burdened the text with additional notes, as many of Patrick's biblical allusions can be understood only in relation to the Vetus Latina or Vulgate versions.

78. The text of the *Vita* is notorious for the problems it causes editors. Cf. A. B. E. Hood, *St. Patrick: His Writings and Muirchú's Life* (Chichester, 1978), pp. 19–21 for a convenient account. The text given here substantially follows that given by L. Bieler in *The Patrician Texts in the Book of Armagh (Scriptores Latini Hiberniae* 10) (Dublin, 1979). Passages that are clearly interpolations, e.g., the passage from a *Vita Basilii* at the beginning have been omitted; cf. T. O'Loughlin, "Muirchú's Vita Patricii: A Note on an Unidentified Source," E 46 (1996), pp. 89–93.

79. Cf. T. O'Loughlin, "St. Patrick and an Irish Theology," *Doctrine and Life* 44 (1994), pp. 153–159.

80. The best overview of Muirchú is in K. Hughes, *Early Christian Ireland: Introduction to the Sources* (Cambridge, 1972), pp. 229–232. For a bibliography, cf. L&S, pp. 84f., n. 303.

81. *Sources*, pp. 273–274.

82. Th. Pal., Vol. 2, p. xxxviii; *Sources*, pp. 267–268.

83. This is the case also with Colum Cille, who is first celebrated in an Old Irish hymn. For a discussion and translation of this poem, see Márkus and Clancy, *Iona: The Earliest Poetry of a Celtic Monastery*, pp. 96–128. The evolution of a hagiographical tradition from oral to written sources is discussed also by Pádraig Ó Riain in his "Towards a Methodology in Early Irish Hagiography," in *Peritia* 1 (1982), pp. 146–159.

84. L. De Paor, *St. Patrick's World* (Dublin, 1993), pp. 119–122.

85. D. Ó Cróinín, *Early Medieval Ireland* (London, 1995), pp. 156–158.

86. Gerald of Wales, *The History and Topography of Ireland* II, 67–68 (Harmondsworth, 1982), pp. 81–82.

87. *Sources*, pp. 357–358. In a difficult passage Cormac seems also to suggest that the name Brigit came to be used as a term for all goddesses in Ireland.

88. When Brigit hangs her garment on a sunbeam, for example. See below, p. 125. There may be some echo of this divine function in the possible derivation of her name from the root "bright arrow." See C. Plummer, *Vitae Sanctorum Hiberniae*, Vol. 1 (Oxford, 1910), p. cxxxvi. For a feminist reading of Brigit as sun goddess, see M. Condren, *The Serpent and the Goddess* (New York, 1989), pp. 65–78.

89. There is a parallel to this in the Welsh persona of Taliesin, who is simultaneously Christian poet, shape-changer, and druid. See *Celtic Christianity*, pp. 77–91.

90. R. Sharpe, "*Vitae S. Brigitae*: The Oldest Texts," in *Peritia* 1 (1982), pp. 86–87.

91. In his *Life of Patrick*, Muirchú refers to Cogitosus as his "father," by which he probably means "spiritual father," since Muirchú was himself in all likelihood an Ulsterman. A Cogitosus is mentioned for April 18th in the Martyrology of Tallaght and the Martyrology of Gorman (*Sources*, p. 359).

92. This was published as the third *Life of Brigid* by John Colgan in his important hagiographical collection *Trias Thaumaturga* (Louvain, 1647).

93. It may be dependent on Cogitosus, as F. Ó Briain ("Brigitana," ZCP 36 [1977], pp. 112–137) and K. McCone ("Brigit in the Seventh Century: A Saint with Three Lives?" in *Peritia* 1 [1982], pp. 107–145) have argued, or itself be one of Cogitosus's sources, which is the view of M. Esposito ("Notes on Latin Learning and Literature in Medieval Ireland, part IV: On the Early Latin Lives of St. Brigid of Kildare," in *Hermarthena* 49 [1935], pp. 120–165) and R. Sharpe ("*Vitae S. Brigidae*: The Oldest Texts," *Peritia* 1 [1982], pp. 81–106). For a useful summary of this debate, see R. Sharpe, *Medieval Irish Saints' Lives* (Oxford, 1991), p. 15.

D. Ó hAodha has suggested that Cogitosus is the earliest *Life*, followed by the Latin sections of the Latin-Irish *Life* (early eighth century), which was a source for about the first third of the *Vita I*. This latter may have been compiled in the early ninth century (*Bethu Brigte* [Dublin, 1978], pp. xxiv–xxv). R. Sharpe has recently edited the later *Vita IV*, which is dependent upon the *Vita I* (*Medieval Irish Saints' Lives* [Oxford, 1991], pp. 139–208).

94. See below, pp. 131–33.

95. See below, p. 134.

96. See below, pp. 146–48. On Brigit as fertility goddess, see P. Berger, *The Goddess Obscured* (London, 1988), pp. 70–74.

97. See below, p. 144.

98. See below, p. 145. On the history of the political connotations of this tradition, see Elva Johnston, "Transforming Women in Irish Hagiography," in *Peritia* 9 (1995), pp. 214–220.

99. E. Hamp, "Imbolc, óimelc," in *Studia Celtica* 14/15 (1979–1980), pp. 106–113. See also the discussion of this in S. Ó Catháin, *The Festival of Brigit* (Co. Dublin, 1995), pp. 7–8.

100. A survey of this material appears in *The Festival of Brigit*.

101. *Sources*, pp. 406–421.

102. David Dumville, "Two Approaches to the Dating of *Navigatio S. Brendani*," *Studi Medievali*, 3rd series, 29 (1988), pp. 87–102.

103. J. Carney, *Studies in Irish Literature and History* (Dublin, 1955), pp. 276–323.

104. *Sources*, p. 409. On voyage literature in general, see J. M. Wooding, ed., *The Otherworld Voyage in Early Irish Literature and History: An Anthology of Criticism* (Dublin, 1999).

105. G. Orlandi has a discussion of the continental influence of the Brendan text in *Navigatio S. Brendani: Introduzione* (Milan, 1968).

106. For a bibliography on the identification of Brendan's Island with America, see *Sources*, p. 408, and J. J. O'Meara, *The Voyage of St. Brendan: Journey to the Promised Land* (Dublin, 1976), pp. xi–xv.

107. Nora K. Chadwick, "Intellectual Life in West Wales in the Last Days of the Celtic Church," in *Studies in the Early British Church*, ed. N. K. Chadwick et al. (Cambridge, 1958), pp. 169–172; J. E. Lloyd, "Bishop Sulien and His Family," *National Library of Wales Journal* 2 (1941), pp. 1–6.

108. There is an account of how Taliesin was able to silence the bards at Maelgwn's court in the *Ystoria Taliesin* (Patrick K. Ford, ed., *Ystoria Taliesin* [Cardiff, 1992], p. 82), which is echoed also in the poem *Buarth beirdd* from the *Book of Taliesin*: "I cause eloquent bards to stumble" (Marged Haycock, *Rhai Agweddau ar Lyfr Taliesin*, University of Wales, Ph.D. [Aberystwyth, 1982], p. 71).

109. James E. Doan develops a structuralist interpretation of four Welsh and Breton saints' *Lives* (though not the "Life of Beuno") along similar lines in his "A Structural Approach to Celtic Saints' Lives," in *Celtic Folklore and Christianity*, ed. Patrick K. Ford (Santa Barbara, 1983), pp. 16–28.

110. Elissa R. Henken, *Traditions of the Welsh Saints* (Woodbridge, 1987), p. 75.

111. Francis Jones, *The Holy Wells of Wales* (Cardiff, 1954). Compare Patrick Logan, *The Holy Wells of Ireland* (Buckinghamshire, 1980), for the Irish material.

112. Huw Pryce, "A New Edition of the *Historia Divae Monacellae*," in *The Montgomeryshire Collections*, Vol. 82 (Welshpool, 1994), pp. 30 and 34.

113. Ibid., pp. 33–34.

114. It is notable also that the few non-Welsh church dedications in pre-Conquest Wales include the traditional Celtic themes of the Holy

Trinity (2) St. Michael (5), and Brigid (2) as well as Mary (1) and Peter (1). See Wendy Davies, *An Early Welsh Microcosm* (London, 1978), pp. 131–132.

115. Hughes, *The Church in Early Irish Society*, pp. 71–74.

116. The problems of monastic terminology in medieval Wales are explored by Huw Pryce in "Pastoral Care in Early Medieval Wales," in *Pastoral Care before the Parish*, ed. J. Blair and R. Sharpe (Leicester, 1992), pp. 41–62.

117. For a description of the *diofrydog* as "one vowed to abstinence" in the context of the Welsh Law, see Huw Pryce, *Native Law and the Church in Medieval Wales* (Oxford, 1993), p. 44.

118. Hughes, *The Church in Early Irish Society*, pp. 157–172. See also Bitel, *Isle of the Saints*, pp. 85–114.

119. Ibid., pp. 51–52.

120. There are also seeming incongruities in the Penitentials, as when the *Penitential of Cummean* advocates a year-long penance for repeated masturbation and a three-year penance for killing someone in anger: 10, 13, and 4, 7.

121. L. Bieler, *The Irish Penitentials* (Dublin, 1975), p. 3.

122. Ibid., p. 6.

123. J. T. McNeill and H. M. Garner, *Medieval Handbooks of Penance* (New York, 1938), pp. 179–182.

124. Bieler, *Irish Penitentials*, pp. 258–277.

125. G. S. M. Walker, *Sancti Columbani Opera* (Dublin, 1970), pp. xlvi–xlviii. On Columbanus's night office, Jane Stevenson remarks: "The prospect of singing psalms continuously for (at a guess) about two and a half hours in the small hours of a winter's night, with barely time to rest one's voice before starting all over again, is a regime which only the most fervent religious devotee could bear to contemplate" (*Liturgy*, p. xlv).

126. For an overview, see Patrick S. Diehl, *The Medieval European and Religious Lyric* (Berkeley, California, 1985).

127. For Anglo-Saxon religious poetic texts, see S. A. J. Bradley, *Anglo-Saxon Poetry* (London, 1982), and for a discussion of the theme of literary catechesis, Judith N. Garde, *Old English Poetry in Medieval Christian Perspective* (Cambridge, 1991).

128. For a woman poet recorded in the Annals of Inisfalen, see F. Kelly, *A Guide to Early Irish Law* (Dublin, 1988), p. 49. Kelly also has an analysis of the legal status of poets and bards (pp. 43–51). On this

theme see also Liam Breatnach, ed., *Uraicecht na Ríar. The Poetic Grades in Early Irish Law* (Dublin, 1987).

129. Ceri W. Lewis, "The Court Poets: Their Function, Status and Craft," in *A Guide to Welsh Literature*, ed. A. O. H. Jarman and G. R. Hughes, Vol. 1 (Cardiff, 1992, rev. ed.), pp. 123–156.

130. James Carney, *The Irish Bardic Poet* (Dublin, 1967), p. 8.

131. For a list of this terminology, see Haycock, *Rhai Agweddau ar Lyfr Taliesin*, pp. 626–629. See also *Celtic Christianity*, p. 143.

132. For a comprehensive discussion of continuity and difference between early Irish and Welsh poets and the bardic tradition of Gaul, see J. E. Caerwyn Williams, "The Court Poet in Medieval Ireland," in *PBA* 57 (London, 1971), pp. 85–135 (also printed separately, London, 1972).

133. Liam Breatnach, ed., "The Caldron of Poesy," in *E* 32 (1981), p. 69. For this theme and its Christian analogues in the Welsh tradition, see *Celtic Christianity*, pp. 28–119.

134. See, for instance, A. T. E. Matonis, "Later Medieval Poetics and Some Welsh Bardic Debates," in *B* 29 (1982), pp. 635–665.

135. Especially passages in "Hostile Alliance" (*Angar Cyfyngdod*), "The Song of Taliesin" (*Cadair Taliesin*), and "The Contest of the Poets" (*Buarth Beirdd*). For translations of the relevant sections, see *Celtic Christianity*, pp. 72, 78–79.

136. Cf. "I do not adore the voices of birds...my druid is Christ the Son of God," attributed to Colum Cille (quoted in J. R. Walsh and T. Bradley, *A History of the Irish Church 400–700 AD* [Dublin, 1991], p. 34).

137. *Sources*, pp. 478–485, and L. Gougaud, "Celtiques (Liturgies)," in *Dictionnaire d'archéologie chrétienne et de liturgie* II, part 2 (1910), cols. 2969–3032.

138. *Celtic Christianity*, pp. 52–56.

139. For a discussion of the *lorica* genre, see below, p. 46.

140. *Celtic Christianity*, pp. 45–48.

141. On the work of these poets, see Catherine A. McKenna, *The Medieval Welsh Religious Lyric: Poems of the Gogynfeirdd 1137–1282* (Belmont, Mass., 1991).

142. On Hiberno-Latin devotions and the Mozarabic influence on them, see Edmund Bishop's "Liturgical Note" in *The Prayer Book of Aedeluald the Bishop*, commonly called the *Book of Cerne*, ed. A. B. Kuypers, (Cambridge, 1902), pp. 234–283.

143. Kathleen Hughes has written interestingly on the development of these texts away from the beseeching of physical defense and bald

listing of parts of the body that is characteristic of the primitive Irish tradition to a more moral and metaphorical context in the later Anglo-Saxon works ("Some Aspects of Irish Influence on Early English Private Prayer," in *Church and Society in Ireland: AD 400–1200* [London, 1987], XVII). On the English prayer books, see also Patrick Sims-Williams, *Religion and Literature in Western England, 600–800* (Cambridge, 1990), pp. 273–327.

144. E.g., *The First Word I Say*, in LlD, pp. 56–57. See also *Celtic Christianity*, pp. 42–45.

145. On *loricae* in general, see M. O'Carroll, DS 9 (1976), cols. 1007–1011; L. Gougaud, "Etude sur les *loricae* celtiques et sur les prières que s'en rapprochent," *Bulletin d'ancienne littérature et d'archéologie chrétiennes* 1 (1911), pp. 265–281, 2 (1912), pp. 33–41, 101–127; and W. Godel, "Irisches Beten im frühen Mittelalter: Eine Liturgie- und Frömmigkeitsgeschichtliche Untersuchung," *Zeitschrift für katholische Theologie* 85 (1963), pp. 261–321 and 389–439.

146. Hughes, *The Church in Early Irish Society*, pp. 48–61; and Michael Herren, *The Hisperica Famina II: Related Poems* (Toronto, 1987), p. 25. Regarding the origins of the *loricae*, W. M. Lindsay asks: "Is it possible that they were adapted by early missionaries as a guard against the spells which the heathen sorcerers directed against them? Such spells often took the form of leaden execration-tablets with malignant specification of the body" (W. M. Lindsay, *Early Welsh Script* [Oxford, 1912], p. 23). Herren quotes this extract and generally supports this thesis, pointing also to the possible influence of apotropaic amulets in the early formation of *loricae* (pp. 26–31).

147. The attribution to Gildas is to be found only in the fourteenth century *Leabhar Breac*.

148. M. Herren, "The Authorship, Date of Composition and Provenance of the So-Called *Lorica Gildae*," in E 24 (1973), pp. 35–51. On Laidcenn, see also *Sources*, pp. 271–272.

149. The debt of the *loricae* to the imagery of the Benedicite is shown by G. S. Mac Eoin, "Invocation of the Forces of Nature in the Loricae," in *Studia Hibernica* 2 (1962), pp. 212–217.

150. D. R. Howlett, "*Orationes Moucani*: Early Cambro-Latin Prayers," in CMCS 24 (1992), pp. 55–74.

151. There are no early medieval liturgical sources for Wales, although we may assume that Irish liturgical practices followed where Irish ecclesiastical culture came to be influential beyond the borders of Ireland (the Antiphonary of Bangor itself survived in Milan). Irish

liturgy may itself have been influenced at its inception by the Celtic British Church, but again no sources are available.

152. One expression of this asceticism is the *laus perennis*, or "perpetual praise" tradition (whereby a community maintained a twenty-four hour cycle of praise). While not unique to Ireland, this was practiced in some Irish monasteries and was viewed, at least by St. Bernard, as being a distinctively Irish tradition (*Liturgy*, pp. xlix–l).

153. Ibid., pp. xlvii–xlix.

154. But it is possible also that the practice of anointing the heads of bishops at their consecration may originate in the Celtic churches (ibid., pp. liii–lvii).

155. Dublin, Royal Irish Academy, ms D.II.3; L&S 537.

156. Jane Stevenson records that this practice was followed "although less elaborately in the Gallican rites of Spain and Gaul" (*Liturgy*, p. lxv).

157. *Liturgy*, p. lxxxii. For an earlier overview of liturgy in Ireland, see also J. Hennig, "Old Ireland and Her Liturgy," in *Old Ireland*, ed. R. E. McNally (Dublin, 1965), pp. 60–89.

158. Jane Stevenson suggests that the latter may have been a continental composition, however (*Liturgy*, p. lxxxvi). I have not included the hymn *Hymnum Dicat*, despite its great popularity in Ireland, on account of its attribution to Hilary of Poitiers.

159. *Sources*, p. 733. Apocryphal material exists also in Welsh, Cornish, and Breton, although these are relatively late and are of less historical interest.

160. Of particular importance are the Irish witnesses to the *Infancy Gospel of Thomas*, the *Gospel according to the Hebrews*, and the *Acts of Thomas* (*Apocrypha*, pp. 1–2).

161. Cf. *The Passion of the Apostle Philip*, in *Irish Biblical Apocrypha* ed. M. Herbert and M. McNamara (Edinburgh, 1989), pp. 106–108.

162. The references are usefully collected by Haycock in her *Rhai Agweddau ar Lyfr Taliesin*, pp. 419–421; in *Apocrypha*, pp. 21–23; and in R. H. Charles, *Apocrypha and Pseudepigrapha of the Old Testament*, Vol. 2 (Oxford, 1913), pp. 448–449.

163. Max Foerster, "Adams Erschaffung und Namengebung," in *Archiv für Religionswissenschaft* 11 (1907–1908), p. 477. See also M. Foerster, "Die mittelirische Version von Adams Erschaffung," in ZCP 13 (1921), pp. 47–48.

164. *The Old Testament Pseudepigrapha*, Vol. I, ed. James H. Charlesworth (London, 1983), pp. 91–213.

165. A variation on this theme occurs in the Irish poem "The Works of the Sixth Day," *Gnimhradha in seseadh lai lain* (ed. M. Carney, in E 21 [1969], pp. 149–166), which can be dated to around A.D. 1000, and again in the figure of Blodeuwedd from the Mabinogion. R. E. McNally records that the derivation of the name of Adam from the four Greek terms for the points of the compass was "a characteristic of Irish biblical exegesis" (*The Bible in the Early Middle Ages*, p. 26; quoted in *Apocrypha*, p. 22). There are parallels also in the Anglo-Saxon world (cf. *The Anglo-Saxon Ritual*, Wasserstein, in PRIA 88).

166. *Apocrypha*, p. 28. See also *Irish Biblical Apocrypha* ed. M. Herbert and M. McNamara, (Edinburgh, 1989), pp. 23–24 and 169–170, for translation and comment.

167. There is a translation, to which I am indebted, in IBA, pp. 137–148. See also C. S. Boswell, *An Irish Precursor of Dante* (London, 1908) and for valuable comment on the sources of this text, David Dumville, "Towards an Interpretation of the *Fis Adamnán*," in *Studia Celtica* 12–13 (1977–1978), pp. 62–77.

168. This is Jane Stevenson's proposal in her "Ascent through the Heavens, from Egypt to Ireland," in CMCS 5 (1983), pp. 21–35.

169. R. E. McNally believes that Pseudo-Isidore, author of *Liber de ordine creaturarum*, may also have been active in this school (*Scriptores Hiberniae Minores* I, in CCSL, CVIII B, p. x).

170. Quoted by M. McNamara in "The Bible in Irish Spirituality," in *Irish Spirituality*, ed. Michael Maher (Dublin, 1981), p. 34.

171. B. Bischoff, "Turning-Points in the History of Latin Exegesis in the Early Middle Ages," in *Biblical Studies: The Medieval Irish Contribution*, ed. M. McNamara, (Dublin, 1976), pp. 75–161.

172. For a valuable overview of Irish commentaries on the Psalter, see M. McNamara, "Tradition and Creativity in Early Irish Psalter Study," in *Irland und Europa* ed. P. Ní Chatháin and M. Richter, (Stuttgart, 1984), pp. 338–389.

173. *Dictionary of the Irish Language*, Royal Irish Academy, s.v. Biáit. Its association with the return from the Captivity in Babylon is explicit in Th. Pal., vol. 1, p. 450 (quoted by O. Bergin, "A Mystical Interpretation of the *Beati*," in E 11 (1932), p. 103). On the place of this psalm in early Irish and Welsh Christianity; see *Celtic Christianity*, p. 46.

174. For the dating and extensive discussion of this manuscript, see M. McNamara, *Glossa in Psalmos*, Studi e Testi (Vatican City, 1986), pp. 1–77.

175. This motif occurs also in a sermon from the *Catechesis Celtica*. In her article "Red, White and Blue Martyrdom," in *Ireland in Early Medieval Europe*, pp. 21–46, Clare Stancliffe shows that this theme originates in early monastic texts, such as the *Life of St. Anthony* and *Life of St. Martin* and perhaps passes to Ireland with a more developed association with colors in the work of the fifth-century Spanish author, Bachiarius. Stancliffe concludes: "Red martyrdom denotes death for Christ's sake; white, the daily martyrdom of ascetic life; and blue, the tears, hardships and fasting of the penitent" (p. 44).

176. One of the features of early medieval Christianity is the importance it attached to the Christian special day: Sunday, and this interest in Sunday is particularly noticeable in Celtic texts. For a general survey, cf. M. Maher, "Sunday in the Irish Church," *Irish Theological Quarterly 61* (1994), pp. 161–84.

177. They were edited by R. E. McNally in *Corpus Christianorum: Series Latina 108B*, pp. 175–86; it is this edition that is translated here. The translation was originally published in *Worship* 64 (1990), pp. 533–544, and a fuller commentary on the three texts can be found there.

178. In his edition, McNally stressed the relationship of these texts to the famous apocryphon, the *Carta dominica,* which claims to have been written by Christ himself and then dropped on one of the great centers of Christendom. But this stress may be misplaced. The *Carta* is a tract strictly commanding the keeping of the Lord's Day by abstinence from earthly work or involvements, backed by threats of punishments for "Sabbath-breakers." Although formally condemned in 745, in the two centuries, at least, during which the *Carta* was in circulation it became so well known that a version of it is found in nearly every European language. A version of it is found in Irish: the *Epistil Isu* (Epistle of Jesus), which forms part of a larger Irish work, the *Cain Domnaig* (The Law of Sunday). However, these texts (apart from two sections in one text: III, xix and xx) do not belong to that tradition of enforcing "the Sabbath," but rather aim at listing the "mysteries" of Sunday. The collection as a whole exhibits a joy over the Lord's Day stemming from its being the day of *magnalia Dei* (the great deeds of God) and their narration by the church. Moreover, with the exception of III, xi, none of the themes are exclusively *Carta* material; all have a wider currency in writings available to the authors, especially Augustine, Jerome, and Isidore of Seville. Cf. McNally, *Corpus Christianorum*, p. 179; and cf. also M. R. James, *The Apocryphal New Testament* (Oxford, 1924), p. 476.

179. The issue of the significance of the cultural and ethnic provenance of the schoolmen is in itself complex. Scholastics of likely Celtic origin include Richard of St. Victor and Duns Scotus, both of whom are believed to have been born in Scotland. For an extensive list of Celtic scholastics, see L&S, pp. 313–345.

180. Opinion is divided on the authorship of *On the Christian Life*. G. de Plinval regards it as being by Pelagius himself (*Pélage: ses écrits, sa vie et sa réforme* [Lausanne, 1943], pp. 27–45), as does R. F. Evans ("Pelagius, Fastidius and the Pseudo-Augustinian *De Vita Christiana*," in *Journal of Theological Studies* 13, [1962], pp. 72–98, and *Four Letters of Pelagius* [London, 1968], pp. 18–20). Others have accepted the ascription to Fastidius, although J. Morris does so tentatively ("Pelagian Literature," in *Journal of Theological Studies* 16 [1965], pp. 32–36). R. P. C. Hanson rejects the authorship of both Pelagius and Fastidius, and denies that there is any evidence for British provenance at all (*St. Patrick: His Origins and Career* [Oxford, 1968], pp. 40–44). All are agreed, however, as to the Pelagian character of the text.

181. Jerome, however, believed that he was an Irishman (*Commentary on Jeremiah*, in PL 24, 680–682 and 757–758). Alypius, Augustine, Orosius, Prosper, and Marius Mercator, on the other hand, all believed him to be a Briton (Hanson, *St. Patrick*, p. 36). J. B. Bury ("The Origins of Pelagius," in *Hermathena* 13, [1905], pp. 26–35) reconciles these two views by suggesting that Pelagius may have come from the Irish settlements of southwest Britain, though Hanson disagrees (pp. 37–38).

182. Peter Brown, *Religion and Society in the Age of St. Augustine* (London, 1972), p. 200.

183. Th. De Bruyn, *Pelagius's Commentary on St. Paul's Epistle to the Romans* (Oxford, 1993), pp. 10–24.

184. The question of its authorship is complex and can be followed in the recent literature notes given with the translation below. The attribution to Columba can probably never be definitively proven; however, neither of the arguments against his authorship cf. Clancy and Márkus, *Iona*, p. 40; and D. R. Howlett in "Seven Studies in Seventh-Century Texts," in *Peritia* 10 (1996), p. 56 conclusively excludes the possibility.

185. This practice was a conscious imitation of Ps 118 (119), which in Hebrew is *abecedarian*.

186. Rabanus Maurus (784–856) used it as a model for his *Aeterne rerum conditor*.

187. This translation is based on the standard Latin edition: J. H. Bernard and R. Atkinson, eds., *The Irish Liber Hymnorum* (London,

1898), Vol. 1, pp. 62–83; and Vol. 2, pp. 23–26; 140–69. A bibliography for the hymn can be found in L&S, n. 580. A partial commentary can be found in Clancy and Márkus, *Iona*, pp. 39–68. Further information is contained in *Sources*, n. 91, pp. 263–265; and its location in other corpora of texts can be found in E. Dekkers, *Clauis Patrum Latinorum* (3e, Steenbrugge, 1995), n. 1131 (where it is ascribed without doubt to Columba).

188. For an introduction to Eriugena's thought, see J. J. O' Meara, *Eriugena* (Oxford, 1988); and Dermot Moran, *The Philosophy of John Scottus Eriugena* (Cambridge, 1989). There is a useful overview of his life and work also in E. Jeauneau, *Jean Scot: Homélie sur le prologue de Jean* (Paris, 1969), pp. 9–77.

189. The *De imagine* is now known as *De hominis opificio*. On Eriugena's use of Greek sources, see I. P. Sheldon-Williams, "Eriugena's Greek Sources," in *The Mind of Eriugena*, ed. J. J. O'Meara and L. Bieler (Dublin, 1970), pp. 1–15.

190. Jeauneau, *Jean Scot*, p. 44.

191. *Periphyseon* 5 (PL 122, 1021A). For an overview of the mystical return in Eriugena, see B. McGinn, *The Growth of Mysticism (The Presence of God: A History of Western Christian Mysticism)*, Vol. 2 (London and New York, 1994), pp. 80–118.

192. Jeauneau, *Jean Scot*, pp. 73–74.

193. On Eriugena's use of scripture more generally, see G. van Riel, C. Steel, and J. McEvoy, eds., *Iohannes Scottus Eriugena: The Bible and Hermeneutics* (Leuven, 1996).

194. I discuss this theme in "'On Divine Love' from *The Food of the Soul*: A Celtic Mystical Paradigm?," in *Mystics Quarterly* 20, no. 3 (1994), pp. 87–95.

195. For a discussion of the context and sources of this work, see Idris Foster, "The Book of the Anchorite," in PBA 36 (1949), pp. 197–226; and *Celtic Christianity*, pp. 120–141.

196. For a recent translation of this work, see R. Sharpe, *Adomnán of Iona: Life of Columba* (Harmondsworth, 1995). Translations of the Iona material can be found in Márkus and Clancy, *Iona*.

PATRICK'S DECLARATION OF
THE GREAT WORKS OF GOD

1. For the rationale of this title, cf. the Introduction.
2. The division of this work, and the Letter to Coroticus, into

sections is the work of N. J. P. White, and has been followed in all subsequent editions and translations.

3. Cf. 1 Tm 1:15.

4. Cf. Eph 3:8.

5. Cf. Dt 32:15.

6. Cf. Gn 26:5.

7. Cf. Dn 9:4–6.

8. The Latin, *qui nostram salutem,* echoes the Nicene Creed *(qui propter nos homines et propter nostram salutem).*

9. Is 42:25.

10. The concept of dispersal among the nations as a divine punishment for infidelity is found in many places in the Old Testament, but especially in the prophets, where it is presented as the just reward of the people: Lv 26:33 and 38; Dt 4:27; Ps 106:27; 1 Chr 16:35; Jer 9:16; Lam 1:3 and 2:9; Hos 9:17; Zec 10:9; Ez 4:13, 5:14, 6:8, 11:16, 12:15–6, 20:23, 22:15, 25:10, 29:12, 30:23 and 26, 32:9, 36:19, and 39:28; and it is found in Jl 2:19 and 3:2—a prophet is echoed in the next section—and in Tb 13:4–7, which seems to be reflected in several ways by Patrick in this section.

11. Acts 13:47.

12. Cf. Jer 45:15 (and Ob 2).

13. A conflation of Lk 24:45 and Heb 3:12.

14. Cf. Ps 24:16–8.

15. Jl 2:12–3.

16. Lk 1:48; and cf. Ps 24:16–8.

17. Cf. Ps 24:5.

18. Cf. Ps 24:7.

19. 1 Kgs 3:9 and Gn 3:5.

20. Cf. Lk 11:11–3.

21. Cf. Wis 4:17.

22. Cf. 2 Cor 12:1.

23. Cf. 2 Chr 6:36–38 (this phrase is also found in Jer 30:16 and 46:27).

24. Cf. Ps 115:12 and 1 Thes 3:9.

25. Cf. Eph 4:14.

26. Ps 88:6.

27. Acts 2:5.

28. Cf. Is 43:10–11.

29. Cf. Col 1:17.

30. Cf. Jn 1:3 and Col 1:16.

31. Cf. Mk 16:19.

32. Phil 2:9–11.

33. Rom 2:6.

34. Ti 3:5–6.

35. The notion of "sons" is found in many places in the New Testament (e.g., Mt 5:9), as is that of "heirs" (e.g., Gal 3:29), but the passage behind this phrase of Patrick appears to be Rom 8:14–9.

36. Ps 50:15.

37. Tb 12:7.

38. Cf. Lk 21:16.

39. 2 Tm 1:8; the implicit statement is that as Paul, the prisoner, warned Timothy "never be ashamed of your testimony to our Lord," so Patrick has taken the apostle's advice and is not ashamed of his testimony.

40. Ps 5:6.

41. Wis 1:11.

42. Mt 12:36.

43. Eph 6:5.

44. Here Patrick echoes the theme of the great and terrible Day of Judgment, which is found in the prophets, e.g., Is 24:21 and Jer 25:33, and again in the New Testament, e.g., Rom 2:16 and Lk 10:12.

45. There is an echo here of Adam and Eve hiding in the garden (Gn 3:10) and of Cain after murdering Abel (Gn 4:9).

46. Rom 14: 12 and 10.

47. Cf. 2 Tm 3:14–5.

48. Cf. Jn 8:43.

49. Sir 4:29.

50. Cf. Eccl 1:8.

51. This sentence, and especially the last part of it, is unclear; it baffled medieval readers, who in turn contributed to the bafflement of modern editors. It has been emended in several ways, none of them wholly satisfactory. What is given here is a rendering that seeks to reflect the overall direction of the sentence's meaning.

52. Ps 118:112; and cf. Ps 115:12.

53. Ex 4:10.

54. Is 32:4 (this is a Vetus Latina/Septuagint reading).

55. This sentence is a conflation of 2 Cor 3:2–3 and Acts 13:47.

56. The manuscripts are corrupt at this point having either *ratum* or *rata* and several editors have held that the text is beyond restoration.

However, if the readings are corrupt, this does not put the text in doubt, for clearly its meaning is linked to both "the letter of Christ" and "written in our hearts." Patrick has combined two verses out of sequence: 2 Cor 3:3 *(quod epistola estis Christi, ministrata a nobis, et scripta non attramento)* with 2 Cor 3:2 *(Epistola nostra uos estis, scripta in cordibus)* to make his point. Hence *rata* in some manuscripts is a legacy of *ministrata;* and *ratum* in other manuscripts is a clumsy attempt to make some sense of *rata.*

57. 2 Cor 3:2–3; Patrick's familiarity with the text of scripture, as well as his competence in handling it, can be observed in this quotation where the elements of Paul's argument are rearranged without loss of meaning, yet in a way that reinforces the exact point he wishes to make. The text of 2 Cor 2–3 reads (RSV): "You yourselves are our letter of recommendation, written on your hearts, to be known and read by all men; and you show that you are a letter from Christ delivered by us, written not with ink but with the Spirit of the living God, not on tablets of stone but on tablets of human hearts."

58. Heb 10:15; the notion of the Spirit bearing witness is found on several occasions in the New Testament (Jn 15:25; Rom 8:16; and 1 Jn 5:7), but the usage here is a more specifically linked linguistically and theologically with Hebrews. Linguistically there is an echo of Hebrews *(Contestatur autem nos et Spiritus sanctus)* in Patrick *(Et iterum Spiritus testatur);* theologically, the Spirit's witness is used in an exactly parallel way: In both a Christological point is witnessed to by the Spirit in that there is a text in the Old Testament to support it, which is then quoted.

59. Sir 7:16.

60. This word, *profuga,* is most translations of Patrick is rendered as "exile," but I am rendering it as "wanderer" as it seems that Patrick, in a foreign land away from his family as a punishment for his sins, is seeing himself as like Cain, who in (the Vetus Latina version of) Genesis is sent off to wander (Gn 4:12); cf. "The Letter to the Soldiers of Coroticus," n. 1.

61. Eccl 4:13.

62. Ps 118:67.

63. Cf. Ps 68:15 and v. 2 of the same psalm.

64. Lk 1:49.

65. Cf. Ps 114:14.

66. Cf. Ps 112:7–8.

67. Rv 19:5.

68. Lk 7:30 (and cf. Lk 10:25, 11:45, 11:46, 11:52, 14:52; and Ti 3:13).

69. Lk 24:19 (and cf. Acts 7:22 and 18:24).

70. Cf. 1 Cor 1:20 and 3:19.

71. Heb 12:28.

72. This notion that one of the qualities of the holy people is living blamelessly is found in many places in the Wisdom literature (Wis 10:5, 10:15, 13:6, 18:21; Sir 8:10) and in Paul (Phil 2:15, 3:6; 1 Thes 2:10, 3:13, and 5:23).

73. Cf. 2 Cor 5:14.

74. Cf. Acts 20:19.

75. Rom 12:3.

76. Jn 4:10.

77. Cf. 2 Thes 2:16.

78. Cf. Phil 2:15.

79. Phil 1:14.

80. 2 Pt 1:15.

81. Cf. Mt 8:8.

82. Cf. Lk 17:5.

83. Cf. Rom 8:14.

84. J. Higgins, in "Two Passages in the Confessio of Patrick," in *Milltown Studies* 35 (1995), pp. 131–133, has shown that this passage (from "And more and more") was written in imitation of the Canticle of the Three Youths in Dn 3:52–90.

85. Acts 18:25, and cf. Rom 12:11.

86. Rom 11:4 (this word *responsus* in Paul (NRSV: "a divine reply") is used by Patrick (and later then by Muirchú) as a technical term for what is said by God during or after a vision—in order to reflect this usage it is translated here, and wherever else it occurs, as "a revelation." When the uses of this word are drawn together, a picture of its meaning appears— i.e., God is explaining what is happening to him in his life.

87. The Latin reads: *Et ueni, lit.* "And I came"; this use of "I came," when the context requires "I went," may be an echo of 1 Cor 2:1: *Et ego, cum uenissem ad uos.*

88. 1 Cor 2:5.

89. Cf. Tb 4:20 and 1 Thes 3:11.

90. Cf. Ps 22:4.

91. This phrase has troubled editors and translators of Patrick for centuries. In fact, "to suck the nipples" is an Old Irish expression, and no doubt a symbolic practice as well, describing the appeal of an inferior for

the protection and friendship of a superior. The significance of Patrick's refusal was that he did not want to enter into a formal agreement of protection with them, and thus deny them his intimate friendship, as they were pagans. It has been pointed out that the use of this Irish phrase indicates that Patrick sailed in a ship crewed by Irishmen. Cf. J. Ryan, "A Difficult Phrase in the 'Confession' of St. Patrick," in *Irish Ecclesiastical Record* 52 (1938), pp. 293–299. However, it could also be an allusion to Is 60:16 as it is found in the Vulgate.

92. Neh 5:15.

93. Patrick uses the word *gentes* in the biblical sense of pagans.

94. Cf. Gn 12:10.

95. Cf. Dt 10:17.

96. 1 2:12.

97. Lk 1:37.

98. This is patterned on the Exodus desert experience, cf. Ex 16:12.

99. This appearance of a herd of swine, on cue, for a demonstration of the power of God has echoes of the herd in the land of the Gadarenes in the Synoptic Gospels: cf. Mt 8:28ff.

100. *Manserunt;* there is an echo here of the *mansiones,* the stopping places, of the people of Israel in the desert.

101. For the basis of this reading cf. J. Higgins, "Two Passages," pp. 130–131.

102. Cf. Mt 15:32.

103. Lk 10:30.

104. This is a motif from several of the prophets (e.g., the Naaman story in 2 Kgs 5) of the God of Israel showing his power, who was then thanked by the pagans, and his prophet held in honor.

105. Cf. Mt 3:4.

106. Lk 24:42.

107. Cf. 1 Cor 10:28.

108. 2 Pt 1:13.

109. This calling on Helias is a one of the knottiest problems in this text: Is he calling on the Sun as a god or as a divine sacrament (the Greek for Sun is *Helios*); or calling on Elijah ([*H*] *elias* in Latin)—some who heard Christ calling out on the Cross thought he was calling on Elijah (cf. Mt 27:47); or is it an echo of the cry of Christ from the Cross (cf. Mt 27:46)?

110. Ps 50:15.

111. Mt 10:19–20.

112. In all the MSS n. 21 follows at this point, where it clearly does not belong as it interrupts the story of what happened on the twenty-eight days in "the desert" from leaving the ship to reaching civilization, hence some editors leave it in sequence but place it in brackets. However, it is clear that it belongs later than the days in the desert, but before he received his mission to Ireland. Therefore, between 22 and 23 seems a logical place. An examination of the language adds some support to this. Having reached civilization, 21 begins: *Et iterum post annos multos...;* and then 23 begins: *Et iterum post paucos annos,...*he is back with his family after his great tribulations.

113. Some MSS read "after ten days."

114. This coincidence of leaving the desert and running out of the food miraculously provided on the journey is modeled on Jos 5:12, which declares that the manna ceased on the day the people entered Canaan.

115. Rom 11:4.

116. Gn 37:21.

117. Dn 7:13.

118. Dn 3:51.

119. Ps 108:16; and cf. Acts 2:37.

120. 2 Cor 12:2.

121. Cf. Jn 10:11.

122. Eph 3:16; and Rom 7:22.

123. Cf. Rom 8:26.

124. Cf. Is 29:9; and Acts 2:12 and 8:13.

125. The same phrase is used in [24] and here: *ad postremum orationis sic efficiatus est.* In [24] I have rendered *oratio* as "speech," but here as "prayer"; this shift in words is to convey a nuance of developing awareness in Patrick. In the first case he seems unclear about what is happening except *(nisi)* for the final part; in the second case he seems clear that it concerns prayer, but he still had a question and *(sed)* it became clearer in the final part—it was the Spirit who was praying.

126. Rom 8:26.

127. Cf. 1 Jn 2:1.

128. Rom 8:27 and 34.

129. Ps 117:13.

130. Ps 106:8, but while the notion of being delivered from trial for the Lord's name's sake is found in the Synoptics, it is the verbal form of Ps 106 that Patrick has in mind; cf. Mt 19:29 and 24:9. Patrick sees himself in the tribulation prophesied in the gospel.

131. 2 Tm 4:16; Patrick sees himself as one opposed in a trial as "Paul" says he was opposed by Alexander the coppersmith: "Alexander the coppersmith did me great harm; the Lord will requite him for his deeds. Beware of him yourself, for he strongly opposed our message. At my first defense no one took my part; all deserted me. May it not be charged against them! But the Lord stood by me and gave me strength to proclaim the message fully, that all the Gentiles might hear it. So I was rescued from the lion's mouth" (2 Tm 4:14–7).

132. Dn 6:5.

133. The text reads *confessus fueram,* which has often been translated as "I had confessed," but this is a false-friend as it suggests something like "aural confession" or "confession" in later Catholic tradition; however, any such formal interpretation would be anachronous.

134. 2 Cor 12:2.

135. Literally: "nor [had I believed] since my infancy."

136. Cf. Ps 117:18.

137. Cf. Dt 28:48 and 2 Cor 11:27.

138. Cf. Ps 117:22.

139. Dn 7:13.

140. Rom 11:4.

141. Zec 2:8.

142. 1 Tm 1:12.

143. The language and ideas reflect Mk 5:27–30.

144. Sir 25:1; and cf. 1 Pt 1:7 and 2 Cor 8:21.

145. Acts 2:29.

146. Rom 1:9 (a phrase used on several occasions by Paul).

147. Cf. Gal 1:20.

148. Cf. Rom 11:4.

149. Cf. Jn 10:29.

150. Cf. 2 Chr 6:36–38.

151. Cf. Sir 33:1; 2 Tm 1:12; combine with a common scriptural expression: Lv 16:21–22; Ps 51:9; Ps 130:8; Ez 36:33 ff.

152. Cf. Rom 8:11.

153. Cf. 1 Cor 12:11 and Phil 2:13.

154. This is a common scriptural expression, e.g., Jos 16:10.

155. Cf. Acts 2:29.

156. Cf. 2 Cor 5:14.

157. Ps 94:9; and cf. Wis 3:18.

158. Rom 12:1.

159. Ps 33:5–7.

160. 2 Sm 7:18.

161. Cf. Ps 33:4; Ps 45:11; and Sir 33:10.

162. This notion is found in many places in the scriptures (e.g., Ps 17:49; Is 12:4; Ez 20:9; Mal 1:11; Rv 15:4; ff.), but Patrick may be thinking especially of 2 Sm 7:23, as this part of 2 Sm is used a few lines earlier.

163. Cf. Jb 2:10.

164. Acts 2:17.

165. This notion of sanctity/discipleship as imitating models of holiness is a theme in Paul, and a particular theme in Patrick's understanding of holiness, cf. nos. 42, 47, and 59 in the text (where there is a fuller comment on the theme).

166. Mt 24:14 (he paraphrases the final phrase using a word from Mt 24:13; there is also an echo of the notion of "the ends of the earth" from Acts 1:8).

167. Jas 2:23; and cf. Mt 24:14.

168. Cf. Acts 1:8.

169. Acts 21:19.

170. Cf. Rom 8:26.

171. Rom 11:4.

172. Mt 13:54.

173. Cf. Ps 38:5; Jb 38:21.

174. Cf. the conclusion of Lk and Acts 1.

175. Sir 29:29.

176. 2 Tm 2:9.

177. Cf. Jn 13:37.

178. Cf. Rom 1:5.

179. Cf. Is 26:15.

180. Cf. 2 Cor 12:15.

181. Cf. Phil 2:8.

182. Cf. Rom 1:14.

183. Cf. Jn 3:5.

184. Cf. Heb 11:40 and Rv 15:8.

185. Jer 16:19.

186. Rom 1:2.

187. Jer 16:19.

188. Cf. Jn 19:37, which is the model for Patrick's use of scripture here. In John two verses are quoted in a *catena* and it is this combination that is brought to fulfillment. Here Patrick uses the same device, and even echoes John's language: John has *Et iterum alia scriptura dicit:...*, while Patrick has *Et iterum:....*

189. Acts 13:47.

190. Acts 1:4.

191. Mt 8:11; it should be noted that Patrick adds the two other corners of the world—south and north—to the gospel text.

192. Mt 4:19.

193. Cf. Jn 19:37.

194. Jer 16:16.

195. Cf. Mk 1:16 and Jn 21:11.

196. Lk 6:17 and cf. Lk 5:6.

197. Mt. 28:19–20; note his added emphasis of urgency: "Go therefore *now....*"

198. Cf. Jn 19:37.

199. Mk 16:15–6; I have rendered *uniuersus mundus* as "entire universe," as this cosmological nuance is present in the original, and in the Latin, but is not captured by a phrase like "whole world" or "all creation."

200. Cf. Jn 19:37.

201. Mt. 24:14; see n. 199 on the words "entire universe."

202. Acts 2:17–8; and cf. Jl 2:28–29.

203. Rom 9:25–26; note that it is Paul who says this is Hosea; cf. Hos 1:9–10, 2:1, and 2:23. Cf. also no. 59 of this text.

204. Cf. Rom 1:28.

205. This notion in Patrick reflects Paul's thinking in Rom 1:19–24 (cf. 2 Kgs 17:12).

206. Cf. Lk 1:17.

207. Cf. 1 Jn 3:1 (and Rom 8:14 and 9:26).

208. The word "virgin" *(uirgo)* means here something similar to our word "nun."

209. Cf. Acts 10:22 (and cf. Rom 11:4).

210. Cf. Mt 11:12.

211. Cf. Lk 21:16.

212. This is an echo of the Pauline notion of imitating Christ as being the guide to Christian behavior; cf. the notes on no. 59 of this text where there is a fuller comment and references.

213. Cf. Ps 118:60.

214. Acts 7:23 and 15:36.

215. Acts 20:22 and 23.

216. The notion is that he would be designated for the future as one who has committed a crime and is in the state of being guilty for this departure; there seems to be an echo of something like the mark that

the Lord imposed on Cain, which continually reminded those who saw him that he was a guilty man (cf. Gn 4:15).

217. Cf. Jas 4:15.

218. Cf. Ps 118:101.

219. Cf. Lk 15:18 and 21.

220. 2 Pt 1:13 and Rom 7:24.

221. The "strong one" is Satan; the identification is based on Mt 12:27 and Mk 3:27.

222. Cf. Rom 8:7.

223. Cf. Prv 24:11.

224. Cf. 1 Cor 13:9.

225. Cf. Rom 1:16.

226. Cf. Eph 1:4.

227. Gal 1:20.

228. Cf. Ps 70:5.

229. 2 Tm 4:7.

230. Cf. Ps 69:17.

231. Dn 3:99 and 6:27.

232. 2 Tm 1:9.

233. Cf. Eph 1:16; 1 Tm 2:13.

234. Cf. Ps 68:6.

235. Cf. Ps 88:8.

236. 2 Kgs 17:18.

237. Cf. 1 Cor 3:9.

238. Jn 14:26.

239. Cf. Ex 20:6.

240. Cf. Ps 118:60.

241. 2 Thes 1:8.

242. Cf. 1 Tm 4:14.

243. This designation of others uses terms frequently found, and linked, in the New Testament, cf. Rv 6:11.

244. 2 Cor 13:2.

245. Cf. Job 4:3–4.

246. This is an echo of the Pauline theme of imitation; cf. the notes on no. 59 for a fuller explanation.

247. Cf. 1 Thes 2:20.

248. Prv 10:1; Lat. *filius sapiens*. This phrase was destined to play an important role in insular Christianity for several learned holy men were given the designation *sapiens*. For example, the theologian

Ailerán (d. c. 665) was known as *Aileran Sapiens* (cf. also Prv 15:20, 17:6; and Sir 3:13).

249. Cf. Ps 70:17.

250. 2 Thes 2:13.

251. 1 Cor 5:8.

252. 2 Cor 12:2; see nos. 24 and 27 in the text.

253. 2 Cor 12:17; and cf. 2 Cor 7:2.

254. Cf. 1 Pt 2:13.

255. Cf. Acts 13:50.

256. This quotation is a combination of Mt 18:7 and Rom 2:24; however, Rom 2:24 is the text that Patrick has in mind for it states that "it is written that 'The name of God is blasphemed among the Gentiles because of you,'" which is Patrick's exact context; in Paul it is an echo of Is 52:5 and Ez 36:20.

257. 2 Cor 11:6.

258. Cf. Acts 13:50.

259. Cf. Wis 3:4.

260. Cf. Eph 5:15.

261. Cf. 1 Pt 2:12.

262. 1 Sm 12:3.

263. 1 Sm 12:3 *(Vetus Latina)*.

264. 2 Cor 12:15.

265. Cf. Mt 22:15; there is irony here on Patrick's part: The allusion is to those who wished to trap Jesus. Patrick wished himself to be trapped by them so that by this they might be entrapped by his message (cp. Horace: "Captured Greece, her brutal capturer captured and brought the arts to rural Rome" [*Epistola* 2,1,156]).

266. Cf. no. 38 of this text.

267. Cf. 2 Cor 12:15.

268. Cf. Jn 7:6.

269. Cf. 1 Pt 2:13.

270. Acts 10:24.

271. Note the discontinuities in the narrative: It seems to be clerics abroad who are criticizing him about a personal sin, and at other times Christians or non-Christians in Ireland giving out about money and brides. Sometimes it seems he has left Ireland, other times that he is writing in Ireland, sometimes that his ideal reader does not know Ireland, sometimes, as here, that readers know all the details of his work.

272. This phrase is used on several occasions in scripture, e.g., Gn 41:46.

273. Cf. Rom 15:24.

274. Cf. 2 Cor 12:15.

275. 2 Cor 12:15.

276. 2 Cor 1:23.

277. Cf. 1 Thes 2:5.

278. Cf. 2 Cor 4:18.

279. Cf. Rom 10:10.

280. Heb 10:23.

281. Gal 1:4.

282. Cf. 2 Cor 8:9.

283. 1 Cor 4:3.

284. Acts 20:24.

285. Cf. Ps 31:5 and Lk 23:46.

286. 1 Chr 29:12.

287. The designation of the psalmist (David) as a prophet is based on Acts 2:30.

288. Ps 54:22.

289. Cf. Ps 31:5; Lk 23:46; Acts 7:59; and 1 Pt 4:19.

290. Eph 6:20.

291. Dt 10:17 and cf. Gal 2:6 (cf. also 2 Chr 19:2; Rom 2:11; Eph 6:9; and Col 3:25).

292. Jn 15:16.

293. Mt 25:40; note Patrick's method: A sequence of identifications with Christ and Paul is presented—what they went through, he too is going through—thus he validates his own position and apostolic identity.

294. Ps 115:12.

295. Cf. Wis 9:17.

296. Ps 6:9 (and cf. Rv 2:23); most modern translations use some phrase like "the depths of the soul" for what I have translated as "inmost parts," but the more graphic nature of the Latin translation should be kept in mind: *renes,* literally, the kidneys.

297. Cf. Ps 118:60.

298. This usage of a phrase from the gospels is most complex. The incident of the disciples' proving their devotion by being prepared to drink the same cup as Christ is found in Mt 20:20–28 and Mk 10:35–41. It is the Marcan account that is most directly relevant, for there the two disciples are named and one of them is John (the "Beloved," cf. Jn 13:23 ff). So as Patrick understands the incident it means something like this: John says he is ready to drink the Lord's cup; this is granted to him and the other disciple, he is the one who loves and is loved by the

Lord. So by identifying himself with these disciples, Patrick displays his discipleship, and expects that the cup will be granted. This will be a demonstration of the love between him and the Lord, and will be a promise of his place in the kingdom in heaven.

299. Cf. 1 Mc 13:5.

300. Is 43:21.

301. Patrick views death as a *transitus*—a move from one sort of life to another, this was a common way of presenting death in both the fathers and the early Middle Ages. It occurs in contemporary Catholic theology only with reference to the Assumption of Mary.

302. Cf. 3 Jn 11; this notion of imitating something good is clearly an echo of this particular text in the New Testament, but it should be remembered that the notion that holiness consists in imitating holiness is a larger theme in early Christian writings, and especially in Paul and writings attributed to him: cf. 1 Cor 4:16, 11:1; Eph 5:1; Phil 3:17; 1 Thes 1:6, 2:14; 2 Thes 3:7, 3:9; Heb 6:12, and 13:7. As a theme is occurs several times in Patrick; cf. nos. 34, 42, and 47 of this text.

303. Cf. Heb 12:4.

304. Links the idea of suffering for the name (Acts 5:41, 9:16) with that of making converts for the sake of the Lord's name (Rom 1:5).

305. Cf. Dt 28:26 and Ps 78:2–3.

306. Lk 8:5 supplies the wording, but the notion is found in the Old Testament: Jer 7:33; Ez 29:5; and especially in 1 Kgs 16:4, and to a lesser degree in 14:11.

307. There is an echo of two phrases from the gospel here: first, of Mt 10:28, which raises the possibility of the destruction of the body independently of the soul ("And do not fear those who kill the body but cannot kill the soul; rather fear him who can destroy both soul and body in hell")—Patrick knows that though the body would be destroyed, the soul would not be harmed, and so he is a follower of Christ's words in that he has no fear for his body, but has a fear for his soul; and second, of Mt 16:26 ("For what will it profit a man, if he gains the whole world and forfeits his life?")—Patrick presents himself as one who would heed this verse's message: He is prepared to lose the whole world, and gain his soul.

308. Cf. Ru 3:13.

309. Cf. Is 30:26.

310. Cf. 1 Cor 15:43 and Phil 3:20–21.

311. Rom 9:26 (and 8:16); cf. Hos 2:1; cf. also no. 40 in the text.

312. Rom 8:17.

313. Cf. Rom 8:29.

314. Rom 11:36. This is one of the great doxology phrases and should be seen primarily as a direct echo of the actual liturgy in which Patrick took part, rather than of Paul who is himself echoing the liturgy in his use of the phrase in Romans.

315. Cf. Mt 5:45, which speaks of God causing the sun to rise on both the righteous and sinners; here Patrick begins with the sun and then described the rewards of both groups.

316. Christ as the sun or the true sun is a complex theme in early Christian writing, which has survived in one or two places in the Latin liturgy even down to modern times. The theme uses a great variety of scriptural passages to develop its mythological coherence, such as Mt 13:43, 17:2; and Rv 22:5, but these and other passages like them should be seen as just elements in a complex development.

317. Cf. 1 Jn 2:17.

318. Cf. Ps 88:37 and 1 Jn 2:17.

319. Rv 11:15.

320. 1 Tm 5:21 (and 2 Tm 4:1 and Ps 118:111, from which he derives the phrase to alter the quotation). Patrick no doubt thinks that the moment when he will give this testimony is when the Son of Man comes in the glory of the Father with his holy angels to repay each according to his deeds (cf. Mt 16:27). See Patrick's "The Letter to the Soldiers of Coroticus," no. 20.

321. This is a Pauline theme, cf. Rom 9:4 and Gal 3:21.

322. Cf. Eph 2:8.

PATRICK'S LETTER TO THE SOLDIERS OF COROTICUS

1. Cf. 1 Cor 15:10.

2. Patrick makes a contrast here between himself and Cain "the wanderer" (Gn 4:12); cf. "Patrick's Declaration," no. 12.

3. Cf. 1 Mc 2:54.

4. Cf. 2 Cor 11:10.

5. Cf. Rom 10:9.

6. Cf. Sir 25:2 and 2 Cor 5:14.

7. Mt 26:38; and cf. Rv 12:11 for the context in which the phrase is used.

8. Several MSS read *uiuo* ("I live"), others *uoui* ("I have vowed"), which seems a far better reading.

9. Cf. Mt 28:19.

10. Phlm 19; writing with one's own hand carries with it a notion of special authority such as that conveyed by Paul at the end of his letters: 1 Cor 16:21; Gal 6:11; Col 4:18; 2 Thes 3:17; and Phlm 19.

11. Three different words are used here: "compatriots," "citizens," and "servants," where Patrick uses *ciues* (literally "citizens" or "those who dwell in the same city with"). The basic idea he wished this word to convey is a notion of alliance with others. This notion of being a fellow citizen with the servants of God or the Devil is an important motif in the development of Latin theology, as in Augustine's *De ciuitate Dei*, and has Eph 2:19 as its basic text.

12. Eph 2:19; Patrick's text reads, somewhat awkwardly: *neque ciuibus sanctorum romanorum.* This is clearly an echo of Eph 2:19: *estis ciues sanctorum et domestici Dei.*

13. This should not be seen as an example of Patrick's political naiveté. The context is the parable of the evil tenants of the vineyard in Mt 21:33–46, where after several warnings the lord of the vineyard sends his son. It is when this son is not respected as the lord expects, but is killed, that the moment of judgment comes for these wicked tenants. Patrick insists that it was not just an ordinary priest he sent to them, but one who was dear to him whom he had instructed since he was an infant; with this messenger rejected the moment has come for the final judgment to be delivered against these evil men.

14. The image of Patrick grieving before the judgment is carried out and is reminiscent of Christ weeping for Jerusalem (cf. Mt 23:37).

15. Cf. Acts 13:10.

16. Jas 3:6 "Gehenna" is used only here in the Latin Bible, but the image is a composite one; cf. T. O'Loughlin, "The Gates of Hell: From Metaphor to Fact," in *Milltown Studies* 38 (1996), pp. 98–114.

17. Jn 8:34.

18. Acts 13:10 (and cf. Jn 8:44). Note that Patrick sees himself as replacing Paul in Acts 13:8–12: Paul preaches, Paul is opposed, Paul judges, Paul condemns, and then punishment immediately follows.

19. Cf. Acts 13:16; Patrick appropriates to himself the whole speech (Acts 13:16–47) for he has been commanded to be a light to the nations and bring salvation to the ends of the earth (13:47 [cf. Is 49:6]). The theme continues in no. 6.

20. Eph 6:20; note his view of ministry. This is not just an image of representative but a full plenipotentiary minister.

21. Cf. Acts 20:29 (and cf. Mt 7:15 and 10:16).

22. Ps 13:4 and cf. Ps 52:5.

NOTES

23. Ps 118:126.

24. Cf. Acts 2:17.

25. There is a distinction here between planting and taking root; this is based on the parable of the sower (cf. Mt 13).

26. Rom 8:30.

27. Cf. Mk 10:29–30.

28. Acts 13:47; cf. no. 5 above.

29. The Enemy is the Devil (cf. Acts 13:10 and 1 Pt 5:8).

30. Mt 16:19. Note the idea of binding the strong man (Mt 12:29), here identified with the devil, and Patrick's image of the priest as the judge.

31. Dn 3:87.

32. 1 Cor 5:11.

33. Cf. Ps 6:6. Patrick refers to the practice of "tearful penance"; cf. T. O'Loughlin and H. Conrad-O'Briain, "The 'Baptism of Tears' in Early Anglo-Saxon Sources," in *Anglo-Saxon England* 22 (1993), pp. 65–83, which also examines fourth- and fifth-century theology.

34. 1 Pt 2:16.

35. Sir 34:23–24.

36. Jb 20:15, 16, and 26.

37. Hb 2:6.

38. Mt 16:26.

39. The notion of "the testimonies of the whole law" is a complex one in patristic theology; for an introduction to the theme, cf. A. C. Sundberg, "On Testimonies," in *Novum Testamentum* 3 (1959), pp. 268–281.

40. This is the only item on his list of basic moral rules that is not taken directly from scripture, but it clearly echoes statements about greed such as Lk 12:15.

41. Ex 20:17. This gathering of crimes is found in Rom 13:9 and is based on the decalogue.

42. Ex 20:13.

43. Cf. 1 Pt 4:15.

44. 1 Jn 3:15.

45. 1 Jn 3:14.

46. Cf. Gal 3:26.

47. Cf. Is 41:9 (and note it invokes the idea found elsewhere in Patrick's writings that he works at "the ends of the earth").

48. 1 Cor 1:17.

49. Acts 20:22.

50. Cf. Gn 12:1.

51. 1 Cor 1:17.

52. Patrick writes "for the benefit of others," which invokes the Pauline notion of utility; cf. Rom 3:1; and 1 Cor 7:35 and 12:7.

53. Rom 6:23.

54. Jn 4:44.

55. Jn 10:16.

56. Eph 4:6.

57. Mt 12:30.

58. Sir 34:28.

59. Cf. 1 Cor 13:5.

60. 2 Cor 8:16.

61. Cf. Jer 16:16.

62. Acts 2:17.

63. Throughout this section of the letter, Patrick draws on the sheep/flock imagery of the prophets (Ez 34 being the *locus classicus* of this imagery) and the gospels (especially Jn 10). This opening remark ("I am despised, so what am I to do?") seems to imply that he is answering a criticism that he was a bad shepherd who left his flock untended and so left them open to attack (cf. Jer 23:1; Ez 34:2; and Jn 10:12).

64. There are echoes of Jn 10:8–12 in this sentence.

65. Cf. Acts 20:29 (and cf. Mt 7:15).

66. This echoes Jn 21:15; the use of the image of being one charged with the love and care of the sheep is additional support for the supposition that Patrick here is defending himself against the charge of being a bad pastor.

67. Sir 9:17; this verse cannot now be found in translations of the scriptures as it belongs to the so-called Expanded Text that stands behind the Vetus Latina/Vulgate. It can only be conveniently found in editions of the Vulgate or old Catholic translations such as the Douay. For an account of these textual problems, the fullest guide is C. Kearns, "Ecclesiasticus" in *A New Catholic Commentary on Holy Scripture*, ed. R. C. Fuller *et al.* (London, 1969), pp. 546–547.

68. Gn 3:6.

69. Cf. 2 Cor 7:10.

70. The word *gentes* is used by Patrick in the technical sense found in the scriptures as denoting the alternative to the People of God: "The nations" means "the pagans"; cf. J. Hastings, F. C. Grant, and H. H. Rowley, *Dictionary of the Bible* (2nd edition, Edinburgh, 1963), s.v. Nations.

71. 1 Thes 4:5.

72. The image is based on Paul (1 Cor 6:15: "Shall I therefore take the members of Christ and make them members of a prostitute? [*meretrix*]"), whose words "members of Christ" are quoted; however, Patrick does not see the members of Christ being handed over to a person, but being handed into a place: *in lupanar.* This word for a brothel carries with it some very strong images. First, it comes from a figurative word for a prostitute, *lupa,* which literally means "a she-wolf" and so the image of the parts of Christ's body being devoured in an evil place is conjured up. Second, this word is used in the scriptures in Latin to describe the places where the Israelites pursued foreign gods (Nm 25:8; Ez 16:24, 31, and 39) and as a result of their dealing with these places they had to face punishment. Thus Coroticus's behavior is in keeping with his status as an apostate.

73. Acts 24:15.

74. Rom 1:32.

75. Jn 12:49.

76. This phrase is used on four occasions in the New Testament (Mt 5:9; Lk 20:36; Rom 8:14 and 19; and Gal 3:26), but since Paul seems to have the argument from Romans in his mind, it probably reflects Paul's usage there where the sons of God are those who have been delivered from slavery by Christ but who have to put up with sufferings in the present life as they await the full revelation of glory at the End.

77. Rom 12:15.

78. 1 Cor 12:26.

79. Cf. Mt 2:18.

80. Cf. Rom 5:20.

81. Patrick used the words *redacti sunt* [literally: they are reduced]. This echoes the Pauline theme in Rom 8: The Christians are those delivered from slavery, and they must not fall back into fear and slavery (Rom 8:15); so Patrick is concerned not only that they are physically the prisoners of the Picts and made into slaves, but that being with these sinful men, they might fall back into a former spiritual slavery.

82. Cf. 1 Cor 4:14–5.

83. Cf. Ps 64:4.

84. Cf. Ps 68:9.

85. Cf. Eph 4:5–6.

86. Mal 2:10.

87. Phil 2:16.

88. Cf. Lk 23:43.

89. This is a conflation of Rv 22:5 and 21:4.

90. Mal 4:2–3.

91. Mt 8:11.

92. Rv 22:15; Patrick intends the whole verse to be understood: "Outside are the dogs and sorcerers and fornicators and murderers and idolaters, and every one who loves and practices falsehood."

93. Rv 21:8: "But as for the cowardly, the faithless, the polluted, as for murderers, fornicators, sorcerers, idolaters, and all liars, their lot shall be in the lake that burns with fire and sulphur, which is the second death." This conflation is a product of memory through similar items in a list triggering a combination of both lists. See also Mal 3:5 and 1 Tm 1:10.

94. 1 Pt 4:18 (and cf. Prv 11:31).

95. Patrick's argument here is based on the idea of the distance between earthy riches and the eternal kingdom as found in texts such as Lk 12:33–34.

96. Cf. 1 Cor 15:52.

97. Cf. Is 44:22.

98. Cf. Wis 5:15.

99. Ps 68:2–3.

100. Wis 3:8.

101. Cf. Rv 20:10 and 22:5.

102. 2 Tm 4:1 and 1 Tm 5:21. See "Patrick's Declaration," no. 61.

103. Patrick uses the forensic tone again: You now stand warned!

104. Mk 16:15–6.

105. This is a phrase used on many occasions in the scriptures, but the two uses in the Psalms (59:8 and 107:8) are especially interesting: "God has spoken through his saint."

106. Cf. 2 Tim 2:25–26.

107. There is an echo here, in that a murderer is allowed to live, of Acts 28:4.

108. In the Book of Armagh there is a colophon giving Patrick's date of death as March 17—this date, also found in seventh-century liturgical calendars, is one of our best-attested "facts" about Patrick's life.

THE SAYINGS OF PATRICK

1. Cf. Rom 3:19 (and Ps 36:2).

2. Cf. Lk 23:43; 2 Cor 12:4; and Rv 2:7.

3. This phrase is found on many occasions in the liturgy and in the writings of Paul, e.g., Rom 6:17.

4. These phrases are in Greek in the *dicta,* indicating their origin in the liturgy, the Kyrie; this form is also found in the New Testament on several occasions, e.g., Mt 17:15.

THE LIFE OF PATRICK BY MUIRCHÚ

1. In the Latin edition by Bieler and many translations this is referred to as "the preface"; however, at the beginning of next section we have the statement "here begins the prologue." It is better to see this as the dedication and apology for writing.

2. Aed of Sletty had gone over to supporting Armagh's claim to be the first church in Ireland. This may have been the occasion for his commissioning of the *vita;* cf. K. Hughes, *The Church in Early Irish Society* (London, 1966), pp. 86 and 113–115.

3. The word *narratio* is used on several occasions in this preface and the word "narrative" springs immediately to mind. I am avoiding that word because when we consider the overall quality of Muirchú's writing it is not fanciful to see in his use of *narratio* the technical sense given to that word by Augustine in *De doctrina christiana,* where it means the careful retelling of the facts so that if there are providential interventions by God in human history these may be clearly seen. On the importance of this concept in insular intellectual life in the late-seventh century; cf. T. O'Loughlin, "Why Adomnán Needs Arculf: The Case of an Expert Witness," *Journal of Medieval Latin* 7 (1997), pp. 127–46.

4. This image is used by others writing saints' lives such as the author of the *Life of St. Samson of Dol* and Cogitosus in his *Life of St. Brigid.* But there may also be a pun here, for *Muir cu* means literally "sea hound."

5. This is the *topos* of humility.

6. Another humility motif; cf. Vincent of Lérins's opening remarks in his *Commonitorium.*

7. This section is garbled in the manuscripts; cf. T. O'Loughlin, "Muirchú's *Vita Patricii:* A Note on an Unidentified Source," in E 46 (1996), pp. 89–93, where this passage is studied in detail.

8. The word used by Muirchu is *magus* and this is often rendered as "druid"; however, since all Muirchú's names for pagan officials are derived from the scriptures, I shall render this word as "wise man," but noting that it has an additional connotation that is something like "magician" or "soothsayer."

9. This list is incompletely extant.

10. The location of Patrick's home, which has exercised so many scholars over the last century, was already a matter of dispute in Muirchú's day.

11. Throughout the work Muirchú distinguishes between barbarians (*barbari*)—i.e., non-Romans, and pagans (*gentiles*)—i.e., non-Christians.

12. Cf. Ex 21:2 and Dt 15:12.

13. Ps 54:6; and cf. Eph 6:5.

14. Mt 22:21.

15. Cf. 2 Cor 11:27 (and compare Paul's account of his trials in 2 Cor 11:24–28).

16. Cf. Rom 11:4.

17. Col 3:9.

18. Cf. Jon 2:1.

19. Allusion to the events of the Exodus in Ex and Nm.

20. Cf. Ex 15:24.

21. The imagery here is related to Jon 1:14–6.

22. Cf. Mt 9:36.

23. Cf. Mt 9:8 and Gal 1:24.

24. Cf. Ex 16:13; Nm 11:31; and Ps 104:40.

25. Cf. Mt 3:4.

26. Cf. 1 Cor 10:28–29.

27. Cf. Dn 1:5–16.

28. Cf. Mk 15:35.

29. Cf. Jl 2:2 and Zep 1:15; and Acts 13:11 as antitype.

30. Cf. Rom 11:4.

31. Cf. Gn 37:21.

32. Eph 4:13; and cf. Lk 3:23.

33. This section more echoes the mentions of "the nations" in the Synoptic Apocalypse (e.g., Mt 24:14) than the commands to evangelize (e.g., Mt 28:19).

34. Cf. Acts 22:3.

35. Cf. Mt 4:18 and 13:47.

36. Cf. Rom 1:1.

37. The technical language for bishops, priests, deacons, and other ministries corresponds precisely to late-seventh-century canonical usage as found in such works as the *Collectio canonum hibernensis.* The translation attempts to echo that language.

38. Jn 3:27.

39. Jn 18:4.

40. Ps 109:4 (and cf. the New Testament uses of this verse: Heb 5:6, 6:20, 7:11, and 7:17).

41. Muirchú presumes this is a known proverb, but I have been unable to find other instances of it; it is possible that it is inspired by Mt 25:26.

42. This chapter is a "flashback" (i.e., it departs from the forward temporal sequence of the account of the saint) and it is placed here to set the scene for something that will happen later when Patrick meets Loíguire.

43. This phrase is taken from Jerome's *Prologue to the Book of Job* (such Prologues were a standard part of the biblical apparatus in scriptural codices in Muirchú's time).

44. This phrase (*Fiat, fiat*) is found in this form in Jdt (10:9, 13:26, and 15:12) and, more importantly, in the more used Latin version (that based on the Septuagint) of the psalms (40:14, 71:19, 88:53, 105:48); it renders the phrase "Amen, Amen."

45. Cf. Mt 24:33.

46. Muirchú, whose native language was Irish and for whom Latin was a learned language, engages in a literary conceit here in telling his audience that *their* language is a foreign one, and *our* language (in this case, Latin) can express this more clearly. To wish to identify himself with Latin to this extent may indicate that he sees this as the Christian language or the language of light and sophistication.

47. The geographical locations of the various places mentioned in the *Vita* are matters of controversy among historians. It would take us too far from our purpose here to enter into these disputes.

48. This sentence is modeled on Acts 1 (especially 1:9); the notion of the angel leaving a visible footprint in the place of his ascension is parallel to a belief that the footprints of Jesus were visible on Mount Olivet (this story is told in Adomnán's *De locis sanctis* 1,23—a work contemporary with Muirchú).

49. There is an echo here of Christ weeping over Jerusalem (Lk 19:41)—the city that would not receive his message and suffered destruction.

50. 2 Cor 12:2.

51. Ibid.

52. Miliucc's throne is contrasted with "the throne of David" (e.g., 2 Sm 7:13–16; 2 Chr 7:18; Ps 88:4, 29, and 36), which is established forever.

53. This is a biblical phrase, e.g., Ex 17:16 or Ps 78:13.

54. There is an echo of what is said in Ex 33:11 about how Moses spoke with God.

55. A gloss in the Book of Armagh adds: "When he said a hundred prayers by day and a hundred by night."

56. See no. 10 of this text above.

57. The word used is *Pascha,* which could be translated as "Easter"; however, in Latin the same word is used for the Christian feast as is used for the Passover in both Old and New Testaments and therefore it calls up a wealth of biblical imagery (as is the case here in Muirchú) that "Easter" does not. Therefore, since the normal biblical translation of *Pascha* is "Passover," this is the word adopted here.

58. In Gn 45:10–50:8 we are told that the Israelites settled in "the land of Goshen" in Egypt, but nowhere in Genesis is there mention of the Passover. The first Passover is described in Ex 12, but it could be inferred from Ex 9:26 that the Israelites were still there at the time.

59. Literally: of these nations.

60. Literally: of their "gentile-ness."

61. Ps 73:14.

62. The imagery is from Jgs 4:17–21.

63. Cf. 1 Pt 5:9.

64. Acts 27:44.

65. Cf. Acts 6:5.

66. Cf. Sir 7:11.

67. Muirchú seems to have in mind Tb 8:19. This verse, present in the Vulgate, is no longer found in modern editions/versions, and reads: "May their hearts, O Lord, always swell with thanksgiving and their lives, which you have preserved, be a sacrifice of praise to you until all of the peoples acknowledge that you alone are God in all the earth." However, it could be simply allusion to Ps 49:14. The actual phrase used by Muirchú about "the word of the prophet" is taken from Lk 3:4.

68. The word *satraps* is used in the Vulgate as the term for officials in several pagan courts (e.g., Jgs 3:3), but the imagery here is that of the gathering of all the officials and powerful in the land that was called by Nebuchadnezzar, king of Babylon, for the great event of idolatry that is found in Dn 3:2–3.

69. Cf. Dn 2:2.

70. Cf. Dn 3:2–3. The image of Nebuchadnezzar as the type of the pagan king stands behind this reference. The image is built up from the stories in 2 Kgs, Jer, and Dn 2 where he receives a dream of what will

happen to him at the end of his days, and many other references. This image was compounded by liturgical references to him such as the collect *Nabochodonosor Rex* in Easter ceremonies.

71. Cf. Dn 6:7–9.

72. For the background to Muirchú's understanding of the Paschal Fire, cf. A. J. MacGregor, *Fire and Light in the Western Triduum* (Collegeville, 1992), pts. 2 and 3.

73. The imagery is that of Herod with the wise men; cf. Mt 2:4–6.

74. Dn 6:6 (and cf. Dn 5:10 and 2:4).

75. Cf. Lk 11:22–25.

76. Cf. Mt 4:8.

77. Cf. Dn 3:7. The point is complex for Daniel, a wise man, tells how all the peoples fell down before the idol at Nebuchadnezzar's feast; here at the idolatrous feast a pagan wise man tells the king how the people will fall down at the feast of the true God. Cf. also Ps 71:11.

78. Rv 11:15.

79. Mt 2:3.

80. The significance of this detail, and other references to "left" and "right," is not understood.

81. Cf. Ps 19:8.

82. The Latin word *adorare* is used; the later verbal distinctions of *adorare/latria* (worship due alone to God) and *uenerare/dulia* (respect, veneration due to the holy) was not yet universal, and it would be anachronous to "correct" the text in translation (e.g., by the use of "venerate") to a later standard of verbal orthodoxy. Such "corrections" are already found in medieval authors who used Muirchú.

83. On this theme of lips and heart, cf. Is 29:13 as used in Mt 15:8 and Mk 7:6; and cf. also Sir 12:15.

84. Ps 19:8.

85. Bieler suggests that this may be a reference to either, or both, of the apocryphal texts known as the *Passion of Saints Peter and Paul*, ch. 56; and the *Acts of Peter with Simon*, ch. 32. Pending a full study of this section, the following points should be noted. First, the work known as the *Acts of Peter and Paul* was used in Ireland at a very early period (cf. M. McNamara, *The Apocrypha in the Irish Church* [Dublin, 1975], pp. 99–101 for comment; and M. Herbert and M. McNamara, *Irish Biblical Apocrypha: Selected Texts in Translation* [Edinburgh, 1989]), pp. 99–105 for text). Second, in this work there is a contest similar in form to that found in Muirchú: Peter the Apostle disputes with Simon the Wise Man *(Magus)* in the presence of the pagan ruler, the Emperor Nero, as to the

truth of Christianity, and the result is the death of Simon. However, third, there is no verbal similarity between these texts, and the death of Simon, while caused by Peter, is not directly a curse; so it could be maintained that the reference by Muirchú to Peter and Simon is only a general reference to the incident in Acts 8.

86. Cf. Is 41:5.

87. Ps 67:2.

88. This imagery of commotion, darkness (cf. the conflict of Paul with Bar-jesus in Acts 13:6–12), and earthquake (cf. Mt 27:54 and Acts 16:26) as a result of a divine intervention is found in several places in the scriptures.

89. Cf. Lk 10:30; and "Patrick's Declaration," no. 19.

90. Cf. Mt 12:25 and 16:8.

91. There are verbal echoes of the description in 2 Kgs 21 of Manasseh, who was proverbially *the* evil king.

92. The phrase "kings and princes" is found on several occasions in the scriptures—e.g., Jer 44:17, Dn 9:6; Neh 9:32; and often there is the sense that they are gathered to witness a divine action—e.g., Is 19:11, 49:7, or Ps 76:12. This seems to be the motive here: They are assembled for their purposes, yet God uses this for his own and their gathering provides a suitable audience for his mighty deeds through Patrick.

93. The imagery is drawn from the description of King Belshazzar's feast in Dn 5.

94. Cf. Jn 20:19–29.

95. Muirchú combines the notion of testifying to all peoples (Mt 24:14 and *Declaration*, no. 3) with that of bearing witness before hostile authorities (Lk 21:12).

96. This notion of believing on the day of hearing the word is modeled on the accounts of large numbers being converted in Acts 2:41 on the first day of preaching (Pentecost).

97. Gn 15:6; and cf. Ps 105:31; 1 Mc 2:52; Rom 4:3, 9, 22; Gal 3:6; and Jas 2:23.

98. Jn 18:4.

99. Mt 26:26.

100. This constitutes a particular kind of text for Muirchú: The saint in accordance with Mk 16:18 cannot be injured by any deadly thing in his drink; and note the incident of Paul with the viper in Acts 28:1–6. Hence I depart from Bieler's text, but stay with two of the manuscripts, in reading "After the cup test *(poculum)*" rather than "after a little while *(paululum)*." Note that Muirchú sees it as a *kind* of test *(hoc probationis genus)*.

101. Mk 1:27.

102. Muirchú's notion of a miracle (*signum*) becomes clear here. He combines the New Testament notion of a miracle as that which produces "amazement" (*stupor*), e.g., at Lk 5:26, in the Synoptics with that found in Jn, e.g., Jn 2:18, where the miracle is a "sign" (*signum*); in both cases it is the recognition of the event that reveals the person who instigates it. The miraculous is testimony to the power that is present; this can be seen in the number of occasions when there is a connection between seeing "signs and wonders" (*signa et prodigia*) and belief in some way or other (Mt 24:24; Mk 13:22; Jn 4:48; Acts 4:30, 5:12, 14:3, 15:12; Rom 15:19; 2 Cor 12:12; 2 Thes 2:9; and Heb 2:4).

103. This might seem to be an unusual humility given what Patrick had already done; however, allowing that it may be a dramatic refusal to encourage the wise man to do what he cannot undo—and so showing a fortiori the relative power of Patrick, it should be noted that sending snow has specific links in the tradition with the will of God; cf. Jb 37:6, 38:22; and Sir 43:14.

104. Mk 1:27.

105. Mt 9:33.

106. Acts 2:37.

107. This miracle appears to be the antitype of that produced by Moses in Egypt (Ex 10:21).

108. Rom 1:21.

109. The phrase is modeled on Ex 20:3.

110. It seems an unequal context for while the wise man has to enter the house himself, Patrick can use a deputy. However, Muirchú may intend to show by this the great power of Patrick: Not only is he mighty in holiness in that he is protected, but his power is such that he can reproduce it in one of his spiritual "sons." Just as Christ's power creates an image in the Christian who then shares in his power, so the mighty saint can reproduce himself in his followers, who in turn become extensions of him (I am indebted to Prof. J. Nagy of UCLA for this suggestion).

111. I translate *uestimentum* with the liturgical term "vestment," as it is clear from the context, and from the later references to chasubles, that it is not ordinary but sacred clothing that is intended here.

112. Sir 39:6.

113. Rv 11:13.

114. The notion of flaming fire seems tautologous, but within Muirchú's physics it is precise statement of what he saw as the facts: "Fire" is one of the four elements—as such it is the inherent heat that

goes to make up material things—and one manifestation of this element is the particular species of fire that we see in a burning fire, i.e., "flaming fire."

115. The whole incident appears to be modeled on the clash between Elijah and the prophets of Baal in 1 Kgs 18:19–40.

116. Dn 3:50 (in modern versions this is sometimes numbered 3:27).

117. Mt 2:16; again the king is being modeled on Herod.

118. Rom 1:18.

119. Cf. 1 Mc 13:49.

120. Cf. Ps 7:17.

121. Cf. 1 Sm 28:5.

122. The phrase is modeled on Mt 2:3, but its language follows Mt 21:10.

123. Cf. Jon 4:8.

124. Cf. Jn 7:31, 8:30, 12:42; and Acts 17:12.

125. Cf. Jer 33:26.

126. Mt 28:19.

127. Mk 16:20.

128. Lk 1:41.

129. Cf. Ps 2:4; Ps 102:19; Is 40:22; and Heb 8:1.

130. Book of Jubilees 11:15–7. McNamara, *Apocrypha*, p. 20, said that it could not be stated "with certainty whether this apocryphon was known in Ireland"; and, at McNamara's suggestion, Bieler in the edition of Muirchú (p. 206) advanced the possibility that this snippet of information was known by way of one of the letters of Jerome.

131. This title is given to several men in scripture: Noah (Gn 6:9), Joseph the husband of Mary (Mt 1:19), and Lot (2 Pt 2:7).

132. Lk 1:41.

133. Cf. Jn 3:5.

134. Echo of Lk 23:46.

135. The expression is found in several places in scripture, e.g., Tb 1:2; Wis 5:6; and 2 Pt 2:2.

136. Cf. Rom 12:18 and Mt 24:24.

137. In the remainder of the text Muirchú gives the impression that Coroticus is a pagan opposed to Christianity; here, by his use of *perfidus* (traitor), he shows his acquaintance with "The Letter to Soldiers of Coroticus" where Coroticus is treated not as a pagan, but as an "apostate," this being equivalent to a grievously sinful Christian.

138. This linkage of "the present" and "future ages" can be found in Mk 10:30 and Eph 1:21.

139. The allusion is to Acts 7, but it should be noted that seeing into heaven is a common saintly attribute and, second, that Muirchú takes the notion that miracles fall into specific categories—and therefore the same miracle can be found in saint after saint—for granted.

140. Cf. Jb 37:14.

141. Cf. Acts 7:55, but note in Acts that Stephen sees the Son of Man at the right hand of the Father, whereas here we have the Son of God and the angels. The text here is a silent conflation of Acts with the promise made by Christ of "the greater things" that will be seen by the disciples in Jn 1:51.

142. The picture created by Muirchú seems to echo the election of Elisha as the successor to Elijah in 2 Kgs 2.

143. This list of the qualities of the evil man allows us to infer what Muirchú considered to be the qualities of sanctity.

144. This incident is set out as a contrast to the faith of the centurion in Mt 8:5–13.

145. Cf. Jn 18:4.

146. Cf. Mt 27:54.

147. Acts 16:31; the addition of "and God" is an expansion of the verse by conflation with Jn 20:28.

148. Sir 4:31.

149. Mt 28:19; the instruction itself (now be baptized) is based on Acts 22:16.

150. Mt 10:19.

151. Cf. Gn 4:15.

152. Such a craft was not only small, but also very flimsy as it could be easily holed. I am indebted to Dr. Jonathan Wooding for this information.

153. This place is identified as the Isle of Man.

154. This reference to the developing notion of refraining from work or travel on Sunday is the earliest indication we have from Irish sources of what would later become a significant element in Christian practice in Ireland as witnessed by the *Cáin Domnaig* (c. A.D. 800). See the translation of "The Day of the Lord," text 1 in *Three Sunday Catecheses*.

155. This is an Irish corruption of Welsh; it means "by the God of judgment."

156. Lk 16:1 and 16:9.

157. Cf. Lk 1:27; Jn 1:6; and Acts 13:6.

158. Ps 37:14.

159. The text is emended here from "you will be well."

160. A colloquial form of *gratias agamus* ("we give you thanks") something like our simple expression "thanks."

161. Cf. Jb 1:21.

162. The imagery is that of the good shepherd from Is 40:11.

163. See no. 27 of this text.

164. Cf. Gn 1:7.

165. Ps 106:34.

166. See, for example, Mt 27:8.

167. The heading reads "sacrifice" (*De sacrificio*), and it is clear from the chapter that this was the Eucharist (*uiaticum*), hence the translation here.

168. Eph 5:19.

169. This curious incident gives us an insight into Muirchú's eschatology. A Christian tomb was considered a place of power, e.g., the tombs of the saints were places for intercessory prayer, as in such a tomb lay someone who was one of the elect while they awaited the resurrection. As such this presence could radiate itself through the sign; but the sign alone, as here where we have the cross but not the waiting soul it should be marking, did not have this radiance. The obverse of this argument is that the dead pagan is just lying there, his soul stuck in the ground and not possessing any power nor awaiting anything, and as such he is one of the damned (see T. O'Loughlin, "The Gates of Hell: From Metaphor to Fact," in *Milltown Studies* 38 (1996), pp. 98–114).

170. Literally: vespers.

171. I.e., Saturday night (the First Vespers of Sunday).

172. I.e., Monday morning. See book 1, 27 above.

173. Jgs 6:36–40.

174. Cf. Lk 11:11–2.

175. This statement echoes Pss 29:11, 24:17, 33:5; and Heb 13:6.

176. Ex 3:2.

177. Cf. Nm 24:11.

178. Mt 10:15, 11:22, 11:24, 12:36; and many other places in scripture.

179. Mt 19:28.

180. Several lists of "the petitions of Patrick" have survived. Here a particular list that links loyalty to Armagh with survival in the judgment is given added authority by being uttered by an angel. While notion of a favored judgment as a result of specific actions (e.g., singing a hymn) may seem very alien to us, we should remember that variants of this

formula (e.g., the "Nine Promises to St. Margaret Mary," where the form of intercession had been theologically sanitized by linking it to the Sacred Heart of Jesus) were still a vibrant part of Roman Catholic preaching in the first half of this century, and still figures in certain eschatological cults within Catholicism.

181. Cf. Gn 31:3; Bar 2:33; and 1 Kgs 19:15.

182. Cf. Virgil, *Aeneid* 8, 369.

183. Cf. 2 Kgs 20, especially verses 8–11.

184. Jos 10:12, but replaces *ne mouearis* in this verse with *stetit* from verse 13.

185. The technical word *viaticum* is used; cf. G. Grabka, "Christian Viaticum: A Study of Its Cultural Background," in *Traditio* 9 (1953), pp. 1–43.

186. Some of the problems associated with the text of this Vita can be seen here. Having described the funeral, the text now returns to the period before Patrick's death; however, such textual problems are beyond the scope of this work.

187. This scene is modeled on Christ in the garden (of Gethsemane) as found in Lk 22:39–46. As that text is found in many ancient witnesses and versions (the Vulgate included), but not in modern editions or translations, there is a contrast between Christ ignored by the sleeping Apostles, while comforted by an angel.

188. Cf. Mt 2:23, and similar phrases.

189. Gn 27:27.

190. See note 114 above on "flaming fire."

191. Cf. 1 Pt 1:9.

192. Cf. 2 Kgs 6:11–20 (in the Vulgate the enemies of Israel are called "Syrians"; in modern versions they are called "Arameans").

PATRICK'S BREASTPLATE

1. There may, however, be a reference here to Eph 3:18 (Th. Pal., p. 357) or, alternatively, the meaning might be "May Christ be wherever I lie down, Christ wherever I sit, Christ wherever I stand up" (Th. Pal., p. 506).

NOTES

THE LIFE OF ST. BRIGIT THE VIRGIN BY COGITOSUS

1. In the north of County Kildare.

2. The following passage is not included in PL, but can be found in Colgan's version (*Acta Sanctorum* 3 [Antwerp, 1658], p. 136).

3. The following passage is not contained in PL, but can be found in Colgan (ibid., p. 137).

4. This is speculative, and I am following Connolly here (S. Connolly, "Cogitosus', *Life of Brigit*: Content and Value," JRSAI 117 [1987], p. 20).

THE IRISH LIFE OF BRIGIT

1. Cf. the white hounds with red ears that occur in the story of Pwyll in the *Mabinogion*, where they are clearly linked with the Other World (J. Ganz, ed., *The Mabinogion* [Harmondsworth, 1976], pp. 46–47).

2. The earliest occurrence of the traditional appellation of Brigit as "Mary of the Gael" can be dated to around the sixth century (D. Ó hAodha, ed., *Bethu Brigte* [Dublin, 1978], p. 42).

3. That is, for the poor or for lepers, who bear the same name as the later monastic reform movement of the eighth century.

4. Grosjean has pointed out that acacia was the wood from which the Ark of the Covenant was made, and he suggests that that an ancient commentary on Exodus may have been influential here (quoted in Ó hAodha, *Bethu Brigte*, p. 48).

5. Alternatively, "on the bank of a river" (ibid., pp. 58–59).

6. For two other references to burning women for sexual incontinence, see M. E. Byrne, in E 11, p. 100, and Ó hAodha, *Bethu Brigte* p. 60.

THE VOYAGE OF BRENDAN

1. For this translation I am using C. Selmer, ed., *Navigatio Sancti Brendani* (Notre Dame, Indiana, 1959); but see also the reviews of this edition by J. Carney in *Medium Aevum* 32 (1963), pp. 37–44, and L. Bieler in *Zeitschrift für Kirchengeschichte* 1 (1961), pp. 164–169. I have also adopted a number of ideas from J. J. O'Meara, *The Voyage of St. Brendan: Journey to the Promised Land* (Dublin, 1976).

2. Kenney makes the point that genealogy was an important and distinctive feature of Irish hagiography on account not only of the role of the genealogists in establishing royal lines but also because of the place of kinship in the inheritance of monastic functions (*Sources*, p. 304).

3. On Barinthus, abbot of Drumcullen, see A. C. L. Brown, "Barintus," in RC 22 (1901), pp. 339–344 (Selmer, *Navigatio*, p. 99).

4. Probably Clonfert in Connacht, county Galway, where Brendan founded his chief monastery.

5. This monastic name is still remembered in the Scottish place-name Kilmarnock (Selmer, *Navigatio*, p. 101).

6. Prior knowledge of the names of others is a common feature of Irish hagiography.

7. See note 5 under "Monastic Texts."

8. Enda was Abbot of Ardmere. Brendan's visit to Enda before commencing his voyage recalls that of Aeneas to Anius, priest of Apollo (Selmer, *Navigatio*, p. 84).

9. St. Brendan's Mountain on the Dingle Peninsular, Kerry.

10. The text *De mensura orbis terrae* also records islands covered with sheep; there may be a remembrance here of the Faroe Islands, whose name is derived from the Danish word for sheep (Selmer, *Navigatio*, p. 86).

11. From Irish *iasc* meaning "fish."

12. Again, the origin of this passage may be a description of one of the many offshore islands that are home to extensive colonies of white sea birds.

13. Ailbe is the patron saint of Munster.

14. Selmer suggests that this passage may be a processional hymn used to greet guests at Irish monasteries (*Navigatio*, p. 87).

15. There may be an echo here of Jerome's account in his *Life of Paul* of the meeting between Anthony the Great and Paul of Thebes, which was attended by a crow bringing a double portion of bread (PL 23, cols. 22–27). See Selmer, *Navigatio*, p. 88.

16. This may be an allusion perhaps to the New Jerusalem decribed in Rv 21:16.

17. That is, the Song of the Three Children, which comes at Dn 3:23 in the Vulgate.

18. The precise meaning of *scalta* (here "vegetation") is unclear.

19. Pss 119–133.

20. The gryphon is a mythological bird known from numerous classical and medieval sources.

21. Selmer suggests that this may have been a shoal of jelly-fish (*Navigatio*, p. 90).

22. This may possibly be the remembrance of an iceberg, although, as Selmer notes, its dimensions recall the description of the temple in Ez 40 and 41 and Rv 21 (*Navigatio*, p. 90).

23. Selmer speculates that this passage, and the following, may be based on the memory of a volcanic island (*Navigatio*, p. 90).

24. Webb translates "like a cauldron of stew boiling over a good fire," but the image here is that of a cauldron heated by the introduction of hot stones; see A. T. Lucas, "Washing and Bathing in Ancient Ireland," in JRSAI 95 (1965), pp. 65–114.

25. The combination of graphic detail and symbolic meanings that we find in this image of Judas Iscariot evidently anticipates the aesthetic principles of Dante's *Divine Comedy*.

26. This is Paul of Thebes, an ancient hermit, whose ascetical surroundings in the Egyptian desert (described by Jerome in his *Life of St. Paul*) have here been transposed to a rocky island in the middle of the sea.

27. This is a reminder that on the bare islands of the western coast, fuel was as much in short supply as food.

THE LIFE OF ST. DAVID BY RHIGYFARCH

1. The name Maucannus may appear again in the title of the *Orationes Moucani (Prayers of Moucan)*, a devotional piece translated below (pp. 301–06).

2. This is a common image for extracting the mystical or spiritual meanings of scripture.

3. It was clearly Rhigyfarch's intention to suggest that Patrick stood to David as John the Baptist to Christ, in order to promote the claims of St. David's see.

4. That is, a site in modern Pembrokeshire.

5. Dew, by virtue of its association with the water of baptism, is an ancient Christian image for the Holy Spirit, an indication again of the parallel Rhigyfarch seeks to draw between David and Christ.

6. The theme of bringing rivals to silence is present also in the Welsh bardic tradition; Taliesin was able to silence the bards at Maelgwn's court (Patrick K. Ford, ed., *Ystoria Taliesin* [Cardiff, 1992], p. 82), a theme that occurs again in "The Contest of the Bards," a poem from

the *Book of Taliesin*, where Taliesin states: "I cause eloquent bards to stumble" (Marged Haycock, *Rhai Agweddau ar Lyfr Taliesin*, University of Wales Ph.D., 1982, p. 71).

7. The site traditionally associated with this place is St. Non's in Pembrokeshire.

8. See also the reference to Ailbe in note 13 under "The Voyage of Brendan."

9. Probably modern Whitland, West Wales.

10. Passages such as this in hagiographical literature are an indication of continuing land disputes between the church and secular rulers.

11. This appears to introduce a section that may be based on a Rule of David still extant in Rhigyfarch's day.

12. The word *apathy* here translates *accidie*. See also Ch. 6 of "The Penitential of Cummean" (p. 238 below).

13. The precise meaning of this sentence is not entirely clear. The term *genuflexionibus* suggests "genuflections" rather than the kneeling posture, in which case Rhigyfarch (or his source at this point) may be describing the typically Celtic and well-attested practice of genuflecting after each Psalm is sung (see also pp. 250–52 below).

14. Cf. "The Life of St. Brigit," p. 125. It was written of St. Ninian too that the book he was reading was unaffected by rainfall (cf. Oliver Davies and Fiona Bowie, *Celtic Christian Spirituality* [London, 1995], p. 71).

15. There is a poem from the *Black Book of Carmarthen* that is attributed to one Ysgolan (LlD, p. 55); see also A. O. H. Jarman, "Cerdd Ysgolan," in *Ysgrifau Beirniadol* 10 (1977), pp. 51–78.

16. The references to David as Archbishop may be a later addition; see D. P. Kirby, "A Note on Rhigyfarch's Life of David," in *Welsh History Review* 4 (1969), pp. 292–297.

17. For the text of this Synod, see Ludwig Bieler, *The Irish Penitentials* (Dublin, 1975), pp. 68–69. The relation of this and *Excerpts from a Book of David*, both of which are attributed to the sixth century, to Rhigyfarch's eleventh-century David is unclear, but it is possible that these or similar texts are the ones that Rhigyfarch refers to below as being "written in the style of the elders."

18. Cf. Eph 5:19, where the Vulgate reads: "Loquentes vobismetipsis in psalmis, et hymnis, et canticis spiritualibus...."

THE LIFE OF BEUNO

1. This is Dahlmann's translation for *bonnhedic* (S. M. Dahlmann, ed., *Critical Edition of the Buched Beuno*, Catholic University of America, Washington, D.C., Ph.D., 1976, p. 45).

2. That is, the River Severn.

3. Although not attested in GPC, the word used here, *dinas* ("city") has the sense of "monastery" (cf. *civitas* in J. W. James, ed., *Rhigyfarch's Life of St. David* [Cardiff, 1967], p. 19).

4. I prefer to read *cymun* ("communion") from Dahlman's B text here rather than "cymyn" meaning "will" or "testament."

5. The *Cywydd i Feuno* has a variant on this in that it is a pagan who cannot pass safely beneath the tree (E. R. Henken, *The Traditions of the Welsh Saints* [Woodbridge, 1987], p. 84).

6. Dahlmann (*Critical Edition*, pp. 129–130) gives parallel references from the *Life of St. Cadog* (A. W. Wade-Evans, ed., *Vita Sanctorum Britanniae et Genealogiae* [Cardiff, 1944], p. 113), the *Life of St. Tatheus* (ibid., p. 179), and the *Life of St. Brynach* (ibid., p. 13).

7. The word *arffed* actually means "lap" or "lower abdomen," suggesting perhaps that the child was strapped to the woman's front, (GPC, s.v. *arffed*).

8. The name *Caer Seint* derives from "the fortress of Segontium" (Dahlmann, *Critical Edition*, p. 136).

9. I have followed B, C, and E here.

10. That is, "Beuno's Home."

THE PREFACE OF GILDAS ON PENANCE

1. I am indebted in many places to Bieler's translation of this and the following text, and for a number of observations in the notes (L. Bieler, ed., *The Irish Penitentials* [Dublin, 1975], pp. 60–65, 108–135). There is a translation of the first text with critical commentary also in J. T. McNeill and H. M. Gamer, *Medieval Handbooks of Penance* (New York, 1938; repr. 1965), pp. 174–178.

2. Bieler takes this to be the meaning of *superpositionem*.

3. That is, between Easter and Pentecost. There is evidence that the Irish Church relaxed its severe discipline during this period (Jn Ryan, *Irish Monasticism*, 2nd ed. [Dublin, 1972], pp. 346 and 387).

4. Bieler takes *ferculo* to be a continental misreading of *serculo*, the Latinized form of Old Irish *sercol* (meaning "tidbit" or "delicacy"),

which occurs in early Irish penitential literature. He argues that this word is evidence for Irish influence both on this text and on the *Excerpts from the Book of David.*

5. That is, the forty days before Christmas and Easter and after Pentecost, which were periods of fasting for all.

6. Bieler prefers the reading in the parallel passage from "The Penitential of Cummean" at this point: "But if after the offense he wants to become a monk he shall do penance in the strict form of exile for a year and a half" (2. 4).

7. I have followed McNeill and Gamer here by translating *superpositio* as "special fast," but for the possible meanings of the term, see McNeill and Gamer, *Medieval Handbooks*, p. 31, and n. 2 above.

8. McNeill and Gamer translate "some of the host" (ibid., p. 176).

9. Bieler has article seventeen following article eighteen, and I have followed the order in McNeill and Gamer (ibid.).

10. Bieler suggests that *misa* (= *missa*) here refers to "the lessons and concluding prayers at matins."

11. But Bieler points out that the meaning here might be "if he does not come a second time," as in Cummean (9. 8).

12. That is, fail to read the prayer of consecration correctly; cf. the Stowe Missal, 65v 24–66r 3, vol. ii (London, 1989, vol. xxxii, p. 40) (p. 312 below).

13. The text actually reads "and is checked as an inconsiderate person" ("et quasi inconsultans refrenatur"), but I have followed Bieler's emendation ("et quasi insultans refragatur").

THE PENITENTIAL OF CUMMEAN

14. Bieler reads "vitae" (rather than "viae"), which is the reading also in the *Codex Amiatinus* and the *Book of Armagh.*

15. That is, the Bible.

16. That is, the mealtime laid down by the Rule.

17. The bracketed sections here are evidently glosses.

18. This passage is evidently borrowed from the beginning of "The Preface of Gildas on Penance."

19. This contrasts with Gildas (2), who states that the measure of bread "shall be increased" but, as Bieler points out, Gildas imposes the same three-year penance on the fornicating monk as he does on the priest or bishop, whereas Cummean imposes a sterner seven-year penance upon the latter.

20. Bieler curiously follows McNeill and Gamer, *Medieval Handbooks*, in translating *sextarium de lacte Romanum* as "a pint of Roman milk."

21. That is, without a bride-price.

22. That is, Wednesday and Friday.

23. Bieler points out that the future tense *dicet* might be the correct reading here, suggesting the reading "for which the Lord shall say" and thus the Judgment at the end of time.

24. Thirty Psalms is a variant in *Pseudo-Cummean* and the *Paenitentiale Bigotianum*, which is to be preferred to the three Psalms of McNeill and Gamer, *Medieval Handbooks*, and Bieler's text here.

25. Bieler wishes to emend this line to "si potest exorare," meaning "if he can prevail."

26. "Apathy" here translates "accidie," suggesting the particular weariness that is associated with the discipline of monastic life.

27. There is some obscurity in the text here, and Bieler suggests "thrice fifty," or the whole psalter, as a possible alternative.

28. Or perhaps "with half his ration of bread," as Bieler suggests.

29. Cf. Bieler *Irish Canons*, II, 6.

30. Also known as the "pyx," or ornamented container for carrying the Host.

31. Bieler points out that this is a reference to the reading of the diptychs after the offertory; see F. E. Warren, *Liturgy and Ritual of the Celtic Church*, 2nd ed. by J. Stevenson (Woodbridge, 1987), pp. 105 and 262.

32. McNeill and Gamer, *Medieval Handbooks*, and Bieler suggest that *animalibus* may have the meaning of "lively" here.

THE RULE FOR MONKS BY COLUMBANUS

33. Walker probably rightly identifies this phrase as a gloss on "psallitis" (G. S. M. Walker, ed., *Sancti Columbani Opera* [Dublin, 1970], pp. 122–143).

34. Jane Stevenson offers a clear summary of Columbanus's Office of Psalms in Warren, *Liturgy*, pp. xliii–xlvii.

35. Walker suggests that these may be the Egyptian monks.

36. The Latin parallel "discretio–discerno" is not so easily reproduced in English.

37. I cannot make sense of the text at this point, and I have followed the variant reading of Walker's C manuscript (*Sancti Columbani Opera*, p. 136, l. 11).

38. In the Irish tradition the ascetical life is regarded as a form of martyrdom (see "The Cambrai Homily" below, p. 370).

IRISH POEMS

1. Cf. Rv 7:12.
2. That is, Christ.
3. This is the Martyrology of Oengus (c. A.D. 800).

WELSH POEMS

4. Ifor Williams suggests: "The Father has wrought such a multitude of wonders in this world…" (R. Bromwich, ed., *The Beginnings of Welsh Poetry: Studies by Ifor Williams,* 2nd. ed. [Cardiff, 1980], p. 102).

5. I am following Ifor Williams's reading of *trylenn* here (ibid., pp. 187–189).

6. Arguably heaven, earth, and hell (ibid., p. 189) or possibly "embracing the three angles of the Cross" (cf. *Blodeugerdd,* p. 244).

7. The word *siric,* or "silk," has caused no little difficulty in the interpretation of this poem. Sometimes it has been taken as it stands (e.g., LID, p. 164) and sometimes it has been omitted (e.g., Joseph Clancy, *The Earliest Welsh Poetry* [London, 1970], p. 113). I am inclined to consider *siric* to be a scribal adaptation of *sedrit* (cf. *perwit*) or "cedar tree." The doublet "the cedar and the sweet apple tree" can then be read as a paraphrase of "ligna fructifera, et omnes cedri" from Ps 148 in its Vulgate form, whose influence can be felt everywhere in the poem. We may explain a scribe's error of this kind on the basis of his ignorance of the cedar tree, which was a Victorian import into the British Isles and was unknown in these islands in the Middle Ages.

8. That is, Paul of Thebes and Anthony the Great, who appear on a number of Irish High Crosses and in certain Irish texts (see also *Voyage of Brendan,* n. 15).

9. A possible alternative reading might be "Tuesday and Monday," or indeed the poet may have both meanings in mind (cf. "Glorious Lord," line 15: "May the seven days and the stars praise you").

10. A reference to the unholy loves found in the "five cities of the plain" of Gn 19.

11. Haycock has "the increase of his mercy" (*Blodeugerdd,* p. 234).

12. The word *devaud* here, which I have translated as "rite," suggests the theme of the Eucharist, which can be felt throughout the poem.

13. The reference to Alexander here may reflect allusions to Alexander the Great in poems that precede and follow this text in the *Book of Taliesin* manuscript itself (Ifor Williams, "Llurig Alexander," in B, 17, 1956–1958, p. 95).

14. Haycock has "the only gentle Son of the strong Trinity" (*Blodeugerdd*, p. 26).

15. I am following Lewis's emendation of *timhyr* to *tymher* here (HGC, p. 116).

16. The word *prostrate* translates *eistedd* here, which does have the secondary meaning of "kneel" in Middle Welsh (s.v. eistedd in GPC). The reference must be to the monastic practice of prostration.

17. In her modern Welsh translation Marged Haycock prefers "Those are the things that shall have turned bitter by Judgment Day" (*Blodeugerdd*, p. 289).

18. I am following Marged Haycock's reading of *fruin guin* as "froenwyn" here (*Blodeugerdd*, p. 278).

19. I have adjusted the final line from "pa divet ae bet am bit" to "pa divet ae bet ae bit," and I read "bit" as meaning "eternity" (*pace* Jarman, who takes it to be the third-person future indicative of "bod"). The text is certainly corrupt in lines three ("ymmared") and five ("credwit" and "kereirhyt": see LlD, p. 109).

20. Marged Haycock tentatively suggests "God shall see the number of the unfortunate" ("Gwêl Duw nifer o ?anffodusion") for this line (*Blodeugerdd*, p. 166), but if we take *trychoed* from "trwch" meaning "stratum" (the "ranks"?), and make this the subject, then we can derive a reference to the Beatific Vision of the blessed in heaven.

21. This is Haycock's ingenious suggestion for this obscure line (*Blodeugerdd*, p. 152).

22. An alternative reading to this is "the mind of God is clear to those who praise him" (HGC, p. 205).

23. McKenna reads "iawn" rather than "ddawn" (HGC, p. 40) and renders this line: "I beseech of God true dedication/To praising my generous, gracious King" (C. McKenna, MWRL, [Belmont, Mass., 1991], p. 165).

24. The text is evidently corrupt and I am following Henry Lewis's amendment of these lines (HGC, pp. 184–185).

25. McKenna points out that there is a lost line somewhere at this point in the poem (MWRL, p. 224).

26. McKenna has "Full mightily He claims the sun's Course" (MWRL, p. 167).

27. Following another reading, McKenna has "Not with awakening have I been concerned" (MWRL, p. 169).

28. Again, following another reading McKenna has "Inappropriate the presumption I have nurtured in my spirit:/Not of enduring penance have I thought" (MWRL, p. 169).

29. These last two stanzas occur also in the *Black Book*, although in a different order, and I am following Jarman at this point (LlD, p. 146). McKenna has "dawn of light" (MWRL, p. 169).

30. McKenna "Do not leave me implicated in the graceless coup" (MWRL, p. 169). See also Jarman in LlD, pp. 161 and 111.

31. Nudd, the son of Senyllt, is a heroic figure from early Welsh tradition. Haycock credibly suggests that *bleidd naf* should read *bleidd blaenaf* ("the leading wolf"; *Blodeugerdd*, p. 32).

32. This too is a speculative emendation. Haycock in *Blodeugerdd* comments on this line but omits it in her translation. It would require the correction of "ae de" to "ade." The form "Ade" occurs in "Alexander's Breastplate" (line 6: "o hil Ade"). The word *rydalwyf* occurs in one of Einion ap Gwalchmai's *awdlau* to God: *Rydalwyf yawn yn radlawn rwyt* (Lewis, HGC, p. 71), where its meaning is "to pay back" (cf. McKenna, MWRL, p. 187: "That I pay compensation graciously, generously"). The particle "ry" can cause aspirate mutation (cf. D. Simon Evans, *A Grammar of Middle Welsh* [Dublin, 1964], p. 62). The reading "those who pay Adam's debt" would pick up the theme of penance that runs throughout this poem.

33. Haycock suggests "gwych" ("fine" or "splendid") for *aduwyn* here, but I cannot see why this should not be "addfwyn" in the military sense of "brave, noble, glorious" (GPC, s.v. addfwyn, 1.b.).

34. If indeed Einion is correct, then it is possible that Einion ap Gwalchmai is intended, who flourished during the early thirteenth century. One of his *Odes to God* bears a certain resemblance to the present poem by virtue of its listing of beautiful things. It is not clear, however, why he should be the "healer of many." Alternatively, the word *eynawn* may simply mean "anvil"—on which many metal objects are hammered into shape. Or, thereagain, the reference may be to a court physician of that name.

35. The word *cerddor* refers to the humblest type of bard, who was known in Latin as *joculator* (cf. French *jongleur*). Its alternative meaning of "musician" is explained by the fact that the poetry of the Welsh bards

would have been sung or chanted to the accompaniment of an early version of the harp.

36. Alternatively, the "beauty of May for the cuckoos and nightingale."

37. Haycock in *Blodeugerdd* suggests that the gift referred to here may be the "cyfarws," which was given to the bard himself at the time of a wedding. Cf. Proinsias Mac Cana, "An Archaism in Early Irish Poetic Tradition," in *Celtica* 8 (1968), pp. 174–181, and "Elfennau cyn-Gristnogol yn y Cyfreithiau," in B, 23 (1968–1970), pp. 316–320 (quoted in *Blodeugerdd*, p. 38).

38. I am following Haycock's suggestion ("cywir") for the term *catholic* here.

39. We find two appreciative references to "fine Welsh" in the *Black Book* (LlD, pp. 4 and 6).

THE BREASTPLATE OF LAIDCENN

1. One manuscript inserts the couplet "And I adjure all virgins, faithful widows and confessors" at this point, which Herren believes to be an interpolation (Michael W. Herren, *The Hisperica Famina II. Related Poems* [Toronto, 1987], p. 117).

2. Herren imaginatively reconstructs the meaning of "patham" and "michinas" here by reference to Old English glosses and to a possible Hebrew source (ibid., pp. 120–121). I have closely followed Herren's translation of this highly unusual text in my own rendering.

3. "Femurs" here is speculative.

4. Literally, "my ten branches."

5. According to medieval custom, the ten orifices here are "the eyes, ears, nostrils, hands (as organs of touch) with the mouth (oesophagus and windpipe) counting as two" (Herren, *Hisperica Famina II,* p. 137).

THE BROOM OF DEVOTION

6. Plummer published the following "Litany of Jesus I" and "Litany of Jesus II" as two adjacent but separate texts (C. Plummer, *Irish Litanies,* London, 1925, pp. 30–45).

7. A variant has "pastors" here (ibid., p. 31).

8. Plummer notes that there is an Irish version of the Passion of the child martyr Cyricus (ibid., p. 112).

NOTES

LITANY OF THE VIRGIN AND ALL SAINTS

9. Plummer translates *eslabrai nainairchis* as "inept loquacity" (ibid., p. 27).

THE LITANY OF CREATION

10. That is, the Church Militant, which, in Irish tradition, was added to the nine grades of heaven. See "The Path I Walk" below, stanza five.

11. Cf. introduction, n. 175.

12. The word *cechuid* is obscure (Plummer, *Irish Litanies*, p. 104).

13. Or possibly "fostering."

14. This may be another reference to the colors of martyrdom. See Monastic Texts, n. 38, above.

MAY THIS JOURNEY BE EASY

15. Or perhaps "against wolves."

THE PRAYERS OF MOUCAN

16. Cf. Lk 18:13. The following eight stanzas are virtually a compendium of biblical references, for which see D. Howlett, "*Orationes Moucani*: Early Cambro-Latin Prayers," in CMCS 24 (1992), pp. 55–74.

17. D. Howlett points out that the reference here is to Thomas, who placed his hand in Christ's wound, as recorded in Jn 20:24–28 (ibid., p. 63).

THE PROTECTION OF THE FATHER AND THE SON

18. The word *gâl* here may also have the sense of "passions" or "hatred" (GPC, s.v. gâl).

19. This is the textual reading in HGC (p. 97); preferring *ddeau* to *deheu*, McKenna suggests "the true, gift-granting Cross" (MWRL, p. 213).

20. I am following HGC (p. 244) here with *geithiw* rather than McKenna's *geithon*.

THE TRACT ON THE MASS IN THE STOWE MISSAL

1. That is, the four gospels, Acts, the Catholic Epistles, the Pauline Epistles, the Apocalypse.

2. The nine households of heaven are the Angels, Archangels, Powers, Dominions, Lordships, Principalities, Thrones, Seraphim, and Cherubim.

3. That is, the Second Sunday in Eastertide.

4. This passage is a reminder that the fraction (breaking of the Host) can be considerably more elaborate than the procedure currently and traditionally used in the Roman Catholic Church (involving three portions). It was the practice in the ancient Mozarabic Rite, for instance, to break the host into nine portions and to arrange seven of them in the form of a cross (*Oxford Dictionary of the Christian Church*, 2nd ed., F. L. Cross and E. A. Livingstone, s.v. "Fraction").

TWO EUCHARISTIC CHANTS FROM THE STOWE MISSAL

5. The source of this verse is unidentified.

6. The source is unidentified.

7. A rubric, in same hand and in black ink.

8. The Vg of Jn 6:56 reads *carnem* [flesh]; our text reads *corpus* [body].

9. A rubric, in same hand and in black ink.

10. A rubric, in same hand and in black ink.

11. A rubric, in same hand and in black ink.

12. The source is unidentified.

COMMUNION HYMN

13. Cf. Jn 4:10.

14. Cf. Rv 1:8.

HYMN AT THE LIGHTING OF THE PASCHAL CANDLE

15. Cf. Ex 13:21.

16. Cf. Ex 3:2–4.

17. Cf. Dt 4:24.

NOTES

18. The process of manufacturing the candle is here compared with the purification through the Holy Spirit of those who are to be baptized.

THE EVERNEW TONGUE

1. Stokes translates *thimthirechtaib* as "services" (W. Stokes, "The Evernew Tongue," in E 2, 1905, pp. 96–162), but the reference is surely to the "motions" of the stars, as Herbert has it (IBA, p. 109).

2. Herbert has "At midnight their voices would reach Jerusalem" (IBA, p. 110). Jerusalem is an image for heaven here (cf. "A Mystical Interpretation of the *Beati*," p. 343 below).

3. The "thought" referred to here is the Second Person of the Trinity or Logos, in whom all things existed as divine ideas prior to their emergence into actuality in the Creation.

THE VISION OF ADAMNÁN

4. The word *long* actually means ship, and hence may refer to the "nave."

5. The word here is *dan*, which combines the idea of a gift or offering to God with particular skill or craft (Royal Irish Academy, *Dictionary of the Irish Language* [Dublin 1983], s.v. *dan*).

6. Herbert translates "with pleasurable utterances" (IBA, p. 139).

7. Cf. the account of the punishment of Judas in *Voyage of Brendan* (pp. 183–185, above).

8. Cf. the birds encountered by Brendan on his voyage (pp. 162–167 above).

A MYSTICAL INTERPRETATION OF THE *BEATI*

1. That is, Ps 119 (Vulgate: Ps 118).

2. The following annotations are an ancient explanatory gloss on the original text.

3. A number of Insular texts depict hell as a place of intense cold (C. D. Wright, *The Irish Tradition in Old English Literature* [Cambridge, 1993], p. 131; and J. Vendryes, "L'enfer glacé," in RC 46, 1929, pp. 134–142).

NOTES

GLOSS ON PSALM 103

4. Cf. *The Julian Epitome* (CCSL 78a, p. 333). Unless otherwise noted this text is the chief source for the gloss (M. McNamara, *Glossa in Psalmos: Gloss on the Psalms of Codex Vaticanus Palatino-Latinus 68, Studi e Testi* 310 [Vatican, 1986], pp. 48–51 and 211–215). I am obliged to the edition by McNamara for the identification of sources.

5. Cf. Augustine, *Commentary on the Psalms* (CCSL 40, p. 1488).

6. Cf. Jerome, *The Book of Interpretation of Hebrew Names* (CCSL 72, pp. 121–122).

7. See also the tradition of the exotic bird *hiruath* in "The Evernew Tongue"; P. Kitson, "The Jewels and Bird *Hiruath* of the 'Ever-New Tongue,'" in E 35 (1984), pp. 113–136.

8. Cf. Augustine, *Commentary on the Psalms* (CCSL 40, p. 1516).

9. Cf. Jerome, *Commentary on the Psalms* (CCSL 72, p. 228).

10. Commentaries on verses 23 and 24 are missing.

11. Cf. Jerome, *Commentary on the Psalms* (CCSL 72, p. 229).

12. Cf. Jerome, *Commentary on the Psalms* (CCSL 72, ibid).

13. Cf. Jerome, *The Book of Interpretation of Hebrew Names* (CCSL 72, p. 133).

14. Commentary on verse 27 is missing.

SERMONS OF COLUMBANUS
SERMON FIVE

1. No translation can capture the force of this phrase: *Via es mortalium et non vita.*

CATECHESIS CELTICA

2. I am correcting *"ui"* here to *"uini."*

3. I read *"obtrussa"* as a variant for *"abstrusa"* (C. T. Lewis and C. Short, *A Latin Dictionary* [Oxford, 1917], s.v. *"obstrusus"*).

AN OLD IRISH HOMILY

4. For *crindel* (an emendation of Strachan's *crinnel*), see ZCP, iv, 243, 8.

5. For *alt* in this sense, see Royal Irish Academy, *Dictionary of the Irish Language* (Dublin, 1983), s.v. alt, 2.

6. The word *finboth* here is obscure.

THE CAMBRAI HOMILY

7. I am following Clare Stancliffe in translating "glas" as "blue" ("Red, White and Blue Martyrdom," in *Ireland in Early Medieval Europe*, ed. D. Whitelock, R. McKitterick, and D. Dumville, [Cambridge, 1982], pp. 28–29).

8. Cf. *Prebiarum de multorium exemplaribus*, 23, in CCSL 108B, p. 163 (quoted in ibid., pp. 37–38).

THREE SUNDAY CATECHESES

9. I have translated the Vulgate here. The NRSV (Ps 118:19) reads: "enter...and give thanks"; while this ideally fits the context of Sunday and the Eucharist, the phrase "give praise" seems closer to the Vulgate: *confitebor Domino.*

10. As Sunday (the church's day) follows the Sabbath (the synagogue's day), so Sunday marks the boundary between the two "ages." This was a common theme in the exegesis of the period.

11. McNally pointed out that certain apocrypha held that Christ was born on a Sunday. However, one can explain this and similar links between events and Sunday (e.g., Cana) by noting that the day the Lord takes possession of by a great event and the day that is the Lord's possession as such (Sunday) are treated within the logic of these texts as convertible items. Such logical "jumps" (the day of a great event is the Lord's Day, and vice versa) are found throughout early medieval exegesis (CCSL, 108B).

12. Our text reads *hominum* while Mt 14:21 has *uirorum* (Jn 6:10 has *uiri*), but this is not evidence of exclusive language as *hominum* is used in contrast to women and children in III, xiii of this work.

13. There is a silent conflation here with Ps 77:24 (*manna*), as Ex 16 calls the divine gift *man.*

14. This question was a famous conundrum between the account of the Six Days (Ex 20:11 says these events took six days) and the statement in Sir 18. It arose in the writings of Augustine and continued to be raised throughout this period; cf. T. O'Loughlin, "Knowing God and Knowing

the Cosmos: Augustine's Legacy of Tension," in *Irish Philosophical Journal* 6 (1989), pp. 27–58. The presence of this rather obscure theological question, which moreover does not conform to the sentence structure of the rest of the text, suggests that it is an interpolation.

15. On the method of the solution, cf. T. O'Loughlin, "Julian of Toledo's *Antikeimenon* and the Development of Latin Exegesis," in *Proceedings of the Irish Biblical Association* 16 (1993), pp. 80–98.

16. These four liquids are found in various combinations in the Old Testament (e.g., Dt 8:7–91, 32:13) and are used in exegesis as symbols of the four Evangelists, the rock being Christ.

17. The text reads that "the Lord gave the *apocalipsin*"; it could refer either to the actual revelation or to the book.

18. These two items (ii and iii) represent a complex exegetical theme from Augustine that continued in early medieval exegesis. It is the conundrum of trying to reconcile Gn 2:3 with Jn 5:17. Cf. T. O'Loughlin, "Tradition and Exegesis in the Eighth Century: The Use of Patristic Sources in Early Medieval Scriptural Commentaries," in *The Scriptures and Early Medieval Ireland,* ed. T. O'Loughlin (Turnhout, 1999, pp. 217–39), which examines this particular problem in detail.

19. Item iv is an interpolation of material from the "weights of Adam" tradition, and reads:
"Adam is made from eight weights (*ponderae*):
first, the weight of mud, whence his flesh is made;
second, the weight of salt, whence his tears are salty;
third, the weight of fire, whence his blood's redness;
fourth, the weight of wind, whence his breathing;
fifth, the weight of flowers, whence the variety of eyes;
sixth, the weight of the clouds, whence the instability of minds;
seventh, the weight of dew, whence he sweat.
These are the weights from which Adam is made, but there is another weight: that of the soul, which is made from heavenly things." See also "The Creation of Adam" (p. 327 above).

20. The fourth "middle" is not mentioned in the text.

21. The notion of Aaron as the first bishop is based on his being High Priest (*Summus sacerdos*) and his sons being the priests. This was held to be a prefigurment of the Christian bishop and his priests, cf. Isidore, *De ecclesiasticis officiis* 2, 5, 2–4 (PL 83, 781) and the *Collectio canonum hibernensis* I, 3 (a version of this collection of law is found in the same manuscript as this text).

NOTES

ON THE CHRISTIAN LIFE BY PELAGIUS

1. Rees points out that this and other passages noted below are paralleled in Pelagius's *Commentary on the Epistles of Paul* (here 20, 8–16, and 19, 25–20, 3). See B. R. Rees, ed., *The Letters of Pelagius and His Followers* (Woodbridge, 1991), pp. 105–126. The *Comm.* can be found in A. Souter, ed., *Pelagius' Expositions of Thirteen Epistles of St. Paul* (Cambridge, 1926). R. F. Evans also has a discussion of parallels between this work and other authentic works of the Pelagian corpus (R. F. Evans, *Four Letters of Pelagius* [London, 1968], especially pp. 18–21).

2. Cf. Souter, *Pelagius' Expositions*, p. 19, 22–25, and p. 20, 3–7.

3. Cf. ibid., p. 194, 3–5.

4. Cf. ibid., p. 76, 20–22.

5. Cf. ibid., p. 202, 13–20.

"THE HIGH FIRST-SOWER"
(THE *ALTUS PROSATOR*) BY COLUMBA

1. The letter of the alphabet in the left-hand margin corresponds to the opening letter of the stanza in Latin. The literary structure of the first verse is analyzed by D. R. Howlett "Seven Studies in Seventh-Century Texts" in *Peritia* 10 (1996), 1–70, p. 56.

2. Cf. Dn 7:9.

3. The biblical sources of the belief in a creation from nothing are explored in T. F. Torrance, *The Trinitarian Faith* (Edinburgh, 1988), pp. 95–98.

4. Cf. Gn 1:1.

5. Cf. Rv 1:4 and 8.

6. Cf. Jn 1:18, 3:16; and 1 Jn 4:9—the word becomes part of the creeds.

7. Here, and in the final stanza, we have an echo of the "Athanasian" Creed (the *Quicumque uult*).

8. Cf. Col 1:16 and Eph 1:21.

9. Cf. Mt 19:26 and Wis 18:15.

10. Cf. Jb 38:7.

11. Cf. Is 14:12.

12. Cf. Lk 10:18; and Rv 9:1.

13. Cf. 1 Tm 3:6.

14. Cf. Sir 10:15.

15. There is a play here on the word *principatus*: On the one

hand this refers to one "choir" of angels, on the other to the first-ranked places.

16. Cf. Rv 12:9.

17. Cf. Gn 3:1.

18. Cf. Gn 3.

19. Going headlong into the depths (*in baratrum*) is an echo of Jgs 5:15.

20. Cf. Rv 12:4.

21. Cf. Jn 1:9 and 1 Jn 2:8.

22. Cf. Jgs 5:15.

23. Howlett, "Seven Studies" p. 2.

24. Cf. Gn 1:1.

25. Cf. Gn 1:2–25.

26. The term *protoplastus* has its origins in Wis 7:1 and 10:1 (LXX), and 1 Tm 2:13.

27. Cf. Gn 1:26–30.

28. Cf. Gn 1:14.

29. The notion of the heavens, and of the heavenly court of angels, praising the Lord is found in many places; among those the first readers of this poem would have recalled are Pss 18, 148, 149, and 150.

30. Cf. Jb 38:7.

31. Cf. 1 Tm 2:14 and 2 Jn 1:7.

32. A gloss in Irish in one of the manuscripts explains that the first fall was from heaven to earth, the second from earth into hell.

33. Cf. Mt 13:30.

34. Cf. Eph 2:2.

35. Following the prophetic notion that sin is fornication with foreign gods, fornication here represents all sinful activity.

36. For the explanation of *dodrans* as referring to the three-quarters of the globe covered by water, I am indebted to D. R. Howlett (personal communication, May 1997).

37. Cf. Ps 134:7.

38. Jb 26:5.

39. There are echoes of 2 Sm 22:12 and of Jb 26:8.

40. Cf. Ps 103:5 and Jb 38:4–6.

41. Cf. Ps 85:13 and Lk 16:22.

42. Cf. Sir 10:13; and note that this would have been read in the light of Mk 9:47.

43. Cf. Rv 19:20.

44. Mt 24:51.

45. Cf., for example, Mt 5:22.

46. Cf. T. O'Loughlin, "The Gates of Hell: From Metaphor to Fact," in *Milltown Studies* 38 (1996), pp. 98–114.

47. The significance of this stanza in later Irish tradition is discussed by J. Szöverffy, "The *Altus Prosator* and the Discovery of America," in *Irish Ecclesiastical Record* 100 (1963), pp. 115–118.

48. The basic image in this line is from Phil 2:10, but it is theme that is picked up here in the context of the same threefold division of human creatures (heaven, earth, under-the-earth) that is found in Rv 5:3 and 5:13.

49. Cf. Rv 5:3.

50. Rv 5:2.

51. Cf. Rv 5:1, 5:5, and 6:1.

52. This possibly refers to the warnings that accompany references to the sealed book in the Old Testament (cf. Is 29:1–16 and Ex 2:9).

53. In Rv 5:5 it is the victorious Lion of the Tribe of Judah (i.e., Christ) who has risen (Rv 5:6: *agnum stantem tamquam occisum*), and as victor (*uicit*) can open the seals.

54. Cf. Is 29:11 and Ez 2:9.

55. Cf. Gn 2:8.

56. Cf. Gn 2:10–14.

57. Cf. Gn 2:9.

58. Cf. Ps 1:3.

59. Cf. Rv 22:2.

60. Cf. Ez 28:13.

61. Cf. 1 Cor 2:9.

62. This whole stanza is inspired by the theophany on Sinai, cf. Ex 24:15–16.

63. The question-form is inspired by Ps 23:3.

64. Cf. Ex 19:16.

65. Cf. Ex 20:18.

66. Cf. Ps 17:15.

67. Cf. Rv 16:18.

68. Cf. Ex 18:13.

69. The Old Testament expression (e.g., Ezr 7:12 or Dn 2:37) becomes a title of Christ the judge in the New Testament; cf. 1 Tm 6:15; Rv 17:14, 19:16.

70. The expression, "The Day of the Lord is near" is found in many places in scripture: Is 13:6; Jl 1:15; Ez 30:3; and several other places.

71. Zep 1:15.

72. Cf. Jer 46:10, which links "the Day of the Lord" and "the Day of Vengeance" and cf. Is 34:8.

73. Cf. Is 8:22.

74. Zep 1:15; and cf. Est 11:8; Ob 12; and Prv 24:10.

75. Cf. Mt 22:30.

76. Cf. 1 Cor 5:5, and 1 Jn 2:17.

77. Cf. Rom 14:10 and 2 Cor 5:10.

78. Cf. Ex 19:16, and Phil 2:12.

79. Cf. Dn 7:10, and Rv 20:12.

80. The notion of the "first" archangel is an addition to 1 Thes 4:16, which may have been inspired by Rv 6:7.

81. The imagery of this chapter is a weaving together of three "pictures" of the resurrection of the dead: 1 Thes 4:16 and 1 Cor 15:51–2, with Ez 38:7–12.

82. Cf. Jb 22:14.

83. Cf. Jb 9:9.

84. This notion that the heavens are a proclamation of Christ is one that has all but disappeared from Christian consciousness, but see 2 Pt 1:19 and the description of Christ as "the Morning Star" in the Easter Proclamation (the *Exultet*).

85. This stanza reflects the liturgical celebrations of the Cross, e.g., the hymn *Vexilla regis* by Venantius Fortunatus.

86. Cf. Mt 24:30.

87. The images here are a combination of Mt 24:29 and Rv 6:12–13.

88. Cf. 1 Pt 3:10.

89. Cf. Rv 6:15.

90. Rv 4:6.

91. Rv 4:4.

92. This stanza follows the sequence of Rv 4, and there (verse 10) the crowns are thrown before "the throne." The image here of them being cast "before the Lamb" is taken from Rv 5:8 ("the four living creatures and the twenty-four elders fell down before the Lamb"); the silent combination of images is no doubt influenced by the several references in Rv (5:13, 7:9, 22:1, 22:3) where the images of the throne and lamb are combined. The image is further developed by identifying the "lamb" of the Rv with the Johannine "Lamb of God" (as a designation for the Christ) (Jn 1:29 and 36), as was invariably done in exegesis.

93. Rv 4:8.

94. Cf. Heb 10:27.

95. Cf. 1 Thes 4:17 and 1 Cor 15:41–42.

96. Cf. Mk 12:35.
97. 1 Pt 1:5; and cf. Jude 1:18.

HOMILY ON THE PROLOGUE TO *THE GOSPEL OF JOHN* BY JOHN SCOTTUS ERIUGENA

1. According to traditional usage based on Ezekiel and Revelation, the eagle represents the fourth Evangelist.

2. Jeauneau points out that the word *superessentialitas* shows the influence of Pseudo-Denys, some of whose work Eriugena translated. See E. Jeauneau, ed., *Jean Scot. Homélie sur le prologue de Jean*, Sources Chrétiennes 151 (Paris, 1969), p. 208.

3. Jerome, *Liber interpretationis hebraicorum nominum*, in CCSL 72, p. 155. See also Jeauneau, *Jean Scot*, p. 209.

4. This reflects an exegetical tradition associated with St. Ambrose, according to which the "created paradise" is understood to be original and pristine human nature (Jeauneau, *Jean Scot*, pp. 219–220).

5. "Substance" here stands for the Greek ὑπόστασις and shows Eriugena's predilection for speaking of the Trinity in typically Greek terms; in the Latin tradition ὑπόστασις usually becomes *persona*.

6. Cf. Augustine, *The City of God*, 11, 6 (Jeauneau, *Jean Scot*, p. 237).

7. Cf. Augustine, *Literal Commentary on Genesis*, II, VI, 12 (Jeauneau, *Jean Scot*, p. 245).

8. Pseudo-Dionysius, *Celestial Hierarchy* IV, 1 (PG 3, 177 D 1–2).

9. The Vulgate incorporates *"omnis"* and *"homo"* at Jn 1:9: *Erat lux vera, quae illuminat omnem hominem venientem in hunc mundum.*

10. Cf. Zec 4:2.

THE FOOD OF THE SOUL

1. Iestyn Daniel has identified the source of this line as Augustine's *De trinitate*: *"quaedam vita duo aliqua copulans, vel copulare appetens"* (viii, 10, 14) (*"Ymborth yr Enaid*-Clytwaith, Cyfieithiad neu Waith Gwreiddiol?" in LlC 17, no. 1 and 2 [1992], p. 16).

2. For an appropriate love of the self, which is particularly associated with the theology of Bernard of Clairvaux, see Etienne Gilson,

The Mystical Theology of St Bernard (London, 1940), pp. 88–89 and 116–118.

3. The nothingness of evil is a Neoplatonic theme that enters Christianity through Augustine's definition of evil as the *privatio boni* or "absence of the good" (e.g., *Contra adversarium legis et prophetarum*, I, 5).

4. The following passage is a Welsh metrical rendering of the ninth-century Latin hymn "Veni Creator," attributed to Rabanus Maurus.

5. The nine orders of angels enter Christian theology in the fourth century with the work of Cyril of Jerusalem, John Chrysostom, and Gregory of Nyssa and represent the biblical themes of seraphim, cherubim, thrones, authorities, dominions, powers, principalities, angels, and archangels. See Andrew Louth's comments on this in his *Denys the Areopagite* (London, 1989), pp. 33–37.

Select Bibliography

I. PRINCIPAL PRINTED SOURCES OF THE TRANSLATIONS

Hagiography:

1. i. N. J. D. White, ed. *Libri Sancti Patricii; The Latin Writings of St. Patrick*, PRIA, 25c (1905), pp. 201–326.
    ii. Ibid., pp. 254–59.
    iii. L. Bieler. *The Patrician Texts in the Book of Armagh (Scriptores Latini Hiberniae* 10). Dublin, 1979, p. 124.
    iv. Ibid., pp. 59–123.
    v. Th. Pal., pp. 354–358.
2. i. Th. Pal., pp. 323–326.
    ii. PL 72, cols. 775–790. J. Colgan. *Trias Thaumaturga*. Louvain, 1647.
    iii. D. Ó hAodha, ed. *Bethu Brigte*. Dublin, 1978.
3. C. Selmer, ed. *Navigatio Sancti Brendani*. Indiana, 1959.
4. J. W. James, ed. *Rhigyfarch's Life of St David*. Cardiff, 1967.
5. S. M. Dahlmann, ed. *Critical Edition of the Buched Beuno*. Ph.D. diss., Catholic University of America, Washington, 1976.
6. Huw Pryce. "A New Edition of the *Historia Divae Monacellae*," *The Montgomeryshire Collections* 82 (1994), pp. 23–40.

Monastic Texts:

1. L. Bieler, ed. *The Irish Penitentials*. Dublin, 1975, pp. 60–65.
2. Ibid., pp. 108–135.
3. G. S. M. Walker, ed. *Sancti Columbani Opera*. Dublin, 1970, pp. 122–143.

SELECT BIBLIOGRAPHY

Poetry:

1. R. I. Best, ed. E 4 (1907), p. 120.
2. R. Thurneyson. "Mittelirische Verslehre," ii, §54. In W. Stokes and E. Windisch, eds., *Irische Texte,* iii. Leipzig, 1891.
3. Th. Pal. 290.
4. K. Meyer. ZCP, xii (1918), p. 297.
5. J. Strachan. E, i (1904–1905), 138.
6. Brian Ó Cuív, ed. E 19 (1965), pp. 4–5.
7. K. Meyer. E, iii (1907), 14.
8. K. Meyer, ed. E 6 (1909), p. 116.
9. M. E. Byrne, ed. E 1 (1904), pp. 225–228.
10. T. P. O'Nowlan, ed. E 2 (1905), pp. 92–94, R. Flower, ed. E 5 (1908), p. 112.
11. I. Williams, *The Beginnings of Welsh Poetry.* Cardiff, 1972, p. 102.
12. *Blodeugerdd,* pp. 241–245.
13. LlD, p. 16.
14. LlD, pp. 17–18.
15. LlD, p. 19.
16. *Blodeugerdd,* pp. 23–29.
17. LlD, pp. 13–14.
18. LlD, p. 58.
19. LlD, p. 45.
20. LlD, pp. 46–47.
21. LlD, pp. 56–57.
22. LlD, p. 15.
23. LlD, p. 54.
24. *Blodeugerdd,* pp. 165–169.
25. *Blodeugerdd,* pp. 151–155.
26. MWRL, pp. 154–156.
27. MWRL, pp. 170–172.
28. MWRL, pp. 164–168.
29. *Blodeugerdd,* pp. 30–40.
30. J. Fisher, ed. *The Cefn Coch MSS.* Liverpool, 1899, p. 238.

Devotional Texts:

1. G. Murphy. *Early Irish Lyrics.* Oxford, 1956, pp. 44–46.
2. Ibid., p. 36.
3. M. W. Herren, *The Hisperica Famina II. Related Poems.* Toronto, 1987, pp. 76–93.

4. C. Plummer. *Irish Litanies.* London, 1925, pp. 29–45.

5. Ibid., pp. 25–26.

6. Ibid., pp. 101–107.

7. K. Meyer. "Four Religious Poems." E 6 (1909), p. 112.

8. J. Carney. "Three Old Irish Accentual Poems," E 22 (1971), pp. 26–29.

9. D. R. Howlett. "*Orationes Moucani*: Early Cambro-Latin Prayers." CMCS 24 (1992), pp. 55–74.

10. MWRL, pp. 212–214.

Liturgy:

1. Th. Pal., pp. 252–255.

2. G. F. Warner, ed. *The Stowe Missal.* Woodbridge, 1989, pp. 17–18.

3. A. S. Walpole. *Early Latin Hymns.* Cambridge, 1922, pp. 344–346.

4. Ibid., pp. 346–349.

Apocrypha:

1. W. Stokes. "The Evernew Tongue," E 2 (1905), pp. 96–162.

2. W. Stokes. "The Irish Text of Adam Octipartite." In *Three Irish Glossaries* (London, 1862), pp. x–xli.

3. J. Pokorny. *A Historical Reader of Old Irish.* Halle, 1923, pp. 12–14.

4. E. Windisch. *Irische Texte mit Wörterbuch.* Leipzig, 1880, pp. 165–196.

Exegesis:

1. O. Bergin. "A Mystical Interpretation of the *Beati.*" E 11 (1914), pp. 103–106.

2. M. McNamara. *Glossa in Psalmos. Gloss on the Psalms of Codex Vaticanus Palatino-Latinus 68. Studi e Testi 310.* Vatican, 1986, pp. 211–215.

Homilies:

1. G. S. M. Walker, *Sancti Columbani Opera, Scriptores Latini Hiberniae* II. Dublin, 1970, pp. 84–86.

2. Ibid., pp. 94–96.

3. Ibid., pp. 106–110.

4. Ibid., pp. 114–120.

5. A. Wilmart, "Catéchèses celtiques." In *Analecta Reginensia, Studi e Testi* 59 (Vatican, 1933), pp. 59–60.

6. J. Strachan. "An Old Irish Homily." E 3 (1907), pp. 1–10.

7. Th. Pal., pp. 244–247.

8. R. E. McNally. CCSL, 108B, pp. 175–86.

Theology:

1. *Liber de vita christiana.* PL 40, cols. 1031–1046.

2. J. H. Bernard and R. Atkinson, eds. *The Irish Liber Hymnorum.* London, 1898, vol. 1, pp. 62–83; and vol. 2, pp. 23–26; 140–69.

3. E. Jeauneau. *Jean Scot: Homélie sur le prologue de Jean.* Sources Chrétiennes 151. Paris, 1969.

4. R. I. Daniel. *"Ymborth yr Enaid," gyda rhagymadrodd a nodiadau.* Cardiff, 1995.

II. OTHER PRIMARY AND SECONDARY SOURCES

Primary Sources:

Bieler, L., ed. *The Irish Penitentials.* Dublin, 1963.

Bischoff, B. "Turning-Points in the History of Latin Exegesis in the Early Middle Ages." In *Biblical Studies: The Medieval Irish Contribution,* edited by M. McNamara, 75–167. Dublin, 1976.

Breatnach, L., ed. *The Caldron of Poesy.* E 32 (1981), 45–93.

Brewer, J. S., Dimock, J. F., and Warner, G. F., eds. *Giraldi Cambrensis Opera.* London, 1861–1891.

Bromwich, R. *Medieval Celtic Literature: A Select Bibliography.* Toronto, 1974.

Carey, J. *King of Mysteries: Early Irish Religious Writings.* Dublin, 1998.

Carney, J. *Medieval Irish Lyrics.* Dublin, 1967.

———."Three Old Irish Accentual Poems." E 22 (1972), 23–80.

Carney, M., ed. *Gnimhradha in seseadh lai lain.* E 21 (1969), 149–166.

Cassian, J. *Opera.* In PL 49 and 50.

Charlesworth, J. H., ed. *The Old Testament Pseudepigrapha,* vol. I. London, 1983.

Colgrave, B., and Mynors, R. A. B., eds. *Bede's Ecclesiastical History.* Oxford, 1969.

de Bruyn, Th. *Pelagius's Commentary on St. Paul's Epistle to the Romans.* Oxford, 1993.

de Paor, L. *St. Patrick's World.* Dublin, 1993.

Dictionary of the Irish Language. Royal Irish Academy, Dublin 1983.

Ford, P. K., ed. *Ystoria Taliesin.* Cardiff, 1992.

Ganz, J., ed. *The Mabinigion.* Harmondsworth, 1976.

Haycock, M. *Blodeugerdd Barddas o Ganu Crefyddol Cynnar.* Cyhoeddiadau Barddas, 1994.

———. *Rhai Agweddau ar Lyfr Taliesin.* Ph.D. diss., University of Wales 1982.

Herbert, M., and McNamara, M. *Irish Biblical Apocrypha.* Edinburgh, 1989.

Hughes, A. *Medieval Manuscripts for Mass and Office.* Toronto, 1982.

Jones, N. A., and Parry-Owen, A., eds. *Gwaith Cynddelw Brydydd Mawr,* vol. I. Cardiff, 1991.

Kenney, J. F. *The Sources for the Early History of Ireland: Ecclesiastical.* Dublin, 1979.

Kuypers, A. B., ed. *The Prayer Book of Aedeluald the Bishop, Commonly Called the Book of Cerne.* Cambridge, 1902.

Lapidge, M., and Sharpe, R., eds. *A Bibliography of Celtic-Latin Literature 400–1200.* Dublin, 1985.

Lewis, H., ed. *Hen Gerddi Crefyddol.* Cardiff, 1931.

Lloyd-Evans, I. *Testun Beirniadol Gydag Astudiaeth o "Fuchedd Beuno."* M.A. thesis, University of Wales 1966.

McNeill, J. T., and Gamer, H. M., eds. *Medieval Handbooks of Penance.* New York, 1938.

Moffat, D. *The Old English Soul and Body.* Cambridge, 1990.

Morris-Jones, J., and Rhys, J., eds. *Elucidarium and Other Tracts from Llyvyr Angkyr Llandewivrevi.* Oxford, 1894.

Morris-Jones, R., Morris-Jones, J., and Parry-Williams, T. H., eds. *Llawysgrif Hendregadredd.* Cardiff, 1933.

O'Meara, J. J. *Gerald of Wales: The History and Topography of Ireland.* Harmondsworth, 1982.

———. *The Voyage of St. Brendan: Journey to the Promised Land.* Dublin, 1976.

Parry, T., and Morgan, M. *Llyfryddiaeth Llenyddiaeth Gymraeg.* Cardiff, 1976.

Plummer, C. *Irish Litanies.* Dublin, 1925; repr. Woodbridge, 1992.

———. *Vitae Sanctorum Hiberniae.* Oxford, 1910, repr. 1968.

Rees, B. *The Letters of Pelagius and His Followers.* Woodbridge, 1991.

Rowland, J. *Early Welsh Saga Poetry: A Study and Edition of the Englynion.* Woodbridge, 1990.

Tierney, J. J. "The Celtic Ethnography of Posidonius," *Proceedings of the Royal Irish Academy* 60, C, 5. Dublin, 1960.

Wade-Evans, A. W., ed. *Vita Sanctorum Britanniae et Genealogiae.* Cardiff, 1944.

Warner, G. F., ed. *The Stowe Missal.* Woodbridge, 1989.

Williams, G. J., and Jones, E. D., eds. *Gramadegau'r Penceirddiaid.* Cardiff, 1934.

Williams, R., and Jones, G. H. *Selections from Hengwrt MSS,* vol. 2. London, 1892.

Winterbottom, M., ed. *Gildas: The Ruin of Britain.* London and Chichester, 1978.

Zwicker, J. *Fontes religiones celticae.* Berlin, 1934.

Secondary Sources:

Allchin, A. M. *Praise above All.* Cardiff, 1991.

Barley, M. W., and Hanson, R. P. C., eds. *Christianity in Britain: 300–700.* Leicester, 1982.

Berger, P. *The Goddess Obscured.* Boston, 1985.

Bertaux, E. S.v. Génuflexions et Métanies, DS, 1965, vol. 6, cols. 213–226.

Bieler, L. "Hagiography and Romance in Medieval Ireland." In *Medievalia et Humanistica,* edited by P. Clogan, Cambridge, 1975, 13–24.

———. *Ireland and the Culture of Early Medieval Europe.* London, 1987.

Bitel, L. M. *Isle of the Saints: Monastic Settlement and Christian Community in Early Ireland.* New York, 1990.

———. *Land of Women: Tales of Sex and Gender from Early Ireland.* New York, 1996.

Bloomfield, M. W., and Dunn, C. W. *The Role of the Poet in Early Societies.* Woodbridge, 1989.

Bosch, D. J. *Transforming Mission.* New York, 1991.

Boswell, C. S. *An Irish Precursor of Dante.* London, 1908.

Bowen, E. "The Cult of St. Brigid," *Studia Celtica* 8 (1973), 33–47.

Bradley, I. *Celtic Christianity: Making Myths and Chasing Dreams.* Edinburgh, 1999.

Bradley, S. A. J. *Anglo-Saxon Poetry.* London, 1982.

Brock, S. "The Dispute between Soul and Body: An Example of a long-lived Mesopotamian Literary Genre." *Aram* 1, no. 1 (1989), 53–64.

Brown, P. *Religion and Society in the Age of St. Augustine.* London, 1972.

———. "The Saint as Exemplar in Late Antiquity." In *Saints and Virtues,* edited by J. S. Hawley, 3–14. Berkeley, CA, 1987.

Brunaux, L. *The Celtic Gauls: Gods, Rites and Sanctuaries.* London, 1988.

Bruning, G. "Adamnáns Vita Columbae und ihre Ableitungen," ZCP 11 (1916–1917), 213–304.

Bury, J. B. "The Origins of Pelagius." *Hermathena* 13 (1905), 26–35.

Carney, J. *The Irish Bardic Poet.* Dublin, 1967.

———. *Studies in Irish Literature and History.* Dublin, 1955.

Chadwick, N. K. *The Celts.* London, 1971.

———. *The Druids.* Cardiff and Connecticut, 1966.

———. *Early Brittany.* Cardiff, 1969.

———. "Intellectual Life in West Wales in the Last Days of the Celtic Church." In *Studies in the British Church,* edited by N. K. Chadwick, K. Hughes, C. Brooke, and K. Jackson, 121–182. Cambridge, 1958.

Chapman, M. *The Celts.* New York, 1992.

Charles-Edwards, T. "The Seven Bishop-Houses of Dyfed." B 24 (1970–1972), 247–262.

Clancy, J. *The Earliest Welsh Poetry.* London, 1970.

Condren, M. *The Serpent and the Goddess.* San Francisco, 1989.

Connolly, S. "The Authorship and Manuscript Tradition of Vita I S Brigitae," *Manuscripta* 16 (1972), 67–82.

———. "Cogitosus's *Life of St Brigit.*" JRSAI 117 (1987), 5–27.

Conran, A. *Welsh Verse.* Cardiff, 1967.

Cowley, F. G. *A History of the Monastic Order in South Wales.* Cardiff, 1977.

Cunliffe, B. *The Celtic World.* London, 1992.

Curtius, E. R. *European Literature and the Latin Middle Ages.* London, 1953.

Daniel, I. "Golwg newydd ar ryddiaeth grefyddol Cymraeg Canol." LlC 15 (1984–1986), 207–248.

———. "*Ymborth yr Enaid*—Clytwaith, Cyfieithiad nei Waith Gwreiddiol?" LlC 17 (1992), 11–59.

Davies, J. *Hanes Cymru.* London, 1990.

Davies, O. *Celtic Christianity in Early Medieval Wales: The Origins of the Welsh Spiritual Tradition.* Cardiff, 1996.

———. "'On Divine Love' from *The Food of the Soul:* A Celtic Mystical Paradigm?" *Mystics Quarterly* 20, no. 3 (1994), 87–95.

———. "Rhetoric of the Gift: Inspiration, Pneumatology and Poetic

Craft in Medieval Wales." in *The Medieval Mystical Tradition in England, Ireland and Wales,* edited by Marion Glasscoe. Cambridge, Boydell, 1999.

Davies, O., and Bowie, F. (eds.). *Celtic Christian Spirituality: An Anthology of Medieval and Modern Sources.* London and New York, 1995.

Davies, P. *Rhwng Chwedl a Chredo.* Cardiff, 1966.

Davies, W. "The Myth of the Celtic Church." In *The Early Church in Wales and the West,* edited by N. Edwards and A. Lane, 12–21. Oxbow, 1992.

———. *An Early Welsh Microcosm.* London, 1978.

———. *Wales in the Early Middle Ages.* Leicester, 1982.

de Plinval G. *Pélage: ses écrits, sa vie et sa réforme.* Lausanne, 1943.

de Waal, E. *A World Made Whole.* London, 1992.

Diehl, P. *The Medieval European Religious Lyric.* Berkeley, California 1985.

Doherty, C. "The Irish Hagiographer: Resources, Aims, Results," *Historical Studies* 16 (1987), 10–22.

Dronke, P. *The Medieval Lyric.* London, 1978.

Dudley, L. "An Early Homily on the 'Body and Soul' Theme," *Journal of English and Germanic Philology* 8 (1909), 225–253.

Dumézil G. *Servius et la fortune: essai sur la fonction sociale de louange et de blâme et sur les éléments indoeuropéens du cens romains.* Paris, 1943.

Dumville, D. *Celtic Britain in the Early Middle Ages.* Suffolk, 1980.

———. "Late Seventh or Early Eighth Century for the British Transmission of Pelagius." CMCS 10 (1985), 39–52.

———. *St. Patrick, AD 493–1993.* Woodbridge, 1993.

———. "Some British Aspects of the Earliest Irish Christianity." In *Irland und Europa,* edited by P. Ní Catháin and M. Richter, 16–24. Stuttgart, 1984.

———. "Towards an Interpretation of the *Fís Adamnán.*" *Studia Celtica* 12–13 (1977–1978), 62–77.

———. "Two Approaches to the Dating of *Navigatio Sancti Brendani.*" *Studi Medievali,* 3rd Series, 29 (1988), 87–102.

Eckenstein, L. *Women under Monasticism.* Cambridge, 1986.

Edwards, N. *The Archaeology of Medieval Ireland.* London, 1990.

Esposito, M. "Notes on Latin Learning and Literature in Medieval Ireland. IV: On the Early Latin Lives of St. Brigid of Kildare." *Hermarthena* 49 (1935), 120–165.

Evans, D. S. *A Grammar of Middle Welsh.* Dublin, 1964.

———. *Medieval Religious Literature.* Cardiff, 1986.

Evans, R. F. *Four Letters of Pelagius.* London, 1968.

———. "Pelagius, Fastidius and the Pseudo-Augustinian *De Vita Christiana.*" *Journal of Theological Studies* 13 (1962), 72–98.

Flower, R. *The Irish Tradition.* Oxford, 1947.

Foerster, M. "Adams Erschaffung und Namengebung." *Archiv für Religionswissenschaft* 11 (1907–1908), 477.

Ford, P. K. "Celtic Women: The Opposing Sex." *Viator* 19 (1988), 417–438.

Foster, I. "The Book of the Anchorite." PBA 36 (1949), 197–226.

Garde, J. N. *Old English Poetry in Medieval Christian Perspective.* Woodbridge, 1991.

Godel, W. "Irisches Beten im frühen Mittelalter: eine liturgie- und frömmigkeitsgeschichtliche Untersuchung," *Zeitschrift für katholische Theologie* 85 (1963), 261–321, 389–439.

Gougaud, L. "Etude sur les *loricae* celtiques et sur les prieres qui s'en rapprochent." *Bulletin d'ancienne littérature et d'archéologie chrétiennes* 1 (1911), 265–281; 2 (1912), 33–41, 101–127.

———. "Some Liturgical and Ascetical Traditions of the Celtic Church. I. Genuflection," *Journal of Theological Studies* 9 (1908), 556–561.

Green, M., ed. *The Celtic World.* London, 1995.

———. *The Gods of the Celts.* New Haven, 1993.

———. *Symbol and Image in Celtic Religious Art.* London, 1989.

Gruffydd, R. G., ed. *Bardos.* Cardiff, 1982.

———. "*Cyntefin Ceinaf Amser* o Lyfr Du Caerfyrddin," YB 4 (1969), 12–26.

Gwynn, A. *The Irish Church in the Eleventh and Twelfth Centuries.* Dublin, 1992.

Hamp, E. "Imbolc, óimelc," *Studia Celtica* 14/15 (1979–1980), 106–113.

Hanson, R. P. C. *St. Patrick: His Origins and Career.* Oxford, 1968.

Harvey, A. "The Cambridge Juvencus Glosses—Evidence of Hiberno-Welsh Literary Activity?" In *Language Contact in the British Isles: Proceedings of the Eighth International Symposium on Language Contact in Europe*, edited by P. S. Ureland and G. Broderick, 181–198. Tübingen, 1991.

Hays, R. W. "Welsh Students at Oxford and Cambridge Universities in the Middle Ages." *Welsh History Review* 4 (1968–1969), 325–361.

Heffernan, T. J. *Sacred Biography: Saints and Their Biographers in the Middle Ages.* New York and Oxford, 1988.

Heist, W. "Irish Saints' Lives, Romance and Cultural History." In *Medievalia et Humanistica,* edited by P. Clogan, 25–40. Cambridge, 1975.

Henken, E. R. *The Traditions of the Welsh Saints.* Woodbridge, 1987.

――――. *The Welsh Saints: A Study of Patterned Lives.* Woodbridge, 1991.

Hennig, J. "Old Ireland and Her Liturgy." In *Old Ireland,* edited by R. E. McNally, 60–89. Dublin, 1965.

Henry, P. L. *The Early English and Celtic Lyric.* London, 1966.

Herbert, M. *Iona, Kells and Derry.* Oxford, 1988.

Herren, M. W. "The Authorship, Date of Composition and Provenance of the So-called *Lorica Gildae.*" E 24 (1973), 35–51.

Higgins, J. "Two Passages in the Confessio of Patrick." *Milltown Studies* 35 (1995), 131–133.

Higley, S. L. *Between Languages: The Uncooperative Text in Early Welsh and Old English Nature Poetry.* University Park, Pennsylvania, 1993.

Hillgarth, J. N. "Ireland and Spain in the Seventh Century." *Peritia* 3 (1984), 1–16.

――――. "Old Ireland and Visigothic Spain." In *Old Ireland,* edited by R. E. McNally, 200–227. Dublin, 1965.

Hughes, K. "The Celtic Church: Is This a Valid Concept." CMCS 1 (1981), 1–20.

――――. *The Church in Early Irish Society.* London, 1966.

――――. *Early Christian Ireland: Introduction to the Sources.* London, 1972.

――――. "Some Aspects of Irish Influence on Early English Private Prayer." In *Church and Society in Ireland: AD 400–1200.* London, 1987. XVII.

Hutton, R. *The Pagan Religions of the Ancient British Isles.* London, 1991.

Jackson, K. H. *A Celtic Miscellany,* rev. ed. Harmondsworth, 1971.

――――. *Studies in Early Celtic Nature Poetry.* Cambridge, 1935.

Jenkins, D. "Pencerdd a Bardd Teulu." YB 14 (1988), 19–46.

Johnston, E. "Transforming Women in Irish Hagiography." *Peritia* 9 (1995), 214–220.

Jones, F. *The Holy Wells of Wales.* Cardiff, 1954.

Jones, G. *Yr Areithiau Pros.* Cardiff, 1934.

Jones, J. Ll. "The Court Poets of the Welsh Princes." PBA 24 (1948), 167–197.

Jones, R. M. *Cyfriniaeth Gymraeg.* Cardiff, 1994.

――――. "Ymryson ac Ymddiddan Corff ac Enaid." YB 5 (1970), 44–61.

Jones, T. "The Black Book of Carmarthen: Stanzas of the Graves." PBA 53 (1967).

Jungmann, J. A. *The Mass of the Roman Rite.* London, 1959.

Kearney, R. *The Irish Mind.* Dublin, 1985.

Kelly, F. *A Guide to Early Irish Law.* Dublin, 1988.

Kirby, D. P. "A Note on Rhigyfarch's Life of David." *Welsh History Review* 4 (1969), 292–297.

Knight, J. K. "Sources for the Early History of Morgannwg." In *Glamorgan County History*, 2, edited by H. N. Savory, 365–409. Cardiff, 1984.

Knott, E., and Murphy, G. *Early Irish Literature.* New York, 1966.

Landgraf, A. "Anfänge einer Lehre vom concursus simultaneus im XIII. Jahrhundert" *Recherches de Théologie Ancienne et Médiévale* 1 (1929), 202–228.

Lapidge, M. "Latin Learning in Dark Age Wales." In *Proceedings of the Seventh International Congress of Celtic Studies,* edited by D. E. Evans, et al., 91–107. Oxford, 1986.

Leclercq, H. S.v. *lorica, Dictionnaire d'Archéologie Chrétienne et de Liturgie* 9 (1930), cols. 2511–2516.

Lindsay, W. M. "A Welsh (Cornish?) Gloss in a Leyden MS." *Zeitschrift für celtische Philologie* 1 (1898), 361.

Lloyd, J. E. *The Story of Ceredigion.* Cardiff, 1937.

Mac Cana, P. "An Archaism in Early Irish Poetic Tradition." *Celtica* 8 (1968), 174–181.

———. *Celtic Mythology.* New York, 1983.

———. "Elfennau cyn-gristnogol yn y cyfreithiau." B 23 (1968–1970), 316–320.

Mac Eoin G. S. "Invocation of the Forces of Nature in the Loricae." *Studia Hibernica* 2 (1962), 212–217.

Mackey, J. P. *An Introduction to Celtic Christianity.* Edinburgh, 1989.

Mackey, J. P. "Magic and Celtic Primal Religion." ZCP 45 (1992): 62–84.

Mason, T. "St. Brigid's Crosses." JRSAI 75, no. 3 (1945), 160–166.

Matonis, A. T. E. "Later Medieval Poetic and Some Welsh Bardic Debates." B 29 (1982), 635–665.

McDonald, M. *"We Are not French": Language, Culture and Identity in Brittany.* London, 1989.

McGinn, B. *The Growth of Mysticism (The Presence of God: A History of Western Christian Mysticism,* vol. 2). London and New York, 1994.

McKone, K. "Brigit in the Seventh Century: A Saint with Three Lives?" *Peritia* 1 (1982), 107–145.

———. "An Introduction to Early Irish Saints' Lives." *The Maynooth Review* 11 (1984), 26–59.

———. *Pagan Past and Christian Present in Early Irish Literature.* Maynooth, 1991.

McNamara, M. *Biblical Studies: The Medieval Irish Contribution.* Dublin, 1976.

―――. "Tradition and Creativity in Early Irish Psalter Study." In *Irland und Europa,* edited by P. Ní Chatháin and M. Richter, 338–389. Stuttgart, 1984.

McNeill, J. *The Celtic Churches: A History AD 200–1200.* Chicago, 1974.

Maher, M. *Irish Spirituality.* Dublin, 1981.

Márkus, G., and Clancy, Th. O. *Iona: The Earliest Poetry of a Celtic Monastery.* Edinburgh, 1995.

Miller, M. "Date-guessing and Dyfed." *Studia Celtica* 12–13 (1977–1978), 33–61.

Moran, D. *The Philosophy of John Scottus Eriugena.* Cambridge, 1989.

Murphy, G. *Early Irish Lyrics.* Oxford, 1956.

Nagy, J. F. *Conversing with Angels and Ancients: Literary Myths of Medieval Ireland.* Ithaca, 1997.

Nash-Williams, V. E. *The Early Christian Monuments of Wales.* Cardiff, 1950.

Ó Briain, F. "Brigitana." ZCP 36 (1977), 112–137.

―――. "The Hagiography of Leinster." In *Féilscríbhinn Eóin Mhic Néill,* edited by J. Ryan, 454–464. Dublin, 1940.

―――. "Miracles in the Lives of Irish Saints." *Irish Ecclesiastical Record* 66 (1945), 331–342.

―――. "Saga Themes in Irish Hagiography." In *Feilscribhinn Torna,* edited by S. Pender 33–42. Cork, 1947.

O'Carroll, M. S.v. *lorica,* DS 9 (1976), cols. 1007–1011.

Ó Catháin, S. *The Festival of Brigit.* Co. Dublin, 1995.

O'Cathasaigh, D. "The Cult of Brigid: A Study of Pagan-Christian Syncretisim in Ireland." In *Mother Worship,* edited by J. J. Preston, 75–94. Chapel Hill, 1982.

Ó Cróinín, D. *Early Medieval Ireland.* London, 1995.

O'Dwyer, P. *Céli Dé: Spiritual Reform in Ireland 750–900.* Dublin, 1981.

O'Loughlin, Th. "The Gates of Hell: From Metaphor to Fact." *Milltown Studies* 38 (1996), 98–114.

―――. "Knowing God and Knowing the Cosmos: Augustine's Legacy of Tension." *Irish Philosophical Journal* 6 (1989), 27–58.

―――. "The Latin Sources of Medieval Irish Culture." In *Progress in Medieval Irish Studies,* edited by K. McKone and K. Simms, 91–105. Maynooth, 1996.

―――. "The Library of Iona in the Late Seventh Century: The Evidence of Adomnán's *De Locis Sanctis.*" E 45 (1994), pp. 33–52.

―――. "Tradition and Exegesis in the Eighth Century: The Use of Patristic Sources in Early Medieval Scriptural Commentaries." In *The*

Scriptures and Early Medieval Ireland, edited by T. O'Loughlin, 217–239. Turnhout 1996.

————. "Unexplored Irish Influences on Eriugena." *Recherches de Théologie Ancienne et Médiévale* 59 (1992), 23–40.

O'Loughlin, Th., and Conrad-O'Briain, H. "The "Baptism of Tears" in Early Anglo-Saxon Sources." *Anglo-Saxon England* 22 (1993), 65–83.

O' Meara, J. J. *Eriugena.* Oxford, 1988.

O'Meara J. J., and Bieler, L., eds. *The Mind of Eriugena.* Dublin, 1970.

Ó Riain, P. "Towards a Methodology in Early Irish Hagiography." *Peritia* 1 (1982), 146–159.

Orlandi, G. *Navigatio S. Brendani: Introduzione.* Milan, 1968.

Pelster, F. "Das Leben und die Schriften des Dominikanerlehrers Richard Fishacre." *Zeitschrift für katholische Theologie* 54 (1930), 518–553.

Pennar, M. *The Black Book of Carmarthen.* Llanerch, 1989.

Picard, J-M. "Structural Patterns in early Hiberno-Latin Hagiography." *Peritia* 4 (1985), 67–82.

Pieris, A. *An Asian Theology of Liberation.* Edinburgh, 1988.

Piggot, S. *Ancient Britons and the Antiquarian Imagination.* London, 1989.

————. *The Druids.* Harmondsworth, 1968.

Pryce, H. *Native Law and the Church in Medieval Wales.* Oxford, 1993.

————. "Pastoral Care in Early Medieval Wales." In *Pastoral Care before the Parish,* edited by J. Blair and R. Sharpe, 41–62. Leicester, 1992.

Rankin, H. D. *Celts and the Classical World.* London, 1987.

Rees, B. *Pelagius: A Reluctant Heretic.* Woodbridge, 1988.

Renfrew, C. *Archaeology and Language.* Harmondsworth, 1987.

Rhys, J. "Celtae and Galli." PBA (1905–1906), 71–134.

Riché, P. "Columbanus, His Followers and the Merovingian Church." In *Columbanus and Merovingian Monasticism,* edited by H. B. Clarke and M. Brennan, 59–72. Oxford, 1981.

Richter, M. *Medieval Ireland: The Enduring Tradition.* London, 1988.

Roberts, B. F. "Llurig Alexander." B 20 (1962–1964), 104–106.

————. "Rhai Swynion Cymraeg." B 21 (1964–1966), 197–213.

Ross, A. *Pagan Celtic Britain.* London, 1967.

Rousselot, P. *Pour l'histoire du probleme de l'amour au moyen âge.* Münster, 1908.

Ryan, J. *Irish Monasticism,* 2nd ed. Dublin, 1972.

Ryan, M. *Ireland and Insular Art AD 500–1200.* Dublin, 1987.

Schupp, J. *Die Gnadenlehre des Petrus Lombardus.* Freiburg im Bresgau, 1932.

Sharpe, R. *Medieval Irish Saints' Lives*. Oxford, 1991.

———. "Some Problems concerning the Organization of the Church in Early Medieval Ireland." *Peritia* 3 (1984), 230–270.

———. "*Vitae S. Brigitae*: The Oldest Texts." *Peritia* 1 (1982), 81–106.

Sheldon-Williams, I. P. "Eriugena's Greek Sources." In *The Mind of Eriugena*, edited by J. J. O'Meara and L. Bieler, 1–15. Dublin, 1970.

Sheldrake, Ph. *Living between Worlds: Place and Journey in Celtic Spirituality*. London, 1994.

Shorter, A. *Toward a Theology of Inculturation*. London, 1988.

Sims-Williams, P. "The Evidence for Vernacular Irish Literary Influence on Early Mediaeval Welsh Literature." In *Ireland in Early Medieval Europe*, edited by D. Whitelock, R. McKitterick, and D. Dumville, 235–257. Cambridge, 1982.

———. *Religion and Literature in Western England, 600–800*. Cambridge, 1990.

———. "Some Celtic Otherworld Terms." In *Celtic Language, Celtic Culture: A Festschrift for Eric P. Hamp*, edited by A. T. E. Matonis, and D. F. Melia, 57–81. California, 1990.

———. "The Visionary Celt: The Construction of an Ethnic Preconception." CMCS 11 (1986), 71–96.

Smyth, M. *Understanding the Universe in Seventh-Century Ireland*. Woodbridge, 1996.

Stancliffe, C. "Red, White and Blue Martyrdom." In *Ireland in Early Medieval Europe*, edited by D. Whitelock, R. McKitterick and D. Dumville, 21–46. Cambridge, 1982.

———. *St Martin and his Hagiographer: History and Miracle in Sulpicius Severus*. Oxford, 1983.

Stevenson, J. "Ascent through the Heavens, from Egypt to Ireland." CMCS 5 (1983), 21–35.

Taylor, T. (trans.) *The Life of St. Samson of Dol*. London, 1925; repr. Llanerch, 1991.

Thomas, C. *Christianity in Roman Britain to AD 500*. London, 1981.

Thomas, P. *Candle in the Darkness*. Llandysul, 1993.

Thompson, E. A. *Saint Germanus of Auxerre and the End of Roman Britain*. Woodbridge, 1984.

Tymoczko, M. "Unity and Duality? A Theoretical Perspective on the Ambivalence of Celtic Goddesses." *Proceedings of the Harvard Celtic Colloquium* 5 (1985), 22–37.

Usher, G. "Welsh Students at Oxford in the Middle Ages." B 16 (1955), 193–198.

Van Riel, G., Steel, C., and McEvoy, J., eds. *Iohannes Scottus Eriugena: The Bible and Hermeneutics.* Leuven, 1996.

Vendryes, J. "L'enfer glacé." RC 46 (1929), 134–142.

Wait, G. A. *Ritual and Religion in Iron Age Britain.* British Archaeological Reports, British Series, 149 (1985).

Walsh, J., and Bradley, T. *A History of the Irish Church: 400–700 AD.* Dublin, 1991.

Ward, B. *The Lives of the Desert Fathers.* Oxford, 1981.

Warren, F. E. *The Liturgy and Ritual of the Celtic Church,* 2nd ed. by J. Stevenson. Woodbridge, 1987.

Watts, D. *Christians and Pagans in Roman Britain.* London, 1991.

Webster, G. *The British Celts and Their Gods under Rome.* London, 1986.

Williams, G. "Fire on Cambria's Altar: The Welsh and Their Religion." In *The Welsh and Their Religion,* 1–72. Cardiff, 1991.

———. "Some Protestant Views of Early British Church History." In *Welsh Reformation Essays,* 207–219. Cardiff, 1967.

———. *The Welsh Church from Conquest to Reformation,* 2nd ed. Cardiff, 1976.

Williams, G. A. *Madoc.* Oxford, 1987.

———. *When Was Wales?* Harmondsworth, 1985.

Williams, I. *The Beginnings of Welsh Poetry.* Cardiff, 1972.

———. "Llurig Alexander." B 17 (1956–1958), 95.

Williams, J. E. C. "The Court Poet in Medieval Ireland." PBA 57 (1971), 85–135.

———. *The Irish Literary Tradition.* Cardiff and Belmont, Mass., 1992.

———. "Medieval Welsh Religious Prose." *Proceedings of the Second International Congress of Celtic Studies, 1963* (1966), 65–97.

———. *The Poets of the Welsh Princes.* Cardiff, 1978.

Wood, I. N. "Forgery in Merovingian Hagiography." In *Fälschungen im Mittelalter. Internationaler Kongress der Monumenta Germaniae Historica, München 16–19 September, 1986,* 369–384. Hanover, 1988.

Wooding, J. M., ed. *The Otherworld Voyage in Early Irish Literature and History: An Anthology of Criticism.* Dublin, 1998.

Wright, C. D. *The Irish Tradition in Old English Literature.* Cambridge, 1993.

Index

References in **boldface** are to introductory material.

Other Volumes in This Series

551

Other Volumes in This Series

Other Volumes in This Series

Other Volumes in This Series

Pseudo-Dionysius · THE COMPLETE WORKS
Pseudo-Macarius · THE FIFTY SPIRITUAL HOMILIES AND THE
GREAT LETTER
Pursuit of Wisdom, The · AND OTHER WORKS BY THE AUTHOR OF
THE CLOUD OF UNKNOWING
Quaker Spirituality · SELECTED WRITINGS
Rabbinic Stories ·
Richard Rolle · THE ENGLISH WRITINGS
Richard of St. Victor · THE TWELVE PATRIARCHS, THE MYSTICAL ARK,
BOOK THREE OF THE TRINITY
Robert Bellarmine · SPIRITUAL WRITINGS
Safed Spirituality · RULES OF MYSTICAL PIETY, THE BEGINNING OF
WISDOM
Shakers, The · TWO CENTURIES OF SPIRITUAL REFLECTION
Sharafuddin Maneri · THE HUNDRED LETTERS
Sor Juana Inés de la Cruz · SELECTED WRITINGS
Spirituality of the German Awakening, The ·
Symeon the New Theologian · THE DISCOURSES
Talmud, The · SELECTED WRITINGS
Teresa of Avila · THE INTERIOR CASTLE
Theatine Spirituality · SELECTED WRITINGS
'Umar Ibn al-Fāriḍ · SUFI VERSE, SAINTLY LIFE
Valentin Weigel · SELECTED SPIRITUAL WRITINGS
Venerable Bede, The · ON THE SONG OF SONGS AND SELECTED
WRITINGS
Vincent de Paul and Louise de Marillac · RULES, CONFERENCES,
AND WRITINGS
Walter Hilton · THE SCALE OF PERFECTION
William Law · A SERIOUS CALL TO A DEVOUT AND HOLY LIFE, THE SPIRIT OF
LOVE
Zohar · THE BOOK OF ENLIGHTENMENT

The Classics of Western Spirituality is a ground-breaking collection of the original writings of more than 100 universally acknowledged teachers within the Catholic, Protestant, Eastern Orthodox, Jewish, Islamic, and Native American Indian traditions.

To order any title, or to request a complete catalog, contact Paulist Press at 800-218-1903 or visit us on the Web at www.paulistpress.com